Concurrences Books

Tributes

Eleanor M. Fox – Antitrust Ambassador to the World, *2021*

Herbert Hovenkamp – The Dean of American Antitrust Law, *2021*

Frédéric Jenny – Standing Up for Convergence and Relevance in Antitrust, (Vol. I & II), *2019 & 2021*

Albert Foer – A Consumer Voice in the Antitrust Arena, *2020*

Richard Whish – Taking Competition Law Outside the Box, *2020*

Douglas H. Ginsburg – An Antitrust Professor on the Bench (Vol. I & II), *2018 & 2020*

Wang Xiaoye – The Pioneer of Competition Law in China, *A. Emch, W. Ng (eds.), 2019*

Ian S. Forrester – A Scot without Borders (Vol. I & II), *A. Komninos (eds.), 2015*

William E. Kovacic – An Antitrust Tribute (Vol. I & II), *2013 & 2014*

Practical Books

Global Dictionary of Competition Law, *D. Healey, W. Kovacic, P. Trevisan, R. Whish, Forthcoming 2022*

Antitrust in the Pharmaceutical Sector, *M. Cowie, G. Gordon M. Thill-Tayara, Forthcoming 2022*

Competition Law Treatment of Joint Ventures, *B Bleicher, N. Campbell, A. Hamilton, N. Hukkinen, P. Khan, Forthcoming 2022 (in collaboration with the IBA)*

State Aid & National Enforcement, *J. Derenne, D. Jouve, C. Lemaire, F. Martucci (eds.), Forthcoming 2022*

Information Exchange and Related Risks – A Practical Guide, *Z. Marosi & M. Soares (eds.), Forthcoming 2022 (in collaboration with the IBA)*

Competition Case Law Digest – 5th Edition, *F. Jenny, N. Charbit (eds.)*

Competition Inspections in 21 Jurisdictions – A Practitioner's Guide, *N. Jalabert-Doury (ed.), 2022*

Perspectives on Antitrust Compliance, *A. Riley, A. Stephan, A. Tubbs (eds.), 2022 (in collaboration with the ICC)*

Turkish Competition Law, *G. Gürkaynak, 2021*

Competition Law - Climate Change & Environmental Sustainability, *S. Holmes, D. Middelschulte, M. Snoep (eds.), 2021*

Merger Control in Latin America – A Jurisdictional Guide, *P. Burnier da Silveira, P. Sittenfeld (eds.), 2020*

Competition Inspections under EU Law – A Practitioner's Guide, *N. Jalabert-Doury, 2020*

Gun Jumping in Merger Control - A Jurisdictional Guide, *C. Hatton, Y. Comtois, A. Hamilton (eds.), 2019 (in collaboration with the IBA)*

Choice – A New Standard for Competition Analysis? *P. Nihoul, 2016*

PhD Theses

Competition & Regulation in Network Industries – Essays in Industrial Organization, *J-M. Zogheib, 2021*

The Role of Media Pluralism in the Enforcement of EU Competition Law, *K. Bania, 2019*

Buyer Power, *I. Herrera Anchustegui, 2017*

General Interest

Women and Antitrust – Voices from the Field (Vol I & II), *E. Kurgonaite & K. Nordlander, 2020*

Conference Proceedings

Antitrust in Emerging and Developing Countries – (Vol I & II), *E. Fox, H. First, 2015 & 2016*

Global Antitrust Law – Current Issues in Antitrust Law and Economics, *D. Ginsburg, J. Wright, (eds.) 2015*

Competition Law on the Global Stage – David Gerber's Global Competition Law in Perspective, *D. Gerber, 2014*

e-Book versions available for **Concurrences+** subscribers

THE INTERNATIONAL COMPETITION NETWORK AT TWENTY

Origins, Accomplishments and Aspirations

Edited by

Paul Lugard
Dave Anderson

INTERSENTIA

Concurrences
Antitrust Publications & Events

Lefebvre Sarrut Belgium NV
Hoogstraat 139/6
1000 Brussels
Belgium

Institute of Competition Law
106 West 32nd Street, Suite 144
New York, NY 10001
USA

Cover design: Danny Juchtmans / www.dsigngraphics.be
Cover image: Mdesignstudio / Shutterstock

ISBN 978-1-939007-09-4

Library of Congress Control Number: 2022936652

FOREWORD

The International Competition Network, ("ICN"), was established in a time which was characterized by a great enthusiasm for the general concept of competition and a blossoming of competition agencies worldwide. We witnessed an impressive momentum and a common understanding that the time was right for the next level, for competition agencies to ride this wave and establish a forum which – as we know today – would provide the basis for 20 years of successful multilateral cooperation.

The first ICN Working Groups dealt with mergers and advocacy as a reaction to the increase in multinational cross-border mergers. But in the member-driven ICN the structure is never more than a snapshot. The ICN follows an inclusive bottom-up approach based on direct input from its membership in the flexible project-oriented working groups, at events and via regular network-wide surveys on topics, tools and structure. Driven by its members' needs, the ICN developed into an international organization covering all areas of competition law enforcement and policy.

"All competition, all the time" has been the ICN's credo from the beginning. We take this approach seriously and look at the pressing questions of our time from the perspective of competition law enforcers. And from the beginning we have done this with an open mind and broad view, considering the interaction with other areas of law. The latest examples include the ICN's Town Hall series dealing with the interaction of competition policy and other government policies. We organized projects and sessions on issues in the context of the COVID-19 pandemic, including the Steering Group statement on competition during and after the pandemic. We launched the ICN Steering Group project on competition law enforcement at the intersection between competition, consumer protection, and privacy, and the 2021 ICN Annual Conference special project dealt with the topic of competition and sustainability. Today this openness plays an increasingly important role as we are confronted with questions of vital, even existential importance. Deliberations on sustainability, in particular, are fueling a debate on aspects to be taken into account in assessments under competition law, and the debate is much wider, bringing in many other economic and socio-political goals. Competition law can adapt to a changing competition environment. It is flexible enough, but it has to be applied stringently and define clear limits. Competition law should remain embedded in and not overlaid with the political context.

This book looks back at 20 successful years, the last of which has been particularly difficult. The ICN has achieved a lot. Founded in October 2001 by antitrust officials from 14 jurisdictions, it currently comprises 140 member agencies from 130 jurisdictions. It has produced a comprehensive encyclopedia of best practices, practical recommendations and other tools. It is obvious that the ICN can rely on a solid foundation. Its virtual structure works and the connection between members is strong. Familiarity and trust built as a result of the multilateral cooperation in the ICN and the global standards established in our work products form the basis for answers to the questions raised by global developments. Now we are entering the ICN's third decade and it is time to look ahead.

Andreas Mundt
President of the Bundeskartellamt and Chair of the ICN Steering Group

ACKNOWLEDGEMENTS

This publication is the result of a collective effort by many people over an extended period of time.

We started this book's journey several years ago, around 2018, when Paul and I first discussed the possibility of co-editing *The International Competition Network at Twenty* book as a follow-up to the *The ICN at Ten* book that Paul conceived of and edited solo (and that I contributed to as an author). Being good friends and sharing a keen interest in international competition law and policy, and the activities of the ICN in particular, it sounded like a great idea to both of us, not only to ensure that the ICN's second decade had its own publication as did the first ten years of the organization, but to also celebrate this great global community that is the ICN. We wanted to take stock again of the organization's accomplishments during the second decade of its existence and to look ahead to the ICN's third decade, especially at a time when the international competition community is working on a number of novel and fundamental questions.

It was at the Annual Conference in Cartagena in May 2019 that we began the project in earnest, talking about the prospect of such a book in the conference hallways with ICN leaders, previous contributors to the first book, agencies, NGAs and others. We received great feedback, and so we took a breath, smiled at each other, and went for it in the belief that we would have this publication ready for the next ICN Annual Conference in 2020 in Los Angeles. Little did we know then of the long and winding road we were about to embark upon to get to the completion of this publication that would take us from Cartagena to Los Angeles, then Budapest, to finally reach our destination in Berlin with the book that you are holding. The road was long of course due to the unexpected repercussions of the COVID-19 pandemic, and winding due to a few other interesting twists and turns during the project that were hard to predict at the start of our journey.

It takes an international village to produce a book like this with so many contributors and moving parts over the extended time it took with the COVID interruption. We would like to say a huge thank you to everyone who helped along the way in ways big and small. In particular, we have had amazing support from the ICN leadership and Secretariat, including from Andreas Mundt, Barbara Schulze, Olaf Wrede and Nigel Caesar – your encouragement and contributions throughout were vital and so kind, we are so grateful. We also received tremendous help from ICN member agency officials around the world who contributed to the project along the way in a variety of ways, we'd like to thank you all here, including Eddy De Smijter, Filip Kubik, Heidi Sada, Paul O'Brien, Shira Gillat, Hiroyuki Kishimoto, Siún O'Keeffe, Cristina Camacho and Nandi Mokoena. We would also like to acknowledge the contribution of a number of key persons who were there at the start of *The ICN at Ten*, without whom this publication would not have appeared: Eleanor Fox, Peter Plompen and Jim Rill. Special thanks go out to Professor Giorgio Monti, Hugh Hollman and Professor Nicolas Petit for their support and guidance.

We are grateful to our firms, Baker Botts LLP, and Bryan Cave Leighton Paisner LLP, for their excellent support during this project. We are particularly indebted to members of our own teams, who worked tirelessly with us throughout the editing and production process, providing editorial, substantive, organizational and other support. A special round of heartfelt thanks from us goes to those team members – Paul Culliford, Thomas Wright, Lucy Hawley, Avani Joshi and to the super Gary Dutry. I know Paul also wanted to thank in particular from his firm Jim Rill and John Taladay, both ICN NGAs and long-time supporters of the ICN, and I'd like to thank from mine Andy Hockley for his great support of our ICN work and Paul Culliford who has served the ICN so well on many projects well beyond this book.

Of course this project would not have gotten off the ground and completed without the content and continuous help we've received from all of our amazing authors whose hard work you will find in these pages. You have hung in there through the many stops and starts of this project with grace, patience and humor – thanks all!

We are very grateful to Intersentia Publishers, in particular Margit Bal, Market Unit Director Legal NL, and Isabelle van Dongen, our editor, who magically brought us to the finish line, for all their support. We are also thankful to Concurrences, in particular Nicolas Charbit, who, alongside Intersentia, supported the project, including financially. Without them, this publication would not have seen the light of day.

And to finish, I would like to acknowledge my co-editor and the original founder of this project, Paul Lugard. Paul, you are such a great friend, lawyer and collaborator, I could not think of a better person to undertake this particular project with given your dedication to the ICN and our friendship. We endured a three-year project that was meant to only take one (!), and we did it together as a team throughout – I wouldn't have had it any other way. I was super lucky to have been there at the start of the ICN (and a bit before!) and this organization has played a big role in my career. I have learned so much from my ICN friends all over the world as we have together, through the ICN, pursued the advancement of competition law and policy globally to the benefit of our economies and consumers. From the hard work of drafting recommended practices and manuals, to the sharing experiences in break-out sessions at workshops, to the small special moments just meeting over coffee around the plenaries in so many places, I've been so honored to have served with this dedicated ICN community over the past twenty years and I'm so happy to have taken this journey with you Paul to complete this book. Here's to the ICN's third decade and beyond!

Dave ANDERSON

CONTENTS

THE ICN AT TWENTY

Origins, Accomplishments and Aspirations: An Introduction

Paul LUGARD

1. INTRODUCTION

In many respects, the ICN is a unique phenomenon: as a virtual and informal network of competition enforcement agencies that spans the globe, it has become the single most authoritative platform in the field of international competition law and policy. And it has accomplished this in less than two decades. As an open organisation based on participation and transparency, it has attracted the vast majority of antitrust authorities and continues to exert a powerful appeal to both existing and potential new members. While the ICN is first and foremost in the business of producing soft law, its recommended practices, manuals, workbooks and other work product have become immensely influential in shaping and developing the system of antitrust enforcement as we know it. Indeed, as "soft law tends to become hard law," as one commentator in this publication observes, it is not surprising that ICN work products have informed legislative changes and enforcement practices around the world.

The compilation of essays included in this book is a testament to the origins of the ICN, the activities that the network has embarked upon during the first two decades of its existence, the accomplishments that it has achieved, and the future directions that the organisation will explore in a challenging but exciting time that sees a resurgence of popular interest in competition law, an almost global backlash against the tech industry and attempts to accommodate sustainability considerations, labour law issues and other policies in competition law and, more recently, some dramatic geopolitical frictions. These issues arise at the time that the members of the ICN – no longer a start-up – as *Leah McCoy* aptly puts it – are already confronted with the fallout of the global Covid-19 pandemic.

Ten years ago, when the ICN celebrated its tenth anniversary, the authors of *The International Competition Network at Ten* looked back at the history of the ICN, its accomplishments during the first decade of its existence and contemplated the future of the organisation. Now, ten years later, at the beginning of 2022, it is tempting to critically look back on the organisation's second decade, take stock of the "acquis" and to again glimpse into the future of the organisation. Has the ICN lived up to the promises that it made a decade ago, gaining importance, legitimacy and effectiveness? Has the ICN been able to integrate and accommodate an impressive number of new members with sometimes diverging views on long-established ICN-practices and work products? Has this led to significant changes of the institutional design of the organisation and the influence that different categories of members have on the functioning of the ICN?

In 2010, we observed that it was a Herculean task to fully capture and analyse the impact and continuing dynamics that the International Competition Network has brought to the substance, procedure and administration of competition law after the first ten years of its existence. Without any doubt, the challenge of assessing and accurately evaluating the ICN's functioning and performance twenty years after it was established in 2001 at Ditchley Park has only become more complex and daunting. However, when digesting the collection of contributions included in this publication, it becomes clear that "*the ICN is a vibrant organisation,*" "*provides for a unique and most valuable platform for peer competition agencies around the world,*" "*has been dramatically successful,*" "*has seen a "phenomenal development*" over the past ten years, and has resulted in "*huge changes to the development of international and national competition laws*" – to cite from just a few of the contributions to this publication.

This, of course, does not imply that the functioning of the organization cannot be further improved or that any criticism towards the ICN would *a priori* be unfounded. On the contrary, while the ICN has, in many respects, been effective and has helped NCAs from younger and more established agencies to instil more competition in their home markets, legitimate questions remain regarding the participation of younger agencies, whose contributions may be limited by lack of funds, time and experience. These questions remain relevant, even in light of the affirmative actions that have taken place in the past decade, in particular under the leadership of the current ICN Chair, Andreas Mundt. While the legitimacy of the ICN is in our view well-guarded, the institutional design and the practical functioning of the network deserves continued attention. Alongside *Yane Svetiev's* article on the governance design of regulatory networks, one contribution that merits specific mentioning in this respect is *Eleanor Fox'* Linked-In article

But this bundle of essays also discusses the effectiveness of the organisation. A number of contributions concentrate on the implementation of ICN work products, in particular the "Survey the Surveys" essay by *Dave Anderson* and *BCLP* and the co-production ("A Century with the ICN"), submitted by *Maria Coppola, Liz Kraus, Cynthia Lagdameo, Paul O'Brien* and *Randy Tritell.* Additionally, a number of country-specific contributions highlight how ICN work products have influenced national competition rules and enforcement practice. In this respect, the insights from *Mateusz Blachucki* into the Polish merger procedure, the reflections of *Paulo Burnier de Silveira* on the Brazilian merger and cartel settlements framework, the impact of the ICN on ACCC cartel settlement discussed by *Rod Sims* and *Marcus Bezzi*, as well as the role of the ICN in the evolution of the Israel Competition Authority commented upon by *Michal Halperin* and *Shira Gillat* are particularly insightful.

We are pleased to see that a number of contributions in this bundle take us back to the origins of the ICN. Indeed, to understand the present and reflect on the future of the ICN, it is helpful to know its past. The contribution of *Eleanor Fox*, *Andreas Mundt's* foreword, as well as the essays written by *Alejandra Palacios* and *Heidi Sada*, by *Oliver Budzinski*, and by *John Pecman* and *Duy D Pham*, remind us of the architectural forces that helped build the ICN two decades ago. Those contributions ideally complement the essays written by *Merit Janow* and *Jim Rill*, *Francois Souty* and *Hugh Hollman* and *Bill Kovacic,* that were included in the bundle of essays that appeared at the occasion of the tenth anniversary of the ICN, *The International Competition Network at Ten.*

It is a daunting task to define the desirable way forward for the ICN or to even formulate the future priorities for the ICN, especially against the backdrop of the uncertain international environment and the many legitimate questions that NCAs are confronted with, both with regard to the scope and application of domestic competition law and the functioning of the ICN. Are we comfortable that the prevailing guiding benchmark of consumer surplus is sufficiently robust to base future antitrust enforcement on? Is that notion broad and flexible enough to accommodate environmental and sustainability initiatives? What is the optimal regulation of platform-based industries and how do we know when to intervene in those high-tech sectors that are particularly vulnerable to the loss of incentives to innovate? How do we balance antitrust intervention with ex-ante regulation of those sectors and, once those sectors are regulated, is there any meaningful residual role to play for "conventional" competition law enforcement? Are we facing new demands that industrial policy objectives should be reflected in competition law enforcement?

This publication presents an account of the many workstreams that the ICN has embarked on during the second decade of its existence. In particular, *Graeme Jarvie* and *Michele Pacillo*'s overview of the work products of the five ICN working groups functions as a beacon when trying to evaluate the accomplishments of the ICN between 2011 and 2021. In many respects, their contribution, together with the essays written by *Maria Coppola, Liz Kraus, Cynthia Lagdameo, Paul O'Brien* and *Randy Tritell; Siún O'Keeffe* and, with respect to cartel enforcement, *Neil Campbell* and *Guy Pinsonnault*, provides an important backbone of this book. And, as *Andreas Mundt* observes, the ICN has a successful track record of taking on new topics if and when the need arises.

However, this publication also looks into the future. Obviously, one key question facing NCAs and the ICN is how best to deal with the digital economy. Not surprisingly, this topic is touched upon by a variety of authors, beginning with *Andreas Mundt*, who notes that the way the ICN will handle the digital revolution will be decisive for its future and *Olivier Budzinski*, who points at the increased risk of cross-border externalities emanating from national competition policies. In their contribution "The role of the International Competition Network in the digital era," *Alejandra Palacios* and *Heidi Sada* discuss how the ICN can foster analysis and discussion about a number of key questions that NCAs are confronted with in this respect.

But there is more: the contribution by *Csaba Kovacs* and *Aranka Nagy* provides valuable insights into the question how sustainability initiatives should be addressed and the survey that the Hungarian Competition Authority conducted in 2021; *Alan Fels* provides particularly interesting views on how competition advocacy can be reconceptualized; *Leah McCoy* and *Neil Campbell* and *Guy Pinsonnault* discuss international cooperation among competition agencies; *Pierre Horna* offers suggestions how UNCTAD and ICN could work together – thereby complementing Frederique Jenny's reflections on collaboration between the OECD and the ICN in *The International Competition Network at Ten* – and *John Pecman* and *Duy D Pham* discuss the next frontier of international cooperation in competition enforcement. Finally, *Huang Yong, Nell Lixia Zhou* and *Tang Jinglun* offer valuable insights into the evolution of competition policy and enforcement in China.

This bundle of essays, which appears at the twentieth anniversary of the ICN, does not purport to present a comprehensive view of the past, present and possible future directions and activities of the ICN. Rather, it offers a collection of views and different perspectives on a number of ICN-related matters which, taken together, provides a kaleidoscopic, yet interesting picture of the state of affairs, the challenges that the ICN faces and possible future directions. The contributions in this bundle are loosely structured around a number of main themes: (i) general perspectives on the functioning of the ICN, its place in the international competition scene and its relationships with other international organisations, (ii) reflections on the work products that have seen the light in the past decade, (iii) the implementation of ICN work products and the impact that the ICN has had on the enforcement practices of NCAs and (iv) future activities and challenges.

The remainder of this introduction provides a brief discussion of a number of key themes which are particularly evident throughout this publication. One key topic is certainly the impressive collection of ICN work product that the organization has produced over the past decade and the related question of implementation. A second main theme relates to due process or procedural fairness, a topic that has been on the ICN-agenda since the early days, but that has recently received renewed attention and which may now herald a new trend of dealing with intricate topics within the ICN context. As briefly mentioned above, the challenges of digitalization are another topic that merits discussion. The fourth and last theme relates to the institutional design of the ICN, the inclusion of its members, diversity and, more generally, the legitimacy of the organisation.

2. ICN WORK PRODUCTS

The output of the ICN in the past decade has been truly impressive.[1] As *Paul O'Brien* c.s. point out, in its second decade the ICN has moved on from its initial focus on merger guidelines, the building blocks of anti-cartel enforcement, the objectives of unilateral conduct enforcement, investigative techniques and other – often broad-based – topics, to more targeted projects, such as tailored advocacy, specific types of unilateral conduct, leniency programs, remedies and settlements and private enforcement. While navigating these new avenues, the ICN has also updated and revisited its existing work on e.g. the ICN Recommended Practices of merger notification rules and on merger analysis, as well as the ICN Anti-cartel Enforcement Manual, to which new sections on case resolution, awareness, outreach and compliance, international cooperation and other topics were added, and many other work streams. To mention other examples: the Competition Agency Practice Manual now includes new chapters, for example on effective project delivery, human resource management and, importantly, the Agency Effectiveness Working Group first issued and then updated the ICN Guidance on Investigative Process. The Agency Effectiveness Working Group has also created a dedicated economist sub-group which advocates the importance of economic insights in competition analysis, something that is highlighted in this publication by *Martin Mandorff* and *Siún O'Keeffe*. The overview of 2010–2020 ICN work products provided by *Graeme Jarvie* and *Michele Pacillo* is particularly helpful to trace the evolution of work product over the past ten years.

---

1 Or an overview of the ICN work product, see ICN2019–2020WPSummary.pdf (international-competitionnetwork.org).

The evolution of ICN work product displays two particularly interesting features. First, compared to the ICN's first decade, which was marked by some fundamentally different views on, for example, the evidentiary requirements for exclusionary conduct by dominant firms, in the second decade the ICN has widened and deepened its guidance documents and other work products and a significant part of these materials are of a practical or technical nature. They offer suggestions for conducting efficient and effective cartel investigations, facilitating inter-agency cooperation, ways to develop advocacy strategies and the identification of key elements for the well-functioning of competition agencies. But for a large part these second decade materials refine and expand on earlier ICN work.

This does not imply that during its second decade the ICN has not embarked on controversial issues and matters that resonate in different ways with different addressees. Indeed, different opinions continue to exist with regard to procedural fairness, the proper treatment of (online) vertical restraints (a topic that the ICN has taken up around the middle of the second decade), exploitative abuses of dominance and, of course, the way to deal with the digitalization of the economy, in particular the best approach towards platform-based companies that enjoy significant market power. But, and this is the second interesting feature when considering the ICN work products of the past ten years, by and large the ICN seems to have successfully catered to the needs of its constituency by addressing salient new issues and topics in a timely manner, ranging from Covid-19-related topics, to price parity clauses included in agreements with platform-based companies, sustainability and a hoist of topics related to the digital economy.

Looking forward, it seems unlikely that the ICN will soon be faced with a paucity of topics on which to concentrate. But as we will see below, new topics may also come with a risk of divergence, especially if there are no established practices in ICN jurisdictions to fall back on. This applies to the treatment of sustainability initiatives, ways to regulate the digital economy, labour market distortions and perhaps other topics that have not yet seen the light of day. It will certainly require ingenuity to navigate these and other discussions in the years to come.

3. IMPLEMENTATION OF ICN WORK PRODUCTS

Implementation of ICN work products is a hotly debated issue. In his contribution, *Andreas Mundt,* noting that implementation of ICN work products is related to inclusiveness, observes that "implementation will only happen if members are involved and convinced that we are doing the right thing.

Implementation is the underlying goal of the ICN. We do not want to produce papers for the sake of it. We work on guidance documents to achieve results and to have an impact. That is what the ICN was created for."

Having said that, it is a well-known adage that there is nothing in the ICN Operational Framework that requires its members to follow or implement ICN recommendations.

It is therefore interesting to witness, as authoritatively laid out by *Paul O'Brien* c.s. in their contribution, that the focus on implementation of ICN work products is slowly but surely increasing and has, to some extent, now been institutionalized in the form of the Promotion and Implementation ("P&I") team, made up of Working Group chairs and other interested members. *Paul O'Brien* c.s. also observe two trends that may spur implementation of ICN work products, i.e. the appearance of opt-in frameworks, a new type of ICN work product that was first utilized to house the CAP within the ICN and, second, indirect implementation of ICN work products in instances where ICN recommendations inform the activities of other international organisations, such as the OECD.

As I already observed when the ICN celebrated its tenth anniversary, NGAs can and, in my personal view, should play a key role in the dissemination of ICN work products. Many of the comments that *Anne Riley* makes in relation to antitrust compliance and the way agencies and NGAs can constructively work together in compliance-related matters, apply more generally: NGAs can be valuable advocates of the ICN and can be instrumental in the dissemination of ICN work products, including in jurisdiction where the ICN has not yet taken root. In this respect, it is worth considering reinforcing the P&I team with one or more NGAs, or representatives of the NGA community, and to reflect on better ways to organize and involve NGAs in the dissemination of ICN work products. Alongside these efforts, I am hoping that over time, courts, both in ICN member and non-member jurisdictions, will prove increasingly receptive to the authoritative nature of ICN products. Again, in these cases, NGAs involved in litigation before those courts, may help to persuade courts to give credit to well-established ICN recommendations, both with regard to procedural fairness and substantive issues.

A number of essays in this publication discuss the implementation of ICN work products. One outstanding contribution is prepared by co-editor *Dave Anderson* and *BCLP*, who analyse the implementation of a number of Recommended Practices for Merger Notification and Review Procedures. While the measurement of any ICN work product implementation is difficult, their conclusions are both heartening and concerning. Importantly, they also suggest a number of easy-to-implement suggestions that may greatly facilitate compliance with the recommended practices. But implementation of work products is also an important theme in the contributions by *Paulo Burnier da Silveira* (Brazil), *Rod Simms* and *Marcus Bezzi* (Australia), *Mateusz Blachuki* (Poland) and *Margarida Matos Rosa* (Portugal).

One thing is certain: while some persons involved in ICN work may wish that the ICN would have some (light) enforcement mechanism, the reality is that such a mechanism may also significantly slow down the consensus building process that is one of the key ICN success factors, most likely resulting in less and lower quality ICN output. In this universe "persuasion through shared experiences" as *Paul O'Brien c.s.* note, may be the preferable approach, certainly if coupled with smart new initiatives, such as opt-in mechanisms.

4. PROCEDURAL FAIRNESS

For many years, procedural fairness has been a focal point in the international competition community. This is not surprising. Indeed, there is widespread consensus that a transparent and fair competition process ensures the impartial and fair treatment of those subject to competition investigations. It also improves the accuracy and comprehensiveness of competition enforcement decisions, by making sure that all arguments are heard and taken into account. Finally, observing due process reinforces the legitimacy of competition enforcement and its credibility vis-à-vis interested parties as well as citizens.

The reader of this book will find that procedural fairness principles have not only permeated ICN work products from the early days of the ICN, but have recently moved to the centre of the debate, in particular as a result of the establishment of the 2019 Framework on Competition Agency Procedures ("CAP"), a multilateral arrangement sponsored by ICN, under which participating competition agencies commit to a set of fundamental procedural fairness principles and agree to participate in cooperation and review mechanisms. By May 2019, the CAP counted 52 initial founding signatures and has now been adhered to by more than 70 NCAs.

In this publication a number of prominent and particularly well-informed authors provide comments on Framework on Competition Agency Procedures and explain why the CAP is such a unique and novel instrument in the ICN toolbox. *Jim Rill* and *Jana Seidl* trace the history of ICN due process undertakings in the past two decades, discuss the work of other international organizations and explain how the ICN's CAP grew out of the work of a U.S Department of Justice's Antitrust Division initiative, the Multilateral Framework on Procedures in Competition Law Investigations and Enforcement ("MFP") and the aspirations of the then Deputy AAG Roger Alford to establish a more robust, international, arrangement for due process principles coupled with an accountability mechanism. The authors also reflect on the future of the CAP and practical ways to further enhance its effectiveness.

In their contribution, *Eddy De Smijter* and *Philip Kubik* highlight the unconventional route that the ICN CAP has travelled: the CAP was only presented to the ICN membership, after it had first been adopted by the ICN Steering Group and to adhere to the CAP, ICN members were asked to explicitly and publicly adhere to the new framework. *Eddy De Smijter's* and *Philip Kubik's* comments on the CAP principles – non-discriminatory treatment; transparency of applicable rules; the opportunity to defend oneself; the protection of confidentiality; publication of written decisions and judicial review – are particularly enlightening and insightful as they place the CAP in a wider context and illustrate the enormous significance of this new type of ICN instrument. In that respect, *Leah McCoy* observes that, while the CAP is not legally binding, it reflects actual commitment by its participants and expect that the CAP will result in benefits arising from enhancing international procedural due process norms across the global antitrust community. But above all she characterizes the CAP as a prominent example of the ICN's willingness and ability to adapt and evolve.

5. DIGITALIZATION

One of the key challenges for competition enforcement agencies that has come up during the second decade of the ICN, is the digitalization of the economy that has transformed many traditional markets and has spurred the rise of global and transnational platform-based companies benefitting from direct and indirect network effects. Looking at the catalogue of ICN work products of the past decade, it is not surprising to see that the ICN has started to dedicate considerable efforts and resources on topics related to the digitization of the economy. Indeed, ICN members have reflected on advocacy efforts in digital markets, ways for NCAs to become better equipped to for the digital age, digital evidence gathering in cartel investigations, vertical online restraints and have launched new workstreams focussing on the assessment of significant market power in digital markets.

A number of contributions included in this book specifically discuss competition enforcement in the digital age. First, *Alejandra Palacios* and *Heidi Sada* discuss which questions NCAs are confronted with and how agencies and the ICN seek to respond to those questions. Their concise and insightful analysis presents an interesting snapshot of the status quo at the beginning of the third decade of the ICN. Next, *Kazuyuki Sugimoto,* the former Chairman of the JFTC, revisits the discussions at the 2008 ICN Annual Conference on the abuse of superior bargaining position, a topic that was of particular relevance to Japan and a limited number of other jurisdictions, such as Korea, Taiwan and Germany. However, it is particularly interesting to see that, fourteen years later, that same concept has, perhaps, under different guises, become a key notion in the regulation of digital markets.

Any reader of this book should certainly also take note of the contribution by *Oliver Budzinski,* who discusses the economics of international competition policy and brings up the question which challenges the digitization of the economy for international competition policy and enforcement. His article is both enlightening, sobering and constructive, as it notes the risk of increased externalities and jurisdictional conflicts, increasing costs from multiple procedures and diverging regimes. He also observes that the novel character of business models and anticompetitive strategies in the digital economy may make it hard to lay down best practices how to adequately deal with the concerns associated with the digital economy and concludes that, "while the ICN approach is definitely superior to an uncoordinated approach," enhanced integration of competition policy regimes may be warranted.

6. INCLUSION, DIVERSITY AND LEGITIMACY

As the family of ICN members extends and includes more and more NCAs from younger jurisdictions with different traditions and economic backgrounds, the pressure on the ICN to accommodate the different interests of those NCAs increases. As *Tembi Bonakele* notes, the number of jurisdictions with competition laws in Africa had almost tripled in fifteen years by 2015 to 32 jurisdictions. And *Paulo Burnier da Silveira* observes that in the past decade a number of South African jurisdictions, including Paraguay, Ecuador and Costa Rica have joined the ICN. It is certainly a difficult balancing act for the ICN to simultaneously cater for the needs of the General Authority for Competition in Saudi Arabia, the State Agency for Antimonopoly and Support of Entrepreneurship of Tajikistan, the European Commission, the US Department of Justice and the Korean Fair Trade Commission.

Having said that, even if the debate around legitimacy is unlikely to stop any time soon, the ICN has a tradition of valuing diversity and inclusion. The current ICN Chair, Andreas Mundt, assumed office with an explicit commitment to inclusiveness and the past decade has seen a number of new initiatives aimed at inclusion of younger agencies, such as the Bridging Project, launched in 2020 to establish special partnerships between members of the ICN Steering Group and young and small agencies to help them identify opportunities for greater participation and their involvement in ICN activities; there is now an ICN Vice Chair for Younger Agencies and Regional Diversity; there are Younger Agencies Sessions at Annual Conferences and the ICN has a modest budget to support younger agencies to participate in ICN events.

All this does not necessarily imply that the ICN is doing enough, or even doing the appropriate things. But it does show commitment to ICN members who may benefit from some additional support to become well-integrated in the ICN.

Inclusion, diversity and legitimacy are likely to remain prominent themes in the third decade of the ICN and it is not surprising that a number of contributions to this book discuss these important topics, in particular *Paul O'Brien* c.s., who note the important work of David Lewis, Bill Kovacic, Alejandra Palacios Prieto and Andreas Mundt in this field; *Eleanor Fox*, who expresses concern that practical ways of working may produce under-representation of developing countries; *Alessandra Tonazzi*, who points at the increasing number of new agencies in the leadership of working groups; *Tembi Bonakele*, who makes a plea for managed change to accommodate more NCAs from developing countries in leadership roles; *Margarida Matos Rosa*, who mentions initiatives to translate ICN work products into Portuguese to stimulate engagement of NCAs from Portuguese -speaking jurisdictions and, finally, *Dave Anderson* and *BCLP*, who also suggest a number of practical measures to support implementation of ICN work products. *Yane Svetiev's* discussion of governance models for regulatory networks, in particular the experimentalist regulatory network model may also inform further thinking about the legitimacy of the ICN, a topic that is also discussed by *Siún O'Keeffe*.

Legitimacy and authority of ICN work products and, more generally, the activities of the ICN are strongly correlated with the willingness of others to consider and accept those practices. Of interest in this respect is the observation made by *Huang Yong*, *Nell Lixia Zhou* and *Tang Jinglun* that discussions among ICN members may impact upon China's domestic competition enforcement system.

One aspect not yet touched upon concerns the increasing interaction of the ICN with other international organisations. The relationship between the ICN and the OECD and UNCTAD, eloquently discussed in this publication by *Pierre Horna*, are relatively well documented. Perhaps less well known are the ICN cooperation with the African Competition Forum, the cooperation with the Lusophone Competition Network, the relationship with ASEAN agencies which are not ICN members and the initiative to intensify relationships with Asia-

Pacific jurisdictions. All of these initiatives contribute to the legitimacy of the work of the ICN.

One contribution merits specific attention in this respect. In his contribution, *Eyad Maher M. Dabbah* takes on the topic of regional cooperation in the area of competition enforcement and discusses in vivid detail the developments in the Middle East, the "only region which has not received any serious attention from the global competition law community." He notes that there are strong incentives for involving the ICN in regionalization efforts based on its characteristics and strengths which would qualify the ICN to perform the role of "coordinator" beyond being a network of competition authorities and concludes that this role will be yet another way for the Network to give an imaginative response to a major international challenge in the field of competition law. As an ICN NGA and a competition law practitioner familiar with competition enforcement practices in a number of Middle East jurisdictions, I could not agree more with Maher Dabbah's plea, which not only has a practical dimension, but also touches upon the legitimacy of the ICN.

A CENTURY WITH THE ICN

Maria Coppola, Elizabeth Kraus, Cynthia Lagdameo, Paul O'Brien, and Randolph Tritell*

Twenty years after its founding, the International Competition Network (ICN) is an active, vibrant network of competition law enforcers, practitioners, and academics from around the world. Twenty years ago, the idea of the ICN as a primary driver of international competition dialogue, development, and convergence was not guaranteed. How did it happen? As the ICN enters its third decade, five ICN participants from the US Federal Trade Commission (FTC) – with 100 years of combined ICN participation – offer their perspectives on the keys to the ICN's accomplishments.

The FTC was a founding member of the ICN and has maintained its participation in the network as a top priority for the agency's international program. With the support of successive agency heads and a major resource commitment, the FTC has: helped lead the ICN's strategic thinking as part of the Steering Group; led the Merger, Unilateral Conduct, and Agency Effectiveness Working Groups as well as the ICN's implementation work and its Training on Demand project; led or co-led the development of recommended practices on merger review procedures, merger analysis, the assessment of dominance, and agency investigative process; organized and co-hosted seven ICN workshops and an annual conference; and participated in dozens of projects across the ICN. It is a privilege to work with counterparts from around the world to support international competition convergence and cooperation through the ICN. For this article, the authors bring to bear 100 years of ICN experience to discuss five pillars of the ICN's success:

- inclusive growth
- innovative tools
- commitment to implementation
- growth of content
- development of a voice as global advocate for competition

---

* The authors work together at the US Federal Trade Commission (FTC), Office of International Affairs (OIA). This article represents their views, not necessarily those of the Commission or any Commissioners.

1. THE ICN'S INCLUSIVE GROWTH

Founded a decade after the fall of the Soviet Union, even the most visionary of ICN's creators could not have anticipated the explosive growth of ICN membership. Established in the Fall of 2001 by 15 competition agencies,[1] ICN membership had already grown to 59 members by the ICN's first annual conference in 2002. By 2004, that number had increased by more than half, to 91 members; 98 members by 2006; 109 members by 2010, and so forth. Today, the ICN counts nearly all of the world's competition agencies as members – with 140 members and hundreds of non-governmental experts (referred to as "NGAs") from around the globe.[2]

This expansion in ICN membership reflected an intentional strategy to be inclusive. The ICN, one of the early chairs said, "is open to everyone."[3] Membership requirements are minimal and largely unchanged since the network's creation: "A member of the ICN is a… competition agency entrusted with the enforcement of competition law(s)."[4] This simple criterion, along with the widespread adoption of competition laws around the world, has facilitated the network's exponential growth.

Although a network of government agencies, members work hand-in-hand with a broad array of NGAs, including academics, in-house counsel, private practitioners, economic consultants, consumer groups, and representatives of international organizations. NGAs help identify projects; produce and offer important comments on work product; contribute to the policy dialogue at conferences and workshops; and help disseminate ICN work product and promote its use.[5] As the ICN's first Chair has described, the ICN "greatly changed the role of non-government advisors. It was decided that non-government advisors should have the same role as agencies in the elaboration of work products of the ICN. They would be welcomed and were needed given the all-encompassing nature of competition. This was a marked deviation from other [international] bodies…"[6] In no other government competition

---

1 Press Release, *U.S. and Foreign Antitrust Officials Launch International Competition Network*, 25 October 2001, available at: https://www.ftc.gov/news-events/press-releases/2001/10/us-and-foreign-antitrust-officials-launch-international.

2 A notable exception is the Chinese competition agency, the State Administration for Market Regulation, which has declined to join.

3 Ulf Boge, ICN Chair, Closing Speech, ICN 4th Annual Conference (2005).

4 ICN Operational Framework 2(i) (2001), "A member of the ICN is a national or multinational competition agency entrusted with the enforcement of competition law(s) or a competition agency of a customs territory entrusted with the enforcement of competition law(s) throughout the customs territory." available at: https://www.internationalcompetitionnetwork.org/wp-content/uploads/2018/07/ICNOperationalFramework.pdf.

5 *See* ICN Operational Framework, 6. Non-Governmental Advisors at 6–7, *supra* note 4.

6 Konrad von Finckenstein, former ICN Chair, *Designing the ICN*, Competition Policy International, ICN Column, January 24, 2021.

fora do non-governmental experts play such an integral role. The network's inclusive approach to membership coupled with the active participation of non-governmental advisors from around the world means that the ICN is truly a reflection of the global antitrust community.

ICN leadership also has underscored a commitment to inclusiveness by ensuring that the network responds to the needs of all of its members. Deep engagement of members and NGAs has been a priority of every ICN Steering Group. Early on, to address the challenges of a growing membership, a Vice Chair for outreach was created in 2007, a position held first by South Africa's David Lewis, followed by FTC Chair Bill Kovacic, and later by the President of the Mexican competition agency, Alejandra Palacios Prieto. David Lewis focused on the needs of newer agencies with the purpose of engaging them more fully in the activities of the ICN. He helped the network intensify the presence and degree of participation of young agencies in the activities of the ICN, including the governance structures, the working groups, and the various conferences and workshops.[7] Fifty-two ICN members responded to his outreach questionnaire, and dozens of NGAs participated in the focus groups Lewis led in 2009. Bill Kovacic continued these efforts and expanded the scope of focus to engagement of a broader range of NGAs – both geographically and professional background-wise (academics and consumer groups), and drafted a proposal for the ICN to engage in self-assessment to determine, among other things, how best to ensure that the ICN is responsive to all of its constituents.

The self-assessment exercise expanded into ICN Chair John Fingleton's signature initiative – the ICN's "Second Decade" project. The project is described more in Section 2 below, but as part of the process of formulating the ICN's Second Decade Vision,[8] almost every member of the ICN was interviewed about its views on the ICN's work and future direction. Feedback was solicited from non-governmental advisers, through a questionnaire and discussions via conference call, with over 70 NGAs contributing. The Second Decade project resulted in institutional change to increase member engagement, for example, by expanding the number of leadership positions and requiring working group leaders to rotate in order to open up leadership opportunities to more members.

---

7 New and young agencies have regularly hosted ICN events, such as working group workshops and the ICN's annual conference, bringing an important voice to the organization and content of such events. For example, agencies in Morocco, Botswana, Ukraine, El Salvador, India, Poland, Mauritius, Colombia, Czechia, Panama, Singapore, and Turkey have all hosted ICN events.

8 The ICN's Vision for its Second Decade (2011), available at: https://www.internationalcompetitionnetwork.org/wp-content/uploads/2018/07/ICN2dDecade2011.pdf.

Current ICN Chair, Andreas Mundt, assumed office with a commitment to three "pillars," one of which was inclusiveness.[9] According to Mundt, broad membership has numerous benefits: "Not only does it ensure that the issues dealt with really matter to the competition law community worldwide, but it also gives the ICN the possibility to advocate its vision on the worldwide playing field of multinational enterprises."[10] Mundt reiterated that inclusiveness is not only about agencies, but "is also about the participation of NGAs who provide extremely valuable input."[11]

The network created structures specifically to support engagement, in the Advocacy and Implementation Network, now known as the Promotion & Implementation (P&I) team. The P&I team aims to raise awareness of ICN work product and promote its implementation by engaging members, working groups, and non-governmental advisors to make the ICN the key element of global convergence in competition law. P&I's work is complemented by the activities of a vice chair, introducing new members to the ICN and encouraging the participation of younger agencies across the network.

To underscore commitment to engaging with all of its members, ICN leadership instituted "town hall" sessions, open to all members and NGAs, for discussion and debate; Steering Group chairs instituted regular updates for members and NGAs via a newsletter; and for nearly a decade, the ICN hosted a blog and now posts updates on its website and Twitter to highlight network and member activity. In addition to these communication initiatives aimed at inclusiveness, ICN chairs and vice chairs have targeted specific groups for deeper engagement, for example, by creating projects for and by competition economists, and by developing a "toolkit" of what to expect and how to get involved for new members and NGAs.

Still other parameters, such as project selection, reflect ICN's commitment to inclusiveness. Every working group, and every ICN project, is open to the participation and input of all members. The network's earliest projects addressed advocacy and capacity building and were selected intentionally for their widespread relevance and responsiveness to the needs of younger agencies, in particular. The ICN regularly has used its resources to examine and address the needs of new and younger agencies. For example, in 2006, it produced a report that identifies the type of challenges young agencies experience and the

9 A statement by Andreas Mundt, President of the Bundeskartellamt, ICN Chair (2013), available at https://www.internationalcompetitionnetwork.org/wp-content/uploads/2018/07/ICNSGMundtVision.pdf.

10 Ibid p. 3.

11 Ibid.

measures these agencies have applied to address the challenges.[12] In 2019, the ICN revisited the topic, with an update to the 2006 report.[13] The ICN's Training on Demand online compilation of training videos also includes a module on competition policy in developing countries.[14]

The ICN has continued its commitment to diversity by addressing a wide portfolio of work: investigative fundamentals and more sophisticated enforcement subjects across the Merger, Cartel, and Unilateral Conduct Working Groups, and a host of operational and institutional matters in the Agency Effectiveness Working Group. In addition, conference hosts and the Steering Group regularly take on special projects to address particular interests such as competition policy in an economic downturn, competition law and policy in small economies, competition issues involving state-owned enterprises, and abuse of superior bargaining position.

Through these concerted efforts that touch on every aspect of the network, today the ICN has mainstreamed the participation of its younger agencies – a reflection of the additional experience gained by the agencies once considered "younger," but equally proof of ICN's integration of members large and small, old and young. The network's approach to membership, participation, leadership roles, work product, and communication has created an actively inclusive body.

2. ICN INNOVATIONS LEADING TO CONVERGENCE AND A COMMUNITY OF COMMON CAUSE

As described in these volumes and elsewhere, the ICN was launched to provide antitrust agencies from developed and developing countries with a more focused network for addressing practical antitrust enforcement and policy issues of common concern.[15] From its inception, the ICN had the lofty goals of facilitating procedural and substantive convergence and cooperation in antitrust policy and enforcement, as a virtual, soft-law network involving the full range

12 ICN Report, Lessons to be Learnt from the Experiences of Younger Competition Agencies (2006) available at: https://www.internationalcompetitionnetwork.org/portfolio/lessons-learned-from-the-experience-of-young-competition-agencies/.

13 ICN Report, Lessons to be Learnt from the Experiences of Younger Competition Agencies, An Update to the 2006 Report (2019) available at: https://www.internationalcompetitionnetwork.org/wp-content/uploads/2019/06/SGVC_YoungerAgenciesReport2019.pdf.

14 ICN Training on Demand, Developing Countries and Competition, available at: https://www.internationalcompetitionnetwork.org/training/developing-countries-and-competition/.

15 *See* for example, https://www.internationalcompetitionnetwork.org/about/; Paul Lugard (ed.): The international competition network at ten. Origins, accomplishments and aspirations (2011); and essays in this volume.

of competition community participants. Its combination of innovative elements related to institutional design, informal, inclusive working methods, and bottom-up approaches to project selection and development has not only helped the ICN to achieve these goals but has also resulted in this virtual network incubating a deeper competition community. ICN's former Chair Sheridan Scott pointed to "the development of a real international culture of antitrust" as a "hugely positive achievement" of the ICN's early years. She explained, "We have all gotten to know each other much better and that allows us to develop the trust you need to do really effective cross-border enforcement."[16]

2.1. INNOVATIVE INSTITUTIONAL DESIGN

Through both foresight and necessity, ICN was founded as a virtual, specialized network based on inclusiveness and consensus. It was conceived as the only international forum dedicated exclusively to competition policy and law. With membership open to all competition agencies – not only those of like mind and experience – working hand-in-hand with non-governmental advisors, private sector experts, interested academics and experts from multilateral organizations engaged in the field, the ICN has proved unique in its capacity to engage all relevant actors on all issues of competition law and policy. Moreover, its novel, virtual nature has prompted ICN members and project participants to engage more directly and frequently with one another in comparison to other international fora that rely on permanent secretariats and established infrastructures.[17] The network's virtual nature also has allowed ICN to adjust its organization flexibly around projects of interest to its participants, over time. Finally, though it lacks rule making functions, the ICN's consensus-based, soft-law approach to developing understanding and convergence has, in fact, complemented and enhanced these attributes to prove one of its strongest features. There is an inextricable link between the ICN's non-binding nature and the scope, content, and value of its work. To achieve consensus, ICN actors engage with one another to understand similarities and differences in approaches in an effort to build common understanding as to the best approaches to competition policy and enforcement issues.[18] This process helps to promote dialogue and the

16 Global Competition Review, *An Interview with Sheridan Scott*, 1 July 2008.

17 For example, the OECD's Competition Committee and related Working Parties, the U.N. Conference on Trade and Development International Group of Experts on Competition Law and Policy. Recognizing the benefits of direct member engagement, the permanent secretariats of these groups also have developed new working approaches for selected projects that promote direct engagement of small groups of interested agencies between meetings.

18 For an excellent assessment of ICN's consensus process and how it has helped to promote convergence, *see* Hugh M. Hollman and William E. Kovacic, *The International Competition Network: Its Past, Current and Future Role*, Minnesota Journal of International Law, Vol. 20, p. 274, 2011.

exchange of experience and learning among all ICN participants. Thus, even before identifying certain approaches as best practice, the consensus process serves to disseminate know-how and experience, providing valuable learning and support to newer agencies.

As described by former ICN Chair David Lewis, at its foundation, the ICN's soft-law approach is founded on persuasion through shared experience rather than coercion.[19] ICN members are free to use and implement its work product within their own legal contexts as they see fit. The lack of binding implementation obligations has a beneficial by-product in terms of work product development. Discussions can focus on the identification of optimal practices without defensiveness from participating members about their non-compliance. Without the threat of binding rule-making authority, members have been open to and accepting of aspirational, forward-looking best practice approaches that may not reflect their own practices.

2.2. INNOVATIVE WORKING METHODS

The ICN established its working methods around these institutional features, providing for flexibility in developing demand-driven projects. Members select projects and produce work product in conjunction with interested NGAs, which helps to ensure that the ICN's work is relevant to all. This has resulted in a long history of work product focused on issues of practical import to the community.[20] While the ICN is guided by a Steering Group composed of representatives of ICN member agencies, its work is developed from the bottom up, in project-oriented Working Groups, currently addressing Advocacy, Agency Effectiveness, Cartels, Mergers, and Unilateral Conduct.[21] Participation in individual projects and working groups is purely voluntary, yet a broad swath of agencies and the NGA community actively engage in the ICN's work. They rely on informal and flexible communications and working methods, focused on e-mails, calls and videoconferences to do so, which allow for timely, frequent, direct discussion. In this way, the scheduling of in-person meetings does not dictate the pace of the group's work, as it has in other international fora. Yet the working groups also benefit from face-to-face meetings, at the ICN's annual conference, at workshops, and on the margins of other international meetings.

---

19 David Lewis, ICN Chair, Introductory Address to 2009 ICN Conference, June 3, 2009 at 5, available at: https://www.internationalcompetitionnetwork.org/wp-content/uploads/2020/01/SpeechChairIntroLewis2009.pdf.

20 *See* current compendium of ICN work product, ICN Work Product Catalog available at: https://www.internationalcompetitionnetwork.org/portfolio/work-product-catalog.

21 *See* https://www.internationalcompetitionnetwork.org/working-groups/ for further information on the ICN's working groups.

The ICN's work product is strengthened by the diversity of views that underlie its creation. Broad-based project participation ensures that the work reflects sound approaches applicable across various legal traditions and experience levels. This further reinforces the relevance of ICN work product, promoting support by newer and more mature agencies as well as the NGA community, and thus providing ready advocates for the adoption and implementation of such work product.[22]

Importantly, working together toward a common goal fosters close relationships and trust among different actors within the community. This has the benefit of not only creating communities of interest related to working group topics, but also of fostering the development of related communities, for example, cartel enforcers or economists focused on antitrust, within the ICN's network. One could think of these sub-communities as overlapping constellations of experts within the broader ICN orbit. As they have developed, so too has the value of the overall network. Moreover, as these communities grow, and relations of trust develop within the network over time, the ICN has been able to move from its initial projects, sometimes deemed low hanging fruit, to tackling more intractable issues, including unilateral conduct concerns and procedural fairness,[23] and addressing some of the most challenging competition issues of our day, including competition challenges posed by the digital economy.

The personal, health, work safety, and economic consequences of the COVID-19 pandemic posed significant challenges to the working methods of the ICN. The ICN's virtual nature allowed its work to continue and provided an opportunity for the network to reinforce and support the operations of its member agencies. The ICN initiated a network-wide effort to share real-time information and experiences with operational, procedural, and policy changes instituted by competition agencies to address the crisis. This initiative to address urgent member needs is consistent with the ICN's role as a forum to collect and exchange ideas, experiences, and best practices. The pandemic also forced the cancellation of the planned in-person 2020 ICN annual conference. As conference co-hosts, the U.S. antitrust agencies led the overall planning and its transition to a

22 Agencies and individuals unable to participate in the ICN's day-to-day work still benefit from ICN work product, which is available free-of-charge, on the ICN's website, and the network, including discussion of work product and issues with experts from around the world either remotely or via participation in the ICN's annual conference.

23 *See* Cynthia Lewis Lagdameo, *Climbing Mount Everest with the ICN Unilateral Conduct Working Group*, Competition Policy International, November 2012, available at: https://www.competitionpolicyinternational.com/assets/Uploads/ICN-11-27-2012-3.pdf; and Paul O'Brien, *Procedural Fairness: Convergence in Process*, Competition Policy International Antitrust Chronicle, November 2018, available at: https://www.ftc.gov/system/files/attachments/key-speeches-presentations/obrien_-_procedural_fairness_convergence_in_process_cpi_11-18.pdf.

virtual format.[24] Nearly 3,000 attendees tuned in to the programming, the largest audience in ICN history, confirming the reach of the ICN and the interest in its work. The ICN has bolstered its experience and capabilities to organize worldwide virtual events, and the 2021 annual conference, hosted by the Hungarian competition authority, was also held virtually. During 2021, the ICN organized its most comprehensive online training event ever, a multi-day virtual workshop for officials from over 60 jurisdictions, using several lines of existing ICN work product targeted to investigative techniques, with live presentations and small group discussions. The ICN continued to promote collaboration within the network on responses to the pandemic and its economic consequences, tailoring its work to address relevant topics such as crisis cartels, horizontal cooperation, agency operational challenges during the pandemic, merger review during the pandemic, and competition advocacy in times of crisis.[25] The network experienced a significant uptick in online seminar participation, and has given more attention to archiving such information for review convenience as well as planning for hybrid in-person/virtual events in the future to increase the reach of its events.

2.3. INNOVATIVE OUTPUTS

Intimately linked to the innovations of its design and working methods are the ICN's outputs. ICN work product generally serves to accomplish one or more functions: promoting transparency and understanding of agency approaches and transference of skills; assessing comparative approaches; and developing and promoting consensus norms and approaches. ICN projects focus on disseminating learning, experience and best practice, and are intended to support the network's overall goals of facilitating procedural and substantive convergence and cooperation in antitrust policy and enforcement. They not only promote the adoption of the ICN's preferred norms and approaches, but also help to support the ICN's less experienced agencies to mature quickly and leapfrog over the failures of others.

The work product developed has been as innovative as the ICN's structure and working methods. Working groups were not and continue not to be limited by prescribed forms of or approach in developing work product. Instead, they consider the most useful format to reach the project's desired goal, from developing online templates to make information on each of the ICN member agency's

24 ICN 2020 Annual Conference materials, available at: https://www.internationalcompetitionnetwork.org/2020vac/.

25 See, for example seminar materials at https://www.internationalcompetitionnetwork.org/news-events/cwg-march-2021/ and https://www.internationalcompetitionnetwork.org/news-events/awg-january-2021/.

policies and practices available and transparent, to creating self-assessment tools for use by agencies. Work product may be written, or presented in other manners, including through interactive, hands-on workshops or web-based seminars. Notably, the ICN has even developed a comprehensive curriculum of training materials, available as video modules and available online, which serves as a virtual university on competition law and practice for competition agency officials and those interested in competition law and policy.[26] The range and evolution of the ICN's project selection and work product is discussed below in Section 4.

We focus here on the innovation of these approaches, recognizing that for each format, the ICN essentially started with a blank slate. For example, consider the ICN's most high-profile work, its Recommended Practices. While ICN recognized the importance of facilitating convergence toward best practice from its earliest stages, the concept of an ICN Recommended Practice did not exist until created by the members and NGAs of the Merger Working Group's Notification and Procedures subgroup. This group determined that they needed not only to identify best practices on the subject, but also had to present the agreed best practices in a manner in which the practices could be best understood and implemented by the ICN's membership. The tool had to be user friendly and applicable across legal traditions. The group determined that the recitation of non-binding, black-letter statements of consensus best practice, followed by explanatory comments would best serve these requirements, and allow for updating and expansion as appropriate. The format proved so successful that it has served as the template for all following ICN Recommended Practices.

Of course, the ICN will not be judged a success based merely on its innovations or the amount of work that it produces. Yet through its innovative design, working methods and work product, the ICN has already brought the broader competition community together and instilled a common purpose. Its success has and will continue to be assessed based on the impact that it has on international competition law and enforcement, and whether it, in fact, meets its goals of facilitating procedural and substantive convergence and cooperation in antitrust policy and enforcement. The implementation of its work is a considerable factor in this assessment.

3. THE ICN'S COMMITMENT TO IMPLEMENTATION

The ICN was set up by its members to be "a project-oriented, consensus-based, informal network of antitrust agencies"[27] that explicitly does not exercise any

---

26 *See* ICN Training on Demand Project, available at: https://www.internationalcompetitionnetwork.org/training/.

27 ICN Operational Framework 1(i), *supra* note 4.

rule-making function. Its "activities take place on a voluntary basis and rely on a high level of goodwill and cooperation among members."[28] The ICN's projected-oriented status plays out in defined working groups, focused on specific areas of competition law and policy, i.e., mergers, cartels, advocacy, unilateral conduct, and agency operations. Working groups are open to all ICN members and non-governmental advisors, and project selection is pursued via open discussion within working groups each year.

The sixth and final clause of the ICN's Mission and Activities provisions in its Operational Framework raises the central challenge of the network: "Where the ICN reaches consensus on recommendations arising from a project, *it is left to its members to decide whether and how to implement the recommendations...*"[29] This is the only mention of implementation in the ICN's founding framework, and it acknowledges the soft spot of a soft law network: there is no commitment, no obligation to follow ICN recommendations. Nonetheless, what the ICN has done to address implementation has been vital to its success. This provision could have been the first and final word on the implementation of ICN work. The network could have chosen to stand down and leave members alone to consider, interpret, and use ICN work. Instead, the ICN chose to actively support and inform member decisions on whether and how to implement ICN recommendations. The network made the challenge of implementation integral to how the ICN operates – from work planning and work product format choices to a variety of other activities such as workshops and seminars. Accepting this challenge has been a crucial factor of the ICN's success.

3.1. THE CHALLENGE OF MEASUREMENT

The aspirational nature of the ICN's work makes measuring implementation difficult. Former ICN Chair David Lewis argued that ICN's "range of activities" and work "do not easily lend themselves to textual consensuses and harmonized implementation."[30] He explained that the development of soft law "is rooted in consensus, rather than majority; in persuasion through shared experience, rather than coercion; in understanding and celebrating differences, rather than suppressing them."[31] This led him to conclude that the ICN should not judge itself by the "norms and standards" of organizations that devise binding rules. Rather, the ICN should judge itself by "a more qualitative and nuanced set of norms: are we developing a deeper understanding of each other's key drivers and practices? Are we providing a framework where the better resourced and more

---

28 Ibid at 1(iii) Mission and Activities.
29 Ibid at 1(vi)(emphasis added).
30 David Lewis, *supra* note 19 at 2.
31 Ibid.

experienced agencies are able to transmit the learnings from their successes and failures to the newer agencies? Are we providing room for the full participation and voice of these newer agencies? Is the ICN a voice for competition on the international stage and in the various national policy debates?"[32]

When the ICN has undertaken the resource-intensive task of tracking the use of its work, the results point to a good deal of influence and success. The ICN's 2010–11 Second Decade review included interviews with most ICN members. The report stated that, "Over the past decade, ICN work products have influenced agency practice of many ICN members and have also influenced legal and policy reforms in many ICN member jurisdictions. For example, 39 ICN members have reported using the Anti-Cartel Enforcement Manual to advance their cartel enforcement programmes. Two-thirds of ICN members that made changes to their merger control regimes cited the ICN Recommended Practices for Merger Notification and Review Procedures as having influenced their reforms. More than a dozen agencies have reported using the ICN's Recommended Practices on Dominance / Substantial Market Power Analysis Under Unilateral Conduct Laws in their casework or staff training."[33] A 2010 Merger Working Group assessment of the use of its work reported that "over 90% of responding agencies indicated that they used MWG work product – dozens reported the use of MWG RPs contributing to change in their merger regimes."[34]

The nature and volume of ICN work has become so vast and varied that real-time, hard statistics on implementation are not available. What is known about use of ICN work tends to be anecdotal – stories and experiences shared by members within the network. Undoubtedly there is a vast amount of ICN work product implementation and influence that is not known – for instance, day-to-day staff investigative choices and practices informed by participation at a workshop, viewing of an ICN online training video, or review of a good practices manual on specific enforcement areas. The ICN encourages members to share these stories, but the reach and impact of ICN work is beyond efficient and easy measure.

3.2. IMPLEMENTATION TAKES ROOT

The ICN's first years focused on creating work product on topics of vital importance. Its first two projects addressed divergence in merger notification rules and competition advocacy basics. Other early work addressed capacity

32 Ibid.

33 ICN's Vision for its Second Decade, *supra* note 8 at 2.

34 ICN Statement of Achievements (2001-2013) at 14–15.

building for new and younger agencies, merger analysis guidelines, and the building blocks of cartel enforcement. No sooner did the working groups accomplish creative new output than questions arose about how to ensure its influence. ICN working groups very quickly realized they were not just in the business of creating work product, but also nurturing, promoting, and advocating for its use.

ICN working groups have been integral to promotion and use of ICN work product. Over the years, ICN working groups have explored creative ways to raise awareness about existing ICN work and encourage its implementation. By nature of its status as drafter of ICN's first recommendations, the Merger Working Group became a pioneer in implementation efforts. After the group completed a groundbreaking set of Recommended Practices for Merger Notification and Review Procedures,[35] it turned to members' experiences with implementation. In 2005, the working group published a report on Implementation of the Recommended Practices for Merger Notification and Review Procedures,[36] identifying implementation challenges and how members addressed them, and in 2006, it compiled examples of conforming language from competition laws and regulations around the globe.[37] The group later introduced a new type of work product developed solely to encourage implementation – the self-assessment tool – that allows agency members to benchmark their own practices against ICN recommendations.[38] Today, working groups routinely promote their work though network teleseminars and workshop sessions based around ICN recommendations and good practices. Annual conferences include sessions that highlight members' stories of using ICN work to inform new laws or agency practices. The ICN newsletter and "town hall" conference calls have been used to promote awareness of ICN work. The ICN's "Training on Demand" set of online videos with agency and academic presenters reinforce existing ICN work in a novel, accessible format.[39]

The ICN also offers formal advice to members when they seek external support for reforms. Former ICN Chair Eduardo Perez Motta called for the ICN to take

35 ICN Merger Notification and Review Procedures (2002–2018), available at https://www.internationalcompetitionnetwork.org/portfolio/merger-np-recommended-practices. The project and group that produced the ICN's N&P recommendations were led by the FTC.

36 ICN Report on Implementation of the Recommended Practices for Merger Notification and Review Procedures (2005) available at https://www.internationalcompetitionnetwork.org/portfolio/implementation-of-the-merger-notification-and-review-procedures-rps.

37 ICN Merger Notification Implementation Handbook (2006), available at https://www.internationalcompetitionnetwork.org/wp-content/uploads/2018/05/MWG_NPImplementationHB.pdf.

38 ICN Merger Notification and Procedures Self-Assessment Tool (2011) and ICN Merger Analysis Self-Assessment Tool (2019).

39 ICN Training on Demand, *supra* note 26.

a "more active role when asked by members for assistance on specific policy initiatives."[40] Over the years, the Steering Group and working groups have authored several letters explaining and promoting ICN recommendations to agency members who have requested advice. There also are many more instances of working groups assisting members by identifying relevant ICN work recommendations for consideration to benchmark internal practices. As Perez Motta explained, "[o]ne should not underestimate the potential influence of 123 agencies speaking with one voice to support one of their own, on the basis of well-founded and time-tested best practices."[41]

3.3. INSTITUTIONALIZING IMPLEMENTATION

The ICN has made institutional decisions to strengthen its advocacy for implementation. In its Second Decade project, the ICN institutionalized its view on the importance of encouraging implementation. In 2012, when the ICN revised its mission statement on the occasion of its tenth anniversary, it embraced the challenge of implementation as part of its top line goal, beginning, "[t]he ICN's mission is to *advocate the adoption* of superior standards and procedures in competition policy around the world…"[42] Taking on this role as an advocate, the ICN confirms that it is not enough to identify, articulate, or create standards, but essential to see them through to implementation. In the words of former ICN Chair John Fingleton, the ICN's work "has to translate into real outcomes."[43] The Second Decade report's long-term vision for the ICN also identified four high level goals for the ICN, including to "encourage the dissemination of competition experience and best practice."[44]

Current ICN Chair Andreas Mundt has maintained the network's emphasis on the value of implementation efforts. His vision statement for the ICN cites implementation as one of three "key factors" to ICN success, emphasizing that if the ICN wants "to ensure that the ICN and its work products matter, we need to make our high-quality products available to everyone and continue our efforts to promote their implementation."[45] The ICN also has tailored its work

40 Eduardo Pérez Motta, ICN Chair, Closing Remarks for the International Competition Network's Eleventh Annual Conference (20 April 2012) at 4, available at: https://www.internationalcompetitionnetwork.org/wp-content/uploads/2020/01/SpeechChairMottaclosing2012.pdf.

41 Ibid.

42 The ICN's Vision for its Second Decade, *supra* note 8 at 4–5.

43 John Fingleton, ICN Chair, The ICN's Vision for its Second Decade, Speech (18 May 2011) at 5, available at: https://www.internationalcompetitionnetwork.org/wp-content/uploads/2020/01/SpeechChairFingleton2011.pdf.

44 The ICN's Vision for its Second Decade, *supra* note 8 at 5.

45 Andreas Mundt, *supra* note 9 at 4.

planning process to emphasize promotion and implementation efforts. Each year, ICN working groups discuss and propose annual and three-year work plans. A network-wide review of the proposals by the Steering Group encourages a category of implementation work that promotes and highlights existing work product.

The single biggest act of institutionalizing the ICN's commitment to encouraging use and implementation of its work came with the establishment of a group dedicated to implementation. The ICN established an "Advocacy and Implementation Network" (AIN), later renamed the Promotion and Implementation (P&I) team. The P&I team is made up of working group chairs and other interested members. It coordinates network-wide implementation initiatives, serving as the first stop for questions from members about existing ICN work and its application. P&I encourages ICN member implementation stories to help inspire members with ideas from their peers about how to use ICN work. It also coordinates ICN advice to members that are contemplating changes to laws, rules, or practices that may be informed by ICN recommendations or other work.

3.4. IMPLEMENTATION SUCCESS IN A NON-BINDING CONTEXT

How has a non-binding network that eschews any obligation to implement its recommendations succeeded in having its recommendations adopted? There are three key aspects of the ICN and its operations that serve to support and promote implementation in the ICN's non-binding context.

First, do not overlook the power of the ICN's working process, as described above in Section 2. ICN work product is developed by a broad range of its membership and non-governmental experts working in dedicated working groups. Its consensus is built on a foundation of best practices, common approaches, and perspectives of member agencies and experts from around the world from a variety of institutional and legal settings. This well-informed input allows members to benchmark their own practices against the best that the competition community has to offer – the direct experiences of similarly situated agencies that share similar needs and missions. ICN work is created for the competition community, by the competition community. Producing work with widespread relevance from sources tested by experience amounts to a very powerful starting point for implementation: by nature of its consensus development and quality content, the work itself is compelling, and worthy of consideration and implementation.

Second, the active commitment of the ICN and its members to promoting ICN work has bolstered interest and implementation. The approach behind the ICN's work is to make best practices accessible to all competition agencies. The many agencies and experts that actively participate in developing ICN work are invested in its success. They realize that a work product has a potential lifespan and utility that far outreaches the time and resources to develop it. They introduce existing work to new ICN members and new staff that become involved in the ICN across its membership. The success of ICN work is linked to its use and implementation, and working groups understand that.

Third, the ICN's success with encouraging implementation can be attributed to the creativity with which it has pursued member implementation. The ICN has a long, innovative history of finding ways to promote and support member decisions on "whether and how to implement" ICN recommendations, as mentioned earlier. As a voluntary, non-binding, non-rule making network, the ICN lacks the proverbial stick or enforcement mechanism. It can only offer carrots. However, the ICN has embraced this spirit with a variety of tools and formats that support and encourage member implementation – offering carrots, broccoli, apples, spinach, berries, pears, and peppers; a virtual cornucopia of healthy recommendations and advice for member agencies to consider.

3.5. FUTURE OF IMPLEMENTATION

The ICN remains a non-binding, virtual, and voluntary network with no impetus to change the nature of the network's soft law convergence mission. Still, the ICN's efforts to encourage agencies to implement its work should not be dismissed as an afterthought. ICN Chair Mundt's vision for the network links the ICN's commitment to implementation and its overall influence by emphasizing the "great importance for the ICN in the future to raise awareness for its work products, promote them and ensure that they are implemented into legislation and everyday work, making the ICN the key element of global convergence in competition law."[46] Implementation efforts in the ICN have evolved and likely will continue to influence global convergence in at least two ways.

First, a review of the ICN's history reveals innovative steps in its implementation efforts, from institutional efforts, work planning and formats, and promotion by working groups. There may be internal innovations in development yet to come.

46 Ibid at 2.

For example, the ICN has developed a novel addition to the ICN work product family: opt-in frameworks. The ICN has promulgated three such frameworks, one on merger enforcement cooperation, one on cartel enforcement cooperation, and one covering procedural fairness principles for competition agency procedures.[47] The idea of these frameworks is to complement the ICN's typical consensus building work but allow participants to affirm additional principles. These ICN frameworks are a creative, evolutionary step in the ICN's approach to the implementation of its work. This is not a move to hard commitments. However, the frameworks have their own built-in implementation tools, permitting additional cooperation and engagement among agencies with the potential to help boost convergence. These frameworks demonstrate the ICN's willingness to expand its toolbox for implementation, allowing for additional opt-in commitments for and among willing agencies on specific topics.

Second, ICN work and consensus building influences the development of norms elsewhere. For instance, the Organization for Economic Co-operation and Development's (OECD's) merger review recommendation[48] took inspiration from ICN recommendations. Likewise, the OECD developed a recommendation on procedural fairness that borrows from ICN consensus principles.[49] Organizations such as Asia-Pacific Economic (APEC) have used or referenced ICN work in their programs and training. Given its development by competition experts, ICN work is likely to continue to influence norm creation in more binding settings, providing a ready-made resource on the competition community's best thinking.

One of the key pillars of the ICN's success has been its insistence that implementation is not an afterthought. The ICN's non-binding nature could have excused the ICN from the hard work of promoting real world impact, but ICN members and leadership have accepted and maintained the challenge to craft compelling, relevant work and promote its use. This has breathed life into the ICN's mission and influence. The ICN's history of prioritizing implementation efforts and its robust and creative practices of encouraging such efforts suggest that the ICN's next twenty years will be filled with many examples, anecdotes, and stories of how the network drives convergence.

---

47 The three ICN Frameworks: for Merger Review Cooperation (2012), for Promotion of Sharing Non-Confidential Information for Cartel Enforcement (2016), and for Competition Agency Procedures (2019), are available at https://www.internationalcompetitionnetwork.org/frameworks/.

48 Recommendation of the OECD Council on Merger Review (2005), available at https://www.oecd.org/daf/competition/mergers/40537528.pdf.

49 OECD, Recommendation of the Council on Transparency and Procedural Fairness in Competition Law Enforcement (2021), available at: https://www.internationalcompetitionnetwork.org/portfolio/work-product-catalog/.

4. THE EVOLUTION OF ICN WORK PRODUCT

Work product is central to the ICN's mission and success. It is the focal point for ICN participation and how the ICN as a virtual network addresses the practical needs of its member agencies. Three general trends characterize the ICN's work topics, types, and formats over its first twenty years: 1) growth from a focus on enforcement fundamentals to incorporating a full-fledged range of topics, 2) organization around a loose hierarchy of types of work, and 3) a creative expansion in terms of the formats used.

4.1. TREND 1: FROM FUNDAMENTALS TO FULL RANGE

In the beginning, the ICN's first two projects addressed the basics of competition advocacy and merger notification rules. These topics were identified for different purposes, both vital to the ICN's mission and success. The first identified and articulated the underpinnings of competition law and policy that are relevant to all agencies: the benefits of competition. The second project had a different purpose: target divergence, compare approaches, and draft consensus recommendations. These projects demonstrated the ability both to reinforce foundational needs shared by all competition agencies and to promote new convergence of specific agency approaches via practical recommendations. From the very beginning, the ICN would walk and chew gum at the same time.

With a growing familiarity with and confidence in its working methods – and the expansion in the number of members – the ICN's annual slate of projects also grew. Within its first five years, the initial Merger and Advocacy Working Groups were joined by working groups on Cartels, Unilateral Conduct, and a work stream focused on agency operations that went through several naming iterations from "Capacity Building" to "Competition Policy Implementation" to today's "Agency Effectiveness" Working Group. Today, a typical working group annual plan includes two or three written projects (a mix of new work and regular revisions to existing work), several seminar topics (often in a themed series), a workshop, and implementation-related efforts to raise awareness of existing work. In total, ICN working groups tackle some 20–25 distinct projects each year.

The topics that the ICN addresses have expanded to match the full range of issues that its member competition agencies address. The ICN's early focus on perceived pressing problems, issues of wide applicability, and the fundamentals of enforcement led to work on topics such as: merger guidelines; the building blocks of anti-cartel enforcement; the objectives of unilateral conduct enforcement; case selection; and investigative techniques. Building upon these initial, often broad-based projects, working groups developed work product on more tailored, related topics such as: advocacy before various stakeholders such as legislatures, business, and the public; market studies; obstruction of justice; various types of single firm conduct; leniency programs; merger notification forms and filing fees; agency ethics rules; remedies and settlements in mergers and cartels; private enforcement; and agency use of social media.[50]

One vehicle for the introduction of new topics is the ability of annual conference hosts to lead a special project or showcase topic. Past conference projects have focused on telecom law and the interaction with telecom regulators, enforcement in small economies, the nature and meaning of consumer welfare, agency interaction with judges, state-owned enterprises, disruptive innovation, online vertical restraints, and environmental sustainability. The ICN has also expanded its work product into important cross-cutting topics that are not easily captured in individual working groups. A seminal example occurred in 2011, with a Steering Group decision to initiate two large-scale projects outside of the working group annual plans: one on enforcement cooperation and one on procedural fairness in competition agency procedures. While each topic was relevant to various working groups, there was a value to projects that could draw experience from multiple competition enforcement and policy areas. Both projects led to significant ICN work product and standalone workshops.[51]

It is important to note that the ICN has not forgotten work on the fundamentals of competition law enforcement and policy. Many of the seminal work products that address the basics of investigation, enforcement, and agency approaches are regularly revisited and updated as needed.

For example, the two sets of ICN Recommended Practices on merger notification rules and on merger analysis have been updated since their creation and many of the ICN Anti-cartel Enforcement Manual chapters have been renewed over its decade-plus lifespan.

---

50 For the best overview of all of the ICN's work product, see the ICN Work Product Catalog, available on the ICN's homepage and regularly updated, *supra* note 20.

51 *See* the OECD/ICN Questionnaire and Report on International Enforcement Cooperation (2013) available at: https://www.internationalcompetitionnetwork.org/working-groups/icn-operations/cooperation/ and Report on 2011 ICN Roundtable on Enforcement Cooperation (Washington DC, 2011) available at: https://www.internationalcompetitionnetwork.org/portfolio/report-on-2011-cooperation-roundtable/; ICN Recommended Practices for Investigative Process (2019) available at: https://www.internationalcompetitionnetwork.org/portfolio/recommended-practices-for-investigative-process/; and Report on ICN Roundtable on Competition Agency Investigative Process (Washington DC, 2014) available at: https://www.internationalcompetitionnetwork.org/wp-content/uploads/2018/09/AEWG_RoundtableReportInvestigativeProcess.pdf.

Over time, in addition to work on shared goals and specific convergence on established enforcement frameworks and approaches, a third strand of work developed: exploring new, developing, and unresolved topics in various formats. Part of effective enforcement is addressing challenges presented by new issues, markets, and theories. Member agencies have brought these challenges to a shared dialogue within the ICN. The discussion of "hot topics" is a purposeful decision by the ICN to facilitate experience sharing and take part in shaping the global competition law dialogue. Examples of this "ICN 2.0" line of topics have included disruptive innovation, competition advocacy in an economic downturn, online vertical restraints, public interest standards and industrial policy, and implications of the digital economy for competition enforcement and policy. These types of topics often are recognized as not ripe for consensus recommendations, but the ICN has valued member discussion and exchange on new developments. Competition agencies created the ICN as their own forum and have increasingly used it to address topical policy issues alongside more traditional work on enforcement fundamentals. The evolution of content is a shining example of how the ICN reflects the needs of its members and chooses meaningful priorities for its work. Today's ICN work program is every bit as vibrant and varied as its member agencies and the full range of issues they face.

4.2. TREND 2: A FOCUS ON PURPOSE

The second trend in ICN work product involves the type of work, or its purpose and intended audience, often reflected in titles such as recommended practices or practical guide. Early ICN work product carried an assortment of titles, including recommended practices, best practices, suggested best practices, good practices, workbooks, handbooks, manuals, booklets, frameworks, toolkits, reports, findings, models, practical guides, guiding principles, and lessons learned. While the titles of ICN work product still evidence this creativity, working groups have settled around three general categories of written work, with different purposes.

"Recommended Practices" or RPs are the ICN's "gold standard" for network approved consensus recommendations, intended as a resource to benchmark agency rules and practices and a driver of convergence. The ICN's RPs include:[52]

- Recommended Practices for Merger Analysis (2002–2017) addressing common legal framework and merger guidelines factors.

[52] *See* list of, and links to, ICN Recommended Practices available at: https://www.internationalcompetitionnetwork.org/working-groups/icn-operations/icn-recs/.

- Recommended Practices for Merger Notification & Review Procedures (2002–2017) addressing notification principles such as nexus between the merger's effects and the reviewing jurisdiction and appropriate criteria for notification thresholds as well as procedural principles such as procedural fairness, transparency, and confidentiality.
- Recommended Practices for Dominance/Substantial Market Power Analysis (2008) addressing the framework and criteria for assessing dominance/ substantial market power.
- ICN Recommended Practices for Investigative Process (2019) promoting fair and informed enforcement through principles of transparency, engagement, internal safeguards, and the protection of confidential information.

Next, working groups developed a category of work that includes "good practices" and other practical work product (often with titles such as guides, manuals, or workbooks) that often are more focused on day-to-day investigative practices. These guides are reference tools for agency staff to enable them to evaluate and compare their own approaches. They detail practices that work well for some, or even many, members but may not be readily applicable for all. More is written in the annals of ICN's work product for the front-line investigator than any other audience. Examples include:

- The Anti-Cartel Enforcement Manual is a compilation of practical discussions, tips, and techniques employed at various stages of enforcement, identifying approaches that have proven effective and successful.[53]
- The Investigative Techniques Handbook for Merger Review describes the tools and techniques used in merger review, such as how to plan a merger investigation, developing reliable evidence in merger cases, economic and econometric analyses, and the benefits of sound economics and including economists in merger review.[54]
- The Unilateral Conduct Workbook explores techniques and approaches to various aspects of unilateral conduct enforcement, covering the analytic framework, assessing market power, and approaches to analyzing specific type of conduct.[55]
- The Agency Effectiveness Competition Agency Practice Manual identifies key elements of a well-functioning competition agency and provides best practices for agency strategy, planning, implementation, and operations.[56]

---

53 ICN Anti-Cartel Enforcement Manual (2008–2019) available at https://www.internationalcompetitionnetwork.org/working-groups/cartel/investigation-enforcement/.

54 ICN Investigative Techniques Handbook for Merger Review (2005) available at https://www.internationalcompetitionnetwork.org/wp-content/uploads/2018/05/MWG_HBInvestigativeTechniques.pdf.

55 ICN Unilateral Conduct Workbook (2011–2017) available at https://www.internationalcompetitionnetwork.org/working-groups/unilateral-conduct/investigation-analysis/.

56 ICN Competition Agency Practice Manual (2010–2017) available at https://www.internationalcompetitionnetwork.org/working-groups/agency-effectiveness/agency-operations/.

Finally, a majority of ICN work makes up a category of informative or comparative reports – often the first line of work when the ICN explores a new topic. These reports often articulate different approaches in different jurisdictions but do not present a consensus recommendation. Examples (just a few) include reports on the objectives of unilateral conduct laws, merger remedies, market studies, competition advocacy, vertical mergers, cartel settlements, merger filing fees, obstruction of justice, and waivers of confidentiality in merger investigations.[57]

One of the reasons that this loose, natural hierarchy of ICN work developed is 'implement-ability,' as RPs represent ICN recommendations for all, good practices and practical guides offer accessible advice for investigative staff and agency investigative practices, and reports provide the opportunity to scan and compare the spectrum of approaches across jurisdictions. Many of the dedicated ICN implementation efforts on issues of procedure, analysis, and policy emanate from the consensus RP category, with investigative techniques training workshops and experience sharing seminars often espousing ICN's practical, investigator-facing work and reports.

4.3. TREND 3: FONT OF CREATIVITY

The third overarching trend or characteristic of ICN work product has been the creativity in delivery. The growth of different formats for ICN work product has matched the expansion of topics addressed. Early ICN work was dominated by the written word, with a project typically starting with a comparative survey and report, the identification of consensus approaches, and ultimately progressing to a written practical guide or recommendation. This is still the tried-and-true working procedure for most topics that are addressed within the ICN. However, over the years, the ICN's written output has been joined by creative complements in a variety of formats.

In 2002, the ICN held its first staff-facing workshop, a merger workshop held in Washington, DC, hosted by the U.S. agencies. It involved a detailed hypothetical case with an agenda built around investigative techniques tips and hands-on exercises. This type of event has been replicated in ICN Cartel and Unilateral Conduct workshops targeted to investigative staff and enforcement managers. All ICN Working Groups, including Advocacy and Agency Effectiveness, regularly organize workshops dedicated to staff training or policy discussions.

---

57 *See* ICN Work Product Catalog available on the ICN homepage for a full list of ICN reports, too numerous to list here, *supra* note 20.

In 2005, the Cartel Working Group introduced the idea of a dedicated, themed teleseminar series as a work product to facilitate experience sharing on topics such as settlements and criminal enforcement. Before then, ICN calls were primarily used for drafting written work and updates. Today, every working group holds substantive discussion calls that complement existing work products or often explore novel issues not addressed in ICN's existing catalog of written work.

The advent and increase of discussion seminars in working groups across the network on a wide variety of topics has provided opportunities for real-time, direct experience sharing and substantive discussion on timely topics. The ICN Chair has also hosted network-wide "town hall" seminars on topical issues, such as public interest review in mergers.

The creativity in work formats can be seen across the ICN's website, with online tools such as the ICN Market Studies Information Store,[58] accessible cartel and merger templates[59] provided by members that explain basic agency rules and practices, online guides to explaining the benefits of competition[60] and advocacy toolkits,[61] and a library of leniency links.[62] Large, new projects, such as the 2012 ICN's Market Studies Handbook[63] (updated in 2016), have undergone a period of "road testing" with a few agencies before they are finalized in order to learn from how agencies use the information. Recommended Practices are now often accompanied by companion "self-assessment tools" – checklists for agencies to benchmark their own practices with the ICN recommendations. Choices about work formatting, planning, and roll outs represent some of the creative ways that the ICN has put the use of ICN work product at the heart of its operations.

The ICN's most significant and prolific creative choice for alternative work formatting is its Training on Demand project, an idea initiated in 2010 by the FTC.[64] The Training on Demand project's library of 32 (and growing) modules

58 ICN Market Studies Information Store available at: https://www.internationalcompetitionnetwork.org/working-groups/advocacy/market-studies/market-studies-information-store/.

59 ICN Cartel Templates available at: https://www.internationalcompetitionnetwork.org/working-groups/cartel/templates/; ICN Merger Templates available at: https://www.internationalcompetitionnetwork.org/working-groups/merger/templates/.

60 ICN Benefits Project Online Resource available at: https://www.internationalcompetitionnetwork.org/working-groups/advocacy/benefits-of-competition/.

61 ICN Advocacy Toolkits available at: https://www.internationalcompetitionnetwork.org/working-groups/advocacy/other-advocacy-work/.

62 ICN Leniency Links available at: https://www.internationalcompetitionnetwork.org/working-groups/cartel/leniency/leniency-links/.

63 ICN Market Studies Good Practice Handbook available at: https://www.internationalcompetitionnetwork.org/working-groups/advocacy/market-studies/.

64 ICN Training of Demand, *supra* note 26.

is an effort to create a comprehensive curriculum of training materials to serve as a virtual university on competition law and practice for competition agency officials. Training modules produced by agency officials, academics and practitioners, consisting of video lectures and accompanying ICN materials, provide an on-line interactive educational center for competition authorities from around the world.

The story of the ICN's output – with well over 100 distinct work products (and counting) – is a vibrant story of purposeful growth to address member needs and creativity to deliver meaningful information and guidance to its members. The ICN's first wave or "1.0-era" work tended to focus on written work products addressing enforcement fundamentals and the basic underpinnings and benefits of competition law. The ICN's "2.0 era" work incorporates more cross-cutting policy topics that overlap with competition, timely debates, cooperation-oriented tools, and a wider variety of work formats. Both aspects are alive and well today within the ICN, and combine to produce a robust, treasure trove of work for ICN members.

5. EVOLUTION OF THE ICN INTO A GLOBAL ADVOCATE FOR COMPETITION

The ICN was established as a project-oriented network to address practical issues facing its member agencies.[65] Thus, its early work focused on promoting convergence on common standards for dealing with challenges such as divergent merger notification thresholds,[66] and fundamentals of enforcement such as investigative techniques.[67] Throughout its history, the large majority of the ICN's work product has fallen into these categories, with best practices work expanding to cover most areas of competition law including merger analysis, unilateral conduct analysis, and anti-cartel enforcement, as well as practical aspects of the design and organization of competition agencies.

As the organization matured and its membership rapidly grew to encompass almost every competition agency in the world, it began to consider whether, in addition to working on internal agency policies and practices, it could assert its voice more widely to advocate procompetitive policies. Although there was some concern about venturing into a realm that could be more political and

65 *See* Press Release on ICN launch, *supra* note 1.

66 ICN merger notification work available at: https://www.internationalcompetitionnetwork.org/working-groups/merger/notification/.

67 For example, ICN Handbook on Investigative Techniques for Merger Review, *supra* note 54, and ICN Anti-Cartel Enforcement Manual, *supra* note 53.

could intersect with other Ministries in members' governments, ICN leadership understood that the collective breadth and expertise of the ICN membership could be an important voice for consumers. The value of moving the ICN in this direction was heightened by the realization that there was no comparable international body that could speak with the authority of the ICN as a voice for competition. Moreover, it became clear that the proposition that competition policy should be a key organizing principle for national economies in many cases needed buttressing and in some cases was under serious challenge.

The movement toward a broader advocacy role was an evolutionary rather than revolutionary step for the ICN. Domestic competition advocacy was a key component of the ICN's work from the outset. Indeed, the Advocacy Working Group was, along with the Merger Working Group, one of the ICN's first projects. The working group shared experiences and developed tools for competition agencies to serve as advocates for competition. Its work has included preparing an advocacy toolkit to enhance the capacity of agencies to influence domestic policy, a project on explaining the benefits of competition, developing recommended practices for assessing the competitive effects of existing or proposed policies, and a report on developing "culture of competition."[68] ICN's fourth Chair, **Sheridan Scott**, recognized the importance of advocating the adoption of the ICN's benchmarks and that to do so, the ICN needed to be known by a much wider audience. Speaking for the network in 2008, she saw the need "to improve our visibility in the business press, our ability to get our messages out further, to be better understood, to influence countries' interaction of merger laws that reflect our recommended practices."[69]

ICN member agencies participate in numerous international bodies that deal with economic issues that directly or indirectly involve competition policy – for example, the OECD, UNCTAD, the G20 and G7, BRICS, and regional bodies such as APEC and the African Competition Forum – and their governments participate in higher-level discussions on broader economic policy. Over time, the ICN recognized that it had the ability and desire to use its experience in formulating and advocating procompetitive policies to advocate procompetitive polices, including in such international bodies, in the media, and elsewhere.

The ICN thus began to spread its wings in several directions. There were occasions when members' legislatures were considering reforms that involved issues on which the ICN had adopted recommended practices, particularly regarding merger review procedures. When the ICN determined that its

68 *See* ICN Advocacy Working Group available at: www.internationalcompetitionnetwork.org/working-groups/advocacy/.

69 *Supra* note 16.

intervention would likely be welcome and effective, it submitted letters on behalf of its Steering Group urging that the legislative body enact rules that were consistent with international standards as reflected in the ICN's recommended practices. The ICN also teamed with the OECD on a project to examine international enforcement cooperation, and with the World Bank on an annual competition advocacy contest that brings member agencies' work promoting competition policy to an audience of global policymakers.[70]

The challenge to competition policy became particularly acute during the financial crisis that began in 2008. As many governments reacted by diminishing the role of competition policy or even explicitly overriding it,[71] ICN Chair David Lewis recognized the issue and the ICN's potential role in confronting it:

> Competition law … is the Magna Carta, the fundamental law, of the market system. As such, it cannot be confined to an island where its relationship with every other branch of economic and social policy – particularly with trade and industrial policy – is studiously ignored. And if anybody seriously believed that this was ever possible, then the financial and economic storm that has battered us all since the latter half of 2007 and the policy responses to these events should have put paid to any such illusions. With industrial policy ascendant and protectionism in the air, can we afford to remain aloof? Must we not rather engage with the concerns of policy makers to ensure that their interventions – many of them necessary – respect and preserve that which is dynamic and creative and democratic in a market system? … [W]e can use the forum of the ICN to discuss the appropriate interface of our work with industrial and trade policy and with the social and developmental needs of our citizens.[72]

As the challenges to competition policy mounted during the financial crisis, the ICN put this call to arms into practice by developing and disseminating to its members "The Case for Competition in Difficult Times." A big step forward for the network, the document was a strong collective statement of how competition has fostered economic growth, how it can aid economic recovery, and how it can support broader government policy objectives.[73] ICN members used the statement to influence public debate and policy to ensure that competition was properly considered by governments as they dealt with the crisis.

---

70 ICN/World Bank Competition Advocacy Contest, available at: https://www.worldbank.org/en/events/2021/04/07/competition-advocacy-contest-2021.

71 *See*, for example, Adrian Croft, UK clears Lloyds TSB takeover of HBOS, Reuters (31 October 2008) available at: https://www.reuters.com/article/lloyds-hbos/update-2-uk-clears-lloyds-tsb-takeover-of-hbos-idUSLV42573620081031; and Michael Reynolds, Sarah Macrory, and Michelle Chowdhury, EU Competition Policy in the Financial Crisis: Extraordinary Measures, Fordham International Law Journal, Vol. 33, Issue 6 (2001) available at: https://ir.lawnet.fordham.edu/cgi/viewcontent.cgi?article=2218&context=ilj.

72 David Lewis, *supra* note 19.

73 ICN, The Case for Competition in Difficult Times (2009) available at: https://www.internationalcompetitionnetwork.org/wp-content/uploads/2018/07/ICNSGCase4competition.pdf

This enhanced role for the ICN was enthusiastically embraced by the ICN's next Chair, Eduardo Perez Motta, who made it a key theme of his remarks to the ICN's 2012 annual conference:

> The recent global financial crisis showcased … the importance of embedding competition principles in the broader policy debate at the national and international level. The ICN did important work in supporting its members' advocacy efforts with products as the *Competition in Times of Crisis* document, but there is no question competition concerns still have, if at all, a rather precarious hold on the minds of most policy makers, locally and globally.
>
> The ICN … is uniquely placed to supplement local efforts by its members with initiatives to place competition issues on the agenda of national and international (regional or global) organizations and fora. If I am allowed to speak of the Mexican experience, we have found that it is often a matter of reminding policy makers over and over again, linking competition concerns with existing policy goals and providing concrete, easily comprehensible and implementable guidance.
>
> Of course, this is not something that can be achieved easily or fast. But it will not happen spontaneously, nor will somebody else do it for us. I believe it is time for us to start making a concerted effort to push competition as an item on the global policy agenda, by using every opportunity to pitch the idea to anyone with potential impact on that agenda – whether it is members of national administrations with a say in international initiatives or international officials of all levels- and by providing guidance on (fairly) general principles for competition-friendly policy formulation.[74]

Perez Motta further elaborated on this theme the following year:

> In addition to efforts in our respective domestic spheres, we need also to use our voice in the international arena. Whether with the G20 or B20 or other groups suggested this week, we must seek to promote sound competition policy… It is my hope that you will individually seek opportunities to promote competition. With your permission, I will work with the ICN's Steering Group to identify additional ways we can reach a new audience as a network.[75]

While these proclamations were in speeches to a competition audience, Perez Motta also joined with EC Vice President and Competition Commissioner Joaquín Almunia in an op-ed in a major media outlet entitled, "The Competition Factor," which appealed to policymakers to include competition on the economic agenda.[76]

---

74 Eduardo Perez Motta *supra* note 40 at 4–5.

75 Eduardo Perez Motta, ICN Chair, Closing Speech to ICN Conference (26 April 2013) available at: https://www.internationalcompetitionnetwork.org/wp-content/uploads/2020/01/SpeechChairMottaclosing2013.pdf.

76 Joaquin Almunia and Eduardo Perez Motta, The Competition Factor (25 April 2013) available at: https://www.project-syndicate.org/commentary/how-pro-competition-policies-can-boost-economic-recovery-by-joaquin-almunia-and-eduardo-p--motta?barrier=accesspaylog.

The ICN has had another, more recent opportunity to showcase its role as a leading venue for influencing global competition practice through agency-led dialogue and convergence. In 2018, there was a proposal for competition agencies to create a multilateral framework on agency procedures.[77] The proposal was envisioned as a standalone, non-binding international arrangement to encourage basic procedural fairness principles with the ability to facilitate agency-to-agency consultations. The framework's content was generally non-controversial, as it largely mirrored work on procedural fairness that the ICN and others had been doing. The structure of the proposal, however, was met with opposition because many ICN members viewed creating a new forum as confusing or inefficient, as well as unnecessary given the ICN's near-universal membership, established working procedures, and existing work addressing the substantive topics. For example, EU Competition Commissioner Vestager argued that such initiatives should be accomplished through existing multilateral bodies like the ICN, and a European Commission official summed up this perspective by stating, "For an agency, I would be probably more willing to join an initiative under the umbrella of the ICN, rather than join now a new self-standing initiative where you don't really know where it will end, what are your obligations, what it will mean in terms of resources and so on."[78]

Ultimately, ICN members, many of whom shared these reservations about the structure, came together to promulgate the principles through the ICN, which issued the Framework for Competition Agency Procedures (known as CAP).[79] The ICN Steering Group "ICN-ized" the proposal by adapting it to its own structure using an opt-in framework for interested participants, an idea pioneered in its Merger and Cartel Working Groups for enforcement cooperation frameworks. For transparency, it added online templates on agency practices, following models in the Merger and Cartel Working Groups. The CAP's novel agency consultation provisions allowed the ICN to expand its toolbox for encouraging convergence.

The evolution of the framework from a standalone mechanism to being housed in the ICN was a vote of confidence in the ICN and its value to member agencies as a preferred venue for competition agency interaction. It is an example of a mature network reaffirming members' investments and their trust in the ICN's tools and capacity to address multilateral issues. This confidence and maturity can serve as a valuable foundation for the ICN, to the extent it decides to

---

77 Makan Delrahim, Remarks on Global Antitrust Enforcement at the Council on Foreign Relations (1 June 2018) available at: https://www.justice.gov/opa/speech/assistant-attorney-general-makan-delrahim-delivers-remarks-global-antitrust-enforcement.

78 Michael Acton, *US global antitrust initiative runs into EU skepticism, but DOJ vows to push ahead,* Mlex (12 November 2018).

79 ICN Framework for Competition Agency Procedures, *supra* note 47.

identify and articulate its own voice on specific issues in international policy discussions.

In April 2020, amid another global crisis – the COVID-19 pandemic – the ICN Steering Group again led an initiative to articulate basic, common considerations for its member agencies related to competition law enforcement in times of crisis. The statement "Competition During and After the COVID-19 Pandemic"[80] recognizes the challenges that competition agencies face to maintain their enforcement missions and reaffirms the importance of maintaining competition to economies in crisis. It urges member agencies to remain vigilant to anticompetitive conduct and calls for transparency of operational and policy changes during the crisis. Importantly, the statement advocates for competition as a guiding principle for economic recovery efforts in the aftermath of the pandemic.

The ICN's first twenty years have lain a firm foundation for the ICN to serve as a global competition advocate. The FTC has been a consistent advocate for the ICN to fulfill this role. The FTC will continue to highlight its importance and to be alert for opportunities for the ICN to perform this critical function, which will serve the interests of consumers in the United States and around the world. With both the need for sound competition policy and the challenges to its role, for example by national industrial policies, greater than ever, it is important that the ICN, as a – many would say the – pre-eminent international competition body, continue to serve as strong voice for competition policy.

6. CONCLUSION

It is hard to imagine today's international competition community without the ICN. It is a key connector and facilitator of global antitrust dialogue, central to international competition agency interaction. We would have to invent something like the ICN if it did not exist. However, it is easier to imagine if a more modest, less ambitious ICN had developed, in terms of its membership, its active participation, its work product accomplishments, its working procedures, and its voice as competition advocate. The first generation of ICN participants made many choices along to the way to invest in and build today's ICN. Their ambitious creativity, stewardship, and enthusiasm pushed the potential of the network far beyond initial expectations. Their vision of an inclusive, active, pragmatic network that addresses the full range of competition agency needs

80 ICN Steering Group Statement: Competition during and after the COVID-19 Pandemic, https://www.internationalcompetitionnetwork.org/featured/statement-competition-and-covid19/.

and challenges in a cooperative, aspirational manner gives the ICN the tools, inspiration, and institutional standing for future success. The authors and the FTC Office of International Affairs look forward to another extraordinary 20 years for the ICN.

2010–2020 ACHIEVEMENTS OF THE ICN WORKING GROUPS

Graeme JARVIE and Michele PACILLO*

1. INTRODUCTION

The International Competition Network (ICN) was founded in October 2001 as a consensus-based, informal network of antitrust agencies that addresses enforcement and policy issues of common interest and formulates proposals for procedural and substantive convergence. The ICN today is a mature network with 141 competition agencies (117 in 2011) from 128 jurisdictions (103 in 2011).

The following sections highlight the main achievements and milestones of the network at working group level.

2. ADVOCACY WORKING GROUP

In recognition of the importance of advocacy to the work of competition authorities, the Advocacy Working Group (AWG) was one of the first groups created by the ICN, first operating between 2001 and 2003. After a 5-year hiatus, the group was reconvened in 2008. Work over the last 10 years has primarily centred around four key areas; competition assessment, market studies, explaining the benefits of competition to stakeholders, and strategies for planning and evaluating advocacy efforts. In recent years, the question of advocacy in digital markets and in times of Covid-19 has had an important role in shaping the AWG's work. The AWG also assists with coordinating an annual Advocacy Contest arranged by the ICN and the World Bank.

---

* Graeme Jarvie is the International Affairs Director at the Swedish Competition Authority. Michele Pacillo is the International Affairs Officer at the Italian Competition Authority (AGCM). The opinions expressed in this article are the authors' own and do not reflect the official view of the ICN or its working groups. The authors would like to thank the 2019–2020 co-chairs of the working groups for their helpful comments and suggestions.

2.1. COMPETITION ASSESSMENT

The working group's work on competition assessment was initiated in 2012 and focused on both procedural and substantive practices. Recommended practices were agreed and adopted in 2014, representing the highest level of consensus among the ICN membership – sometimes referred to as the "gold standard" of ICN work product. A year later, a Framework of Competition Assessment was produced, which summarises different competition assessment regimes among a range of different member agencies.

The area of competition assessment is a particularly good example of the way in which ICN and OECD work can complement each other. Together with the OECD Recommendation and Toolkit on Competition Assessment, the ICN work offers a comprehensive set of recommendations and best practices for competition authorities.

2.2. MARKET STUDIES

Market studies are a central component in many competition authorities' toolboxes when conducting advocacy work. Reflecting this, the topic has been a recurring theme of work over the last decade. An extensive handbook of good practices for carrying out market studies was first published in 2012, after substantial consultation and information-gathering from ICN member agencies and NGAs. The handbook was subsequently revised and consolidated in 2016. A user-friendly companion booklet with high-level guiding principles was also published in 2017.

In 2013, an "Information Store" containing details of agencies' market studies was published, with a subsequent update in 2017–18. The information store is the result of an ambitious effort to catalogue various market studies carried out by member agencies. This catalogue can assist agencies in understanding how studies have been conducted in particular sectors across the ICN membership, and encourage further informal information exchange between agencies. At the time of writing, more than 700 market studies from 45 jurisdictions are catalogued in the Information Store.

2.3. EXPLAINING THE BENEFITS OF COMPETITION

The last ten years have also seen the AWG give priority to developing practical tools and guidance to support competition authorities' advocacy efforts to explain the benefits of competition to government and non-government stakeholders. This work was broadly carried out under the auspices of a multi-year project called the "Benefits Project". Work focused principally on identifying messages and arguments that competition authorities can employ to effectively communicate the benefits of competition, based on case studies provided by member agencies and other materials. In recognition of the fact that different messages may be relevant or resonate in different ways depending on the stakeholder in question, work was divided into three chapters focusing on different target groups: 1) government and legislators, 2) businesses, and 3) the general public through the media and academia.

Related work was also carried out in the first half of the decade to chart the level of competition culture within ICN member agency jurisdictions and establish techniques with which to promote competition culture within different groups in society. The work culminated in a report on competition culture in 2015.

2.4. ADVOCACY STRATEGIES

The AWG has also looked at broader strategic aspects of competition authorities' advocacy work. In 2016–2017, the group gathered information from member agencies about their advocacy strategies with regard to the planning and the monitoring and evaluation of advocacy work. Member agency experiences were compiled in reports outlining results and lessons learned from the information provided. In 2019 the AWG began compiling detailed case studies of advocacy strategies that had been successfully implemented. With the outbreak of the Covid-19 emergency in 2020, the AWG has started a reflection on the advocacy strategies and messages that competition agencies can adopt to support their government's response to the public health crisis and its impacts on competition.

2.5. DIGITALISATION

Common to all ICN working groups in the latter half of the decade has been the growing importance of digitalisation to the work carried being out. In 2019, the AWG published a report compiling member agency experiences of advocacy efforts in digital markets over the period 2015–2018. Among other things the report looked at the objectives, strategies and messages relevant to these advocacy efforts, and addressed the question of whether digital markets require different approaches to non-digital markets when it comes to advocacy work.

2.6. ICN / WORLD BANK ADVOCACY CONTEST

The World Bank launched an Advocacy Contest in 2013–2014 to showcase successful advocacy stories by competition authorities. Since that inaugural contest, the ICN and the World Bank have jointly coordinated the initiative on an annual basis, and over the years it has grown in size and prominence. Each year, an overarching topic and specific sub-themes are identified, about which competition agencies and other non-governmental organisations are invited to submit successful advocacy stories. For example, the topic of the 2020–2021 contest is "building forward better: how competition advocacy can support countries with Covid19 crisis response, relief, and resilient recovery." The submissions are considered by a panel of competition experts, who identify winners and honourable mentions for each sub-theme. These submissions are recognised in an awards ceremony at the ICN's annual conference, while specific experiences and lessons learned from the winning submissions are shared during a break-out session during the conference or in subsequent teleseminars.

The Advocacy Contest has proven to be an extremely successful way of drawing attention to innovative and effective advocacy initiatives from a broad range of competition authorities around the world. Importantly, the Contest benefits from a significant level of input from younger competition authorities and authorities in developing countries, which gives a platform for these initiatives and allows different voices and ideas to come through. In turn this helps to promote the ICN's stated goals of diversity and outreach.

2.7. WORKSHOPS AND TELESEMINARS

Workshops and teleseminars have been employed to great effect by the AWG in the last decade. They have been used to disseminate knowledge and good practices identified in the projects carried out by the working group to a broad audience of agencies and NGAs. Teleseminars have also been employed as a method of information-gathering as part of ongoing projects. Five advocacy workshops have been held in Paris (2012), Rome (2013) Mauritius (2014), Mexico City (2016) and Kyiv (2019).

3. AGENCY EFFECTIVENESS WORKING GROUP

The Agency Effectiveness Working Group (AEWG) was launched in 2009 as a successor to the Competition Policy Implementation Working Group (CPIWG). It has the core mission of identifying the key elements of a well-functioning competition agency as well as developing best practices for agency strategy, planning, operations and procedures. In recent years, the AEWG has additionally focused on encouraging and facilitating the greater engagement of competition agencies' chief and senior economists in ICN activities.

Over the last ten years, the AEWG has explored a variety of factors that affect how competition agencies achieve their objectives in an efficient and effective way. It has achieved an impressive level of output in this time, centred on three predominant areas: developing a competition agency practice manual, engaging in work related to investigative process, and promoting the role of economics in competition enforcement. For some years the AEWG was also responsible for the coordination of the ICN's online training materials, now called ICN Training on Demand.

3.1. COMPETITION AGENCY PRACTICE MANUAL

Since its formation, the AEWG has undertaken the considerable task of developing a handbook on competition agency operations. The resulting Competition Agency Practice Manual is a broad-ranging practical guide containing tools, procedures and best practices to enhance agency effectiveness. The Manual is a "living" document, with new chapters added to incorporate the results of the latest work produced by the AEWG. There are currently nine chapters in the Manual, each drawing on input and survey responses provided by ICN member agencies:

- Strategic Planning & Prioritization (2010);
- Effective Project Delivery (2012);
- Effective Knowledge Management (2014);
- Human Resources Management (2014);
- Competition Agency Evaluation (2016);
- Ethics Rules in Competition Agencies (2016);
- Competition Agency Staff Training Programmes (2017);
- Competition Agency Use of Social Media (2017);
- Agency Effectiveness through Organisational Design (2019).

3.2. INVESTIGATIVE PROCESS

The AEWG has also been at the forefront of the ICN's consensus-building work on procedural fairness in competition law enforcement. In 2015, the AEWG's multi-year project on compiling information about competition agencies' investigative processes culminated in the ICN Guidance on Investigative Process.

It included recommendations on enforcement tools, agency transparency, agency-party engagement, and the protection of confidential information with a view to promoting fair and informed competition law enforcement. In 2017–2018, the AEWG bolstered its role as a proponent of due process with work that supplemented and updated the Guidance on Investigative Process:

(1) the ICN Guiding Principles for Procedural Fairness in Competition Agency Enforcement;
(2) an addition to the ICN Guidance entitled "Internal Agency Safeguards" exploring recommended internal safeguards and agency practices that help ensure sound and effective competition enforcement; and
(3) an annotated version of the ICN Guidance with specific implementation tips for competition agencies.

The following year, the AEWG took a further significant step in its work on procedural fairness by developing the existing ICN Guidance into Recommended Practices for Investigative Process, which were adopted by the ICN membership in May 2019. As such they represent the highest possible level of consensus among ICN member agencies as regards principles for fair and effective investigative process.

3.3. THE ROLE OF ECONOMICS IN COMPETITION ANALYSIS

While economics and economists have an indispensable role in the work undertaken across the board by the ICN, for some time there was for a lack of explicit provision in the ICN framework for competition economists to discuss economic insights in a specific forum. In recent years the AEWG has filled this gap by creating a dedicated economist sub-group which advocates the importance of economic insights in competition analysis.

As part of this work-stream, the AEWG organises regular ICN Economist Workshops, which bring together chief and senior economists of competition agencies from around the world to discuss current issues. Leading professors have also been invited to lead discussions. The very first workshop was held in Vancouver, Canada in 2016. Building on the success of this event, another fruitful workshop was organised in Seoul, South Korea (2018) in conjunction with the OECD. Another workshop is planned for Bergen, Norway (2020). To increase the involvement of chief and senior economists in ICN work further, the AEWG has also organised teleseminars on various topics of interest, e.g. Non-Horizontal Mergers (2018), and Challenges in Market Definition (2019).

3.4. DIGITALISATION, INNOVATION AND AGENCY EFFECTIVENESS POST COVID-19

In recent years, the AEWG has started a discussion about possible ways to increase the effectiveness and efficiency of competition agencies, in order to help them become better equipped for the digital age. The 2021 report on "Digitalisation, Innovation and Agency Effectiveness" shares practical experiences for member agencies to learn from to improve agency effectiveness, by looking at three key areas: agencies' digital environments and digital tools, digital goals and strategies, as well as adoption of new digital skills. Building on the report's findings, the AEWG will further explore the different strategies used by competition agencies to digitalise and innovate their agencies, also in light of the changes brought about the consequences of the Covid-19 on their institutional design and processes.

3.5. ICN TRAINING ON DEMAND (ITOD)

ICN Training on Demand (ITOD) is the ICN's collection of online training materials, intended to function as a virtual university on competition law and practice for competition agency officials. ITOD's first incarnation was launched in 2010 under the name ICN Curriculum Project, within the mandate of the Vice Chair for Outreach and subsequently the Agency Effectiveness Working Group. Latterly, the project has been a free-standing initiative within the ICN coordinated by the US FTC and involving input from member agencies and NGAs. In recent years the American Bar Association's Section of Antitrust Law has provided financial support to the project.

Training modules typically involve presentations, discussions or vignettes involving agency staff and NGAs with expertise in the topic being presented. In line with the ethos of the ICN as a whole, the modules strive to find a diversity of voices and perspectives, and often involve a broad range of ICN jurisdictions from around the world.

Modules are available in an interactive format where users can navigate between scenes and click on links to materials. In recent years videos have also begun being uploaded to YouTube. Transcripts of the presentations are often available, which facilitates understanding by users whose first language is not English. Member agencies have also begun cooperating to provide subtitles of modules in other languages, particularly Spanish and French.

The content has expanded over the last ten years to cover 32 modules at the time of writing, grouped into broader topics: competition fundamentals, horizontal restraints, dominant firm conduct, mergers, state impediments to competition, investigative techniques and agency effectiveness.

Outreach and implementation are cornerstones of ICN work, and ITOD modules are an effective and enduring way of providing ICN member agency staff from around the world with access to high-quality training materials. They can be a particularly useful and cost-effective way of providing on-going professional development.

3.6. WORKSHOPS AND TELESEMINARS

In addition to specific ICN economist workshops organised under the auspices of the AEWG, the working group has organised agency effectiveness workshops to promote the implementation of ICN work. The Botswanan Competition Authority hosted a workshop in Gaborone in 2016, while the AEWG cooperated with Association of Southeast Asian Nations (ASEAN) and the Competition Commission of Singapore to organise a regional workshop focused on due process, transparency and investigative practices in 2017. Teleseminars have, meanwhile, featured regularly as a method of information sharing and dissemination of ICN work.

3.7. SUMMARY

The AEWG's work has been instrumental in encouraging effective and efficient competition enforcement and good practices for well-functioning competition agencies across the world. ICN member agencies can draw on methods and experiences captured in the Competition Agency Practice Manual and ICN Recommended Practices for Investigative Process, while the AEWG's efforts in the area of competition economics have generated a greater involvement of chief and senior economists in the ICN's work.

4. CARTEL WORKING GROUP

The Cartel Working Group (CWG) aims at reducing obstacles that antitrust agencies face in deterring and detecting national and international cartels through the examination of important legal and policy issues and the exchange of effective investigative techniques.

4.1. ANTI-CARTEL ENFORCEMENT MANUAL

In the last ten years, the CWG has continued to develop the Anti-Cartel Enforcement Manual which is a compilation of investigative approaches used by ICN members and it is intended to be a reference tool for agencies to enable them to evaluate and benchmark their own approaches. The Manual is divided in chapters exploring measures employed at various stages of anti-cartel enforcement. Since 2010 it has been enriched with new chapters on: Case Resolution (2011); Awareness, Outreach and Compliance (2012); International Cooperation and Information sharing (2013), Relationship between Competition Agencies and Public Procurement Bodies (2015) and Development of Private Enforcement of Competition Law (2019).

These new chapters reflect new policy developments for antitrust agencies such as the importance of outreaching key stakeholders like policymakers, public procurement agencies, media and the public in general in order to increase awareness of and compliance with the anti-cartel laws. In 2014, two existing chapters of the Manual have been updated to consider latest developments in the practice of the ICN members on leniency programs (Drafting and implementing an effective leniency program) and digital evidence (Digital Evidence Gathering). All the good practices identified in the Manual were summarised in a document (Compilation of Good Practices) in 2011 and revised in 2017.

4.2. LENIENCY WORK

In recognition of the challenges faced by competition authorities in incentivising leniency programs due to the diffusion of private enforcement and individual sanctions, the CWG has focused its attention on the topic of leniency programs, by delivering in 2017 the Checklist for Efficient and Effective Leniency Programmes and in 2019 a report on Good practices for incentivising leniency applications.

4.3. INTERNATIONAL COOPERATION WORK

Given the growing importance of international cartel investigations, the CWG has delivered an impressive number of outputs in order to facilitate effective and efficient cooperation among competition authorities. In 2016, it has established a framework intended to assist competition agencies in knowing how to and whom to contact when seeking non-confidential information to foreign counterpart agencies.

This framework complements other tools created in the previous years: in 2012, the CWG published charts on the types of mechanisms allowing information sharing (Charts Summarizing Information Sharing Mechanisms); in 2014, it elaborated a template for confidentiality waiver to be used by leniency applicants with an explanatory note on the use and usefulness of waivers; finally, in 2016 the CWG updated templates providing public access to information about ICN members' anti-cartel enforcement regimes.

These templates are of great use for both competition authorities and parties under investigation in promoting mutual understanding of the main features of the various jurisdictions, including the process for filing a complaint, decision-making, sanctioning cartel conduct, investigative tools, leniency, rights of defendants and confidentiality regimes. In 2016 the template was enriched with new sections on commitments and settlement, and more recently it was agreed to add a section on private enforcement.

In 2020, the CWG published the first piece of guidance on the coordination of multijurisdictional leniency applications. Recognising that, despite convergence, generation gap exists between agencies that have had leniency programs for many decades and agencies that have recently adopted programs and are working to implement them, the CWG released a "Guidance on Enhancing Cross-Border Leniency Cooperation", to provide practical advice to younger agencies and foster international coordination.

4.4. BIG DATA AND CARTELS

More recently, the CWG has undertaken a project on big data and cartels to discuss the main practical and legal challenges in cartel enforcement raised by the use of big data, algorithms and artificial intelligence. The project led to the update of three chapters of the Anti-cartel enforcement manual (Digital Evidence Gathering, Cartel Case Initiation and Investigative Strategy).

4.5. WORKSHOPS AND WEBINAR SERIES

Over the last ten years, the CWG has continued to strengthen and enlarge the network of its members by organising a striking number of workshops and webinar series with the intent of assisting agencies in improving their operational and practical skills and facilitating periodic discussions of important policy issues related to cartel enforcement.

The workshops organised by the CWG are a continuation of the successful series of agency-led international cartel conferences that began in 1999 in Washington. This annual event provides a venue for agencies' anti-cartel enforcers to share experiences and best practices. Since 2010, workshops were held in: Bruges (2011), Panama (2012), Cape Town (2013), Cario (2014), Cartagena (2015), Madrid (2016), Ottawa (2017), Tel Aviv (2018) and Foz do Iguacu (2019) and Lisbon (2021).

To boost experience sharing and participation from the wider community, the CWG organises webinar series (6 events per year) focusing each year on different topics of interest, for instance: cartel awareness and outreach (2010–2011), bid-rigging (2011–2012), leniency (2012–2013), investigative powers to fight international cartels and sanctioning international cartels in the context of multi-jurisdictional investigations (2014–2015), investigative tools, detection methods and disclosure and discovery (2016–2017), parental liability, international cooperation to fight against cartels and ex officio investigations (2017–2018), digital cartels, compliance, cooperation with public procurement agencies, information sharing gateways and leniency (2018–2019). The 2010–2011 webinar series on cartel awareness and outreach was complemented by a collection of examples of public messages and materials used by ICN members in cartel-related outreach efforts. This information amounts to the world's largest compilation of cartel awareness and outreach materials and is available through the ICN website. The 2020–2021 webinar series on horizontal collaborations and crisis cartels at times of Covid-19 will be accompanied by a document collecting agencies' guidelines and practice in assessing horizontal agreements and drawing lessons learnt from past crisis cartels.

ICN Cartel workshops and webinar series have attracted unprecedented participation and large numbers of speakers. They have become the largest, longest-running and most participatory group discussions within the ICN, and have contributed to build and foster the sense of "community" within the ICN.

5. MERGER WORKING GROUP

Founded in October 2001, the Merger Working Group (MWG) is the first working group of the ICN and its mission is to promote the adoption of best practices in the design and operation of merger review regimes in order to: (i) enhance the effectiveness of each jurisdiction's merger review mechanisms; (ii) facilitate procedural and substantive convergence; and (iii) reduce the public and private time and cost of multijurisdictional merger reviews. Looking back over the past ten years, the MWG has successfully addressed the following focus areas: international cooperation and remedies, notification and review procedures, and substantive matters (non-horizontal mergers and economic analysis).

5.1. INTERNATIONAL COOPERATION WORK

The increasing globalization and complexity of transactions, which more frequently raise data-related issues, together with the growing number of merger review regimes around the world have called for greater cooperation and coordination of competition authorities' review of multijurisdictional transactions, in order to avoid inconsistent if not conflicting outcomes, especially in the field of remedies. For these reasons, the MWG successfully created tailored solutions to facilitate effective and efficient cooperation between and among ICN member agencies.

In 2012, it established a non-binding framework for facilitating enforcement cooperation through identifying each agency's liaison officers and possible ways to exchange information in multijurisdictional merger review; in 2015, it delivered a practical guide to merger enforcement cooperation which provides guidance to agencies on how cooperation in individual cases can be structured; and finally, in 2019 it advised on practical tools and tips on how to use the 2012 framework.

5.2. MERGER REMEDIES WORK

In parallel, the MWG has conducted important work on the topic of remedies, by updating a 2005 document which now provides conceptual and practical guidance for agencies and merging parties seeking to address competition issues raised by domestic and multijurisdictional mergers (Merger Remedies Guide). Both the work on international cooperation and remedies allowed to take stock of the agencies' good practices in order to update the corresponding Recommended Practices released by the MWG in their first ten years. In 2020–2021, the MWG explores in greater details all issues related to design implementation and ex-post review of merger remedies, also in multijurisdictional context, through a webinar series and a virtual workshop.

5.3. UPDATE OF RECOMMENDED PRACTICES

In the area of notification and review procedures, the MWG has devoted the last ten years in the update of its Recommended Practices on Merger Notification and Review Procedures, whose main bulk was approved at the First Annual ICN Conference in Naples in September 2002.

As revealed by a survey in 2010, ICN members showed a high degree of satisfaction with the MWG and its impressive array of accomplishments, with several agencies identified the Recommended Practices for Merger Notification and Review Procedures and Merger Analysis as contributing to change in their merger regimes. Indeed, ICN members' use of these Recommended Practices is usually either as a benchmark to review their own practices or as a means of support for reform or both. For instance, in May 2012, Brazil introduced a drastic overhaul to its merger regime which now envisages, in line with the ICN practices, a pre-merger notification regime, with a fast track system for non-problematic mergers and new notification thresholds.

Given their importance, over the period 2017–2018 the MWG has remarkably updated the best practices in relation to several aspects of a merger notification regimes: the notion of reviewable transactions, the definition of an agency's jurisdiction and its nexus, the main criteria for setting notification thresholds and the timing and stages of the review periods. In 2019, the MWG has started a new work on procedural infringements in merger review, given the growing members' and merging parties' interests in the topic. The project aims to cover mainly two areas of infringements: infringements of mandatory notification obligations (e.g. failure to file, gun-jumping), and infringements of compliance with review procedure (e.g. RFI compliance).

On the substantive issues, in 2017 the MWG enriched the Recommended Practices on Merger Analysis with a new section on efficiencies, to provide guidance on how agencies should assess efficiency claims and the types of evidence to consider in the evaluation.

5.4. NON-HORIZONTAL MERGERS AND ECONOMIC ANALYSIS

Another milestone of the MWG was to deepen members' understanding of non-horizontal mergers, such as vertical mergers (e.g. Vertical Mergers Survey Report 2018) and more recently conglomerate mergers, with a particular focus on issues arising in the context of high-tech industries, digital markets and multi-sided platforms. At the same time, the MWG worked on consolidating the analytical skills of member agencies by updating in 2013 the 2005 Investigative Techniques Handbook for Merger Review, in the section related to the use of economic thinking and quantitative techniques in assessing horizontal mergers (Chapter 4).

5.5. WORKSHOPS AND TELESEMINARS

In the last ten years, the MWG has organized eight ICN Merger Workshops, hosted in Rome (2010), Bogotá (2012), New Delhi (2014), Brussels (2015), Washington (2017), Mexico City (2017), Tokyo (2018) and Melbourne (2020). These workshops have highlighted MWG work on notification and procedures, investigative techniques, and merger analysis. The MWG's workshops were the first within the ICN to use comprehensive, real-world styled hypotheticals throughout multi-day training exercises for investigators. Many member agencies have adapted and used the merger workshop materials in their own internal training.

Since 2010, the MWG has started a series of teleseminars on topics of interest to the MWG members, such as challenges for analysing innovation in mergers (2017) and digital mergers (2019). These teleseminars provide a forum for promoting the MWG work products among its members and for experience sharing so that ICN members identify shared standards and techniques as well as areas of difference. More recently, the MWG has launched "regional" teleseminars to promote interaction among members and NGAs active in the same geographical area on common topics (e.g. retail mergers in 2018, decision making in 2020 and impact of Covid-19 on merger control in 2021).

6. UNILATERAL CONDUCT WORKING GROUP

The Unilateral Conduct Working Group (UCWG) was established in May 2006, at the Fifth Annual ICN Conference. Its primary objectives are to examine the challenges involved in analysing unilateral conduct of dominant firms and firms with substantial market power, to facilitate greater understanding of the issues involved in analysing unilateral conduct, and to promote convergence and sound enforcement of law and policy governing unilateral conduct.

6.1. RECOMMENDED PRACTICES ON PREDATORY PRICING ANALYSIS

In the last ten years, building on the consensus gathered around the best practices on the assessment of dominance/substantial market power and state-created monopolies, in 2014 the UCWG delivered the first recommendations focused on a specific conduct, predatory pricing, which represented an important step to promote convergence toward sound enforcement of laws governing unilateral conducts.

6.2. UNILATERAL CONDUCT WORKBOOK

Another achievement is the Unilateral Conduct Workbook, which the UCWG began developing in 2011 as a practical tool for case-handlers in assessing dominance and specific types of unilateral conduct. The practical guidance of the Workbook is based on previous work which outlined agencies' approaches to assessing the conduct and the criteria used to distinguish pro-competitive from anti-competitive conduct.

The Workbook begins with a section on principles and objectives underlying unilateral conduct laws, followed by chapters on the assessment of dominance and of the following unilateral conducts: predatory pricing (2012), exclusive dealing/single branding (2013) and tying and bundling (2015). The most recent chapter (2017) takes a step back and provides an analytical framework which poses and explores basic questions an agency must address in formulating its enforcement policies, in particular on two key questions in unilateral conduct enforcement: 'what is dominance?' and 'what makes conduct exclusionary?'.

6.3. WORKSHOPS AND WEBINARS

To explore in greater depth the issues raised in the Workbook and to promote the implementation of the Recommended Practices, the UCWG began organising interactive workshops in which case handlers could discuss practical as well as substantive aspects of a particular conduct, with the help of hypothetical case scenarios. The Working Group has now organized a total of eight such events: Washington, D.C. (2009), Brussels (2010), Singapore (2012), Stockholm (2013), Istanbul (2015), Rome (2017), Cape Town (2018) and Mexico City (2019).

The workshops have been complemented by webinars designed to increase mutual understanding of different approaches. These programs enable ICN members to delve into discrete issues of mutual concern, identify commonalities and differences in agencies' approaches, and better understand the relative advantages and drawbacks of different policies. Webinars are an opportunity to discuss challenging areas of the unilateral conduct laws, for instance laws addressing exploitative abuses such as excessive pricing.

6.4. VERTICAL RESTRAINT PROJECT

In response to a growing concern about the spread of old and new forms of vertical restraints in online markets, the UCWG began in 2016 a multi-year project examining the effects on competition of online vertical restraints, in order to promote increased understanding, and where differences exist, to work towards convergence. The project was based on an innovative comparison initiative: jurisdiction-specific responses around two hypothetical scenarios (online parity clauses and online selective distribution models), were collected and formed the basis of a report (Vertical Restraints Report 2019) which highlights commonalities and divergent factors in the assessment of the scenarios.

6.5. ASSESSING DOMINANCE IN DIGITAL ERA PROJECT

As competition agencies are increasingly confronted with the need to assess unilateral conduct in digital markets, in 2019, the UCWG launched a new workstream focusing on the assessment of dominance/substantial market power in the digital markets. It seeks to understand whether the experience suggests that digital markets exhibit specific characteristics that would warrant reconsideration of the traditional approach of assessing dominance/substantial market power. It will also provide useful information on whether the existing ICN documents on market power/dominance are "fit for purpose" or need to be updated to reflect the specific features of digital markets and provide more effective guidance to enforcers around the world.

In 2020, after publishing a "Report on Dominance/Substantial Market Power in Digital Markets" based on a survey among its members and NGAs, the UCWG further deepened two main topics, namely markets shares and barriers, by producing a paper which provides key information on the most important features that are relevant for the assessment of these two crucial elements in competition cases. In 2021, the UCWG will explore the main issues and challenges connected with analysis of theories of harm and design of remedies concerning unilateral conduct with dominance/substantial market power in digital markets.

6.6. OUTREACH

The UCWG work products have been well received and continue to have an impact on the agencies' enforcement practice. Today, agencies around the world are using the UCWG Recommended Practices and Workbook to help analyse cases or as a reference guide. Several members and NGAs use UCWG work products and hypothetical case studies for in-house staff training and technical assistance missions, like capacity training in the course of assistance for younger competition agencies, to benchmark their practices against those of other agencies or as reference material for speeches and meetings at international level. The UCWG work has proven to be a useful guide also for academics who have utilized the hypothetical case studies as a teaching tool in their class room, reporting large success and appreciation by the students.

THE ROLE OF THE ICN IN THE EVOLUTION OF THE ISRAEL COMPETITION AUTHORITY

Michal HALPERIN and Shira GILLAT

1. INTRODUCTION

The Israel Competition Authority (the "ICA") has evolved and changed substantially in its 26 years of existence. It started with the main purpose of enforcing the Israeli Economic Competition Law-1988 (the "Competition Law") (until January 2019, the Competition Law was known as the Restrictive Trade Practices Law-1988). Hence, most of its resources in its initial years were dedicated to merger reviews and enforcement against violations of the Competition Law. From its very beginning, the ICA had the power to criminally investigate and indict violations of the Competition Law. This power was used almost exclusively for enforcement against cartels and bid rigging. Only more recently has the ICA started imposing administrative fines on non-cartel violations of the Competition Law, including vertical restraints and abuses of dominance. In the last decade the ICA has also started to invest much of its resources into advocacy.

This unique evolution of the ICA stands in contrast to the way in which many other young competition authorities evolved. This unique evolution makes the ICA's interface with the International Competition Network (the "ICN")'s activities more enriching and valuable than for many other agencies. Notwithstanding its size, ICA has a lot to contribute to the ICN and its members in terms of criminal enforcement of cartel and bid rigging. At the same time, the ICA has learned a lot from the experience of other competition authorities on how to advocate effectively for competition goals. This two-sided process is an excellent example of how the ICN can benefit its members.

This essay discusses the valued role that the ICN has played in the development of the ICA. We address this role, particularly, in view of the manner in which ICA has evolved over its history into its powers and authorities – which differs somewhat from what may be considered as the natural process of evolution of competition authorities.

2. HOW THE ICA BECAME WHAT IT IS TODAY

The ICA was established in 1994 as an independent authority. Its mandate includes enforcement against anticompetitive restrictive arrangements and abuse of dominance, merger control, regulation of collectively dominant firms, as well as market research and competition advocacy roles. The ICA has the power to prosecute criminal cases and its Director General can impose administrative fines for violations of the Competition Law. A Competition Tribunal has exclusive jurisdiction over non-criminal regulatory antitrust proceedings. The District Court of Jerusalem has exclusive jurisdiction over criminal antitrust matters.[1] Both criminal and civil antitrust rulings are subject to appeal before the Supreme Court of Israel. In addition, the ICA's mandate includes enforcement of the Law for Promotion of Competition and Reduction of Concentration 5774–2013, the Law for the Promotion of Competition in the Food Sector, 5775–2014 and the Law for Fuel Industry Law – 1994.

From the outset, the ICA held criminal enforcement powers as well as the authority to review mergers. In 1994 the ICA had already initiated a complicated criminal investigation against the leading insurance companies in Israel for price fixing.[2] This case ultimately exposed an industry-wide cartel of the major insurance companies in Israel. Those companies, together with their directors, were indicted, convicted, and ultimately sentenced. Since this investigation, the Investigations Department in the ICA has initiated over 100 criminal investigations of cartels and bid rigging in many different markets. The Legal Department of the ICA has indicted over 50 cartels and bid rigging cases; and over 350 participants (individuals and corporations) have been found guilty. In 2002 the Israeli court decided for the first time to send executives of entities that were involved in criminal cases to jail.[3] Since then executives served imprisonment

1 According to a temporary order (one year as of 31 March 2019), excluding pending cases, criminal antitrust matters shall be deliberated before the Central District Court of Lod.

2 *See* CrimC (Jer) 417/97 *State of Israel v. Israel Phoenix, Insur. Co.* ISRDC (Sentencing Decision), 33(4) Dinim Mehozi 708, 2002 Antitrust 3013681 (sentencing Israel Phoenix Insurance Company to a fine of NIS 12 million and another company, Ayalon Insurance Company to a fine of NIS 6.6 million NIS; the Supreme Court ultimately affirmed one sentence but did not review the other sentence).

3 In 2002, the ICA successfully concluded the prosecution of a nation-wide floor tile cartel, which had endured for over a decade. This resulted in criminal convictions of several tile manufacturers including significant jail sentences. For example, in one of the proceedings, CrimA 2919/02 *Aloni v. State of Israel* ISRSC, 62 Dinim Elyon 729, 2002 Antitrust 3015629 (a CEO of a floor tile company was sentenced, among other things, to 21 months imprisonment, of which nine months were to be served in prison and the remainder as a suspended sentence).

sentences in five more cartel and bid rigging cases.[4] From its establishment and until today, the criminal prosecution of cartels and bid rigging is one of the stone pillars of the ICA's activity. Many financial and human resources are dedicated to the investigation and indictment of such cases. This is an ongoing effort in which the ICA invests in order to renew its methods, improve and excel.

During its early years, the ICA also had administrative powers directed towards vertical restraints and unilateral conduct. However, those administrative powers were limited.[5] During this period, the ICA used these powers on several occasions, but due to their limited scope, they had a limited degree of effectiveness. In 2012, the ICA received, in addition, the power to impose administrative fines. In 2019, the maximum administrative fine that the General Director is authorised to impose on corporations increased from NIS 24 million to NIS 100 million.[6]

During the first 17 years of its existence the ICA rarely engaged in advocacy work. The ICA was consulted on different matters by other governmental agencies and issued its opinion on a selection of issues but such involvement and activity were limited and no structured work on advocacy was engaged in. This changed after the large scale civil protests against the high cost of living that took place in Israel in the summer of 2011.

The protests of 2011 changed the attitude of and the way of thinking within the ICA. The need to have the ICA involved in the ongoing government activity and the need for the ICA to actively promote competition started to become clearer. As a result, the ICA started investing a growing proportion of its resources into advocacy activity and initiatives. The Committee for Economic and Social Change, which was nominated by the government as an outcome of the 2011 protests, made far reaching recommendations on competition issues and on the need to promote competition in Israeli markets. It went further to recommend that the ICA have the power to research markets and to recommend to the government how to promote competition in these markets. As an outcome,

4 The cooking gas cartel, the bakeries cartel, the water meters cartel, the school books cartel and the tree pruning cartel.

5 The ICA's administrative powers included: the power to determine that violation of the law has occurred (the Competition Law, section 43); the power to declare that a monopoly in a defined market exists (the Competition Law, section 26); the power to impose instructions on a monopoly or request the Competition Tribunal to do so (the Competition Law, sections 30 and 31) and the power to ask for a judicial order from the Competition Tribunal (the Competition Law, Section 51).

6 In addition, since 2012, the ICA developed this area of activity. It *inter alia* published guiding papers, including, the Director General's Guidelines on the Use of Enforcement Proceedings of Administrative Fines (Guidelines 1/12); and the Director General's Considerations in Determining the Amount of Administrative Fine (Guideline 1/16), which replaced Guideline 2/12. ICA also imposed administrative fines, in several cases throughout the years since.

the Competition Law was amended to allow the General Director to conduct examinations of the level of competition in various sectors of the economy, including an examination of failures in competition and barriers to competition. Additionally, the General Director may forward the reasoned conclusions to the relevant authorities and publish the conclusions of the ICA examinations on the website and in any other manner they see fit. This area of activity began development as a separate unit in the ICA in 2018 with the ICA's reorganisation and the establishment of the Markets Department. This Department (in addition to the review of merger transactions and restrictive arrangements brought before the General Director for their approval), is entrusted with advocacy: including consultations with the government and advancing knowledge of competition law in various sectors of Israeli industry.

3. AN INTERNATIONAL POINT OF VIEW

Other young authorities may develop in a different manner to that of the ICA. As time goes by, such authorities gain experience, as well as the confidence of the public and the government, and accordingly they are often granted with, and are able to make use of, enforcement tools, including administrative and criminal tools.

William Kovacic has made the following comment on the development of young competition agencies, particularly in developing and transitioning economies:

> "[...]well before it begins bringing cases, the competition agency can use its education, publicity, and research activities to criticize government restrictions on entry and market access. Particularly for a new agency facing severe resource constraints, advocacy provides a way to promote the adoption of pro-competitive policies without the extensive commitment of personnel that the prosecution of cases often entails"[7],

Young competition authorities, which at early stages, made use of consulting and advocacy tools and authorities, while in parallel held limited enforcement tools, include, for instance Argentina[8], India[9], and the Philippines. Notably, challenges

---

7 William E. Kovacic "Getting Started: Creating New Competition Policy Institutions in Transition Economies" 23 *Brooklyn Journal of International Law* 403 (1997), 439.

8 See the United Nations Conference on trade and development UNCTAD guidebook on competition systems at (https://unctad.org/en/Docs/ditcclp20072_en.pdf) (p. 2), with reference to Background of Argentina, stating that *"Although the tribunal has not been constituted, the National Commission for the Defence of Competition (CNDC) continues operating without having independent decision-making authority. CNDC is only an advisory body, within the ministry. Its decisions must be ratified by a secretariat within the Ministry of Economy and Production"*.

9 Ibid., p. 65 stating with reference to competition policy in India at its initial stages, that *"presently, the Competition (Amendment) Bill, 2006 is before the Parliament. It is expected that once it is passed, the Competition Law will become enforceable in India. Until then, the Competition Commission of India is engaged in competition advocacy with all stakeholders,*

pertaining to young agencies acquiring criminal enforcement tools were also discussed in ICN's report of 2019 on "Lessons to Be Learnt from the Experience of Young Competition Agencies an Update to the 2006 Report".[10] Scanning through challenges faced by young agencies, this report addresses enforcement challenges, and how they are dealt with, in such young authorities. Some challenges relate to administrative and criminal enforcement tools, particularly regarding investigation processes, gathering of evidence, the absence of search and seizure authority, and more.

4. ICA'S CO-OPERATION WITH COMPETITION AGENCIES WORLDWIDE

The ICA ascribes great importance to establishing and strengthening its foreign relations. It devotes considerable resources and efforts to this purpose. Participation in international fora dealing with competition as well as fostering working relationships with peer competition authorities around the world enables the ICA to take part in leading discussions in the field, to regularly keep up-to-date and with innovations in law and policy, as well as assist and consult with peer authorities as appropriate.

Indeed, the ICA regularly conducts consultations with peer competition authorities, worldwide. Whether with reference to particular cases (e.g. review of cross border mergers and cartel enforcement), or concerning broader policy and other issues. In particular, the ICA finds great value in learning from the experience of competition authorities around the world, and more so, in areas of activity in which ICA gained its powers or developed its expertise in, as described above, relatively late, such as advocacy and administrative enforcement. At the same time, in areas in which the ICA has considerable experience, notwithstanding its size and age, the ICA enjoys sharing its experience, and finds itself many times in a position to counsel and guide competition agencies. This is the case in particular concerning consultations provided by ICA's experienced cartel investigation and prosecution force; guiding workshops and training sessions in aspects pertaining to criminal enforcement and bid-rigging. One example in this regard is the ICA hosting the 2018 ICN cartel work shop on *"How to Crack a Cartel Step By Step"*. Intense discussions, which took place at the ICN cartel workshop in Tel-Aviv, over three days, focused on developing the capabilities required to uncover a cartel, and the legal issues that

such as academia, professionals and government authorities/bodies, regulators, etc. It is also being prepared for readiness as and when the enforcement provisions are notified".

10 See https://www.internationalcompetitionnetwork.org/wp-content/uploads/2019/06/SGVC_YoungerAgenciesReport2019.pdf.

require attention at every step from the beginning of the investigation until the final sentencing. The workshop tackled various issues which ICA has acquired significant experience in, such as intelligence, digital evidence gathering, cloud computing and the unique legal challenges faced by agencies during legal enforcement. A hands-on practice session, led by ICA's investigations teams, aimed at sharing experience on the conduct of effective questioning and dawn raids.

5. THE ICN: A DUAL PLATFORM FOR LEARNING AND TEACHING

The ICA is honored to take part in the ICN, which provides for a unique and most valuable platform for peer competition agencies around the world. The ICA has been active, throughout the years, in ICN's working groups, and has also served as a member of the organization's steering group.

Looking back, and into the future, throughout its years of activity, one of the ICN's most significant and extraordinary features, for the ICA and for agencies worldwide, is providing them with the opportunity to both learn from experience of one another, and at the same time to share their knowledge and experience where relevant.

The unique development of the ICA – significant enforcement tools including criminal powers from the outset, to acquiring additional administrative and advocacy authorities throughout the years – highlights this feature of the ICN: as a dual-purpose platform. In the framework of ICN, the Israel Competition Authority, often has the opportunity to share its experience in criminal enforcement, and at the same time, ICA gains great benefit learning from the immense experience collected by peer agencies worldwide, in such areas where the ICA is less experienced in. In this regard, from ICA's standpoint, the ICN effectively serves to foster relevant and valuable professional consultations and co-operation in various fields of activity; alongside fruitful, enriching and long-lasting international relationships in the global competition community.

THE IMPACT OF THE ICN ON THE ACCC

Rod SIMS and Marcus BEZZI

1. INTRODUCTION

The Australian Competition and Consumer Commission ("ACCC") is a founding member of the ICN and has been heavily involved with the ICN since its inception. The ACCC served on the interim steering group for the creation of the network, and thereafter has remained heavily involved in ICN working groups and workshops. Creating the ICN was an important step towards achieving common ground on enforcement matters and protecting competition worldwide – a significant achievement in a globalised economy.

Over the past 20 years, the ICN has continued to grow in influence and membership. The scale and reach of the present day ICN was demonstrated palpably for the ACCC in May 2015, when the ACCC hosted the ICN annual conference, an event that was attended by more than 400 international delegates from over 70 countries, including staff from competition agencies, academics, and legal and economic representatives. The conference took place during an important time domestically for Australia's competition law, when competition issues were front-page news, with the Australian Government considering its response to the final report of an independent Competition Policy Review.

While staying true to its mandate of "all competition, all the time", the ICN has continued to consider a steadily increasing range of competition issues, some of which are outlined below.

2. INFLUENCE ON ACCC CARTEL ENFORCEMENT

Since the ICN's founding 20 years ago, combatting cartels has been at the forefront of its agenda. By bringing different competition agencies from around the world together, the ICN has helped to strengthen the proficiency of individual agencies as well as deepen the cooperation between agencies and ensure collaboration by agencies worldwide on cartel law enforcement. Over the past 20 years, the ACCC has significantly expanded its capacity to detect and prosecute cartels with assistance from the ICN and its member agencies.

Even when confined to a single country, cartels cause widespread economic and consumer harm and are difficult to detect and prosecute. However, over the life of the ICN the world's economy has grown closer and increasingly globalised. Nowadays cartels are often international operations capable of harming consumers around the world while also being even harder than ever to detect and prosecute. Cartel agreements that affect Australian consumers are often reached outside of Australia and the evidence required to bring a matter before an Australian court is often all located off-shore.

This global problem requires a global solution. Over the past 20 years, the ICN has been instrumental in harmonising approaches to cartel detection and investigation through sharing of best practices, global cooperation and information exchange. The ACCC's cartel enforcement capacity has drastically improved thanks in no small part to the persuasive guidance and knowledge sharing facilitated by the ICN and its Cartel Working Group ("CWG"). The development and introduction of the ACCC's leniency policy is a telling example of the huge value the ACCC has derived from its ICN membership.

The ICN has facilitated the development, implementation and revision, from time to time, of the ACCC's cartel leniency policy (now called the Cartel Immunity and Cooperation Policy). The ACCC launched its leniency policy in June 2003. The content of the policy was based largely on the United States Department of Justice's Cartel Leniency Policy. The ACCC also incorporated aspects of the European Union, United Kingdom, Canadian and South Korean leniency policies and learned from their respective institutional knowledge. The ICN was central to allowing the ACCC to access international expertise and developing the relationships we needed to leverage that expertise and institutional experience.

Before launching our leniency policy, the ACCC had maintained a general cooperation policy to secure participant cooperation across all enforcement matters. However, through engagement with other ICN member states, the ACCC recognised that a leniency policy in cartel matters, which created the right incentives for applicants, was necessary to adequately detect and prosecute cartel conduct due to the especially pernicious nature of cartel conduct.

As the ACCC's leniency program evolved over time, the ICN has continued to play an integral role in its development through direct feedback on ACCC proposals and close institutional cooperation between member states. These processes have continued to strengthen the ACCC's cartel immunity program, with the introduction of a 'marker' system for cartel immunity applicants and the recent streamlining of the immunity application process directly resulting from consultation with the ICN and its member states.

The ACCC's cartel leniency and immunity policies have been a successful tool for us in combatting cartel conduct in Australia. Shortly after launching the first review of our leniency policy at the 2004 Cracking Cartels workshop in Sydney, the ACCC received a leniency application that led directly to the successful ACCC case against Visy for a price fixing cartel in relation to the supply of cardboard products. Visy was fined AU$36 million for the leading role it took in this case, which until 2019 was the record fine for any competition law contravention in Australia and highlights how influential collaboration between ICN member states has been for us in improving our cartel work.

The ICN was also central in the ACCC's successful advocacy for the criminal prohibition on cartel conduct within Australia. Its knowledge and expertise added to the evidence base that eventually led the Australian Government to make serious cartel conduct a criminal offence in 2009. Since the criminal prohibition of cartel conduct entered into force, the ACCC has supported the successful prosecution of three international shipping lines, NYK, K-Line and WWO, for involvement in a cartel arrangement leading to total fines of AU$83.5 million being imposed.

Australia's independent criminal prosecutor ('the CDPP') also commenced criminal proceedings against individuals for the first time in 2018 in the Country Care matter, which was followed later in 2018 by further charges against individuals from ANZ, Deutsche Bank and Citigroup. The CDPP has also laid charges against Alkaloids of Australia and an individual (who have subsequently entered guilty pleas) and against companies and individuals relating to currency exchanges between Australia and Vietnam. The Country Care Matter was the first criminal cartel trial before a jury. It resulted in an acquittal. The CDPP in late 2021 and February 2022 decided not to proceed with the prosecution of ANZ, Deutsche Bank and Citibank. The ICN's advocacy and support for criminalisation has greatly improved the ACCC's institutional capacity to prosecute cartel conduct and provided us with a greater array of tools to address the harms cartels cause to consumers.

The CWG has provided a forum for the ACCC to discuss our policies and practices to ensure they reflect international best practice. The CWG is the largest working group within the ICN, and attracts a significant amount of interest from practitioners and competition agencies around the globe. For around 10 years until 2018, the ACCC co-chaired the CWG and found the

Working Group to be an invaluable forum to discuss innovative topics in cartels enforcement, provide for cross-pollination between different cartel enforcement agencies, and build and maintain strong relationships going forward.

The CWG has been indispensable for the ACCC in helping us develop and refine our cartel leniency policy. At the 2013 Cartel Workshop in Cape Town, Scott Hammond from the US Department of Justice Antitrust Division gave a closed session presentation on the hallmarks of successful cartel enforcement programs. Following that, we arranged for Mr Hammond to review our leniency policy procedures and criminal investigation practices to ensure they were consistent with international best practice. Mr Hammond's feedback was the catalyst for an update to our leniency policy and a number of other procedural changes at the core of our cartels enforcement program, to build a more effective criminal investigation capability.

A small but useful project that emerged from the CWG has been the Anti-cartel Enforcement Template, which provides ICN members, as well as international businesses, transparent information about each jurisdiction's legislation concerning hard-core cartels. Due to the increasingly globalised world economy, having a repository of countries' domestic laws readily available allows for greater harmonisation of laws around the world and facilitates greater cooperation between competition agencies.

In addition, having each country's steps for gaining immunity in their jurisdiction displayed in an accessible document incentivises further immunity applications because applicants can be assured they are following the correct procedure in each country, therefore minimising the overall risk of prosecution. This development, along with the development of the leniency program outlined above, has significantly increased the amount of immunity applicants to the ACCC, particularly in international cartel matters. The ICN has been critical in providing and promoting this tool amongst the different competition agencies and this has greatly assisted the ACCC with our international cartel investigations over the past few years.

The ICN has also played a pivotal role in developing and maintaining the ACCC's relationships with our international counterparts. Fostering these relationships has been one of the most important achievements of the ICN throughout the past 20 years. Through the early years of the ICN, the ACCC was able to use our relationships with members to grow our institutional knowledge and increase the effectiveness of investigations. The ACCC has greatly benefited from training opportunities provided by ICN member states to improve our capacity to detect and prosecute cartel conduct. In regards to cartel enforcement, this collaboration prominently resulted in the first criminal cartel prosecutions in Australia in the international shipping matter, as the relationships we had developed through the ICN were central in the investigation and subsequent prosecution of NYK, K-Line and WWO in Australia.

The ICN's Immunity Waiver Template has proved a valuable resource for the ACCC and other members in improving our cartel detection work. In the ACCC's experience, the ICN model waiver is used by many law firms when applying for immunity, demonstrating the high regard that both regulators and private firms have for the ICN's cartel materials. It also facilitates witnesses gaining immunity across multiple jurisdictions using a consistent template and in that way has ensured that competition agencies can detect and prosecute more harmful global cartels.

3. INFLUENCE ON ACCC MERGER ENFORCEMENT

Over the last 20 years, while the number of mergers the ACCC assesses annually has remained relatively stable, we are faced with increasingly complex and contentious mergers. This is not a unique experience; but rather reflects the global trend of increasing complexity brought on, in part, by the development of technology that opens up new markets and has changed the ways businesses compete.

Although the ACCC needs to focus on the impact of mergers and acquisitions on Australian consumers, the reality is that a significant proportion of these have an international nexus. This highlights the ever-increasing importance of international cooperation in merger matters. The number of cross-jurisdictional mergers affecting Australia continues to increase as we become more interconnected, and barriers to trade, whether legal, physical, or technical, are broken down.

Since the ICN was formed in 2001, we have seen significant changes to the international mergers landscape. At the turn of this century, only around 60 jurisdictions had a merger control regime. A mere two decades on, there are now over 130 separate regimes. This generally aligns with a proliferation of competition law regimes around the world, but is a stark reminder that while we have come a long way in a relatively short time, merger control is still in its relative infancy worldwide. The ICN, which aims to instil best practices and push toward global convergence, is critical in ensuring the growing number merger regimes around the world are consistent, fit for purpose, and adaptable to the rapid creation of new markets in the modern, digital economy.

The ACCC has been a member of the ICN's Merger Working Group ("MWG") since its inception. In February 2020, the ACCC hosted its first ICN Merger

Workshop and is now busy applying the bountiful learnings obtained at the workshop to its day-to-day merger assessments. Now is a fitting time for the ACCC to reflect on some of the significant benefits the ICN's Merger Working Group has given us, principally through promoting consistent approaches to merger regulation worldwide and developing relationships that foster international cooperation on merger investigations.

4. MARKET STUDIES

The ICN is heavily involved in bringing together best practices in market studies, which are a key tool of competition agencies. Notably, the ICN recognises that market studies can help to build authorities' capacity and, if done well, both enhances their reputation and promotes better market outcomes. Drawing from the experiences of its members, the ICN's Good Practice Handbook identifies the key features of good market studies, without trying to prescribe the particular powers or purposes of market studies.

The role of market studies in competition advocacy and enforcement has been a key issue for the ACCC over the past few years. The issue was considered in depth as part of an independent review of Australia's competition law and policy in 2015 ("the Review").[1] That Review noted the importance of market studies, recognising that they are one means though which policymakers can delve deeper into the workings of a market, in an effort to identify changes that would lead to more competitive outcomes. In particular, the Review noted the absence of a formal market studies power in Australia. In contrast, in 2012 the ICN noted that 40 ICN member authorities were using market studies – a number that has continued to grow.

The Review recommended that Australia's competition agency should not be responsible for conducting competition studies of Australian markets, and that the function should instead lie with a new and separate competition policy agency with no enforcement responsibilities. Ultimately, the Australian Government noted that the ACCC already performs a market studies function for competition matters. For its part, the ACCC had increasingly undertaken "informal" market studies, resulting from both directions from government under existing powers, and through self-initiated research into matters within the ACCC's jurisdiction. Guidance from bodies with international experience such as the ICN and OECD has proved very valuable in building our capacity in this important role, and in reinforcing that message to the market.

1 *The Australian Government Competition Policy Review*, 2015.

5. ENHANCED RELATIONSHIPS

One of the key objectives of the ACCC's international engagement is to enable subject matter experts, investigators, case officers, managers and agency officials to share experiences, investigation and enforcement expertise, practices, and strategies for dealing with particular sectors or types of anticompetitive practices. This type of relationship building is incredibly beneficial in all competition matters, not the least in merger reviews.

International cooperation with other agencies in cross-jurisdictional merger reviews facilitates quick and efficient assessment of merger applications, and allows agencies to leverage off the remedies imposed in other jurisdictions. This ultimately helps to minimise the public and private costs of assessing cross-border mergers. However, this type of cooperation is not possible without a strong relationship built on mutual understanding and trust with a counterpart agency. These relationships have been developed through informal cooperation and engagement with our counterparts. The ACCC's active participation in MWG projects and our participation in the annual workshops over the years has played a significant part in building the close relationships we have established with other agencies and key personnel.

Building on the relationships we have formed and strengthened through our ICN engagement, we strive to share the Australian experience, and our practices and perspectives on merger control and learn from the experiences of other agencies. Developing and reinforcing these relationships with international counterparts would not be possible without an organisation like the ICN to bring competition agencies from around the world together.

Attendance at ICN workshops and meetings is also hugely beneficial from a learning and development perspective. It is critical for our ability to develop as an agency in how we assess mergers, and has a very practical day-to-day impact when we engage with our international peers on global mergers. Face-to-face and virtual engagement through the MWG events and projects allows us to:

- Exchange information relating to merger enforcement and remedies;
- Contribute to international best practice discussions about international cooperation on substantive merger reviews and remedies;
- Help support capacity building of developing agencies; and
- Draw upon international benchmarking, trends and developments to inform the ACCC's merger regulation.

6. IMPROVED INTERNATIONAL PRACTICES

Recognising the importance of international cooperation in ensuring effective merger enforcement, the MWG has developed extensive guidance for competition agencies on nearly every aspect of an effective merger review framework.

Foremost among these are the ICN are the Recommended Practices for Merger Analysis, and the Recommended Practices for Merger Notification and Review Procedures. The ICN's recommended practices are the highest-level consensus statements that the ICN produces, and therefore represent the established view of best practice amongst the vast majority of the world's competition agencies on each aspect they cover.

Because the ICN is the largest global network of competition agencies, its recommended practices are incredibly persuasive. They are relied on and referred to around the world by governments in developing competition frameworks, and also by international organisations in promoting competition policy. In mergers this is no different, as demonstrated by the Organisation for Economic Cooperation and Development incorporating the principles of the Recommended Practices on Merger Review into its 2005 Recommendation on Merger Review.[2] This is a testament to the ICN's ability to reach consensus and guide on best practices in mergers around the world.

Underpinning and complementing these recommended practices are additional guidance materials and tools, such as the merger guidelines workbook, handbook on investigative techniques, and the practical guidance on international cooperation. All of these resources are available publicly to anyone, whether an ICN member or not.

These resources are incredibly valuable, especially to jurisdictions with new frameworks or young competition agencies. They allow competition agencies to quickly understand and implement procedures and practices that are known to be effective, enhancing their capability as a regulator.

Beyond recommended practices and guidelines, the tools the ICN produces are practical and useful. For instance the MWG produced a model waiver to help facilitate confidential information sharing across borders in merger matters. Voluntary waivers are an important part of international merger cooperation. Most competition agencies do not have the ability to share confidential

2 Organisation for Economic Cooperation and Development, Competition Committee, *Report on Country Experiences with the 2005 OECD Recommendation on Merger Review*, 2013.

information with other jurisdictions. In isolation, this would hamper cross border merger enforcement that another agency had already looked at, and lead to additional expense and difficulty for competition agencies in pertinent information relevant to the merger. Waivers can be given to merger parties for them to then grant permission to share confidential information across borders. Developing a model waiver that has proven application is just one of the many examples of how the ICN contributes to the improved functioning of competition agencies through by providing practical tools.

7. PROMOTING CONVERGENCE AND THE ICN'S WORK ON VERTICAL RESTRAINTS

There are some aspects of competition law where it is easy to reach consensus. Take cartels for example. It would be hard to find anyone in the global competition community who would disagree that cartels are bad for competition. They are immoral and harmful because they not only cheat consumers and other businesses, but also restrict healthy economic growth and prosperity. This makes most endeavours that aim to strengthen our ability to tackle cartels uncontroversial.

However, not all issues the ICN grapples with are this clear cut. Jurisdictions have varied approaches to certain types of conduct based on their local jurisprudence and economic schools of thought. This poses a clear challenge: how can we promote convergence in a global network when there are strong and divergent views between jurisdictions about the economic harms involved? The pragmatic and collegiate approach of the ICN means agencies are able to navigate these challenges and still produce beneficial guidance and practical tools in the face of differing views. One example of this is the ICN's extensive work on online vertical restraints over the past five years, an emerging issue in the global economy.

The significant growth in e-commerce in the modern economy presents opportunities for expanded choice, competition, and efficiency. Likewise, it also poses a challenge to competition agencies to ensure these benefits are not undermined by anti-competitive conduct. Recognising an emerging area of online competition, the ICN Steering Group decided to commence a multi-year project on practical issues relating to the application of competition law to online vertical restraints. The ICN sought to understand if online vertical restraints should be a priority for ICN members, whether existing legal frameworks, investigative and analytical tools in member jurisdictions were effective for online vertical restraints, and what recommendations could/should the ICN make in response.

As the host of the 2015 ICN Annual Conference, the ACCC undertook the first phase of the project, which was a stocktake on the current climate for online vertical restraints among ICN members. We wanted to understand differences in legal frameworks around the world, the prevalence of vertical restraints across jurisdictions, and the extent to which competition agencies considered tackling vertical restraints a priority. To get to the heart of these issues, we conducted a literature review and a survey of ICN members.

The final report on the project identified that many members' considered their legal and analytical frameworks were generally sufficient to deal with most vertical restraints. However, members believed they would benefit from additional analytical work on certain types of vertical restraints, for example, 'across platform parity agreements' (otherwise known as 'most favoured nation' clauses), which remain common in several industries including online travel booking services.

With the findings of the report as a backdrop, the ICN's work on vertical restraints continued in the Unilateral Conduct Working Group ("UCWG"). The UCWG's project sought to promote increased understanding of vertical restraints, and where differences exist, to work towards convergence. It did this by developing hypothetical scenarios and asking members to answer questions about how that scenario would be dealt with in their jurisdiction.

The hypotheticals project produced a wealth of information in response, and highlighted the differing views agencies had about the detriment to competition arising from vertical restraints. The UCWG will now be able to use this information to determine future work products to guide agencies through assessing and dealing with vertical restraints, and also promote future convergence. Currently this project is ongoing within the UCWG and we are excited to see how it develops in the near future.

What this vertical restraint project shows us is that the ICN is able to pick up emerging competition issues as they arise, even those that are controversial, and develop novel approaches to understanding and addressing them. The ACCC has benefited substantially from this project by being able to assess our own legal and analytical framework, and therefore identify gaps in our knowledge and approach. But we also benefitted by gaining an understanding of how other agencies approached these issues, which gave us the ability to explore cross border cooperation on our own vertical restraint investigations.

8. WORK WITH ASEAN JURISDICTIONS

At the ACCC we consider cooperation and capacity building with other competition agencies overseas to be critical to our ability to effectively tackle anticompetitive conduct in our own backyard. The ICN has been influential and beneficial to the success of our own capacity building activities. This is no more apparent than in our capacity building efforts in South East Asia.

Since 2010, the Australia/New Zealand and the Association of Southeast Asian Nations ("ASEAN") Free Trade Area ("AANZFTA") agreement has formed the backbone of Australia's efforts to promote and support competition policy and cooperation in the region. AANZFTA contains a competition chapter that focusses solely on cooperation. This paved the way for a capacity building program known called the Competition Law Implementation Program ("CLIP").

Commencing In 2014, CLIP aims to promote competition in markets through support for ASEAN economies to develop their legal frameworks, build competition enforcement capacity, and strengthen their law enforcement institutions. CLIP has been enormously successful in developing strong competition frameworks in ASEAN Member States, and enhancing the capability of ASEAN competition agencies. When CLIP commenced in 2014, just five of the ten ASEAN Member States had national competition laws in place. This has now increased to nine. The ICN's established principles for organisational design, investigative process, as well as many other materials have been valuable in developing and delivering capacity building activities under CLIP.

The ICN Training on Demand is another ICN initiative that the ACCC has found to be incredibly valuable over the years. These modules provide competition agencies around the world with an online interactive educational centre, including video lectures and accompanying materials such as case studies from the US or EU. Topics covered include competition fundamentals, horizontal constraints, dominant firm conduct, investigative techniques, and agency effectiveness. By focussing on the basic elements and economics of these issues, the resources can be utilised by competition agencies to provide staff with a consistent understanding of the mechanics of competition and working within a competition authority.

This consistency ensures that ICN members are able to quickly understand competition problems and draw upon relevant practices by other jurisdictions when needed. When we help administer CLIP to members of ASEAN, the ACCC provides the ICN Training on Demand modules to staff within ASEAN competition authorities as a valuable source of information for building capacity among emerging competition agencies. By providing these educational resources, the ICN ensures that staff around the world share a similar knowledge base, and that all member agencies are able to learn best practices from each other.

9. COMPETITION AGENCY PROCEDURES

We recognise that improved cooperation in the promotion of competition enhances economic efficiency and consumer welfare to those within a market, and those seeking to do business within that market. Our experience with CLIP has also been a tangible example of the benefits to consumers, businesses and trading partners that developing norms of procedurally fair and transparent competition law frameworks can bring. The ICN has been integral in promoting the value of consistent procedural fairness and transparency principles among competition agencies around the globe. Particular examples include the ICN's Guiding Principles on Procedural Fairness, Recommended Practices for Investigative Process, and the Framework on Competition Agency Procedures ("CAP").

The CAP originated from a 2018 proposal by the US Department of Justice called the Multilateral Framework on Procedures. Late in the development of this initiative, the agencies developing it recognised there was the potential for increased scope and reach if the framework was implemented through the ICN, highlighting its influence and credibility. CAP was launched with the United States Department of Justice, Germany's Bundeskartellamt, and the ACCC as the inaugural co-chairs, responsible for promoting the CAP and helping to meet its strategic objectives.

By implementing the CAP, the ICN clearly recognises the benefits that come with creating global norms of procedural fairness, including for developing competition agencies and competition agencies operating in different political and legal environments. The establishment of these norms can help improve the quality and consistency of global competition law enforcement, and importantly, provide better conditions for improved cooperation between agencies.

The ICN CAP will help provide greater transparency over how each agency manages its enforcement procedures, which in turn can aid willingness between agencies to both informally and formally exchange information and provide assistance. Improving competition agency procedures in other jurisdictions also aids Australian business interests in these jurisdictions by helping ensure higher quality, procedurally fair investigations of Australian business by participating agencies.

As at August 2021, the CAP has 73 members, and the CAP page on the ICN website makes the templates of all participating agencies available. Going forward, 2021/22 is shaping up to be an exciting year for the ICN CAP, with a range of opportunities for discussion and sharing of best practices between participants.

10. CONCLUSION

As a voluntary network, the ICN relies entirely on the dedication and efforts of its members. The fact that the ICN has been able to produce so many high quality, useful, work products since its inception is a testament to the collective efforts of the global competition community to advance the interests of competition law and policy, and enhance the capability of regulators outside their own jurisdiction.

The ACCC has greatly benefitted from its involvement with the ICN. That involvement culminated in March 2017 with the ACCC receiving an international award from the World Bank and the ICN, for its role in elevating competition policy to the national economic agenda. The ACCC won the award for its advocacy work in promoting pro-competition measures when governments are privatising public assets.

Evolving markets and new ways of doing business will always give rise to new competition and regulatory issues. With its motto of "all competition, all the time", the ICN is uniquely placed to meet these future challenges, drawing inspiration from and delivering support back to its membership.

20 YEARS OF SOUTH AFRICA'S PARTNERSHIP WITH THE ICN

Tembinkosi BONAKELE*

1. INTRODUCTION

The Competition Commission of South Africa (CCSA) is one of three bodies established in 1999 to regulate competition in South Africa. It serves as an investigative and prosecutorial body. The other two are both adjudicative bodies, namely the Competition Tribunal of South Africa (CTSA) and the Competition Appeal Court (CAC). The CCSA and the CTSA have actively participated in the International Competition Network (ICN) in various capacities since its inception in 2001. This report details:

- South Africa's participation in the ICN since its founding;
- the extent to which South Africa makes use of ICN materials, including guidelines and video manuals; and
- suggested areas for development within the ICN, in particular: broadening participation, working with developing economies and increasing ICN representation on global forums.

2. SOUTH AFRICA'S PARTICIPATION IN THE ICN SINCE ITS FOUNDING

2.1. THE BEGINNINGS

The South African competition authorities take pride in being founding members of the ICN. Established barely a year after the CCSA and the CTSA, the timing could not have been better. In a jurisdiction with almost nothing to start with in terms of competition technical expertise – where former liberation activists who fought apartheid, most of whom were Marxists and trade unionists, combined with some elements who shared a mutual suspicion of free markets

* Commissioner, South African Competition Commission.

and a few lawyers who received a few days of training by European and North American experts, found themselves at the helm of the competition authorities, the search for international companionship was almost desperate. South Africa threw itself whole heartedly into the ICN, a tradition it upholds to this day. South Africa gave so much to the ICN, and received so much more. For us, the last twenty years have been a labour of love.

2.2. OUR PARTICIPATION

CCSA is a founding member of the ICN and today, 20 years later, still actively participates in its working groups. David Lewis chaired the ICN for a period when he was chairman of the CTSA. The CCSA and CTSA have hosted ICN events over the last 19 years, including the ICN's annual conference. To this day, we receive flattering comments about a memorable annual conference in Cape Town, with some – to our embarrassment – describing it as the best party ever held under the banner of the ICN, while some think the wine producing region of Stellenbosch in South Africa should be a permanent home for the Unilateral Conduct Working Group, for understandable reasons.

Two Commissioners of the CCSA sat on the ICN Steering Committee and the CCSA has either chaired or co-chaired various ICN working groups over this time. Moreover the CCSA has facilitated the participation of several South African non-governmental advisors (NGA's) in the ICN and has actively encouraged members of the African Competition Forum (ACF) to participate in the ICN. Table 1 lists some of the highlights of South Africa's participation in the ICN for the last 12 years. As mentioned, the CCSA's participation in the ICN pre-dates 2006 however Table 1 contains information available from our annual records.

Table 1. Highlights of the CCSA's participation in the ICN for the last 12 years

Year	Level of participation in the ICN
2006	– South Africa was the first African country selected to host the annual conference of ICN. It was held in May 2006. – David Lewis, chairperson of the CTSA was elected deputy chair of the ICN.
2007	– CCSA was participating in a number of the ICN's working groups – Senior CCSA staff attended the annual ICN conference in May 2007, held in Moscow. – CCSA staff participated in working group discussions and made written submissions to the ICN about strategic planning and prioritisation. – CCSA staff participated in the unilateral conduct working group.

Year	Level of participation in the ICN
2008	- CCSA staff: - submitted two papers to the ICN; - made one presentation at an ICN conference; and - made one presentation at the ICN cartel workshop. - CCSA staff were active in the following working groups: (1) advocacy; (2) mergers; (3) cartels; (4) unilateral conduct; (5) competition policy implementation.
2009	- Shan Ramburuth, the Commissioner of the CCSA, was a member of the steering group of the ICN. - A senior CCSA and CTSA delegation attended the ICN's eight annual conference in Zurich, Switzerland in June 2009. - CCSA submitted written contributions to the ICN working groups on agency effectiveness, cartels and advocacy. - CCSA staff participated in the ICN's cartels workshop held in Egypt in October 2009. - CCSA staff took part in a teleseminar of the ICN, several teleconferences of the ICN and attended working group meetings.
2010	- CCSA staff actively participated as presenters, moderators and panellists in various ICN conferences, workshops and tele-seminars. - CCSA staff contributed to the work product of the following working groups: (1) advocacy; (2) agency effectiveness; (3) cartels; (4) mergers; and (5) unilateral conduct. - A CCSA delegation attended the ninth annual conference of the ICN in Istanbul, Turkey in April 2010.
2011	- CCSA staff participated in: - the ICN's 10th annual conference; - the ICN cartel workshop; and - the ICN agency effectiveness roundtable for agency heads. - CCSA staff contributed to the ICN's curriculum project.
2012	- A senior delegation attended and participated in the ICN's 11th annual conference in Rio de Janeiro in April 2012. - CCSA staff actively participated on panels at various ICN workshops including the mergers workshop in Colombia in November 2012, the cartel workshop in Singapore in June 2012 and the advocacy workshop in Paris in June 2012. - CCSA staff assisted in the development of a new module for developing countries for the ICN curriculum project. - In August 2012 the CCSA won the bid to host the 2013 annual ICN cartel workshop. - CCSA staff continued to actively participate in ICN working groups.
2013	- CCSA staff participated in the ICN advocacy working group conference held in Rome, Italy, sharing its experiences on 'competition policy assessment' and 'bid rigging'. - CCSA hosted the 2013 annual ICN cartel workshop in Cape Town October. - CCSA staff continued to participate in ICN working groups.
2014	- CCSA staff participated in ICN conference in Morocco in April 2014. - CCSA continued to serve as a member of the ICN steering group. - CCSA maintained its active participation in five working groups of the ICN.

Year	Level of participation in the ICN
2015	- CCSA staff attended the annual ICN conference in Sydney, Australia in April 2015. - CCSA continued to serve as a member of the ICN steering group. It also served as co-chair of the cartels working group. - CCSA maintained its active participation in five working groups of the ICN.
2016	- CCSA participated in six ICN working groups, namely the steering group where it was co-chairing; the mergers group; the unilateral conduct group; the cartels group, where it was also a co-chair; the advocacy group; and the agency effectiveness group. As such the CCSA participated in calls and contributed to the work product of these groups. - CCSA planned and participated in the ICN's agency effectiveness workshop in Botswana, Gaborone in March 2016. It did so in collaboration with the ACF. - CCSA took part in the roundtable on the second decade of the ICN, Washington, USA, in April 2016. - CCSA took part in the ICN annual conference and launch of ACF/World Bank research into competition in Africa. The event took place in Singapore in April 2016. - The CCSA along with the Netherlands and Colombian authorities were co-chairs of the ICN cartels working group. As such the CCSA participated in numerous conference calls to discuss the progress of the working group and to plan for the annual conference. - The CCSA had two NGA's on the ICN's official list of NGA's: John Oxenham and Kasturi Moodaliyar.
2017	- CCSA participated in the ICN's annual conference held in May 2017 in Porto, Portugal. In particular, the CCSA contributed to the sessions on agency effectiveness, the session on strategic thinking in communicating for deterrence and the steering group meeting. - The CCSA, as outgoing co-chair of the cartels working group, participated in the cartel working group plenary on *"Leniency, incentives and deterrence"*. The CCSA also participated in the work of the unilateral conduct working group in addition to its work on the other ICN working groups. - CCSA was announced as co-chair of the ICN's unilateral conduct working group for the 2018 and 2019 calendar years and as host of the unilateral conduct annual conference in November 2018.
2018	- The CCSA participated in the 2018 ICN Annual Conference hosted by the Competition Commission of India in Delhi in March 2018. - CCSA hosted the ICN unilateral conduct working group workshop in Stellenbosch, Cape Town, in November 2018. - CCSA hosted the ICN merger working group regional teleconference in November 2018. - CCSA participated in more than 20 teleconferences and webinars of the ICN.

2.3. INTERNAL STRUCTURES

Internally the CCSA allocates dedicated resources to promoting and maintaining a relationship with the ICN. Our international relations officer ensures that the CCSA participates in the ICN and monitors staff contributions to the various

ICN working groups. In this regard the international relations officer monitors who participates on our behalf and what our position is on various issues. Moreover the international relations officer keeps track of written submissions and speaking roles at workshops and other ICN events. The international relations officer also serves as a liaison between the ICN and the CCSA.

ICN workshops take place annually and are coordinated by the relevant working groups. CCSA staff are usually nominated to attend the workshops based on a number of factors including their role at the workshop, the work they have contributed to the relevant working group and the relevance of topics under discussion for the CCSA's work.

The ICN's work product consists of guidance, best practice recommendations, good practice and other practical tools for competition authorities. CCSA staff can access these materials on the internal knowledge management system, or KMS, which is an internal database of information necessary for staff to carry out their day to day tasks. This international relations site on the KMS is updated and circulated to staff as and when new product is published.

3. EXTENT TO WHICH SOUTH AFRICA MAKES USE OF ICN MATERIALS

3.1. LEARNING BY DOING

The ICN has been one of the primary learning centres for our people at all levels, whether through its guidelines, ICN training-on-demand videos, webinars, working group workshops and teleconferences, participation in the annual conferences, or being a part of its major initiatives such as ICN's Next Decade 2016 initiative, CALEP or being at the cusp of its major debates such as the place of excessive pricing or public interest objectives in competition law, or participating in its leadership structures.

We conducted a simple survey amongst staff which revealed that ICN materials are in regular use in the CCSA and they are typically referenced in final case reports presented to the CCSA's decision making body. The CCSA is represented on seven ICN working groups and staff receive notifications and updates on ICN materials from the CCSA's library. For the most part staff make most use of the ICN guidelines when assessing cases, especially when cases present new competition concepts or new markets not previously dealt with in the CCSA. ICN guidelines also form part of the information pack new staff receive when they join the core departments of the CCSA. CCSA staff clearly view ICN materials as a convenient single platform from which to gain insights into the approach of multiple jurisdictions.

However, CCSA staff mentioned two shortcomings with ICN materials: (1) that they do not offer enough diversity in the types of markets featured in the materials which makes it difficult for CCSA staff to "*compare apples with apples*" should they seek to apply learnings from other jurisdictions to the South African context of a developing market; and (2) while guidelines for case work are widely publicised and widely used, the availability of ICN training-on-demand is not well publicised which causes agencies to develop their own training material without much guidance in this area from the ICN.

CCSA staff have extensively used ICN materials when assessing mergers, abuses of dominance and cartels. Staff highlighted the following examples.

- While conducting the CCSA's health market inquiry, staff made extensive use of ICN materials to determine the approach of multiple jurisdictions to competition issues arising in health care markets and to benchmark South Africa's thinking against that of jurisdictions that have confronted similar issues.
- Also while conducting the CCSA's health inquiry, staff found the ICN's own compilations of multi-jurisdictional approaches to health care very useful.
- New staff have consulted ICN materials in order to understand the basics of competition regulation.
- Beyond casework, staff find ICN materials to be useful for understanding competition policy on a broader level.
- ICN materials have been particularly helpful in the area of excessive pricing. The assessment of excessive pricing has been challenging for the CCSA and ICN materials have helped CCSA staff determine the approach of other jurisdictions to excessive pricing and the various cost measures applicable to the concept.
- ICN materials have been useful for CCSA staff assessing new and complex concepts not previously encountered. One example was the ICN guidelines on vertical co-ordination which came in handy when the CCSA assessed a global merger involving Sinopec and Chevron South Africa. Another example was the ICN guidelines on vertical assessments in mergers which guide staff on the factors to take into account when assessing mergers which present foreclosure concerns.
- When compiling internal guidelines for assessing cases, ICN materials served as an example for CCSA staff to model their guidelines against.

Specific materials highlighted by staff are listed in Table 2 below.

Table 2. Key ICN materials regularly used by CCSA staff

Field	Key ICN Material
Merger review	i. Recommended Practices for Merger Notification and Review Procedures ii. Recommended Practices for Merger Analysis iii. Framework for Merger Review Cooperation
Abuse of dominance enforcement	i. Recommended Practices on assessment of dominance/substantial market power ii. Unilateral Conduct Workbook
Anti-cartel enforcement	i. ICN Framework for Sharing Non-Confidential Information for Cartel Enforcement ii. Anti-Cartel Enforcement Manual iii. Leniency work

3.2. NETWORK EFFECTS

While the materials generated by the ICN are most helpful in the CCSA's day to day work, perhaps the greatest contribution of the ICN is bringing enforcers together as people – creating lasting bonds and fellowship that has become part of the culture among enforcers today. Through the ICN, an investigator in a small jurisdiction is able to pick up the phone and discuss a merger with her counterpart in a large jurisdiction. They share experiences of their work in various sectors, and they develop trust. Such interactions are the priceless gift that is the ICN to the world of competition enforcement, a gift so rare in other public sector international endeavours.

The schedule at international conferences is filled with bilateral or regional meetings organised on the side-lines of these events. Over the years the ICN has been an unofficial platform for agencies to meet and discuss collaboration on investigations, research, capacity building and staff exchanges. Moreover the participation of NGA's expands on the network and promotes better understanding across the usually fortified divide.

While Table 2 sets out the extent to which the CCSA makes use of ICN materials, as stated the benefits we have derived from our ICN interactions reach further than these interactions alone. It is the international relations we have forged on the ICN platform and in conference side meetings that have led to the bilateral relations we now enjoy with competition agencies around the world. Over the years we have also collaborated on joint research programs, staff exchange programs and capacity building initiatives with other competition agencies. We have also observed the formation and organisation of the ICN, making use of those lessons in the formation and organisation of newer competition bodies such as the ACF.

4. AREAS FOR DEVELOPMENT WITHIN THE ICN

The ICN was founded in October 2001 and has grown tremendously over this time from just 16 competition agencies to over 100 member agencies today. As mentioned the CCSA was a founding member and so has proudly observed this growth and contributed to the position the ICN finds itself in today. However, the CCSA believes there are some areas of the ICN's operation that require further development.

The ICN has been an inspiration and encouraged regional collaboration such as the African Competition Forum or ACF. As the chair of the African Competition Forum, we have seen the growth of competition law in Africa, and how the ICN has worked to bring new agencies within the international community through various ways, including financially sponsoring their participation in ICN events. We have also seen earnest discussion and exploration of how to get the ICN agenda to incorporate the needs of smaller and young agencies. With these outreach initiatives, the ICN has emerged a membership driven organisation responsive to the needs of its wide and diverse membership, which is a no mean feat.

Having said that and not taking away from the achievement, a 20 year anniversary is also an opportunity to explore areas of improvement. We now briefly reflect on these.

4.1. BROADENING COUNTRY PARTICIPATION

It is conceivable that part of the reason for the ICN's growth has been its ability to function by consensus and its ability to stay relevant to growing needs. The growth within the ICN is indicative of the influence of competition policy around the world and the resulting establishment of new competition agencies or strengthening of existing competition agencies. On the continent of Africa, for instance, the number of jurisdictions with competition laws almost tripled in 15 years. In 2000, 13 jurisdictions had adopted competition laws. By 2015, this number had increased to 32 jurisdictions. (*Breaking Down Barriers*, a report by the World Bank and the African Competition Forum, 2015).

Broadening participation at the ICN is a work in progress. While much work has been done to bring agencies within the ICN, there is a notable absence of the People's Republic of China, a jurisdiction most members are unfamiliar with but which has the second largest economy of the world, i.e. a very important jurisdiction. The CCSA believes that the ICN should actively encourage China to join and remove all obstacles that prevent it from doing so. In this respect the world has changed and we believe it is time for the ICN to reflect this global shift.

The ICN must create more space for participation of developing countries and share geographic spread of representation in its leadership structures. This means that some developing countries have to give way in some structures such as the Steering Group in order to accommodate this change. Of course, this change has to be managed in view of the resources that are required to play the leadership role, so that representation does not mean appointing countries that may not be able to fulfil obligations in an organisation surviving through membership voluntarism.

4.2. BROADENING GENDER PARTICIPATION

The ICN activities are dominated by men. The ICN must not be indifferent to the global struggle against gender inequality and must deliberately promote representation of women in its structure and activities. These matters must also find expression in the discussions at the ICN.

4.3. BROADENING THE SUBJECT MATTER

The need to broaden participation at the ICN goes beyond gender and identifying more countries for membership. It extends to the ICN's leadership and its discourse. The ICN has itself recognised this need and has already embarked on initiatives to ensure broader participation. However from the perspective of a developing market, there is still room for further and faster development in this area. In this regard the CCSA would advocate for the establishment of more working groups tackling concerns faced by competition agencies in developing markets. There remains a gap in policy, law and practical application within the area of developmental competition and the ICN is well positioned to advance learning and contribute to the body of knowledge in this area. Given its extensive membership and its existing infrastructure, the ICN is also well positioned to serve as a platform for exchanging ideas with alternative market structures such as the Chinese market and developing or mixed economies.

During 2016 the CCSA undertook an informal analysis of the speakers proposed by agencies for the cartels working group plenaries and break-out sessions at the annual conference of the ICN. The CCSA sought to determine the state of affairs concerning diversity in gender, geographical spread and the age of agencies represented. The survey showed, among other things, that over 70% of proposed speakers were male, 49% were from European agencies and one international agency was more represented than other agencies attending the annual conference. It had speakers in five out of the seven sessions. Africa had only one speaker (Makgale Mohlala of the CCSA). Given the ICN steering group's emphasis on more inclusivity and on drawing expertise from younger agencies the co-chairs of the working group convened an urgent conference call to discuss the composition of the speakers and thus addressed this concern.

Such initiatives by the working groups, as well as the sensitivity and speed with which the ICN has responded to changing needs, have assisted the ICN to grow and to remain relevant. In the CCSA's view, opening up participation, broadening the subject matter, actively encouraging participation amongst newer agencies, agencies in developing markets and agencies in alternative market structures will go some way towards ensuring the ICN's continued effectiveness over the next 20 years.

4.4. VOICE IN THE GLOBAL DIALOGUE

The voice of the ICN is relatively absent in global fora that debate global economic challenges such as the World Economic Forum. Debates about business practices should not be confined to multilateral state bodies such as the UN and OECD. It is the CCSA's view that the ICN must engage in platforms where these debates are held.

5. CONCLUSION

I want to conclude these brief reflections by paying tribute to successful generations of enforcers who founded and or participated in the activities of the ICN throughout. Their foresight in establishing a membership driven virtual organisation proved its genius with the remarkable growth of the ICN from a handful of countries into well over a hundred. There are no strings attached – no one is compelled to join the ICN, there is no membership fee, no one is forced to participate in its activities, no one is stopped from leaving – it is a friendship with benefits only. We all owe the ICN a debt of gratitude – long live the ICN!

Revised Aug. 19, 2021

LINKED-IN: ANTITRUST AND THE VIRTUES OF A VIRTUAL NETWORK – LOOKING BACK AND FORWARD

Eleanor M. Fox*

1. INTRODUCTION

This article is an intellectual history of ICN. It examines its background and birth, its early years, and its maturity at 20. It assesses its performance, it glimpses its future, and it closes with a recommendation: While the ICN has thus far limited itself to national law, its convergence, and cooperation in its implementation, it is time for it to grapple with world competition problems that require global vision, albeit implemented at national level. This article is based on my article to commemorate the 10th anniversary of ICN.[1] As I noted then, the International Competition Network is an outstanding example of networking, which is the new world order.[2]

---

* Eleanor Fox is the Walter J. Derenberg Professor of Law at New York University School of Law. The author thanks John Fingleton, Barry Hawk, Alberto Heimler, Merit Janow, David Lewis, Daniel Sokol, Maria Coppola, and Randy Tritell for extremely helpful conversations and comments. She acknowledges research assistance from the Filomen D'Agostino and Max E. Greenberg Faculty Research Fund.

1 Published in THE INTERNATIONAL COMPETITION NETWORK AT TEN: ORIGINS, ACCOMPLISHMENTS AND ASPIRATIONS (P. Lugard ed. 2011).

2 *See* ANNE-MARIE SLAUGHTER, A NEW WORLD ORDER (2004). Slaughter conceptualizes networking across borders, and particularly networks of government officials, as a key feature of the new world order and a phenomenon that is "underappreciated, undersupported, and underused to address the central problems of global governance." *Id.* at 1. See, for an updated iteration, Anne-Marie Slaughter and Gordon LaForge, Opening Up the Order: A More Inclusive International System (Foreign Affairs March/April 2021), p 154.
The ICN differs from networks in other fields of law, which often are engaged in explicit rule-making and standard-setting. See Slaughter, *supra*; Kal Raustiala, *The Architecture of International Cooperation: Transgovernmental Networks and the Future of International Law*, 43 VA. J. INT'L L. 1 (2002); Pierre-Hugues Verdier, *Transnational Regulatory Networks and Their Limits*, 34 YALE J. INT'L L. 113 (2009) (comparing the Basel Committee on Banking Supervision, the International Organization of Securities Commissions, and the International Competition Network).

2. ANTITRUST, THE WORLD, AND THE STALLED POSSIBILITY OF A GLOBAL SYSTEM

The ICN is a network that was invented to fill a void. It arose in the presence of global competition and the absence of an international law of antitrust. In the background were intense discussions, in the 1990s, of the need for a global framework and how to achieve it.

In modern times, the Europeans were the first to articulate and promote a world antitrust agenda.[3] Europe has spent half a century studying and implementing modes of establishing community among nations, having in mind the benefits of community-wide vision while being mindful of the realm preserved to the non-parochial sovereignty interests of each Member State. It is not surprising, therefore, that the European Union was the first jurisdiction to study the need for global vision in competition policy and to make recommendations to achieve it.

The Directorate-General for competition of the (then) European Community convened a "Committee of Wise Men." The Committee outlined a model of a competition law for the world, which they placed institutionally within the World Trade Organization (WTO). Under this proposal, designed for transactions or conduct with cross-border effects, the project for a world antitrust framework would begin slowly and from the ground up. It would start with building blocks of cooperation among nations' antitrust authorities, principles of transparency, non-discrimination and due process, and a program for capacity building and technical assistance to developing countries. It would multilateralize existing bilateral cooperation agreements. The system would advance to the adoption of common substantive principles against abuse of dominance and cartels, eventually encompassing the substantive law common to antitrust systems, and would put into place a process for dispute resolution within the WTO framework.[4]

The proposal was vetted within the Competition Directorate-General and then within the European Commission and European Council. It became the basis

---

3 For a useful account of the development of international competition policy as launched by the European Commission, see also Alberto Heimler, *Competition Policy as a Tool of EU Foreign Policy: Multilateralism, Bilateralism and Soft Convergence, in* The European Union Foreign Policy: Myth or Reality? (F. Bindi ed., Brookings 2009).

4 *Commission of the European Communities, Report of the Group of Experts, Competition Policy in the new Trade Order: Strengthening International Cooperation and Rules*, COM (1995) 359 final (Dec. 7, 1995) [hereinafter Van Miert Report]. *See European Commission, XXVIth Report on Competition Policy*, at 95, COM (1997) 628 final (1996), *available at* http://ec.europa.eu/competition/annual_reports/rap96_en.html.

for the Singapore antitrust initiative adopted by the WTO in December 1996, which established the WTO Working Group on the Interaction between Trade and Competition Policy.[5] The Working Group, which met many times over the course of seven years, became a vehicle for discussions and submissions from scores of nations, developed and developing, on the benefits and drawbacks of a world competition-policy initiative.[6] Reactions of the various non-European nations differed widely. The United States expressed strong skepticism toward a world initiative for fear that developing and other countries' protectionist goals would be enshrined, that consensus would be formed at the lowest common denominator, that disputes would be resolved by uninformed bureaucrats, and that the competition agencies of the various nations would lose their prerogative of prosecutorial discretion.[7] Europe, Japan, Korea, and Canada favored a WTO framework for antitrust as the natural next step. Hong Kong (which then had no antitrust law) would support only a regime against state restraints of trade, while India and various developing countries opposed a world antitrust initiative for fear that resulting rules would favor the West and further colonize and marginalize developing countries. Developing countries feared also that they lacked the technical knowledge and sophistication to protect their interests in the course of negotiations and that they lacked the resources and other capacities to establish and carry on the work of a competition agency.[8]

Despite the doubts, the idea of a competition initiative within the WTO gained traction and held its grip for some years. Reactively, the United States introduced a different idea.

U.S. officials proposed a recommendation against cartels in the Organization for Economic Development and Cooperation (OECD). The OECD is an organization of developed nations, and has no dispute resolution powers. While

---

5 See European Commission, *XXVIth Report on Competition Policy, supra* note 4, at 95.

6 *See* World Trade Organization, *Annual Report 1997. Trade and Competition Policy*, Vol. 1, Ch. 4, 29–91 [hereinafter WTO 1997 Report]. For more information, *see* also the annual reports of the working group and the underlying documents, *available at www.wto.org/english/tratop_e/comp_e/wgtcp_docs_e.htm*. For the history and early evolution of the WTO initiative, *see* Clifford A. Jones, *Come the Millennium (Round)? Competing Visions of International Antitrust Policy in the European Union and the United States, in* International Antitrust Law & Policy: 2001 Fordham Corporate Law ch. 3 (Barry Hawk ed., 2001). For reflections on the work of the WTO Working Group, see Robert D. Anderson & Frederic Jenny, *Competition Policy, Economic Development and the Possible Role of a Multilateral Framework on Competition Policy: Insights from the WTO Working Group on Trade and Competition Policy, in* Competition Policy in East Asia (E. Medalla ed., 2005).

7 *See* Joel Klein, *Anticipating the Millennium: International Antitrust Enforcement at the End of the Twentieth Century, in* International Antitrust Law & Policy: 2001 Fordham Corporate Law Institute ch. 1 (Barry Hawk ed., 1998).

8 *See* World Trade Organization [WTO], Documents of the Working Group on the Interaction Between Trade and Competition Policy, Countries' Submission, www.wto.org/english/tratop_e/comp_e/ wgtcp_docs_e.htm (last visited Apr. 5, 2009).

the Europeans had prioritized abuse of dominance, and vertical restraints at national boundaries, as the most heinous of antitrust offenses, Americans prioritized cartels. Americans regarded single firm (non-conspiratorial) acts and vertical restraints as usually efficient and good. They wanted to shift focus from abuse of dominance and vertical restraints to cartels.

The American enforcers were not pleased with the WTO as an antitrust forum, for the WTO caters to the trade community. Agreements are negotiated among more than 140 (now 164) nations, including many developing countries, many of which were unsure of the virtues of competition and preferred interventionist industrial policy. A recommendation against cartels in the OECD would have three benefits: it would prioritize hard core cartels (price fixing and market division among competitors); it would mute the stress on abuse of dominance and vertical restraints; and it would move the forum from the WTO to one comprised of more nearly like-minded countries and to one without enforcement powers. The OECD was "safe." No nation would risk being disciplined by a remote world organization and by decision-makers who might dislike multinationals, disregard economics, and distrust free markets.[9]

The two initiatives – the cartel-focused one in the OECD and the broader one in the WTO – proceeded side by side. The OECD initiative led to adoption of the Hard Core Cartel Recommendation.[10] The Hard Core Cartel Recommendation urges that nations adopt and maintain an anti-cartel law. It allows derogations from the anti-cartel principle, but it urges that nations limit and review their derogations. The signatory nations undertake to report new derogations to the OECD.

Meanwhile, in the face of U.S. criticism of its WTO initiative, the European Commission streamlined its proposal for a world competition framework, limiting the substantive undertaking of states to adopting and maintaining an anti-cartel law[11] and all but eliminating dispute resolution. Dispute resolution would be available only for certain objective defaults such as failing to maintain an anti-cartel law. Certain recommendations were left unmodified: that nations cooperate in matters of common interest, ensure transparency and procedural

---

9 *See* Daniel Tarullo, *Norms and Institutions in Global Competition Policy*, 94 AM. J. INT'L L. 478 (2000) (recommending that the OECD, not the WTO, be the forum for antitrust convergence).

10 Organisation for Economic Co-operation and Development [OECD], *Recommendation of the Council Concerning Effective Action Against Hard Core Cartels*, C(98)35/Final (Mar. 25, 1998), *available at* http:// strategis.ic.gc.ca/pics/ct/1998oecd_hccrec.pdf.

11 This change effected a sharp shift of focus from vertical restraints and abuses by dominant firms to cartels. *See* THE SINGAPORE ISSUES AND THE WORLD TRADING SYSTEM: THE ROAD TO CANCUN AND BEYOND (State Secretariat of Economic Affairs & Simon Evenett, eds., WTI 2003); Heimler, *supra* note 3. The shift was a U.S. victory.

fairness in application of their competition laws, and support capacity building and technical assistance for developing countries. This slimmed-down proposal became a part of the provisional agenda of the round of the WTO introduced at the ministerial meeting at Doha, Qatar, in 2001 – a round dubbed the Doha Development Round in recognition of the fact that the developed countries had been the big winners of the recent trade rounds and the developing nations had not received a fair share of the gains. The Doha Agenda was meant to focus on measures that would especially help developing countries.

At the ministerial meeting of the new round in Cancun in fall 2003, however, Europe and the United States made insufficient offers to reduce agricultural tariffs and subsidies, and the whole round faltered.[12] The negotiators considered it necessary to jettison the more tangential aspirations, and the antitrust agenda was sacrificed to the hoped-for success of the round, which has now substantially failed.[13]

At present, there is no active agenda for world antitrust law, and the enterprise is not likely to be revived in the foreseeable future. While the competition committees of the OECD and the United Nations Conference on Trade and Development (UNCTAD) continue to thrive in their research and programmatic activities, attention has shifted to the ICN.

3. THE RISE OF THE NETWORK

3.1. THE BIRTH OF THE ICN

By the late 1990s, the surge in global business activity exposed the need for deeper transnational coordination in vetting mergers and rooting out cartels. In 1997, U.S. President Clinton's Attorney General Janet Reno convened the International Competition Policy Advisory Committee (ICPAC) to the U.S. Attorney General and Assistant Attorney General for Antitrust to study the implications of globalization on antitrust cooperation and enforcement. The Committee was co-chaired by James Rill, former Assistant Attorney General for

---

12 *See* Joseph Stiglitz & Andrew Charlton, Fair Trade for All: How Trade Can Promote Development 1–6 (2005).

13 In the wake of the Cancun Ministerial Meeting, the European Commission issued a Communication considering how the EU could contribute to a revival of negotiations on competition and the other Singapore issues (investment, trade facilitation, and government procurement). As to the development dimension of the Doha Development Agenda, it said: "The integration of developing countries into the world economy is a necessary condition for development. Such integration will be deeper and fairer if anchored in the multilateral trading system." Communication from the Commission to the Council, to the European Parliament, and to the Economic and Social Committee, at 15, 26 Nov. 2003.

Antitrust, and Paula Stern, former Chair of the International Trade Commission. Its executive director was Professor Merit Janow of Columbia University. The Committee was comprised of ten other members, including seven business or foundation executives and three professors (including the author) of law, business, and economics. At the time, the debate about a competition initiative in the WTO was active and gaining traction, and the U.S. Assistant Attorney General in charge of Antitrust, Joel Klein, strongly opposed.[14]

The Committee held hearings, received submissions, and deliberated. In 2000, it issued a report containing numerous recommendations for increased coordination and cooperation and modes for convergence of law and process, in particular regarding multinational mergers and world cartels. It recommended a Global Competition Initiative (GCI).[15] The GCI was envisioned as a virtual, voluntary forum with no ground address or secretariat, no power to make binding rules, and no power of adjudication. The idea for the enterprise stemmed from the realization that antitrust authorities, business people, and experts lacked a forum for the sharing of views and experiences, for close cooperation, and for exploration of common issues that could lead to convergence or harmonization of legal standards. Although competition problems were increasingly global, these issues had no antitrust home.

No existing organization filled the need.[16] The OECD is an organization of developed nations and is therefore – despite its successful outreach efforts, including a Global Forum – exclusive or limited. The UNCTAD caters to developing countries and was not a satisfactory forum to developed countries. The WTO is a trade organization at which trade representatives have the seat at the table. Moreover, success at the WTO entails bargaining and trade-offs, in contrast to the (sometimes) "purer" antitrust rule-of-law. Antitrust authorities lacked a table of their own. Further, in the WTO the mere prospect of committing their nations to obligations made the representatives reluctant to talk freely about solutions to common problems.

The GCI would by-pass the limits of each of these organizations. It would be a roots-up forum. It would include developing as well as developed countries. It would be purely voluntary, with no binding action. The logic of GCI, said the ICPAC Report, "stems in part from a recognition that countries may be prepared

14 *See* Klein, *supra* note 7.

15 U.S. Dep't of Justice, Antitrust Div., Report of the International Competition Policy Advisory Committee to the Attorney General and Assistant Attorney General for Antitrust 281–85 (2000), *available at* www.usdoj.gov/atr/icpac/chapter6.htm [hereinafter ICPAC Report].

16 *See* Eleanor Fox, *Competition Law and the Millennium Round*, 2 J. Intl Econ. L. 665, 677 (1999) (proposing a World Competition Forum).

to cooperate in meaningful ways but are not necessarily prepared to be legally bound under international law."[17]

The ICPAC submitted its report to Attorney General Reno and Assistant Attorney General Klein in February 2000. In September 2000, at the Tenth Anniversary Conference for European Merger Control, Assistant Attorney General Joel Klein made a proposal:

> [W]e all realize that bilateral efforts, while absolutely essential, are not a complete answer... There is still a lot of work to be done without an obvious unifying forum in which to do it. Our Advisory Committee recognized the problem and called for a Global Competition Initiative. I have been giving this considerable thought and believe that, whatever happens on antitrust at the WTO... we should move in the direction of a Global Competition Initiative, cautiously and on an exploratory basis, but in the end I think such a development is almost inevitable.[18]

Klein's proposal came as a surprise to his counterparts, heads of competition agencies from around the world, for until this moment American unilateralism had held sway. European Competition Commissioner Mario Monti almost immediately welcomed the idea as a positive move towards multilateralism. But Klein's proposal was met with skepticism. Why yet another forum? Would the GCI only tread on the toes of the OECD and the UNCTAD? Was the GCI an empty vessel, a "headless horseman," only meant to take the wind out of antitrust sails in the WTO?[19]

Gradually, however, the idea of a virtual global antitrust initiative gained acceptance. In February 2001, the International Bar Association, with support from the American Bar Association Antitrust Law Section and the Fordham Corporate Law Institute, convened a meeting at Ditchley Park near London, under the leadership of William Rowley. The meeting resulted in support for an international competition initiative, which was to be useful to "multiple audiences: government, business, legal and other communities,"[20] inclusive

17 ICPAC Report, *supra* note 15, at 284.

18 *See* Joel Klein, Assistant Attorney Gen., Antitrust Div., Dep't of Justice, Address at the EC Merger Control 10th Anniversary Conference: Time for a Global Competition Initiative? (Sept. 14, 2000), *available at* www.usdoj.gov/atr/public/speeches/6486.pdf. *See also* Merit Janow, *Observations on Two Multilateral Venues: The International Competition Network (ICN) and the WTO*, *in* International Antitrust Law & Policy: 2002 Fordham Corporate Law Institute 49 (Barry Hawk ed., 2003); Jones, *supra* note 6.

19 *See* Lawson Hunter & Susan Hutton, *Global Competition Initiative: A "Headless Horseman?,"* *in* International Antitrust Law & Policy: 2000 Fordham Corporate Law Institute ch. 3 (Barry Hawk ed., 2001); *U.S. and Canadian Antitrust (Panel Discussion)*, *in* International Antitrust Law & Policy: 2000 Fordham Corporate Law Institute 45–59 (Barry Hawk ed., 2001).

20 Janow, *supra* note 18, at. 51.

of developing as well as developed jurisdictions, and a forum in which participants could speak in their individual capacities. Rationalizing the merger process was to be high on the agenda. Indeed, rationalizing the burdensome, uncoordinated premerger filing regimes of scores of jurisdictions seemed to be the business lawyers' motivating passion. The bar associations offered resources and analytical support and offered to host an initial meeting to consider how to proceed.[21] This offer was not accepted by the antitrust authorities, who would not cede control to business, but the Ditchley meeting and the support it engendered were to be crucial factors in the eventual launch of the ICN.

The increasing but still tentative enthusiasm for the global project coincided with the change in presidential administrations in the United States, from Bill Clinton to George W. Bush. U.S. support was crucial to the project. But "in early 2001 it was... not yet clear how the incoming U.S. [Bush] administration would view the proposed initiative."[22]

Charles James was confirmed by the U.S. Senate as Assistant Attorney General in Charge of Antitrust in June 2001. He consulted with Timothy Muris, newly appointed Chairman of the U.S. Federal Trade Commission, and both gave their support to the Global Competition Initiative. James was especially attracted to the idea that the initiative would be "all antitrust, all of the time"[23] (i.e., not trade), and that the project would focus on practical tasks where solutions were achievable (i.e., ICN was not to be or to auger a lofty antitrust code for the world). The collaborators in the new initiative would pick the "low-hanging fruit" that touched no raw nerves. For example, they would seek consensus as to the earliest date on which merger parties could file pre-merger notifications, thus eliminating inefficiencies of multiple uncoordinated filing requirements and waiting periods for multinational mergers.

By fall 2001, sufficient consensus among competition authorities had been achieved. At the annual Fordham International Antitrust Conference, representatives of fourteen jurisdictions[24] came on stage and announced the launching of the initiative. What would it be called? Global Competition Initiative (as proposed by ICPAC) had been its notional name. The word "global" was dropped. In the wake of the rioting at the G8 summit in Genoa, "global" had become a red flag to anti-globalization activists. "International" was a less-

---

21 *Id.* at 52–53.

22 *Id.* at 53.

23 *See* Charles James, *Reconciling Divergent Enforcement Policies: Where Do We Go From Here?*, *in* INTERNATIONAL ANTITRUST LAW & POLICY: 2001 FORDHAM CORPORATE LAW INSTITUTE 1, 5 (Barry Hawk ed., 2002).

24 Australia, Canada, European Union, France, Germany, Israel, Italy, Japan, Korea, Mexico, South Africa, United Kingdom, United States, and Zambia.

charged descriptor. "Network" added an interactive, non-hierarchical flavor. Thus, the International Competition Network was named.

By the time of the launching at Fordham, some contours of the enterprise were clear and others soon became clear. The members of the ICN were to be the government antitrust (competition law) authorities. Representatives of international organizations such as the OECD, the UNCTAD and the World Bank were to be invited to participate in the work and meetings (but not the voting) as non-governmental advisors (NGAs). NGAs were to be drawn, also, from the legal, business, academic, and consumer communities. The individual NGAs would be designated by the antitrust authorities of their nation. There would be a steering group, with a chair and vice-chair, who would facilitate activities including the annual conference and telephone conference calls on issues and procedures, and who would manage a web site. The work was to be project-based. Working groups would do research, draft memos, formulate proposed recommended practices, guidelines and other recommendations for consideration at the annual meetings, and engage in other projects such as (as it developed) informal technical assistance. The ICN would facilitate the sharing of information and experience, facilitate cooperation, and work towards consensus rules, principles, methodologies, and procedures.

Thus, the ICN was born. As events took their course in Cancun,[25] the WTO competition agenda dissolved into the background (and later fully dissolved), and the ICN emerged center stage.

3.2. THE FUNCTIONING AND EVOLUTION OF THE ICN

One of the first tasks of the ICN steering group was to launch a work plan. Projects were to be prepared for the first annual meeting, which, it was decided, would be held in Naples in September 2002. To qualify, the subject matter of the project was to be of broad general interest and likely to engage a large portion of the membership, and the project was to be capable of achieving practical outcomes that would make a difference. A project on merger process was inevitable.

The project work would be carried out by working groups. Each working group would be guided by a chair or by co-chairs, often pairing (as it later developed) a developed and a less developed nation. All interested members of the ICN and the NGAs would be invited to participate in the work of the working groups.

25 *See* Stiglitz & Charlton, *supra* note 12.

In the initial stages of the ICN, working groups were formed: on multijurisdictional mergers and on advocacy. The project of the Advocacy Working Group was designed to highlight the important but daunting work competition authorities can do within their own governments: supporting pro-market policies where the market can work, advocating against unnecessary regulation and statism, and helping to develop a culture of competition.

The Advocacy Working Group devised and distributed questionnaires to all members, synthesized the answers, and wrote a report, which was distributed at the first annual conference in Naples and posted on the ICN's website. The report addressed the role of advocacy, the fruits of advocacy in terms of tangible benefits for consumers and respect for the competition authority, political influences on advocacy, and the importance of institutional settings in either facilitating or obstructing the authority's advocacy efforts. This work was, reportedly, of significant aid to competition authorities.

The Merger Working Group was divided into three subgroups: notification and procedures, the analytical framework of merger review, and investigation techniques in merger review. In the first year, the investigative techniques subgroup planned and soon thereafter held a workshop. The analytical framework subgroup sent questionnaires to all members, with a view to comparing the substantive tests for merger prohibition of each jurisdiction. The subgroup compiled the information for each jurisdiction and wrote a discussion paper on the objectives of analytical frameworks. This subgroup was later to compile a handbook consolidating the analytical methodologies of all responding jurisdictions, with case examples.

The subgroup on notifications and procedures was charged with the subject at the core of the defense bar's support for ICN. Leading members of the bar had been decrying chaos in merger control.[26] At the time, approximately sixty-five nations required merger review, and the jurisdictions had different timing, different informational requirements, arbitrary filing deadlines, and often a long-arm reach to mergers with little relationship with the regulating jurisdiction.

The subgroup included leading merger lawyers from the private sector, who were active and indeed essential participants and became the reliable backbone of the work. The subgroup studied merger notification requirements in all member jurisdictions. It deliberated on practical possibilities for coherence.

---

26 *See* Global Forum for Competition and Trade Policy, Special Report, *Policy Directions for Global Merger Review* (1999) (organized by J. William Rowley, then Chairman of the International Bar Association's Section on Business Law and Director of the Global Forum on Competition and Trade Policy) [hereinafter Global Competition Review 1999].

For the first annual meeting, it proposed that the ICN members adopt eight guiding principles to make the process more transparent, fair, and efficient, and it proposed three recommended practices to address needs for clarity, efficiency, and limits on excessive jurisdiction. It organized a "weblinks" project that posted links to the merger laws and guidelines of all members; it prepared a report on the costs and burdens of merger notification and review; and it later published a report on confidentiality waivers with a model form and a survey and report on merger filing fees. Also, the subgroup devised and facilitated a common template for the presentation of information about merger review procedures from the various jurisdictions. The group requested the member authorities to fill out the template with their own information for posting on the ICN website. Scores of jurisdictions posted their information in template form, which is a form very friendly to practitioners and other users.[27]

The eight guiding principles proposed were: recognition of each jurisdiction's sovereignty; transparency; non-discrimination on the basis of nationality; procedural fairness; efficient, timely and effective review; coordination among agencies reviewing the same transaction; convergence of processes to agreed best practices; and protection of confidential information. The three recommended practices were: an appropriate nexus with the reviewing jurisdiction; clear and understandable notification thresholds based on objectively quantifiable criteria such as sales and assets (not market share); and a recommendation on the timing of merger notifications. The latter has two aspects: flexibility as to the earliest date of notification so as to permit parties to coordinate multijurisdictional filings, and elimination of filing deadlines.

The guiding principles were adopted at the first annual conference. The recommended practices were discussed, and later amended and adopted, along with others, at the second annual conference.

The first two years set the tone. A modus operandi developed. More working groups were formed. Some have been consolidated. The current working groups are: Advocacy, Agency Effectiveness, Cartels, Mergers and Unilateral Conduct. Each has two co-chairs, usually from a more mature and from a younger agency. In addition, a group on curriculum (ITOD, or ICN Training on Demand) prepares or organizes creation of curriculum training videos, developed for the agencies' staffs. The subjects of these training modules range from market power to competitive effects to merger remedies to dawn raids to interviewing witnesses. The modules are freely available on the ICN website.

27 *See* International Competition Network [ICN], *Merger Working Group 2008–2009 Work Plan, available at* www.internationalcompetitionnetwork.org/media/library/mergers/Merger_WG_3.pdf.

Most of the work is done or launched through the working groups, with policy questions surfacing to the Steering Group. For example, the Unilateral Conduct Working Group has recently hosted a webinar on the assessment of dominance in the context of multi-sided platforms, hosted a workshop on assessment of power and conduct in digital markets, and launched a project collecting experience of ICN members and NGAs in assessing dominance in digital markets. The ICN has an on-going project with the World Bank Group which is a contes. The agencies are asked to submit their best success stories on given themes, which has included such topics as aligning industrial policies with competition principles, and promoting pro-competition data regulation. In 2021, the topic of the contest was: How competition advocacy can support countries with Covid19 crisis response, relief, and resilient recovery. The contest draws extraordinary examples and is a testament to the achievements of the agencies.

4. ASSESSMENT: EFFECTIVENESS, LEGITIMACY, SUFFICIENCY

In this section we ask: Is the ICN effective? Is it legitimate? Is it sufficient? Does it have power or influence?

4.1. EFFECTIVENESS: IS THE ICN EFFECTIVE?

Effectiveness is a function of ambitions. The ICN's stated ambitions were modest. It aspired to provide "competition authorities with a specialized yet informal venue for maintaining regular contacts and addressing practical competition concerns,"[28] with a view also to facilitating consensus on issues of law and procedure, thereby bringing antitrust enforcement practices, techniques, and interpretations into greater alignment.

The ICN was designed to be informal, to have no ground location, and to make no binding rules. The ICN was meant to have no power. The ICN was designed *not* to be antitrust governance.

The question at the outset was not whether the ICN would fulfill tasks of governance but whether it would do anything at all; whether it would be a "headless horseman;"[29] whether it would be redundant; whether it could and

---

28 ICN, About the ICN, www.internationalcompetitionnetwork.org/index.php/en/about-icn (as of Mar. 18, 2009).

29 *See* Hunter & Hutton, *supra* note 19.

would have any momentum given its humble virtual aspirations; and whether, even if it got traction, it would quickly wither away.

Judged by its own aspirations and against a chorus of skeptics, but also judged by virtually any measure, the ICN has been an enormous success. It is stable and rooted. It has leadership and momentum. It is a unique connector of people around the world committed to a common task. It inspires hard work and devotion. It provides information, perspective, and contacts. It provides guidance and moral support to newer and more vulnerable agencies pursuing the lonely and often resisted task within their nation of creating a competition culture. It provides a blueprint or referent for agencies in drafting or revising their rules or regulations.[30] And it gives anchor to the officials of the newer agencies appearing before legislators and jurists. "This is the way it is done in the world" or "This is the international standard of good practice" is powerful testimony.

The ICN has created a unique work product. Its leaders and cadre of volunteer workers are continually adding to the work product, virtually all of which is posted on the website. The templates for merger analysis and cartel enforcement convey important information about each jurisdiction in a common form, and the merger guidelines handbook of principles, analysis, and methodologies is both an informative comparative document and a guidance document. The competition advocacy toolkit and the cartel handbook, including methods of detection and enforcement, are deeply informational and useful sources for knowledge and skills. The various authorities' answers to questionnaires, for example, on the objectives of their law and on their framework for analyzing unilateral practices, are all posted on the website and form a unique trove of information for research and under- standing of comparative antitrust law. The guiding principles and recommended practices in merger review are a particular achievement. Nations' implementation of the recommended practices and use of the guiding principles have rationalized the global merger process, reducing costs, eliminating conflicts, and facilitating transactions. The annual workshops on cartels and periodic workshops on mergers and unilateral practices, educate, and facilitate convergence. Periodic webinars organized by working groups explore the most important issues of the day. Close professional relationships are forged in the working groups and at annual workshops and the annual meetings. These networks of relationships deepen understanding, respect, and trust; build community; and provide ready-made avenues for mutual assistance and cooperation.

---

30 The ICN has, for example, given advice to officials of the new antitrust regimes in China and India. India explicitly linked revisions to its draft merger rules to the ICN recommendations.

It appears that, as a result of the ICN, merger process in the world has improved; cartel enforcement in the world has improved; and the mutual understanding of laws, policies, and cultures among the myriad participants has reached a new level. Moreover, ICN has been the venue for the exploration and launch of inquiries into new economy issues. Panels on big tech and big data, with Germany's Bundeskartellamt as the leader, pioneered the now galvanized attention focused on the platforms.

One may also assess the effectiveness of the ICN in relation to other organizations. Recall that skeptics had argued that existing organizations were already performing or could easily perform the tasks targeted by the ICN. The worry of redundancy never materialized. The ICN is doing work that neither the OECD, nor the UNCTAD, nor the WTO (which once was a possible player in this space) could do or could do as well, given the nature, the constituency, and the orientation of each of these bodies.[31] The very informality of the ICN, with its antitrust-only agenda, noncontroversial initial agenda (merger filing rules and modes of advocacy), and lack of power to make rules or enforce them, conduced to the fruitful interchange that characterizes the ICN.

Should the ICN's effectiveness be assessed also in terms of the extent to which its recommended practices have been adopted and implemented? Some argue that implementation is the measure of the ICN's success.[32] This author disagrees, but observes nonetheless that there has been a substantial degree of implementation of the ICN's merger process recommendations.

4.2. LEGITIMACY: IS THE ICN LEGITIMATE?

The ICN is built around values of participation and transparency.[33] All antitrust jurisdictions of the world are invited to belong to the ICN. Virtually all have

---

31 The ICN's unique networking approach, which harnesses immense energy of private stakeholders, is a distinguishing feature. Also, there is a complementarity among the organizations. The ICN's active and dynamic work has acted as a competitive spur to enliven the competition policy work of the OECD.

32 *See* William Rowley & Wakil Omar, *The ICN Five Years On*, Global Competition Review, May 2007, at 29, available at www.mcmillan.ca/Upload/Publications/WRowley_OWakil_TheICN_five_years_on.pdf. The authors decry the fact that "the merger review provisions of a considerable number of ICN member regimes do not conform with, or even fall below, the ICN's recommended practices." They list non-conforming jurisdictions and their thresholds. *Id.* at 30–31.

33 *See* Eleanor Fox, Report on the First Annual Conference of the ICN (Naples, Italy, Sept. 2002) (summarizing the remarks of William Kovacic regarding efforts of the ICN fund-raising commit- tee to attract sufficient funds to enable the attendance of representatives of the developing countries), *available at* www.internationalcompetitionnetwork.org/media/library/conference_1st_naples_2002/icn_naples_ report.pdf. Most systems, however, do

joined except China – which is a loss on both sides; representatives of ICN try to find a path for entry suitable and acceptable to China. Representatives of all members are invited to attend the annual meetings and workshops and to take part in all working groups. A substantial number of non-governmental advisors (from the defense bar, business community, academics and others) actively participate. Consumer groups and representatives of the private plaintiffs' bar were initially under-represented but that problem may be cured. Attendance at the annual meetings is high. More than 500 delegates, representing more than 70 agencies, NGAs, observers, and guests, took part in the 7th Annual Conference in Kyoto in April 2008. The 18th Annual Conference, held in Cartagena in May 2019, hosted nearly 500 participants from more than 80 jurisdictions. The ICN prides itself on its open, inviting, inclusive, and transparent process.

The depth of participation by other than a central core of mature antitrust jurisdictions is predictably limited by lack of funds (despite some funding by the ICN), lack of time, sometimes by lack of expertise, and sometimes by language. (The lingua franca of the meetings is, most often, English).[34] The numerous round-the-world telephone conferences are scheduled for times convenient for most of the world. This often means 8:00 a.m. eastern time, disadvantaging Australia, New Zealand, and the Far East, but sometimes calls of duplicative content are launched from the East. Less well-resourced authorities have constraints against aspiring to be chair of the steering group and even serving as a member of the steering group. This means that authorities from resource-strained nations have less opportunity to participate in setting the agenda and to write first drafts of recommendations, as a practical matter. Individuals not confident of their English language abilities or their level of technical knowledge are sometimes reluctant to speak and may remain silent. These practical considerations may produce underrepresentation of developing countries, and by default greater voice of the two leading antitrust models in the Western world – the United States and the European Union.[35]

---

not follow the United States procedure but limit challenges to notifiable mergers. For the importance, generally, of transparency, *see* William Kovacic, Remarks Before the Seoul Competition Forum: Achieving Better Practices in the Design of Competition Policy Institutions (April 20, 2004), *available at* www.ftc.gov/speeches/other/040420comppolicyinst.pdf. *See also* Slaughter, *supra* note 2; Raustiala, *supra* note 2.

34 The host country language may be available. The documents are mostly in English. The merger recommended practices are posted also in French and Spanish. Workshop sessions and break-outs may be held in more than one language.

35 *See* Daniel Sokol, *Monopolists Without Borders: The Institutional Challenge of International Antitrust in a Global Gilded Age*, 4 Berkeley Bus. L.J. 37, 106–07 (2007). Sokol notes that the concern is mitigated by membership of several developing countries on the ICN steering committee. Indeed, in January 2009, David Lewis of South Africa became the interim chair of ICN.

4.3. SUFFICIENCY: IS THE ICN SUFFICIENT?

By definition, the ICN is not sufficient as antitrust global governance; it was never meant to be. It is not sufficient to solve world competition problems that arise from the internationalization of markets such as the disconnect between anti-dumping laws and predatory pricing, jurisdictional gaps allowing export cartels, parochial uses of state measures that immunize private action, and the lack of a coherent view of world competition and trade-and-competition problems.[36] The ICN limits itself to facilitating dialogue, mentoring, and nudging applications of national laws to be more alike.

By facilitating convergence of procedures, process, and legal principles, the ICN could pave the way towards a future international antitrust system.[37] Perhaps more likely, the ICN and the work of the sister institutions, think tanks, and international conferences and training programs, will sufficiently soften rough edges to alleviate the urgency of an international law of antitrust. The work of the ICN may tend to confirm the perspective that only an informal process without legal consequence can achieve trust, respect, and sharing, and thereby produce soft consensus.[38]

Opportunities may yet be taken by the ICN to help fill the cross-border gap, as discussed in the concluding section.

4.4. DOES THE ICN HAVE POWER?

Some observers speculated, in the first decade, that the ICN might become the international antitrust standard-setting organization for the world (even while others feared the opposite – it would amount to nothing; it would have no effect). If ICN is becoming the standard setter for the world, that would have bearing on all three of the factors examined: effectiveness, legitimacy, and (in part) sufficiency.

---

36 *See* Eleanor Fox & Janusz Ordover, *Internationalizing Competition Law to Limit Parochial State and Private Action: Moving Towards the Vision of World Welfare*, 24 Int'l Bus. Law. 458 (1996); WTO 1997 Report, *supra* note 6; Heimler, *supra* note 3.

37 The degree of divergence of the law of the various nations was cited as one reason why the world was not ready for an antitrust regime in the WTO. *See* Douglas Melamed, *Promoting Sound Antitrust Enforcement in the Global Economy*, *in* INTERNATIONAL ANTITRUST LAW & POLICY: 2000 FORDHAM CORPORATE LAW INSTITUTE ch. 1. (Barry Hawk ed. 2001).

38 These accomplishments, however, do not imply that the ICN meets the unfilled need for a coherent trade-and-competition perspective. *See* Fox & Ordover, *supra* note 51; WTO 1997 Report, *supra* note 6. *See* Chris Noonan, THE EMERGING PRINCIPLES OF INTERNATIONAL COMPETITION LAW (2008), suggesting that "[t]he work of the ICN could formally and informally feed into the WTO processes." *Id.* at 563.

We have seen in other fields, such as banking, the migration of soft law standards set by discrete and even secretive bodies into harder international standards.[39] We have noted the use of soft antitrust law to influence legislators and jurists. And we have noted the claim that if the ICN does not achieve convergence, it has failed. In its first decade, the ICN merger recommendations influenced, and continue to influence, the drafting and revision of merger laws of member nations[40], and they informed an OECD recommendation on merger notifications.[41] It is therefore not fanciful to consider that the ICN's output could develop into soft law with some influence.[42]

Some early signs might have indicated a hegemony of the West. For example, in early days, ICN set about to draft a best practice on how to prove "substantial market power" – a first step in determining whether economic power was abused. The working group confronted several questions: In proving substantial market power, may significant or even controlling weight be appropriately given to the putative dominant firm's large market share? May and should proof of a large market share satisfy the plaintiff's prima facie case?

Most of the mature jurisdictions and their NGAs participating in the project argued that proof of substantial market power is a very complex matter; that market shares mean little in themselves, and that significant economic evidence is necessary to hurdle this first stage in an abuse of dominance case. They expressed concern that a market share test for market power would label too many firms "dominant," and an effect would be to cause large firms to pull their punches and thus to chill their pro-competitive, inventive behavior.

The South African representative, David Lewis, then Chair of the South African Competition Tribunal and later to become Chair of the ICN Steering Group, strongly disagreed with rejection of a market share proxy. He especially disagreed with the proposed recommendation as applied to South Africa, where

---

39 Roman Grynberg & Sacha Silva, *Harmonization Without Representation: Small States, the Basel Committee, and the WTO*, 34 World Dev. 1223 (2006) (noting that small states, excluded from the process, were put at a competitive disadvantage by banking standards).

40 *See* Rowley & Wakil, *supra* note 32.

41 OECD, Recommendation of the Council on Merger Review, OECD Doc. C(2005)34 (Mar. 23, 2005), *available at* http://webdomino1.oecd.org/horizontal/oecdacts.nsf/linkto/c(2005)34.

42 There is a balance to be struck between convergence and informed diversity. Moreover there is an interest of developing countries to adopt standards that emerge from their roots, context and needs. *See* Dani Rodrik, *Institutions for High Quality Growth: What Are They and How to Acquire Them?*, Stud. In Comp. Int'l Dev., Sept. 2000, at 3, 5 ("I emphasize the importance of 'local knowledge' and argue that a strategy of institution building must not overemphasize best-practice 'blueprints' at the expense of local experiementation."). Yet, there are trade-offs between blueprints and experimentation; there is opportunity for "institutional arbitrage"; much technical legislation can be borrowed wholesale or at least be a source for learning. *Id.* at 13–14.

the statute dictated a market share threshold. He argued for ICN standards flexible to the context of the country, and offered that developing country authorities cannot bear a heavy burden of proof at this first stage of proceedings against an apparently dominant firm; that authorities should be able to use high market share as a proxy for market power; and that a rule requiring complex economic evidence and analysis to determine whether a firm with a high market share was dominant would tend to put beyond the ability of developing countries' competition authorities the power to challenge the persistent monopolistic conduct that blights their economies.[43]

A document emerged from the process and was adopted at the annual conference. It states that proof of substantial market power is a complex inquiry; "[a] firm should not be found to possess dominance/substantial market power without a comprehensive consideration of factors affecting competitive conditions in the market under investigation."[44] While "[m]arket shares should be used" as a starting point for analysis, they "fail to reflect certain important features of the competitive environment, in particular market dynamics, [and therefore] should be put into perspective by consideration of other factors…"[45] The recommendation identifies the various indicia that should influence analysis.

South Africa lost the battle for a recommendation flexible to accommodate the developing country context. However, the participating developed country agencies and (most of) their NGAs lost their quest for a rule that even very large market share is no sign of economic power and should never be a basis for burden-shifting.

Developing countries and poorly-resourced authorities might have been better satisfied by an ICN endorsement of the use of a high market share, or persistent high market share in the context of a high-barrier market, as a proxy for substantial market power. They might have been better satisfied by an ICN document stating that a high market share accompanied by barriers to entry

---

43 *See* David Lewis, *Chilling Competition*, *in* International Antitrust Law & Policy: 2008 Fordham Corporate Law Institute (Barry Hawk ed., 2009). Under South African competition law, "[a] firm is dominant in a market if – (a) it has at least 45 percent of that market…" Competition Act of 1989 §7. *See* Michal S. Gal, *Extra-territorial Application of Antitrust – The Case of a Small Economy (Isreal), in*, Cooperation, Comity, and Competition Policy (A. Guzman ed., Oxford 2009) (noting that ICN rejection of the market share proxy may imply that small jurisdictions will not have the practical ability to bring abuse of dominance cases; "in reality small jurisdictions are mostly, once again, rule takers rather than rule makers.").

44 ICN, Unilateral Conduct Working Group, *Dominance/Substantial Market Power Analysis Pursuant to Unilateral Conduct Laws* 2 (May 9, 2008), *available at* www.internationalcompetitionnetwork.org/media/ library/unilateral_conduct/Unilateral_WG_1.pdf.

45 *Id.* at 3.

may give rise to a presumption of economic power, which is in fact the law in many jurisdictions.[46] The recommendation is more conservative than the law.

An unastounding observation can be drawn. The voices of the major players in the developed world are likely to be more influential than the voices of developing and small economies. Even so, the leaders of the ICN have shown consistent resolve to include, involve, and respond to all voices. Moreover, for those who may have hoped for "law development" in ICN that would become law for the world, that has not happened. Countries apply the law that is theirs. ICN standards are helpful referents.

5. CONCLUSION

The ICN has been dramatically successful. Its limits have also been its success. It has carved out a space for itself that no other organization could have achieved. Its own success has muted calls for a global framework for antitrust, perhaps limiting a future WTO project – if ever one might be – to trade-competition issues such as export cartels that have been left unaddressed.[47] The agenda of "all antitrust all the time" has paid off.

Neither the worry that ICN would be a headless horseman nor the worry that ICN would write the antitrust standards for the world came to pass. The inspirational flame has not stopped burning. The successive chairs of the Steering Committee have blazed strong and pro-active paths, and ICN is robust and relevant.

In its first two decades, ICN examined national competition principles, convergence of those principles, and modes of cooperation so that nations can best protect the integrity of their own law and their businesses can better compete across national lines. It shied away from issues that are truly trans-national or global. The time has come for it to confront global issues. Let me give two examples.

First, mergers whose effects span many borders. Here there are at least two opportunities; one about process and one about substance. It is time to consider

---

46 Caselaw in most jurisdictions, including the United States, provides that very high market shares (such as in excess of 70 percent) shifts the burden to the putative dominant firm to show that it does not have significant market power. *See Market Share as an Indicator of Monopoly Power, in* ANTITRUST LAW DEVELOPMENTS 230 (8th ed. 2017). For Europe, see Case C-62/86, AKZO Chemie BV v. Commission, 1991 ECR 3151.

47 Trade/competition issues include the flanking issues of dumping/predatory pricing, market access, export cartels, and state shields that protect private anticompetitive conduct.

a common clearing house for global mergers with a common first filing, to eliminate huge unnecessary costs imposed by the scores of pre-merger notifications required for even harmless mergers. Second and more important is treatment of mega-mergers that span many nations' borders and have global anticompetitive effects, such as the merger of two leading cement companies in the world, Holcim and Lafarge. These mergers need to be examined through a world lens, and their prohibition – as opposed to nation-limited ad hoc spinoffs, should be seriously considered. This can be done without international law, but we need better consortia of the authorities of affected markets, and we need authorities who do not insist that cross-border harms are not their problem.

The second example is big data/big tech. Abuses of the leading big tech platforms have galvanized the attention of competition authorities around the world. A multitude of jurisdictions are developing their own antitrust and regulatory responses, with significant inconsistencies with one another in both concept and detail. Yet the businesses, their benefits and restraints, are quintessentially global. A national-only perspective is not enough. Bi-lateral cooperation is not enough.[48] A forum for the world, with world vision, is sorely needed, and ICN, with the OECD and UNCTAD, is positioned to craft an agenda.

If ICN is to be the vehicle of tomorrow, ICN must engage the world.

48 See Eleanor Fox, Antitrust: Updating Extraterritoriality, in Antitrust and Public Policies Review, inaugural issue (Italian Competition Authority Dec. 2019), based on Antitrust and the Clash of Sovereigns, November 2019, Concurrences N° 4–2019, pp. 73–80, https://papers.ssrn.com/sol3/papers.cfm?abstract_id=3835242.

THE REGIONALISATION OF COMPETITION LAW

A Future Role for the International Competition Network (ICN)?

Eyad Maher M. DABBAH*

1. INTRODUCTION

The International Competition Network (ICN) will soon be celebrating its twentieth anniversary. Since its launch in October 2001, the Network has secured a score of phenomenal successes which, frankly, no one at that time had anticipated or even imagined would be possible to achieve over a relatively short time period. Not only the ICN broadened its base from the handful of its founding competition authorities to around 137 members, its agenda became stretched in parallel, beyond merger control and competition advocacy – the Network's central pillars – to include the important areas of cartels, abusive conduct and effective enforcement (what the ICN refers to as 'agency effectiveness').

Within an anniversary volume devoted to the ICN – like the present one – it is unlikely any ink will be spared marking the Network's many achievements. Furthermore, it is likely that some contributions will reflect on what the ICN's agenda for the next decade should feature. The present essay falls more into the latter category than the former one, given that the topic at hand is one to which the ICN has devoted hardly any attention. Yet, it is a topic which, as will be demonstrated in what will follow below, should be seriously considered by both ICN leadership and membership as they determine that agenda.

Regional cooperation, or regionalisation, in the field of competition law is an articulation of the very ideas expressed in the ICN's mission statement[1], according to which:

---

* Chair, Competition Law and Policy; Director, Institute for Competition and Consumers (formerly, the Interdisciplinary Centre for Competition Law and Policy) (ICC), Queen Mary University of London; Barrister (of the Middle Temple).

1 See www.internationalcompetitionnetwork.org.

'The ICN's mission to advocate the adoption of **superior standards and procedures** in competition policy around the world, formulate proposals for **procedural and substantive convergence**, and seek to facilitate **effective international cooperation** to the benefit of member agencies, consumers and economies worldwide.' (Emphasis added)

One needs not look further than the European Union (EU) competition law regime[2] to see what this particular example of regional cooperation has resulted in: the adoption of *superior standards and procedures*; *procedural and substantive convergence and harmonisation* among very divergent national competition law regimes; and *effective cooperation* to the benefit of millions of European consumers and the domestic economies of all EU member states.[3] Regional cooperation in the EU has meant that many harmful practices (particularly international cartels and abusive conduct) *and* harmful merger operations, not to mention illegal state aid, have been possible to address which otherwise would probably have escaped proper scrutiny.

This essay has been inspired by the importance of regional cooperation in the field of competition law. It offers a critical assessment of the potential role of the ICN in, and the contribution the Network can make to, promoting this cooperation. The central argument of the essay is that the ICN is well-placed, after twenty years of its existence, to open this 'new' front in its work for the next decade. This will serve the Network's interests and particularly those of the majority of its members who belong to regions in which regional cooperation is clearly desired and desirable. Such involvement will be in the best interests of the competition law community globally.

The essay is structured as follows. The following part, part 2, gives an overview of regional cooperation. Part 3 debates the difficulties surrounding this form of cooperation. This paves the way for the discussion in Parts 4 and 5 which – respectively – present a 'case study' using the Middle East region and highlight a number of aspects of regional cooperation which deserve attention. Part 6 assesses the role the ICN could play in helping different regions realise the full potential of cooperation. Finally, Part 7 contains concluding thoughts.

---

2 The EU competition law regime is not the only European example to be mentioned. Other examples include: the European Free Trade Association (EFTA); the European Competition Authorities (ECA); and the Nordic Agreement on Cooperation in Competition Matters.

3 The literature coving the EU competition law and policy, including their success, is vast. See generally L. McGowan and S. Wilks, 'The first supranational policy in the European Union: Competition policy', (1995) *European Journal of Political Research* 141; A. Papadopoulos, *The International Dimension of EU Competition Law Policy* (Cambridge University Press, 2010); G. Amato, *Antitrust and the Bounds of Power* (Hart Publishing, 1997).

2. AN OVERVIEW OF REGIONAL COOPERATION

Regional cooperation is an important form of cooperation in the field of competition law.[4] Considerable efforts have been made by a number of communities over the past two decades in particular to develop competition law and policy regionally. Some form of regional cooperation has been attempted or exists within every region of the world: Africa[5]; Asia (including the Middle East)[6]; Oceania; and the Americas and Caribbean[7]; this is in addition to Europe, the region with the most successful type of regional cooperation (the EU competition law regime).[8] In some regions, other than Europe, impressive steps have been taken towards the 'crown-jewels' of regional cooperation: building a supranational competition law regime.[9]

The number of initiatives seeking to develop a regional approach to competition law and policy has been relatively, perhaps astonishingly, high. These initiatives – like the regions within which they were launched – are at different stages of development. The fact that all world regions have devoted particular attention to regional competition law and policy is highly interesting, not least because in the case of some regions several of the member countries actually lacked *effective* competition law regimes and sufficient competition expertise domestically at the time those initiatives were launched.[10]

---

4 See generally *Regional Cooperation Agreements: Benefits and Challenges* (OECD, 2018); M. Dabbah, *International and Comparative Competition Law* (Cambridge University Press, 2010); D. Melamed, 'International cooperation in competition law and policy: what can be achieved at the bilateral, regional, and multilateral levels (1999) *Journal of International Economic Law* 423; Q. Tong, 'On the regional cooperation mechanism of competition policy: a comparative research among APEC, NAFTA and EU' (2007) *The International Law Review of Wuhan University* 1; M. Gal, 'Regional cooperation law agreements: an important step for antitrust enforcement' (2010) *University of Toronto Law Journal* 239; F. Jenny, 'International cooperation on competition: myth, reality and perspective' (2003) *Antitrust Bulletin* 973.

5 See the *Economic and Monetary Community of Central Africa* (CEMAC), the *Common Market for Eastern and Southern Africa* (COMESA), the *West African Economic and Monetary Union* (UEMOA or WAEMU), the *Southern African Customs Union* (SACU), the *East African Community* (EAC) and the *Southern African Development Community* (SADC).

6 See the *Association of South East Asian Nations* (ASEAN), the *South Asian Association for Regional Cooperation* (SAARC), and the *Asia-Pacific Economic Cooperation* (APEC). Middle Eastern initiatives are discussed in detail in part 4 below.

7 See the creation of the *Southern Common Market* (MERCUSOR), the *Andean Community*, *Caribbean* Community and Common Market (CARICOM), the *North American Free Trade Agreement* (NAFTA), the *Central America-Dominican Republic-United States Free Trade Agreement* (CAFTA-DR) and the various Latin American Free Trade Agreements.

8 See notes 2 and 3 above and their accompanying text.

9 See some of the examples mentioned above, such as COMESA competition law regime. See M. Elfar and M. Momtaz, 'Egyptian competition enforcement: putting COMESA and LAS cooperation into practice' (2017) *Journal of European Law and Practice* 586.

10 See *Competition Regimes in the World: A Civil Society Report* (CUTS International, 2006).

Broadly speaking, regional cooperation can be of different types. The *first* is where the cooperation is used as a 'forum' for consultation and experience sharing which would facilitate the building of effective domestic competition law regimes and support these regimes through technical assistance and capacity building channels. The *second* type revolves around achieving convergence and harmonisation – whether in substantive or procedural terms – among the domestic competition law regimes of the countries concerned. The *third* type of regional cooperation is considerably ambitious and much more 'long term' and complex than the first two types: it involves adopting binding regional competition law to be enforced by a regional competition authority, whether exclusively or in a shared manner with the domestic competition authorities of the relevant member countries. These three types are not mutually exclusive and may be pursued simultaneously or successively within a given regional cooperation framework. This is demonstrated by the EU experience which has inspired all regional communities around the world in their pursuit of competition law cooperation.

Communities have differed in their reasons for developing competition law within a regional cooperation setting.[11] Broadly speaking, these reasons include: the fact that competition law is seen as complementary to rules on trade, which regional cooperation often, if not always, incorporates; the fact that it is considered to be a natural component of economic cooperation, which is usually sought when regional cooperation is opted for; the fact that there is, sometime, particular interest to enhance the status and importance of competition law domestically whilst ensuring harmonised standards at regional level; the fact that regional cooperation may help facilitate the provision of technical assistance between the different (participating) competition authorities and their capacity building; and the fact that regional solutions can be seen as necessary to address cross-border competition problems.

In relation to the last point in particular – as demonstrated so succinctly by the EU experience – regional cooperation (or more accurately the building of a regional competition law regime) can help achieve more effective competition law enforcement both domestically and regionally. This is particularly beneficial where cross-border anticompetitive behaviour, conduct or transactions have significant regional and international consequences or implications. In relation to some of these situations – most notably the regulation of cross-border merger operations – regional cooperation can have enormous benefits for business firms whether in terms of harmonisation of substantive and procedural rules; reducing costs; enhancing legal certainty; creating similar regulatory environments

11 See Dabbah, note 4 above; M. Matsushita, 'International cooperation in the enforcement of competition policy' (2002) *Washington University Global Studies Law Review* 463.

among different countries; and minimising the risk of inconsistent findings by more than one competition authority.[12]

3. THE DIFFICULTIES SURROUNDING REGIONAL COOPERATION

Pursuing regional cooperation in the field of competition law is a task fraught with difficulties of both extrinsic and intrinsic nature. *Extrinsically*, other than the need to have political will and agreement among the participating countries to engage in regional cooperation, many parts of the world where regional cooperation has been attempted face serious challenges, which tend to dominate both domestic and regional agendas. These challenges include bitter conflicts and regional tensions, poverty, and natural disasters and diseases. *Intrinsically*, other than the fact that an interest must exist on the part of the domestic competition authorities of the relevant countries to cooperate, sufficient competition law expertise and resources must exist domestically and an appropriate portion of these will need to be devoted to building a viable regional cooperation framework.

The existence of such hurdles means that fields such as competition law many times end up being pushed not to the *fore* but to the *background* in regionalisation efforts, and, occasionally, such fate may be encountered at domestic level.[13] It must be appreciated, therefore, that the journey from formulating an idea of regional cooperation to converting this idea into a fruitful initiative is long and features extremely tough terrain. Even if it were assumed that the destination would eventually be reached, realising coherent and practicable competition *enforcement* within a regional framework is a highly challenging task. Among other things, it would be important to have in place practical mechanisms to ensure that the regional framework and the domestic competition law regimes of the relevant countries would operate in harmony and support each other in a way that would prevent possible clashes, whether in terms of actual outcomes of cases or at a policy formulation level. Similarly, careful efforts should be made in

---

12 One of the ways this is achieved is through using a one-stop shop principle, under which when a transaction is regulated at the higher regional level it will be excluded from the jurisdiction of competition authorities at the lower national level. See the existence and the operation of this principle under the merger Regulation in the EU competition law regime. For an account on the benefits of cooperation in the area of merger control, see J. Galloway, 'Convergence in international merger control' (2009) *Competition Law Review* 179; *Cross-border Merger Control: Challenges for Developing and Emerging Economies* (OECD, 2012).

13 See generally M. Dabbah, 'Competition law and policy in developing countries: a critical assessment of the challenges to establishing an effective competition law regime' (2010) *World Competition Law and Economics Review* 457.

order to avoid having the domestic regimes undermine the regional framework and vice versa. This requires the existence of an appropriate system defining the relationship between the regional and domestic level as well as between the national competition law regimes of the countries concerned.

It should not be surprising in light of this – and notwithstanding its considerable advantages and the significant regionalisation efforts made by many countries over the years – that regional cooperation in the field of competition law, on the whole, has not achieved its full potential. This perhaps obvious conclusion raises a most basic, yet fundamental question, namely: how could one promote regional cooperation and support the efforts of individual countries and their competition authorities who are clearly interested in cooperating regionally?

This is where this author believes the ICN has a role to play. The present essay will address this role by the ICN in part 5 below. Before doing so however, the essay offers a suitable case study of regional cooperation in the following part.

4. THE MIDDLE EAST

The choice of the Middle East region as a case study was made because – among all world regions – the Middle East suffers from the hardest conflicts, the deepest divisions and the most extreme of political and religious sensitivities and tensions. In many ways, it is the one region which desperately needs regional cooperation in all arenas, especially economic and political ones, as well as being the one region within which, normally, people would least expect any form of regional cooperation.[14] In relation to competition law, expectations were never high that competition law could develop and flourish in Middle Eastern countries even when such countries formally adopted domestic competition rules. In light of this, making any kind of progress in the field of competition law and more importantly pursuing regional cooperation in the field would be remarkable, unique and warmly welcome. Furthermore, the Middle East has enjoyed far less attention within international competition law circles – than any other region in the world. All this makes the region a most suitable case study for present purposes. This view becomes strengthened when the Middle East is compared with other regions, which – although have their fair share of difficult challenges and problems – have seen significant progress in the areas of domestic and regional competition law. Africa is one such region to compare to the Middle East.

---

14 See generally C. Harders and M. Legrenzi (eds.), *Beyond Regionalism? Regional Cooperation, Regionalism and Regionalization in the Middle East* (Routledge, 2016).

4.1. GEOGRAPHICAL DELINEATION

When discussing the Middle East, it would be important, regardless of the issue at hand, to, first, give a geographical definition. In the context of the present essay, this is important not least because, from an ICN's perspective, a rigid Asian/African division appears to be followed in relation to the Middle East.[15]

A (never settled) debate has evolved for many years now over how to define the region known as the 'Middle East' in geographical terms. This debate has spanned different academic, political and diplomatic circles. This author does intend to contribute to this debate on this occasion but rather to offer a definition, which is neutral in geographical terms. For the purposes of the present discussion, therefore, the 'Middle East' is taken to include the following countries: Algeria, Bahrain, Egypt, Iran, Iraq, Israel, Jordan, Kuwait, Lebanon, Libya, Morocco, Oman, Palestine, Qatar, Saudi Arabia, Sudan, Syria, Tunisia, Turkey, United Arab Emirates and Yemen. Obviously, in certain quarters, these selected countries are referred to geographically as the 'Middle East and North Africa'.[16] However, there are many uniting factors justifying grouping all of these countries together as Middle Eastern ones, most notably in terms of culture, language and religion.[17]

4.2. NOTABLE DEVELOPMENTS

Competition law exists in the majority of Middle Eastern countries.[18] Judged objectively, various Middle Eastern countries have been making highly notable efforts in the field of competition law through instituting competition law regimes and seeking to build a 'portfolio' of effective enforcement.[19]

Regionally, the most significant competition law development has been the drafting of a set of *Arab Competition Regulations* which were prepared within the framework of the League of Arab States.[20] The *Regulations* essentially take

---

15 See the ICN's divisional map used in identifying and listing different ICN members, available at: www.internationalcompetitionnetwork.org/members.

16 As noted in the previous paragraph, the ICN appears to be one example according to its divisional map. See *ibid*.

17 The author has discussed elsewhere this question of geographical definition and such factors. See M. Dabbah, *Competition Law and Policy in the Middle East* (Cambridge University Press, 2007).

18 See *Promoting Fair Competition in the Middle East and North Africa* (World Bank, 2019).

19 Examples of these efforts exist across the region, including within: Turkey, Tunisia, Morocco, Saudi Arabia, Jordan, Israel, Qatar, and Kuwait, among others.

20 The League came into existence in 1945 and aimed to coordinate the economic affairs of its members, which are Arab countries. It is the oldest attempt to achieve regional cooperation in the Middle East.

the form of a 'competition law', the provisions of which have been informed by three sources: EU competition law; the competition laws of Arab countries which at the time had enacted domestic competition legislation; and UNCTAD's *Set of Multilaterally Agreed Equitable Principles and Rules for the Control of Restrictive Business Practices.* The declared aim of the *Regulations* is to protect and encourage competition and to supervise monopolistic practices for the purposes of increasing economic activity. The *Regulations* apply to collusion, abuse of dominance and harmful mergers, though acts involving the sovereign or the exercise of prerogatives of public powers and/or the exercise of public tasks and activities fall outside the scope of the *Regulations.*[21]

Though still not approved[22], the *Regulations* amount to a major step taken towards creating some form of regional cooperation mechanism in the Middle East. The *Regulations* are not intended to have the binding force of the law when implemented and therefore their role is to serve as a set of guidelines for the member states to follow for the purposes of adopting domestic competition laws or modifying their existing laws in line with the wording and spirit of the *Regulations.* They provide that enforcement should be handled by domestic competition authorities[23], which, according to the *Regulations*, should be established in each member state and be armed with a wide range of powers and responsibilities enabling them to effectively enforce domestic competition laws.[24]

The decision to draft the *Regulations* as a set of guidelines followed a lengthy debate, which focused on whether the *Regulations* should serve as a blueprint for an enforceable regional competition law at the Arab League level. At the time this debate emerged, a dissimilar position to the present one had existed throughout the Arab world, namely that competition law and policy were absent

21 See Article 3 of the *Regulations.*

22 A detailed set of explanatory notes was also drafted. This set of explanatory notes is intended to serve as an accompanying document to the *Regulations* for the purposes of explaining the different provisions in the *Regulations* and their application. Both the *Regulations* and the explanatory notes will need final approval of the League prior to their implementation.

23 Under Article 2 of the *Regulations*, an authority is defined as the competent body with responsibility to implement and enforce the *Regulations* in accordance with the internal rules in operation within each member state.

24 See Chapter 4 (Articles 12–23) of the *Regulations.* Among the powers listed in Article 12 are conducting investigations (including searches); reviewing notified concentrations (mergers); engaging in competition advocacy and building a culture of competition; cooperation with foreign competition authorities; preparing annual reports to be submitted to the relevant bodies or persons in the country; and making decisions. Other provisions in Chapter 4 worth noting are those dealing with issues such as the expertise and qualifications of individuals to be appointed as competition officials (Article 13), the obligation on officials to observe confidentiality in internal agency proceedings (Article 22) and the obligation on those officials to avoid conflict of interest (Article 21).

from the vast majority of Arab countries.[25] Admittedly, opting for the regional regime option would have been problematic. Apart from the fact that this option represents an ambitious attempt requiring political approval at the level of heads of states (which was not possible in the case), the *domestic* competition issues of Arab countries outnumber those with cross-border element. The regional model would not have addressed such domestic problems effectively or comprehensively. Furthermore, at the time, there was lack of sufficiently robust and widespread competition culture in all Arab countries and to a large degree insufficient recognition of competition or even an understanding of it. A regional model would have contributed very little to spreading such culture given the daunting task a regional competition authority would have faced when attempting to deal with a large number of local economies and markets. The regional model would not have, thus, been an appropriate substitute for having domestic competition law regimes become established in the different countries.

Nonetheless, one should acknowledge the merit to the regional regime option as argued by its proponents. The intention was to avoid a situation where some Arab countries would, through delaying the enactment of domestic competition rules, eventually derail the creation of a regional competition law regime. Such a regime was seen as desirable in the case of the Arab world and beneficial for the purposes of addressing cross-border competition problems. Additionally, those proponents argued that – by choosing this option – it would have been possible to guarantee that the same rules and standards would prevail throughout the Arab world as opposed to a situation where domestic rules and standards would have to be 'adjusted' to a common approach at a later stage. This was largely a pragmatic approach adopted by the supporters of the regional regime option. Clearly, those supporters had anticipated divergences between the *Regulations* and future domestic competition laws of member countries. Admittedly, such divergences are possible to identify when considering the competition law regimes in existence within Arab countries at present (which did not exist at the time the *Regulations* were drafted). For example, the provisions of the *Regulations* on enforcement are markedly different from some of those regimes. The *Regulations* themselves acknowledged the potential for divergences in this regard; hence the reason the provisions contained in Chapter 4 of the *Regulations* provide that they do not prejudice the right of each member state to determine the nature, composition and operation of its domestic competition authority.[26]

Any future *formal* adoption and implementation of the *Regulations* can make an important contribution on several fronts, ranging from providing a common

25 At that time, various Arab countries – notably Saudi Arabia, Egypt, Jordan, United Arab Emirates, Kuwait and Qatar – had not adopted domestic competition law; only Algeria, Morocco and Tunisia had domestic competition legislation.

26 See Article 23.

ground to which all domestic competition law regimes of Arab countries would be linked, to opening a new chapter in competition law and policy in the Arab world and the Middle East more generally. The mere existence of the *Regulations* in a draft form has placed competition law and policy firmly on the regional map in the Middle East. Obviously, any formal adoption and implementation of the Regulations depends on the political support individual countries are willing to offer and the ability of existing Arab competition authorities to work together. Neither can be taken for granted at present. This in itself is an indication towards the potential role a third party or platform – such as the ICN – could perform especially in assisting Middle Eastern competition authorities on the regional cooperation front.

5. PARTICULAR ASPECTS OF REGIONAL COOPERATION DESERVING ATTENTION

Every regional cooperation in the field of competition law globally would benefit from appropriate support, fresh input and further development. Even in the case of the EU competition law regime, it is perfectly possible to propose – theoretically and practicably – ways in which the regime and its network of competition authorities, the European Competiton Network (ECN), could be improved further: whether in substantive or procedural terms.

The room for improvement is particularly generous and such improvement is mostly necessary among regional communities of the developing world. These form the greater majority of the ICN membership. Many of the competition authorities in these regions, which are young institutions, face considerable challenges, whether in the form of: lack of suitable expertise and/or financial resources; insufficiently developed rules and procedures; or wider political constraints.

The present essay identifies several aspects of regional cooperation which deserve attention, and which need improvement in order to help the relevant communities benefit from (more) meaningful competition law cooperation. Admittedly, a list of such aspects can never be exhaustive since it is always possible to identify further aspects, though these are likely to be exclusive to individual communities. The aspects discussed below are relevant to almost all regional cooperation initiatives in the field of competition law.

5.1. LACK OF CLEAR DIRECTION

Most of the regional efforts launched in the field of competition law have in essence been attempts to identify directions in which regional cooperation could be pushed. Much of what has been achieved as a result of these efforts could be considered to have been largely *exploratory* in nature and shows a degree of uncertainty among the participating countries or competition authorities in relation to what can be realistically expected. This can be seen in light of how considerable hopes were attached to a number of regional initiatives when these were first introduced, though for a long time little progress was made in practice.[27] In the case of some initiatives, resources have been wasted on endless discussions on how these initiatives should be revised.[28]

The lack of clear direction has resulted in a noticeably heavy borrowing from the EU experience by virtually all regional communities around the world with hardly any attention given to any other regional experience. Some of the communities have set themselves extremely over-ambitious goals to achieve in a few years what took European nations over 70 years to achieve in their EU cooperation (and probably would be correct to say what the EU continues to achieve until the present time).[29]

Undoubtedly, it is good for the different regional communities to be inspired by the EU experience. It would also be correct to argue that it is necessary for these communities when seeking regional cooperation to consult and learn from this experience. Nonetheless, one should be aware that it has been neither suitable nor useful for different regional communities to attempt an almost 'copy' and 'paste' exercise when consulting the EU experience when the circumstances and history of the relevant regions differ significantly from those of the European region. It is always worth remembering that the experience the EU has had in the field of competition law – like its experience in all other fields – has been very much 'European', inspired by historical events and conditioned by developments unique to EU member states.[30] Interestingly, it is possible to identify a paradox when studying the position of those regional communities, which have opted to copy the EU experience. On the one hand, by following the EU model these communities have opted for a far-reaching form of regionalism. On the other hand, the countries within these communities have been very reluctant to surrender sovereignty and to transfer competence to the regional level (as has been the case with the EU).[31]

---

27 See for example the ASEAN cooperation, note 6 above. See P. Porananond, *Competition Law in the ASEAN Countries: Regional Law and National Systems* (Kluwer, 2018).

28 Both the Middle East and Africa regions are examples in point.

29 See *ibid.*

30 See A. Weitbrecht, 'From Freiburg to Chicago and Beyond – the First 50 Years of European Competition Law' (2008) *European Competition Law Review* 81.

31 The Arab League initiative, discussed in the previous part, is an example in point. In relation to the EU, one must acknowledge that some of the founding member states reluctantly accepted the limitation of sovereignty and some of them have questioned, and continue to,

Pursuing cooperation in the different regions – especially those within which, at the relevant time, domestic competition law and policy did not exist or had not reach a sufficiently advanced level – reveals an openness or acceptance of a 'top-down' approach. This is a significant point to note since it means an opportunity does exist for input from a higher level such as the ICN and for guidance to be offered at this level which the relevant countries and their competition authorities are likely to welcome, especially when they lack clear direction in their cooperation efforts. Such input and guidance can help these countries and their competition authorities achieve the necessary clarity on the direction in which their regionalisation efforts should move, as well as how they should approach 'foreign' experiences (mostly, the EU experience) and use these experiences in a coherent and useful manner.

5.2. HARMONISATION

Regionalisation efforts around the world show an express desire by many communities to achieve harmonisation of competition rules. However, even with a most comprehensive regional approach to harmonisation, full success cannot be guaranteed if major discrepancies exist between the domestic competition laws and policies of the relevant countries; not to mention discrepancies in the wider legal, political and economic environments of those countries. Looking at all countries which are members of regional communities or organisations, it is obvious that significant differences exist between them and this is bound to make any harmonisation initiative considerably hard. Moreover, the countries within one and the same community may be at different stages of economic development and may enjoy varying degrees of economic and trade strengths. Any attempt to achieve harmonisation – regardless of the mechanism used in this case – is likely to result in one or a small group of countries 'dominating' the process, and this is likely to trigger objection on the part of weaker countries. This highlights the need for these countries to learn how harmonisation should be pursued and in parallel how to engage in convergence among their competition law regimes.

5.3. DIVISION IN COMPETENCE

The different regional communities seem to lack the necessary understanding and tools to deal with all questions concerning the exercise of jurisdiction and the likely problems following the exercise of such jurisdiction by regional

---

question the whole legitimacy of limitation on their sovereignty. See F. Bignami (ed), *EU Law in Populist Times* (Cambridge University Press, 2020).

authorities.[32] These questions concern, among other things: the division in competence between the regional level and national level; the exact role to be fulfilled by regional authorities especially in the arena of enforcement (for example whether they will have the ability, and if so how, to access and gather information in actual cases from firms operating in the different countries; and the necessary safeguards needed to have in place to deal with a possible expansion of the workload of regional authorities to an extent that they are no longer able to handle such workload (for example, whether in this case national competition authorities may become involved).

5.4. SUB-REGIONAL COOPERATION

In various regions around the world, countries have opted for building 'sub'-regional cooperation, which represents a longer route for establishing a wide regional framework, including one with a competition law dimension. This appears to have been used as an alternative to pursing such a framework directly. Examples of sub-regional cooperation in fact exists in the Middle East.[33] This can be seen in the case of: the Gulf Cooperation Council (GCC)[34]; the Agreement for the Establishment of a Free Trade Zone between the Arabic Mediterranean Nations (Agadir)[35]; the Greater Arab Free Trade Area (GAFTA) which effectively has rendered Agadir somewhat redundant[36]; and even the Arab League, discussed in the previous part.

It is doubtful that sub-regionalisation is viable for the purposes of consensus building and for achieving wide regional cooperation. As far as competition law is concerned, doubts exist that introducing competition law in sub-regional initiatives will prove workable or helpful whether in the short or long terms. In some parts of the world, countries have been highly reluctant to subscribe to the idea of sub-regionalism in the field of competition law (especially the idea of creating a sub-regional competition authority).[37] Sub-regionalism may prove to be problematic if the overall objective of the countries concerned is to achieve harmonisation in the competition law regimes of *all* countries in the region.

---

32 See *The Attribution of Competence to Community and National Competition Authorities in the Application of Competition Rules* (UNCTAD, 2008).

33 It should be noted that the Middle East is not an exception here since other examples can be found in the rest of the world. See Dabbah, note 4 above.

34 The GCC is made of the following Arab Gulf countries: Saudi Arabia, Kuwait, United Arab Emirates, Bahrain, Qatar and Oman.

35 Agadir nations include: Egypt, Jordan, Morocco and Tunisia.

36 GAFTA members include: Bahrain, Egypt, Iraq, Kuwait, Lebanon, Libya, Morocco, Oman, Qatar, Saudi Arabia, Sudan, Syria, Tunisia, and the United Arab Emirates.

37 See for example the views expressed by some Mercosur countries; see *Competition Law and Policy in Brazil: A Peer Review* (OECD, 2005).

5.5. OVERLAP IN MEMBERSHIP

The issue of sub-regionalisation has triggered an interesting situation of overlap in membership, in which some countries are parties to more than one regional community. Among other things, this situation causes confusion and raises wide speculation over whether a given country found in a cross-membership position will give priority to one community over another and, consequently, whether it will favour the competition law framework of one community over that of another.

It is probably correct and safe to assume that an overlap in membership is bound to dim the prospects for achieving proper and meaningful regionalisation in the field of competition law and is likely to lead to failure in turning the declared objectives of the relevant communities within a given region into a reality. The likelihood of failure is enlarged considerably due to the overambitious goals some of these communities set for themselves.[38] This calls for clarification of the relationship, and definition of the interplay, between regional communities whose memberships overlap. Suitable illustrations can be found around the world which highlight the need for such clarification and definition.[39] Equally, suitable illustrations also exist which prove that when such clarification and definition are secured this will lead to positive outcomes.[40]

6. THE ROLE OF THE ICN

In light of the discussion above – and with the clear desire by various world communities, including the Middle East, to establish regional cooperation – this part will consider why and how the ICN could offer valuable support and input as part of a future role to promote regionalisation.

---

38 Suitable illustration of can be found

39 Other than the example of the Arab League and Agadir/GAFTA within the Middle East referred to in the previous section, a particularly good example showing the need for clarification of the relationship between regional communities where an overlap in membership exists concerns the relationship between the Caribbean Community (CARICOM) and the Organisation of Eastern Caribbean States (OCES). The Competition Commission of CARICOM has jurisdiction in cases with cross-border effects. However, the interplay between it and the proposed OCES Competition Commission (OCC) has not been defined.
For a discussion on the Caribbean experience, see J. Molestina, *Regional Competition Law Enforcement in Developing Countries* (Springer, 2019).

40 The most high profile example is the relationship between the EU and EFTA within the European Economic Area framework.

6.1. SUITABILITY

The central 'thesis' of the present essay is that the ICN is suitably positioned to help different regional communities and their competition authorities explore regional cooperation fully; do so in an effective, efficient and meaningful manner; and reap the benefits of such cooperation. A contribution by the ICN is likely to be well-received by the relevant competition authorities of those communities and it should, ultimately, make a material difference in the entire landscape of regional competition law and policy.

As noted in part 1 above, the regionalisation of competition law reflects the very essence of the ICN. The topic therefore fits perfectly and naturally within any future ICN agenda. In making this statement, this author believes that the question, curiously, is not whether the ICN should take up this new challenge and become involve in promoting regional cooperation but rather why the ICN has not done this until now, especially when regionalism is inherent within it. The latter is evident from the way the Network presents its membership base and from its use of a divisional map, which is clearly regional in orientation[41], as well as in light of how the Network conducts its activities, especially its various events. This shows that – while the ICN's outlook is 'international' – it is somewhat sensitive to the regional dimension of competition law and policy. Whether the ICN leadership or membership are aware of this, however, is unclear, though it would not be unreasonable to believe that such regional sensitivity is likely to have been more inadvertent than intentional.

6.2. CHARACTERISTICS AND OPERATION

What places the ICN in a unique, if not ideal, position to pursue the regionalisation of competition law as part of its future endeavours are the Network's special characteristics and method of operation?

Launching the ICN was a novel development. For the first time, competition authorities from around the world were brought together to discuss and share ideas in a meaningful way on their difficulties and problems in addressing international competition issues and to seek ways in which they may improve their domestic regimes and achieve convergence between their procedural and substantive rules.[42]

41 See notes 15 and 16 above.

42 See M. Todino, 'International Competition Network *the state of play after Naples*' (2003) *World Competition Law and Economics Review* 283.

The work of the ICN has been of particular orientation and focus, determined by the objectives of the project(s) at hand. This has enabled the Network to achieve important consensus among a highly divergent membership, which brings together mature and young, developed-economies and developing-economies competition authorities from around the world. Over the years, the ICN has develop two key advantages, namely: *credibility* of output due to the large number of competition authorities engaged in its work; and the *incentives* it offers to competition authorities to implement its recommendations and best practices. The ICN's pragmatism and largely neutral stance helped it tremendously in securing these two advantages. In fairness, no other international initiative is a match for the ICN. For example, if one looks at the Organisation for Economic Cooperation and Development (OECD) or the United Nations Conference on Trade and Development (UNCTAD) – arguably the closest ICN's peers – it is easy to see how such comparison favours the ICN. Whereas the OECD lacks a sufficiently broad membership base, UNCTAD – whilst enjoying a broad membership base – does not provide sufficient incentives to all countries and their competition authorities to implement its output due to the fact that this output is often seen as too general and more academic than practical in nature.

The ICN has been remarkably imaginative in its treatment of the challenges facing competition law enforcement in a globalised economy. Its work has focused on areas in which convergence and harmonisation among different competition law regimes are considered to be possible and desirable to achieve. The ICN has always proceeded on the basis of a realistic and appropriately-ambitious agenda which is guided by the need to achieve consensus. The Network's *modus operandi* – using the model of steering and working groups – has enabled competition authorities, regardless of age and level of expertise, to both 'teach' and 'learn'.

6.3. STRENGTHS WITH SHORTCOMINGS

The characteristics and way of operating enjoyed by the ICN have helped its membership achieve an unprecedented level of wealth of competition expertise, an impressive 'know-how' in forging cooperation and handling technical assistance and capacity building activities, and a vastly rich experience with the concept and tool of competition advocacy. These assets are of major value to the regionalisation of competition law. At the same time, they reveal a shortcoming in the work of the ICN. The tool of competition advocacy offers an interesting illustration in this regard.

From the point of view of regionalisation, there is wide scope for developing and operating a proper competition advocacy mechanism within the different regional initiatives. Such mechanism sits comfortably within a regional setting and can easily serve as a 'centre of gravity'. A regional use of competition advocacy gives it *context*. This can only help the competition authorities of the relevant countries build a competition culture and competition law agendas which suit their own circumstances whilst ensuring harmony between competition law and developments in the domestic and regional economic, social and political arenas.

When considered carefully, each region of the world has its own special features and circumstances, both within and outside the competition law arena, which distinguish it from other regions. The Middle East, which served as a case study in part 4 above, is a good example. Not only the commonalities of language, religion and culture of the Middle East do not exist elsewhere, the politics of the region is also unrivalled.[43] Within the 'Middle Eastern competition law arena', two points in particular are crucial to highlight.

First, the experience of various countries in the Middle East with the concept of competition has been interesting. Other than competition has been considered as both a means to an end *and* as an end in itself throughout the region[44], it has been conditioned by a regional mentality of 'Middle Eastern style' which is one of *Modarabah* as opposed to *Monafasah*.[45] The former is a form of *negative* competition according to which the goal is always to undermine rivals through all means possible. *Monafasah*, on the other hand, is a form of *positive* competition in line of how it is understood in the field of competition law, namely 'winning' on the merit by striving for the custom of people through legitimate means. The prevalence of a mentality of *Modarabah* remains in existence in the region even with almost all countries having adopted competition law. This highlights the need to facilitate a cultural transformation.

Secondly, a common policy approach exists among different Middle Eastern countries. This approach revolves around the twin pillars of: heavy intervention by the state in the market place; and giving domestic competition rules a social 'orientation'. In particular, there is an interest throughout the region to *regulate* the prices of certain commodities as well as the behaviour of powerful firms in the market. Such 'competition-regulation' model is normally unlikely where

43 See generally M. Dabbah, *A Promising Middle East* (Contento, 2014).

44 On the one hand, a declared goal of the competition law regimes of these countries is to have competition in the domestic economy. On the other hand, in practice competition has been treated as a tool to achieve a variety of objectives, ranging from economic efficiency and the maximisation of consumer welfare to ensuring economic development and sustainable growth. This applies to all countries in the region without exception. See Dabbah, note 17 above.

45 *Modarabah* and *Monafasah* are Arabic terms.

there is increasing reliance on the market mechanism and a growing belief in the desirability of competition – as has been the trend around the Middle East in recent years. The approach clearly shows that Middle Eastern countries have been reluctant to relinquish their control of their domestic markets. As a result, these countries seem interested in reaping the benefits of competition without a readiness to accept its possible ramifications, such as a possible increase in prices to reward additional innovation and investment on the part of firms or the difficulties heated rivalry may create for some market players, whether inefficient or small firms. It would be fair to say that competition has not been embraced fully throughout the Middle East, notwithstanding the many declared statements by some national governments and competition authorities on its importance.

These points show – not only the vitality and importance of competition advocacy – but also the need for contextual, region-specific approach when engaging in competition advocacy both at the level of promoting it and at that of practicing it. Without such an approach, any competition advocacy initiative or effort is likely to be of limited relevance or benefit. The ICN experience shows this.

As noted in the introduction, competition advocacy was one of two pillars on which the ICN stood at the time of its launch. Today, the *ICN Advocacy Group* – which handles the ICN competition advocacy 'portfolio' – is a large group with over 70 ICN members and over 130 non-governmental advisors (NGAs). The *Group* has conducted various activities, including publishing advocacy reports, over the years. Arguably, but for the purposes of the present essay at least, the most important output by the *Group* has been *Competition Culture Project Report* (2015).[46] Nonetheless, this output reveals a shortcoming in the work of the *Group* and the ICN as a whole. This author has no particular desire to be overly-critical of the *Report* especially with him being a supporter of the ICN and its involvement in competition advocacy activities. However, it is difficult to see the value of the *Report* both after almost 15 years of such involvement *and* in general, not least with it being based on 'estimates' given by far less than half of ICN members.[47] Whilst, in fairness, the *Report* could have served a purpose in 2002 when the ICN began to execute its agenda, in 2015 the *Group* should be producing more concrete and analytical output, which presents competition advocacy as a 'problem-solving' tool whilst offering a *regional* road-map. The emphasis is put on 'regional' in this case not because the present essay deals with regionalism but because – at such advanced stage of ICN existence – the regional

46 The *Report* is available at www.internationalcompetitionnetwork.org/wp-content/uploads/2018/09/AWG_CompetitionCultureReport2015.pdf.

47 According to the *Report*, 48 members participated in the survey conducted.

level is the most appropriate level of all three possible levels for doing so. On the one hand, offering a road-map at the lower national level is not feasible because of the extremely wide ICN membership base. On the other hand, using the higher international level will mean that this road map will largely be of general and superficial nature.

What is said here regarding the need for a contextual, region-specific approach to the topic of competition advocacy, is also applicable in relation to other topics of competition law, whether those of technical assistance and capacity-building, convergence and harmonisation or agency effectiveness. In simple terms, such an approach is the most effective means available to promote competition law and policy within a given community, in particular where the desire is to do this at domestic and regional levels. The *OECD Latin American and Caribbean Competition Forum* (LACCF) amply demonstrates this.[48] The *Forum* has enabled its participants – who are senior officials from countries in the region and the OECD as well as selected international experts – to discuss on an annual basis issues of competition policy that are of interest to these countries and to do so in a concise and precise fashion. The work of the *Forum* shows how following a contextual, region-specific approach leads to concrete benefits. Many of the major successes Latin American (and more recently Caribbean nations) have scored in the field of competition law are, in a significant part, attributed to the *Forum*. A simple comparison between the Latin American and Caribbean competition and competition law landscapes *before* and *after* the Forum's launch in 2003 (and its expansion to the Caribbean region in 2015) would support this.[49]

Whilst the LACCF has been a remarkable achievement on the part of the OECD, the ICN is in an even more favourable position than the OECD to become involved in regionalisation efforts. There is no reason to doubt that such ICN involvement would not be certain to match, if not most probably exceed, the success of the LACCF. If anything, the LACCF should inspire and motivate the ICN leadership and membership to follow suit in other regions of the world. African, Middle Eastern or wider Asian communities would certainly benefit from a future region-specific approach by the ICN. Having said that, this author does not argue that the ICN should launch its regionalisation efforts across all these communities at the same time. Whilst theoretically this would not be an impossible task for the ICN to fulfil (in light of the nature and size of its membership and its formidable capabilities), it would be more sensible for the ICN to focus on one region as a starting point.

48 See www.oecd.org/competition/latinamerica.

49 See in general I. De Leon, *Latin American Competition Law and Policy* (Kluwer, 2001).

The present essay used the Middle East as a case study in part 4 above for the reasons given in that part. These reasons should qualify the region to be the first to benefit from ICN attention. This author is fully aware that many people might consider suggesting or choosing the Middle East as a candidate region for exploring regionalisation comes with a high probability of failure. Any fear of failure in this case is understandable and it is not without validity. It is difficult to dismiss such fear when, for example, one considers the idea of establishing a supranational competition law regime in the Middle East or of making *all* countries within the region sit around the same table. Having said that, it is important to recognise that a great deal of regionalisation of competition law can always be achieved below the threshold of a supranational competition law regime[50], and that regionalisation does not have to involve forcing people, whether politicians or competition officials, to sit around the same table.

The neutrality of the ICN and its various capabilities, coupled with the clear interest in regionalisation among Middle Eastern countries, are key assets for making an *ICN Middle East Initiative* not a myth, nor a dream but a realistic prospect. In this author's view, these assets allow for a generous margin of imaginative tools to be developed effectively. It is rather obvious that these countries are unable to pursue regionalisation meaningfully on their own as can be seen from the Arab League experience, which reveals how – even with a 'brotherhood' link – cooperation can easily stall. An ICN involvement is certain to make a difference especially when a pragmatic approach will be followed and when competition authorities within the region will see that this involvement bears the necessary sensitivity towards their needs and circumstances and comes to serve their sole benefit. The chances that every single competition authority in the region, whether one already in existence or conception, will take a regional ICN initiative seriously are high.

Recently, the United Nations Economic and Social Commission for Western Asia (ESCWA), UNCTAD and the OECD decided to launch a *Competition Forum for the Arab World*. It is understood that the first (annual) *Forum* meeting will take place in early 2020. Whilst it is a welcome development that the OECD in particular has decided to focus on the Middle East as part of its work, the launch of the *Forum* does not render an *ICN Middle East Initiative*, as proposed here, irrelevant or unnecessary. As a matter of fact, this development strengthens the case for an ICN involvement. The following five points in particular should be made in this regard.

First, the *Forum* seems to lack sufficient clarity in terms of its exact goals. Nor does the *Forum* appear to have concrete ideas which are directly linked to the competition law experience of Arab countries.

---

50 See part 2 above for the different types of regionalisation.

Secondly, although it is launched as an Arab world initiative, the *Forum* does not have a regional dimension in the shape of ideas or plans for regionalisation of competition law. As such, the *Forum* is easily distinguishable from the proposed *ICN Initiative*.

Thirdly, the Forum appears to lack the necessary participation of key Arab countries, including: Morocco; Qatar; United Arab Emirates; and the most important Arab country, Saudi Arabia. It is in fact rather intriguing and controversial that the agenda for the *Forum*'s first meeting does not include any consideration of the competition law experience of these countries, especially that of Saudi Arabia.

Fourthly, that agenda appears to be highly theoretical and academic in nature with hardly any practical orientation due to the decision to address issues such as: competition and economic development; institutional design; competition and private sector development; partnership for development; and public procurement. The current stage/state of competition law development within Middle Eastern countries, including Arab ones, requires a far more practical approach and consideration of 'issues of the moment' in competition enforcement. It is this approach and issues which are of interest and relevance for the region and its countries and in turn for the competition authorities of those countries. The kind of topics featuring on the *Forum*'s agenda are ones which would have been suitable for the region and the Arab world perhaps at the turn of the century. It is difficult to see how it could ever be useful at present to engage competition authorities of the relevant countries in a debate on such topics when their needs and interests dictate otherwise. The needs and interests of these countries are more along the lines of the ICN output and the practical work conducted by the OECD as part of its Competition Committee and LACCF.

Fifthly, this point follows directly from the previous one and it comes to explain the academic approach and nature of the *Forum*. The *Forum* and its agenda appear to reflect the outlook and orientation of ESCWA and UNCTAD which are closer to theory than practice. Obviously, the *Forum* is led more by ESCWA (and UNCTAD) and less by the OECD. It is perfectly understandable, thus, that the *Forum*'s agenda is of such nature.

7. CONCLUDING THOUGHTS

Every good reason exists for celebrating the ICN and its achievements 'at twenty'. The Network is reaching an important milestone. Any assessment of what has been achieved during the second decade of the Network's existence – which is conducted objectively and in an overall manner – is bound to be highly favourable.

It is hoped that the present essay would be seen as a modest attempt confirming this. Equally, however, it is hoped that the ICN leadership and membership will use such an important occasion not for a 'pat on the back', but for serious 'head-scratching' over what the third decade of the ICN's existence should look like.

The ICN at twenty is widely considered as the best forum within which competition authorities from different economies and world regions can interact deeply and fruitfully. A large number of these authorities view the ICN as the most significant aspect of their international operations and cooperation. The ICN at twenty enjoys a more-established and more-credible position globally than the ICN 'at ten', an occasion marked just under a decade ago. The question that should be posed, genuinely and seriously, on this occasion is how the ICN community – which is in effect the global competition law community at large – could ensure that such good progress will continue towards the further milestone of the ICN 'at thirty'.

In discussing the regionalisation of competition law, the present essay selected the Middle East as a suitable case study not only to ensure the analysis conducted above is concrete, but also to bring the topic of regionalisation and the region to the attention of the ICN leadership and membership. When looked at through comparative lenses – unlike all other regions in the world – the Middle East has been the only region which has not received any serious attention from the global competition law community. Yet, especially in recent times, many competition law practitioners have been experiencing, first hand, the importance of competition law and policy in the region and the ambiguities, complexities and difficulties of handling competition law matters in different Middle Eastern countries.

The essay sought to make the case for a future ICN role in regional cooperation and for this role to follow a contextual, region-specific approach. There are strong incentives for involving the ICN in regionalisation efforts based on its characteristics and strengths which would qualify the ICN to perform the role of a 'coordinator' beyond being a network of competition authorities. This is the kind of role that will be most effective for a third party to play in the Middle East region. The ICN as a coordinator in this case will be yet another way for the Network to give an imaginative response to a major international challenge in the field of competition law. An awareness of the value of both this new role and the topic of regionalisation on the part of the ICN leadership and/or the vast majority of the Network's membership (for whom regionalisation is in fact material) is an opportunity for the Network to prove that it is indeed the champion of: superior rules and standards; convergence; and international cooperation. This will also prove how fitting it is for the ICN's mantra to be 'All Competition, All the Time' and for this mantra to possibly become at some point: 'All Competition, All the Time, *All over the World*'.

RETHINKING ADVOCACY

Allan Fels

1. INTRODUCTION

When the history of competition policy comes to be written, it will be seen to have been relatively effective in dealing with private sector anticompetitive behavior, but relatively ineffective in dealing with government restrictions on competition. The success of competition advocacy will be seen as, at best, modest.[1]

In every country there is a vast number of highly anticompetitive government laws, rules and actions. They exist in every sector from agriculture to public services and at every level of government, whether national, regional or local.

The causes of these restrictions and their survival are numerous. To roll them back as much as possible and to minimise the number of new restrictions requires a multifaceted political approach. Traditional advocacy by competition authorities is one facet of these approaches.

The International Competition Network ("ICN") defines competition advocacy as 'those activities conducted by the competition authority related to the promotion of a competitive environment for economic activities by means of non-enforcement mechanisms, mainly through its relationships with other governmental entities and by increasing public awareness of the benefits of competition'.[2]

---

1 Much of this article draws on A. Fels and W. Ng in A. Ezrachi (ed), *Handbook of International Competition Law*, Cheltenham – Northampton: Edward: Edward Elgar Publishing, 2012, 185–202 and A. Fels and W. Ng, *Rethinking Competition Advocacy in Developing Countries in Competition Law and Development*, Stanford: Stanford University Press, 2013, *182–198*.

2 ICN Advocacy Working Group, 'Advocacy and Competition Policy', International Competition Network Conference, Italy, 2002, 25; ICN Competition Advocacy Work Group Sub-Group 1, 'Report on Assessment of ICN Members' Requirements and Recommendations on Further ICN Work on Competition Advocacy', Eighth Annual Conference of the International Competition Network, Switzerland, 2009.

The essay proceeds by setting out the nature of the ICN approach to advocacy identifying its limitations, considering institutional and policy alternatives and raising policy options for future ICN consideration of this topic.

We conclude that traditional advocacy by competition authorities on its own, although valuable and important, will not overcome the problem of government restrictions on competition. The ICN approach to advocacy should recognise the broad nature of the problem and look to expand advocacy and identify wider policy options for the future.

2. TRADITIONAL ADVOCACY APPROACH

The ICN's definition of competition advocacy focuses on those activities of the competition authority that are not enforcement related. Under this approach, there are generally two main perceived roles of competition advocacy. First, competition advocacy aims at building a competition culture, which is generally thought of as an awareness by economic agents and the public at large about competition rules.[3] In this capacity, competition advocacy is intended to educate and persuade other government institutions, the judiciary, economic agents and the general public of the benefits of competition to society and the role of competition law and policy in promoting welfare.[4] Second, competition advocacy is seen as a way to influence other government authorities from adopting anticompetitive laws and regulations.[5] In this role, competition advocacy is aimed at assisting other government authorities in their consideration of the relative competitive impact of various policy options and provides technical expertise on particular industries or markets to other policy makers.

2.1. COMPETITION ADVOCACY TO BUILD COMPETITION CULTURE

Competition agencies often engage in activities to raise general awareness of the benefits of competition and competition laws, regulations and policies because a strong competition culture helps both competition enforcement and advocacy. A strong competition culture also enhances the credibility and convincing power of the competition agency, which, in turn, reinforces the agency's enforcement and advocacy efforts.[6]

---

3 Ibid 31–32.

4 Ibid 25.

5 ICN Advocacy Working Group, 25.

6 R. Shyam Khemani (ed), *A Framework for the Design and Implementation of Competition Law and Policy,* Washington D.C. – Paris: The World Bank and the Organisation for Economic

As noted above, competition advocacy aimed at building and enhancing competition culture is directed towards other government agencies, the judiciary, economic agents and the general public. Government agencies that are more familiar with the benefits of competition might be less inclined to adopt anticompetitive laws and regulations. Judges who are more educated about competition principles, law and policies will be better equipped to handle competition law cases which come before them and improve the effective enforcement of competition law. A business com- munity and public that are informed about the benefits of competition and competition rules could help competition agencies in their enforcement role. They might bring more instances of anticompetitive conduct to the competition agency's attention or even initiate private actions to enforce the law themselves. A strong competition culture might even prevent economic agents from engaging in anticompetitive conduct in the first place.[7] Overall, this aspect of competition advocacy can foster conditions that will promote a more competitive market and competitive market behaviour without the direct intervention of the competition agency.[8]

The activities that are typically undertaken by competition agencies to raise public awareness of the benefits of competition and competition law and policy include:

(i) distributing publications such as annual reports, official gazettes, guidelines, newsletters, discussion papers, journal articles and surveys;
(ii) using mass media such as websites, press releases, radio and television;
(iii) conducting seminars and workshops;
(iv) making speeches, giving public lectures and participating in conferences;
(iv) undertaking and publishing economic studies of competition, including the impact of regulation in markets and industries;
(v) undertaking market studies (discussed further below);
(vi) conducting public consultation exercises; and
(viii) creating education and compliance programmes.[9]

2.2. COMPETITION ADVOCACY TO INFLUENCE GOVERNMENT

Apart from private anticompetitive conduct, government activities such as regulatory rule-making and intervention can also have anticompetitive

---

Co-operation and Development, 1998,Ch 6. 'Competition Advocacy' 99; ICN Advocacy Working Group, 32, 77, 89.

7 ICN Advocacy Working Group 31–32.

8 Khemani 93.

9 Ibid 99; ICN Advocacy Working Group, 31, 81–84; ICN Advocacy Working Group, 'Advocacy Toolkit: Part I: Advocacy Process and Tools', Tenth Annual Conference of the ICN, Amsterdam 2011, 13–14; ICN Competition Advocacy Work Group Sub-Group 1, 6, 22.

effects.[10] The traditional advocacy approach regards consultation on legislative or regulatory procedures as one of the primary tasks of competition agencies and the most important component of competition advocacy.[11] In this capacity, competition agencies review existing and proposed laws and regulations in order to provide recommendations and advice on whether certain government policies or measures promote anticompetitive practices or inefficiencies.[12]

Competition advocacy is considered to be especially relevant and necessary in those sectors that are subject to sector-specific regulation (such as public utilities) or that are undergoing or have recently undergone privatisation or deregulation.[13] Competition advocacy efforts targeting these sectors attempt to influence the content of the rules that govern the sector and the implementation of those rules.[14] In those sectors subject to sector-specific regulation, interest groups may have a particular interest in lobbying the government for protection or engage in other rent-seeking behaviour.[15] Here, competition advocacy efforts are directed at regulatory agencies and the legislature to convince them not to adopt anticompetitive measures that protect specific interest groups but harm public interest and to delineate the boundaries of economic regulation.[16] Sectors that are undergoing privatisation or deregulation, or that have recently done so, are new to competition and here the impact of competition advocacy can be the greatest. Competition advocacy can help to promote and develop a competition-friendly regulatory framework, both in design and implementation.

Competition authorities use a variety of tools to undertake competition advocacy vis-à-vis other government agencies. One of the most commonly used tools is consulting with other government bodies, which includes issuing opinions and recommendations, making submissions on proposed or new legislation and regulations, having one-to-one meetings with influential stakeholders and conducting workshops.[17] In particular, executive and legislative bodies are the most common targets of competition advocacy efforts due to the importance of being able to influence the drafting of legislation and regulations that impact on competition. This consultation may be formal or informal. In addition, the mechanisms typically used to advocate in particular sectors include providing comments, opinions and recommendations on draft legislation or projects,

10 ICN Advocacy Working Group 30.

11 Ibid 58, 93; ICN Competition Advocacy Work Group Sub-Group 1, 20.

12 Capacity Building & Competition Policy Implementation Working Group, 'Competition Advocacy in Regulated Sectors: Examples of Success', *Report*, International Competition Network, 2004, 47–48.

13 ICN Advocacy Working Group 67–69.

14 ICN Competition Advocacy Work Group Sub-Group 1, 22.

15 Khemani 93.

16 16 ICN Advocacy Working Group 31.

17 ICN Competition Advocacy Work Group Sub-Group 1, 20–22, 42.

advising on market definition, entering into cooperation agreements with sector regulators and drafting guidelines and sector codes of conduct.[18]

A recent development has been the focus on conducting market studies. Market studies are 'research projects conducted to gain an in-depth under- standing of how sectors, markets, or market practices are working'.[19] Market studies are generally considered to be useful tools to examine the anticompetitive features of a particular market and might result in: intervention in the legislative or regulatory process by the competition agency; further competition advocacy efforts; or even the initiation of enforcement actions (although there is some difference of opinion amongst competition agencies as to whether market studies should be used to base enforcement action). Market studies might also serve as a means to increase the transparency of the competition authority, educate the public, build sector expertise or bring about reform.[20] Whilst the notion of market studies is not new[21], it is a relatively new tool for most competition authorities.[22] In particular, the ICN has recently placed emphasis on the use of market studies and the Office of Fair Trading (the predecessor to the Competition and Markets Authority) in the United Kingdom has been especially vocal in advocating their use.[23] The increasing use of market studies is a welcome development as they provide a systematic study of the anticompetitive features of a particular industry, partly for enforcement reasons but also for the purposes of reform. Advocates also claim that market studies have had some impact on reform.[24] However, market studies are still limited in scope as they do not comprehensively identify anticompetitive laws nor address nor engage with the wider political causes of anticompetitive laws. In addition, market studies may be abstract economic studies and not targeted towards particular areas of government.

Some factors that influence the effectiveness of competition advocacy directed at other government agencies include: the timeliness of the consultation; whether the consultation is mandated by law or is discretionary; whether the opinions issued are binding on the government agency or the decision maker[25]; and

---

18 ICN Advocacy Working Group 72; Capacity Building & Competition Policy Implementation Working Group 58–59.

19 ICN Advocacy Working Group, 'Market Studies Project Report' (Eighth Annual Conference of the ICN, Switzerland, 2009) 28.

20 Ibid 31–33.

21 Market studies have been conducted in the United States since the early 20th century and in Japan since 1947.

22 ICN Advocacy Working Group 3.

23 Ibid; Office of Fair Trading, 'Market Studies – Further Information', <www.oft.gov.uk/OFTwork/markets-work/market-studies-further-info/>.

24 ICN Advocacy Working Group 87–89.

25 ICN Advocacy Working Group 60–67.

whether other government agencies hold different objectives and opinions.[26] Each of these factors will be discussed in the remainder of this section.

The timing of the competition agency's consultation in the legislative or regulatory process is relevant to competition advocacy in at least two respects. First, the competition agency needs sufficient time to assess the proposed activity's impact on competition; otherwise it is unable to provide useful advice or its consultation risks being a mere procedural formality.[27] Second, the timing of the competition agency's feedback into the legislative or regulatory process is important.[28] For example, if a draft law or regulation has already been presented to the executive or legislature, the competition agency's recommendations are much less likely to be considered and incorporated as compared to a law or regulation which is still in the early stages of drafting. Therefore, the earlier in the legislative or regulatory process the competition agency is consulted, the more likely that competition advocacy will be effective.[29]

Competition advocacy is also more effective if it is mandatory to consult the competition agency.[30] Mandatory consultation enhances the competition agency's access to the regulatory decision-making process. It may range from the competition agency receiving notice of the proposed regulatory activity, which then triggers its competition advocacy efforts, or it may receive a formal request for a recommendation.

Another factor that affects the effectiveness of competition advocacy is whether the competition agency's recommendation is binding.[31] Clearly, if the competition agency's recommendation must be followed, then the impact of competition advocacy is significant and provides the competition agency with some power. However, this is generally not a realistic option.[32] A more realistic option, which would improve the effectiveness of competition advocacy, at least where competition advocacy is directed at a government agency as opposed to the legislature, is to require government agencies to provide the competition agency with reasons why its advice was not taken up.[33]

Further, other government agencies might prioritise the achievement of their own objectives over competition.[34] These objectives may include those related

26 Ibid 72.
27 Ibid 60.
28 Ibid 60–61.
29 Ibid 61.
30 Ibid 63.
31 Ibid 65–67.
32 Ibid 65.
33 Ibid.
34 Ibid 72.

to revenue, investment, environmental, labour, social or other concerns. The government agency might want to protect its own regulatory domain and constituencies. Moreover, these government agencies might be subject to political influences. These issues present challenges to the competition agency's competition advocacy efforts.[35]

3. LIMITATIONS OF THE TRADITIONAL ADVOCACY APPROACH

Two principal limitations of the traditional advocacy approach are discussed in this section. First, the traditional advocacy approach fails to explicitly recognise and incorporate strategies for dealing with the magnitude of the political challenge involved in overturning anticompetitive laws. There are deep political drivers for these anticompetitive laws, which are broad in their scope and nature. Second, the traditional advocacy approach does not sufficiently consider the impact of institutional arrangements on the method and effectiveness of competition advocacy. The traditional advocacy approach assumes that the competition agency is a decentralised agency of the executive branch of government with a certain amount of independence[36], when, in reality, there is a range of institutional arrangements in different countries that bring competition agencies into varying degrees of closeness with their interaction with government.[37]

3.1. THE MAGNITUDE OF THE POLITICAL CHALLENGE IS GREATER THAN THAT RECOGNISED UNDER THE TRADITIONAL ADVOCACY APPROACH

The political drivers of anticompetitive behaviour are strong and numerous. The most important are in the interests of those businesses which benefit from the regulation on competition. Second, there may be competing and conflicting government policy objectives, for example, industry development brought about in the past by restrictions on competition. Third, there may be ideological factors, for example, the commitment in some countries to the support of state-owned enterprises.

35 ICN Competition Advocacy Work Group Sub-Group 1, 17–18.

36 Ibid 40, 93; ICN Competition Advocacy Work Group Sub-Group 1, 8.

37 ICN Advocacy Working Group 44–52.

3.2. SOME POLITICAL DRIVERS FOR COMPETITION REFORM

Nonetheless, there are forces that support and promote the development and enforcement of competition law. First, governments have incentives to support and promote competition. Since the fall of the Berlin Wall, virtually every country depends principally on markets to supply the goods and services that its citizens need. As governments generally recognise that, for markets to work well, competition is needed and that they need to promote it, competition law has taken on a quasi-constitutional status as a near fundamental law of all economies. Moreover, a government's performance is judged by the electorate, in part, on how efficiently the economy operates and this is partly determined by how well competition policy works. There is also a degree of public support for competition reform. Business interests often recognise that competition policy is to their advantage – and the national advantage – if it applies to all participants in the economy.[38] For example, when Australia embarked on its national competition policy, export industries supported the reforms as they recognised that they could gain from internal reform. There is also some recognition of the benefits of competition reform to consumers; a significant part of the community welcomes action against big businesses (without necessarily being supporters of competition policy as such).

The fact that competition law has spread around the world (despite frequent opposition by businesses) and that enforcement has become more vigorous is itself a sign of political support.[39] The proliferation of competition laws internationally is due to a combination of factors, one of which is international pressure to adopt competition laws, whether it is from trading partners, donor agencies, international organisations or international agreement.[40] However, the support is strongest for competition law enforcement rather than the repeal of anticompetitive laws.

3.3. IMPLICATIONS FOR COMPETITION ADVOCACY

Although it is clear (at least to competition agencies and advocates) that laws that restrict competition are very harmful, the political forces supporting anticompetitive laws are strong, complex and hard to overturn. Moreover, the breadth of these anticompetitive laws means that very large resources are

---

38 Khemani 99.

39 Competition laws exist in over 100 jurisdictions: D. J. Gerber, *Global Competition: Law, Markets, and Globalization*, Oxford: Oxford University Press, 2010, 85.

40 W. E Kovacic, 'Getting Started: Creating New Competition Policy Institutions in Transition Economies' (1997) 23 *Brooklyn Journal of International Law*, 403, 407.

required for these laws to be addressed comprehensively and such resources may not be available. This presents a challenge for competition advocacy.

When faced with these political challenges involved in overturning anticompetitive laws, it is clear that the traditional advocacy approach alone is inadequate for the task. The role of the competition agency under the traditional advocacy approach consists largely of advising and educating government departments about the public interest aspects of their laws. There is a need for a more fundamental analysis of the challenge and analysis of deeper and broader policy approaches to these issues.

3.4. IMPACT OF INSTITUTIONAL ARRANGEMENTS ON THE TYPE AND EFFECTIVENESS OF COMPETITION ADVOCACY

The traditional advocacy approach assumes that the competition agency is a decentralised agency of the executive branch of government with a certain amount of independence.[41] However, in reality, a wide range of institutional arrangements exist for competition agencies. This affects how the competition agency conducts competition advocacy and how effective it may be.[42] Some of these arrangements include:

(i) Independent agency: the competition agency is an independent agency and tends not to be engaged in government processes. An example is the Federal Trade Commission in the United States. Its main role is to enforce competition laws, although it may engage in competition advocacy on the periphery. Typically the competition agency has limited resources to expend on competition advocacy.

(ii) Ministerial system: if the competition agency is situated within a ministerial system, the competition agency is the responsibility of a government minister and the head of the competition agency reports to that minister. Hence competition agencies are meant to work through their sponsoring department, which may see itself, not the agency, as the policy advocate within government.

(iii) Agency inside the government: the head of the competition agency is a member of the high-ranking members of government or the executive branch. For example, the European Union's Competition Commissioner is a member of the European Commission[43] and the chairman of the Korea

---

41 ICN Advocacy Working Group 8.

42 F. Jenny, 'Competition Authorities: Independence and Advocacy' (IDRC pre-ICN Forum on Competition and Development: Alliance Building for a Culture of Compliance, 2011) 8.

43 R. Whish, *Competition Law* (5th edn), Oxford: Oxford University Press, 2005.

Fair Trade Commission is a minister and a member of South Korea's cabinet.[44] Therefore the competition agency is inside and at the top of government. An advantage of this model is that the competition agency is present when major decisions are being made that affect all areas of the economy; therefore, it can bring its knowledge to enhance the quality of those government decisions. On the other hand, there may be a conflict between the independence of the agency (due to its enforcement role) and the competition agency's involvement in the political process.

(iv) Independent advocate: most of the advocacy is done by an agency that is independent of the competition law enforcement body. However, the scope of the agency's powers may be limited. For example, Australia's Productivity Commission, which is an independent research and advisory body on a range of economic, social and environmental issues, is empowered only to act upon matters that are referred to it by the government and cannot initiate enquiries.

(v) Advocate inside the government: a government agency will engage in competition advocacy. That agency will generally be controlled by a minister and may, or may not, have areas of responsibility outside of competition. If it is an agency engaged solely in competition matters, it will tend to be small and have limited resources and political power, all of which hamper its ability to engage in competition advocacy. If that agency possesses an area of responsibility wider than competition policy, such as tax or climate change policy, then competition advocacy is but one of many competing priorities and the agency may or may not engage in competition reform. In both cases, the agency will tend to be susceptible to politics.

(vi) Direct prohibition of anticompetitive laws, *regulations and other government actions*: government agencies are directly prohibited from misusing their administrative powers to promote, manipulate, impede or prevent economic activities and intervene in market activities. Therefore, anticompetitive laws are prohibited as a matter of law under this model. An example of this model is China's Anti- Monopoly Law 2007.[45] There are, however, some practical issues surrounding the enforcement of this prohibition on administrative monopoly, for example whether it is appropriate for an agency to override its parliament by enforcing the prohibition against administrative monopoly or whether the matter needs to be brought before the court. In China, if a government agency abuses its administrative powers, it is up to its superior authority to make the correction and impose the punishment.[46]

---

44 S. H Jacobs, 'Regulatory Reform in Korea'. *Organisation for Economic Co-operation and Development*, 2000 187–88.

45 Anti-Monopoly Law of the People's Republic of China (People's Republic of China) National People's Congress, 30 August 2007, Articles 32–37.

46 Ibid Article 51.

(vii) Neutral umpire: the government undertakes the reform itself and establishes an independent body to ensure the proper implementation of those reforms. This body might also have a continuing role in reviewing new legislation. An example is Australia's National Com- petition Council (discussed in Section 4 below).

(viii) Regulatory impact statement *review bodies*: an independent agency is established to ensure the quality of new regulations whilst reducing the regulatory burden on businesses.

(ix) Government departments: competition advocacy is left to individual government departments.

Therefore competition agencies must be more aware of their institutional environment and role in the political process if they are to increase their effectiveness as advocates for competition. Some strategies for enhancing the effectiveness of the competition agency within its institutional environment, and hence its advocacy efforts, may be to:

(i) align itself with powerful government departments to boost its political power;

(ii) talk to departments generally about competition rather than pursue them on individual matters;

(iv) try to be involved in advance of competition issues;

(v) recognise that generally it is outside pressure that leads to change, not meetings inside the government;

(vi) consider using publicity as a weapon (although this might be unwelcome and it may be punished, such as by reduced resources and loss of jurisdiction); and

(vii) employ consultation mechanisms but recognise that they have their limitations.

Another way to improve the effectiveness of competition advocacy would be to move the competition agency closer to the centre of government where the real political power lies (such as departments of the prime minister or treasury). Typically competition agencies are located at the fringes of government, for example as attachments to departments of law (or Attorneys General) that have minimal involvement in law-making and economic reform. Their influence at the State and local level is also slight if they are national bodies and generally politically weak. They also generally do not have the authority, let alone the power acting on their own, to make substantial inroads. It is true that some competition agencies are positioned to exert considerable power, such as in the European Union and South Korea, but even then their power has limits as a 'voice of one' in the government. Competition agencies also often find it difficult to get access to ministers or political leaders (as opposed to bureaucrats), especially outside their own sponsoring department. Moving the competition agency closer to the centre of government might improve its access to ministers or political leaders.

Further, there are some challenges that competition agencies may face, regardless of their institutional setting. Where the competition agency has both enforcement and advocacy roles, there may be a trade-off between the agency's independence and its ability to advocate effectively.[47] On the one hand, an independent competition agency, or one that maintains arm's length relationships with other government institutions, will have relative freedom in carrying out its enforcement role. The perception of independence and neutrality increases the public's confidence in competition enforcement and enhances the competition agency's credibility.[48] However, an independent agency may lack good access to ministers and political leaders, not be involved in or consulted upon in decisions that affect competition or have little influence in general, thus hindering its ability to have its recommendations adopted and advocate effectively.[49] However, if a competition agency is involved in the political process, either because it is not an independent agency or due to its advocacy efforts, it may lose credibility with consumers, businesses and the general public and thus compromise its effectiveness as an enforcement agency.

The balance between advocacy and enforcement must also be addressed. Competition agencies have limited resources and there is generally a trade-off between devoting resources to enforcement as opposed to advocacy.[50] Generally speaking, the primary role of most competition agencies is the enforcement of competition laws, whilst advocacy tends to be a relatively minor task. However, this type of competition advocacy is inadequate to address the problem of anticompetitive laws. Therefore a dilemma arises: on the one hand, traditional advocacy is insufficient to address the problem of anticompetitive laws and there needs to be a more comprehensive approach to competition policy. On the other hand, a more comprehensive approach will likely require more resources, which may detract from the competition agency's enforcement efforts. Moreover, as noted above, competition agencies are not elected and their job is to enforce the law, not be advocates, and so the legitimacy of

---

47 J. Clark, 'Competition Advocacy: Challenges for Developing Countries' (2005) 6 *OECD Journal of Competition Law and Policy* 69, 70–71.

48 Clark 78–79.

49 See for example the observations by one member of the ICN at ICN Advocacy Working Group, 'Advocacy and Competition Policy' 54–55; Clark 70–71.

50 For example, in the context of developing countries, there is some debate over whether competition agencies should, during the early stages of implementing a competition law, devote more resources to advocacy over enforcement. See for example ICN 34–37; Kovacic 439–40.

advocacy may be questioned. There is thus a choice that must be made and a balance struck between the dual roles of competition agencies and their closeness to the centre of government.

4. BEYOND TRADITIONAL ADVOCACY: A POLICY APPROACH

From the preceding discussion, it is apparent that the task of competition advocacy is more complex and resource-intensive than that understood under the traditional advocacy approach. If a nation is to seriously address the problem of harmful anticompetitive laws, it will need to go well beyond the normal scope of advocacy activities typically undertaken by a competition regulator. It is therefore necessary to rethink the concept of competition advocacy. Rather than general actions that competition agencies might take to influence competition decisions within the government, competition advocacy could instead be a comprehensive programme that targets underlying anticompetitive laws. The role of a competition law enforcement agency in this context could range from marginal to central.

This approach was taken by Australia in the mid-1990s and is considered to be one of the most successful examples of pro-competition reform.[51] The national competition policy approach has since been adopted more widely, with Mexico having committed to a national competition policy in 2007 and now beginning to embark on those reforms and India has seriously considered its adoption. Further, Australia's national competition policy approach has been endorsed and largely adopted in the Competition Assessment Toolkit that has been developed and promoted globally by the Organisation for Economic Co-operation and Development ("OECD"), although the OECD presents it as a purely technical exercise and does not address the political nature of the task.[52]

This section discusses Australia's experience in conducting a national competition policy. Australia's experience demonstrates that the task of competition law reform is a much broader undertaking than suggested by the traditional advocacy approach and requires substantial political and administrative support. The point in this essay is not so much to advocate the comprehensive Australian approach; rather it is to indicate the demands of a complete policy.

---

51 Working Party No 2 of the Competition Committee of the Organisation for Economic Co-operation and Development, 'Competition Assessment Toolkit: Volume 1: Principles', *Organisation for Economic Co-operation and Development*, 2011, 3.

52 Ibid.

4.1. AUSTRALIA'S NATIONAL COMPETITION POLICY

Australia introduced its National Competition Policy in 1995.[53] All Australian governments – federal, state and territory – agreed to a series of agreements that set out a comprehensive and nationally coordinated microeconomic reform programme; that is, a national competition policy. The guiding principle underlying the National Competition Policy was that nothing limiting competition was warranted unless it could be demonstrated at an independent public inquiry that the restriction was justified and that the public interest objectives could not be achieved in any other manner, including a less anticompetitive manner.[54]

One of the key components of Australia's National Competition Policy was legislation review and reform, which involved the federal, state and territory governments each identifying, reviewing and, where appropriate, reforming legislation that restricted competition. Another key component was the adoption of the principle of competitive neutrality, whereby governments ensured that their publicly owned businesses would not enjoy any net competitive advantage due to them being publicly owned and committed to applying the Trade Practices Act (Australia's competition statute as it was then called) to all businesses and all levels of the economy. The National Competition Policy also introduced sector-specific reforms.[55]

This process placed substantial political, legal and administrative demands on Australia's national, state and territory governments. In fact, this was a ten-year process of review and reform of a mass of anticompetitive laws and government actions. A large majority of the planned reforms were achieved, and Australia's National Competition Policy is recognised as having delivered substantial benefits to the Australian community; benefits which have, overall, greatly outweighed any transactional or adjustment costs.[56] Elements of this approach, which contributed to its success, included:

(i) a serious attempt to change the competition culture of the community;
(ii) enlisting the support of top political leaders and their governments;

---

53 National Competition Council, 'National Competition Policy: Overview', <http://ncp.ncc.gov.au/pages/overview>.

54 Competition Principles Agreement, 11 April 1995, section 5(1). See also Australian Government Productivity Commission, 'Review of National Competition Policy Reforms', *Inquiry Report*, Commonwealth of Australia, February 2005, xiv; J. Feil, 'Up a Down Escalator: National Competition Policy – A Little History and a Glance Forward', 2010, 35 *Network* 1, 1.

55 National Competition Council, 'National Competition Policy: About the NCP', <http://ncp.ncc.gov.au/pages/about>; Australian Government Productivity Commission (n 68) xv.

56 Australian Government Productivity Commission (n 68) xvi–xxiii.

(iii) the adoption, in advance, of critical principles of competition policy;
(iv) the establishment and resourcing of institutional machinery to identify and review all anticompetitive laws;
(iv) a process for evaluation of those reviews; and
(v) financial rewards for governments that complied with those principles.[57]

The Australian experience reinforces the view expressed in this essay that the task of securing national competition reform is much broader than that suggested by the normal statement of tasks for competition advocacy.

5. BEYOND TRADITIONAL ADVOCACY: AN INCREMENTAL APPROACH

For many countries, a national competition policy approach, similar to that undertaken in Australia, might not be feasible or realistic. However, there remains a wide spectrum of possibilities that are more comprehensive than the traditional advocacy approach but less demanding than the national competition policy approach. An incremental approach to competition policy reform, discussed in this section, might be more suitable in such circumstances.

5.1. SET THE SCENE FOR REFORM

First, the competition agency should quantify the costs of the status quo and potential benefits of reform and communicate these to stakeholders and the public.[58]

Second, it helps if the competition agency is able to identify the potential reform winners and organise them to affect policy, as potential reform losers are more likely than potential reform winners to mobilise themselves.[59] Related to this, appropriate transition and compensation arrangements should be devised to avoid the experience of abrupt changes in economic conditions and to ease the concerns and resistance of the potential reform losers to reform.[60]

Third, international competitive pressures and international organisations and agreements can play a very large role in driving policy change, often in

---

57 Feil 5–6.
58 M. Wise, 'Opening Markets to Competition' in Organisation for Economic Co-operation and Development, 2005, 57–59.
59 Ibid 57–58.
60 Ibid 58.

conjunction with major crises.[61] Not only can international pressures lead to 'at the border' reforms, but they may also result in 'behind the border' reforms.[62] Also, if there is international trade liberalisation, the sequencing of behind the border reforms may be particularly important.[63] Sectors exposed to international competition may press strongly for greater efficiency and policy reform in the non-traded goods sector that supplies many of their inputs.

Fourth, whilst crises can create significant opportunities for reform by 'demonstrating the unsustainability of the status quo and by disrupting the interest coalitions that have previously resisted reform'[64], they can also promote anticompetitive laws.

5.2. SOME FURTHER GENERAL OBSERVATIONS

It is important to remember that there is no 'one size fits all' formula for overcoming obstacles to competition reform or even identifying the most urgent reform priorities. Both reform design strategies and reform adoption need to reflect the specific institutional and cultural context of the country. The transplant of policies and institutions from one environment to another rarely takes root and some degree of adaptation is usually required. Nonetheless, most countries face some common problems, especially in the field of competition policy and there has been a degree of policy convergence with respect to product market regulation and competition policy. There are also a number of commonalities in the way reform processes unfold, which suggests that those contemplating reform need to address a certain number of basic issues. Successful reform tends to be characterised by an electoral mandate for reform, effective political leader- ship and strong institutions that are capable of supporting reform.[65] It may be worthwhile for the competition agency to identify and engage with the potential opponents of reform and consider the feasibility, extent and nature of any compensation for potential reform losers.[66]

6. CONCLUSION

The concept of competition advocacy requires reconceptualisation. The ICN should promote analysis and discussion of this. The prevailing concept of

---

61 Ibid 42–45.

62 Ibid 46.

63 Ibid 55, 63.

64 W. Tompson 'Reform Beyond the Crisis' in Organisation for Economic Cooperation and Development (ed), *Making Reform Happen: Lessons from OECD Countries* (OECD Publishing 2010), 31.

65 Ibid 16–18.

66 Ibid 18–19.

competition advocacy – which is also the approach typically adopted by competition agencies in their roles as advocates for competition and the one that is discussed and promoted by the ICN – is one that involves the competition agency making speeches, issuing press releases, making submissions, providing briefings and writing papers about particular issues requiring competition reform. There are, however, other approaches that one could take to the task of competition advocacy. These approaches, as discussed in this essay, start by identifying the nature of the problem, the broad challenges presented to government and some of the possible responses (which may or may not ultimately include a role for a competition agency).

As shown in this essay, there is a vast range of anticompetitive laws at all levels of government, driven by major complex political forces, many of which are resistant to pressure for change. To deal with these laws properly and comprehensively, there needs to be a careful consideration of how a country can best eradicate anticompetitive laws. Whilst a national competition policy, representing a comprehensive approach to eliminating anticompetitive laws, is desirable, it might be unrealistic for many countries. If so, an incremental approach to competition reform, as outlined above, can and should be adopted. Admittedly, an incremental approach still represents a difficult, large and lengthy challenge that requires a considerable investment of political and bureaucratic time. However, as we have argued in this essay, there are many potential benefits from the adoption of such an approach.

Of course, we are not saying that the traditional advocacy approach should be abandoned completely. Traditional competition advocacy remains a worthwhile exercise, especially to build and enhance a competition culture, to complement other competition advocacy efforts and in situations where it is not realistic to adopt a national competition policy or an incremental approach. That being said, we argue that, regardless of which approach to competition advocacy one might take, it is essential that some consideration is given to both the political drivers and obstacles that are associated with anticompetitive actions and the institutional arrangements of the relevant actors so that advocacy efforts can be tailored to maximise their effectiveness. Moreover, it must be remembered that competition policy is but one component of broader economic policy that encompasses matters such as deregulation, trade liberalisation, monetary policy and tax policy. Competition advocacy efforts should also be framed with the wider economic reform agenda in mind. This is an important future agenda item for the ICN.

ANTITRUST COMPLIANCE – ENCOURAGING CORPORATE COMPLIANCE EFFORTS*

Anne RILEY**

1. INTRODUCTION

The last decade has seen some dramatic (and welcome) changes to the approach of several ICN member antitrust agencies to assessing and evaluating genuine compliance efforts by companies.

Certainly, in the first decade of the ICN's existence, the focus of antitrust agencies was on enforcement, ever increasing penalties and the use of leniency programmes to "encourage" compliance rather than encouraging companies to invest in compliance.

Enforcement obviously has an important place, as the absence of any enforcement action might encourage complacency in the corporate world. But enforcement and increasingly heavy penalties do not by themselves encourage a real compliance culture, but perhaps a fear of "getting it wrong" – or perhaps (in a very small percentage of cases) a fear of "being caught". Yet antitrust infringements still occur, so it is time to rethink the approach to "encouraging" compliance.

---

* This article is based in part on an article by the author that appeared in the November 2019 edition of *Competition Policy International* under the title "Antitrust Compliance – reluctance to embrace and recognise corporate compliance efforts".

** The views in this article are personal to the author, and do not necessarily represent the views either of Shell or of the International Chamber of Commerce.

2. ATTITUDE OF ANTITRUST AGENCIES TO COMPLIANCE EFFORTS – THE EARLY YEARS

The attitude of many (but not all) antitrust agency members of the ICN to corporate antitrust compliance efforts has developed considerably over the last two decades.

For many years, Canada and Australia were "ahead of the game" in terms of providing guidance on (and in the case of Canada, credit for) credible compliance efforts by companies when assessing the appropriate sanction to impose.

As early as 1996 – even before the genesis of the ICN – the Australian Competition and Consumer Commission ("ACCC") had issued a media release saying that corporate Australia needed a culture of compliance.[1] At the time of the media release in 1996 Professor Allan Fels (the then Chair of the ACCC) stressed that corporate compliance was not merely about adopting good tools, but about changing corporate culture. This is undoubtedly correct.

The Canadian Competition Bureau, too, was a very active promoter of corporate compliance, publishing extensive guidelines (in the Bulletin on Corporate Compliance Programs) in September 2010. This Bulletin was extensively revised and update in June 2015[2] and is an admirable document that sets out detailed guidance on the essential elements of a credible antitrust compliance programme.

Other ICN members were also starting to explore the benefits of compliance programmes as an additional enforcement tool. The UK's Office of Fair Trading (now the Competition and Markets Authority or "CMA") issued guidelines in 2011 entitled "How your business can achieve compliance with competition law".[3]

Despite these guidance documents, in the early days of the ICN there remained a significant degree of scepticism (and even positive distrust) amongst even some of the sophisticated antitrust agencies about the true purpose of antitrust compliance efforts.

---

1 Https://www.accc.gov.au/media-release/corporate-australia-needs-culture-of-compliance and https://www.accc.gov.au/business/business-rights-protections/implementing-a-compliance-program.

2 Competition Bureau of Canada, "Bulletin – Corporate Compliance Programs", June 2015, https://www.competitionbureau.gc.ca/eic/site/cb-bc.nsf/eng/03927.html.

3 OFT document 1341, https://www.gov.uk/government/publications/how-your-business-can-achieve-compliance-with-competition-law.

The US Department of Justice ("DOJ") Antitrust Division and the European Commission's Directorate-General for Competition ("DG COMP") were historically amongst the most sceptical of the leading antitrust agencies on the benefits of encouraging compliance (or, to their minds, "rewarding compliance failure").[4] Possibly this view was driven in part on a reliance on amnesty and leniency as the primary enforcement incentive (and perhaps an underlying belief that antitrust compliance efforts were "self-serving" and not likely to be genuine).

However, DG COMP was starting to consider the importance of compliance programmes in developing and sustaining a culture of compliance – issuing its "special first edition" booklet "Compliance Matters" in November 2011– this was revised and reissued in February 2013.[5] Whilst this was a welcome move by DG COMP showing at least some movement in its approach to corporate compliance programmes, given the historic scepticism of DG COMP to compliance efforts, the document was understandably focussed primarily on enforcement, penalties and leniency.

3. FURTHER WORK BY THE ICN ON COMPLIANCE

The second decade of the ICN saw real efforts by ICN members to engage with non-governmental advisers ("NGAs") and the wider business community on compliance.

Compliance issues regularly featured as Teleseminars and Working Group Workshops of both the Cartel Working Group[6] and Advocacy Working Group.[7] The Advocacy Working Group also undertook its valuable "Benefits" project which looked at explaining the benefits of competition to the general public through media and academia, explaining the benefits of competition to business and explaining the benefits of competition to governments and legislators. Valuable resources were collected from agency members of the ICN and from

4 J. Almunia, "… a company involved in a cartel should not expect a reward from us for setting up a compliance programme, because that would be a failed programme by definition." SPEECH/11/268, 14 April 2011.

5 European Commission, "Compliance Matters", 8 February 2013, https://op.europa.eu/en/publication-detail/-/publication/78f46c48-e03e-4c36-bbbe-aa08c2514d7a/language-en.

6 For example, the CWG Teleseminar on 27 January 2016 on Compliance and Deterrence, and another CWG Teleseminar on 05 December 2018 on Compliance programmes.

7 For example, the AWG Teleseminar on 27 October 2011 "Explaining the benefits of competition to business" and the AWG Workshop in Mauritius on 6–7 November 2014 on Advocacy Foundations, Strategy and Assessment which included break sessions on compliance advocacy.

participating NGAs. Those resources can be accessed online on the ICN's website.[8]

It is to be hoped that the ICN continues its valuable work in looking at compliance and perhaps follows the lead of Canada, the DOJ Antitrust Division and other agencies in providing some substantive guidelines (and perhaps best practices) on credible compliance programmes in the coming years.

4. WHAT HAVE COMPANIES BEEN DOING TO ENCOURAGE ANTITRUST COMPLIANCE?

Compliance programmes and codes of ethics have become a fundamental part of not merely antitrust compliance but compliance overall for companies.[9] Whilst most major companies invest significant amounts of time, effort and resources in trying to ensure that they have a credible and robust antitrust compliance programme, business organisations such as the International Chamber of Commerce ("ICC") have been working tirelessly to advocate the of benefits of competition and the importance of antitrust compliance to all businesses, both large and small.

In 2013, the ICC launched the Antitrust Toolkit for companies.[10] The purpose of the Toolkit is to provide practical tools for companies wishing to build a robust antitrust compliance programme. It seeks to complement materials produced by antitrust agencies and other sources of guidance[11], by focusing on practical steps companies can take internally to embed a successful compliance culture. To ensure that the Toolkit can be easily accessed by business, it is currently available free of charge online, and has been translated into several languages, including several European languages, Chinese Mandarin and Russian. The main Toolkit was followed in 2015 by a very short and simple Toolkit specifically designed for SMEs.[12]

Since the publication of the Toolkits, the ICC has organised (or has participated in) more than 100 workshops and conferences around the world, ranging from Canada in the north to Australia in the south, and also across the globe

---

8 Https://www.internationalcompetitionnetwork.org/working-groups/advocacy/benefits-of-competition/.

9 D. Sokol,, "Cartels, Corporate Compliance and What Practitioners Really Think About Enforcement", *Antitrust Law Journal*, Vol. 78, 2012, https://ssrn.com/abstract=2079336.

10 Https://iccwbo.org/publication/icc-antitrust-compliance-toolkit.

11 See for example the publication by the Society of Corporate Compliance and Ethics (SCCE): J. Murphy, "A Compliance & Ethics Program on a Dollar a Day: How Small Companies Can Have Effective Programs" 2010, www.corporatecompliance.org/Portals/0/PDFs/Resources/ResourceOverview/CEProgramDollarADay-Murphy.pdf.

12 Https://iccwbo.org/publication/icc-sme-toolkit-complying-competition-law-good-business.

from east to west, to explain to businesses the benefits of competition, and to encourage agencies to give more guidance on their expectations of what a robust antitrust compliance programme would entail. The advocacy work of the ICC continues, and the ICC is considering updating the main Toolkit (as an online-only version) in 2020.

The pre-ICN roundtable (organised jointly by the ICC and International Bar Association, with support and encouragement from the ICN Secretariat) now regularly features a panel on compliance, where ICN members and NGAs share perspectives on encouraging compliance. It is to be hoped that this round table continues in the future, and continues to discuss how to promote a culture of compliance.

Through ICC members who are also NGAs, the ICC hopes to continue to work closely with the ICN in promoting compliance and advocating for investment in antitrust compliance programmes and the building of a real culture of compliance.

5. IS ANTITRUST THE "POOR RELATION" IN THE COMPLIANCE WORLD?

Antitrust has been described as an "outlier" when it comes to how antitrust agencies treat compliance compared with other enforcement agencies.[13]

Antitrust compliance cannot be viewed in isolation or exist in a vacuum. In today's world, companies must comply with a vast array of compliance topics, including Anti-Bribery and Corruption ("ABC"), Anti-Money Laundering, Data Privacy, Trade Controls and Sanctions laws and Health and Safety laws to name but a few.

Companies and their internal advisers can feel overwhelmed at the sheer range of compliance requirements and confused at the (very) different approaches some enforcement agencies take in terms of positively encouraging and rewarding genuine compliance efforts.

In relation to Foreign Corrupt Practices Act ("FCPA") enforcement, the DOJ has a long history of taking account of ABC compliance programmes.[14] This

---

13 A. Riley and D. Sokol, "Rethinking Compliance", *Journal of Antitrust Enforcement* 31, 2015), University of Florida Levin College of Law Research Paper No. 16-3, http://ssrn.com/abstract=2475959.

14 In fact, when it came to criminal enforcement, antitrust was (until the recent change of policy in the Antitrust Division) the only area in the entire DOJ that did not recognise the value of compliance programmes.

constructive approach by the DOJ's FCPA enforcers has been at least partly driven by the policy objective that a key goal of enforcement is to achieve a compliance culture in practice.

The FCPA enforcers have indeed gone further than "merely" giving credit by way of a reduction in a fine or criminal sentence for credible compliance efforts. In April 2012, the DOJ for the first time declined to prosecute an FCPA violation by a corporation, whilst prosecuting an individual within the corporation. The declination related to Morgan Stanley, and was on the grounds that a Morgan Stanley employee had[15]:

> ".. used a web of deceit to thwart Morgan Stanley's efforts to maintain adequate controls designed to prevent corruption. Despite years of training, he circumvented those controls for personal enrichment".

The same policy objective (that a key goal of ABC enforcement is to achieve a compliance culture in practice) motivated the UK's Ministry of Justice to include a compliance defence of "adequate [compliance] procedures" in the UK Bribery Act[16] and to provide significant amounts of guidance on what compliance "adequate procedures" would entail.[17]

Recently a number of commentators have advocated that antitrust agencies should give more credit for genuine compliance efforts, since rewarding robust and genuine compliance programmes in the context of an investigation can improve the effectiveness of corporate sanctions in providing ex ante incentives to companies to deter and detect illegal behaviour internally.[18]

Certainly, these approaches of the authorities to giving compliance guidance and giving positive incentives for companies to invest in ABC/FCPA compliance (including the possibility of a complete defence for the corporation) have had a very dramatic impact on how much time, effort and (above all) resources that companies dedicate to this area of compliance. Whilst it would be comforting to think that all companies will invest significant amounts of money and time in a compliance programme from a sense of public spiritedness, that is perhaps a little naïve. The reality is that corporate resources – even in large companies – are limited, so that the in-house Legal and Compliance functions have to "compete" internally for precious resources (and the resource of employee and management

---

15 DOJ Press Release, 24 April 2012, https://www.justice.gov/opa/pr/former-morgan-stanley-managing-director-pleads-guilty-role-evading-internal-controls-required.

16 UK Bribery Act 2010, s7(2).

17 Https://www.gov.uk/government/publications/bribery-act-2010-guidance.

18 See F. Thepot, *The Interaction Between Competition Law and Corporate Governance*, Cambridge University Press, 2019.

time) that could otherwise be devoted to other matters – such as investing in the organic or inorganic growth of the business to increase profitability.

This does not mean that companies are not serious about antitrust compliance – generally they are, and most companies want to comply. But the reality is that they also want to invest in their business – so anything agencies can do to encourage and incentivise companies to devote sufficient and appropriate resources to the important area of antitrust compliance will support the policy objective of reducing antitrust violations.

Although there is little empirical evidence to support the following statement (as companies are understandably reluctant to discuss their compliance spend publicly), the author believes that the reluctance of antitrust agencies to engage actively in a dialogue with companies on the financial benefits of investing in a credible antitrust compliance programme (in terms of mitigation of fines) has meant that antitrust might be "left behind" in some companies (but not in all) when it comes to a decision whether to invest (for example) in ABC compliance (where the benefits of the investment are tangible) or in antitrust compliance, where the benefits of the resource allocation may not be immediately obvious to management, since mitigation of fines by antitrust agencies is rare.

6. THE WINDS OF CHANGE – THE DEPARTMENT OF JUSTICE ANTITRUST DIVISION'S NEW APPROACH TO CORPORATE COMPLIANCE PROGRAMMES

The scepticism of antitrust agencies in the early days of the ICN has been mentioned above – but times, however, are changing. In April 2018 the DOJ Antitrust Division held a public Roundtable[19] to consider antitrust compliance programmes – and, specifically, how the Division's (then) policy of giving no credit to credible compliance programmes "sat" with the US Federal Sentencing Guidelines and with the rest of the DOJ's policy (outside the Antitrust Division) of recognising and crediting robust compliance programmes.

Following this roundtable, on 11 July 2019, Makan Delrahim, the Assistant Attorney General in the Antitrust Division announced a new policy to incentivise corporate antitrust compliance.[20] The Antitrust Division will in future consider genuine and robust compliance efforts at the charging stage

19 Https://www.justice.gov/atr/public-roundtable-antitrust-criminal-compliance.

20 Https://www.justice.gov/opa/pr/antitrust-division-announces-new-policy-incentivize-corporate-compliance.

in criminal antitrust investigations, and the Division published a guide to prosecutors[21] to assist them in evaluating corporate compliance programmes at both the charging and sentencing stages. This guidance document will provide a useful "roadmap" to companies of the Division's expectations of antitrust compliance programmes.

The DOJ's policy change is very much to be welcomed (and long wished for), as is AAG Delrahim's statement that *"the Antitrust Division is committed to rewarding corporate efforts to invest in and instil a culture of compliance"*. It is to be hoped that this policy change – which is a dramatic shift for the Antitrust Division – will be followed in other jurisdictions, including those that only have a system of administrative rather than criminal enforcement (such as the EU).

As noted above, other ICN member agencies give some sort of credit (or at least incentives) for antitrust compliance programmes[22], notable amongst them is Canada, where an antitrust compliance programme can be a mitigating factor, and the implementation of compliance measures may be imposed as part of alternative forms of resolution. As mentioned above, the Canadian Competition Bureau also gives detailed and useful guidance on the necessary elements of an effective (or robust) antitrust compliance programme.

The interest of ICN member agencies in considering compliance programmes as a possible mitigation factor continues to grow. In September 2019 the Peruvian Competition Authority (Indecopi) issued a public consultation on antitrust compliance programmes (including detailed guidelines similar to the Canadian Competition Bureau guidelines) indicating that it may be prepared to take into account genuine compliance efforts when considering an infringement that has already occurred.[23]

7. A WAY FORWARD IN TERMS OF RECOGNISING ANTITRUST COMPLIANCE EFFORTS?

In considering the optimal approach to assessing (and perhaps even rewarding) genuine compliance efforts, it is worth recalling that EU Competition Commissioner Almunia famously (and rightly) observed in 2010[24] that the purpose of antitrust enforcement is not in itself to impose high fines and other

21 Https://www.justice.gov/atr/page/file/1182001/download.

22 See F. Thepot at fn 20 *supra*.

23 See Section 9.3, Indecopi draft Guidelines on Antitrust Compliance Programs, September 2019.

24 Speech at the Business Europe & US Chamber of Commerce Competition Conference, 25 October 2010, https://europa.eu/rapid/press-release_SPEECH-10-586_en.htm.

penalties – rather the ultimate policy goal of antitrust is to have no need to impose penalties at all. Whilst Mr Almunia was undoubtedly thinking about the benefits of imposing fines and encouraging the EC's leniency/immunity programme in uncovering covert cartels, Mr Almunia (almost certainly unintentionally) highlighted a fundamental truth which antitrust agencies should consider and take to heart: the ultimate (and the proper) policy goal of antitrust enforcement is to encourage and to achieve genuine compliance by changing behaviours and culture. Behavioural research into organisation ethics demonstrates that culture can be used as a tool to improve compliance as a law-abiding culture creates norms that push for more effective compliance.[25]

Whilst enforcement will remain an important tool, focussing only on penalties and not on behavioural expectations will do little to change societal norms. This involves antitrust agencies in the ICN, academia and business organisations such as the ICC working together to change compliance values, so that businesses "doing the right thing" when it comes to fair competition becomes normal and accepted – and even expected – by society at large.

If a company has made sincere and consistent efforts to comply, the antitrust agencies should understand that a company compliance programme has not "failed" because one or more employees have circumvented company policy. Companies should rather be encouraged by the agencies to learn from any past compliance incidents and continuously improve their compliance efforts. ICN member agencies need recognise that there is no such thing as zero risk – a company with even the best approach to compliance and with a good corporate culture may still have individuals within the organisation who, despite a company's best efforts, decide to flout the law and ignore the company's own culture and policies.[26]

Perhaps a "perfect" compliance programme, whilst undoubtedly a laudable goal, may be an unrealistic goal, given that "humans are human". Ultimately it is not inanimate companies that decide to break the law – it is the human beings within those companies – and each person will have his/her own personal drivers – whether these are positive, such as the desire to behave ethically and with integrity, or negative such as ego, hubris, arrogance or greed.[27]

25 L. Sharp Paine, "Managing for Organizational Integrity", *Harvard Business Review*, March–April 1994, at 106.

26 T. Banks and J. Murphy, "*But it is also an inescapable fact of our human existence that people are fallible, and that in some cases people will ignore instructions and do things that they were expressly forbidden to do*" 40 *Denver Journal of International Law & Policy* 368, 2012, http://ssrn.com/abstract=2787970.

27 This view of human nature is not universally accepted by all commentators – see W. Wils, "*Because companies benefit from the antitrust infringements engaged in by their employees, companies would have an incentive to encourage violations. Companies would have an*

There is a credible argument (in terms of encouraging compliance in practice) for antitrust agencies to think more creatively about how corporate antitrust compliance programmes could help enforcement[28], for example by antitrust agencies:

- Giving credit for pre-existing genuine antitrust compliance efforts and a truly robust programme, as the US DOJ Antitrust Division has indicated it will now do;
- Actively and openly requiring the adoption of an antitrust compliance programme in decisions and settlements, and for companies benefitting from immunity or leniency[29]; and /or
- Acknowledging genuine compliance efforts, in looking at parental liability for acts of a wayward subsidiary, such as by not fining the parent company.

Given the DOJ Antitrust Division's recent policy change in relation to genuine antitrust compliance efforts, ICN member agencies may be inclined to move their position slightly closer to that of the DOJ (even if it is not minded yet to give credit for antitrust compliance programmes).

8. CONCLUSIONS

There are many pressures facing businesses today – and many compliance challenges, both in relation to antitrust and in relation to the myriad of other laws they need to comply with. Research has shown that most businesses want to "do the right thing" – they want to act with integrity and protect their reputation – they just need to understand how to do that. Research by the CMA demonstrates that the knowledge of the requirements of competition law amongst small and micro businesses (in particular, but also amongst some medium sized and even some larger companies) is deplorably low. ICN member agencies as well as NGAs and business organisations have a vital advocacy role in changing this.

---

incentive to recruit those employees most likely to engage in antitrust infringements, and to give them the authority necessary to do so.", Journal of Antitrust Enforcement, Vol. 1, No. 1, April 2013, pp. 52–81, http://ssrn.com/author=456087.

28 Bloom M. and Riley A, "Antitrust Compliance Programmes – Can Companies and Antitrust Agencies Do More?", *Journal of Competition Law* 21, 2011.

29 An argument sometimes put forward by antitrust agencies is that they do not have the resources to monitor compliance on an ongoing basis, but that could be resolved in appropriate cases by appointing an independent antitrust compliance monitor– perhaps the appointment of a monitor should be limited only to the more egregious cases such as *United States v Apple* Inc 952 F. Supp. 2d 638 (S.D.N.Y. 2013).

Encouraging antitrust compliance is not just about programmes and processes – although these are helpful and perhaps even necessary to provide structure. Antitrust compliance is fundamentally about encouraging companies to do the right thing. It is about achieving and sustaining the right corporate culture.

An antitrust compliance programme is not an "end in itself" – it is merely a tool to help businesses achieve a culture of ethics and integrity. On the other hand, an antitrust compliance programme on its own that is not underpinned and reinforced by a culture of compliance – involving "Tone at the Top", "Tone in the Middle" and "Tone all the way down" the organisation – will be unlikely to be effective. So, a robust antitrust compliance programme needs appropriate policies and procedures that reflect and enforce the company's real commitment to conducting business ethically and in compliance with the law. If ICN member agencies continue (or start) to regard genuine compliance efforts more positively and do more to encourage compliance efforts, antitrust compliance efforts are likely to increase, and hopefully more compliant behaviour will be the outcome. This can only benefit business, society and consumers generally.

THE DEVIL IS IN THE ENFORCEMENT: POLISH MERGER PROCEDURE IN THE LIGHT OF THE ICN GUIDING PRINCIPLES AND BEST PRACTICES*

Mateusz Błachucki**

1. INTRODUCTION

The establishment of the International Competition Network has resulted in huge changes to the development of international and national competition laws. The ICN has also fostered unprecedented growth in international cooperation among national competition authorities. On the verge of the third decade of the ICN's existence, it is fully justified to analyse how the functioning of the network has shaped national antimonopoly laws and competition enforcement, and what the possible scenarios are for the further development of the ICN. This essay will undertake this aim by looking at the ICN's legacy on merger procedures, and its impact on Polish merger proceedings. Merger control has remained at the core of the ICN's activities since the very beginning, and its achievements in this area are especially impressive. The Polish merger procedure has also evolved substantially since 1990, so it would be interesting to investigate how this evolution has been influenced by the ICN's recommendations and guidelines.

The aim of this essay is to compare the guiding principles and recommendations on merger procedure issued by the ICN, the largest network of competition authorities, with the relevant Polish provisions. This comparison will show the possible impact of the soft law adopted by the ICN on Poland's domestic legal order. Its results will be relevant for discussions on how the ICN can ensure that its members comply with the soft law rules that they approved collectively. The analysis provided in this essay is limited to procedural issues. Substantive issues are also relevant, but examining these would require extensive additional

* The essay forms part of research financed by the National Science Centre, Poland, in accordance with grant agreement No UMO-2016/23/B/HS5/03605.

** Institute of Law Studies, Polish Academy of Sciences, ORCID: 0000-0001-5805-048X.

research and which would be impractical to present within one essay.[1] This essay is structured as follows: first, a brief presentation of the ICN guiding principles and recommendations on merger procedure. This will be followed by a concise description of the Polish merger control system and its main developments in relation to merger proceedings. Subsequent sections offer a detailed analysis of Polish merger procedure, before turning to the level of compliance of Polish rules with the ICN's recommendations. This is followed by an analysis of the ICN's possible detection tools for inconsistencies between the network's recommendations and national laws and an examination of measures that can be taken to remedy this situation. The concluding section attempts to confirm the importance of enforcement for the formal harmonisation of laws.

2. ICN GUIDELINES ON MERGER PROCEDURE

Merger control involves important transaction costs for companies, which are usually obliged to suspend their transactions until consent is given by the relevant competition authority. Transaction costs may rise significantly in cases of multijurisdictional mergers, which require multiple notifications. The more aligned national competition laws are, the easier the analysis of potential competition problems is for companies. At the same time, where national competition authorities cooperate more, there may be more coherent outcomes from a merger analysis. Therefore, it is in the interest of companies, and to a significant extent for competition authorities as well, to have harmonised competition rules and solid international cooperation with other authorities. Those aims may be achieved through participation in transnational competition networks, the most prominent of which is the ICN. The achievements of the ICN in relation to fostering cooperation between authorities and the harmonisation of laws in the area of merger procedure are considerable.

The ICN is primarily a soft law network that has adopted numerous recommendations and best practices, as well as handbooks and manuals for the competition community.[2] Those documents are ultimately aimed at the progressive convergence of the administrative practice of national competition authorities and national competition laws. The ICN is probably the most successful network of competition authorities and offers the best solution for the

---

1 For analysis of the substantive issues please refer to M. Błachucki, The Consistency of Polish Competition Law with ICN Recommendations – the Example of Merger Notification Obligation, (2018) 3 *Studia Prawnicze*, 103–129.

2 The list of the ICN's soft law documents may be found in *ICN Work Products Catalogue (September 2019)*, https://www.internationalcompetitionnetwork.org/wp-content/uploads/2019/11/ICNWPCatalog9–2019.pdf (accessed 11/01/20).

development of international antitrust rules and cooperation in the absence of an international antitrust treaty.[3]

There are two fundamental soft law documents from the ICN related to the construction of merger procedure: 1) the ICN Guiding Principles for Merger Notification and Review[4]; and 2) the ICN Recommended Practices for Merger Notification and Review Procedures.[5] There are also documents providing practical tools for merger proceedings, such as 1) the Practical Guide to International Enforcement Cooperation in Mergers[6]; 2) the Model Confidentiality Waiver for mergers[7]; and 3) the Merger Remedies Guide.[8] Those documents are varied in character and length, but they are all relevant for the analysis of the subject. The ICN's Recommended Practices are accompanied by comments prepared by the ICN Merger Working Group. Those comments are updated periodically and offer a more detailed analysis of particular standards.

The first document has historically been the first and the most general document in the area of merger control. The ICN Guiding Principles for Merger Notification and Review are a short set of basic and fundamental guidelines for merger control regimes. The document expresses the desire to achieve consistency, predictability and fairness in the merger review process. These aims should be achieved by following certain procedural rules, such as: 1) procedural fairness; 2) efficient, timely, and effective review; 3) coordination; and 4) protection of confidential information. Furthermore, members of the ICN should abide by the general rule of transparency and convergence. Those rules should guide national legislators when adopting relevant provisions and competition authorities when enforcing them. Even though the above-mentioned principles are general, they provide enough clarity to be easily comprehensible and applicable for relevant national authorities.

The second document is the ICN Recommended Practices for Merger Notification and Review Procedures. It is the most comprehensive soft law

---

3 For more analysis on the ICN please refer to P. Lugard (ed.), *The International Competition Network At Ten. Origins, Accomplishments and Aspirations*, Antwerp – Oxford – New York: Intersentia, 2011.

4 Https://www.internationalcompetitionnetwork.org/portfolio/guiding-principles-for-merger-notification-review-procedure/ (accessed 01/12/2019).

5 Https://www.internationalcompetitionnetwork.org/portfolio/merger-np-recommended-prac tices/ (accessed 01/12/2019).

6 Https://www.internationalcompetitionnetwork.org/portfolio/merger-cooperation-guide/ (acces-sed 07/12/2019).

7 Https://www.internationalcompetitionnetwork.org/portfolio/model-confidentiality-waiver-f or-mergers/ (accessed 01/12/2019).

8 Https://www.internationalcompetitionnetwork.org/portfolio/merger-remedies-guide/ (acces-sed 01/12/2019).

document adopted by the ICN relating to merger control obligations and merger procedure. It contains thirteen sets of recommendations, of which vast majority (10 of 13) concern merger procedure. They propose basic principles for designing crucial elements of merger procedure regulations, such as: 1) timing of notification; 2) review periods; 3) requirements for initial notification; 4) conduct of merger investigations; 5) procedural fairness; 6) transparency; 7) confidentiality; 8) interagency enforcement cooperation; 9) remedies; 10) competition agency powers; and 11) review of merger control provisions. Each set of best practices provides for specific guidelines accompanied by comments prepared by the Merger Working Group. Due to the detailed character of the Recommended Practices, they are able to serve as the most comprehensive blueprint for national legislators when adopting laws, and for national competition agencies when preparing guidelines or implementing relevant merger provisions.

The remaining three documents constitute practical tools and are aimed at influencing the administrative practice of competition authorities. They are not formal guidelines, but they still have important practical value. These documents provide for flexible and comprehensive tips on how to coordinate investigations with other agencies, use waivers and construct and adopt remedies. Also, importantly, they can direct not only competition authorities but undertakings as well. This dual application is a result of the less formal and practical character of those documents. Therefore, their impact on administrative practice should not be underestimated.

This brief summary of the ICN's guiding principles, Recommended Practices and practical tools on merger procedure shows that the ICN is attempting to achieve a coherent level playing field for merger control systems around the world. The network promotes clear and objective rules to achieve consistency, predictability and fairness in the merger review process. The inevitable consequence of applying the ICN recommendations is a subsequent reduction in transaction costs and increased speed and predictability of reviews of multijurisdictional mergers. It is also clear that the ICN is trying to limit merger control to purely competition-related principles, which leaves any non-competition-related questions out of the picture. Procedural rules are often more related to general national procedural norms than is the case with substantive provisions. Hence, such an ambitious goal will not always fit into the national legislators' agenda. Furthermore, in spite of the ICN's absolutist approach to merger control, in practice merger control systems are often part of a broader enforcement and procedural framework of national administration. Therefore, some inconsistencies between the ICN recommendations and national provisions should be expected in all jurisdictions.

3. MERGER CONTROL IN POLAND – OVERVIEW OF THE SYSTEM

The merger control system in Poland is based on the Competition Act[9] and two implementing regulations.[10] Furthermore, there are two sets of guidelines issued by the Polish competition authority: one devoted to the jurisdictional and procedural aspects of merger control[11], and one dealing with substantive merger analysis.[12] The case law of Polish courts in relation to merger control is scarce and offers very little, if any, useful guidance. Therefore, the key role in the development of the Polish merger control system lies in the hands of the Polish competition authority, which is solely responsible for merger control in Poland.[13] The President of the Office for Competition and Consumer Protection ("OCCP") is the competition authority in Poland. The competition authority is a central public administration authority that has two main domains of activity: first, 'traditional' antitrust matters connected with the protection of competition (in the public interest); and second the protection of consumer interests. The competition authority in Poland is not independent and the President of the OCCP has no fixed term of office and may be dismissed at any time and for any reason by the Prime Minister. The OCCP has exclusive jurisdictional powers and relies entirely on an inquisitorial system of proceedings. The authority initiates, investigates and decides on merger cases. The OCCP has powers to clear a merger, order remedies or prohibit a transaction. Appeals against the rulings of the competition authority are heard by the antimonopoly court.[14] Administrative courts play only a subsidiary role in antimonopoly adjudications.

---

9 The Act on Competition and Consumer Protection of 16 February 2007, *Journal of Laws* 2018, item 798 (the "Competition Act").

10 Regulation of the Council of Ministers of 23 December 2014 on the notification of intended concentration of undertakings, Journal of Laws of 2018, item 367 and Regulation of the Council of Ministers of 23 December 2014 on the calculation of the turnover of undertakings participating in the concentration, *Journal of Laws* 2015, item 79.

11 Office for Competition and Consumer Protection – Guidelines on the criteria and procedure of notifying the intention of concentration to the President of the OCCP ("Procedural Guidelines"), available in Polish at http://uokik.gov.pl/wyjasnienia_i_wytyczne.php (accessed 01/12/2019).

12 Office for Competition and Consumer Protection – Clarifications concerning the assessment by the President of the OCCP of the notified concentrations, available in Polish at http://uokik.gov.pl/wyjasnienia_i_wytyczne.php (accessed 01/12/2019).

13 There are sectoral regulators (for example, the Office for Electronic Communications, the Financial Supervisory Authority and National Council for Radiophone and Television) that may review mergers in parallel to the competition authority, but their review is limited exclusively to regulatory issues.

14 The official name of the antimonopoly court is the Court for Competition and Consumer Protection.

The OCCP is composed of the central office in Warsaw and nine regional offices. The central office consists of 21 divisions, one of which is the Department of Concentration Control. This department deals exclusively with merger control, with the regional offices playing no role in merger control in Poland.

This brief introduction shows that merger control in Poland is based on a centralised and inquisitorial system, with the competition authority playing a pivotal role. The basic weaknesses of Polish public enforcement of competition law are the wide jurisdictional portfolio of the OCCP, which has an adverse effect on the actual number of official interventions, along with the weak position of the competition authority in the Polish public administration system.[15]

4. POLISH MERGER PROCEDURE – KEY SOLUTIONS

Polish merger procedure is a special administrative procedure employed by the Polish competition authority when reviewing notified mergers. The purpose of this section is to briefly present key aspects of this procedure in the light of the above-mentioned ICN guiding principles and Recommended Practices.

4.1. TRANSPARENCY OF THE MERGER PROCEEDINGS

The Polish competition agency is probably one the most transparent government agencies in Poland as regards access to laws, soft law and decisions. All applicable laws are easily accessible on the OCCP's webpage. Moreover, general guidelines and interpretations are also available. Furthermore, there is constantly updated news of all pending cases, with information on the status of all cases. All the decisions of the OCCP may be freely downloaded from the OCCP's webpage. The OCCP is largely unique in this regard when compared to other Polish public bodies. This practice is in line with the ICN's Recommended Practices (VIII.C).[16] The only problem is that applicable laws, and especially guidelines, are updated only very rarely, which makes them outdated in certain areas. Those rare periodical changes tend to occur for internal reasons. Unfortunately, external recommendations (from academics, stakeholders or the ICN) are not very persuasive for the authority. This practice is hardly in line with the ICN's Recommended Practices (XIII.A-B).

---

15 For a general overview of Polish competition law, please refer to M. Błachucki, *Polish Competition Law – Commentary, Case law and Texts*, Warsaw: UOKiK, 2013.

16 The numbers in brackets refer to the relevant ICN Recommended Practices.

4.2. DEADLINE FOR NOTIFICATION

In the 1990s, Polish competition law required undertakings to notify transactions within one week from the day when the intention to concentrate materialised, i.e. signing an agreement. However, it has since moved towards abolishing the fixed deadline for notification. In point II.2 of the OCCP Procedural Guidelines, the Polish competition authority indicated that in most types of concentrations the entry in the official company register is regarded as the moment when the concentration is consummated. Hence, the merger should be notified at any time before that moment. It should be noted that Polish law does not require that the agreement at the source of the concentration be definite. Any document[17] expressing the intention of companies to enter into a transaction is permissible. However, the OCCP Procedural Guidelines make it clear that *the intention to concentrate should be real and precise. For this reason, the notifications based solely on the subjective belief of the undertaking or on nonbinding negotiations are treated as untimely and subject to return.*[18] This regulation is in line with the ICN's Recommended Practices (III.A-B).

4.3. PRE-NOTIFICATION PHASE

In many jurisdictions, the pre-notification phase constitutes a voluntary or even compulsory part of merger proceedings. The Polish merger procedure takes the opposite position. Neither the Competition Act nor the OCCP Procedural Guidelines provide for the basis to conduct the pre-notification phase. The OCCP Guidelines state that the Polish competition authority allows only limited contact with the authority before formal notification. The OCCP Guidelines state as follows: *in situations requiring the clarification of particularly complex issues, the President of the OCCP permits the possibility of their verbal presentation by the notifying entity at a specially organised meeting with authorised representatives of the President of the OCCP (this possibility also exists prior to the initiation of the proceedings)* (II.3.2).[19] In practice, such pre-notification meetings are rare and depend on the discretionary decision of the authority.

Polish regulation and administrative practice of the OCCP in relation to pre-notification phase/contacts remain contrary to the ICN's Recommended

17 In practice it may be a conditional agreement, preliminary agreement, letter of intent or public invitation to sell stocks in the case of public companies. At the same time, the Polish competition authority claims that draft agreements, statements of the undertaking's managing authorities, announcements or press statements are not regarded as sufficient to demonstrate the required intention.

18 Procedural Guidelines, p. 29.

19 Procedural Guidelines, p. 30.

Practices. The ICN clearly advocates pre-notification discussions (III.D and V.C). As the ICN rightly points out, these discussions can also help the agency and the parties prepare for any required review. As a result, the authority misses the possibility to prepare for complex cases. Another consequence is that a resolution of any jurisdictional issues or the correction and supplementation of the notification may take place during proceedings, which may prolong the merger process extensively. These negative consequences may be found in many merger cases conducted by the OCCP.

4.4. PARTY TO THE MERGER PROCEEDINGS

Only an undertaking may be a party to merger proceedings. The Competition Act regulates strictly who can be party to merger proceedings. Article 94 of the Competition Act determines that every person who notifies the intention of concentration is a party to the proceedings. There is an explicit list of entities who are both entitled and obliged to notify the intention to concentrate: 1) the merging undertakings jointly; 2) the undertaking taking over control; 3) jointly, all the undertakings participating in the creation of a joint venture; and 4) the undertaking acquiring the assets of another undertaking. It is also noticeable that the legal concept of a party to a concentration is narrower in scope than the concept of a participant in such cases.[20] Contrary to European competition law, Polish merger proceedings lacks the concept of 'undertakings concerned' and only the party acquiring the control has a standing before the competition authority. Furthermore, target companies, competitors, contractors or consumers are not parties to merger proceedings.[21] As a result, none of those entities have the right to access the case files or to challenge the merger decision.

This issue is not regulated directly in the Recommended Practices. There is only a general point that *procedural fairness should be afforded to merging parties and third parties with a legitimate interest in the merger under review* (VII.A). Moreover, in many points (i.e. III, V, VI, VII, IX, X) the Recommended Practices refer to merging parties. Those observations suggest that both the active and passive parties to the merger should have standing during proceedings before the competition authority. It is worth mentioning that the passive party to the transaction used to enjoy the status of 'interested person' with some limited procedural rights. However, this institution was abolished in 2007 in Poland

---

20 E. Modzelewska-Wąchal, *Ustawa o ochronie konkurencji i konsumentów. Komentarz*, Warsaw: Twigger 2002, at 309.

21 The order of the Antimonopoly Court of 11 March 1991, XVII Amr 5/91, Wokanda 1992, No 4, item 37.

for no apparent reason.[22] It is justified to say that the Polish regulation of party status limits the rights of certain undertakings and restricts transparency of merger proceedings. It is only partially in line with the ICN's Recommended Practices.

4.5. PUBLIC INTEREST INTERVENTION

Polish administrative law provides for extensive possibilities for public interest interventions during administrative proceedings. Such public interest interveners are called persons vested with the rights of a party. Their legal position is very similar to the position of the parties to proceedings, although their rights are limited. This regulation applies to merger proceedings, as well. There are three categories of public interest interveners: public prosecutor, Ombudsman and social organisation. In practice, public interest interventions are very rare. Under the present Competition Act, there has never been a case where a social organisation was admitted to merger proceedings. In March 2021, for the first time in its history, the Polish Ombudsman challenged in court a decision of the Polish NCA to approve a concentration. There was also one intervention by the public prosecutor, who unsuccessfully challenged one merger.[23] This issue is not tackled by the ICN's Recommended Practices or any other network document.

4.6. INITIATION OF MERGER PROCEEDINGS

Merger proceedings may be instituted exclusively by the notifying undertaking or undertakings. If the merger is implemented and the undertaking subsequently notifies the competition authority of the merger, the notification is returned and the authority initiates proceedings to levy a fine for a failure to notify the merger. Merger proceedings are instituted upon the merger notification by the notifying undertaking. Detailed conditions of the notification of an intention to concentrate are ascertained by the Regulation of the Council of Ministers.[24]

---

22 For a critical analysis of these changes, please refer to M. Błachucki, *Postępowanie skargowe jako próba zastępczej regulacji ochrony interesów faktycznych osób trzecich w postępowaniu administracyjnym po likwidacji instytucji osoby zainteresowanej* [w:] M. Błachucki, G. Sibiga (eds), *Skargi, wnioski i petycje – Powszechne środki ochrony prawnej*, Presscom, Wrocław 2017, pp. 289–314.

23 M. Błachucki, Glosa do postanowienia Sądu Apelacyjnego w Warszawie z 23 kwietnia 2018 r. (VII AGz 523/18), Orzecznictwo Sądów Polskich 2019, No 12, pp. 110–119.

24 Regulation of the Council of Ministers of 17 July 2007 concerning the notification of the intention of concentration of undertakings, Journal of Laws of 2007, No 134, items 936 and 937.

The notification form is uniform – there is no short or complete version.[25] It is the result of the fact that Polish merger proceedings are uniform and there is no simplified procedure. One notification form applies to all types of concentrations. However, the notification form consists of two parts and the second part needs to be completed only if there are affected markets. This may be regarded as a rationalisation of information obligations.

The scope of the required information is relatively standard, and even more limited when compared to some other jurisdictions. For example, the notifying party is not obliged to list mergers or acquisitions that took place in a certain period before notification. Furthermore, the OCCP has, to date, never demanded internal documents during merger proceedings. There has been a tendency to limit the amount of required information. Since 2015, undertakings are no longer obliged to provide certificates from the company registry, and they only need to provide financial statements for one year (previously it was two). Unfortunately, this positive tendency is contradicted by the practice of the authority in relation to documents showing the intention of undertakings to engage in the concentration. Previously, the OCCP allowed an undertaking to provide just the key provisions of the agreement, such as the names of the parties, the subject of the agreement, or conditions precedent. Currently, the authority demands a translation of the entire document. This creates an additional unnecessary, costly and time-consuming burden on undertakings. The scope of information requirements in the notification form is formally in line with the ICN's Recommended Practices (V.D).

The merger notification is subject to a fee of PLN 15,000.[26] The fee is not significant and in most European jurisdictions undertakings are obliged to pay higher administrative fees. No additional fees are levied, even in the case of second phase merger proceedings. This issue is not tackled directly by the ICN's Recommended Practices or any other network document.

4.7. STATUTORY DURATION OF MERGER PROCEEDINGS

Timing is a crucial aspect of all merger proceedings. The regulation of time limits concerning merger proceedings has changed considerably in Poland. Until 2015, there was a uniform time limit of two months. At present, merger proceedings must be completed within one month in phase one, or within an additional four months during phase two. Additionally, there are "stop the clock" provisions. The most important time-suspension provision allows the authority to stop

25 For a detailed presentation analysis of the notification form, see *Guidelines on the criteria and procedure of notifying the intention of concentration to the President of UOKiK*, p. 3.4.

26 Approximately EUR 4,150.

the clock whenever the OCCP asks the party to the proceedings to supplement the notification and provide additional information. It is noteworthy that the initiation of phase two is rather easy for the OCCP. The Competition Act allows the authority to open a second phase whenever "the case is complicated". This ambiguous provision does not create any real obstacle against the initiation of phase two whenever the OCCP wishes to do so. When initiating the second phase, the OCCP informs the parties about the legal grounds for an in-depth investigation. In practice, this information is rather short and the party has no legal means of challenging it.

Time limits in merger proceedings must be adhered to, and so if they lapse the OCCP is no longer legally able to adjudicate on the case.[27] If a merger decision is not issued within the prescribed statutory time limit, it is presumed that the competition authority has issued a positive decision. Although merger proceedings must, on their face, be concluded within one month, that only happens in rare cases. Given the use of "stop the clock" provisions, the average time of phase one proceedings ranges from 32 to 37 days (depending on the year), whereas second phase proceedings are concluded on average within 220 to 225 days (depending on the year).

The regulation of time limits may be regarded as being in line with the Recommended Practices (IV.C). However, the enforcement of these provisions clearly does not allow for *expedited review and clearance of notified transactions that do not raise material competitive concerns* (IV.B). This is a result of inadequate resources and imperfect internal procedures. When the time limit for merger proceedings (in simple cases) has been shortened, no additional resources were allocated to deal with the increasing time pressure and the flow of new cases. In some cases, this resulted in prolonging the merger review i.e. multiple requests to supplement notifications, or the need to initiate second phase proceedings. As a result, merger cases are not *always completed within a reasonable period of time* (IV.A). It is interesting that the inconsistency with the ICN's Recommended Practices is primarily a result of imperfect enforcement and not necessarily inadequate legislation.

4.8. EVIDENCE IN MERGER PROCEEDINGS

The OCCP relies primarily on information provided by parties and data already in the authority's possession. In the vast majority of cases, such sources of information are enough to clear the merger. Should additional information be

[27] The resolution of the Supreme Court of 26 November 1993, III CZP 63/93, *Orzecznictwo Sądu Najwyższego – Izba Cywilna* 1994, No 4, item 13. See also the comment of T. Woś to this resolution, *Państwo i Prawo* 1995, No 1.

required, the OCCP may ask the party to supplement the information. When a market survey is necessary, the authority sends a compulsory request for information ("RFI") to third parties. It is interesting to note that RFIs in Poland are always sent as a compulsory decision safeguarded by heavy fines in the event of a failure to respond. The recipient is therefore obliged to respond fully to the RFI, and its scope cannot be challenged.[28] Such a complaint may, however, form part of an appeal to the antimonopoly court if a fine is levied for non-compliance with the RFI. However, the competition authority cannot demand information unnecessary for adjudicating the case.[29] Moreover, the competition authority cannot demand that the undertaking perform any special analyses or studies that are not required by law, since such work is to be carried out by the authority.[30] Similarly to undertakings, other public administration bodies are obliged to cooperate. They are under an obligation to provide the OCCP with access to the files in their possession, along with information relevant to the pending merger proceedings. Finally, third parties are always allowed and encouraged to express their views during merger investigations. This regulation is in line with the ICN's Recommended Practices (VII.C and XII.A). Until 2015, the OCCP had the competence to conduct dawn raids during merger investigations, but the authority is currently legally precluded from performing such searches. This change is contrary to the ICN's Recommended Practices (XII.A).

4.9. ACCESS TO FILES AND INFORMATION RIGHTS

The right of the party to access files is a fundamental right in merger proceedings. The merger procedure is inquisitorial by nature and a public hearing takes place very rarely. If the authority fails to respect this fundamental right, it is treated as a grave violation of the procedural rules and may lead to the proceedings being invalidated.[31] The right to access the file is laid down in Articles 72 and 73 of the Administrative Procedural Code. It includes the right to: 1) examine the files[32]; 2) make notes and copies of the files; and 3) certify notes and copies of the files. The regulation of access to files is old-fashioned and does not answer the needs of modern administrative procedure. What is especially problematic is that the OCCP does not provide for any access to source data or organise

28 The judgment of the Antimonopoly Court of 16 December 1998, XVII Ama 62/98, Wokanda 2000, No 4.

29 The judgment of the Antimonopoly Court of 19 November 1992, XVII Amr 24/92, Wokanda 1993, No 5.

30 The judgment of the Antimonopoly Court of 6 September 1993, XVII Amr 22/93, Wokanda 1994, No 2.

31 G. Rząsa, *Nieważność postępowania sądowoadministracyjnego jako podstawa skargi kasacyjnej*, C.H. Beck, Warsaw 2011, p. 310.

32 Z. Janowicz, *Kodeks postępowania administracyjnego. Komentarz*, Wydawnictwo Prawnicze PWN, Warsaw 1995, p. 185.

data rooms.[33] The right to access the files fully applies to the parties and public interest interveners. However, it is possible to gain access to certain information contained in case files under the Act on Access to Public Information of 6 September 2001.[34] It should be stressed, though, that the mentioned Act does not provide access to all files, but only to those materials that contain public information.[35] The party may access the files at any time during the merger proceedings, or at any time after the conclusion of the proceedings. The only condition concerns prior consultation with the case handler on the technical conditions for presenting the files to the party. Should the files be transferred to the court, it is the court that is obliged to provide the party with access to them.

Access to the file is important, but only one of the means designed to guarantee the transparency of merger proceedings. Another important means is the information flow between the competition authority and the party to the proceedings. This is especially important when reporting competition concerns identified during the merger investigation. Proper and accurate information should enable the party to explain the position and produce relevant evidence. Since 2015, the Competition Act provides for the obligation to inform the party about any identified market problems. The information is to be presented to the party whenever the competition authority decides to open a thorough investigation and initiate the second phase of the merger proceedings. Last but not least, the party is always informed who the case handler is and may contact them at any time. It should be stressed that only informal contacts are possible via email or phone. Any formal communication between the competition authority and the party, and vice versa, must be in writing. This regulation is partially in line with the ICN's Recommended Practices (VI.B, VI.C and VII.B).

4.10. PROTECTION OF BUSINESS SECRETS

During merger proceedings, confidential business information generally has to be provided to the OCCP. Such business secrets need to be protected from public disclosure. The OCCP may restrict access to business secrets upon request from the undertaking, or on an *ex officio* basis. This happens when the undertaking fails to submit a request for confidentiality, but the evaluation of

---

33 It is widely criticised – J. Łukawski, *Prawo strony do obrony w postępowaniu w sprawie kontroli koncentracji prowadzonym przez Komisję – glosa do wyroku Trybunału Sprawiedliwości z 16.01.2019 r., C-265/17 P, Komisja Europejska przeciwko United Parcel Service, Inc.*, Europejski Przegląd Sądowy 2019, No 10, p. 38.

34 *Journal of Laws* 2001 No 112, item 1198 with further amendments.

35 M. Błachucki, *Dostęp do akt sprawy administracyjnej na podstawie Kodeksu postępowania administracyjnego a dostęp do informacji publicznej znajdującej się w aktach sprawy administracyjnej,* [in:] *Dostęp do informacji publicznej w Polsce i w Europie – wybrane zagadnienia prawne,* E. Pierzchała, M. Woźniak (eds), Uniwersytet Opolski, Opole 2010, p. 135.

documents leads to the conclusion that they contain business secrets. Moreover, employees of the OCCP are under an obligation to protect business secrecy and any other secrets that they might acquire during the proceedings. The restriction of access to files may vary in relation to different entities. For example, such a restriction may take place between the parties to the proceedings, or even between the party to the proceedings and its mother company. The information acquired in the course of the merger proceedings cannot be used for other proceedings conducted on the basis of separate provisions, excluding other proceedings conducted by the OCCP, the exchange of information with the European Commission and relevant authorities of the European Union Member States pursuant to Regulation No 2006/2004/EC, or when providing competent authorities with information that may indicate the infringement of separate provisions. It may come as a surprise to learn that the OCCP has never used or accepted waivers from parties in a merger process, even when cooperating with foreign counterparts. This regulation is mostly in line with the ICN's Recommended Practices (IX.A and IX.B).

4.11. REMEDIES

Should the merger investigation reveal potential market problems, the party is officially presented with a document expressing competition concerns related to the transaction. The party has 14 days (which may be extended by another 14 days) in which to respond. This is the time when the party may propose remedies. It is interesting to note that prior to 2015, when the OCCP did not send competition concerns to parties, it was the authority who initially offered remedies. Currently, the initiative lies in the hands of the parties. The findings of the authority made on the basis of a market survey set out the framework for negotiations. Surprisingly, the statutory timing for negotiations is very tight. The competition authority enjoys wide discretionary powers when deciding on remedies in merger cases. These remedies can be structural and behavioural, as well as any combinations thereof. In practice, the decisions issued by the OCCP show an unequivocal preference for structural conditions. When analysing remedies accepted by the authority, it is striking that they are rather simple and that the OCCP has never used trustees to implement or monitor the execution of remedies. In some occasions, this has resulted in remedies that may not have been properly implemented. This regulation is mostly in line with the ICN's Recommended Practices (XI.A-D).

4.12. DECISION-MAKING PROCESS – OVERVIEW

The decision-making process within the OCCP is rather typical of Polish public administration. There is one case handler for each case. The case handler is responsible for preparing all documents during the proceedings, including draft decisions. The parties may contact the case handler directly, and, if necessary, the head of unit or the director of the department. Holding meetings with the parties is not an integral part of the standard rules of conduct – the authority decides on a case by case basis whether such meetings are, from its perspective, useful for the proceedings. In practice, such meetings are quite rare, which is not in line with the ICN's Recommended Practices (VI.B). All the documents prepared by the case handler are verified by the head of unit and ultimately approved and signed by the director of the department or regional office. When preparing a decision, the legal department (in certain cases) and the department of market analyses (in all cases) are consulted. Those departments are consulted at a late stage of proceedings. There may be serious delays in completing the review if there are any diverging views on the draft decision. Stakeholders have pointed out that the lack of coordination of the analysis between the Merger and the Market Analysis Departments *in many instances prolongs the assessment on merits. Moreover, in practice we have encountered situations in which even the most straightforward concentrations, with a marginal impact on markets covering Poland, were diligently analysed by Market Analysis Department from the point of view of overlapping horizontal and vertically linked markets.*[36] All draft decisions must be checked and approved by the President of the OCCP. As stated earlier, all decisions are issued on behalf of the President of the OCCP. The decision-making process is rather formal and not always transparent to undertakings. Moreover, the decision-making process in merger cases may be regarded as (at least) partially inefficient. The framework does not *promote an effective, efficient, transparent and predictable merger review process* (VI.A). It is noteworthy that the decision-making process is primarily a result of the internal organisation of the authority.

5. COMPATIBILITY WITH AND DISCREPANCIES BETWEEN THE ICN RECOMMENDATIONS AND THE POLISH REGULATION

An analysis of Polish provisions on merger proceedings shows that they are mostly compatible with the ICN's recommendations. It is the enforcement of these that may be problematic on certain occasions. It is undeniable that the merger procedure has evolved immensely over recent decades. This evolution has been marked by a tendency to modernise merger proceedings and make them more compatible with the ICN recommendations. The Competition Act, implementing regulations, guidelines and decisions provide a solid basis for

36 K. Kanton, J. Łukawski, Sz. Murek, *Merger control proceedings in Poland in 2018*, www.skslegal.pl.

undertakings preparing to engage in merger proceedings. The transparency of merger proceedings is much better than it used to be. Parties to the merger proceedings are kept informed at every important stage of the process – there are no longer any surprises about second stages or negative conclusions from market investigations. Third parties may easily learn about notified proceedings and have an opportunity to express their opinions. Changes in the notification form have overall led to a limitation of information obligations. Business secrets are well protected – sometimes even too well. The duration of proceedings has shortened and undertakings may notify mergers without any strict deadline. The general progress is undeniable.

The core regulation of merger procedure is in line with the ICN's recommendations, but there are also visible discrepancies between the Polish provisions and these recommendations. My personal belief is that this is due to the fact that Polish merger procedure is burdened with the original sin of formality. This sin is universal for Polish administrative proceedings and the merger procedure is no exception. It is visible when we analyse the areas of discrepancies: the lack of pre-notification phase, the rarity of meetings during investigations, the lack of willingness to provide access to source data justified by the rigid protection of confidential information, the imperfect regulation of remedies including poor negotiations and formalistic remedies, an overly static and traditional internal decision-making process, and the lack of instruments for interagency coordination to change and update laws or guidelines. What is striking is that most of these divergences from the ICN recommendations result from imperfect enforcement, which is too heavily influenced by the traditional administrative Polish culture.

These discrepancies should be a starting point for a discussion on future amendments to the Polish merger control system. Such discussions should be as comprehensive as possible and include not only the ICN recommendations, but also OECD recommendations together with the views of Polish academics, practitioners and the business community. The ICN guiding principles, Recommended Practices and practical tools constitute the most comprehensive proposal for change, and the OCCP should thoroughly analyse them before presenting well-reasoned proposals. Ignoring the ICN or OECD proposals, not to mention opinions from Polish academics and practitioners, is a long and controversial practice of the Polish competition authority and the Polish legislator. Such conclusions should not be understood as full support for complete compliance of the Polish merger control provisions with the ICN recommendations.[37] I argue for the Polish legislator making a conscious decision

37 I believe that when it comes to procedural laws there will always be some national divergences stemming from general national administrative procedure regulations.

on the future amendment of the Polish merger control system, taking into consideration all possible experiences and opinions.

6. ICN DILEMMA – HOW TO MAKE THE RECOMMENDATIONS EFFECTIVE

The ICN is a virtual and informal trans-governmental network of competition authorities. It is an information network that relies primarily on soft law documents adopted by the ICN. However, the visible and impressive achievements of the ICN in the area of adopting recommendations and best practices are mirrored by equally visible inconsistencies between the ICN recommendations and the national merger provisions of its members. Studies have been undertaken exploring the reasons given by network members when deciding not to follow network recommendations.[38] There might be objective and subjective reasons behind these discrepancies, and some of them are independent of competition agencies involved in the work of the ICN. Even though no one expects full compliance by all jurisdictions with the ICN recommendations, the level of inconsistencies remains significant. The results of a study on the compliance of member jurisdictions with the ICN's merger recommendations were not very optimistic.[39] The conclusions of this study pointed out that *a clear majority of jurisdictions have not yet made implementation a priority* and *it is clear that achieving implementation will be a significant challenge, notwithstanding the consensus and momentum arising from their development and adoption.*[40] A subsequent ICN survey also identified similar inconsistencies, but concluded that the situation had improved and that there have been *a tiny fraction of agencies who have made changes that do not conform to the Recommended Practices, and no agency has engaged in reforms that change an ICN-compliant regime to a non-compliant one.*[41] The most recent survey on implementation of Recommended Practices was completed in 2016.[42] The report indicated that *52 of the 80 responding agencies indicated that*

38 S.J. Evenett, A. Hijzen, *Conformity with International Recommendations on Merger Reviews: An Economic Perspective on "Soft Law"*, University of Nottingham, Research Paper 2006/04, pp. 30–39.

39 J.W. Rowley QC, A.N. Campbell, Implementation of the International Competition Network's Recommended Practices for Merger Review: Final Survey Report on Practices IV-VII, *World Competition* 2005, Vol. 28(4), pp. 533–588.

40 *Ibidem*, p. 559.

41 M. Coppola, C. Lagdameo, *Taking Stock and Taking Root: A Closer Look at Implementation of the ICN Recommended Practices for Merger Notification & Review Procedures* [:] P. Lugard (ed.), *The International Competition Network At Ten. Origins, Accomplishments and Aspirations*, Intersentia, Cambridge – Antwerp – Portland 2011, p. 315.

42 *ICN Recommended Practices Self-Assessment 2016: Report on Survey Results*, https://www.internationalcompetitionnetwork.org/wp-content/uploads/2019/04/MWG_NPRPssurveyreport2017.pdf (accessed 11/01/2020).

they had used the ICN N&P RPs in reviewing their merger regime.[43] As regards Poland, the survey showed a 61% level of conformity of Polish merger control rules with Recommended Practices. Those surveys show that the ICN is aware of its Achilles heel, i.e. the insufficient level of implementation of the network's recommendations.

There are a number of ways in which the ICN may encourage greater convergence among its members. The ICN may call for greater involvement of non-governmental advisors, who could indicate deficiencies in the national merger control systems. Furthermore, the network may engage in direct contact with particular agencies to assist them in the development of national merger control rules. The ICN may push for changes to be directly implemented by agencies themselves, without the involvement of the national legislator or government. The network may also take a step-by-step approach, meaning that it should encourage its members to comply with more general recommendations, before gradually passing on to more detailed ones. Last but not least, the ICN may begin conducting peer reviews of particular countries on a voluntary basis. When advocating for a more active approach from the ICN to the implementation of the network's recommendations, one should be aware that this may adversely affect the willingness of particular jurisdictions to engage in the work of the ICN. The success of the ICN lies within its informality, elasticity and the lack of enforcement powers. Therefore, varying levels of implementation of particular recommendations by national jurisdictions may be directly connected to the nature of this trans-governmental network.

Merger procedure is crucial for the effective enforcement of the merger control system. The ICN recommendations may serve as an important source of assistance for national authorities when designing relevant national provisions. The Polish legislator has been very reluctant to admit any foreign influence over legislative changes. The only exception is the influence of the *acquis communautaire*. The OCCP has never officially acknowledged the influence of the ICN recommendations on Polish legislation or administrative practice. This is especially surprising, given how many of the Polish competition authority's resources have been invested in the Polish competition authority participating in the network (including organising the ICN annual conference in 2010). What is even more worrying is that the OCCP has never expressed any desire in pursuing convergence with the best practices and international standards of merger control (the OCCP similarly ignores the recommendations and conclusions from peer reviews undertaken by the OECD[44]). Despite

43 Report on Survey Results, p. 16.

44 M. Błachucki, The role of the OECD in development and enforcement of competition law, *e-Pública – Revista Eletrónica de Direito Público*, 2016, Vol. 3, No 3, p. 190.

this official denial of the ICN's influence, it is possible to speculate that its informal influence has shaped Polish merger provisions. When analysing the history of Polish merger rules, there is a visible tendency towards greater conformity of those rules with the ICN recommendations. This tendency may suggest that participating in the work of the ICN has indeed stimulated Polish officials and resulted in alterations to their administrative practice, ultimately encouraging the amendment of Polish merger control provisions. On the other hand, the absence of any official recognition of external influence from the ICN may be driven by political considerations. Furthermore, there may also be a practical side to the policy. By officially ignoring the influence of the ICN recommendations, the OCCP does not need to explain why there are so many discrepancies between them and the Polish provisions. This may provoke a relevant question – why does the Polish competition authority support the adoption of recommendations by the ICN, while simultaneously refusing to follow them? The answer to this question would require more of a political analysis rather than a legal one.

Even though many jurisdictions have problems with implementing the ICN recommendations, this should not be treated as an excuse for the OCCP to ignore the network's soft law. Should the Polish competition authority decide to deviate from previously agreed best practices, such a decision ought to be made consciously and after careful consideration of international recommendations. In addition, in recent years (especially 2016–2020) the Polish competition authority has presented a rather passive attitude towards the ICN, which has been reflected by a low level of participation in the network's activities. Therefore, a more active approach is advisable. Officials from the OCCP should more eagerly engage in particular working groups of the ICN that correspond to the particular needs of the Polish competition authority. The greater involvement of the OCCP in the work of the ICN will lead to a greater chance of achieving cognitive convergence among all cooperating officials.[45] Such cognitive convergence is often a prerequisite for the administrative convergence of practices of national competition authorities. The final stage of this convergence process is likely to be the harmonisation of hard law national rules. Last but not least, the greater the participation of the OCCP officials in the work of the ICN, the greater the chance for the development of daily international administrative cooperation between national competition authorities from different jurisdictions.

45 D.K. Tarullo, Norms and Institutions in Global Competition Policy, *The American Journal of International Law* Vol. 94, No 3, July 2000, pp. 479 and 495.

7. CONCLUSIONS

This essay has shown that the Polish merger procedure is generally in line with the ICN recommendations. However, this formal compliance is not always supported by enforcement in practice. There is a lot of room for improvement in the administrative practice of the OCCP. This conclusion should not underestimate the general positive assessment of the current state of merger proceedings in Poland. *L'appétit vient en mangeant* – since there have been so many positive changes to Polish merger proceedings, there is a desire for this to be continued in order to catch up with recognised international standards. The ICN delivers such standards, but it lacks any powers to enforce them. Nonetheless, the ICN should invest more resources in monitoring compliance with the adopted recommendations and continue to place persuasive pressure on national jurisdictions for greater convergence. The last word will still be with national legislators, who may choose to retain full sovereignty over inefficient national merger control systems, but the cost of this choice will be incurred by undertakings and consumers. The Polish example shows that monitoring and peer reviews should go beyond the formal analysis of the compliance of laws to also cover qualitative research on enforcement. Only a careful analysis of the administrative practice of competition authorities may lead to justified conclusions on the compliance of national legal systems with the ICN recommendations. The devil is in the… enforcement.

ICN DUE PROCESS INITIATIVES OVER THE DECADES AND THE CAP'S PROMISE OF ACCOUNTABILITY

James F. RILL and Jana I. SEIDL*

Beginning in 1980, the number of countries with active competition law enforcement grew dramatically to today encompass more than 130 jurisdictions.[1] While there are shared fundamental principles across established and developing regimes, there are also critical differences in terms of substance, procedure, remedy, institutional framework, and other aspects of competition law enforcement. Fundamental due process rights are unfortunately not universally available, sometimes leaving companies in the crosshairs of a competition law investigation without even a basic written charge, the absence of meaningful access to enforcers' records in a matter, the absence of an opportunity to engage and defend against a charge, or even without a final written decision and a basis or venue for appeal. As a result, companies today can face considerable disruption and difficulty in attempting to defend against competition law charges across several foreign jurisdictions.

Given these challenges, increasingly, a principal focus of the International Competition Network's (ICN) program has been the promotion of global standards of due process in agency investigation and enforcement undertakings. Although some modest steps were taken with regard to due process in the first decade, the ICN's second decade has reflected increased guidance to foment agency recognition of due process principles. The continuation of the ICN's

---

* James F. Rill is Senior Counsel in the Washington, D.C. office of Baker Botts L.L.P. Jana I. Seidl is a Senior Associate in the Washington, D.C. office of Baker Botts LLP. The views are those of the authors and do not necessarily reflect the views of the firm or any client. The authors are grateful for the assistance of Senior Regulatory Analyst Jane Antonio in the preparation of this essay.

1 *See* European Commission, Competition Policy Brief at 1 (May 2016) ("In the past 25 years, the number of competition regimes around the world has increased from around 20 at the beginning of the 1990s to around 130 today."), http://ec.europa.eu/competition/publications/cpb/2016/2016_002_en.pdf; *see also* FED. TRADE COMM'N, Competition & Consumer Protection Authorities Worldwide, https://www.ftc.gov/policy/international/competition-consumer-protection-authorities-worldwide.

work to make due process rights universally available would be a substantial step towards convergence – and a substantial step in the correct direction. Not only is due process critical for companies navigating global operations, but jurisdictions adhering to these norms benefit from the enhanced likelihood of reaching the correct decision from a competition law perspective, and the confidence of other stakeholders in the give and take of the global sphere, which bolsters open lines of global commerce, and of course principles of international comity and respect.

The current challenge is to determine the extent to which the ICN, as a voluntary organization, can or should establish mechanisms to evaluate implementation of these norms by its members, and even non-members. Ensuring actual implementation (i.e., compliance rather than promises or aspirations) is the critical next step towards true convergence that has long been a focus of the ICN and its mission "to advocate the *adoption* of superior standards and procedures in competition policy around the world."[2]

1. PRINCIPAL ICN DUE PROCESS UNDERTAKINGS TO DATE

As the end of the second decade of the ICN's existence approaches, a scan of the landscape reveals major accomplishments in due process initiatives over the past ten years and invites sharper focus on the next initiatives to strengthen further the ICN's contributions to international convergence around accepted antitrust principles with regard to due process norms.

The initiatives of the ICN to promote global convergence toward accepted standards of due process actually predates the body's second decade. As early as 2002, the ICN adopted *Recommended Practices for Merger Notification and Review Procedures*.[3] Paralleling an undertaking by the Competition Committee of the Organisation for Economic Cooperation and Development (OECD),[4] the ICN focused on suggesting common standards of due process covering a broad spectrum of practices. The ICN document sets forth merger review recommendations dealing with jurisdictional and parties' nexus for notification,

2 *About the ICN*, Int'l Competition Network, https://www.internationalcompetitionnetwork.org/ (emphasis added).

3 Int'l Competition Network, ICN Recommended Practices for Merger Notification and Review Procedures (2018), https://www.internationalcompetitionnetwork.org/wp-content/uploads/2018/09/MWG_NPRecPractices2018.pdf.

4 The OECD Competition Committee undertook a project in parallel to the ICN's, which resulted in a recommendation of the OECD Council. *See* OECD, Recommendation of the OECD Council on Merger Review, C(2005)34-C/M(2005)7/PROV (2005), https://www.oecd.org/daf/competition/mergers/40537528.pdf.

the content of notification, review period, frequency of consultation, and independent review of staff determinations, as well as other procedural elements. The central themes are transparency and procedural fairness to the party under investigation. The document has been supplemented with subsequent working group comments.[5]

In our view, the most important ICN contribution to the convergence of due process principles is the *ICN Guidance on Investigative Process* developed by an investigative practices subgroup of the Agency Effectiveness Working Group and approved by the ICN at the 2015 conference in Sydney.[6]

This document promotes a broad set of basic principles underlying the affordance of due process to a party in the investigative stage of agency action. The overriding themes are transparency and meaningful engagement in the interface between the agency investigatory staff and the party involved in the inquiry. In particular, the guidance document encourages notification to the party of the legal and factual basis for agency concern, consultation at appropriate intervals (including a discussion of the relevant evidence), and a working description of supporting theory. In addition, the guidance paper endorses the disclosure of evidence to the party at the time the allegations of violation are made and advocates a review of the matter by a source independent of the investigative staff.

The issue of confidential treatment of materials being ruled on by the agency is also addressed. The document includes a suggestion of procedures for making such materials available under appropriate safeguards. This process is set forth, however, only where the agency has made a determination regarding the disclosure of confidential materials. There does not appear to be any recommendation that such disclosure procedures be put in place. Finally, unlike the designation of the merger notification and procedure recommended practices, the extent of the strength of the ICN's advocacy of the initial guidance document was unclear. Additionally, the document itself seems to acknowledge, perhaps excessively, the fact that each agency may be guided by its own statutory and procedural instruments that could appropriately impair its adherence to the guidance.

---

5 While the ICN's *Recommended Practices for Merger Notification and Review Procedures* was originally released in September 2002, it continues to be strengthened with the addition of new practices and supplemental commentary to original practices. The most recent revisions were completed in April 2018.

6 Int'l Competition Network, ICN Guidance on Investigative Process (2018), https://www.internationalcompetitionnetwork.org/wp-content/uploads/2018/09/AEWG_Guidance_InvestigativeProcess.pdf. The 2015 document was revised in 2018.

The guidance document has received further attention from the working group and the ICN Steering Committee. In March 2018 at the Annual Conference in New Delhi, a set of guiding principles was adopted that, among other elements, strengthened the advocacy of transparency, including timely disclosure of agency concerns, communication on central issues at key points in the process, the opportunity to respond to adverse findings, and independent review.[7] At the same time, the underlying document was supplemented by issue-by-issue commentary designed to further illuminate the specific points.[8]

Recently, the force of the guidance document was strengthened by its being designated as "recommended practices."[9] As a result, it now has the mantle of the stronger statement of ICN endorsements. Although the guidance on investigative process is an important contribution to the ICN's second-decade accomplishments, there remains the question of the extent to which the recommendations are followed or any degree of accountability in that regard.

2. LEARNING FROM THE WORK OF OTHER ORGANIZATIONS DURING THE ICN'S SECOND DECADE

The work of the ICN going forward could be complemented by and draw support from the focus on due process in antitrust enforcement proceedings by other organizations, both governmental and private sector, during the ICN's second decade. Several examples are noteworthy.

The most comprehensive international undertaking relating to due process has been the work of the OECD Competition Committee. Working Party 3 of the Committee conducted three roundtables on the topic in 2010 and 2011. These proceedings resulted in a report, *Procedural Fairness and Transparency--Key Points*, issued by the OECD in April 2012.[10] The report described in detail the roundtable discussions, with contributions by national agency presentations. According to the report, the central theme of the roundtables was a concern

---

7 Int'l Competition Network, ICN Guiding Principles for Procedural Fairness in Competition Agency Enforcement (2018), https://www.internationalcompetitionnetwork.org/wp-content/uploads/2018/09/AEWG_GuidingPrinciples_ProFairness.pdf.

8 Int'l Competition Network, *Annotated* ICN Guidance on Investigative Process (2018), https://www.internationalcompetitionnetwork.org/wp-content/uploads/2018/09/AEWG_GuidanceAnnotated_InvestigativeProcess.pdf.

9 Int'l Competition Network, ICN Recommended Practices for Investigative Process (2019), https://www.internationalcompetitionnetwork.org/wp-content/uploads/2019/05/RPs-Investigative-Process.pdf.

10 OECD, Procedural Fairness and Transparency–Key Points (2012), https://www.oecd.org/daf/competition/mergers/50235955.pdf.

acknowledging the need for transparency and procedural fairness in agency enforcement.

National agency contributions are cited across the due process report landscape, including transparency of agency concerns, access to information and documents, right of response, and judicial review. Although not designed to characterize agency efforts, the report does provide a basis for evaluation of contributing agencies' self-described adherence to due process principles. Significantly, the report concludes that "work [on due process] is never done."[11] Subsequently, the OECD Competition Committee has sponsored several sessions focusing on due process as an aspect of a broader discussion.[12]

The U.S. Chamber of Commerce sponsored a private sector study of competition policy and practice in the international context.[13] The group's report, issued in March 2017, covers a wide range of issues relating to antitrust enforcement having international dimensions, including the intersection between trade and competition. Regarding due process, the report recommends that intergovernmental organizations, specifically the OECD, undertake a peer review of national agency adherence to accepted global standards of due process, notably, not necessarily with the consent of the subject agency.[14] The expert group also recommends that OECD adopt a due process code.[15]

In addition, the U.S. Chamber has conducted four practitioner surveys relating to due process.[16] One, in particular, seeks to obtain an assessment of national agency compliance with the ICN's investigatory process guidance document.[17] The International Chamber of Commerce (ICC) Commission on Competition also issued a document, *Effective Procedural Safeguards for Competition Law*

11 *Id.* at 7.

12 *See, e.g., Access to the Case File and Protection of Confidential Information*, OECD, https://www.oecd.org/daf/competition/access-to-case-file-and-protection-of-confidential-information.htm; *Treatment of Legally Privileged Information in Competition Proceedings*, OECD, https://www.oecd.org/daf/competition/treatment-of-legally-privileged-information-in-competition-proceedings.htm; and *Investigative Powers in Practice*, OECD, *available at* https://www.oecd.org/daf/competition/investigative-powers-in-practice.htm.

13 U.S. Chamber of Commerce, International Competition Policy Expert Group–Report and Recommendations (Mar. 2017), https://www.uschamber.com/sites/default/files/icpeg_recommendations_and_report.pdf.

14 *Id.* at 15.

15 *Id.*

16 *See Competition Policy and Antitrust*, U.S. Chamber of Commerce, https://www.uschamber.com/international/global-regulatory-cooperation/center-global-regulatory-cooperation/competition-policy.

17 U.S. Chamber of Commerce, Adherence to ICN Guidance on Investigative Process: A Practitioner Survey (Apr. 2017), https://www.uschamber.com/sites/default/files/023172_adherencetoicnguidancereportfn.pdf.

Enforcement Proceedings, in June 2017.[18] The submission consists of guiding principles to promote due process with accompanying clarification. The ICC's report calls for procedures that may exceed those contained in the ICN guidance document. Salient among these are a recommendation for nearly unlimited access to a complete case file, including exculpatory materials,[19] and an admonition to balance claims of confidentiality against the rights of the investigated party to the opportunity for an informed defense.[20]

The most direct effort to target agency adherence to due process principles was undertaken most recently by the Antitrust Law Section of the American Bar Association. A task force of the Section, the Procedural Transparency Task Force, assessed the extent to which specific agencies, selected with a new geographic diversity, had implemented procedures in harmony with the Section's International Task Force's 2015 *Best Practices for Antitrust Procedure.*[21] The 2019 procedural transparency report identifies the relative standing of specific national agencies with respect to their adherence to the specific elements of due process set forth in the Section's 2015 *Best Practices.*[22]

The high degree of agency and private sector attention to the topic of due process in competition agency investigations has resulted in a clear framework for international best practices. As the ICN's second decade draws to a close, it would be desirable for the organization to take into account the work and recommendations of these bodies in designing the next steps toward developing and encouraging acceptance and adoption of sound principles of procedural fairness. Each of them suggests some mechanism to enhance adoption of such principles and accountability of their implementation in practice. The ICN's newest adopted program, *Framework for Competition Agency Procedures* (CAP),[23] may provide a vehicle for this end that can draw on the work of those other bodies.

---

18 Int'l Chamber of Commerce, Effective Procedural Safeguards for Competition Law Enforcement Proceedings (June 2017), https://iccwbo.org/content/uploads/sites/3/2017/07/ICC-Due-Process-Best-Practices-2017.pdf.

19 *Id.* at 5.

20 *Id.* at 6.

21 Am. Bar Ass'n, Section of Antitrust Law, Best Practices for Antitrust Procedure (May 22, 2015), https://www.americanbar.org/content/dam/aba/administrative/antitrust_law/at_comments_bestprac_20150522.pdf.

22 Am. Bar Ass'n, Section of Antitrust Law, Assessment of Global Competition Agency Implementation of ABA Best Practices for Antitrust Procedure (Apr. 29, 2019), https://www.americanbar.org/content/dam/aba/administrative/antitrust_law/sal-procedural-transparency-2019–04–29.pdf.

23 Int'l Competition Network, ICN Framework on Competition Agency Procedures (2019), https://www.internationalcompetitionnetwork.org/wp-content/uploads/2019/04/ICN_CAP.pdf [hereinafter CAP Framework].

3. THE ICN'S THIRD DECADE SPENT FOSTERING THE CAP AD LEADING IT TO HARNESS ITS FUTURE POTENTIAL

The ICN's CAP grew out of a U.S. Department of Justice's Antitrust Division initiative announced in June 2018: the Multilateral Framework on Procedures in Competition Law Investigation and Enforcement (MFP).[24] At the time, then DOJ's Assistant Attorney General for Antitrust, Makan Delrahim, stressed that "[r]ather than simply encourage good behavior, the time is now for us to embrace meaningful mechanisms that encourage *compliance*."[25] Fundamentally, the goal of the MFP is to recognize and incorporate the prior work done by competition regimes and private organizations – especially with respect to due process norms – and go one step further to focus on actual implementation.

Following multiple discussions among international competition stakeholders, the DOJ agreed to submit its MFP to the ICN "to take advantage of existing institutions and to reduce administrative burdens."[26] From there, the ICN announced in early April 2019 that it was creating the CAP, rooted in the MFP and lauding the prior work on which it builds.[27] After agency consideration and approval by the ICN's Steering Group of 20 members, the CAP opened for registration and went into effect in May 2019.[28] The CAP had its inaugural meeting in June 2019 at which the first-term Co-Chairs were confirmed as the Australian Competition and Consumer Commission, the German Bundeskartellamt, and, fittingly given the CAP's origins, the U.S. DOJ.[29] We understand the CAP currently has over 70 signatories, signaling widespread support.[30]

---

24 Makan Delrahim, Fresh Thinking on Procedural Fairness: A Multilateral Framework on Procedures in Antitrust Enforcement, Address Before the Council on Foreign Relations (June 1, 2018), https://www.justice.gov/opa/speech/file/1067582/download [hereinafter MFP Announcement].

25 *Id.* at 3 (emphasis added).

26 Press Release, U.S. Dep't of Justice, New Multilateral Framework on Procedures Approved by the International Competition Network (Apr. 5, 2019), https://www.justice.gov/opa/pr/new-multilateral-framework-procedures-approved-international-competition-network [hereinafter DOJ MFP Press Release].

27 Press Release, Int'l Competition Network, New ICN-led Framework to Promote Fair and Effective Agency Process (Apr. 3, 2019), https://www.internationalcompetitionnetwork.org/wp-content/uploads/2019/04/CAP_PR.pdf.

28 Press Release, Int'l Competition Network, ICN's 18th Annual Conference Concluded Today in Cartagena Colombia (May 17, 2019), https://www.internationalcompetitionnetwork.org/featured/2019-annual-conference-press-release/.

29 Press Release, Int'l Competition Network, Participants of the ICN Framework for Competition Agency Procedures Hold Inaugural Meeting (June 7, 2019), https://www.internationalcompetitionnetwork.org/news/icn-framework-for-competition-agency-procedures-update/.

30 Int'l Competition Network, ICN CAP Participants (as of August 2019), https://www.internationalcompetitionnetwork.org/wp-content/uploads/2019/08/CAPparticipants.pdf.

The challenge now is how to ensure that the CAP's signatories follow those fundamental pillars of due process in practice. To be sure, the CAP's somewhat unique structure and envisioned mechanisms enable it to bring about such compliance if its signatories take full advantage, work cooperatively and transparently, and consider some further advancements down the line.

First, the CAP is set up as one of only three opt-in frameworks within the ICN. The ICN functions as an administrative host, or as one commentator has described it, a "sponsor,"[31] rather than an "owner" of the CAP. Additionally, CAP participation is open to both ICN members and non-members.[32] In other words, the CAP is an active choice for each competition regime. An agency's being a signatory signals that agency's intention to adhere to the principles laid out in the CAP[33]; participants are publicly listed[34] and must submit a template,[35] which is also publicly posted by the ICN, demonstrating endorsement of the CAP program.

Second, the CAP has two major components: (1) an annex of fundamental, consensus principles for sound agency procedures,[36] and (2) dedicated implementation tools – a "cooperation process" and a "review process"[37] – to help promote use of the principles.

Unsurprisingly, the consensus principles are rooted in experience gathered to date and reflect the critical nature of due process in any type of proceeding. By way of example, in the United States, due process protections are deeply ingrained in U.S. jurisprudence. They originate in the Fifth Amendment to the U.S. Constitution, which guarantees that "[n]o person shall be... deprived of life, liberty, or property, without due process of law."[38] Due process is meant to protect against abusive, arbitrary action by the government.[39] Thus, procedural due process requirements in the U.S. include notice of the charges brought and

---

31 Paul O'Brien, *ICN's Framework for Competition Agency Procedures, Part 1: What Does the CAP Mean for the ICN Today?* 3 (Apr. 17, 2019), https://www.ftc.gov/system/files/attachments/key-speeches-presentations/obrien_-_icn_column_4-19.pdf.

32 CAP Framework, *supra* note 24, §1(b).

33 *Id.* §1(i).

34 *Id.* §1(h).

35 *Id.* §§3(a–b).

36 *Id.* at 4–7.

37 *Id.* at 2–3.

38 U.S. Const., amend. V.

39 Carey v. Piphus, 435 U.S. 247, 259 (1978). *See also* Mathews v. Eldridge, 424 U.S. 319, 344 (1976) ("[P]rocedural due process rules are shaped by the risk of error inherent in the truthfinding process as applied to the generality of cases.").

an opportunity to be heard,[40] a timely hearing,[41] that the hearing be conducted before an impartial arbiter,[42] an opportunity to confront and cross examine witnesses,[43] access to the evidence in the case,[44] and a decision on the record.[45] Similarly, the CAP's provisions call for non-discrimination, transparency and predictability, timely investigative notice, timely resolution, confidentiality, impartiality, access to information and opportunity to defend, representation by legal counsel, written decisions, and independent review.[46]

A major challenge to the CAP going forward is whether signatories will avail themselves of the agency-by-agency limitations the CAP allows and if so, to what degree. Rather than requiring all or nothing from its members, the CAP is non-binding and flexible to a degree. Members can elect limitations on the CAP due process provisions, which must be outlined in the competition regime's template.[47] This provision perhaps aims to attract CAP member signatories who are interested in participating but not yet fully compliant. Alternatively, perhaps it allows for some modifications to account for cultural relativism so

---

40 *See* Mullane v. Cent. Hanover Bank Tr. Co., 339 U.S. 306, 314 (1950) ("An elementary and fundamental requirement of due process in any proceeding which is to be accorded finality is notice reasonably calculated, under all the circumstances, to apprise interested parties of the pendency of the action and afford them an opportunity to present their objections.").

41 *See Mathews*, 424 U.S. at 333 ("[S]ome form of hearing is required before an individual is finally deprived of a property [or liberty] interest."); Armstrong v. Manzo, 380 U.S. 545, 552 (1965) (explaining that notice and a hearing "must be granted at a meaningful time and in a meaningful manner"); Baldwin v. Hale, 68 U.S. 223, 233 (1863) ("Parties whose rights are to be affected are entitled to be heard.").

42 *See* Goldberg v. Kelly, 397 U.S. 254, 271 (1970) ("an impartial decision maker is essential"); Marshall v. Jerrico, 446 U.S. 238, 242 (1980) ("The Due Process Clause entitles a person to an impartial and disinterested tribunal in both civil and criminal cases. This requirement of neutrality in adjudicative proceedings safeguards the two central concerns of procedural due process, the prevention of unjustified or mistaken deprivations and the promotion of participation and dialogue by affected individuals in the decisionmaking process. The neutrality requirement helps to guarantee that life, liberty, or property will not be taken on the basis of an erroneous or distorted conception of the facts or the law. At the same time, it preserves both the appearance and reality of fairness... by ensuring that no person will be deprived of his interests in the absence of a proceeding in which he may present his case with assurance that the arbiter is not predisposed to find against him.") (internal citations omitted).

43 *Goldberg*, 397 U.S. at 269 ("In almost every setting where important decisions turn on questions of fact, due process requires an opportunity to confront and cross-examine adverse witnesses.").

44 The Supreme Court has suggested such access must be granted as a matter of course. *See* Greene v. McElroy, 360 U.S. 474, 496 (1959) ("where governmental action seriously injures an individual, and the reasonableness of the action depends on fact findings, the evidence used to prove the Government's case must be disclosed to the individual so that he has an opportunity to show that it is untrue").

45 *Goldberg*, 397 U.S. at 271 ("the decision maker should state the reasons for his determination and indicate the evidence he relied on").

46 CAP Framework, *supra* note 24, at 4–7.

47 *Id.* §§1(j), 3(a).

that differences in various competition regimes' structures, proceedings, or legal systems in which they operate are respected.

Notably, to date, 64 competition agencies have provided templates for public review.[48] This is an area where signatories can do more in the future to foster cooperation toward full compliance; they could consider mandating a timeframe in which signatories must certify full compliance after joining or a process that requires active discussion and a joint membership decision allowing the rare exception if a competition regime insists on any permanent limitations.

With respect to the CAP's "cooperation process" and "review process," we are encouraged by the more prominent and on-demand accountability mechanisms. In this manner, the CAP embodies the approach of the MFP that it is critical that the institution not only provide guidance but also provide a mechanism by which to measure and evaluate the extent to which nations implement due process norms.

The cooperation process calls for ad hoc agency-to-agency dialogue "regarding any issue of Competition Law procedure that is material" to the CAP.[49] A point of clarification from which the CAP could benefit involves the inherent tension between its mandate that "[p]articipants will discuss the issues raised in *general terms*" and the suggestion that "[t]o facilitate the dialogue, Participants are encouraged to discuss procedural issues related to a *relevant* Investigation or Enforcement Proceeding."[50] We are hopeful that participants will avail themselves of opportunities to discuss specific proceedings and potential questions raised in conjunction with these proceedings to drive progress through concrete examples and applications of due process norms. And while the CAP makes dialogue between participants confidential unless otherwise agreed by the parties themselves, we are hopeful that the CAP will progress to require public disclosure of such dialogue or at the very least any takeaways or outcome. Peer review is a critically important factor in bringing about change. It "create[s] the opportunity for reflecting on decisions that may help enhance reputational standings among peers."[51]

This type of interaction is already envisioned by the Federal Trade Commission and DOJ's joint 2017 *Antitrust Guidelines for International Enforcement and Cooperation*, which calls for more active U.S. agency guidance to foment

---

48 *CAP Templates*, Int'l Competition Network, https://www.internationalcompetitionnetwork.org/frameworks/competition-agency-procedures/cap-templates/. The U.S. Federal Trade Commission and DOJ submitted separate templates.

49 CAP Framework, *supra* note 24, §2(d).

50 *Id.* §2(f) (emphasis added).

51 MFP Announcement, *supra* note 25, at 4.

crucial convergence in the international antitrust arena on due process: "An Agency may continue that cooperation when either it or the foreign authority has closed its investigation. The Agencies may also engage in *general discussions* with foreign authorities on matters in which only one authority has an open investigation."[52]

The "review process" itself calls on the CAP participants, in addition to submitting the previously discussed templates, to engage in a process of self-assessment and policing. This provision is laudable but could also benefit from future modification. Currently, it calls for a session for review of implementation and functioning of the CAP Framework "at least every four years" and envisions that "[t]he Framework may report on general trends, but will not identify individual Participants without consent."[53] What the competition law forum needs to promote real convergence is a mechanism that can shine light on the extent to which nations implement due process norms. In the future the review process should consider introducing a measure of public accountability, which could take the international antitrust community further along the path of this important and promising direction.

4. CONCLUSION

The MFP's major promise – the distinguishing feature that took the proposal beyond what has been accomplished to date – was its envisioned more prominent and regular accountability mechanisms. Then AAG Delrahim lauded the CAP as carrying on this legacy, being "equivalent in all respects to the principles of the MFP that was originally proposed by the Antitrust Division. By combining strong substantive principles with meaningful review mechanisms, it goes well beyond anything competition agencies have ever done before."[54] We urge the ICN and the CAP's signatories to heed these words as the program is tested and evolves over the ICN's next decade. The ICN has a timely opportunity to cement its role as a leadership forum for a much-welcomed step forward in cementing due process in competition proceedings. The crux of actual rather than aspirational convergence, as emphasized by then Deputy AAG Roger Alford, is that "[t]o retain the confidence of both the business community governed by [a competition regime's] laws and the public [that competition enforcers] protect, [agencies] must be willing to expose [their] policies and practices to

52 Fed. Trade Comm'n & Dep't of Justice, Antitrust Guidelines for International Enforcement and Cooperation §5 n.138 (2017), https://www.ftc.gov/system/files/documents/public_statements/1049863/international_guidelines_2017.pdf (emphasis added).

53 CAP Framework, *supra* note 24, §3(c).

54 DOJ MFP Press Release, *supra* note 27.

aggressive scrutiny and challenge."[55] It bears repeating: sunlight (i.e., external transparency) is the best disinfectant.

55 Roger Alford, Charting a Straight Course: Promoting Transparency and Procedural Fairness in Competition Enforcement, Address Before the 6th China Competition Policy Forum 8 (Aug. 30, 2017), *available at* https://www.justice.gov/opa/speech/file/994671/download.

ICN FRAMEWORK FOR COMPETITION AGENCY PROCEDURES (ICN CAP)*

Eddy DE SMIJTER and Filip KUBÍK**

1. ICN CAP ORIGINS AND THE WIDER CONTEXT

1.1. THE ICN AND ITS PREVIOUS WORK IN THE FIELD OF PROCEDURAL FAIRNESS

The International Competition Network ("ICN") is an informal network of some 140 competition authorities from around the world. It is not an intergovernmental organisation, but rather a peer-to-peer network, which makes it an ideal forum for competition enforcers to discuss in depth topical issues in a flexible and timely way, to exchange experiences from across jurisdictions, to learn from each other, and to globally promote sound and coherent enforcement of competition rules, including through issuing practically oriented and non-binding ICN guidelines, best practices and other work products.[1]

While the work of the ICN is primarily driven by the five working groups dedicated to particular fields (cartels, unilateral conduct, mergers, advocacy, and agency effectiveness), the ICN Steering Group takes care of coordinating the overall ICN efforts and promoting horizontal topics relevant for competition enforcement across the particular fields.

* The authors wish to thank Kris Dekeyser, former Director of Policy and Strategy at DG Competition, for his useful comments on an earlier version. Obviously, in this paper they express their own views, i.e. the paper cannot be read as presenting any official position of the European Commission. This paper is a reworked version of the one that appeared in Competition Law & Policy Debate.

** DG Competition, European Commission.

1 Pursuant to its website (https://www.internationalcompetitionnetwork.org/), the ICN's mission is "to advocate the adoption of superior standards and procedures in competition policy around the world, formulate proposals for procedural and substantive convergence, and seek to facilitate effective international cooperation to the benefit of member agencies, consumers and economies worldwide."

Procedural fairness has had a firm place among such topics ever since the creation of the ICN back in 2001, as the ICN has recognised that fair and effective procedures are essential to sound competition law enforcement, and that they can increase opportunities for international cooperation.

The ICN 2003 and 2004 Recommended Practices for transparency and procedural fairness during merger review were the first international consensus principles on the topic. In 2015, the ICN approved its Guidance on Investigative Process ("Guidance"), which was further developed in the ICN Agency Effectiveness Working Group and amended in 2018 at the ICN annual conference in New Delhi.[2] Simultaneously, the amended Guidance was complemented by the ICN Guiding Principles for Procedural Fairness in Competition Agency Enforcement, which articulate a common framework of high-level procedural fairness principles to inform and guide the investigations and enforcement practice of ICN members.[3] At the 2019 ICN annual conference in Cartagena, the Guidance was further refined and upgraded to ICN Recommended Practices for Investigative Process.[4]

1.2. THE OECD'S WORK IN THE FIELD OF PROCEDURAL FAIRNESS

The Organisation for Economic Co-operation and Development ("OECD") Competition Committee held three roundtable discussions on transparency and procedural fairness during 2010 and 2011. A key theme emerging from the discussions was a broad consensus on the need and importance of transparency and procedural fairness in competition enforcement despite the many differences amongst jurisdictions. These discussions are summarised in a 2012 OECD publication titled "Procedural Fairness and Transparency".[5]

In 2018, the OECD Competition Committee produced a Scoping Note on transparency and procedural fairness as a long-term theme for 2019–2020.[6] This has triggered a number of roundtable discussions on specific topics within this theme, including on treatment of legally privileged information in competition

---

2 Https://www.internationalcompetitionnetwork.org/portfolio/guidance-on-investigative-process/.

3 Https://www.internationalcompetitionnetwork.org/portfolio/guiding-principles-for-procedural-fairness/.

4 Https://www.internationalcompetitionnetwork.org/portfolio/recommended-practices-for-investigative-process/.

5 Https://www.oecd.org/competition/abuse/proceduralfairnessandtransparency-2012.htm.

6 Www.oecd.org/officialdocuments/publicdisplaydocumentpdf/?cote=DAF/COMP/WD(2018)6&docLanguage=En.

proceedings[7], the standard of review by courts in competition cases[8], or access to the case file and protection of confidential information.[9] On 6 October 2021, the OECD Council adopted a Recommendation on Transparency and Procedural Fairness in Competition Law Enforcement.[10]

1.3. THE 2018 MFP INITIATIVE AND ITS EMBEDDING WITHIN THE ICN

In early 2018, the Antitrust Division of the US Department of Justice ("US DoJ") approached a handful of competition authorities from around the world with a draft initiative titled "Multilateral Framework on Procedures in Competition Law Investigation and Enforcement" ("MFP").

The MFP's stated goal was to promote global due process in antitrust enforcement and thereby further improve cooperation among antitrust agencies around the world. The MFP would combine a set of universally accepted fundamental principles of procedural fairness with an adherence and review mechanism, under which the participants commit to observe these principles and agree to cooperate with each other regarding their compliance.

Ideas about the exact format of the MFP have developed over time. The European Commission ("Commission") and many other competition authorities which were involved in the talks – and many of which were at the same time members of the ICN Steering Group – believed that the most sensible way to implement the MFP idea was to embed it within the well-established international structures existing in the competition field, be it the ICN or the OECD.

Gradually, as the shape of the initiative crystallised, a consensus was built that the flexible peer-to-peer structure and the wide and truly global membership base of the ICN would be the ideal platform to give maximum effectiveness and efficiency to the MFP idea. Besides, on substance, the MFP fundamental principles were virtually identical with those included in the ICN 2018 Guiding Principles for Procedural Fairness in Competition Agency Enforcement (referred to in section 1.1 above).

7 Https://www.oecd.org/daf/competition/treatment-of-legally-privileged-information-in-competition-proceedings.htm.

8 Https://www.oecd.org/daf/competition/standard-of-review-by-courts-in-competition-cases.htm.

9 Https://www.oecd.org/daf/competition/access-to-case-file-and-protection-of-confidential-information.htm.

10 Https://www.oecd.org/mcm/Recommendation-of-the-Council-on-Transparency-and-Procedural-Fairness-in-Competition-Law-Enforcement.pdf.

1.4. THE ICN CAP

The ICN Framework for Competition Agency Procedures ("ICN CAP")[11] was adopted by the ICN Steering Group in April 2019 and presented to the ICN membership during the ICN annual conference in Cartagena in May 2019.

This was the result of in-depth discussions within the ICN Steering Group, which focused in essence on two goals. First, to ensure that the ICN CAP is fully consistent with existing ICN work products and makes the best use of the ICN infrastructure to maximise visibility and impact while minimising the administrative burden for participants operating in different legal regimes and enforcement systems and with different resource constraints. Second, to ensure that the ICN CAP integrates innovative features that allow it to emphasise the commitment of ICN CAP participants to respecting the fundamental principles of procedural fairness covered by the ICN CAP, to being transparent about the way in which these principles are implemented in their respective jurisdictions, and to being ready to engage in a dialogue with other participants with regard to questions and issues concerning the implementation.

2. MEMBERSHIP AND INSTITUTIONAL SET-UP

2.1. A WIDE-REACHING MEMBERSHIP

Different from other ICN documents, the ICN CAP is not from the outset endorsed by the ICN as a whole. Rather, it is a document that was first adopted by the ICN Steering Group, before being presented to the ICN membership. Since the ICN Steering Group is composed of competition authorities from all continents with different legal and institutional enforcement mechanisms, the ICN CAP can be considered to reflect a broad consensus within the global competition community of the fundamental procedural fairness principles.[12] That does not mean, however, that the other ICN members are automatically deemed to have implicitly acknowledged the ICN CAP. Rather on the contrary: to join the ICN CAP, they have to do so explicitly and publicly. This opt-in mechanism underlines the active engagement of the participating authorities to implement and adhere to the basic principles of due process laid down in the ICN CAP. At the time of writing, 73 ICN members from the four corners of the globe, have signed up to the ICN CAP.[13]

---

11 Https://www.internationalcompetitionnetwork.org/frameworks/competition-agency-procedures/.

12 For the composition of the ICN Steering Group, see https://www.internationalcompetitionnetwork.org/working-groups/icn-operations/steering-group/steering-group-members.

13 Https://www.internationalcompetitionnetwork.org/wp-content/uploads/2019/08/CAPparticipants.pdf.

To underline the universal nature of the agreed due process principles and the equally worldwide need to respect these fundamental principles when enforcing competition rules, the ICN CAP is also open to competition authorities that are not (yet) members of the ICN. It thus gives those authorities that are not considering full ICN membership an opportunity to publicly demonstrate that in their enforcement activities, they nevertheless pledge to adhere to the ICN CAP principles. However, at the time of writing, no non-ICN member has yet joined the ICN CAP.

With over half of the world's competition authorities having expressed their readiness to respect the ICN CAP's due process principles, the latter are now clearly confirmed as globally recognised standards, independent of the part of the world that the authority is located in and independent of the kind of enforcement mechanism that the authority is operating in (administrative or judicial) and independent of the authority's level of maturity in enforcing the competition rules. With every new participant in the ICN CAP, the latter bolsters its reputation as the benchmark for appropriate competition law enforcement, thus making it increasingly difficult for the shrinking minority of non-participants to justify their absence. Such absence also cannot be justified by the assertion that domestic law prevents the authority from respecting one or more of the ICN CAP principles. Indeed, for competition authorities in such a situation, the ICN CAP provides for an exemption: they can at any moment in time indicate that they are not in a position to respect a particular (part of a) ICN CAP principle, and possibly later withdraw such limitation.[14]

As global minimum standard, the ICN CAP may also help both the business community and the domestic competition law enforcer when requesting that the competent domestic legislator ensures that these due process principles are explicitly provided for in the relevant legislation. Equally, one could imagine that the ICN CAP serves as a point of reference when negotiating the competition chapter in bilateral trade or investment agreements.

2.2. A LIGHT AND FLEXIBLE INSTITUTIONAL SET-UP

In June 2019, the ICN CAP participants held their inaugural meeting. At that occasion, they confirmed three of the Steering Group members that lay at the foundation of the ICN CAP, namely the Australian Competition and Consumer Commission, the German Bundeskartellamt and the US DoJ, as the CAP co-chairs for a first three-year term. The co-chairs not only function as the depository of participation registration and, when needed, of the limitations to

14 See point 1.j of the ICN CAP.

that participation. They are also the guarantors of the smooth functioning of the ICN CAP mechanisms, such as the timely publication of the information templates[15] and the maintenance of the contact list of the ICN CAP participants' liaison officers.[16] The ICN CAP co-chairs will also regularly organise live discussions, e.g. during the ICN annual conference, or teleconferenced meetings of the ICN CAP participating authorities to take stock of the implementation of the CAP principles and to assist participants in the operation of the cooperation processes established by the ICN CAP.[17] The ICN CAP co-chairs are also well-placed to ensure the reporting on general trends in the implementation of the ICN CAP principles.[18]

3. THE PRINCIPLES

It is quite easy to agree that sound competition law enforcement needs to go hand-in-hand with the respect of fundamental due process principles that guarantee that the subject of such enforcement can appropriately defend itself. However, when determining which are these due process principles that are so fundamental that they should be respected globally, one may be tempted either to focus on one's own procedural rules or to limit oneself to the common denominator of the procedural rules of the jurisdictions that one knows best. Whereas the first approach risks losing sight of the diversity of competition law enforcement models that exist around the world, the second approach risks leading to a minimalistic list that is not representative of the world's competition agencies.

The ICN CAP avoided both of these traps by being able to rely on the many existing international documents on the topic (see the first section) and by the collective determination of the competition agencies that are represented in the ICN Steering Group to establish an as ambitious as possible list of due process principles. That being said, given the ubiquitous divide between administrative and judicial enforcement models, the ICN Steering Group made sure that all principles would equally apply to both models.

The ambitions of the ICN Steering Group are best illustrated by the fact that instead of looking for an absolute consensus on each of the principles, it rather chose (in case of dissent on a given principle or a constitutive aspect thereof)

15 More information on the information templates in section 4 below.

16 More information on the ICN CAP participants' liaison officers in section 5 below.

17 More information on the cooperation processes in section 5 below.

18 See point 3.c of the ICN CAP, where it has been specified that the reporting will not identify individual ICN CAP participants without their consent.

to maintain that principle in the ICN CAP, and to allow a participating agency to indicate that its "Competition Laws and Procedural Rules prevent it from applying one or more of the Principles, as a limitation on its participation."[19] Not only did this let-out option lead to a more ambitious formulation of the due process principles, but this methodology is surely also more conducive to an eventual convergence of fundamental due process principles than a mere enumeration of the lowest common denominator principles.

Turning to the principles themselves, these can largely be grouped around 6 rules: (1) non-discriminatory treatment, (2) transparency of the applicable rules, (3) the opportunity to defend oneself, (4) the protection of confidentiality, (5) the publication of written decisions and (6) judicial review.

Below, we summarise these principles in a non-exhaustive manner, without necessarily doing full justice to the nuances and exceptions provided for in the ICN CAP itself. It may thus be worthwhile checking this summary against the actual text of the principles. Also, the below describes the way in which the European Commission is respecting each principle in its enforcement of the EU competition rules. It should be read as a synopsis of the detailed EU information template published on the ICN CAP website.[20]

(1) Non-discriminatory treatment

The first principle prescribes that non-domestic undertakings that are the subject of a competition law proceeding should not be treated worse than domestic undertakings, both in terms of the applicable substantive and procedural rules, and as to the application of those rules in a concrete proceeding. This principle of non-discrimination is a cornerstone in an economy that aspires to be open to foreign investments and it is at the same time key to achieving a level-playing field between domestic and foreign undertakings that are providing goods or services on the same open (domestic) market.

In the EU, the substantive and procedural competition rules are formulated irrespective of the nationality of the undertakings concerned: they apply in the same terms to both domestic and foreign undertakings.[21] This equality of the rules also implies that in the enforcement of these rules, the European

19 Point 1.j of the ICN CAP.

20 Https://www.internationalcompetitionnetwork.org/frameworks/competition-agency-procedures/.

21 The use of languages is worldwide a notorious nuance to this principle of non-discrimination: in the EU, undertakings have to address the Commission in an official language of the EU, see Article 2 of EEC Council Regulation No 1 determining the languages to be used by the European Economic Community, OJ 17, 6.10.1958, p. 385; consolidated version of 1.1.2007.

Commission is bound to respect the principle of non-discrimination on grounds of nationality.[22]

(2) Transparency of the applicable rules

According to the second principle, the applicable substantive and procedural rules have to be publicly available. Competition authorities may also wish to issue guidance documents to further clarify the applicable rules. This principle ensures the predictability of the legal context in which businesses operate. It allows both undertakings and third parties to verify that the competition authority has indeed acted in accordance with the applicable rules.

The EU has published its rules both in the Official Journal of the European Union and on the website of DG Competition.[23] On the latter, one can find the applicable rules, as well as Commission guidelines on how it is interpreting substantive provisions and it is applying those rules in its proceedings.[24]

(3) The opportunity to defend oneself

The ICN CAP participating competition authorities agreed to inform undertakings as soon as legally possible of the fact that they are subject to an investigation. They will also clarify the legal basis of such investigation and what conduct of the undertaking is at stake. Throughout the investigation, undertakings should have the opportunity to engage with the authority on the factual, legal, economic and procedural aspects of the investigation.

If, following the investigation, the competition authority suspects a violation of the competition rules, the undertaking should be informed thereof, as well as of the facts and legal and economic arguments to support the allegations. The undertaking concerned should then have the opportunity to access the competition authority's file and, on that basis, to defend itself against these allegations.

These principles are at the very heart of the respect for due process: undertakings should know that they are the subject of an investigation, they should know on which facts and arguments allegations of an infringement are based, and

22 For the non-discrimination on grounds of nationality of one of the EU Member States, see also Article 21(2) of the Charter of Fundamental Rights of the European Union and in Article 18 of the Treaty on the Functioning of the European Union (TFEU).

23 Https://ec.europa.eu/competition.

24 See e.g. the Commission notice on best practices for the conduct of proceedings concerning Articles 101 and 102 TFEU: https://eur-lex.europa.eu/legal-content/EN/ALL/?uri=CELEX:52011XC1020(02).

they should have access to the incriminating and exculpatory evidence the competition authority has collected in order to enable them to defend themselves against the alleged infringement. These are the core due process principles that ensure transparency and protect against arbitrary and capricious enforcement of the competition rules.

The central role of the due process principles in an enforcement that is based on the rule of law does not prevent, however, that they need to be carefully balanced against the effectiveness of the investigation. No right should be construed or used in a way that surpasses its objective and rather becomes a vehicle to obstruct the enforcement of the law. Only a nuanced calibration of both due process principles and effective enforcement will prevent both an abuse of power by the competition authority and an abuse of rights by the undertakings under investigation.

As a further emanation of this delicate equilibrium, the ICN CAP set forth the objective for competition authorities to conclude their proceedings within a reasonable period of time, taking due account of the complexity of the case.

In the EU, the respect for these principles and how they relate to the effectiveness of the enforcement, are firmly enshrined in Article 41 of the Charter of Fundamental Rights of the European Union and in EU legislation. It has been extensively elaborated upon in the Commission's best practices on the conduct of antitrust and merger control proceedings.[25]

(4) The protection of confidentiality

Confidential exchanges can take place at two levels, a first between the undertaking under investigation and its legal counsel, and a second between that undertaking and the investigating competition authority:

(a) an undertaking that is under investigation by a competition authority should be able to communicate in confidence with the legal counsel of its choosing. That communication will thus, in principle, be protected by legal professional privilege and considered confidential as regards the investigating authority. This confidentiality is an essential corollary to the full exercise of the rights of defence.
In the EU, communications between an undertaking and its external legal counsel are protected by legal professional privilege. The European Court of Justice has deemed, however, that this legal professional privilege only

25 See the previous footnote for the antitrust best practices text and for best practices in merger control, see https://ec.europa.eu/competition/mergers/legislation/proceedings.pdf.

covers written communications with "an independent lawyer entitled to practise his profession in an [EU] Member State." Moreover, it only covers those communications that are made for the purpose and interest of the exercise of the undertaking's rights of defence in competition proceedings.[26]

(b) information that does not fall under legal professional privilege can still be confidential as regards third parties. The competition authority should protect such confidential information that it obtains during the proceedings from unlawful disclosure. At the same time, the authority needs to consider the public interest in a fair, effective and transparent enforcement.
In the EU, the protection of the confidentiality of information obtained during competition proceedings falls under each of its officials' obligation of professional secrecy.[27] The confidentiality of certain information can, however, be outweighed by other interests, such as the need to prove an infringement[28], or the need to safeguard the rights of defence of another party, for whom the confidential information may constitute exculpatory evidence.[29]

(5) Publication of written decisions

Competition authorities also agreed that they will issue their final decisions finding an infringement, imposing a prohibition, a remedy or a fine, or accepting commitments, in writing. This should allow the addressed undertaking to have full knowledge of the factual, legal and economic arguments on which the decision is based. In case the undertaking would want to challenge the findings of authority, the written decision will also provide the basis for the undertaking's request for review.

Competition authorities are also encouraged to publish their final decisions, subject to confidentiality rules and applicable legal exceptions. Such publication not only enhances their wider deterrent effect, it also informs possible victims of the infringement who may subsequently claim damages, and it fits well with the public accountability of competition authorities.[30]

---

26 See Case 155/79 AM&S Europe Limited v Commission, ECLI:EU:C:1982:1575. The quote is taken from paragraph 35.

27 Article 339 TFEU and Article 28 of Regulation 1/2003 on the implementation of the rules on competition laid down in Articles [101] and [102 TFEU], OJ L 1, 4.1.2003, p. 1.

28 See Article 27(2) in fine of Regulation 1/2003.

29 See point 24 of the Commission Notice on the rules for access to the Commission file in cases pursuant to Articles [101] and [102 TFEU], Articles 53, 54 and 57 of the EEA Agreement and Council Regulation (EC) No 139/2004, OJ C 325, 22.12.2005, p. 7.

30 See point 78 of Case T-198/03, *Bank Austria Creditanstalt AG v Commission* (ECLI:EU:T:2006:136): "the interest of an undertaking which the Commission has fined for breach of competition law in the details of the offending conduct of which it is accused not being disclosed to the public does not warrant any particular protection, given the public

The European Commission issues all of its competition decisions in writing. The adoption of a decision is widely announced through a press release and the decision itself is published, with due regard to the legitimate interest of undertakings in the protection of their business secrets.[31] As the addressed undertakings may contest the confidentiality of some information that the Commission intends to publish, the Commission would publish a provisional version of the decision excluding all information for which confidentiality has been requested, in anticipation of a final version after resolution of the disputed parts.[32]

(6) Judicial review

As a final principle, the ICN CAP provides that undertakings that are the subject of a prohibition, remedy or fining decision, should have the opportunity to seek review of that decision by an independent and impartial court. Such judicial review is the ultimate guarantee for undertakings that competition authorities are bound to respect the due process principles throughout their competition proceedings.

In the EU, this principle of judicial review is secured by Article 263 of the Treaty on the Functioning of the European Union (the "Treaty"), which gives the Court of Justice jurisdiction to annul the decisions of the Commission on the grounds of lack of competence, infringement of an essential procedural requirement, infringement of the Treaty or of any rule of law relating to its application, or misuse of powers, and by Article 31 of Regulation 1/2003, which gives that Court the unlimited jurisdiction to review decisions whereby the Commission imposed a fine or a periodic penalty payment.

4. TRANSPARENCY AND REVIEW

The competition authorities that are adhering to the ICN CAP also agreed to publish the relevant information about their domestic rules and procedures, to demonstrate that they indeed respect the principles that they have subscribed to. Such information may consist of a reference to existing legislation or administrative guidance, but it may also refer to the case practice of the authority

---

interest in knowing as fully as possible the reasons behind any Commission action, the interest of the economic operators in knowing the sort of behaviour for which they are liable to be penalised and the interest of persons harmed by the infringement in being informed of the details thereof so that they may, where appropriate, assert their rights against the undertakings punished, and in view of the fined undertaking's ability to seek judicial review of such a decision."

31 Article 30(2) of Regulation 1/2003.

32 See point 149 of the Commission notice on best practices for the conduct of proceedings concerning Articles 101 and 102 TFEU.

or case law of its review court. The participating competition authorities committed to keep these so-called information templates (the "CAP Templates") up-to-date to reflect significant modifications to their rules or procedures. The CAP Templates are publicly available on the website dedicated to the ICN CAP[33] – there are currently 66 of them, while new ones are arriving regularly from agencies having joined the ICN CAP.

By making the information about how they respect the ICN CAP principles publicly available on the ICN website, the participating competition authorities not only underline their adherence to the principle of transparency (see above), they also make it easier for their sister authorities and for the undertakings that are subject of their procedures, to retrieve and understand the applicable rules and procedures. Such awareness of the applicable rules is obviously a *sine qua non* to trigger the bilateral consultation process, which aims to clarify how an adhering competition authority is respecting the ICN CAP principles, either in general terms or in the context of a concrete investigation or enforcement proceeding. The next section provides further detail on this dialogue.

As mentioned in section 2.2 above, the ICN CAP participating authorities will regularly take stock of the implementation of the ICN CAP principles and of the functioning of the ICN CAP framework itself, e.g. during dedicated sessions at the ICN annual conference. At least every four years, such a stock-taking session will be used to discuss the appropriateness of modifying the ICN CAP principles. This review process allows the ICN CAP participants to either update some of the principles, to bring further nuance to their formulation, to elaborate on existing principles or to introduce new ones. Though the ICN CAP does not specify the precise procedure or voting mechanism for such review, it can be assumed that any amendment to the ICN CAP framework, or to the principles themselves, requires consensus amongst the then ICN CAP participants. Then again, the possibility for adhering competition authorities to indicate that they cannot apply (part of) a particular principle, should prevent the further development of the principles being hampered by the participants' common denominator.

5. COOPERATION PROCESS: DIALOGUE BETWEEN ICN CAP PARTICIPANTS

The ICN CAP's transparency rules described in the previous chapter are complemented by the establishment of a direct communication channel between ICN CAP participants, which is dedicated to discussing questions

33 Https://www.internationalcompetitionnetwork.org/frameworks/competition-agency-procedures/cap-templates/.

and issues concerning the implementation of the fundamental principles of procedural fairness covered by the ICN CAP. The participants are encouraged to communicate directly with each other with regard to any such questions and issues. To facilitate the communication, each ICN CAP participant is committed to name a dedicated liaison officer to be featured in a contact list managed and updated by the ICN CAP Co-chairs.

The cornerstone of the direct communication is a novel cooperation process, which allows any ICN CAP participant to request another participant to engage in a dialogue regarding any question or issue that is material to the ICN CAP. It is an exclusively participant-to-participant dialogue, i.e. third parties have no right to participate therein, nor to initiate it. In other words, it is entirely up to each competition authority participating in the ICN CAP to decide whether it wishes to request a dialogue and, if so, what the subject-matter and the scope thereof should be. Concerning the scope of the cooperation process, the ICN CAP provides, in general, that it is to be undertaken only for matters that fall within the responsibility of the requested participant, although participants may raise broader issues related to investigation and enforcement of competition rules.

ICN CAP participants commit to engage in a dialogue in good faith, according full and sympathetic consideration to the questions and issues raised, in a mutually convenient manner compatible with their respective laws and in light of the need to effectively enforce such laws. Unless otherwise agreed by the participants involved, the dialogue will be kept confidential.

While the procedural questions and issues are typically to be discussed in general terms (e.g. how a competition agency applies a particular principle of procedural fairness in its enforcement practice), the ICN CAP encourages participants to discuss also the specific circumstances of the investigation concerned, if relevant for understanding the concrete way in which a principle has been applied in that context.

Participants are also encouraged to share relevant information in accordance with applicable laws, but there is obviously no obligation to disclose confidential information. Finally, the ICN CAP clarifies that any measures taken by the requested participant as a result of the dialogue are within the discretion of that participant.

6. ASSESSMENT OF THE ICN CAP

The ICN CAP adds another layer to the various instruments produced at the international level with the objective of promoting respect for fundamental principles of procedural fairness in competition investigations and enforcement.

It is novel in many respects:

- Being a peer-to-peer instrument, the ICN CAP is particularly well suited to exercise gentle, yet profound peer pressure on competition authorities to observe fundamental principles of procedural fairness in their investigations and enforcement practice. The more competition authorities that join the ICN CAP, the harder it becomes for those staying outside to justify why they hesitate to subscribe to respecting the fundamental principles of procedural fairness covered by the ICN CAP. This effect is further facilitated by the fact that the ICN CAP allows each participant to opt out from complying with a particular ICN CAP principle if it is prevented from compliance by the existing legal rules in its jurisdiction;
- Thanks to the transparency – each participant sharing (and updating where necessary) a written explanation of the practical implementation of the ICN CAP principles in its jurisdiction – and cooperation – dialogue between participants – mechanisms, the ICN CAP does not stop at proclaiming certain principles. Rather, it is designed to be a living instrument with continuous relevance for – and influence upon – the practical implementation of those principles in the investigations and competition enforcement practice of each participant. The living character of ICN CAP will be further strengthened by the fact that its participants will regularly hold sessions to discuss topical issues concerning its implementation, e.g. at ICN annual conferences;
- Given that the ICN CAP is not an instrument that automatically applies to all ICN members but requires each interested competition authority to actively opt in, it underlines the commitment aspect. By joining the ICN CAP, its participants commit not only to respect the relevant principles, but also to be transparent about their implementation and willing to engage in a dialogue with other participants when there are questions or issues concerning such implementation;
- The ICN CAP is open to non-members, i.e. even competition authorities from countries that for various reasons are not (yet) part of the ICN are welcome to participate in the ICN CAP and thus actively contribute to the promotion of procedural fairness worldwide; and
- Last but not least, the ICN CAP is an open-ended instrument, as the participants can, at any time, consider whether it might be appropriate to include new principles in the ICN CAP and/or to modify/expand the principles already covered, in reflection of the discussions to be held regularly, and to be facilitated by the structure of rotating ICN CAP co-chairs.

THE SECOND DECADE OF ICN IN BRAZIL: AN OVERVIEW AND PERSPECTIVES FOR LATIN AMERICA

Paulo Burnier da Silveira*

1. INTRODUCTION

The International Competition Network (ICN) was created in 2001 and it will complete two decades in 2020. Initially composed of 14 competition authorities, it is nowadays includes more than 135 members. It is the largest international organization in the field of competition in the world. Although it faces different challenges compared to those of its early years, including the challenge to work with an increasingly diverse membership base, its success is widely recognized. It is also remarkable how much ICN has achieved since its conception as an alternative to a forum within the World Trade Organization (WTO).[1] Moreover, its unique design adds a special flavor to the study of international organizations, which has led experts to comment on its similarities and complementarities with other multilateral bodies.[2]

This contribution will focus on the second decade of the ICN in Brazil including an overview and perspectives for Latin America. During 2010–2020, the Brazilian competition framework has changed significantly: first, with

* Paulo Burnier da Silveira is a Senior Competition Expert at the Organization for Economic Cooperation and Development (OECD) and Manager of the OECD Regional Center for Competition in Latin America. He is also a former Commissioner at the Brazilian Competition Authority (CADE) and former head of CADE's International Unit, with an active participation in ICN activities during 2011–2019. He holds a PhD from the University of Paris and is a Law Professor at the University of Brasilia. E-mail: pburnier@unb.br. The opinions expressed are personal and do not necessary reflect the opinions of the related organizations.

1 Merit E. Janow. "Observations on two multilateral venues: the International Competition Network (ICN) and the WTO". *Annual Proceedings of the Fordham Corporate Law Institute*. Barry E. Hawk (ed.). New York: Juris Publishing, 2002. pp. 49–50.

2 For instance, see: Frédéric Jenny. "The International Competition Network and the OECD Competition Committee: Differences, Similarities and Complementarities". *The International Competition Network at Ten. Origins, Accomplishments and Aspirations*. Paul Lugard (dir.). Cambridge: Intersentia, 2011. pp. 93–104.

the approval of a major competition legislative reform in 2011; then, with an implementation phase of the new legislation; and, finally, with the improvement of the legislation including the publication of guidelines (soft law) and minor legal adjustments (hard law). Many dimensions of the Brazilian current competition regime were inspired by ICN experience and materials, which have indeed played a key role in Brazil throughout the last decade.

In order to address the second decade of ICN in Brazil, this contribution will first demonstrate how the Brazilian competition reforms were positively influenced by ICN work products and activities, including on issues related to substance, procedure and competition policy. Then, it will do the inverse and describe how the Brazilian competition authorities, in particular CADE, have contributed to the ICN. This part includes the planning of the ICN Annual Conference in 2012 and the ICN Cartel Workshop in 2019. Last, this paper will attempt to shed some light on future perspectives for the ICN in Latin America.

2. ICN ACTIVITIES IN SUPPORT OF COMPETITION ENFORCEMENT IN BRAZIL

In May 2012, a new Competition Act entered into effect in Brazil. The main changes were the unification of all competition enforcement competences into one single competition authority (CADE) and the adoption of a pre-merger control system. These two changes resulted in a substantial transformation of the Brazilian competition framework. During the *vacation legis* of the new competition legislation, which lasted for six months, the ICN contact points facilitated the planning of technical visits abroad to benchmark a number of aspects related to the procedure, the substance and agency effectiveness (i.e. a division of units and tasks, in particular a screening unit to review fast-track transactions). A senior merger team from Brazil was thus able to collect important information and practical experience from sister agencies before the new legislation entered into effect.

In a number of respects, these changes were inspired and supported by the ICN.[3] In particular, in the last decade, there are two specific reforms in the Brazilian competition regime, that had a clear "ICN touch": the first one is related to the pre-merger control system, while the second reform concerns the current

---

[3] For instance, see the participation of Mr. Bruno Lasserre in a hearing at the Brazilian Senate during the public discussions of the Brazilian Bill of Law. CADE's Press Release from 10.11.2009: www.cade.gov.br/noticias/antigas/encontro-franca-brasil-de-defesa-da-concorrencia-debate-projeto-de-lei-que-reforma-o-cade. Mr. Bruno Lasserre is former President of the French Competition Authority and former Vice-Chair of the ICN.

framework for cartel settlements, which includesstronger incentives for first applicants.

2.1. REFORM OF THE MERGER CONTROL SYSTEM

In effect since 2012, the Brazilian current merger control system today serves as a successful case story for ICN's recommended practices in this area. This is clear when considering the procedure, as well as substantive and practical issues.

In terms of procedural rules, the Brazilian legislation addresses the main sections of "ICN's Recommended Practices for Merger Notification & Review Procedures" from 2002, including the (1) definition of a merger transaction; (2) nexus to the reviewing jurisdiction; (3) timing of merger notification; (4) merger review periods; (5) requirements for initial notification; (6) conduct of merger investigations; (7) procedural fairness; (8) transparency; (9) confidentiality; (10) interagency enforcement cooperation; (11) remedies; (12) competition agency powers; and (13) review of merger control provisions.[4] In particular, a great effort was given to procedural fairness and transparency in relation to CADE's online system which is often used for merger proceedings, including the notification of transactions (*Sistema Eletrônico de Informações – SEI*).

The same is true for substantive aspects, which were laid down by ICN members in a set of recommended practices for merger analysis. In a nutshell, they address: (1) the Legal Framework for Competition Merger Analysis; (2) Market Definition; (3) the Use of Market Shares: Thresholds & Presumptions; (4) Competitive Effects Analysis in Horizontal Merger Review: Overview; (5) Unilateral Effects; (6) Coordinated Effects; (7) Entry and Expansion; (8) Efficiencies; and (9) Failing Firm/Exiting Assets. As this area has been subject to wide convergence efforts around world, including with other national or regional guidance, the Brazilian Merger Guidelines follow a similar ideas approach.[5]

As for the practical dimension, one may also note that CADE's international cooperation in merger review is backed by the ICN Framework for Merger Review Cooperation (2012), which intends to facilitate effective and efficient cooperation between and among ICN member agencies by identifying

---

4 ICN Recommended Practices for Merger Notification & Review Procedures (2002–2018): https://www.internationalcompetitionnetwork.org/portfolio/merger-np-recommended-practices/.

5 For the ICN Recommended Practices for Merger Analysis (2002–2018), see: https://www.internationalcompetitionnetwork.org/portfolio/recommended-practices-for-merger-analysis/. For CADE's Merger Guidelines, see: www.cade.gov.br/acesso-a-informacao/publicacoes-institucionais/guias_do_Cade/guia-para-analise-de-atos-de-concentracao-horizontal.pdf.

each agency's liaison officers and possible ways to exchange information.[6] Moreover, the frequent ICN web conferences serve as an important source of information for Brazilian case handlers, for instance on how to define relevant markets, how to assess market power, how to deal with coordinated effects and so forth.

2.2. REFORM OF THE FRAMEWORK FOR CARTEL SETTLEMENTS

The ICN also inspired an important reform of CADE's settlement policy in 2013. It started when the topic of settlements was chosen in 2011 as Special Project for the ICN Annual Conference to be organized in Rio de Janeirothe following year. The Special Project is a topic traditionally chosen by the host country in consultation with ICN's Steering Group. It offers an opportunity for the host country to develop a specific topic that it considers important for the development in the field of competition law and policy at that particular moment in time.

For Brazil, this meant that a special part of the 2012 ICN Annual Conference in Rio de Janeiro was to be dedicated to discussions around settlements. Brazil could then enjoy the valuable input from the international expertise present at the Annual Conference, including high quality of benchmarking and technical exchanges. After this exercise with the international antitrust community, Brazil was able to transform its competition settlement The topic was initially chosen to cover both mergers and anticompetitive practices. Accordingly, dedicated panels were organized to bring together experts to discuss settlements in mergers, cartels and unilateral conduct cases.

After the ICN Annual Conference, Brazil chose to prioritize settlements in cartel enforcement. A public consultation was released a few months after the event, which proposed to stagger the discounts of fines based on the moment of the application. This was an innovative approach in Brazil. The national antitrust community submitted a number of contributions during the period of public consultation. The overall feedback was positive, which gave greater comfort to move forward with the idea and to implement a new framework for cartel settlements in Brazil. The system entered into effect in 2013 and it is still in place today. It can be summarized by the chart below:

6 For the ICN Framework for Merger Review Cooperation (2012), see: https://www.internationalcompetitionnetwork.org/portfolio/icn-framework-for-merger-review-coopeation/.

Framework for settlements in cartel investigations in Brazil

Phase of case	Order of requests	Discount in fine
Superintendence (investigation phase)	1st applicant	between 30% and 50%
	2nd applicant	between 25% and 40%
	3rd applicant	up to 25%
Tribunal (adjudication phase)	all applicants	up to 15%

The objective was to increase incentives for defendants to request for settlements in a speedy manner, as well as to bring new evidences to cartel investigations. The overall success is astonishing, with numbers of settlements application and fines effectively collected having strongly increased in the following years. The chart below provides a snapshot of the success of the settlement policy in cartel cases:

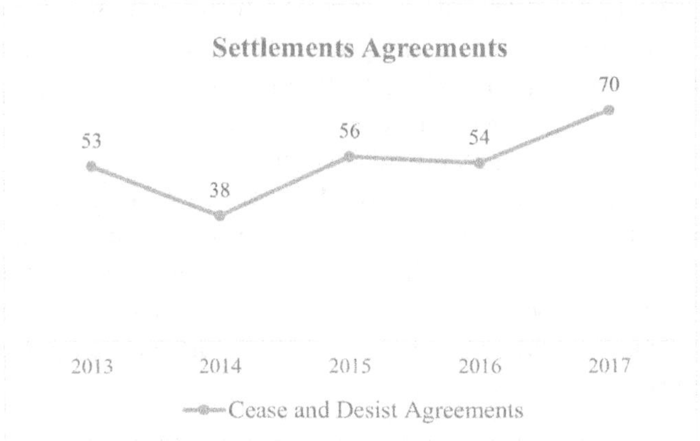

Source: Brazilian Competition Authority (CADE)

The introduction of the system was followed by a training session on negotiation techniques to competition enforcers in order to prepare civil servants to these new tasks. The process of learning by constant evolution was consolidated in the Guidelines on Settlements available in both Portuguese and English.[7]

The new framework was largely inspired by international best practices and benefitted from a comparison with similar policies in other jurisdictions. In this regard, the ICN has provided a great platform for convergence and international cooperation amongst competition authorities around the world. The Brazilian experience illustrates ICN's success in achieving these objectives.

7 Guidelines "Cease and Desist Agreements for Cartel Cases": www.cade.gov.br/acesso-a-informacao/publicacoes-institucionais/guias_do_Cade/guidelines_tcc-1.pdf.

3. THE BRAZILIAN EFFORTS IN SUPPORT OF ICN ACTIVITIES

During the past decade, the active role of Brazil in the ICN activities is expressed in various ways. It reflects the prioritization of the goals of the organization, which includes the convergence of practice and rules in competition enforcement around the world. As CADE provides important resources to the ICN activities, the relationship with the ICN can be considered as a form of cooperation. This section will highlight the Brazilian efforts in ICN activities which includes in particular the active participation in the management of the organization and the planning of both the ICN Annual Conference in 2012 and the ICN Cartel Workshop in 2019.

3.1. ACTIVE ROLE IN MANAGEMENT POSITIONS

The *Steering Group* is ICN's main executive body. It is composed of around 18 competition authorities and it sets de agenda of the organization, in particular by coordinating the work agenda of ICN's Working Groups on Advocacy, Agency Effectiveness, Cartels, Mergers and Unilateral Conducts. As it does not hold a permanent secretariat, each member is expected to contribute its own capacity and resources. Accordingly, it is a relative burden to have an active role in ICN's activities in particular in light of its management tasks and hosting its annual conferences and workshops. At the same time, these efforts enable a greater participation in the development of guidelines and recommendations, which play a key role in the convergence of competition enforcement policies as they are often used as soft law instruments.[8]

In this context, Brazil has played an important role in management positions. It has been a member of the ICN Steering Group with CADE since 2004 and has acted as Vice-Chair with Mr. Vinicius Marques de Carvalho (2013–2015). Interestingly, also Mexico has played an impressive leading role in ICN since its very beginning. It has been one of ICN's founding members (the only one from Latin America at the stage of conception[9]) and a member of the ICN Steering Group during the last two decades. It has also acted in the Steering Group as Chair with Mr. Fernando Sánchez Ugarte (2003–2004) and Mr. Eduardo Perez Motta (2012–2014), as well as Vice-Chair with Ms. Alejandra Palacios (since

8 Paul Lugard. *The International Competition Network at Ten.* Cambridge: Intersentia, 2011, p. 10.

9 The ICN was created on 25 October 2001 with the following countries as founding members: Australia, Canada, European Union, France, Germany, Israel, Italy, Japan, Korea, Mexico, South Africa, United Kingdom, United States, and Zambia. It was launched at a meeting in New York.

2016). Both Mexico and Brazil have also co-chaired ICN's Working Group together with sister agencies from other parts of the world.

3.2. ACTIVE ROLE IN HOSTING ICN EVENTS

Another example of Brazil's efforts in relation to ICN activities in the last decade is reflected in the organization of key ICN events. The ICN Annual Conference held in Rio de Janeiro in 2012 and the ICN Cartel Workshop held in Foz do Iguaçu in 2019 were highlights in this respect.

The 11th ICN Annual Conference took place on 17–20 April 2012 in Rio de Janeiro. In total 532 persons registered and 489 attended the event. Most of them represented competition authorities and non-governmental advisers (i.e. academics, economists and lawyers).

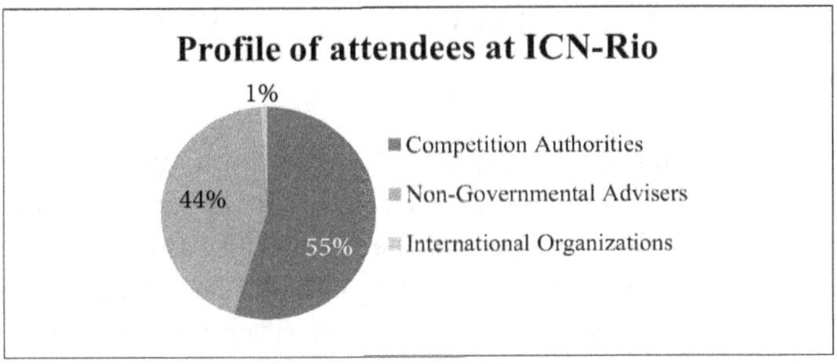

Source: Brazilian Competition Authority (CADE)

A clear effort was made to increase the number of academics at the conference, as they tend to bring a pair of fresh eyes and research to the daily life of competition enforcers. This effort seems to continue until today in particular involving academics who act at universities and research centers as full scholars.

During the 2.5 days of the annual conference, many discussions took place with a special emphasis on settlements as the topic that was selected as a special project for that year. At the end of the event, a survey indicated that the conference had achieved a satisfaction record of 90.3% considering the answers of attendees that were either satisfied or very satisfied with the overall planning and discussions of the event in Rio de Janeiro. The planning of the ICN annual conference consumed a budget of around € 150,000.00. Most of the budget was allocated to the rental of a venue that could accommodate almost 500 attendees, as well as to an organizing company selected through a national public procurement proceeding.

The organization of the largest competition event in the world offered a great impetus for competition law and policy in Brazil. On the one hand, it drew political attention to the importance of sound competition policy. And, on the other hand, the event enabled a direct exchange between national enforcers and other competition enforcers around the globe. In a number of respects, the atmosphere created by hosting the event contributed a positive wave that led to the approval of the Brazilian new and current competition law (Law n. 12.529/2011).

The ICN Cartel Workshop was hosted by CADE in November 2019. The event focused on the topic of digital economy and gathered more than 200 attendees, including competition enforcers and non-governmental advisers from 46 jurisdictions. One highlight was the participation of 12 competition authorities from Latin America and the Caribbean.[10]

4. THE FUTURE PERSPECTIVES FOR ICN IN LATIN AMERICA

The process of the internationalization of competition law and policy seems unstoppable. In the past two decades, a great number of competition authorities were created. During the same period, the number of cases with international dimensions has also increased, which led to a greater need for convergence and cooperation around the world. In Latin America, several competition authorities have emerged during the last decade, for instance Paraguay, Ecuador and Costa Rica. In the context of proliferation of competition laws and regimes in the region, he ICN objective of convergence is particular relevant and welcome. For this reason, the trend of active participation of Latin American competition authorities in ICN activities is likely to continue.

A glance at the hosts agencies of ICN Annual Conferences helps to understand the importance of the ICN in the region: in 19 editions, the ICN Annual Conference was hosted 3 times in Latin America: Mexico (2003), Brazil (2012) and Colombia (2019).[11] It represents approximately 15% of the total number of ICN's Annual Conferences. Considering that competition law is still a relatively

---

10 See Noemy Melo, "Cartels in the Age of the Data-driven Economy: Outcomes from the 2019 ICN Cartel Workshop". CPI, 2019. Available at: https://www.competitionpolicyinternational.com/cartels-in-the-age-of-the-data-driven-economy-outcomes-from-the-2019-icn-cartel-workshop/.

11 List of hosts of ICN Annual Conferences: Italy (2002), Mexico (2003), Korea (2004), Germany (2005), South Africa (2006), Russia (2007), Japan (2008), Switzerland (2009), Turkey (2010), Netherlands (2011), Brazil (2012), Poland (2013), Morocco (2014), Australia (2015), Singapore (2016), Portugal (2017), India (2018), Colombia (2019) and US (2020).

new field in the region, this number reflects the great support that is given by Latin American members to the ICN activities and objectives.[12] A recent example was the presence of Mr. Iván Duque Márquez, President of the Republic of Colombia, as a keynote speaker in the opening session of the ICN Annual Conference held in Cartagena in 2019. His presence, in addition to the contents of his speech, underlines the support at the highest level of government of sound competition policy and the values promoted by the ICN.

Indeed, new challenges lie ahead during ICN's third decade. One of these challenges will be to deal with convergence in a scenario of greater diversity due to the enlargement of the ICN. The organization encompasses nowadays members with small/large sizes and new/old regimes. In addition, many new ICN members are at different levels of economic and social development when compared to most of its founding members. The co-existence of this diverse member profiles is both a challenge and an opportunity for ICN. An opportunity to foster convergence with an effort of understanding local particularities, which may lead to local nuances in the application of competition policy in a particular country of region, for instance a greater role for advocacy instead of enforcement.

In Latin America, the ICN will continue to benefit from a large mandate in terms of promoting convergence and international cooperation in the area of competition law and policy. Competition authorities in the region know that they may rely on international organizations such as ICN and the OECD to promote a better environment for competition. Considering that the ICN is older than most of Latin American competition authorities, it will likely continue to serve as a safe family refuge, in particular for young members to meet and exchange with sister (and brother) agencies.

5. REFERENCES

FINGLETON, John. The International Competition Network: Chair's update. *Competition & Antitrust Review – 2011*. Colchester: Euromoney Yearbooks, 2011.

FOX, Eleanor. Linked-In: Antitrust and the Virtues of a Virtual Network. *The International Competition Network at Ten. Origins, Accomplishments and Aspirations*. Paul Lugard (dir.). Cambridge: Intersentia, 2011.

12 As reminder, hosting an ICN Annual Conference requires a large amount of human and financial resources, in total or large part originated from public budget. As a result, the decision to host an Annual Conference is usually preceded by the highest support of national government. As reference, this is the list of countries in Latin America that have a competition authority: Argentina, Bolivia, Brazil, Chile, Colombia, Costa Rica, Dominican Republic, Ecuador, El Salvador, Honduras, Mexico, Nicaragua, Panama, Paraguay, Peru, Uruguay and Venezuela. This number does not include the Caribbean countries and its competition agencies.

INTERNATIONAL COMPETITION NETWORK. ICN: The ICN'S vision for its second decade [Internet]. 2011. Available at: <www.internationalcompetitionnetwork.org/uploads/library/doc755.pdf>.

INTERNATIONAL COMPETITION NETWORK. ICN: Current Working Groups [Internet]. International Competition Network. Available at: <www.internationalcompetitionnetwork.org/working-groups/current.aspx>.

JANOW, Merit E.. Observations on two multilateral venues: the International Competition Network (ICN) and the WTO. *Annual Proceedings of the Fordham Corporate Law Institute*. Barry E. Hawk (dir.). Nova Iorque: Juris Publishing, 2002.

JENNY, Frédéric. The International Competition Network and the OECD Competition Committee: Differences, Similarities and Complementarities. *The International Competition Network at Ten. Origins, Accomplishments and Aspirations*. Paul Lugard (dir.). Cambridge: Intersentia, 2011.

KALBFLEISCH, Pieter. From Ditchley Park to The Hague – A Journey Worthwhile. *The International Competition Network at Ten. Origins, Accomplishments and Aspirations*. Paul Lugard (dir.). Cambridge: Intersentia, 2011.

LUGARD, Paul. *The International Competition Network at Ten. Origins, Accomplishments and Aspirations: an Introduction*. Paul Lugard (dir.). Cambridge: Intersentia, 2011.

MELO, Noemy. "Cartels in the Age of the Data-driven Economy: Outcomes from the 2019 ICN Cartel Workshop". CPI, 2019. Available at: https://www.competitionpolicyinternational.com/cartels-in-the-age-of-the-data-driven-economy-outcomes-from-the-2019-icn-cartel-workshop/.

MOTTA, Eduardo Pérez. My roadmap as ICN Chair. ICN [Internet]. Available at: <www.internationalcompetitionnetwork.org/uploads/library/doc792.pdf>.

SILVEIRA, Paulo Burnier; and BAKAJ, Giovanna. "A segunda década da Rede Internacional da Concorrência: os desafios da promoção da convergência na diversidade". *Revista de Defesa da Concorrência*, n°1. Brasilia: May 2013.

ENGAGING ECONOMISTS IN THE ICN: UNITING UNDER A COMMON LANGUAGE

Martin MANDORFF

1. INTRODUCTION

The enforcement of unilateral conduct law is arguably the most challenging task of antitrust. Nowhere do the controversies run as deep as when determining whether a certain type of unilateral conduct is pro- or anticompetitive. Add to this the differences in legal standards and policy objectives and achieving international convergence of unilateral conduct policy stands out as a herculean task.

The ICN Unilateral Conduct Working Group (UCWG) has nevertheless made important progress since its formation in 2006, as laid out a CPI ICN column, "Climbing Mount Everest with the ICN Unilateral Conduct Working Group".[1] That column also suggested that by engaging more economists in the UCWG, the working group could help improve agency decision-making and promote convergence in the longer term. In essay, I provide an economist's viewpoint on how economists can contribute to, and benefit from, enhanced participation in the ICN in general, and in the UCWG in particular.

2. HOW ECONOMISTS CAN CONTRIBUTE TO THE ICN

This section uses the UCWG to illustrate how enhanced participation of member and Non-Governmental Actor (NGA) economists at the project level contributes to furthering the principle goals of the network: cooperation and convergence.

1 Cynthia Lewis Lagdameo,"Climbing Mount Everest with the ICN Unilateral Conduct Working Group", https://www.competitionpolicyinternational.com/assets/Uploads/ICN-11-27-2012-2.pdf.

In the area of unilateral conduct, as in other areas of competition law enforcement, agencies are increasingly bringing cases that safeguard the competitive process and not cases that protect competitors. The tools for enforcement actions to protect the competitive process are more explicitly grounded in economic theory, using primarily the economics of exclusionary behavior developed by the Chicago and post-Chicago schools. Agency decision-makers, therefore, rely more on economists' input in deciding whether to bring a case than in previous times.

This increased reliance on economics begins at the stage of considering whether to open an investigation and continues throughout the entire investigative process. Thus, for case handlers to be able to incorporate the findings of economics and develop coherent theories of harm during the investigation, they increasingly seek substantial guidance from economists.

The UCWG, like other ICN working groups, is currently drafting a multi-chapter workbook, which will function as a practical manual for case handlers. Case handlers will stand to benefit greatly if the UCWG workbook clearly describes prevalent economic thinking and details what findings to look for that are consistent with anti-competitive exclusion. To achieve this, economists need to be involved at all stages of producing the workbook.

While nearly all ICN work products can benefit from economists' input, this input is particularly essential in the area of unilateral conduct, since the economics of vertical conduct (to which unilateral conduct normally belongs) are much less intuitive than the economics of horizontal conduct.[2] For example, tying can, in some circumstances, be a profitable means to an anti-competitive end, but not for the "intuitive" reason that tying diverts sales from the competitors' products to one's own – a fallacy disproved long ago by the Chicago-critique. Instead, anticompetitive tying works through much subtler mechanisms, for example, by being a commitment device. The relevance of these mechanisms however depends entirely on whether specific criteria are satisfied, as set out by economic theory.

In the longer term, greater participation by economists in the creation of ICN work product will likely translate into greater policy convergence. Economists have the advantage of all sharing the same analytical toolbox. So, whereas legal standards and policy objectives differ, economists in different jurisdictions can

2 Whereas horizontal arrangements (such as cartels) allow the combination of substitute goods, which provides incentives to worsen the product-offering, vertical arrangements (such as between a producer and a retail outlet) allow the combination of complement goods, which in fact provides incentives to improve the product-offering.

often agree on what tools to use in their analyses. For example, the legal criteria for finding significant market power and dominance differ somewhat across jurisdictions, but economists' understanding of these concepts are more likely to be in agreement, since market power is rather clearly defined in economic theory (i.e. the ability to price profitably above marginal cost). Similarly, while in some jurisdictions the possibility of recoupment is a legal prerequisite for pricing to be predatory, and in others it is not, economists are nevertheless likely to agree that a coherent theory of harm requires a likelihood of higher consumer prices at some point (if higher prices were unlikely, why would the predator incur losses now, and who would be harmed?). What this shows is that the methods used in the economic analysis of unilateral conduct, such as predatory pricing, are likely to be more convergent than the legal analysis of the same conduct.

Economists can also contribute to convergence by participating in the overarching policy discussion. As new research is developed within the field of industrial organization, economists can inform the wider antitrust community of potential enforcement implications. This is especially relevant in the policy debate about when effects may be presumed and when they must be established (i.e., the per se approach vs. the effects-based approach). Here, economists can inform decisionmakers as to what the current state of economic theory and empirical evidence predicts and identify the types of conduct where there is enough evidence pointing in one direction to warrant a per se approach.[3]

Typically, working groups have a handful of agency economists that may participate on calls and the development of work product, but more participation is needed. Another model that would allow economists to make these contributions to policy convergence, in a more structured setting, would be to create a dedicated working group for economists. Such a working group could then provide analytical input to the different ICN working groups.

3. HOW ECONOMISTS CAN BENEFIT FROM PARTICIPATING IN THE ICN

The ICN holds great promise for antitrust economists, who tend to speak a more similar language across borders than lawyers, investigators, and case handlers, but who nonetheless have remained more in siloes than the other disciplines. The ICN can provide a cross border platform for economists to engage with one another, both for more experienced and less experienced economists.

---

3 See the section Risk of Enforcement Errors, p.13–15, in the Unilateral Conduct Workbook Chapter 1: The Objectives and Principles of Unilateral Conduct Laws, www.internationalcompetitionnetwork.org/uploads/library/doc827.pdf.

For an economist who has just entered the field of unilateral conduct enforcement, for example, finding the right analytical framework for a particular case can be a nearly overwhelming task. The economics of vertical conduct are, as mentioned above, difficult to master in comparison to, for example, the economics of cartels. Without guidance from the relevant research literature, it is almost impossible to develop a coherent theory of harm. And even knowing what constitutes the relevant economic literature, the additional difficulty occurs that for every type of conduct there are a multitude of theoretical models that attempt to explain it – all with different policy implications.

The ICN could contribute by facilitating an exchange between new and more seasoned antitrust economists. Existing working groups or a dedicated economist group could, for example, replicate existing ICN methods to promote cooperation and convergence – such as a workshop for economists (much like the Merger Working Group held in 2012, or the economist panels at UCWG workshops on competitive effects), panel discussions at annual conferences, and/or a webinar series dedicated to economic issues. Topics could cover the basics of economic analysis, a more advanced seminar series, case studies, and "hot topics".

Economists from smaller agencies, or agencies that only recently added economics-capacity to their unilateral conduct enforcement, particularly stand to benefit from such an exchange since they will likely have less experience gained from actual cases.

Case studies can be used both as a teaching tool for less experienced economists, as well as to stimulate a high level discussion of economic models. The exchange of ideas on hot topics – areas where new research results have particular relevance for enforcement, such as new methods established for dealing with two-sided markets, could be particularly beneficial for more experienced antitrust economists.

Through interaction in ICN working groups or tailored workshops or webinars, agency economists will get to know one another, much like their legal and investigative counterparts. This familiarity is likely to lead to enhanced cooperation, both for specific cases as well as for policy issues, as it has in other disciplines.

The ICN has benefitted from private sector participation in all areas of work product, and while initial efforts should be made to reach out to agency economists, private sector economists also could contribute to discussions and debate.

4. CONCLUSION: THE ROAD AHEAD

In conclusion, the benefits from enhanced participation by agency economists accrue to the ICN, to member agencies, and to individual agency economists. By providing practicing antitrust economists with a platform to engage generally and on specific topics, the ICN facilitates the constructive relationships forged across competition agencies for other disciplines. By integrating economists more fully in the network's activities, the ICN will quicken the pace and depth of convergence by making use of the more unified view of antitrust offered by economics.

THE ICN AT 20 – LOOKING AHEAD

Margarida Matos Rosa*

1. ORIGINS AND KEY ASPECTS OF THE ICN

The International Competition Network ("ICN") is a rather unique case of informal project-based cooperation between competition agencies on a global scale. Its origins trace back to the work of the International Competition Policy Advisory Committee ("ICPAC"), a group which addressed global competition issues and cooperation in the context of economic globalization, following the Uruguay Trade Round in the late 1990s. In its final February 2000 report,[1] ICPAC proposed the creation of a Global Competition Initiative – a ground zero for the future ICN – focused on promoting convergence of competition rules worldwide.

Following international recognition of the necessity and viability of promoting cooperation and advocating for best practices in competition matters around the globe, in an era of economic globalization, the ICN was created in October 25th, 2001.[2] The creation of the ICN was directly linked to the liberalization of, and resulting increase in, world trade, which led to a call by the international community for a global competition agenda.[3] Its establishment followed that of the World Trade Organization ("WTO") in 1995, and took place somewhat later than other global standard-setters, such as IOSCO[4] (launched in 1983), IAIS[5] (founded in 1994) or ICER[6] (2000, as WFER).

---

* Portuguese Competition Authority.

1 See International Competition Policy Advisory Committee, Final Report (2000): https://www.justice.gov/atr/final-report.

2 See https://www.internationalcompetitionnetwork.org/about/.

3 P. Lugard (ed), *The International Competition Network at Ten – Origins, Accomplishments and Aspirations*, Cambridge – Antwerp – Portland: Intersentia, 2011, p. 10.

4 See International Organization of Securities Commissions (IOSCO): https://www.iosco.org/about/?subsection=about_iosco.

5 See International Association of Insurance Supervisors (IAIS): https://www.iaisweb.org/page/about-the-iais.

6 See International Confederation of Energy Regulators (ICER): http://icer-regulators.net/history/.

The ICN was initially founded by 14 competition agencies.[7] Since then, the ICN has grown with an overarching success in developing both advocacy and enforcement cooperation strategies, alongside a global proliferation of competition regimes. It has seen its membership increase to nearly 150 member agencies – a remarkable growth for a specialized – yet informal – network about to reach the end of its second decade of existence.

As a global network of competition agencies, organized *by* and *for* member agencies, the scope of the ICN's portfolio of projects inevitably has to embrace challenges in different jurisdictions – including challenges that both "newer" and "established" agencies face. In its early years, the ICN focused on three goals: establishment, working modes and expansion of the organization.[8] This was a prolific period in defining areas of mutual interest, promoting recommended practices and finding different methods of promoting coordination between member agencies. Later, during its second decade of existence, four high-level goals were identified by the ICN: (1) encouraging the dissemination of competition experience and best practices; (2) formulating proposals for procedural and substantive convergence through a results-oriented agenda and structure; (3) supporting competition advocacy; and (4) facilitating effective international cooperation.[9] These objectives have been the premise for the core work of the ICN in recent years and have allowed the network to distinguish itself from the work of other international networks, which include the Organisation for Economic Co-operation and Development ("OECD") or United Nations Conference on Trade and Development ("UNCTAD") – producing complementary policy products.

The ICN, as a project oriented network that does not rely on a permanent secretariat, carries out much of its activities in working groups which bring together member agencies and non-governmental advisors ("NGAs"). Once a year, the ICN gathers at its annual conference to discuss working group projects, which include both advocacy and enforcement policies. Member agencies are able to participate in these working groups without committing to specific amendments to their law or policy – a "soft law" approach that fosters a wider participation. As such, the ICN's work is effective in providing added value in the

---

7 Australia, Canada, the European Union, France, Germany, Israel, Italy, Japan, Korea, Mexico, South Africa, the United Kingdom, the United States, and Zambia. See International Competition Network (ICN): https://www.internationalcompetitionnetwork.org/about/.

8 Andreas Mundt, *Focus, inclusiveness and implementation – The ICN as a key factor for global convergence in competition law*, ICN Chair's Vision Statement, 2013: https://www.internationalcompetitionnetwork.org/wp-content/uploads/2018/07/ICNSGMundtVision.pdf

9 International Competition Network, *The future of the ICN in its second decade – Final Report*, Presented at the ICN Steering Group Meeting, 15 June 2016, Paris, p. 4: https://www.internationalcompetitionnetwork.org/wp-content/uploads/2018/09/ICN2dDecade2016.pdf

exchange of experiences, in the development of convergence and in international enforcement cooperation between members. This has boosted the discussion on handling competition matters that have cross-border impacts, such as mergers, cartels, unilateral conduct, agency effectiveness and advocacy. Overall, the ICN has been a ubiquitous network in the promotion and discussion of the most significant and trending global competition issues.

The ICN's vibrant work has resulted in clear achievements, including recommended practices,[10] case-handling and enforcement manuals, reports, templates on legislation and rules in different jurisdictions, databases, toolkits and workshops, proving itself to be an increasingly relevant actor in the global competition scene.[11]

The Portuguese Competition Authority (*Autoridade da Concorrência*, or "AdC") has been an active participant in the production of a wide range of ICN work products and has shared its experience in the promotion of competition rules, contributing to an increasingly effective competition legal framework. Simultaneously, it has also benefitted from several landmark work products produced in the ICN context.

The steady growth of the ICN did not occur without an extensive reflection on its work by its members and various stakeholders, conducted throughout its existence – the ability to adapt to the different challenges of globalization impacting its members has always been one of the key reasons for the network's success. In that regard, in 2010, reaching the end of the first decade of existence of the ICN, former Chair John Fingleton requested ICN members and participating NGAs to assess the network's accomplishments and identify further objectives for the future.[12] In May 2011, the ICN presented the Second Decade Project reflecting on a new vision for the ICN. Following the Second Decade Project, in 2015, ICN's Chair Andreas Mundt proposed a reassessment of the ICN's goals. The final report on "The future of the ICN in its second decade", presented at the ICN Steering Group Meeting on the 15th of June 2016, in Paris, contained several suggestions from ICN members and NGAs, both on goals and process, as well as on topics and type of work products. An example of a successful feature of the ICN's work product, driven by the network's innovative spirit, is the implementation of the ICN Training on Demand, which

10 See https://www.internationalcompetitionnetwork.org/working-groups/icn-operations/icn-frecs/

11 ICN Factsheet and Key Messages, April 2009, p. 8–9: https://www.internationalcompetitionnetwork.org/wp-content/uploads/2018/09/Factsheet2009.pdf

12 International Competition Network, *The future of the ICN in its second decade – Final Report*, Presented at the ICN Steering Group Meeting, 15 June 2016, Paris, p. 3: https://www.internationalcompetitionnetwork.org/wp-content/uploads/2018/09/ICN2dDecade2016.pdf.

created a comprehensive curriculum of virtual training materials, organized in different modules. These materials have been widely acceptance and used in the international competition community.[13] This ability of the ICN to be creative and responsive to the circumstances of globalization has been key in its continued success in both addressing enforcement and policy issues, as well as in providing avenues for substantive and procedural convergence.

The ability of the ICN to sustain and increase its relevance on a global scale necessarily depends on its proximity to the needs of members and being as flexible and dynamic as possible in order to face multiple globalization challenges. A clear example is the challenges brought by the digitalization of the economy, which have an increasingly global impact on the scope of agencies' work, as we reach the end of the second decade of the ICN's existence. The ability of the ICN to actively foster the discussion and the sharing of experiences and policies – as well as mutual work between agencies – on recent trending phenomena, such as, for instance, issues in digital ecosystems, data or algorithms – to which the AdC has contributed,[14] in the midst of a global discussion – is certainly the path to increase its relevance and further attract participation from its members and NGAs.

That is one of the true challenges for the ICN: to bolster its vigorous spirit and ability to promote the discussion of innovative issues, improving enforcement and advocacy of competition law on a global scale, while respecting differences that may exist or emerge between legal frameworks.[15] However, and while innovation should play a key role in the ICN's agenda, its members should not overlook "newer" agencies' challenges and should continuously embrace their needs, thereby promoting wider global cooperation.

2. WHAT THE FUTURE COULD BRING

The ICN has built its strengths and distinctive features on what could be have been considered its weaknesses: informality, project-based work, and diversity of its members (in terms of size, maturity, geography, political, economic and social context). Instead, this has made the ICN rather unique in the landscape of international cooperation, let alone in the field of competition policy.

---

13 See https://www.internationalcompetitionnetwork.org/training/

14 See AdC, *Issues paper on Digital Ecosystems, Big Data and Algorithms*, 2019: www.concorrencia.pt/vPT/Estudos_e_Publicacoes/Estudos_Economicos/Outros/Documents/Digital%20Ecosystems,%20Big%20Data%20and%20Algorithms%20-%20Issues%20Paper.pdf

15 H. M. Hollman and William E. Kovacic, "The International Competition Network: Its Past, Current and Future Role", (2011) *Minnesota Journal of International Law*, p. 284.

Those idiosyncrasies are also the key to the challenges that lie ahead for the next decade, namely (i) enlargement, (ii) implementation; and (iii) the ICN's institutional role. Some thoughts on each of these challenges are shared below.

2.1. ENLARGEMENT AND THE IMPLICATIONS OF A GLOBAL NETWORK

The ICN is rightly a global network that has expanded to all continents. Each year, new agencies join the network, adding further nuance and experience, as well as challenges.

New members are encouraged to join as soon as a competition agency is established in a given jurisdiction. Even before a competition agency is formally established, the ICN may play a role in offering guidance to the setup of new agencies, by means of its work products and by allowing observers to attend its events.

However, the expansion of the network poses the challenge of language barriers. In order for ICN work products to become everyday tools within an agency, language barriers may need to be addressed so as to maximize the effectiveness of competition policy enforcement.

As ICN members become more numerous, the challenge of encouraging the participation of NGAs on a global level also becomes more prominent. When a competition agency joins the ICN, it is desirable that the NGAs from that jurisdiction become active members as well. The ICN benefits greatly from the participation of NGAs, as does the full competition ecosystem. NGA engagement enriches the discussions both at the level of the ICN and internally, fostering the maturity of local competition communities. Again language issues may impair NGA participation.

With a view to addressing such concerns, the AdC has volunteered its resources by translating a set of work products into Portuguese as a means to amplify their usefulness and impact among Portuguese-speaking jurisdictions. Furthermore, it has promoted sessions in Portuguese language in key ICN events so as to enhance participation from Portuguese-speaking countries.

2.2. IMPLEMENTATION – EXTRACTING VALUE FROM THE ICN

The ICN work product portfolio has greatly expanded over the years, both in terms of format and substantive issues covered. The obvious ensuing challenge is to promote its awareness and implementation, closing the gap between ICN guidance and practice by agencies. Implementation is a long-standing priority of the ICN, and there have been many successes in this regard, resulting in legislative reform or overhaul of internal procedures.

The ICN Promotion and Implementation ("P&I") group, currently co-chaired by the AdC, Mexican Federal Economic Competition Commission ("COFECE") and the United States Federal Trade Commission, is tasked with the mission of *"raising awareness of ICN work product and promot[ing] its implementation, engaging members, working groups, and non-governmental advisors"*[16], using simple but effective tools, such as the work product catalogue, peer-to-peer contacts, and sessions in key ICN events to showcase successful implementation stories.

However, awareness and implementation are wider ICN concerns which are also taken into account by Working Groups. Working Groups provide self-assessment tools for member agencies (e.g. self-assessment tools of the Merger Working Group on the Recommended Practices for Merger Notification and Review Procedures), that are instrumental in identifying areas of reform and sparking internal debate on whether amendments of legislation or agencies' practice are in need. Awareness and implementation are as important to the success of the ICN as the production of new work products.

The challenge of engagement and participation in ICN events is also linked to a wider membership. Geographic dispersion of members calls for ensuring regional diversity in the hosting of ICN events. It is clear that events' geographic dispersion is key to maximizing attendance and awareness from a wide array of regional stakeholders. Formats and contents of ICN events are made relevant to the region hosting them. Nevertheless, ICN events combine overarching goals which make sure that each agency can benefit from such events; such goals include substantive discussions, experience-sharing, training and networking. Agendas and speakers thus ensure that each event is relevant for all agencies, irrespective of their maturity. Thorough discussions among members while planning each event are therefore the right approach so as to ensure that the goals of inclusiveness and relevance are attained.

2.3. INSTITUTIONAL ENGAGEMENT AND POSITIONING

The ICN interacts with global, regional and domestic competition communities and networks, such as the OECD, UNCTAD or, at regional levels, the Association of Southeast Asian Nations, the African Competition Forum or

16 See https://www.internationalcompetitionnetwork.org/working-groups/icn-operations/implementation/.

European Competition Network. This allows the ICN to enhance its relevance for its membership and reach a wider audience. But as competition policy evolves worldwide – alongside a proliferation of *fora* for debate – exploring synergies, complementarity and experience-sharing with other institutions and networks is a motto for the future.

Meanwhile, the ICN also reaches out to other areas of regulation and public policy. But in order to attain a higher impact, and higher effectiveness of competition policy, that dialogue may need to be strengthened in coming years. Competition policy does not develop in a vacuum in any jurisdiction. The interplay of competition policy with consumer policy, privacy and data regulation, or sector regulation is a topical issue, which poses the challenge of preserving the advantages of a specialized network while allowing for dialogue with other policy areas.

Moreover, the ICN may reflect on playing a wider institutional role, namely when approaching policy-makers. As technical and methodological issues of competition policy (re)enter the political debate, the ICN may be called to play a role in developing expert consensus. The ICN may contribute to communicate a competition point of view in wider policy. For instance, the ICN may be the international expert voice on issues such competition and trade, or competition and industrial policy, or even competition and financial stability.

Recently, the ICN served as a platform to reach a wider policy consensus on due process – i.e. the ICN Framework on Competition Agency Procedures ("CAP")-, reaching out to non ICN members. As other policy concerns emerge, there may be areas where the ICN could wish to provide a specific platform for members and non-members to adhere to particular principles.

2.4. EMBEDDING COMPETITION IN OTHER POLICIES

The advancement of institutional engagement discussed above finds a rare opportunity in the aftermath of the Covid-19 pandemic and consequent economic shock. As countries endeavour to support – whether financially or through other means – their economies while triggering reform in areas such as climate change and digitalization, the ICN and its members may find it important to voice the benefits of competition principles.[17] Competition

17 See for example, *The role of competition in implementing the economic recovery strategy*, Autoridade da Concorrência (AdC), June 2021 www.concorrencia.pt/vEN/Estudos_e_Publicacoes/Estudos_Economicos/Other/Documents/2021%20-%20AdC%20contribution%20on%20economic%20recovery.pdf.

as a catalyst for economic recovery, across sectors and across countries, is the message that the ICN can lever on with other institutions. In this rare occasion of economic recovery across the globe, the ICN may significantly induce an increased adherence to principles of competition policy such as reducing unnecessary barriers to entry and expansion, promoting competitive and efficient public procurement procedures and ensuring competitive neutrality in state support.

3. FINAL WORDS

The ICN has developed over time as a success story of a global, flexible, and competition-agency-based network. It has crafted its very own identity. More importantly, it has achieved its goals of promoting convergence, implementation of internationally recognized recommended practice and exchange between authorities, colleagues and with the wider community.

As a mature – yet vibrant – group, the ICN is now well-positioned to have a stronger and much needed institutional presence in the policy-making sphere, alongside other global and regional actors. In this manner, ICN will more effectively voice the benefits of competition policy, particularly in a post-pandemic economic recovery scenario.

THE ICN'S ROLE IN TRANSFORMING CARTEL ENFORCEMENT

Neil Campbell and Guy Pinsonnault

Cartel activity has long been recognized as the most clear-cut concern of competition laws. Over the past two decades, the scope and effectiveness of anti-cartel enforcement has increased dramatically. The International Competition Network ("ICN") has played a vital role in this transformation by contributing to the proliferation of modernized competition laws, increasing the effectiveness of enforcement agencies, building connectivity between enforcers, and fostering widespread consensus on the use of leniency programs as a primary enforcement tool.

1. PROLIFERATION

In the 1990s there were a modest number of jurisdictions with vigorous and effective competition law regimes. In the cartel area, only the United States ("US"), European Union ("EU"), Canada and a few other jurisdictions were actively pursuing both domestic and international cartel activity.

The ICN's role in competition law proliferation is well known. Its membership has grown from 16 founding agencies in 2001 to more than 140 competition agencies in 2020. Much of this growth correlates with the introduction or modernization of competition laws in jurisdictions on every continent. This phenomenon has broad economic and political drivers such as globalization, deregulation, trade liberalization and technological development. But the ICN was not merely a passive beneficiary of such developments; it established credibility as a "virtual network" that was important to belong to. Participation in this "competition club" brings incentives and "peer pressure" to introduce or upgrade the three fundamental pillars of competition laws: cartel, unilateral conduct and merger rules. Most of the vastly expanded ICN membership has embraced cartel enforcement as a core component of agency mandates.

2. AGENCY EFFECTIVENESS

From its earliest days, the ICN's primary focus has been on helping agencies to do their enforcement work more effectively. The ICN's annual conference and the Agency Effectiveness Working Group have been critical elements of this mission, working alongside its substantive working groups.

The Cartel Working Group ("CWG"), along with the Merger Working Group and the Unilateral Conduct Working Group, have ensured that the ICN's substantive work is anchored on practical enforcement issues and challenges in each of these key areas. The CWG has produced a tremendous portfolio of work products, including recommended practices, manuals, reports, checklists and templates.

The CWG's core 'Anti-Cartel Enforcement Manual' has steadily been expanded to address a wide range of enforcement issues ranging from evidence gathering and case strategy to broader system design and policy issues:

- Searches, Raids and Inspections (2009)
- Drafting and Implementing an Effective Leniency Program (2014)
- Digital Evidence Gathering (2014)
- Cartel Case Initiation (2010)
- Investigative Strategy (2008)
- Interviewing Techniques (2008)
- Case Resolution (2011)
- Cartel Awareness, Outreach and Compliance (2012)
- International Cooperation and Information Sharing (2013)
- Relationship between Competition Agencies and Public Procurement Bodies (2015)
- Development of Private Enforcement of Competition Law (2019)
- Compilation of Good Practices from the Anti-Cartel Enforcement Manual (2017)

The CWG has also been prolific in generating other work product that catalogues and supports expanding agency enforcement efforts. Examples include:

- 'Report on Building Blocks for Effective Anti-Cartel Regimes' (2005)
- 'Report on Obstruction of Justice in Cartel Investigations' (2006)
- 'Interaction of Public and Private Enforcement in Cartel Cases' (2007)
- 'Cooperation Between Competition Agencies in Cartel Investigations' (2007)
- 'Cartel Settlements' (2008)
- 'Trends and Developments in Cartel Enforcement' (2010)

- 'Charts Summarizing Information Sharing Mechanisms' (2012)
- 'Leniency Waiver Templates' (2014)
- 'Online Compilation of Cartel Awareness and Outreach Materials' (2014)
- 'Catalogue of Investigative Powers for Cartel Investigations' (2016)
- 'Checklist for Efficient and Effective Leniency Programmes' (2017)
- 'Setting of Fines for Cartels in ICN Jurisdictions' (2017)
- 'Good Practices for Incentivizing Leniency Applications' (2019)
- 'Anti-Cartel Enforcement Templates' (revised as needed)
- 'Framework for the Promotion of the Sharing of Non-confidential Information' (continued operation)

Producing work products is not itself an overriding goal; rather, it is a building block towards achieving the goal of improving and advocating for sound competition policy and its enforcement around the world. The value of the ICN's work products have been confirmed and enhanced through their widespread use by member and even non-member agencies.

This effort has been reinforced by an enormous number of professional development programs and events including teleseminars, webinars (the ICN's website contains an extensive list of CWG webinars which illustrates this activity), and annual workshops. Such programs disseminate, review, and extend the CWG work products. The CWG annual workshops have made a particularly significant contribution to upgrading the skills and effectiveness of developing agencies.

3. CONNECTIVITY

The annual conference and workshop events, and the ongoing working group projects, generate a continuous flow of professional and social interactions among agency personnel. Importantly, such relationship-building opportunities are occurring not only at the leadership level, but also across a wide range of management and staff personnel. The importance of these interactions on the ICN platform (as well as at the OECD, bar association and other international conferences – the ICN does not have a monopoly!) should not be underestimated. They help to foster common understandings of enforcement challenges, facilitate exchanges of know-how, and encourage cooperative approaches on international cases. While impact is difficult to quantify, the significant "soft convergence" in competition law design and enforcement that has occurred over the past two decades is undoubtedly partly enabled by the familiarity and trust that come from repeated and meaningful personal contact and relationships fostered over the past two decades.

The presence of non-governmental advisors ("NGAs") from the private sector has amplified these phenomena. NGA's provide "real-world" perspectives on how policies and practices are likely to function or have been functioning, as well as the ways in which they are responded to by companies and their advisors. The expansion of professional and personal relationships between officials and NGAs has also contributed to greater levels of communication and trust that manifest in enforcement cases. In particular, leniency programs have benefited from strengthened working relationships facilitated in part through the ICN.

One of the most important enablers for this collegial environment is the originating principle that the ICN focus will be "all antitrust, all the time". Another is that agencies and officials are participating in their own capacities, in contrast to the formal, cautious style of interaction that occurs when statements or actions are viewed as official commitments or positions. Such government-to-government communications potentially need to be coordinated with an array of officials with responsibilities related to economic policies (as, for example, can be seen in the failed efforts to develop an agreement on competition law and policy framework) and are antithetical to open-ended discussions and explorations of enforcers' challenges and areas of mutual interest. As a corollary, it is explicit that ICN guiding principles, recommended practices, guides and other outputs are non-binding. Collectively, these ground rules create a "safe space" in which competition enforcers have been able confer and collaborate candidly, even on issues that may involve heavy potential cartel penalty exposures for companies and citizens from their own jurisdictions in cross-border cases.

4. COOPERATION

In the 1970 and 1980s, the OECD's 'Recommendation on Restrictive Business Practices Affecting International Trade' was, in part, an effort to build a consensus that cartel conduct has no redeeming qualities and that enforcement should be encouraged. However, much of the focus was on sovereignty, conflict avoidance and comity, as manifested through the commitments to notify and consult other jurisdictions when enforcement action would affect their firms and interests. Various bilateral "memoranda of understanding"-type instruments adopted similar approaches.

Beginning in the 1990s, perhaps because of the increasing frequency and scope of mergers being reviewed in multiple jurisdictions, agencies began to explore opportunities for more positive cooperation and collaboration on cross-border cases. Such efforts soon emerged in cartel investigations as well, with cases such as lysine, citric acid and vitamins representing early break-throughs. By

Valentine's Day of 2006, numerous agencies had developed an unprecedented plan for coordinated dawn raids and related enforcement actions around the world in the air cargo cases (neatly timed to coincide with the ABA/IBA bi-annual International Cartel Workshop!).

While the ICN is certainly not the only driver of this remarkable evolution from comity to cooperation, it was one of the critical building blocks. Following the CWG's 2007 work on cross-border cooperation, a chapter was added to the 'Anti-Cartel Enforcement Manual' in 2013 which documented and promoted mechanisms for international cooperation and information sharing by agencies that are interested in undertaking cooperation in cross-border investigations. The CWG has also established frameworks related to sharing of non-confidential information and assisting agencies in knowing how and who to contact when seeking information from counterparts, charts that summarize the mechanisms available to share information, and confidentiality waiver templates for cooperating parties, among other measures to promote cooperation.

5. THE LENIENCY PROGRAM CONSENSUS

In the early 1990s, the US Department of Justice, under Gary Spratling's leadership, pioneered the design of a first-in "amnesty" (referred to as "immunity" or "leniency" in various other jurisdictions) program that reduced the uncertainty related to investigator / prosecutor discretion and established strong "carrot and stick" incentives for cartelists to break ranks and cooperate with enforcement authorities. It proved to be spectacularly effective. Early adopters of this approach included the Canadian Competition Bureau and the European Commission.

Gradually, over a quarter of a century, this model has been elaborated and fine-tuned – particularly in respect of "paperless processes" to reduce disincentives arising from private/class actions for damages, and the incentives provided to induce subsequent cooperating parties ("leniency applicants"). This general approach has subsequently been incorporated into the vast majority of modernized anti-cartel regimes, albeit with assorted local procedural variations.

Of the many agencies, bar associations (IBA, ABA, etc.) and other institutions that have played a role in this extraordinary, non-negotiated international convergence, the CWG surely ranks as one of the most important. Its annual workshops and projects provided a prominent and stable environment in which agencies could discuss the design, operation and outcomes of leniency programs as a domestic enforcement tool. They also provided the primary forum for considering how cooperation in cross-border cases could be enhanced using such programs.

The 'Anti-Cartel Enforcement Manual' addressed 'Drafting and Implementing an Effective Leniency Program' at an early stage and this important chapter was updated in 2014. In 2017, the CWG issued the 'Checklist for Efficient and Effective Leniency Programs', which sets out various considerations when designing or amending leniency regimes. In April 2019, the CWG published 'Good Practices for Incentivizing Leniency Applications', which discusses the interface between leniency and the potential exposures flowing from private litigation and sanctions for individuals in addition to agency enforcement proceedings. This initiative is an initial response to perceptions that the cumulative international public and private legal exposures facing parties that have been involved in international cartel activity, and the time and cost burdens of cooperation, may be contributing to the significant decline in leniency applications observed around the world in recent years.

6. CONCLUDING OBSERVATIONS

The decline in international cartel cases may in part reflect that the concerted global efforts to investigate, penalize and compensate parties injured by cartel conduct are having some deterrent effect in the international business community. To the extent this is the case, the ICN can properly claim a portion of the credit for progress on this shared objective of governments and their competition enforcement authorities. However, it is likely that there is still considerable anti-competitive conduct that is not being self-reported or detected. As the ICN's CWG enters its third decade of work, it is well-placed to make further contributions to leniency regimes and to agency effectiveness in detecting and taking enforcement action against problematic conduct that is not self-reported.

WHO IS GLOBAL IF NOT THE ICN?

ICN Milestones and the Future of the Agencies Network

Andreas Mundt*

1. INTRO

Even after nearly 20 years, I am still impressed that our network of agencies is not a vision but reality. Every year when all member agencies and NGAs come together at the ICN Annual conference to reflect on what we have done and to define the future, we can really see what we have created. Looking back on the birth of the ICN in Naples in 2001 and comparing that time to today's conferences, we realize that the ICN has taken us a long way. The ICN is unique in the way it operates on a purely informal and voluntary basis and is nonetheless the most important organisation for competition agencies in the world today.

2. FIVE MILESTONES

The ICN is a vibrant organisation. Every year we have many in person, or as in the last year, virtual events – workshops, teleseminars and webinars. The working groups develop work products that serve as a basis for global standards. When the ICN was established and took up operation, I was involved as Head of the International Unit of the Bundeskartellamt which is a founding member of the ICN and I was a member of the MWG group in 2001 on its way to establishing the first ICN Recommended Practices. The foundation of the ICN was a formative experience for everyone involved and when I look back on special steps in the development of the network, I also look at highlights in the context of my work in international business.

---

* Andreas Mundt has been President of the Bundeskartellamt since December 2009, member of the Bureau of the OECD Competition Committee since 2010 and the Steering Group Chair of the ICN since 2013.

Given the dynamic nature of the network, there are many ICN highlights, but I will pick only five milestones, which I think illustrate the unique features of our network:

1. The first milestone is the foundation of the ICN. That was a big step. We take today's status for granted, which shows how well the system works. However, things did not go as smoothly at that time.
2. The ICN's first Recommended Practices are the second milestone. They stand for two ICN characteristics: speed and impact.
3. Opening up the ICN to new topics is the third milestone, which illustrates the member-driven nature of the network.
4. The forth milestone, the ICN Framework for Competition Agency Procedures (ICN CAP) could only be accomplished because of the level of trust and confidence members have in the ICN, as well as their willingness to break new ground.
5. The fifth milestone is the focus on digital topics, which marks the transition to the ICN's future.

2.1. 1ST MILESTONE: HOW IT ALL STARTED

At the Steering Group Meeting at the first ICN Annual Conference in Naples on 29 September 2002, it was observed that the conference was the first item on CNN's business news. However, it was by no means a given that we would get there. ICN was a novel idea: a group of competition authorities formed to satisfy the need for a forum that would help further cooperation and facilitate convergence as an answer to overambitious unsuccessful attempts by governments.

Improvement in cooperation had been discussed for years and the debates on how to address competition in the context of globalisation were at times emotional and sophisticated. There was a common understanding that competition agencies needed to cooperate more closely, the question was how. When discussions started in the early 1990s, several well-established organisations dealing with competition issues already existed: the OECD, UNCTAD, and cooperation also took place at regional level. However, despite the fact that well-respected international organisations already operated successfully, there was a strong desire to take multilateral cooperation to the next level. However, it was unclear which direction to take.

Very different approaches were discussed, sometimes in parallel for years, including the most ambitious vision of all, a global competition law, an international antitrust authority and a dispute resolution panel. An international competition framework within the WTO was considered and this really got underway at the Singapore WTO Ministerial in December 1996, when the EU initiated a Working Group on the Interaction between Trade and Competition Policy. Shortly afterwards, a whole new plot strand was initiated: The International Competition Policy Advisory Committee (ICPAC) was established in November 1997 "to address the global antitrust problems of the 21st Century". This time, the driving force was not Europe but the US. In its final report, issued in February 2000, ICPAC proposed the creation of a new venue, a Global Competition Initiative, where government officials, private firms and non-governmental organisations could consult on antitrust matters. ICPAC recommended that this Global Competition Initiative be directed towards greater convergence of competition law and analysis, common understanding, and common culture. Then things happened fast. ICPAC's recommendation for a Global Competition Initiative was embraced. Joel Klein and Mario Monti expressed their support for the initiative. Following these endorsements, the International Bar Association convened the Ditchley Park meeting in February 2001 to discuss feasibility and on 25 October 2001, top antitrust officials from 14 jurisdictions – Australia, Canada, the EU, France, Germany, Israel, Italy, Japan, Korea, Mexico, South Africa, the UK, the US, and Zambia – launched the ICN.[1] Shortly before the first ICN Annual Conference in Naples, a new name for the new organisation had to be found. The initial idea and working title of the ICN had been "Global Competition Network". After the riots at the G8 meeting in Geneva in 2001, the word "Global" had become a somewhat taboo word and the Italian Competition Authority feared new protests at the first Annual Conference if a "Global" organisation was to hold a conference in Naples. In a quite spontaneous teleconference, the new organisation was renamed the International Competition Network, the ICN we know today.

The first few years of the organisation resulted in fast growth and very lively discussions, and even though the ICN has a superlight structure and no headquarters and staff like other organisations, it has managed to develop its own stable institutional framework. Indeed, the growth of the ICN is quite impressive and we take pride in the fact that the organisation is attractive not only to mature agencies but also to young agencies. Today the ICN's membership is as diverse, in terms of agency size, organisation, enforcement environment, geographic diversity etc., as our tasks, and this factor is one of the main assets of the ICN.

2.2. 2ND MILESTONE: THE FIRST ICN RECOMMENDED PRACTICES

The first flagship project and earliest success story was the adoption of the Recommended Practices for Merger Notification and Review Procedures. Multi-

---

1 ICN, "About > History", www.internationalcompetitionnetwork.org/about/history.aspx, accessed 6 Aug 2018.

jurisdictional mergers had become one of the main challenges for competition authorities and companies and they were a key factor in the decision to establish the ICN. The first Annual Conference in Naples in September 2002 focused on issues arising in the context of mergers subject to multi-jurisdictional review. In Naples, the Merger Working Group's Notification and Procedures Subgroup presented a set of Guiding Principles and Recommended Practices for Merger Notification and Review Procedures which were the starting point for procedural convergence in international merger control regimes and encouraged competition authorities to further coordinate their approach and to create a level playing field for business, legal certainty and efficiency. The subgroup was chaired by Randy Tritell, US FTC, who is one of the few people to have joined all the ICN annual conferences and who has been a member of the ICN steering group ever since. I remember the discussions very well as I participated in the subgroup in my capacity as Head of the International Unit together with about a dozen other agencies and the OECD.

The Recommended Practices of the Merger Working Group are an example of the direct influence that the ICN's work products have on antitrust regimes, including mature agencies. After the first annual conference, the then President of the Bundeskartellamt received a letter from a representative of the Studienvereinigung Kartellrecht, the association of German-speaking lawyers from Germany, Austria, Switzerland and Brussels specialising in competition law, who had joined the conference, and emphasised in his letter that if the Recommended Practices really were implemented, this would prompt legislative changes. Indeed, living up to the ICN's recommendations was one facilitating factor in bringing about a domestic reform in Germany, which strengthened the local nexus of merger control. Taking stock at the 5th Annual ICN Conference in Cape Town in May 2006, the ICN Chair observed in his opening speech that notwithstanding the non-binding nature of the Recommended Practices, by March 2006 already 33 ICN member jurisdictions had made changes to their merger control regime, bringing their system into greater conformity with the Recommended Practices.

2.3. 3RD MILESTONE: OPENING THE ICN TO NEW TOPICS – FLEXIBLE AND MEMBER-DRIVEN

In identifying the content of its work and accomplishing it, the ICN is member-driven in every sense. The high degree of participation in the ICN has never impaired the ICN's flexibility. The ICN works very well without a formal secretariat, permanent employees or its own budget, relying only on very dedicated staff in the various competition agencies and many Non-Governmental Advisors around the world. No other relevant organisation is so closely geared to the desires and needs of its members. The ICN's flexible and member-driven bottom-up approach can realize ideas quickly and has enabled the ICN to take on new topics and adapt its structure accordingly. This bottom-up approach is a unique feature of the ICN, a feature I consider extremely important to preserve. This observation still fits today, but it was made in Bonn in 2004 by Ulf Böge,then President of the Bundeskartellamt and ICN Chair in his closing speech at the 4th ICN Annual Conference.

The first ICN Working Groups dealt with mergers and advocacy because it had become apparent that the increase in multinational cross-border mergers meant that the competition authorities had to increase their efforts. After the first Annual Conference in Naples, the ICN established the Working Group Capacity Building and Competition Policy Implementation chaired by DG COMP and the South African competition agency. Taking into account the responses of members to new topics to be taken up by the ICN, the 2nd ICN Annual Conference in Merida, Mexico, in June 2003, decided to set up the Antitrust Enforcement in Regulated Sectors (AERS) Working Group chaired by the French and the Italian authorities. The 3rd ICN Annual Conference in Seoul in 2004 marked a crucial step for the network. At that time there were different views on the areas of competition law enforcement that should be covered by ICN, and one view was to focus on mergers. However, the Steering Group came to the conclusion to open up the network to new topics, which is best illustrated by the foundation of the Cartel Working Group in Seoul, inter alia in response to queries from Ulf Böge. Already only one year later, at the Annual Conference in Bonn, the Cartel Working Group presented two chapters of the Anti-Cartel Enforcement Manual. More ICN Working Groups followed. The ICN Working Group on Telecommunications Services, co-chaired by the Canadian Competition Bureau, the Italian Antitrust Agency and the South Africa Competition Tribunal, was set up in 2005 just six weeks after David Lewis proposed the topic and presented its report at the 5th Annual Conference in Cape Town in 2006. In Cape Town the ICN established the Unilateral Conduct Working Group chaired by the US FTC and the Bundeskartellamt which in its first year saw a level of participation unprecedented in the ICN, with 40 working group member authorities and 80 non-governmental advisors. The group elaborated questionnaires and compiled a Report on the Objectives of Unilateral Conduct Laws and Assessment of Dominance, and State-Created Monopolies. Then the group took a bold step and decided to set forth in developing Recommended Practices on the Assessment of Dominance based on this report. At the beginning of this project, quite a few people thought it was very doubtful that the group would ever achieve this aim. Given that dominance analysis is discussed controversially even within jurisdictions and their agencies, it seemed all the more difficult, if not impossible, for a number of agencies from different legal traditions and systems to agree on Recommended Practices. However, each and every member of the Working Group made great efforts and in long and controversial but also highly interesting, constructive and fruitful discussions the group eventually reached consensus and presented the Recommended Practices at the 7th Annual conference in Kyoto.

Today we have five operative working groups, but the current structure is never more than a mere snapshot. Agencies are confronted with issues different to those identified when ICN was established. ICN projects follow its members' needs and the ICN's structure ensures direct input from its membership. All ICN working group members are involved when work plans are drafted, and the whole ICN membership is asked to provide input at regular intervals. Shortly before completing its first decade of existence, the ICN took stock and asked its members to consider the benefits of ICN participation and to identify any improvements needed. The results of this process helped establish the Second Decade report, a long-term vision and strategy paper for the ICN. Five years later, in 2015, we conducted a follow-up and invited ICN member agencies to complete surveys addressing their participation, views on work products and implementation, and ideas for the ICN's future. The corresponding report provided valuable impulses for our network and again demonstrated the ICN's practical relevance and real-world impact. It turned out that more than half of the respondents had used ICN guidance documents to develop or revise internal procedures, guidelines and best practices, and that agencies frequently refer to ICN work products when engaging in competition advocacy and use ICN products as an important source of information and inspiration to support, advance, or improve proposals to review or amend national competition laws. Now it is time for the Third Decade-Project to assess the tools, topics, and operations of the network in order to provide a roadmap for the ICN's work during its third decade.

2.4. 4TH MILESTONE – THE ICN CAP

In 2019, the ICN established a new instrument on procedural fairness in competition law investigations and enforcement proceedings, the ICN Framework for Competition Agency Procedures (CAP). At the Annual Conference in Cartagena a remarkable panel with speakers from the US DOJ, FAS Russia, JFTC Japan, DG COMP, COFECE Mexico, South African Competition Commission and the Bundeskartellamt presented the CAP to the ICN membership and it went into effect with over 60 agency participants. The ICN CAP is an opt-in framework, open to all agencies including those that are not ICN members. It builds on fundamental principles of fair and effective agency procedures fully consistent with the extensive work of the ICN in this field such as non-discrimination, transparency, notice of investigation, timely resolution, confidentiality protections, impartial enforcement, opportunity to defend, representation, and judicial review, reflecting the broad consensus within the global competition community. It allows for agency-to-agency dialogue to increase understanding of differences in agency procedures, and promotes transparency about agency procedural rules through templates that explain how each participant's procedures match ICN CAP principles. The starting point was the MFP project brought forward by the US DOJ in June 2018, which has been developed into the ICN CAP as an ICN Steering Group project.

Fair and effective agency investigative process is essential to sound competition law enforcement and important for the legitimacy and acceptance of our work as competition enforcers; it is important for the acceptance of the entire system worldwide. The The Merger Working Group developed the first set of principles on procedures. Procedures have also been addressed by other working groups and by an overarching long-term project on investigative process that produced Guiding Principles and Recommended Practices for Investigative Process. With the CAP the ICN has taken a next step and now offers a comprehensive package of classic ICN work products and the innovative CAP.

There are two more reasons that make the CAP an ICN milestone. First, the ICN CAP again showed the network's ability to act flexibly and quickly. Second, and maybe more significantly, it illustrates the trust which competition agencies place in their network – in their natural habitat as one Steering Group member put it. The ICN CAP is the result of intensive and at times controversial discussions around a core issue: should it stand alone or under the umbrella of ICN? The ICN Steering group put a lot of effort into the project in order to keep it within the established multilateral framework of the ICN where it is easily accessible and acceptable to as many countries as possible and to avoid the fragmentation of multilateral competition agreements and organisations.

And is it relevant? If the International Chamber of Commerce (ICC), the Association of Corporate Counsel (ACC), the Association of in-house competition lawyers (ICLA) and the United States Council for International Business (USCIB) decide to publish a joint press release to welcome the ICN CAP, it clearly shows that it is well received.

2.5. 5TH MILESTONE – THE DIGITAL ECONOMY

Finally, I consider the ICN's work on digital topics a milestone because the question of whether the ICN is able to handle the revolution we are witnessing today will be decisive for its future. Digital technology is transforming the global economy; new services are rapidly changing existing industries. Competition agencies are called upon to act and provide answers. They are in the spotlight and as the head of a competition agency, I can confirm that if you have to be in the front line, it is a great advantage if you are not alone. The digital economy raises many new issues about competition law and related policy areas. There are big challenges for enforcers: we have to be quick in order to prevent irreparable harm; some market areas are already highly concentrated, which makes abuse control our main tool, and finally, large parts of our established legal framework are not tailored to data-driven business models. These challenges are supranational in scope, which makes it so important to keep exchanging on them and establish standards together.

The ICN recognized these challenges early. At the 2015 ICN Annual Conference in Sydney, the ACCC presented a special project on online vertical restraints, the plenary discussed "Unilateral Conduct in the New Economy" and breakout sessions were dedicated inter alia to cross-platform parity agreements and the hotel booking platform cases. In Porto the Unilateral Working Group looked at the challenges of big data. In India, ICN members and NGAs discussed among other issues effective advocacy in the digital world and merger reviews in the digital economy. ICN kept this focus and the digital economy became one of the overarching themes of the 2019 event in Cartagena, and at the 2020 ICN Annual Conference in Los Angeles more plenary topics than ever before dealt with the digital economy. At the 2021 Annual Conference hosted by the Hungarian competition authority, the Cartel Working Group discussed the role and challenges of digitalisation in a cartel investigation and the Unilateral Conduct Working Group addressed dominance in digital markets.

In February 2020, the ICN Steering Group started a new project on competition law enforcement at the intersection between competition, consumer protection, and privacy. This was in response to the fact that the relationship between these areas of law and policy was brought into increasing focus by changes in information technology and the growth of large technology platform ecosystems, which revolutionize the collection, and use of personal and non-personal data.

As all working groups conduct projects touching on digital issues, the Steering Group decided to introduce a new Vice Chair for Digital Co-ordination and in September 2021 confirmed Rod Sims, Chair of the Australian Competition and Consumer Commission, in this position to ensure the overarching co-ordination of projects and discussions on competition in the digital economy within the ICN.

3. WHAT CAN YOU EXPECT FOR THE FUTURE OF ICN?

As nice as it is to enjoy what has been achieved in the past, what is more important is to look at what we have in mind for the future. If I were asked what I would expect for the future of ICN, I would answer: It will take hard work, it will take courage, but it is worth it.

The ICN is still needed despite what has been achieved: the many good work products, the well-established relationships. We are well advised to keep our eyes open, to look ahead and to use what we have achieved as a firm and foundation because things are not getting easier. Globalisation and digitalisation create winners but also losers. They create fears. The fear of losing jobs, the lack of economic stability, the lack of sustainability. When governments try to address these issues, I do not see many endeavours to strengthen competition. What I see instead is a tendency to limit competition. I witness a general discussion about exceptions to competition and about public interest. I do believe that the ICN is quite different. When we as competition agencies address these issues, we have a common interest: competition and consumers worldwide. ICN is not a network of governments, it is not political, it is competition all the time – and should remain this way. Itis voluntary, all members are equal and there is no lead authority or primus inter pares, just consensus. This will also help us when dealing with the second topic, which will lead to the major transformation of industries and business models and will require our greatest attention: sustainability. This is not just about whether environmental concerns can be taken into account, it is about advocating for competition, which will be part of the solution.

Compared to a compulsory system, voluntary implementation logically leads to a limited impact. However, this view somewhat misses the point. First, the ICN has impact as the examples above show, and second, a little change of perspective makes the situation very different. The ICN system gives us the opportunity to aim higher, to be ambitious, to agree on recommendations even if our legal system does not – yet –meet them, rather than having to agree on the lowest common denominator. However, a healthy sense of reality is always appropriate. Do we really change entire systems by demanding due process for antitrust law if we draft principles and recommendations and establish an opt-in framework? Systems that face many challenges that are more fundamental? I do not think there is a reason to give up. The ICN's achievements allow us to view the future with optimism.

When I took over the position as ICN Chair, I concentrated on three major aspects – focus, inclusiveness and implementation. Focus means that we want to make sure that the ICN chooses the topics that matter most and sets the right priorities. Inclusiveness refers to the impressive growth of the ICN, which makes it more important to get everyone involved. It is also about the participation of our non-governmental advisors and inclusiveness is linked to the third aspect, implementation, because implementation will only happen if members are involved and convinced that we are doing the right thing. Implementation is the underlying goal of the ICN. We do not want to produce papers for the sake of it. We work on guidance documents to achieve results and to have an impact. That is what the ICN was created for.

What does that mean for ICN members and NGAs? We praise the ICN's super-light structure and the opportunities it offers. However, flexibility and freedom come at the price of responsibility. We authorities have not delegated responsibility for the ICN to an external organisation; we have to make sure ourselves that the system is up and running. This is true for the practical work in the working groups, for the administration of the network and for the selection of topics. When it comes to substance, we have to remain ambitious and determined. Globalisation, digitalisation, and sustainability will continue to raise questions and pose new challenges. Agencies will have to explore new approaches and appropriate measures. However, this does not mean that the relevant and partly unanswered issues should be kept out of the ICN. On the contrary, this is exactly why we should address them together in the ICN. The ICN is a mirror of the activities of its member agencies. Currently, agencies all around the world are restructuring and evolving to keep pace. Agencies have fresh ideas; they review their positions in the legal regime and in relation to other areas of law. As ICN members, we view our cases from our perspective as competition law enforcers, but as then, ICN Chair David Lewis put it when opening the 2009 ICN Annual Conference, competition law as the fundamental law of the market system cannot be confined to an island where its relationship with every other branch of economic and social policy is ignored. The rapidly developing world is forcing agencies forward, and pushing the ICN to help create a transparent level playing field for all actors. I am confident that the ICN provides its members with a strong basis and anchor.

DEVELOPMENT OF COMPETITION LAW AS REFLECTED IN THE ICN

Siún O'KEEFFE*

1. INTRODUCTION

The International Competition Network (ICN) is a unique organisation. It is an informal, virtual, network organisation that relies for its success on the goodwill and interest of over 130 competition agencies across the globe. Looking back at the ICN's phenomenal development over the last 10 years, and at the work that was done on the Second Decade project, it becomes evident that it is an organisation which, in its structure and in the topics on which it focuses, provides an interesting reflection of the developments in competition law in that period. This can be said of other organisations too, from universities to economic think-tanks and commercial law firms,[1] but arguably it is more pronounced in ICN, perhaps because the network's lack of a hierarchical structure permits, facilitates and even encourages the organisation to respond to changes on the ground, as they are experienced by the agencies.

This organisational response results in an interesting dynamic, whereby economic changes alert the agencies to a potential gap in their expertise, and they then look to the ICN to provide them with information from their peers in other states, relating to that knowledge-gap. The ICN responds with a webinar, or a workshop. Other agencies recognise the significance of the topic. More members and Non-governmental advisors (NGAs) join the calls and maybe a survey is conducted. A break-out session is organised at the annual

* Siún O'Keeffe, Manager Academy, Netherlands Authority for Consumers and Markets, former Strategy advisor of the ACM and international advisory at the NMa since 2008. My sincere thanks to Olaf Wrede and Joost van Zwet for their valuable advice and assistance. Opinions expressed are my own and not attributable to the ACM or any other organisation.

1 See for example, Posner, R.A., *Overcoming Law* (Harvard University Press, 1995), on the changes to the legal profession in the U.S.A. since the 1950's. See also Lundberg, K., "Convenor or Player? The World Economic Forum and Davos" (Kennedy School of Government Case Study 1741.0; April 1 2004), discussing how the World Economic Form, by convening meetings of experts, established an international policy network and helped set an agenda of policy issues for consideration by leaders in academia, business and government.

conference. A case arises at national level, and because of their ICN engagement, the agency knows which other agencies are dealing with the topic, allowing it to consult and learn from their mistakes. The following year there is a panel on the topic at the ICN annual conference, and then work continues in the relevant workgroup to the stage of a report or a recommendation. The subsequent year, the national ministry expresses an interest in passing legislation on the topic, and the agency has a ready source of information from the ICN facilitating it in advising government. In this way, the ICN leads incrementally, (sometimes surprisingly swiftly, and sometimes agonisingly slowly!) but always inexorably, if not to converging systems of competition law, to systems that are increasingly well-informed and coherent in their assessments of the trade-offs involved in effective enforcement.

Turner refers to horizontal networks like ICN as having little coercive power, observing that they depend on soft-law mechanisms and informal sanctions to achieve their goals.[2] Sokol is more lenient and credits ICN with helping to create a consensus about competition norms, while Botta goes further, linking ICN's success to its large output of soft law instruments.[3] In his book on experimentalism in competition law, Svetiev devotes a chapter to exploring whether the ICN has provided the basis for an evolution of an experimentalist global antitrust regime.[4] The idea behind experimentalism in governance is to seek solutions to difficult, multifaceted problems in an open, cooperative structure, using a recursive process of rule-making and revision. Svetiev sees experimentalist elements in ICN, but reflects that as the exchanges and mutual learning within ICN are informal it does not constitute an experimentalist regime. In this article, I explore how ICN's organisational development reflects wider changes in competition law, using three illustrative topics; economic analysis, vertical restrictions and the relevance of institutional or agency design, also referring briefly to other issues that support this idea of organisational development.

These are topics which are approached differently in the varied jurisdictions of the ICN Member States. There is no general consensus as to how they should be tackled. Despite their controversial nature, and the lack of consensus as to

---

2 Turner, J.I., "Transnational Networks and the International Public Order", in Miller, R.A., and Bratspies, R.M., *Progress in International Law* (Nijhoff, Leiden, 2008), p. 407.

3 Sokol, D.D., "Monopolists Without Borders: The Institutional Challenge of International Antitrust in a Global Gilded Age", (2007) 4 Berkerley Bus. L.J. 37, and Botta, M., "Competition Policy", in Falkner, G., and Muller, P., *EU Policies in a Global Perspective Shaping or Taking International Regimes* (Routledge, 2014).

4 Svetiev, Y., *Experimentalist Competition Law and the Regulation of Markets*, (Hart 2020). See also Sabel, C.F., and Zeitlin, J., "Experimentalist Governance" in Levi-Faur, D., *The Oxford Handbook of Governance* (OUP, 2012).

how they should be dealt with, the ICN has incorporated them into its body of work products. This shows how the functional impetus that thrives within ICN to tackle problems that spill beyond national borders is more powerful than the national desire for self-rule that can so easily dampen cooperation. It also shows that the ICN may be a far more powerful force than any of us realises.

2. THE ROLE OF ECONOMIC ANALYSIS IN COMPETITION LAW

The role of economic analysis in competition law has long been a subject of debate. From the outset, the EU seemed focused more on the principle of upholding the competitive process, rather than on promoting consumer welfare as US competition policy professes to do. In line with Bork's assertion that the US Sherman Act was concerned with consumer welfare, the US Supreme Court made it clear in *Continental TV Inc* v *GTE Sylvania Inc*, that modern economic theory underlies US antitrust law.[5] In Europe, in *Glaxo Smith Kline*, the European Court of Justice stated that there is nothing in Article 101(1) of the TFEU to indicate that agreements must deprive consumers of certain advantages in order to have an anti-competitive effect, as had been stated by the General Court. Rather, Article 101 TFEU aims to protect not only the interests of competitors or of consumers, but also the structure of the market.[6]

Even today, while the vast majority of agencies and many courts, make use of economic expertise, the way in which economic analysis is used by competition authorities is not undisputed. Economic theories can sometimes be incomplete and are often unable to give an explanation for observable facts. Occasionally, effects are predicted in theory, but in practice this prediction is not observable. Wils states that the (post-) Chicago (consumer) welfarist approach to competition takes a unduly narrow view of the benefits of undistorted competition, by considering only the value of maximal achievement (consumer welfare or efficiency), while neglecting the process values of undistorted competition (including the right to compete on the merits, and equality of opportunity between economic operators).[7] Add to this the arguments put forward by behavioural economists, that economic decisions are not always based on rational behaviour, and it might seem that some economic analyses could be counterproductive rather than helpful to decision-making. This discussion on

5 433 U.S. 3 (1977). See further Bork, R., *The Antitrust Paradox* (1978).

6 Joined Cases C-501/06P, C-515/06P and C-519/06P, *GlaxoSmithKline Services Unlimited, formerly Glaxo Wellcome plc* v *Commission*, 6 October 2009.

7 Wils. W., "The judgment of the EU *General* Court in *Intel* and the so-called 'more economic approach' to abuse of dominance", (2014) 37 4 *World Competition*, 405.

the role of economic analysis in competition law is observable in how ICN has devoted increasing attention to this topic over the last decade.

Former ICN chairman, John Fingleton, CEO of the UK OFT and himself a prominent economist, played a major role as chairman of ICN in increasing the acceptance of economics as a topic of discussion within the network. With his encouragement, the Canadian Commission, a strong steering group member and vice-chair of the ICN, hosted in November 2008, a small meeting of approximately thirty participants from Asia, North and South America, Europe and the Middle East in Ottawa to discuss topics such as (i) Empirical Methods in Antitrust, (ii) Appropriate tests in Anticompetitive Exclusion; and (iii) the Role of Economists in Enforcement Agencies. The attendees found the sessions and networking productive and valuable.[8]

Over the next few years, more and more agencies began to appoint chief economists as the recognition of the role economics could play in competition law grew. In several significant merger cases, *Airtours*, *Schneider* and *Tetra-Laval*, the European Commission had its decisions overturned by the then EU Court of First Instance. Following these judgments, the European Commission appointed a chief economist in 2003.[9] This counteracted criticism, whether objectively justified or not, that had highlighted the fact that whereas the US Department of Justice and the Federal Trade Commission had chief economist teams, the European Competition had no chief competition economist. The UK Office of Fair Trading (now the CMA), the Netherlands Competition Authority (now the ACM), the South African Competition Commission and the French Autorité de la Concurrence followed suit in 2006. The Bundeskartellamt began to use the term formally around 2012/2014. The Australian Competition and Consumer Commission appointed its first chief economist in 2015. By the 2010's large companies such as Google, Microsoft and Facebook were also appointing chief economists. The ICN Second Decade report also referred to the calls from members to devote ICN resources to this topic.[10]

ICN did some work on the relevance of consumer-welfare for competition law in 2011, in preparation for the 10th annual conference hosted by the Dutch Competition Authority. At that stage, it was clear that there was some debate as to whether consumer welfare meant consumer surplus or total surplus. Also, most competition authorities which participated in the study were reluctant

8 See Report on ICN Chief/Senior Economists Workshop, Canada September 12–13, 2016.

9 In Case T-42/99 *Airtours* v *Commission*, 6 June 2002, Joined Cases T-310/01&T-77/02 *Schneider Electric SA* v *Commission*, 22 October 2002 and Joined Cases T5 & 80/02 *Tetra-Laval BV* v *Commission* 25 October 2002, the Court of First Instance struck down the European Commission's merger decisions.

10 The Future of the ICN in its Second Decade (Final report, Paris, 2016).

to go further than acknowledging that competition should ultimately benefit consumers either directly or indirectly.[11] At the ICN Annual meeting in Warsaw in 2013, during an optional breakout session on competition economics, and the role of economists in authorities, participants expressed an interest in seeing more ICN-related activities focused on economics. Eventually, with the approval of the ICN Steering Group, a decision was made to move forward with an ICN Chief/Senior Economists Workshop in September 2016. The first Economists workshop was hosted in Vancouver. In 2017, the Agency Effectiveness Working Group ran a survey on the role of economists in ICN member agencies. In 2018, a second Economists workshop was held in Seoul and co-hosted by the OECD. In the meantime, increasing numbers of ICN NGAs are economists. That economists play an important role within competition policy and the ICN seems now undisputed. Some may argue that as their role becomes so mainstream and accepted that economic work has been absorbed into the normal work of all the ICN workshops. This holds true to a degree, and most workshops and annual conferences devote sessions to specialised economic topics, especially those hosted by the Merger Working Group.

However, there have been recent waves alleging an exaggerated focus by competition agencies on neo-classical economics associated with Chicago ideology.[12] Counter-waves, arguably unfairly, brand such critics as neo-Brandeisians and advocates of 'hipster antitrust'.[13] Both waves bypass the fact that most competition agencies worldwide employ mainstream industrial economics theory rather than strict Chicago School. In any event, it seems clear that the role of economics in antitrust analysis remains an issue that requires special attention. The economists it seems, are here to stay, also in the ICN!

3. VERTICAL AGREEMENTS

The place of vertical agreements in ICN had long been a topic of discussion within the Network. Vertical agreements, made between parties at different levels of the production chain, are common and practical instruments for the organisation of business, but there are different views on the degree to which they may be economically harmful. Antitrust policy in the USA has traditionally been far more accepting of the efficiencies of vertical agreements than the

11 Competition Enforcement and Consumer-welfare, Setting the Agenda (ICN, 2011).

12 See for example, Khan, L., "Amazon's Antitrust Paradox" (2017) *Yale Law Journal* 126(3) 710 and Katz, M.L., "Platform economics and antitrust enforcement: A little knowledge is a dangerous thing" (2019) *Journal of Economics* Volume 28 Issue 1.

13 Wright, J.D., et al., "Requiem for a paradox: The Dubious Rise and Inevitable Fall of Hipster Antitrust" (2019) *Arizona St. Law Journal* 293.

EU.[14] In *Leegin*, the US Supreme Court abandoned the per se prohibition of minimum resale price maintenance.[15] Following the modernisation of European Competition Law in 2004, there was evidence of a growing acceptance in European states that many vertical agreements had efficiencies, at least in some situations. At EU level, the initial approach of having different block exemptions for different types of vertical agreement was changed to allow for a new-style block exemption that covers the great majority of vertical agreements. Nevertheless in the wake of 2010, cases concerning vertical restraints continued to cause problems in some member states and as Big Tech took off, the potential of vertical agreements to cause problems became increasingly evident.[16]

The issue of vertical restraints was frequently discussed at ICN, but did not explicitly fall under any one of the working groups of the network. There were occasional suggestions that the Cartel Working Group should deal with vertical restraints. Such suggestions were firmly rejected by most NGAs and a majority of ICN Steering Group members who asserted that the Cartel Working Group should confine itself to hard core cartels. Indeed, the Cartel Working Group itself also made the point that it already had its hands full simply dealing with hard core cartel detection and fines, especially as the work of that group expanded to deal with deterrence, leniency, compensation issues and alternative methods of case settlement.

One issue on which there was broad agreement was that vertical restraints could be problematic in situations of monopoly. This led to an interest in this area emerging in the ICN Unilateral Conduct Working Group. As E-commerce continued to develop, new online business models emerged, leading to the growth and importance of online platforms. This provided more choice for consumers and opened up new markets for businesses. However, it also raised concerns about consumer protection, dominance and (big) data issues. Online price transparency enabled businesses to easily monitor each other's prices. Online distribution also led to new kinds of vertical restrictions such as price parity clauses and online platform bans.

The 2015 ICN Special Project, which was run by the Australian Competition and Consumer Commission considered online vertical restraints, in particular: the extent to which online vertical restraints are, or should be, prioritised by the ICN membership; whether, and to what extent, existing legal frameworks, investigative tools, and analytical tools in ICN member jurisdictions are able to

14 For criticism of the European Commission's approach, see Hawk B., "System Failure: Vertical Restraints and EC Competition Law", (1985) 98 *Harv. L Rev.* 983, 1001.

15 *Leegin Creative Leather Products, Inc.* v. *PSKS, Inc.*, 127 S.Ct. 2705 (2007).

16 See OECD Policy Roundtable Vertical Restraints for Online Sales 2013.

deal with online vertical restraints effectively; and what recommendations could or should be made by the ICN in relation to online vertical restraints. Eventually, the ICN Unilateral Conduct Working Group emerged as a suitable home for work on vertical restraints within ICN. The Unilateral Conduct Working Group committed to prepare an issues paper on the treatment of vertical restraints by ICN members.[17] The issues paper was supplemented by interactive webinars which were used to explore key issues arising with ICN members and NGAs. A temporary group was formed to deal with these projects on vertical restraints within the unilateral conduct group, and eventually the work on verticals was subsumed within the main body of the unilateral conduct working group. Not everyone was initially content with this compromise, but it fitted well with the recognition of the fact that vertical agreements and their associated network effects were prominently visible in the BigTech industry with its accompanying problems of dominance. In addition, it was a compromise that suited the balance of the workload between the working groups. A new comparative evaluation of approaches to common hypothetical cases studies was presented to the ICN Annual Conference 2018 in Colombia and today, work on vertical restraints is firmly established as part of the workplan of the ICN Unilateral Conduct Working Group.[18]

4. THE RELEVANCE OF INSTITUTIONAL DESIGN

Competition agencies throughout the world have different systems when it comes to institutional and agency design. This leads to questions pertaining to the comparative advantages of multifunction agencies, independence from government, different decision-making powers (e.g. the administrative or the prosecutorial model) and internal governance issues. These can be sensitive, even political, questions that come close to the sovereign heart of the state. As such, these topics do not immediately lend themselves for discussion in a voluntary forum for technical agencies, such as ICN, where the goal is one of increasing convergence. Nevertheless, over the last number of years, more of these topics are being discussed at the ICN, either directly or indirectly.

One reason for this change could be that globalisation and technological development have granted agencies an increased awareness of each other's

17 Vertical Restraints Multi Year Project 2016–2019, ICN Unilateral Conduct Working Group, April 2019.

18 See the Unilateral Conduct Working Group 2019–2022 Work Plan which refers specifically to the goal of promoting greater understanding regarding standards for assessing vertical restraints, and continuing the discussion on vertical restraints, based on the Vertical Restraints Report presented at the 2019 annual conference in Cartagena and through sharing of experiences.

systems. Many agency experts have studied abroad and this has enhanced their comprehension of alternative systems, leading to an information symmetry that facilitates open dialogue. Kovacic makes the point that by far, most of the 80 or so jurisdictions that have adopted new competition laws in the past 30 years have civil law systems. Their competition systems usually rely on an administrative enforcement model that resembles the EU regime. Few civil law countries have established competition systems that use the adversarial prosecution model employed by the US Department of Justice. Because the EU institutional platform is more compatible with the institutional arrangements in most civil law countries, many transition economies have an inclination to look first to EU models in designing and implementing their competition systems. This condition means that EU norms, more than US norms, tend to be more readily absorbed into the newer competition policy regimes.[19] It could be that these changes have led to an increased acceptance of the fact that we are dealing with different systems on the global stage, and have led organisations such as the ICN to focus rather on identifying basic norms on which the different types of agencies agree, which eases the discussion on the underlying differences between their systems.

Also, within the EU, there has been a further movement towards increased legislative convergence within the European Competition Network, as the agencies of the EU member states move to improve the effectiveness of their enforcement by coming closer and closer on issues such as the power of the agency to issue administrative fines and the power of independent decision-making in cases.[20]

Reflecting these changes in the competition landscape globally, the ICN has worked on topics such as Recommended Practices for Investigative Process[21] and Principles of Procedural Fairness,[22] This work reveals an implicit acceptance that regardless of the different decision-making powers of different agencies, we have nevertheless found principles on which convergence can be reached. The Principles set an overarching goal that regardless of internal structure, competition agencies should conduct enforcement matters in a consistent, impartial manner, free of political interference. It also reinforces institutional checks and balances by noting the right to seek impartial review

19 Kovacic, W.E.. "Competition Policy in the European Union and the United States: Convergence or Divergence?" Bates White Fifth Annual Antitrust Conference Washington, D.C. June 2, 2008.

20 Directive 2019/1 to empower the national competition authorities of the EU Member States (NCAs) to be more effective enforcers and to ensure the proper functioning of the internal market [2019] OJ L11/3.

21 ICN Recommended Practices for Investigative Process 2019.

22 ICN Guiding Principles for Procedural Fairness in Competition Agency Enforcement 2018.

by an independent judicial body. The Recommended Practices describe internal agency safeguards to bolster investigative integrity and support informed and robust decision making. These include consistent internal rules or practices, objective application of legal and economic analysis meaningful opportunities for parties to be heard, enforcement proceedings pursuant too timely notice and transparent rules, and written reasoned decisions.

Working together within ICN to identify areas on which there is common ground inevitably renders the issue of the advantages and disadvantages of administrative or prosecutorial models less sensitive. By focusing on fundamental principles that any agency should pursue in the operation of its enforcement mandate, the ICN implicitly recognises that impartial enforcement of competition rules can be achieved in various types of institutional design.

Similarly, surveys such as the ICN Agency Effectiveness survey on organisational design, while it focuses on internal organisation, reveals an awareness of the variety of agency forms within the ICN. Its approach is factual rather than judgmental. The survey goes no further than to reveal a correlation between size and multifunctionality as it observes that there is a tendency that small agencies work with a more limited number of activities, and larger agencies often have hybrid functions.[23] The initiation in 2015 of a series of "Town Hall" discussions for all members and NGAs on topics at the intersection of competition and other policies showed an openness within ICN members to engage in discussions going beyond politically uncontroversial technical and jurisprudential issues, and approaching issues such as independence in decision-making. Topics such as public interest considerations in merger decisions and the interaction of competition and industrial policy were discussed, often by heads of agencies, during these tele-seminars.

All of the above are small changes. Nevertheless, as convergence in less controversial areas increases, we may see ICN discussions delving deeper into constitutional issues of independence and agency design that have traditionally been carved out as more suitable for discussion in other fora.

5. AND THERE'S MORE...

There are many other topics of competition law and policy which have slowly been gaining acceptance as topics of discussion within ICN. For example, for many years, when it came to discussion among competition agencies in ICN, there was little appetite for issues such as compliance or private damages

23 Report on Agency Effectiveness through Organisational Design 2019.

actions. These were seen as issues pertaining to the interests of the private bar, rather than agency issues. This has changed in the last ten years, as agencies acknowledge the close relationship between compliance, effectiveness and deterrence, and also between public and private enforcement. The ICN began to refer to the importance of compliance in its work products from about 2012. A chapter on private damages actions was added to the Anti-Cartel Enforcement Manuel in 2018. Guidance and advocacy have become mainstream business for all agencies.

Other examples of changes in the organisation reflecting changes in competition law and policy, include the increased attention within the ICN of the importance of cooperation with national agencies involved in different types of detection and a push for joined-up thinking on ex officio investigations. For example, a new chapter on Relationships between Competition Agencies and Public Procurement Bodies was added to the Anti-Cartel Enforcement Manual in 2015. More recently, the ICN has proved an excellent forum to share experiences on abuse of dominance cases, allowing members to contrast different approaches in the digital sphere between jurisdictions. For example at the Annual Conference in 2019, there was a session on exploring new challenges in the assessment of dominance in light of recent developments in the digital and high tech sectors, with a focus more driven by empirical insights and by the technical aspects of the cases, rather than on their political (in)desirability. This makes the competition law debate less abstract and less polarised, ensuring its continued relevance in an economy and a society marked more than ever by disruptive developments.

6. CONCLUSION

In 2013, ICN Chairman, Andreas Mundt was asked whether in 2021, we would still require an ICN. He answered; "Now, do I think that in 2021 we will still require an ICN? Yes, I do. Competition authorities are faced with multinational players that operate on worldwide markets. This globalisation assigns the competition authorities with new tasks and challenges and will require the ICN to help create a transparent and level playing field for all actors. I don't know in detail what challenges we will be facing nor what tasks the ICN will have, but I am confident that our flexible hands-on approach and our practical guidance documents and other work products will help ICN members to meet the forthcoming demands".[24]

24 "Focus, implementation, inclusiveness – The impact of the ICN", *Concurrences* interview, 15 November 2013.

As the examples dealt with in this essay illustrate, the flexible hands-on approach to which Mundt refers has allowed ICN to develop its scope to deal with new topics, reflecting their growing importance in competition law as it develops and changes over times. Slowly, these new and at least initially controversial areas, have become part of the ICN's body of work. They are not areas in which there is consensus. Nevertheless, the sheer fact that they are on the ICN agenda leads to a greater convergence. This involves agencies genuinely engaging with one another on the day-to-day issues of effective enforcement. Hollman and Kovacic referred to how ICN 's promotion of a broad adoption of superior techniques improves the performance of individual jurisdictions. Decentralisation of authority within the network, coupled with the sharing of experimentation and techniques, through webinars and workshops allows the voluntary adoption by agencies and eventually by states of the most effective practices.[25]

It begins with the adoption of common terms, a willingness to translate and identify equivalent concepts and an acknowledgement of the existence of different systems. Without forcing any state to accept the legitimacy of another system, the ICN's discussion of each other's systems contributes to a common understanding of each other's substantive norms, procedural standards, and operational techniques. The former Director of DG Comp at the European Commission, Johannes Laitenberger, explained this well, saying that "the ICN is a unique forum in the sense that it exists with a minimum of organizational and institutional operators and a maximum... of intense discussion, exchanges of best practices, and mutual support".[26] This bottom up approach of the Network means that the working groups deal with the issues that are of importance to the agencies. Coupled with the personal contacts, facilitated by the Network, and the increased access to each other's literature and jurisprudence, facilitated by modern technology, this allows the ICN to promote interoperability and increases the likelihood of convergence. Indeed, the ICN's strength seems to lie in the very lack of an obligation to converge. Simply ensuring that agencies are continually exposed to how others tackle similar competition problems, results in increased inclusiveness. The constant exchange of experience and knowledge exposes agencies to an expectation from their peers, from business, from politicians and more recently from consumers, that they be open to adopting best practices and standardised enforcement methods. Its status as an informal network belies its power as a force for convergence.

---

25 Hollman, H., and Kovacic, W.E., "The International Competition Network: Its Past, Current and Future Role" in Lugard, P, *The International Competition Network at Ten* (Intersentia, 2011).

26 Interview with Johannes Laitenberger, *ABA The Antitrust Source*, 1 June 2017.

SPECIAL PROJECT ON SUSTAINABLE DEVELOPMENT AND COMPETITION LAW: THE BEGINNING OF AN EVEN MORE BEAUTIFUL FRIENDSHIP?

Csaba Kovács and Aranka Nagy*

1. INTRODUCTION

In a world where consumer preferences are shifting towards consumption with less environmental impact, competition is a driver of innovation and investment into greener products and services. Thus, simply protecting competition, without any special regard to sustainability, in general, contributes to achieving sustainability objectives.[1] In this sense, "*competition policy is already a green policy*".[2]

However, it is subject to debate whether competition law could and should be made even greener by taking into account sustainability considerations, and if

* Csaba Kovács is Deputy Head of the Competition Economics and Market Research Section of the GVH. Aranka Nagy is Senior Associate at CMS Cameron McKenna Nabarro Olswang LLP, Hungarian Branch Office and was Chief Advisor at the International Section of the GVH at the time of the special project. The views expressed here are those of the authors and are not necessarily identical with the official position of the ICN or any of its members, including the GVH. The authors are grateful to Miranda Molnár for her assistance. All errors solely belong to the authors.

1 A recent example is the intervention of the Competition and Markets Authority (CMA) aimed at opening up competition in the motorway chargepoint services in the UK to ensure that "*drivers [of electric vehicles] have a greater choice of chargepoints where they need them, and for a fair price*". (CMA to open up electric vehicle charging competition on motorways, CMA press release of 17 November 2021.) https://www.gov.uk/government/news/cma-to-open-up-electric-vehicle-charging-competition-on-motorways.

2 "*Il est très facile de réconcilier le droit de l'environnement et le droit de la concurrence car la politique de la concurrence est déjà une politique verte. En maintenant les marchés ouverts, compétitifs et innovants, la politique de concurrence soutient pleinement les objectifs du Pacte vert*" Alexander Wintersten, Head of the Communications Policy Unit at DG Competition. https://www.linkedin.com/posts/alexander-winterstein-a5130a206_il-est-tr%C3%A8s-facile-de-r%C3%A9concilier-le-droit-activity-6872567003249475585-xKxh.

yes, what is the most appropriate way to do so. The issue has been raised and further explored by various members of the competition community, including competition agencies, private practitioners, businesses, and international organisations.[3]

While the ongoing debate is often about prescriptive ideas, the Hungarian Competition Authority (GVH)[4] decided to contribute by stocktaking the existing experience of incorporating sustainability considerations into competition enforcement, when designing its special project as the host of the 20th ICN Annual Conference in 2021.

We surveyed ICN members, that is competition agencies, and non-governmental advisors (NGAs) of the ICN worldwide. Our survey focused on restrictive agreements, as the most promising area of enforcement, but also covered other issues, such as market studies and various institutional aspects. 52 agencies and 41 NGAs responded to the questionnaire, and we believe that our survey covers experience well.[5]

In the rest of our essay, we give a selective and non-technical overview of the findings of the survey as well as the connecting high-level panel discussion of

3 A few examples:
The advice of the UK Competition and Markets Authority to government:
https://www.gov.uk/government/news/cma-publishes-environmental-sustainability-advice-to-government.
The draft guidelines of The Netherlands Authority for Consumers and Markets.
https://www.acm.nl/en/publications/draft-guidelines-sustainability-agreements
The project of the Hellenic Competition Commission.
https://www.epant.gr/en/enimerosi/competition-law-sustainability.html
https://www.epant.gr/en/enimerosi/sandbox.html
The project of the European Commission. https://ec.europa.eu/competition-policy/policy/green-gazette_en
The survey of Linklaters.
https://www.linklaters.com/en/insights/blogs/linkingcompetition/2020/esg/competition-and-sustainability
The hearing and the subsequent roundtable discussion of the OECD Competition Committee.
https://www.oecd.org/daf/competition/environmental-considerations-in-competition-enforcement.htm
The book edited by Simon Holmes, Dirk Middelschulte and Martijn Snoep, published by Concurrences, collecting a wide range of perspectives, including business in various industries. https://www.concurrences.com/fr/les-livres/competition-law-climate-change-environmental-sustainability.

4 Hungarian Competition Authority: Gazdasági Versenyhivatal (GVH).

5 Sustainable Development and Competition Law (Special Project for the 2021 ICN Annual Conference – Survey) Survey Report dated 30 September 2021 (the 'Survey Report'). The survey report and all its appendices are available at the website of the GVH.
https://www.gvh.hu/en/gvh/Conference/icn-2021-annual-conference/special-project-for-the-2021-icn-annual-conference-sustainable-development-and-competition-law.

the conference.[6] First, we describe case experience, its outlook, and the challenge that emerges at multiple levels. Then, we present potential means of meeting that challenge as well as the international aspects, including convergence. Finally, we draw a few broad conclusions.

2. LIMITED, BUT EXPANDING CASE-EXPERIENCE

Environmental sustainability is not a newcomer to competition law enforcement, as some decades-old EU cases attest: *Exxon/Shell* and *CECED* in fact predate the ICN.[7] Responses to our survey also reveal experience that is older than six years: a large portion of NGAs report such experience and one agency mentioned a case prior to 2015, even though that period was not covered by the competition agencies' survey.

Yet, case law has hardly evolved at present. It is telling that in competition policy press and newsletters the term "sustainable" is much more often used as a byword for "viable" in the context of merger remedies than in the sense of more modest environmental impact.[8]

This is not surprising in light of our results, which do not show a great deal of experience in the field. Few agencies reported sustainability cases and even the cumulative number of such cases remains low in the 2015–2021 period. All those agencies are European, but even in Europe, a large majority of responding agencies did not have cases where sustainability was the sole or main consideration, either in terms of competitive concern or in terms of defence. Only one agency that reported sustainability cases also reported that one or more of its cases were tested in court.

---

6 Participants of the panel discussion at the International Competition Network Annual Conference (October 2021) ("ICN Annual Conference Panel"): Martijn Snoep (moderator), Chair of the ACM; Tembinkosi Bonakele, Commissioner of the South African Competition Commission; Nicole Kar, Partner, Head of Antitrust and Foreign Investment UK and Ireland at Linklaters; Andreas Mundt, President of the German Federal Competition Authority, Chair of the ICN Steering Group; Delia Rickard, Deputy Chair of the Australian Competition and Consumer Commission (ACCC); Csaba Rigó, President of the GVH.
The video recording of the panel discussion is available at the website of the conference under "Program & Recordings of Wednesday, 13 October 2021, Host's Special Plenary Session: Sustainable Development and Competition Law". https://icn2021budapest.hu/.

7 *Exxon/Shell* ((94/322/EC) Commission Decision of 18 May 1994 (IV/33.640 – Exxon/Shell)) and *CECED* (2000/475/EC: Commission Decision of 24 January 1999 relating to a proceeding under Article 81 of the EC Treaty and Article 53 of the EEA Agreement (Case IV.F.1/36.718. CECED)).

8 At least this is what we observed when checking for the media footprint of our survey and of the conference in the subsequent weeks.

As we move from cases to market studies, sector inquiries and research where sustainability was a major issue, the low numbers remain in place and so does Europe's predominance, although it is less extreme.

At the same time, we have found that a much larger portion of agencies expect to encounter cases that will raise sustainability considerations in the future. This anticipation goes beyond Europe, although it is stronger there.

The number of cases with a sustainability defence is already growing: it increased threefold to tenfold – depending on whether we count all cases or only those where the sustainability aspect played a major role – between the first and second half of 2015–2021.

In other words, the topic is on the rise. This influences agency and stakeholder planning. About half of those agencies that responded to the question indicated that the issue of sustainability and competition is on their strategic agenda. NGAs also tended to regard it as one of the major topics of the coming years. The views concerning international organisations reinforce all of this, as discussed later.

3. THE CHALLENGE

While the reasons behind the above statistics are not all revealed by our survey, corporate activity seems to be an underlying factor, and the business case for sustainability claims, especially those that are connected to "green agreements", is likely to go from strength to strength.

As Martijn Snoep put it in his opening remarks of the panel, "*the world is preparing for a massive transition to a net zero economy, and this transition will require a drastic change in production processes, in consumption patterns, and will require an enormous adaptation of the world economy. […] And most of the change indeed will need to come from […] companies and consumers.*"[9]

Later in the panel discussion, Nicole Kar named a few types of private "green initiatives", which are often various horizontal self-regulations to move away from polluting technologies and non-sustainable packaging, and towards more sustainable inputs and greater use of recycled materials.

She also explained why they may be risky in a competition law context: joint commitments may lead to higher prices and less choice, or may be perceived as

9 ICN Annual Conference Panel (Snoep comments).

doing so, especially if they increase costs, possibly triggering cartel allegations; agreeing to stay away from non-sustainable inputs, such as those linked to illegal deforestation, may trigger collective boycott allegations; and reporting about keeping such commitments to other participants may trigger allegations of exchanging sensitive information between competitors. The possibility of "*killer acquisitions in the sustainability sector*" was also mentioned in the panel.

Competition agencies will need to deal with these types of, possibly proliferating, arrangements in one way or another. As societal priorities are shifting – even if sometimes in turbulent ways – towards demanding public policy support for sustainability business initiatives, they might feel mounting pressure in the future to make it clear when they accept those arrangements and when they do not, and to explain why.

In the panel discussion Tembinkosi Bonakele went on to say that sustainability "*has become a survival issue for humanity, but also it has become a survival issue for agencies*", noting that "*if competition authorities were seen to be a hindrance to environmental sustainability, and policymakers have a choice to make between having competition and sustainability, […] competition may come second best*".[10]

Still, there are no ready-made answers as to how to deal with sustainability.

One question is whether the legal framework should be readjusted and, if so, by how much. While almost all responding NGAs in our survey supported the idea that competition law enforcement has a reasonable role to play in achieving sustainability goals, their comments suggest that they think this should not entail changes in the standards and objectives of competition law, and that competition law should not replace regulation.

The same view was reiterated in the panel discussion. For example, Delia Rickard highlighted that "*the ACCC's focus is on protecting the process of competition across the economy and enforcing laws in the interest of the broader public.*"[11] On the one hand, "*this is opposed to the idea of promoting competition in line with specific public interest consideration such as sustainability*", which "*require their own policy instruments*". On the other hand, "*our exemptions regime provides us with a transparent and effective lever*" for not letting enforcement "*obstruct […] positive initiatives that may technically contravene competition laws but are in a broader public interest.*"

10 ICN Annual Conference Panel (Bonakele comments).
11 ICN Annual Conference Panel (Rickard comments).

Our results on case records show that sustainability cases were not less common in jurisdictions where the welfare/efficiency objective was present and were not more common in jurisdictions where competition law contained special provisions related to sustainability. This does not mean that those provisions or a public interest objective may not be helpful, and it may be too early to draw strong conclusions. Nonetheless, our results indicate that the "traditional" legal framework is likely to be able to accommodate those sustainability considerations that are thought to be relevant.

However, what exactly are those relevant sustainability considerations and how should they be taken into account? In particular, how should they be measured against other important variables in trade-off situations? Sorting out these analytical issues is the core substantive challenge. This would, in turn, lead to more complete answers to higher-level questions.

Analytical methods were covered by our survey through descriptions of cases and methodological documents provided by the respondents. We collected those descriptions in Appendix B of the survey report, even if existing experience was too limited to identify and analyse best practices.

In contrast, a number of agencies reported that they have either encountered an "expertise gap" or anticipate encountering one in terms of sustainability in competitive analysis. Responses also revealed that casework, market studies, sector inquiries and research as well as competition advocacy were equally affected. Given how limited actual experience is, we suspect that many agencies that replied to our question about "expertise gap" with "no" are either extremely optimistic or yet to realise the true nature of the challenge.

All of this is consistent with the responses of NGAs, showing that, on average, they have a significantly better opinion of the legal framework than of enforcement, including analysis. NGAs also observe "expertise gaps" of agencies, or at least they, on average, tend to assess current agency preparedness as mediocre. At the same time, several of them recognise the difficulty of agency adaption.

4. MEANS OF AGENCY ADAPTION

We asked agencies about their actual and planned efforts to overcome current or expected "expertise gaps". Our results are consistent with the idea that co-operation with foreign sister agencies – that is utilising others' experience and brainpower – tends to be the most effective option in the beginning, while later internal capacity building catches up, and may become even more effective.

Indeed, frequently needed knowledge may be worthy of internalisation. For example, one “more experienced” agency hired environmental economists and established an in-house “sustainability team”.

Many competition agencies faced similar challenges in the past. Market openings in telecommunications, energy and transport brought these sectors into the domain of competition law enforcement, which required the acquisition of new skills to understand these markets and to be able to apply the general analytical framework properly to conducts that were sometimes previously unknown to competition agencies. Andreas Mundt mentioned digitalisation as a more recent example in the panel discussion. Institutional memory may be extremely valuable when trying to find the best combination of available tools.

One way to fill an “expertise gap” is co-operation with other parts of the (domestic) public administration, for example with energy regulators concerning green energy. Thus, it may matter if those parts of the public administration are already in-house. Therefore, we asked agencies about synergies with their other activities.

Activity portfolios vary, but one certainly could imagine synergies between dealing with sustainability cases and state aid, energy, transport, or perhaps consumer protection. Responses, however, suggest that such synergies either do not exist or are not realised. This may point towards a more general problem than sustainability.

Case selection is sometimes also proposed as a tool to support sustainability: competition agencies could prioritise those cases where the restrictive practice also harms sustainability, and de-prioritise those cases where there might be competition law infringement, but also significant sustainability benefits. This may bring flexibility into otherwise rigid laws.

We had three main findings in this respect. First, the majority of agencies reported that they have no such discretion in the first place – rigid laws may also be rigid procedurally. Moreover, the majority of the remaining agencies are neutral.

Second, agencies, on average, indeed, favour launching formal proceedings that involve sustainability related competitive concerns, rather than proceedings that involve a sustainability defence, although the difference is moderate.

More importantly, however, even the presence of a sustainability defence seems to increase the likelihood of launching a formal proceeding. It appears that a number of agencies are not prepared to disregard sustainability defence cases, at least for now. Perhaps they want to gain experience before adopting rules of thumb in terms of prioritisation. This attitude may be strengthened by the fear of greenwashing.

The Hungarian greenwashing "defence" attempt presented by Csaba Rigó in the panel discussion is a case in point. Cartel members "*based their claims [about exemption] on environmental benefits but without any serious substantiation, thus resulting in the plain and simple refusal of the GVH*"[12], even though the Hungarian Competition Act explicitly recognises environmental benefits.

In other cases, however, greenwashing may not be so obvious at first sight, which may make agencies cautious about upfront case selection as a tool. They may want to double check sustainability benefits and their relationship to competitive effects. More sustainability sensitive agencies may be more likely to think so, narrowing the prioritisation gap between defence and offence cases.

Guidance to and informal consultations with parties of "green agreements" are often mentioned as a means of adaption in the context of providing legal certainty in a timely, flexible and tailor-made fashion. Our survey covered informal consultations only implicitly, as the terms "case" and "case law" included them, and we know from the comments that such consultations actually happened and were a substantial part of the case record of certain agencies.

A real-life example given by Nicole Kar in the panel discussion provides further insight.[13] Her law firm contacted 14 competition agencies with "*a detailed briefing paper with market share information and analysis [...] on whether there were competition concerns*", but got only one reply on the merit. "*13 agencies said a mix of 'this is a self-assessment issue, we cannot give you an answer', 'we will not give advance guidance, you have to commence your collaboration before we will give you guidance', and others said 'thank you, but we would need to market test this and deal with this publicly'.*" Apparently, informal consultations are not always straightforward due to procedural constraints and institutional attitudes.

This is significant because responding NGAs did not have a very favourable view about the transparency of agency analysis. Their responses also suggest that guidance documents are even more important for them than interactions in particular enforcement contexts, formal or informal. In any event, the demand for more and better guidance is expressed very strongly in responses throughout the whole NGA survey.

---

12 ICN Annual Conference Panel (Rigó comments). Collective passing-through of battery treatment fee (Energizer et al.) (VJ/43/2015). Further information on the case can be found in Appendix B of the survey report.

13 ICN Annual Conference Panel (Kar comments).

5. THE INTERNATIONAL DIMENSION

International convergence in dealing with sustainability cases would be extremely important – not only many environmental crises are of global nature, but also certain types of private "green initiatives" easily affect consumers in multiple countries and continents, given that supply chains are increasingly global.

Convergence, however, cannot be taken as granted. Our results show a current, and perhaps widening gap between Europe and the rest of the world, and only time will tell if that gap narrows or widens in the long run. European agencies may or may not be followed by others – anticipation and interest extend beyond the old continent, but this does not necessarily imply that cases will be approached in the same way across jurisdictions in the future. Even Europe is diverse right now, albeit there are signs of regional convergence around ongoing and possible future EU initiatives.

International co-operation is expected and likely to be instrumental in this context, according to our survey results. Direct co-operation between competition agencies, as discussed earlier, is a well-recognised way to meet challenges, and inherently facilitates convergence.

Responses also suggest that international organisations are supposed to play an important role. A clear majority of respondent agencies – and a large majority of those who responded to the particular question – believe that sustainability and competition should be among the top five topics that international organisations engage in. NGAs were even more supportive of the idea. Respondents would welcome recommendations and the collection of good practices the most. These contributions may be crucial for agencies with more modest resources and capacity.

6. CONCLUSIONS

The challenge of dealing with sustainability in competition enforcement is here to stay. One should keep it in mind, however, that, in the words of Andreas Mundt, "*sustainability and competition go hand in hand*",[14] and the question is rather whether there is a greater potential in competition policy, without compromising its benefits to society.

---

14 ICN Annual Conference Panel (Mundt comments). Mundt emphasized this not only in the panel discussion, but also in his speeches in the opening and closing sessions of the conference, by repeating the same phrase.

This may be the beginning of an even more beautiful friendship, but relationships require effort.

At the heart of the problem lie the unanswered questions of technical analysis. Experience is limited so far, and it is largely yet to explore whether, when and how to take sustainability considerations into account in competition enforcement. Research and development in competition policy is needed to move ahead: difficult analytical and measurement issues need to be resolved to get the right metrics that can serve as a basis for both better guidance and international convergence.

Competition agencies in all likelihood will need to adapt, most importantly, acquire new skills. Institutional memory about similar challenges in the past – such as market openings in network industries or digitalisation – can be especially valuable in this endeavour.

International co-operation is a crucial ingredient of the whole process, and – if its twenty-year history is any guide – the ICN is well placed to do its bit in its third decade.

SURVEYING THE SURVEYS: THE DRIVE FOR IMPLEMENTATION OF THE ICN'S RECOMMENDED PRACTICES FOR MERGER NOTIFICATION AND REVIEW PROCEDURES

Dave ANDERSON and Paul CULLIFORD

1. INTRODUCTION

1. Let's take a quick trip back in time to the late 1990s before there was an International Competition Network ("ICN"). There was a merger boom and a boom in the number of merger control regimes around the world. The proliferation occurred in an uncoordinated fashion and there was no consensus on global "best practice" with regard to the key issue of procedure – which deals should be notified, when, where, why or how. This rapid and uncoordinated expansion of merger control globally inevitably led to a divergence of approaches to the notification requirements and review procedures across jurisdictions. This, in turn, led to significant difficulties and uncertainties for advisors and companies trying to assess the notifiability of a transaction and coordinating multiple filings globally. Agencies also faced difficulties during this time, many receiving too many filings with limited or no nexus to their jurisdiction, thereby unnecessarily draining scarce resources, while others saw procedural divergence affect their ability to cooperate on deals that could have benefitted from international agency collaboration. The situation was viewed as chaotic and needed an international fix. Multiple efforts were launched by both the public and private sectors to address the global procedural divergence, all striving for consensus and harmonisation.

2. The international merger control divergence problem was one of the contributing factors that inspired the formation of the ICN in 2001 and led to the adoption of one of the ICN's earliest (and perhaps most enduring) convergence work products – the Merger Working Group's ("MWG") Guiding Principles for Merger Notification and Review Procedure, which were then followed by the Recommended Practices for Merger Notification and Review Procedures

(the "N&P RPs").[1] A three-step procedure (that has since been used in many other working groups) emerged from the ICN's N&P RP creation experience with agencies and their non-governmental advisors[2] ("NGAs") – namely (i) surveying jurisdictions and NGAs to identify agency practices and rationales (ii) where consensus could be found, developing and agreeing on the best or "recommended practices" and finally (iii) seeking implementation of those N&P RPs to drive global convergence where possible.

3. This last and key step of implementation has always been part of the ICN's culture and is key to ensuring that the ICN delivers tangible results. This has been true from its earliest days through to today as evidenced by the relatively recent creation of the "Promotion and Implementation" ("P&I") initiative.[3] The ICN's Mission Statement includes a goal "*to advocate the adoption of superior standards and procedures in competition policy around the world.*" To this end, the ICN's Chair, Andreas Mundt, has said that the ICN needs "*to raise awareness for its work products, promote them and ensure that they are implemented into legislation and everyday work, making the ICN the key element of global convergence in competition law.*"[4]

4. However, implementation and compliance measurement will always be challenging for an organisation like the ICN that produces non-binding recommendations leading to hoped-for voluntary adherence. Ensuring hard-won work products are utilised, influential and implemented is key for the ICN – it's where the "rubber hits the road" in terms of its effectiveness and significance. Throughout its history, the MWG has sought to promote implementation of the N&P RPs, and thereby global convergence in merger procedure rules, in a variety of ways. Examples of the MWG's work on implementation have included conducting annual workshops focussing on procedural issues, producing implementation self-assessment tools, providing direct assistance to agencies on reforms where requested and, importantly, on three occasions, "counting our numbers" by seeking to measure implementation of the N&P RPs through various forms of compliance surveys.

---

1 For further detail of the origin and development of the Recommended Practices, *see* M. Coppola & C. Lagdameo, Taking Stock and Taking Root: A Closer Look at Implementation of the ICN Recommended Practices for Merger Notification & Review Procedures, in P. Lugard (ed.), *The International Competition Network at Ten: Origins, Accomplishments and Aspirations* (Intersentia, 2011).

2 D. Anderson, Reflections on the ICN and its NGAs: Advocacy and Implementation, in P. Lugard (ed.), *The International Competition Network at Ten: Origins, Accomplishments and Aspirations* (Intersentia, 2011).

3 *See* the description of the Promotion and Implementation Group's mandate on the ICN website here: https://www.internationalcompetitionnetwork.org/working-groups/icn-operations/implementation.

4 A. Mundt, Focus, inclusiveness and implementation – The ICN as a key factor for global convergence in competition law, 2013.

5. The three N&P RP implementation surveys came in different forms in 2007, 2011 and 2016, each progressively increasing the scope and detail of the review, including in this last decade the most comprehensive survey ever. The important next step is to use the data obtained to continue to drive implementation and convergence, and help agencies towards the goal of even greater global harmonisation. This essay outlines the key aspects of the Recommended Practices, before going on to review the implementation of the N&P RPs to date, by reference to three separate surveys that have been conducted since they were first adopted. The essay concludes by considering what further steps could be taken in order to continue to move towards full implementation of the N&P RPs and convergence across merger control regimes globally, as well as areas where research and potential reform of the N&P RPs could assist these efforts. It is hoped that this "survey of the surveys" on N&P RP implementation will help the ICN members and NGAs remember their good work over the last two decades on this important convergence project while looking ahead to the work yet to be done in the ICN's next decade, in order to continue the convergence mission of the N&P RPs, one of the ICN's earliest and most influential work products.

2. THE N&P RPS

6. At the ICN's Second Annual Conference in 2003, three N&P RPs were adopted. A further 10 were adopted over the following years. The N&P RPs have been amended and added to a number of times since then.

7. As at January 2020, there are 13 categories of recommendation:

N&P RP I	Definition of a Merger Transaction
N&P RP II	Nexus to Reviewing Jurisdiction
N&P RP III	Timing of Notification
N&P RP IV	Review Periods
N&P RP V	Requirements for Initial Notification
N&P RP VI	Conduct of Merger Investigations
N&P RP VII	Procedural Fairness
N&P RP VIII	Transparency
N&P RP IX	Confidentiality
N&P RP X	Interagency Enforcement Cooperation
N&P RP XI	Remedies
N&P RP XII	Competition Agency Powers
N&P RP XIII	Review of Merger Control Provisions

8. Each wider N&P RP contains a number of specific recommendations and includes commentary, reflecting best practice and experiences across the ICN membership, as well as the views of NGAs to the ICN, from private practice and the business community.

9. The N&P RPs only cover questions of notifiability and procedure – i.e., the question of which transactions might require notification, and the procedure that applies to that notification. They do not, in particular, cover the substantive review of a transaction, which is covered by a separate set of recommendations.[5]

10. While the substance of a merger review will, of course, be crucial in some cases, the requirements for a notification obligation to arise and review procedures are important in all cases. The significant majority of notified transactions do not raise any substantive issues and are relatively routine – for example, in 2019, around 78% of transactions notified to the European Commission were notified and cleared at Phase One under the Commission's "simplified procedure,"[6] meaning they did not raise substantive issues. However, while such transactions do not raise substantive issues and Phase I clearance is more or less guaranteed, they still require notification and (in most jurisdictions) suspension until clearance is received. This has an important bearing on overall deal timelines, and in some cases on the viability of a deal at all.

11. In the modern economy merging companies will often have sales in multiple countries around the world, meaning it will often be necessary to assess notification thresholds and potentially notify a transaction in several jurisdictions. In order to give businesses certainty of where filings are required and, consequently, the effect on deal timelines, and also to assist parties and their advisors to coordinate filings across multiple jurisdictions, it is of crucial importance that merger rules across the world are clear and, as much as possible, consistent. This is what the N&P RPs aim to achieve.

12. However, while the drive for conformity with the N&P RPs is an important aspect of the ICN's work, it has its limits and it is important to remember that they are just that – recommendations. Not all global competition agencies are members of the ICN, and ICN members are not obliged to adopt them. Indeed, many aspects of the N&P RPs involve matters that are set out in legislation that agencies do not have direct power to control, and to implement them would require political buy-in and changes to that legislation, a key barrier to implementation.

---

5 ICN, Recommended Practices for Merger Analysis.

6 *See* European Commission Merger Statistics: https://ec.europa.eu/competition/mergers/statistics.pdf.

13. It must be kept in mind that these factors do not mean the ICN membership should not strive towards implementing the N&P RPs and, indeed, as is set out below there is evidence of a gradual move towards conformity with the N&P RPs across the ICN membership. However, there is also still a way to go.

3. ASSESSING CONFORMITY WITH THE N&P RPS

14. Because implementation of ICN work products is so key to the ICN's mission, tracking the success of the ICN's work products – in particular, the extent to which they have been implemented across the ICN membership – is crucial. To this end, since the initial iteration of the N&P RPs in 2002, the ICN MWG has carried out two systematic surveys of ICN members' compliance with the N&P RPs.

15. Between 2006 and 2007, ahead of the ICN's 2007 Annual Conference in Moscow, 57 ICN members were surveyed on their conformity with N&P RPs II and III ("the 2007 Survey"). In 2016, the ICN MWG implemented a "member self-assessment" survey where ICN members were asked to complete most of the N&P RP "Self-Assessment" tool (initiated in 2011) in a survey form to measure conformity with the N&P RPs ("the 2016 Survey").[7] The 2016 Survey was initiated in late 2015 by a small group of agencies and NGAs working within the MWG. The group started work after the 2015 ICN Merger Workshop in Brussels featured a panel commemorating the 10-year anniversary of the N&P RPs and a suggestion was made by a panellist that it was time to more fully "count our numbers" on implementation and that the existing N&P RPs self-assessment online tool could be used as a vehicle for the survey.[8] The 2016 Survey achieved a very high response rate that resulted in 80 of the 100 jurisdictions surveyed responding, and, to date, the 2016 Survey stands as the most comprehensive dataset and account of compliance with the N&P RPs.

16. In addition, in 2011, around half way between the 2007 and 2016 Surveys, Maria Coppola and Cynthia Lagdameo published an essay in the ICN's edited volume celebrating its tenth anniversary.[9] This essay reported the results of a review of ICN members' conformity with N&P RPs I to IV that had been carried out by a small project group.

---

7 ICN Merger Working Group, ICN Recommended Practices for Merger Notification and Review Procedures Member Self-Assessment: Report on 2016 Survey Results, April 2017.

8 This suggestion was made by one of the authors (Dave Anderson) and taken up energetically by the MWG co-chairs at the time, the United States Federal Trade Commission and the French Autorité de la concurrence. The suggestion to do a comprehensive N&P RP implementation study was also raised by the author at the time of the ICN's tenth anniversary (*see* Anderson, *supra* n. 2, p. 284).

9 *See* Coppola & Lagdameo, *supra* n. 1.

17. Given the evolution of the N&P RPs over time, and the more subjective nature of some N&P RPs, it is difficult to try to assess substantive conformity of ICN members across all N&P RPs. With that in mind, we have focussed the discussion in the following paragraphs on compliance with N&P RPs II, III and IV, which deal with the nexus to the reviewing jurisdiction, notification timing and review periods. These N&P RPs deal with some of the most important issues in practice for business and advisors, as they are crucial to determining whether a transaction will require notification and also the timing impact of that notification obligation.

4. THE GOOD NEWS: A STEADY MOVE TOWARDS IMPLEMENTATION AND CONFORMITY

4.1. N&P RP II

18. N&P RP II is aimed at ensuring ICN members' merger control laws only capture transactions that have a material "nexus" to that jurisdiction before a notification is triggered. That is, merger parties should only be put to the task of preparing a notification, and suspending their transaction until clearance is received, in jurisdictions where the merging parties have material business operations. To this end, N&P RP II makes a number of different recommendations, including:

- Recommending that thresholds incorporate appropriate standards ensuring that there is a material nexus to the reviewing jurisdiction[10];
- Recommending that the nexus to the reviewing jurisdiction should be based on the business activities of at least two parties and/or the acquired business in that jurisdiction[11]; and
- Recommending that notification thresholds should be based on clear and understandable[12], and objectively quantifiable[13], criteria.

19. This is one of the most important N&P RPs for business and advisors as it will, in most cases, be the determinative factor in ascertaining whether a notification, and associated obligations, are required. N&P RP I covers the definition of a merger transaction. However, in reality, in most transactions (particularly straight mergers or acquisitions of majority shareholdings), there will not be any doubt that the transaction is of the type that is, subject to the

10 N&P RP II(B).
11 N&P RP II(C).
12 N&P RP II(D).
13 N&P RP II(E).

relevant thresholds being satisfied, covered by merger control. Further, N&P RPs III through to XIII all cover questions of procedure (such as timing, information requirements and due process), all of which are only relevant if there is a filing obligation in the first place. So, it is the issues covered by N&P RP II that will in most cases be the "gateway" to whether merger control applies. This makes it even more important that the ICN and its members work towards convergence and conformity with N&P RP II.

20. There have been some positive moves toward greater conformity between 2007 and 2016. For example, in 2016, 91% of respondents commented that their thresholds for reviewing a merger required a substantial nexus to their jurisdiction.[14] This compares to only 69% in the 2007 Survey. Similarly, in the 2007 Survey, just 41% of respondents said that their thresholds only took into account the activities of the target business, rather than the selling entity. In the 2016 Survey this had risen to 71%.

21. N&P RP II(E) states that mandatory notification thresholds should be based on objectively quantifiable criteria, such as sales values (i.e., revenue) or asset values. The 2016 Survey found that 70% of respondents' jurisdictions used objectively quantifiable criteria within their merger notification thresholds. This represented a modest increase from the 66% who responded accordingly in the 2007 Survey.

22. In the 2007 Survey, respondents whose jurisdictions did not use objectively quantifiable criteria were asked to indicate the method that they used to measure whether a merger met the threshold for notification. This question was not repeated in 2016. Sixteen respondents determined whether a threshold was triggered by assessing the market share, five used market power and four assessed both the market share and market power. While, as noted, this same question was not asked in the 2016 Survey, our experience assessing merger control thresholds globally suggests that those jurisdictions that do not use objectively quantifiable criteria continue to use similar concepts of market share and market power.

4.2. N&P RP III

23. The time at which merger parties can, or are obliged to, make a notification can be crucial to ensuring tight deal timelines can be met, and to ensuring that

14 Although, as set out in Section V below, it is likely this figure is somewhat overstated as the "local nexus" requirement identified by many jurisdictions is unlikely to be consistent with the ICN's view on what constitutes a relevant local nexus.

multiple merger filings across the world can be coordinated. Two elements of rules relating to timing can be important in this regard:

- The earlier parties can make a filing, the earlier they can usually obtain clearances. Having to wait until a binding agreement is signed before filing, for example, can mean that such merger control procedures will lead to an unnecessarily long time between signing and closing a transaction.
- If the parties are obliged to make a filing within a specified deadline (for example, a specified number of days after signing), this can impact their ability to prepare a complete filing (particularly in cases where there are substantive issues to address), as well as their ability (and the ability of the agencies) to coordinate timing across jurisdictions.

24. To this end, N&P RP III sets out a number of best practices for the timing of notifications. The two principal recommendations are that:

- The parties should be able to notify a merger on the basis of a good faith intention to consummate a transaction (i.e., it should not be necessary for the parties to have entered into a binding agreement before they are able to notify)[15]; and
- In jurisdictions where closing a transaction is prohibited prior to clearance, there should not be a deadline for notification (i.e., the regime should not require notification within a specified time period following signing).[16]

25. This is an area that has seen significant improvement in terms of conformity between the 2007 and 2016 Surveys. With regard to N&P RP III(A), relating to notification on the basis of a good faith intention to consummate a transaction (meaning that the parties do not have to wait until they have a signed agreement before notifying), conformity increased from 57% to 81% between the 2007 and 2016 Surveys.

26. A greater number of jurisdictions also comply with N&P RP III(B), which suggests that suspensive merger control regimes should not include a deadline to file. In the 2007 Survey, 59% of jurisdictions with these suspensive rules did not impose a pre-merger notification deadline. By 2016, this had also risen to 81%.

27. Of course, not all jurisdictions have suspensive merger control regimes. To this end, N&P RP III(C) applies specifically to non-suspensive jurisdictions, where parties are permitted to close notified transactions before the relevant competition authorities have completed their review. This N&P RP acknowledges

15 N&P RP III(A).
16 N&P RP III(B).

that filing deadlines are legitimate in such jurisdictions, but recommends that parties be allowed a reasonable time in which to notify the transaction following a clearly defined triggering event. The reasonableness of a deadline is subjective, making it difficult to measure jurisdictions' conformity with this N&P RP. However, in the 2016 Survey only half of the respondents whose jurisdictions were non-suspensive stated that they imposed a filing deadline at all. Furthermore, just over half of these respondents had a clear definition of "triggering event" and just under half allowed extended filing deadlines where parties faced objective difficulties in satisfying notification requirements. In the 2007 Survey, only a third of the respondents with non-suspensive jurisdictions imposed a filing deadline.

28. One other important timing issue that is covered by N&P RP III is in relation to pre-notification discussions. Such discussions can be valuable to both agencies and merger parties to, first of all, ensure that a filing obligation actually arises, and if so, on the information the agency requires. This ensures that, once formal filing occurs, the filing can be quickly accepted as "complete," and the clock can start. N&P RP III(D) suggests that agencies should provide for this possibility. In the 2007 Survey, 70% of agencies allowed for such pre-notification discussions. At the time of the 2016 Survey, this had risen to 86%.

4.3. N&P RP IV

29. N&P RP IV relates to the review period for transactions. Again, this is of crucial importance to the business community, as the time periods during which their transactions may be subject to suspension obligations can have a crucial bearing on overall deal timing and, in many cases, they can make or break a deal. Further, in the few jurisdictions around the world where the merger control rules are not suspensive, businesses require certainty as to how long a review may run post completion so as to be able to begin truly integrating their businesses. Certainty of review periods also allows merging parties and their advisors to coordinate reviews across multiple jurisdictions simultaneously. Having convergence and consistency can also benefit agencies – by having consistency in review timings, agencies are better able to coordinate and cooperate on merger reviews with their peers.

30. To this end, N&P RP IV makes a number of recommendations relating to review periods. Most importantly, it is recommended that reviews are completed in a reasonable time[17], that expedited reviews are available for cases that do

[17] N&P RP IV(A).

not raise significant issues[18] and that waiting periods should expire within a specified period.

31. Over time, N&P RP IV has generally seen a high degree of conformity across ICN members. While the 2007 Survey did not assess the compliance of ICN members with N&P RP IV, Maria Coppola and Cynthia Lagdameo's 2011 essay considered some statistics in relation to N&P RP IV. In particular, Coppola and Lagdameo's survey of the 87 ICN members that had merger control rules in 2011 concluded that around 91% of jurisdictions' review periods expired within a determinable timeframe.[19] In 2016, 93% of respondents confirmed that their jurisdictions had merger review periods with definitive and readily ascertainable deadlines, while 96% of respondents added that their competition agencies completed their reviews in a determinable time period.

32. The allowance for expedited review for non-problematic transactions is another core limb of N&P RP IV. Coppola and Lagdameo's 2011 essay concluded that at least 31% of jurisdictions conformed with this N&P RP in 2011, by allowing non-problematic transactions to proceed following a preliminary review undertaken during an abbreviated initial review period.[20] By 2016, this figure had increased significantly, with 79% of respondents confirming that their jurisdictions provided for expedited reviews of non-problematic transactions.[21] It should, however, be noted that this apparent increase may be overstated and there is some subjectivity in determining whether an agency's procedures conform with this recommendation. For example, many jurisdictions' (including the European Commission's) procedures allow for a "short form" filing, with lower information requirements, in non-problematic cases. While in practice clearance is usually received much more quickly than in a "full" filing, there is often no formal difference in the statutory review period. As such, these jurisdictions could arguably fall either side of the line. It is, however, now clear that the vast majority of ICN member jurisdictions provide some form of relief to parties facing merger control obligations in non-problematic transactions.

4.4. CONFORMITY WITH AND USE OF THE N&P RPS GENERALLY

33. While neither the 2007 Survey nor Coppola and Lagdameo's 2011 essay covered all N&P RPs, the 2016 Survey did cover the majority of N&P RPs in one

18 N&P RP IV(B).

19 Coppola & Lagdameo, *supra* n. 1, p. 303.

20 Ibid.

21 N&P RP IV(B).

form or another. A full summary of compliance with all N&P RPs is not possible in the context of the current article. However, the 2016 Survey did show some high levels of conformity with various other N&P RPs – including some relating to due process and procedural fairness. A selection of such figures includes:

- 76% of respondents to the 2016 Survey confirmed that the merging parties will be provided with an explanation of the competition concerns that motivate an in-depth review no later than the beginning of a Phase II inquiry.[22]
- 95% of respondents to the 2016 Survey confirmed that parties have the opportunity to respond to material competition concerns before the agency makes a final enforcement decision.[23]
- 96% of respondents to the 2016 Survey confirmed that third parties are permitted to express their views on a merger during the review process.[24]

34. The 2016 Survey also demonstrates that, over time, ICN members have made changes to their merger control regimes that reflect the N&P RPs. It also demonstrates that many agencies actively consider the N&P RPs when reviewing their regimes.

35. The 2016 survey concluded with questions on how jurisdictions use the N&P RPs, with 65% of respondents confirming that they had used the N&P RPs when reviewing their merger notification and review regimes. Many of the jurisdictions that had used the N&P RPs in this way did so to identify areas for internal reform or legislative change. Others used them to draft specific notification or process rules and, in some cases, entirely new merger control regimes. For others, the N&P RPs were useful for building a consensus of opinion in support of the need for change.

36. ICN members were also asked to identify barriers that prevented the implementation of the N&P RPs. The most common obstacles were the cost and difficulty of both implementing legislative change and gaining external consensus for specific areas of reform.

22 N&P RP VI(C) reads: "Merging parties should be advised not later than the beginning of a second-stage inquiry why the competition agency did not clear the transaction within the initial review period."

23 N&P RP VII(B) reads: "Prior to a final adverse enforcement decision on the merits, merging parties should be provided with sufficient and timely information on the facts and the competitive concerns that form the basis for the proposed adverse decision and should have a meaningful opportunity to respond to such concerns."

24 N&P RP VII(C) reads: "Third parties should be allowed to express their views during the merger review process."

37. The final question of the 2016 survey asked ICN members whether any of the N&P RPs should be revised. Only 35% felt that there should be modifications. These respondents were then asked to identify which N&P RPs in particular should be revised. No N&P RPs were identified in greater numbers than the others. So, it appears that most ICN members are content with the N&P RPs in their current form. However, as we set out below, we believe there are a number of aspects of the N&P RPs that warrant revision or additions.

5. THE NOT-SO-GOOD NEWS

38. Having read the foregoing discussion, one could be forgiven for thinking that the picture is great – ICN members are using the N&P RPs and conformity is gradually improving, and so the N&P RPs are doing their job. While there is without doubt a lot that the ICN can be proud of, it is important to also consider the picture from the other angle – that is, the proportions of agencies that, in the 2016 Survey, still did not conform with the N&P RPs. When looking at the figures from this perspective, it is clear that there is still a lot of work to do.

39. Again, questions of local nexus and thresholds are some of the most important aspects of the N&P RPs. As set out above, there has been a steady increase in conformity with these N&P RPs since the 2007 Survey. However, significant proportions of the ICN membership still do not conform with some of the key recommendations in this area. For example:

- Although 91% of respondents stated that their thresholds require a substantial local nexus, over one third (38%) of respondents to the 2016 Survey confirmed that the local activities of the acquirer alone can trigger a notification requirement. That is, in 38% of ICN member countries, a merger notification obligation can be triggered even if the target has zero presence (in terms of sales or assets) on the local market. This shows that the 91% figure is likely to be somewhat overstated, as, if only the acquirer has a local presence, it is something of a stretch to suggest that the transaction in question truly has a local nexus. Indeed, the survey question itself defined "local nexus" as both parties, or the target business, having local activities.[25]
- Almost one third (30%) of jurisdictions surveyed in 2016 confirmed that their thresholds do not use objectively quantifiable criteria (such as sales or asset values) when determining notifiability. In our experience, most commonly this will mean that thresholds will be based on a subjective concept such as market share as is the case in some significant jurisdictions in Europe (for example Spain, Portugal and the United Kingdom – albeit that

[25] 2016 Survey, Question 1.

notification in the United Kingdom is voluntary), and further afield (such as Israel and Taiwan). Since 2016, conformity with this recommendation has arguably gone backwards, with Germany and Austria recently introducing new "transaction value" thresholds which contain a number of subjective elements – both in terms of actually determining the true "consideration" for a transaction and in determining whether the target is active "*to a significant extent*" in the relevant country. The fact that the joint guidance[26] of the Austrian and German agencies on these new thresholds runs to over 30 pages underlines the difficulties faced by the parties and the agencies in determining whether they are satisfied.

40. It is, however, not just in relation to thresholds and nexus where there remains work to do. There are also concerns in relation to the review periods in certain jurisdictions. The 2016 Survey showed, for example, that more than 80% of jurisdictions did not have specific procedures for companies in financial distress[27] (such as allowing for derogations from the suspension obligation, as is the case in jurisdictions such as the EU). The significant lack of such procedures across the ICN membership is concerning – although always the exception, the ability to provide respite from the suspension obligations of merger control can in some circumstances be the difference between a business (along with potentially thousands of jobs) being saved or failing. More than one third (37%) of respondents in the 2016 Survey also noted that their merger review procedures do not allow for early termination of applicable waiting periods (meaning that even in non-problematic transactions, parties are likely to have to see the full clearance timeline run its course before they can proceed with their transaction). This can have an unnecessarily significant impact on transaction timelines in non-problematic transactions.

41. The 2016 Survey also provided some worrying results as regards issues of due process and rights of defence. More than a quarter (26%) of jurisdictions responding said that the agency would not provide the merging parties with an explanation of their concerns prior to an in-depth review[28], and 39% of jurisdictions stated that parties could not withhold disclosure of materials that are subject to legal privilege or similar concepts.[29]

42. More generally, it is worth noting that no single respondent to the 2016 Survey demonstrated 100% conformity with the N&P RPs, with conformity

---

26 Bundeskartellamt & Bundeswettbewerbsbehörde, Guidance on Transaction Value Thresholds for Mandatory Pre-merger Notification (Section 35 (1a) GWB and Section 9 (4) KartG), July 2018.

27 N&P RP IV(E).

28 N&P RP VI(C).

29 N&P RP VI(F).

across the totality of those N&P RPs ranging from as low as 34% to as high as 95%. While having 100% conformity across the ICN may be an unrealistic goal, it is clear that there are many jurisdictions where significant work can be done in order to bring their regimes into greater conformity with the N&P RPs over the coming years. The next section considers how this can be achieved.

6. CONCLUSION: CONTINUE THE DRIVE TOWARDS CONVERGENCE – SOME SUGGESTIONS FOR THE NEXT DECADE

43. Andreas Mundt, the chair of the ICN, has said that "[i]*f we want to ensure that the ICN and its work products matter, we need to make our high-quality products available to everyone and continue our efforts to promote their implementation.*"[30] It is clear that further steps are required to promote the implementation of the N&P RPs. These promotion and implementation initiatives are key in assisting this drive towards convergence and conformity – having the N&P RPs freely available is one thing, but promoting them and encouraging their use and implementation is another story.

44. The MWG (including its NGAs) must continue to devote time and resources to the promotion and implementation of the N&P RPs (and, indeed, other work products). The MWG's efforts to date have borne fruit, as is evidenced by the significant improvements in conformity with a number of the N&P RPs worldwide. However, the job is not done. The fact that some agencies conform with as little as one third of the N&P RPs that were surveyed in 2016, and the fact that significant proportions of ICN members, in particular younger agencies, do not conform with some of the most important recommendations means that the MWG should be vigilant in ensuring the N&P RPs remain on the ICN's agenda and on the radar of non-compliant jurisdictions. The data generated by the 2016 Survey is a gold mine to help the ICN target its resources towards helping to improve conformity generally, but with a particular emphasis on those agencies that the data shows need significant assistance with implementation.

45. There is no "one way" to improve implementation efforts, but we offer a few concrete suggestions here as we enter into the ICN's next decade:

- **Survey using the Self-Assessment tool periodically**: We suggest that the 2016 Survey format using the N&P RPs Self-Assessment tool be used to survey conformity on a periodic basis now that it has been shown to be a

[30] Mundt, *supra* n. 4.

successful vehicle for assessing conformity. Its mostly "yes/no" design format is not burdensome for agencies and thus the 2016 Survey obtained a high response rate. The significant amount of useful jurisdiction-specific data on conformity also shows the 2016 Survey model to be a solid one for the MWG to continue to use. Also, surveying periodically and more frequently using the same format means that we will obtain comparable data across surveys thus enabling us to track trends and movements across the network and individual jurisdictions. The ICN should set itself target dates to re-review conformity with the N&P RPs at regular intervals. Running these surveys semi-regularly (for example, every three to five years) will help the MWG and P&I group determine whether the revised efforts are actually working and, if necessary, alter their strategy. It will also help identify any particular agencies that continue to lag behind, and that may therefore merit specific attention and discussion.[31]

- **Use the valuable survey data surgically**: The 2016 Survey provides an N&P RP-by-N&P RP account of agency compliance. Thus, we can see clearly which agencies need the most help and which need less. This should help the MWG target its implementation resources more surgically and efficiently, taking advantage of the detailed Self-Assessment Survey data to focus on assisting with compliance in those jurisdictions that need it the most.
- **Be creative with the "P&I" initiative**: The relatively new P&I group is perfectly placed to take a key role. The P&I group's mandate does not currently extend to engaging in promotion efforts itself. Rather, the group's aim is to work with the various working groups to share best practices for promotion and implementation, with a view to ensuring the ICN's work products are promoted and used to their full potential across the ICN membership (and, indeed, more widely). In this respect, given the fundamental importance that the N&P RPs play in ensuring the efficiency and viability of global merger control (and, in turn, global transactions), there may be room for the P&I group to use experiences across other working groups and more widely to assist the MWG to target agencies where conformity lags behind (and particularly those younger agencies from developing countries where the work product may not be as easily accessible), and also to push for greater conformity on a collection of what may be seen as "core" N&P RPs.
- **Some easy implementation wins**: We think there is merit in starting with some very simple steps to improve the accessibility and promotion of the N&P RPs. This could be as simple as translating the N&P RPs (or even just

31 Currently the Self-Assessment tool for N&P RPs has not been updated and at the time of writing is not operational on the ICN's website – this is an easy thing to fix and we would encourage the MWG to update the tool and put it back online so it can be used for self-assessment and survey purposes again.

a summary of them) into languages that will make them more accessible to some agencies. There may also be merit in considering targeted workshops or sessions at ICN conferences or merger workshops to work through key aspects of the N&P RPs with those agencies that are lagging behind. Relaunching the Self-Assessment tool for conformity may also assist agencies to re-engage with this issue, and identify where they have room to improve.

46. In addition to working on implementation of the N&P RPs, the MWG has periodically reviewed and amended the N&P RPs to keep up with evolving best practices and as a result improve the N&P RPs based upon the ideas and experiences of the ICN members and NGAs through the years. The authors have been a part of this ongoing reform process and believe that there may be a number of possible review and reform projects to promote best practice and convergence in the ICN's next decade, including:

- **Joint ventures**: There continues to be a multitude of approaches around the world to defining what constitutes a notifiable joint venture. These range from "EU-style" approaches, where both "joint control" and "full functionality" are required, to approaches that require just joint control, and others where the acquisition of a given (even very small) proportion of the shares or voting rights in a target is sufficient. Indeed, many jurisdictions do not even have a special "joint venture" test, meaning joint ventures need to squeeze into definitions of a merger that are best designed to capture straight acquisitions. This divergence globally on the fundamental issue of whether a deal is notifiable leads to different results and treatment of the same transaction around the world. This in turn leads to a significant and unnecessary burden on merging parties and their advisors when assessing notifiability globally. While the MWG has studied the differing approaches in the past[32] and has enhanced the N&P RPs by including for the first time an RP on the "Definition of a Merger Transaction" in the new N&P RP I in 2017, the comments relating to control and joint ventures could be enhanced to the benefit of agencies and parties given the divergence we currently have globally. We suggest that a "joint venture convergence project" should be undertaken in order to survey anew and capture best practices for defining what constitutes a notifiable joint venture. The MWG's 2020/21 Joint Venture survey report is a great first step to understand the current outlook on members' regimes within the network. The MWG should then, based on that initial survey and report, seek to provide more guidance in this area to drive greater legal certainty and convergence in the laws and practices worldwide.
- **Thresholds**: data/digital: At the time of the latest revision to the N&P RPs, the MWG expressly decided that it was too early to make any amendments

32 ICN, Defining "Merger" Transactions for Purposes of Merger Review, 2007.

in relation to the issue of catching transactions in the digital space, where the target may have little or no revenue.[33] This issue has been discussed at various ICN MWG workshops and at annual conferences in recent years while some agencies have moved ahead by introducing new "deal value" thresholds (e.g., in Germany and Austria) and others are considering introducing similar thresholds seeking to capture acquisitions involving "low revenue/high value" targets. In some cases, this involves a clear step away from conformity with N&P RP II regarding nexus, clarity and/or objectively quantifiable criteria in notification thresholds. It is also not necessarily clear that there is a problem to fix given the experience so far of jurisdictions employing such thresholds. There are also other models that are less burdensome to address any jurisdiction "gap" concerns. Given the overall focus within the ICN agency membership on digital issues in mergers, we think the time has now come to tackle this issue within the MWG by carrying out work to document global best practices in this area and, in particular, setting out alternative approaches (such as residual "call in" powers) that can allow such transactions to be captured while avoiding the introduction of deal value thresholds that are overly broad and based on non-objective criteria that increase compliance costs and risks for parties and guidance and consultation costs for agencies.

- **Information requirements**: While N&P RP V provides guidance to agencies on the requirements for initial notification, including recommending that initial requirements should be limited to avoid imposing unnecessary burdens in light of the fact that most transactions do not raise material competitive issues, agency practice worldwide varies considerably with regard to initial notification requirements and is even more varied in connection with further "requests for information" ("RFIs") during in-depth investigations. For example, some agencies "front load" initial requirements while others require less initially and then "back load" requests if issues are found. During in-depth investigations some agencies are willing to discuss and agree the scope of a draft RFI while others will not. The wide variety of procedures and practices in this area can give rise to inefficiencies and unnecessary burdens both for parties and agencies, particularly in multijurisdictional mergers. It would therefore seem that initial notification and ongoing information requirements and practices could be an ideal project for the MWG. Indeed, this was discussed by members of the MWG at the Merger Workshop in Melbourne in February 2020. Such a project could follow the traditional ICN model of first surveying agency procedures and practices with a view to determining the areas of consensus and divergence. The survey results could then give rise to guidance or recommended practices (e.g., enhancing N&P RP V) with a view to reducing burdens on agencies and parties by making information requirements in merger notifications

33 *See* N&P RPs, *supra* n. 1.

and RFIs more harmonised, effective and targeted, while possibly even facilitating better international cooperation in investigations.

- **Pre-notification** procedures: As noted above, N&P RP III(D) states that jurisdictions should provide for the possibility of pre-notification discussions. N&P RP V(C) covers this issue to some extent as well. While the increased conformity with this recommendation that we noted above is to be commended, we think that the practice of pre-notification procedure has evolved in an uncoordinated fashion worldwide resulting in a wide variety of practices worldwide leading to timing and other procedural divergences. As such, we believe that this is a clear area for research on "best practices" to help agencies and parties understand the different procedures employed globally and to see if there is scope for convergence through guidance or recommended practices in relation to pre-notification procedures. It is important to recall that N&P RP V(C) was drafted at a time when few agencies used a formal or informal pre-notification process and since then many agencies have developed such procedures while other agencies may be considering such procedures in future. During the review of N&P RP III that led to the 2018 amendments, the MWG drafting team (of which the authors were members) considered including more guidance on pre-notification procedure than appears in the new RPIII(D) but that part of the amendment process did not proceed. We believe that this is an area ripe for international best practice development given the expansion of the procedure in merger control globally and that an enhancement of RP III(D) and/or RP V(C) could help agencies and parties with more guidance based upon possibly an ICN MWG survey to identify best practices in this area. NGAs can assist in a material way from their experience of the various approaches, procedures and policies and their impact on notification timing and other aspects for parties involved in multijurisdictional filings in particular. It is crucial for agencies to remember that pre-notification engagement is voluntary and should only be intended to first confirm whether a transaction is notifiable and, secondly, confirm that the notification is complete before the formal "clock" begins ticking. In our experience, some agencies utilise pre-notification as an extension of their formal review period, meaning substantial RFIs are sent to the parties, and, in some cases, market testing even begins during this period. This can lead to the amount of time taken to obtain clearance significantly exceeding the formal review period, meaning that conformity with N&P RP IV(A) (which says merger reviews should be completed within a reasonable time) may be overstated in reality. In practice, as the vast majority of mergers are not problematic, pre-notification in most cases should not be an extended procedure but simply a brief one to help both the agency and the parties to agree on jurisdiction and notification requirements.

47. As can be seen by the above, there is plenty for the MWG and its NGAs to do in the ICN's third decade in the N&P RP area. We hope that the above "survey of the surveys" shows that the MWG is committed to the ICN's goal of implementation and that while we have come a long way since 2001, there is more to do to enhance implementation and thus deliver a key promise of the ICN to have an impact in practice. As we move into the ICN's third decade, such work within the MWG needs to continue energetically with a view to improving the efficacy and efficiency of the ICN members' merger regimes, helping private parties navigate and comply with the global network of regimes through enhanced convergence and, as a result, contributing positively to the economies of the ICN members.

THE NEXT FRONTIER OF INTERNATIONAL COOPERATION IN COMPETITION ENFORCEMENT

John Pecman and Duy D Pham*

1. INTRODUCTION

The practice of international cooperation among competition agencies has come a long way. One of the earliest cooperation instruments was the first OECD Recommendation on international cooperation in enforcement (OECD Recommendation) introduced in 1967.[1] The OECD Recommendation has been progressively refined with the most current version coming out in 2014.[2] An early example of a bilateral cooperation instrument is the 1976 US–Germany Antitrust Accord.[3] As of April 2017, the OECD's inventory of memoranda of understanding (MOUs) between competition agencies lists 145 such

---

* Competition Bureau of Canada.
John Pecman was appointed Canada's Commissioner of Competition in June 2013 for a five-year term. He also acts as ICN/OECD coordinator, OECD Bureau member and ICN steering group member. Mr Pecman is an economist with an MA from McMaster University and has worked at the Competition Bureau of Canada as an investigator, manager and executive for more than 30 years. Duy Pham is a Competition Law Officer with the Competition Bureau. He has an LLM from Georgetown University Law Center and a JD from the University of Ottawa, Faculty of Law. Prior to joining the Bureau, Duy consulted for the World Bank and US Federal Trade Commission and articled at a leading Canadian law firm. The views expressed in this article are the personal views of the authors. A substantially identical version of this contribution appeared in the Liber Amicorum for Frederique Jenny. We thank Concurrences for kindly agreeing to a reprint in this bundle of essays.

1 See OECD, *Challenges of International Co-operation in Competition Law Enforcement* (OECD 2014) 12 (OECD, Challenges).

2 OECD, *Recommendation of the OECD Council concerning International Co-operation on Competition Investigations and Proceedings*, C(2014)108 (16 September 2014) (OECD Recommendation).

3 Agreement between the Government of the United States of America and the Government of the Federal Republic of Germany Relating to Mutual Cooperation Regarding Restrictive Business Practices, 23 June 1976 www.ftc.gov/sites/default/files/attachments/international-antitrust-and-consumer-protection-cooperation-agreements/agree_germany.pdf.

instruments.[4] Modern cooperation instruments now cover a broad range of areas, including notifications, investigative assistance and information sharing.

Although significant progress has been made by the international competition community to facilitate cooperation, the reality is that the drivers that initiated the necessity for cooperation have only increased. One of the main drivers of international cooperation is the increasing globalisation of commerce.[5] Globalisation has resulted in business practices in one jurisdiction having the potential to negatively affect another jurisdiction.[6] However, there has been a recent populist backlash against international trade.[7] Scepticism toward international trade notably led the United States to withdraw from the Trans-Pacific Partnership.[8] Nevertheless, international trade is unlikely to significantly recede.[9] Mega-regional trade agreements, such as the Regional Comprehensive Economic Partnership, continue to move forward.[10] The Trans-Pacific Partnership has also been revived by the remaining parties as the Comprehensive and Progressive Agreement for Trans-Pacific Partnership.[11]

---

4 OECD, "Inventory of International Co-operation MOUs between Competition Agencies" (OECD 2017) 1 www.oecd.org/daf/competition/mou-inventory-list.pdf.

5 See John Pecman, "Better Together: The Importance of Cooperation Amongst Competition Authorities" (Remarks at the North American Antitrust Authorities Conference, 21 May 2015), <www.competitionbureau.gc.ca/eic/site/cb-bc.nsf/eng/03940.html>.

6 For an elaboration of effects-based conflicts, see Duy D Pham, "Resolving Conflicts in International Merger Reviews through Merger Remedies" (2016) 39(2) *World Competition* 267, 272–75.

7 See Andrew Sentance, "This Popular Backlash to Global Trade Threatens Mass Instability" *The Telegraph* (London, 30 September 2016) <www.telegraph.co.uk/business/2016/09/30/this-popular-backlash-to-global-trade-threatens-mass-instability/>.

8 See David Smith, "Trump withdraws from Trans-Pacific Partnership amid flurry of orders" *The Guardian* (London, 23 January 2017) <www.theguardian.com/us-news/2017/jan/23/donald-trump-first-orders-trans-pacific-partnership-tpp>.

9 See World Economic Forum, "Strategic Brief for the Annual Meeting of Stewards of International Trade and Investment" <www3.weforum.org/docs/WEF_DAVOS_BRIEF.pdf> ("It is true that global merchandise trade in value has been roughly flat for two years … [but] merchandise is hardly all that is traded. Services trade continues to grow, and new services are becoming tradable thanks to advances in communications. Digital trade reaches record highs every day, contributing to innovation, growth, and jobs. While cross-border capital flows are down, knowledge-intensive and long-term direct investment has held up well. Even some of the slow merchandise trade figures are due in part to weak commodity prices. The global value chains operated by many multinational corporations will continue to underpin international trade flows, even as they reorganise in response to policy and structural changes. So globalisation, in many important senses, is likely to continue in the upcoming years."). See also, HSBC, "Trade Winds: Shaping the Future of International Business" (2015) 2–3 <https://globalconnections.hsbc.com/grid/uploads/trade_wind_report.pdf> (projecting world trade in goods to quadruple in value by 2050).

10 Association of Southeast Asian Nations, Regional Comprehensive Economic Partnership (3 October 2016) <http://asean.org/?static_post=rcep-regional-comprehensive-economic-partnership>.

11 See Global Affairs Canada, Comprehensive and Progressive Agreement for Trans-Pacific Partnership (CPTPP) <www.international.gc.ca/trade-commerce/trade-agreements-accords-commerciaux/agr-acc/tpp-ptp/index.aspx?lang=eng>.

Jurisdictions continue to enter into expansive bilateral trade agreements, such as the Comprehensive Economic and Trade Agreement between Canada and the EU.[12] Although there has been a slight dip recently, international trade in merchandise and commercial services has nevertheless increased significantly from 2007 to 2016, according to World Trade Organization (WTO) data.[13]

Other drivers of international cooperation are the international competition institutions, such as the OECD, the International Competition Network (ICN) and the United Nations Conference on Trade and Development (UNCTAD).[14] These institutions provide a platform for cooperation and have become even more important due to the growing number of jurisdictions with competition laws and agencies. Between 1990 and 2013, the number of jurisdictions with competition agencies increased more than 500% (16 in 1990 compared with 120 in 2013).[15] Similarly, when the ICN first launched in 2001, it only had members from 14 jurisdictions.[16] As of 2017, it can boast having members from 122 jurisdictions. The explosion of competition agencies creates greater risk of conflict because each agency enforces a competition law that has different historical, economic and legal origins, as well as there being differences in procedures.[17]

A new development that may increase the potential for conflict is the increasing digitalisation of the global economy.[18] Firms that operate in the digital economy are often large businesses that operate across borders. Notable examples include Google, Amazon, Facebook and Apple. Furthermore, competition enforcement

12 See Global Affairs Canada, Canada–European Union Comprehensive Economic and Trade Agreement (CETA) <www.international.gc.ca/trade-commerce/trade-agreements-accords-commerciaux/agr-acc/ceta-aecg/index.aspx?lang=eng>.

13 World merchandise exports increased from US$14 trillion in 2007 to US$16 trillion in 2016, while imports increased from US$14.3 trillion to US$16.2 trillion over the same period. Similarly, world commercial services exports increased from US$3.5 trillion in 2007 to US$4.8 trillion in 2016, while imports increased from US$3.4 trillion to US$4.7 trillion over the same period. See WTO, "Statistics Database" http://stat.wto.org/Home/WSDBHome.aspx?Language=E.

14 See Hugh M Hollman and William E Kovacic, "The International Competition Network: Its Past, Current and Future Role" in Paul Lugard (ed) *The International Competition Network at Ten: Origins, Accomplishments and Aspirations* (Intersentia 2011) 51, 61–79.

15 OECD, Challenges (n 3) 26.

16 ICN, "History" <www.internationalcompetitionnetwork.org/about/history.aspx> The original 14 jurisdictions were Australia, Canada, the EU, France, Germany, Israel, Italy, Japan, South Korea, Mexico, South Africa, the UK, the US and Zambia.

17 For an elaboration of substantive conflicts, see Pham (n 8) 275–78.

18 See James Manyika, Susan Lund, Jacques Bughin, Jonathan Woetzel, Kalin Stamenov and Dhruv Dhingra, "Digital Globalization: The New Era of Global Flows" (McKinsey Global Institute February 2016) <www.mckinsey.com/business-functions/digital-mckinsey/our-insights/digital-globalization-the-new-era-of-global-flows> ("Remarkably, digital flows – which were practically nonexistent just 15 years ago – now exert a larger impact on GDP growth than the centuries-old trade in goods.").

against digital firms often involves novel and complex issues, such as two-sided markets, network effects and algorithms.[19] These features of digital firms, in conjunction with rising populist concerns[20] and differences in competition laws, increase tension among competition agencies and the risk of divergent approaches to enforcement.

Divergence, however, is not a new phenomenon. Indeed, the conflicting results in the GE/Honeywell and Boeing/McDonnell Douglas mergers provided the impetus for greater cooperation and convergence between competition agencies.[21] But all jurisdictions should agree on several fundamental principles in competition law. For example, a widely accepted economic standard such as the consumer welfare standard should be used to guide enforcement.[22] Relying on amorphous public interest considerations would only increase uncertainty and hurt consumers and businesses.[23] Relatedly, economics should be the primary tool of agencies. Overly formulistic approaches to enforcement can discourage procompetitive business practices.[24] Furthermore, enforcement should complement competitive neutrality – the idea that private and public enterprises should compete while facing the same set of rules and without government actions that would provide a competitive advantage to a market participant.[25] Competition can only truly flourish when both private and public distortions of competition are eliminated.

Another concern is the cost and uncertainty imposed on businesses that arise from increased multi-jurisdictional competition enforcement. This concern affects all three primary categories of enforcement – mergers, cartels and unilateral conduct. Competition practitioners have long lamented that multi-

---

19 See, generally, Antonio Capobianco and Anita Nyeso, "Challenges for Competition Law Enforcement and Policy in the Digital Economy" (2017) 1 *JECL & Pract* 1.

20 See James C Cooper, "A Return to Antitrust Populism?" *Antitrust Source* (February 2017).

21 See Merit E Janow and James F Rill, "The Origins of the ICN", in *The International Competition Network at Ten* (n 16) 21, 26–27.

22 See John Pecman, "Remarks at Weir Foulds" (24 October 2013) <www.competitionbureau.gc.ca/eic/site/cb-bc.nsf/eng/03622.html> ("[P]romoting consumer welfare is well aligned with the direction other prominent competition agencies are taking.").

23 See, arguing against non-economic considerations in merger control, OECD, "Public Interest Considerations in Merger Control: Note by BIAC" DAF/COMP/WP3/WD(2016)33 (6 June 2016) <www.oecd.org/officialdocuments/publicdisplaydocumentpdf/?cote=DAF/COMP/WP3/WD(2016)33&docLanguage=En>.

24 See (describing how through economic learning competition law has evolved from being formalistic to more effects-based) OECD, "Safe Harbours and Legal Presumptions in Competition Law: Background Note by the Secretariat" DAF/COMP(2017)9 (9 November 2017) 5–7 <https://one.oecd.org/document/DAF/COMP(2017)9/en/pdf>.

25 See OECD, "Roundtable on Competitive Neutrality in Competition Enforcement: Note by the European Union" DAF/COMP/WD(2015)31 (2 June 2015) 2 <www.oecd.org/officialdocuments/publicdisplaydocumentpdf/?cote=DAF/COMP/WD(2015)31&docLanguage=En>.

jurisdictional merger filings impose significant costs. A 2003 IBA/ABA survey revealed that a typical international merger required six filings, took an average of seven months to complete and generated an average of € 3.3 million in external merger review costs.[26] For international cartels, practitioners are concerned that having to comply with different leniency programmes creates undue burdens and uncertainty, ultimately reducing the incentive to apply for leniency.[27] Lastly, the concern with international unilateral conduct cases is the increased risk of divergent outcomes. Since unilateral conduct cases are often fact-intensive and analytically complex, there is less of an international consensus on the proper approach.[28] The risk of divergent outcomes in unilateral conduct cases results in unique challenges and costs for global businesses, while chilling innovation and investment.[29]

Consequently, the time is ripe for the international competition community to reinvigorate approaches toward cooperation. The purpose of this paper is to canvass and assess ideas on how competition agencies may be able to engage in even deeper and closer cooperation and to develop these ideas by fleshing out the issues that need to be addressed if they are to be implemented. Before we know where we want to take cooperation, we need to be able to envision its possibilities.

Part 2 of this paper discusses joint investigative teams (JITs), with a focus on the EU framework. Part 3 examines the potential for a multilateral MOU based on the International Organization of Securities Commission's (IOSCO's) Multilateral Memorandum of Understanding Concerning Consultation and Cooperation and the Exchange of Information (MMOU). Part 4 considers a common marker system inspired by the international patent filing system. Part 5 discusses enhanced extraterritorial application of competition laws based on

26 International Bar Association Press Release, "IBA/ABA Survey Identifies Costs to Business of Competition Referrals on Cross-Border M&A Deals" 23 June 2003, <www.ibanet.org/Article/NewDetail.aspx?ArticleUid=7a18abb4-4da0-4f31-b606-86c21b211a49>.

27 See, *e.g.*, Andreas Schwab and Christian Steinle, "Pitfalls of the European Competition Network – Why Better Protection of Leniency Applicants and Legal Regulation of Case Allocation is Needed" [2008] 29 *ECLR* 523, 526–27; Christof R. Swaak and Rein Wesseling, "Reconsidering the Leniency Option: If not First In, Good Reasons to Stay Out" (2015) 36 ECLR 346, 352. Part IV of this paper provides a more detailed discussion of the costs and uncertainty facing leniency applicants filing in multiple jurisdictions.

28 See Edith Ramirez, Chairwoman FTC, "Keynote Remarks" (at Problems with Global Antitrust Enforcement Conference, 20 February 2016) <www.ftc.gov/system/files/documents/public_statements/933593/160220yaleremarks.pdf>; Renata B Hesse, Principal Deputy Assistant AG, Antitrust Division, US DOJ, "Can There Be a 'One-World Approach' to Competition Law?" (Remarks at Chatham House Conference on Globalization of Competition Policy, 23 June 2016), <www.justice.gov/opa/file/897731/download>.

29 See A Neil Campbell and J William Rowley, "The Internationalization of Unilateral Conduct Laws – Conflict, Comity, Cooperation and/or Convergence?" (2008) 75 *Antitrust LJ* 267, 30911.

the unique and innovative Australia–New Zealand model. Part 6 argues that competition agencies should renew their commitment to using comity, when appropriate, to dispose of multijurisdictional competition cases. Although not a new concept, the ever-increasing internationalisation of competition enforcement suggests comity may become more relevant. Lastly, Part 7 provides concluding remarks.

Before going further, an important point to keep in mind is that several of these proposals may require more robust international competition institutions. The ICN, OECD and UNCTAD play important roles but they have limited resources, tools and mandates. For instance, these institutions currently do not have the ability to settle disputes between competition agencies, issue rulings, or act as a central repository for filings and applications. The WTO has some of these powers but its participation in international competition policy discussions has greatly diminished.[30] Thus, furthering international cooperation may require pushing existing institutions to do more or creating a new supranational body with greater powers.

2. JOINT INVESTIGATIVE TEAMS

Competition agencies may want to explore the use of cross-border JITs to deepen cooperation. The EU has an extensive legal and institutional framework governing JITs, since it has often combated transnational crimes such as terrorism and drug trafficking.[31] At EU level, the framework legislation governing JITs is the Convention on Mutual Assistance in Criminal Matters 2000 (the Convention).[32] Most EU Member States also have domestic legislation in place that implements the Convention.[33] In addition, participating Member States negotiate agreements to govern the operation of a particular JIT.[34]

---

30 See Hollman and Kovacic (n16) 72–73.

31 See Judit Nagy, "About Joint Investigation Teams in a Nutshell" (2010) 2 *Issues Bus & L* 105, 105. In 2016, 148 JITs were supported by Eurojust, 69 of which were newly formed. Eurojust, *Eurojust Annual Report* 2016 (Eurojust 2017) 18 <http://eurojust.europa.eu/doclibrary/corporate/eurojust%20Annual%20Reports/Annual%20Report%202016/AR2016_EN.pdf>.

32 Convention on Mutual Assistance in Criminal Matters between the Member States of the European Union (29 May 2000) OJ C 197/1, Article 13.

33 See Conference of the Parties to the UN Convention against Transnational Organised Crime, "Informal Expert Working Group on Joint Investigations: Conclusions and Recommendations" 5, CTOC/COP/2008/CRP.5 (2 October 2008) (Conclusions and Recommendations).

34 For a model agreement, see Network of National Experts on Joint Investigation Teams, *Joint Investigation Teams: Practical Guide* (14 February 2017) 28–7, 6128/1/17 Rev 1. The agreement covers topics including the purpose, duration and composition of the JIT, the jurisdictions where the JIT will operate and the procedures for the gathering, access and exchange of information and evidence.

Several EU institutions play a role in the formation and operation of JITs. Eurojust, the EU's judicial cooperation unit, assists Member States in identifying whether a JIT is suitable for a particular case and in negotiating JIT agreements.[35] During the operation of a JIT, Eurojust provides ongoing assistance through legal and practical advice, funding and the lending of technology. Another important institution is Europol, the EU agency responsible for supporting law enforcement agencies.[36] Member States can use Europol's databases, networks, facilities and expertise when forming and operating JITs.

Under the EU model, a JIT is formed when two or more Member States agree to participate in a joint criminal investigation in some or all of the participating jurisdictions.[37] One Member State will act as the lead jurisdiction and primary base of operations for the JIT.[38] The JIT is required to follow the laws of the lead jurisdiction. Other participating Member States will second members to the JIT.[39] Seconded members may be permitted to undertake investigative measures under the direction of the team leader.[40] When the JIT requires investigative measures to be undertaken in a participating Member State, the seconded member from that Member State may request the authorities in that jurisdiction to undertake the investigative measures; this request will be treated as though it was for a national investigation.[41] Seconded members may provide information to the JIT as long as it is for the purposes of carrying out the joint investigation and it is in accordance with the seconded member's laws and competence.[42] Conversely, information lawfully obtained as part of the JIT, which would not otherwise be available, may be used by the other participating Member States for the following purposes:

1. the purposes for which the JIT was formed;
2. for detecting other criminal offences if prior consent is given from the Member State where the information was obtained;
3. for preventing an immediate and serious threat to public security as long as a subsequent criminal investigation is opened; and
4. for other purposes if agreed to by the participating Member States.[43]

The major benefit of the EU JIT model over current forms of competition cooperation is its superior ability to facilitate the gathering and sharing of

---

35 Ibid 20–22.
36 Ibid 22–24.
37 Convention (n 34) Article 13(1).
38 Ibid Article 13(3).
39 Ibid Article 13(4).
40 Ibid Article 13(6).
41 Ibid Article 13(7).
42 Ibid Article 13(9).
43 Ibid Article 13(10).

information and evidence. First, a JIT can request investigative assistance from participating Member States more quickly and flexibly since such requests are treated as though they are for a national investigation.[44] Traditionally, a Member State would have to send a letter rogatory each time it required investigative assistance. This would not be a significant issue if a cross-border investigation required only a few discrete and predictable instances of assistance. However, if the investigation requires assistance dynamically and frequently, having to exchange letters rogatory would become quite burdensome and could even hamper the investigation. Second, as a result of the Convention, domestic implementing legislation and JIT agreements, JIT members can share information and evidence with each other more freely but in a way that is consistent with the laws and expectations of each participating Member State.[45]

Newer competition agencies that struggle to enforce their competition laws could benefit greatly from JITs. For instance, in many developing countries, agencies often lack the resources, expertise and tools (particularly, effective leniency programmes) to adequately combat international cartels.[46] In these situations, a newer agency could defer investigating an international cartel to a lead agency from a mature jurisdiction that has formed a JIT to prosecute the cartel. The newer agency would then second a member to the JIT. In addition to ensuring that the anti-competitive effects in its jurisdiction are being taken into account by the JIT, an ancillary benefit of the secondment is that it would serve as an opportunity for the newer agency to gain experience and expertise from the more mature agency and for them to build a relationship of trust and understanding.

But even mature agencies may benefit from JITs. For instance, a mature agency may be thinking about applying comity to defer enforcement against a cross-border cartel to a better-placed lead agency.[47] Such a situation arose between the Netherlands' Authority for Consumers and Markets (ACM) and Germany's Bundeskartellamt in a cross-border towage cartel case.[48] A mature agency may be more willing to defer enforcement, as the ACM did in the towage case, if it is able to second a member to the lead agency. The secondment would provide the

44 See Toine Spapens, "Joint Investigation Teams in the European Union: Article 13 JITS and the Alternatives" (2013) 19 *Eur JCrime CrLCrJ* 239, 247–48.

45 See ibid 249.

46 See UNCTAD, "Cross-border Anti-competitive Practices: the Challenges for Developing Countries and Economies in Transition" TD/B/C.I/CLP/16 (19 April 2012) 3–11.

47 Part VI of this paper contains a more in-depth discussion of comity.

48 See Mattijs Baneke and Ruben Elkerbout, "Towage Services Cartel: a New Chapter in the Collaboration between Competition Authorities?" (Kluwer Competition Law Blog 6 February 2018) <http://competitionlawblog.kluwercompetitionlaw.com/2018/02/06/towage-services-cartel-new-chapter-collaboration-competition-authorities/>.

agency with another means to ensure that its interests and concerns are being fully considered by the lead agency.

Despite the potential benefits of JITs, several significant obstacles need to be overcome before they can be used for cross-border competition enforcement. One major issue is complying with disclosure obligations. Since information and evidence are coming from and being sent to members from multiple jurisdictions, JITs may complicate competition agencies' ability to comply with disclosure obligations when engaging in litigation. This issue was recently considered in *United States v Matthew Connolly and Gavin Campbell Black*.[49] The case was part of the US Department of Justice's (US DOJ's) prosecution of the global LIBOR rate-fixing conspiracy. The defendants attempted to argue that the US DOJ, as part of its disclosure obligations, was required to, among other things, disclose exculpatory evidence in the possession of foreign agencies that had also prosecuted LIBOR cases. As part of their arguments, the defendants claimed that the US DOJ had engaged in joint investigations with these other agencies based on press releases indicating they had cooperated and, in one instance, an agency had provided legal assistance. The judge ultimately rejected the defendants' arguments, holding that they provided insufficient evidence to establish there was a joint investigation. Furthermore, the judge held that even if there was a joint investigation, for sovereignty reasons the US DOJ would only be required to make a good faith effort to obtain the exculpatory evidence from the other agencies to comply with its disclosure obligations.

Another issue is the substantial legal and institutional framework that may be required to implement JITs. Competition agencies wanting to employ JITs would have to ensure their laws, for example, permit foreign officials to participate in investigations in their jurisdiction; allow their authorities to provide investigative assistance to JITs as though it was for a national investigation; and permit the exchange of information and evidence between the participating jurisdictions.[50] Furthermore, international competition institutions, in their current form, are unlikely to be able to provide the type of institutional support for agencies wanting to implement JITs that Eurojust and Europol currently provide EU Member States.

Nevertheless, it is important to note that several of the mechanisms required for JITs are already in place in limited forms for some jurisdictions. For example, competition agencies already engage in staff exchanges[51] and cross-

---

49 *United States v Matthew Connolly and Gavin Campbell Black*, No. 1:16-cr-00370 (SDNY, 2 March 2017) (order denying defendants' joint motion to compel).

50 See Conclusions and Recommendations (n 35) 19.

51 See FTC, International Fellows Program <www.ftc.gov/policy/international/international-fellows-program>.

appointments.[52] In merger cases, agencies have even conducted joint interviews and remedy negotiations.[53] Going forward, agencies may want to consider using these mechanisms more strategically to emulate some of the functions of JITs.

A way to address some of these concerns, while also maintaining some of the benefits gained from JITs, is for competition agencies to engage in more parallel investigations. With parallel investigations, agencies conduct their own investigations but do so with frequent uses of investigative assistance and exchanges of information and with closely coordinated investigative steps. As with JITs, agencies conducting parallel investigations could negotiate agreements to set out the obligations and expectations of each participating agency.

Greater use of parallel investigations could facilitate closer cooperation in unilateral conduct cases where competition agencies have historically engaged in relatively less cooperation.[54] One of the major obstacles to cooperation on unilateral conduct cases is the lack of alignment on procedural timetables, such as there is for mergers.[55] Parallel investigations may address this problem by aligning investigative timetables without the need for procedural amendments. Suppose an agency begins a unilateral conduct investigation and is aware that another jurisdiction could also be significantly affected by the conduct. The initial agency could invite the potential partner agency to open an investigation. If the initial agency is significantly further ahead in its investigation, it could bring the partner agency up to speed on the investigation.

Another issue that parallel investigations may help to resolve is the inadmissibility of evidence from international investigations. This issue arose recently in another LIBOR case, *United States v Allen*.[56] In that case, the defendants had been compelled to provide testimony by the UK Financial

---

52 See Winnie Agbonlahor, "Australian and New Zealand competition watchdogs announce new cross-appointment" Global Government Forum 11 December 2015, <www.globalgovernmentforum.com/australian-and-new-zealand-competition-watchdogs-announce-new-cross-appiontment/>.

53 See Canada–US Merger Working Group, "Best Practices on Cooperation in Merger Investigations" (25 March 2014) <www.competitionbureau.gc.ca/eic/site/cb-bc.nsf/vwapj/Canada-US-Best-Practices-en-2014–03–25.pdf/$file/Canada-US-Best-Practices-en-2014–03–25.pdf> (discussing how the Competition Bureau and US antitrust agencies will conduct joint interviews and remedy negotiations).

54 In the OECD/ICN survey on international cooperation that collected data from 2007 to 2012, only 13 competition agencies out of the 55 responding agencies had any experience with cooperation in unilateral conduct cases. In contrast, 19 and 21 agencies had experience with cooperation in cartel and merger cases, respectively. OECD, Secretariat Report on the OECD/ICN Survey on International Enforcement Co-operation [2013] 66 (OECD/ICN Survey).

55 See Ramirez n 30; Cynthia Lewis Lagdameo, "Climbing Mount Everest with the ICN Unilateral Conduct Working Group" [2012] *Competition Policy International* 1, 8 <www.competitionpolicyinternational.com/assets/Uploads/ICN-11–27–2012–2.pdf>.

56 *United States v Allen* No. 16–898 (2d Cir, 19 July 2017).

Conduct Authority (UK FCA) for its investigation. A witness relied on by the US DOJ for the US proceedings had been exposed to this compelled testimony. The US Court of Appeals for the Second Circuit held that the US DOJ's use of this witness had violated the defendants' US constitutional right against self-incrimination. If the US DOJ and UK FCA had been more closely cooperating as part of a parallel investigation into LIBOR rate-fixing, the US DOJ may have been able to prevent the witness from being tainted by the testimony compelled by the UK FCA. At the very least, the US DOJ would have been more alive to the potential issues because it would have been closely cooperating with the UK FCA.

3. MULTILATERAL MOU

Cooperation between competition agencies has primarily been facilitated through bilateral cooperation instruments.[57] Instruments with broader coverage have been developed, such as the OECD Recommendation[58] and several regional agreements created as part of trading blocs, but most of these have been limited in their coverage and relative success at encouraging enforcement cooperation.[59] Agencies thus lack a true multilateral cooperation instrument with near universal coverage.

A multilateral cooperation instrument that can serve as inspiration is the Multilateral MOU (MMOU)[60], which was negotiated by IOSCO.[61] Initially, IOSCO did not take a central role in the negotiation of cooperation instruments,

57 Cooperation instruments often take the form of MOUs signed between agencies. See, e.g., Memorandum of Understanding between the Commissioner of Competition, Competition Bureau of the Government of Canada and the Competition Commission of the Hong Kong Special Administrative Region of the People's Republic of China Regarding the Application of Competition Laws and the Sharing of Information (2 December 2016) <www.competitionbureau.gc.ca/eic/site/cb-bc.nsf/vwapj/MOU-Bureau-CC-Hong-Kong-e.pdf/$file/MOU-Bureau-CC-Hong-Kong-e.pdf> On occasion, these instruments can also come in the form of state-to-state agreements. See, e.g., Agreement between the Government of the United States of America and the Commission of the European Communities Regarding the Application of their Competition Laws (23 September 1991) 1995 OJ L 95/47, <http://eur-lex.europa.eu/legal-content/EN/TXT/PDF/?uri=CELEX:21995A0427(01)&from=EN>.

58 OECD Recommendation, n 4.

59 See UNCTAD, "Review of the Experience Gained so Far in Enforcement Cooperation, Including at the Regional Level" (10 May 2011) TD/B/C.I/CLP/10, 7–9.

60 Multilateral Memorandum of Understanding Concerning Consultation and Cooperation and the Exchange of Information (May 2002, revised May 2012), <www.iosco.org/library/pubdocs/pdf/IOSCOPD386.pdf> The International Association of Insurance Supervisors has also instituted a multilateral cooperation instrument: IAIS Multilateral Memorandum of Understanding on Cooperation and Information Exchange (February 2007, revised July 2014) <www.iaisweb.org/page/supervisory-material/mmou/file/34363/iais-mmou>.

61 See IOSCO, "About IOSCO" <www.iosco.org/about/?subsection=about_iosco>.

leaving that up to the prerogative of its members.[62] At the urging of the US, this approach to cooperation instruments began to change after the events of 9/11 due to concerns that financial markets were being used to finance terrorism.[63] In October 2001, IOSCO formed a project team to consider expanding cooperation and information-sharing among financial regulators and enforcement authorities. The project team introduced the MMOU in 2002. Adoption of the MMOU was initially lacklustre, with only 25 signatories by the end of 2004. However, from April 2005 IOSCO began to commit significant resources to push members to become signatories of the MMOU and decided to pursue a policy of full implementation by IOSCO members. As of November 2016, of the 140 eligible IOSCO members, 109 were signatories of the MMOU.[64] Consequently, the MMOU has been used more frequently, with the number of information requests increasing from 56 in 2003 to 3,330 in 2016.

IOSCO uses several positive and negative incentives to encourage its members to become signatories of the MMOU. First, IOSCO makes available to non-signatory members a comprehensive programme of technical assistance and political support to ensure they can make the necessary legal changes to sign onto the MMOU.[65] Second, IOSCO publishes a watch list on its website of members who are not signatories of the MMOU.[66] The watch list serves as a way of applying indirect pressure by publicly identifying non-signatories, since being part of the MMOU may offer a member legitimacy and prestige.[67] Lastly, IOSCO has measures that allow it to restrict non-signatory members from nominating candidates for IOSCO leadership positions, participating in certain committees and exercising voting rights. It has also suggested that members take precautions when engaging in securities transactions with entities or individuals from non-signatory jurisdictions.[68]

IOSCO's use of aggressive tactics to encourage the adoption of its MMOU contrasts greatly with the ICN's more inclusive approach toward the adoption of its work product. The ICN has traditionally encouraged members to implement its numerous work products but has not resorted to providing either positive

62 See Janet Austin, "The Power and Influence of IOSCO in Formulating and Enforcing Securities Regulations" (2015) 15 Asper Rev 1, 4–5 (Austin, IOSCO).

63 See Janet Austin, "IOSCO's Multilateral Memorandum of Understanding Concerning Consultation and Cooperation and the Exchange of Information: A Model for International Regulatory Convergence?" (2012) 23:4 *CrimLF* 393, 402–6 (2012) (Austin, MMOU).

64 IOSCO, "About MMOU" <www.iosco.org/about/?subsection=mmou>.

65 See n 66.

66 IOSCO, "2013 List of Non-signatories to the MMoU" <www.iosco.org/about/?subSection=mmou&subSection1=2013_list>.

67 See Austin, MMOU (n 65) 406.

68 See IOSCO media release, "IOSCO Reinforces Standard on Cross-Border Cooperation" 18 September 2013 <www.iosco.org/news/pdf/IOSCONEWS299.pdf>.

or negative incentives.[69] Indeed, this approach to implementation is set out in the ICN's foundation document.[70] Consequently, if competition agencies decide to pursue a multilateral MOU through the ICN, that MOU may not be able to obtain as wide coverage as the MMOU unless the ICN adopted a similarly aggressive approach toward implementation. But if the ICN did take such an approach, the risk is that this would alienate members of the ICN that did not want to sign onto a multilateral MOU.[71]

Another notable feature of the MMOU is the institutional framework in place to oversee applications and compliance. To sign onto the MMOU, an IOSCO member must go through a rigorous application process to demonstrate it is able to implement the provisions of the MMOU.[72] This process involves submitting an application that goes through various bodies within IOSCO that screen, verify and ultimately make a decision on the application. The following are the bodies involved and their respective roles in this process:

- The Secretary General provides general administrative support and initially verifies that the application is complete.
- The Screening Group, which is composed of representatives of IOSCO members in the Monitoring Group, assesses whether an applicant has the legal authority to comply with each of the MMOU's provisions and provides an overall recommendation to the Decision-Making Group.
- The Verification Team, a small team composed of IOSCO members with substantial enforcement expertise, prepares a report in which it makes a recommendation on whether the applicant is able to comply with the MMOU.
- The Decision-Making Group, which is comprised of chairmen from several of IOSCO's committees, makes a final decision on the application.[73]

In addition, there are procedures in place to ensure continuing compliance with the MMOU.[74] All MMOU signatories are members of the Monitoring Group, which makes recommendations to the Decision-Making Group on a course of action if a signatory is determined not to be in compliance with the MMOU. If a

69 See Paul Lugard, "The ICN at Ten. Origins, Accomplishments and Aspirations: An Introduction", in Paul Lugard (ed) *The International Competition Network at Ten: Origins Accomplishments and Aspirations* (Intersentia 2011) 5, 12–13.

70 ICN, Memorandum on the Establishment and Operation of the International Competition Network 1 <www.internationalcompetitionnetwork.org/uploads/library/doc579.pdf>.

71 See Austin, IOSCO (n 64) 11 (expressing similar concerns regarding IOSCO's aggressive approach to implementation of the MMOU).

72 See IOSCO, "MMOU: Frequently Asked Questions" 8–10, <www.iosco.org/library/mou/pdf/MoU-FAQS.pdf>.

73 See n 74, 10–12.

74 See n 74, 20–21.

signatory is concerned that another signatory is not complying with the MMOU, it can bring up the issue with the Monitoring Group. Potential sanctions for non-compliance include suspension and termination from the MMOU.[75]

This robust institutional framework is a feature that the ICN currently lacks. While IOSCO has a physical headquarters in Madrid[76], the ICN has operated as a "virtual network" rather than a "bricks-and-mortar" organisation from its inception.[77] Substantial resources would thus be required to transform the ICN into an organisation that could provide the necessary institutional support for a multilateral MOU in the way that IOSCO has for the MMOU. Otherwise, the ICN would not be able to adequately receive and process applications and verify and monitor compliance of a multilateral MOU.

Nevertheless, one of the major strengths of a potential multilateral MOU over bilateral cooperation instruments is the former's ability to facilitate convergence in the way competition agencies cooperate. Since every IOSCO member interested in becoming a signatory has to go through a rigorous screening process, the MMOU ensures that each signatory has the necessary powers to collect and share information with its enforcement partners.[78] In other words, the MMOU facilitates the proliferation of common powers among securities regulators so that they can cooperate effectively with each other. Furthermore, the MMOU ensures that all the signatories cooperate using harmonised procedures. For instance, the MMOU provides a standard form for requests for information.[79] Harmonised procedures would simplify cooperation, potentially benefiting newer agencies that do not have as much experience of cooperating with other agencies.

Consequently, greater convergence in the way competition agencies cooperate could encourage more collaboration on enforcement. In the OECD/ICN survey on cooperation, the top reasons inhibiting cooperation included legal limitations, lack of willingness to cooperate and lack of resources.[80] Since agencies would be expected to have similar powers regarding the collection and sharing of information, a multilateral MOU could reduce the amount of legal limitations to cooperation. Additionally, a lack of willingness to cooperate could be overcome

---

75 MMOU (n 62) Annex B, Part III(c).

76 See IOSCO, Annual Report 2016, 80 <www.iosco.org/annual_reports/2016/pdf/CompleteAnnualReport2016.pdf>.

77 See Alexander Schaub, "Co-operation in Competition Policy Enforcement between the EU and the US and New Concepts Evolving at the World Trade Organization and the International Competition Network" (Remarks at Mentor Group, Brussels, 4 April 2002) <http://ec.europa.eu/competition/speeches/text/sp2002_013_en.pdf>.

78 See Austin, MMOU (n 65) 409–10.

79 MMOU (n 62) Annex C.

80 See OECD/ICN Survey (n 56) 104.

if there was a mechanism to monitor the extent of cooperation, which could most effectively be achieved with a multilateral cooperation instrument. Lastly, a harmonised approach to cooperation would ensure that working with other agencies becomes more routine and therefore less resource and time intensive.

4. COMMON MARKER SYSTEM

For most competition agencies, leniency programmes are central tools for detecting cartels.[81] However, concerns have been raised that the incentives for businesses to apply for leniency are decreasing. Reasons for this include the difficulties businesses face in making informed decisions on whether to apply for leniency, agencies applying more discretion in how they apply leniency procedures and the growth of private enforcement.[82] Furthermore, for businesses contemplating applying for leniency, there is a tension between the speed and the accuracy of an investigation.[83] When conducting an internal investigation over suspected cartel behaviour, a business would want to get a comprehensive view of the facts (i.e., information about the conduct and its potential extent and scope). A thorough investigation, however, takes time and could inhibit a business's ability to be, crucially, the first leniency applicant. The fact that there can be different first-in applicants in different jurisdictions also creates problems. A business that is the first-in applicant in one jurisdiction but not in another has conflicting incentives because it would want to divulge information of its involvement in a cartel in the former jurisdiction but downplay involvement in the latter jurisdiction to limit its potential liability.

A way to address these issues is to introduce a common marker system.[84] First, such a system would exponentially increase the incentive to be the first-in applicant because establishing priority in one jurisdiction would establish it in others. Second, the system would reduce the tension between speed and accuracy because it would make filing in multiple jurisdictions significantly less time-consuming, complex and costly. Lastly, by ensuring a common date of priority when filing in multiple jurisdictions, the system would reduce the risk that a first-in applicant in one jurisdiction would not be the first-in applicant in others.

---

81 See OECD, "Competition and the Use of Markers in Leniency Programmes: Note by Secretariat" (16 December 2014) DAF/COMP/WP3(2014)9, 23 (OECD, Secretariat).

82 See Romina Polley, "Is the Continued Success of Leniency in Cartel Cases in Danger? Some Comments from a Private Practitioner's Perspective" (2015) 1 *CPI Antitrust Chron* 1, 2–3.

83 See John M Taladay, "Time for a Global 'One-Stop Shop' for Leniency Markers" (2012) 27 *Antitrust* 43, 44–45.

84 See Antonio Capobianco and Aranka Nagy, "Developments in International Enforcement Co-operation in the Competition Field" (2016) 7 *JECL & Pract* 566, 577–79.

Furthermore, a common marker system would benefit competition agencies if it results in more and better-quality leniency applications and improves their ability to cooperate through better alignment of investigative timelines.[85] Newer agencies that do not currently present a credible risk of enforcement for international cartels could particularly benefit because they would be less ignored by potential leniency applicants.[86]

A type of common marker system endorsed by several commentators is a one-stop shop system.[87] Under this system, an applicant could apply for a marker at a supranational body, in any of the participating jurisdictions or at a designated jurisdiction that acts as a clearing house. Once the marker is granted, this would immediately be notified to all the jurisdictions where the applicant wishes to obtain leniency. The date of notification would establish the date for determining priority. It would still be up to each agency, however, to ultimately grant leniency in accordance with their respective laws. The benefit of a one-stop shop system is that it could reduce costs and uncertainty for applicants since they would only have to apply for a single marker.[88] By contrast, applicants currently have to go through the difficult task of obtaining a marker in multiple jurisdictions. Nevertheless, a one-stop shop system may be difficult to implement because it would require all the participating agencies to agree on harmonised information requirements and timelines for perfecting a marker, and to have mutual trust that other agencies will be able to keep the information in a marker confidential.[89]

Inspiration for a common marker system can be taken from the international patent filing system, since establishing priority is also a concern for patents.[90] One way an applicant can obtain a patent in multiple jurisdictions is to go through the system enacted by the Patent Cooperation Treaty (PCT)[91], which

---

85 See OECD, Secretariat (n 83) 27.

86 See OECD, "Use of Markers in Leniency Programs: BIAC" (16 December 2014) DAF/COMP/WP3/WD(2014)38, 3 (OECD, BIAC).

87 For one-stop shop marker proposals, e.g., Taladay (n 85) 46–48; ICC, "Proposal to the International Competition Network for a One-Stop-Shop for Leniency Markers" (March 2016) 225/752.

88 See OECD, Secretariat (n 83) 26.

89 See OECD, Secretariat, n 83, 27–28. It is important to mention that a one-stop shop system does not need to be put in place all at once. Competition agencies could begin by agreeing on a uniform marker application and then work toward aligning their timelines for perfecting markers. Even in the absence of a one-stop shop system, such harmonisation could benefit businesses through reduced compliance costs.

90 Establishing priority is important in patent law because an inventor generally cannot obtain a patent for an invention that another inventor has already filed a patent for. See Graeme B Dinwoodie, William O Hennessey and Shira Perlmutter, *International and Comparative Patent Law* (Matthew Bender, 2002) 115–116.

91 Patent Cooperation Treaty (10 June 1970) 1160 UNTS 231.

was introduced in 1970 and currently has 152 contracting states.[92] The PCT system involves an international stage and a national stage. The international stage involves an application process that establishes the date of priority and consists of up to five steps (the first three are mandatory while the last two are optional):

1. the filing and processing of the application by a receiving office;
2. the establishment of the international search report and written opinion by an international search authority;
3. the publication of the international application together with the international search report by the World Intellectual Property Organization's International Bureau;
4. a supplementary international search carried out by one or more international search authorities, other than the authority that conducted the original search; and
5. the establishment of an international preliminary examination and international preliminary report on patentability by an international preliminary examining authority.[93]

National and regional patent offices carry out the functions of the various offices and authorities.[94] During the national stage, the applicant submits its international application to a national or regional patent office in accordance with that office's procedures, and the office ultimately determines whether to grant a patent under its patent laws.

Although applicants still have to go through each patent office in the jurisdictions where they want a patent, the PCT system benefits applicants for two primary reasons. First, with only one application, an applicant can establish a globally recognised date of priority and go through the five steps in the international stage only once, regardless of the subsequent number of patent offices where applications for a patent are filed.[95] Second, with the information, reports and assessments obtained at the international stage, applicants can avoid filing applications at patent offices if they conclude they are unlikely to be granted a patent.[96]

---

92 World Intellectual Property Organization (WIPO), "The PCT now has 152 Contracting States" <www.wipo.int/pct/en/pct_contracting_states.html>.

93 WIPO, PCT Applicant's Guide – International Phase (2017) 4 <www.wipo.int/pct/guide/en/gdvol1/pdf/gdvol1.pdf>.

94 See Jay Erstling and Isabelle Boutillon, "The Patent Cooperation Treaty: At the Center of the International Patent System" (2006) 32(4) *WmMitchell LRev* 1583, 1587–88.

95 WIPO, n 95, 6.

96 Ibid.

In addition, applicants who want to obtain patents in multiple jurisdictions can use an alternate procedure. Under article 4 of the Paris Convention for the Protection of Industrial Property, if an applicant properly files a patent application in one contracting state, it can file in other contracting states within 12 months and the date of the initial filing will be the one considered to determine priority.[97]

A common marker system based on this reciprocal procedure could provide some of the benefits of a one-stop shop system without the need to harmonise leniency programs. Under such a system, a leniency applicant can initiate a marker with one agency and mention that it intends to apply to other participating agencies. The initial agency would then immediately notify the other agencies of the marker, which would establish the date of priority for these jurisdictions.[98] The applicant would then have a set period of time, such as three months, to obtain markers under the procedures of each agency. This system would provide more time and flexibility to applicants as well as greater certainty regarding their priority in different jurisdictions. Smaller jurisdictions could particularly benefit from this system because one of the difficulties applicants face when seeking leniency in these jurisdictions is that there are fewer local law firms with the right expertise and experience.[99] As a result, finding a firm that is free of conflicts of interest is significantly more difficult. A reciprocal system for markers would provide applicants with more time to find proper local competition counsel, thus making leniency more accessible in these jurisdictions.

5. ENHANCED EXTRATERRITORIAL APPLICATION OF COMPETITION LAWS

Jurisdictions have generally resisted the extraterritorial application of another jurisdiction's competition law to conduct that occurred within their own borders.[100] In contrast to this, Australia and New Zealand have created a legal framework to facilitate the extraterritorial application of each other's

97 Paris Convention for the Protection of Industrial Property (20 March 1883, last revised at Stockholm, 14 July 1967) 828 UNTS 30.

98 Some competition agencies under this reciprocal marker system may be reluctant to take on the responsibility of having to notify the other agencies. If that is the case, a supranational body could be tasked with notifying the relevant agencies.

99 See OECD, BIAC, n88, 2.

100 Indeed, US attempts to apply its antitrust laws extraterritorially caused several jurisdictions to enact "blocking statutes" to limit such encroachment. See Roger P Alford, "The Extraterritorial Application of Antitrust Laws: A Postscript on *Hartford Fire Insurance Co v California*" (1993 34 *VaJInt'l L* 213, 215.

competition laws. This enhanced extraterritoriality framework is worth considering since it fosters more efficient and effective application of Australian and New Zealand competition laws in cross-border cases.[101]

First, Australia and New Zealand have explicit provisions in their competition laws that prohibit the misuse of trans-Tasman market power.[102] For example, section 46A of Australia's Competition and Consumer Act 2010 provides:

> (2) A corporation that has a substantial degree of market power in a trans-Tasman market must not take advantage of that power for the purpose of:
> (a) eliminating or substantially damaging a competitor of the corporation, or of a body corporate that is related to the corporation, in an impact market; or
> (b) preventing the entry of a person into an impact market; or
> (c) deterring or preventing a person from engaging in competitive conduct in an impact market.

This provision gives the Australian Competition and Consumer Commission (ACCC), or a private party[103], explicit legal authority to bring a case against anti-competitive conduct that has an effect in Australia, New Zealand or Australia and New Zealand collectively. Extraterritorial enforcement is further supported by section 155A of the Act, which gives the ACCC the power to obtain information and documents in New Zealand for investigations relating to trans-Tasman markets.

Second, Australia and New Zealand introduced innovative features relating to judicial proceedings to further extraterritorial enforcement of their competition laws. For instance, under the Federal Court of Australia Act 1976, the Federal Court of Australia can sit in New Zealand to conduct trans-Trasman market proceedings.[104] New Zealand lawyers are entitled to practice before the Federal Court when it sits in New Zealand.[105] The Federal Court can issue injunctions

101 See Productivity Commission, *Australian and New Zealand Competition and Consumer Protection Regimes: Productivity Commission Research Report* (2004) 20–21.

102 A trans-Tasman market is defined as "a market in Australia, New Zealand or Australia and New Zealand". Competition and Consumer Act 2010 (Cth) s 46A(1) (Austl.). To ease explanation of the enhanced extraterritoriality framework, citations in this paper will be made to provisions relevant for initiating trans-Tasman proceedings from the Australian perspective. It is important to keep in mind, however, that there are equivalent provisions that allow for trans-Tasman proceedings to be initiated from the New Zealand perspective. For a more detailed description of how Australia and New Zealand have created a trans-Tasman judicial area for a broad range of matters including competition, see generally Reid Mortensen, "A Trans-Tasman Judicial Area: Civil Jurisdiction and Judgments in the Single Economic Market" (2010) 16 *Canta LR* 61.

103 Competition and Consumer Act 2010, ss 80, 82.

104 Federal Court of Australia Act 1976 (Cth) s 32C.

105 N 108, s 32D.

against conduct in New Zealand.[106] Furthermore, under New Zealand's Trans-Tasman Proceedings Act 2010, Australian judgments in trans-Tasman market proceedings are enforceable in New Zealand if they are registered with the High Court of New Zealand.[107]

Notably, the introduction of this enhanced extraterritoriality framework allowed Australia and New Zealand to abolish the enforcement of their anti-dumping laws against each other.[108] Arguably, the two countries' competition laws now deal more effectively with problems that were previously dealt with by the anti-dumping laws.[109] Proponents of this approach argue that the only economically justifiable application of anti-dumping laws is to deter international predatory pricing, but that this practice can be dealt with more effectively through predatory pricing provisions in competition laws.

The fact that this enhanced extraterritoriality framework was instituted as part of the Australia–New Zealand Closer Economic Relations Trade Agreement[110], which has the goal of significantly deepening economic integration between Australia and New Zealand, suggests there are likely several important preconditions that have to be met for such a framework to become viable.[111] First, there likely has to be a substantial degree of legal convergence between the jurisdictions to reduce the risk of inconsistent application of their respective laws.[112] Greater divergence between the laws would also increase the difficulty of instituting the necessary legal changes. Second, there likely needs to be a high degree of trust between the jurisdictions.[113] Otherwise, there would be a fear that extraterritorial enforcement would be used to serve one jurisdiction's interests at the expense of the other. Lastly, the jurisdictions likely need to have

---

106 N 108, s 32E.

107 Trans-Tasman Proceedings Act 2010, ss 69–72 (N.Z).

108 Protocol on Acceleration of Free Trade in Goods (18 August 1988) [1988] ATS 18, Article 4 (entered into force 18 August 1988).

109 For the argument that competition laws should take the place of ant-dumping laws, see, e.g., Presley L Warner, "Canada–United States Free Trade: The Case for Replacing Antidumping with Antitrust" (1992) 23 *Law & Pol Int Bus* 791; Michael J Trebilcock and Thomas M Boddez, "The Case for Liberalizing North American Trade Remedy Laws" (1995) 4 *MinnJGlobal Trade* 1. But see Terence P Stewart and Timothy C Brightbill, "Some 'Heretical' Observations on the Interaction of U.S. Trade and Competition Laws: A Defense of U.S. Antidumping and Countervailing Duties" (1996) 4 *US-Mex LJ* 35 (arguing that competition law and anti-dumping law are complementary).

110 Australia–New Zealand Closer Economic Relations Trade Agreement (28 March 1983) [1983] *ATS* 2 (entered into force 1 January 1983).

111 See Mortensen n104, 62–66; Geoffrey Palmer, "International Trade Blocs – New Zealand and Australia: Beyond CER" (1990) 1 *PLR* 225.

112 See Palmer, n115, 228 ("Australia and New Zealand share the same legal history. We share the same legal tradition. We share a reliance on the common law, and we have developed common legal institutions.").

113 See Palmer, n 115, 222 ("New Zealand and Australia have a unique relationship. No other pair of neighbouring countries have been touched by so little distrust or mutual suspicion.").

a strong trade relationship.[114] In the absence of such a relationship, it would be unlikely that the economic benefits to instituting an enhanced extraterritoriality framework would outweigh the substantial implementation costs.

6. RENEWED COMMITMENT TO COMITY

As businesses become more global, there is a greater risk that competition enforcement in one jurisdiction will have unintended negative effects in another. For instance, concerns have been raised that competition agencies are employing remedies with extraterritorial effects which may be inconsistent with another jurisdiction's laws or policies.[115] To reduce the potential for conflict, agencies must enforce their competition laws in a manner that is mindful of the effect their decisions will have on other jurisdictions.

A way to approach competition enforcement in this manner is through the application of comity. Although it has several different meanings, in the context of enforcement, comity often refers to the practice of competition agencies standing "aside in appropriate cases where other authorities were better placed to take charge of the matter and where interests of the deferring authority would otherwise be protected".[116] The 1967 OECD Recommendation on cooperation recognised early on the need for agencies, in accordance with the principle of comity, to exercise moderation and self-restraint in the interest of cooperation.[117]

114 See Parliament of the Commonwealth of Australia, *Report 116: Review into Treaties Tabled on 24 and 25 November 2010, 9 February and 1 March 2011 and Treaties Referred on 16 November 2010 (Part 3)* (11 May 2011) 74, <www.aph.gov.au/Parliamentary_Business/Committees/House_of_Representatives_Committees?url=jsct/1march2011/report.htm> ("In 2009, two-way bilateral investment between the two countries totalled $110 billion and it continues to increase annually. The greater movement of people, assets and services across the Tasman also increases the prospects for litigation with a trans-Tasman element. The implementation of the [Agreement between the Government of Australia and the Government of New Zealand on Trans-Tasman Court Proceedings and Regulatory Enforcement] should reduce the time and costs involved in such litigation.").

115 See, e.g., Koren Wong-Ervin, Bruce H Kobayashi, Douglas H Ginsburg and Joshua D Wright, "Extra-jurisdictional remedies involving patent licensing", [2016] *Competition Policy International* 1, <www.competitionpolicyinternational.com/wp-content/uploads/2016/12/CPI-Wong-Ervin-Kobayashi-Ginsburg-Wright-Final.pdf>.

116 Terry Calvani and Justin Stewart-Teitelbaum, "Is There Too Much Traffic on the Competition Law Enforcement Autostrada?" (Draft Paper Presented at the Fordham Competition Law Institute 43rd Annual Conference on International Antitrust Law & Policy, 22 September 2016) <https://awards.concurrences.com/IMG/pdf/negative_comity_--_2016.11.30_--_calvani_stewart-te.pdf>.

117 See Deborah Platt Majoras, "Convergence, Conflict, and Comity: The Search for Coherence in International Competition Policy" (Remarks at the Fordham Competition Law Institute 34th Annual Conference on International Antitrust Law & Policy, 27 September 2007) <www.ftc.gov/sites/default/files/documents/public_statements/convergence-conflict-and-comity-search-coherence-international-competition-policy/070927fordham_0.pdf>.

However, despite the growing number of multi-jurisdictional competition cases, comity is seldom employed in this manner.[118]

Comity and cooperation should be complementary ideas.[119] For instance, if a competition agency is considering deferring to another agency's remedy, closely coordinating on the investigation ensures the deferring agency can be confident that the remedy adequately addresses the competition concerns in its jurisdiction. Further, when agencies closely cooperate on cases, they build the necessary trust and understanding that serves as the foundation for comity.

For multi-jurisdictional competition cases, comity is important because it allows for efficient and harmonious enforcement.[120] If a remedy imposed by Agency A addresses the competition concerns in Agency B's jurisdiction, then Agency B imposing its own remedy would simply increase the costs of enforcement for both the agency and the affected business without providing much additional benefit. Furthermore, when an agency accepts another's remedy, it eliminates the risk of conflicting remedies.

It is important to emphasise that comity is not about a competition agency abdicating its responsibility to enforce its laws.[121] Prior to relying on another remedy, an agency would have conducted its own initial investigation and collaborated with the other agency to know the degree of competitive harm done to its jurisdiction and whether the remedy sufficiently resolves those harms. Indeed, if it is properly applied, comity will help an agency better enforce its laws.[122] By not wasting resources on a matter that was adequately addressed by another agency, agencies can focus their resources on pursuing matters that they are best placed to deal with.

The ACCC and the Canadian Competition Bureau (Bureau) have created frameworks that guide their application of comity and thus offer useful models that other agencies could consider adopting. The ACCC applies comity in cases where it has concluded that:

(i) the nexus to Australia of the competitive harm being investigated was not sufficient (including considerations of the level of involvement of Australian businesses); and

---

118 See Calvani and Stewart-Teitelbaum, n 120.

119 See Sheridan Scott, "Canadian Perspectives on the Role of Comity in Competition Law Enforcement in a Globalized World: To Defer or Not To Defer? Is that the question?" (Remarks at American Bar Association's Section of Antitrust Law 2006 Spring Meeting, 29 March 2006).

120 See Calvani and Stewart-Teitelbaum, n 120.

121 See Sheridan Scott, "A Canadian Perspective on the Role of Comity in Competition Law Enforcement in a Globalised World" (2012) 1 *Competition LRep* 103, 106.

122 Scott, n 123.

(ii) possible enforcement actions by sister agencies would nevertheless result in the termination of the offending conduct and protection for Australian consumers.[123]

The ACCC has even established an internal benchmark of dedicating only 50% of its cartel caseload to international cartels so that it can focus its resources on investigating national cartels.[124]

With respect to the Bureau, it set out its approach to comity in merger cases in the "Information Bulletin on Merger Remedies in Canada".[125] The Bureau may apply comity and defer to another agency's merger remedy when the following conditions are met:

1. the assets that are subject to divestiture, or the conduct that must be carried out as part of a behavioural remedy, are primarily located in another jurisdiction;
2. the Bureau is confident that the foreign agency's remedy is effective and viable and that it will enforce the remedy; and
3. the Bureau is satisfied that the actions taken by the foreign agency are sufficient to resolve the competition issues in Canada.[126]

For international mergers, these conditions provide useful guidance for determining when a local remedy would be required or when another agency's remedy would be adequate. When considering comity in other areas of competition enforcement, the Bureau would apply the same general principles as it does for mergers.[127]

The Bureau has several examples that illustrate how it has used comity in each enforcement area. An international merger example is the GlaxoSmithKline (GSK)/Novartis transaction.[128] The transaction contained three parts: (1) GSK and Novartis would create a joint venture containing their over-the-counter and consumer healthcare products; (2) Novartis would sell its global vaccine business

123 Calvani and Stewart-Teitelbaum, n 120.

124 See Calvani and Stewart-Teitelbaum, n 120.

125 Competition Bureau, "Information Bulletin on Merger Remedies in Canada" (22 September 2006) <www.competitionbureau.gc.ca/eic/site/cb-bc.nsf/eng/02170.html>.

126 See ibid, para 78.

127 See Vicky Eatrides, "The Competition Bureau's Approach to International Cooperation and Comity" (Remarks at USC Gould's Center for Transnational Law and Business Inaugural Conference on Antitrust Enforcement in a Global Context: Extraterritoriality and Due Process 23 January 2017) (on file with authors).

128 See Competition Bureau, "Competition Bureau Statement Regarding the Three-part Inter-conditional Transaction between GlaxoSmithKline plc and Novartis AG involving their Consumer Healthcare, Vaccines and Oncology Businesses", 23 February 2015, <www.competitionbureau.gc.ca/eic/site/cb-bc.nsf/eng/03874.html>.

(with the exception of its influenza business) to GSK; and (3) GSK would sell its global portfolio of oncology products (excluding manufacturing assets) to Novartis. The Bureau decided that a Canadian-specific remedy was not required after it investigated the transaction and ultimately determined that the US Federal Trade Commission's requirement that Novartis divest its pipeline cancer treatment therapy was sufficient to address the competition concerns in Canada with respect to the oncology part of the transaction.

A notable example of the Bureau's application of comity to international cartel enforcement can be seen in the auto parts case involving Nishikawa.[129] In that case, after extensively consulting with the US DOJ, the Bureau determined that the bid-rigging primarily targeted US consumers. Further, the Bureau was satisfied that the US$130 million fine imposed by the US DOJ effectively addressed the adverse effects of the conduct in both Canada and the United States. It is important to note that Nishikawa took a proactive approach and brought this situation to both enforcers simultaneously. When considering comity in cartel cases, of upmost importance to the Bureau is whether another jurisdiction's sanction sufficiently denounces the Canadian offence and deters others from committing similar offences in Canada.[130]

Lastly, the Microsoft case is an example of the Bureau applying comity in the context of an international unilateral conduct case.[131] Given the integrated nature of the North American market, the Bureau decided to await the outcome of the case in the United States rather than impose its own remedy first. This approach allowed the Bureau to have its concerns addressed without needlessly duplicating efforts. It also ensured that the Bureau's enforcement action did not conflict with the enforcement action of a jurisdiction that had a significantly greater nexus.

7. CONCLUDING REMARKS

The international competition community should receive this paper as a call to action to be more imaginative in our thinking and more ambitious in our proposals. The challenges we face in an increasingly globalised and digital world make it imperative that we find new ways to cooperate in order to make competition agencies more efficient, to better protect consumers and to reduce

129 See Competition Bureau News Release, "Unprecedented Cooperation with US Antitrust Enforcement Authority Leads to Major Cartel Crackdown" 20 July 2016, <www.canada.ca/en/competition-bureau/news/2016/07/unprecedented-cooperation-with-us-antitrust-enforcement-authority-leads-to-major-cartel-crackdown.html>.

130 See Eatrides, n 131.

131 See Scott, n 123.

undue costs on businesses. This paper offers several ideas to stimulate further discussion and debate. We invite the international competition community to engage with these ideas at forums such as the OECD, ICN and UNCTAD.

HOW ICN AND UNCTAD CAN WORK TOGETHER IN INTERNATIONAL CARTEL ENFORCEMENT BEYOND 2020

Experiences of the UNCTAD Discussion Group on International Cooperation

Pierre M. HORNA*

The rising protectionism in both developed and developing countries has sparked cross-border anticompetitive practices such as hard-core cartels to flourish. These actions have impacted a vast majority of jurisdictions including developing countries and countries with economies in transition, which form the majority of agencies in 2019 (roughly 100 out of 140).

As a result, UNCTAD Member States and relevant stakeholders have convened various consultations on the topic of international cooperation in the area of competition law enforcement since 2017 in Geneva. The main focus of the discussions was particularly on how to deter the harmful effects of cross-border anticompetitive practices within and on vulnerable domestic markets.

Throughout the durations of the consultations, UNCTAD Member States have decided to strengthen the available tools and procedures to fight against international forms of anticompetitive practices. As such, the Section F of the UN Set on Competition was chosen to provide additional avenues as the way forward to combat anticompetitive practices at the international level. This

* Legal Affairs official at the Competition and Consumer Policies Branch of the United Nations Conference on Trade and Development (UNCTAD). Dr. Horna was the Lead Coordinator of the UNCTAD Discussion Group on international Cooperation at the UNCTAD Competition Branch since 2017 and is grateful to the contribution of the 10 Member States that were part of the Drafting Committee of the Guiding Policies and Procedures that was agreed in July 2019. The author wishes to thank the comments sent to an earlier version of this draft from David Anderson, Anna Pozdnyakova, Sofia Puteri and Sophie Hunter. The views expressed and remaining errors are the author's responsibility and are not to be taken as the official views of the UNCTAD Secretariat or its Member States. Comments and suggestions can be made to author at: Pierre.Horna@un.org

is particularly important for the young competition agencies and also to the competition agencies that lack familiarity with international cooperation schemes. The reason being that much of provisions were developed by mature and bigger competition agencies and mostly by developed countries and some BRICS competition agencies.

The purpose of this paper is to provide some suggestions as to how UNCTAD and ICN could work together in international cooperation in dealing with competition enforcement cases. This is particularly relevant since UNCTAD Member States have adopted an important instrument that will be formally included as an annex to the Set of Multilaterally Agreed Equitable Principles and Rules for the Control of Restrictive Business Practices (The UN Set on Competition) during the 8th Review Conference of the UN Set on Competition to be held in July 2020.

The paper, firstly, presents the work of UNCTAD in international cooperation in competition enforcement cases, and then of the ICN. Subsequently the paper will provide insights on the relevance of the latest instrument entitled 'the Guiding Policies and Procedures under Section F of the UN Set on Competition' (GPPSF), which has already been triggered twice by Member States. Finally, the paper ends with conclusions and suggestions as to how ICN and UNCTAD mechanisms can complement each other in the next decade of work (2020–2030).

1. THE WORK OF THE UN AND UNCTAD ON INTERNATIONAL COOPERATION[1]

From 1946 until the establishment of UNCTAD in 1964, the United Nations worked under the framework of the Economic and Social Council (ECOSOC). The United Nations has established an ad-hoc committee on Restrictive Business Practices (RBPs) that produced reports throughout the years, particularly in the 1950s.[2]

1 This section has been greatly enriched by an interview with the former head of UNCTAD's Competition Branch. Interview with Qaqaya, Hassan, 'Interview with the Former Head of the Competition and Consumer Policies Branch of the United Nations Conference on Trade and Development (UNCTAD)' (30 May 2017).

2 The founding members of this Ad-hoc Committee were 10 States (Belgium, Canada, France, India, Mexico, Pakistan, Sweden, UK, US and Uruguay) and were entrusted to prepare and submit to ECOSOC no later than March 1953, proposals on methods to be adopted by international agreement for implementing the recommendation on how to control RBPs. On 26 May 1955, ECOSOC resolution 568(XIX) reaffirmed its continuing concern with the existence in international trade of RBPs which have harmful effects; urged governments to continue the examination of RBPs with a view to the adoption of laws, measures and policies which will counteract such effects; and recommended Member States to continue to

In 1946, the US delegation prepared the initial blueprint on RBPs within the framework of Committee III on Restrictive Business Practices. At the first session of the preparatory committee of the UN Conference on Trade and Employment (UNCTAE), the US delegation informed the committee of the US antitrust experience in dealing with RBPs which were restraining trade within the Federal Union. Thus, it was no surprise when the brief statement given by Mr. Wilcox, Head of the US delegation, highlighted the reasons as to why a chapter on RBPs should be included in a World Trade Charter known as the Havana Charter.

In 1976 at the UNCTAD IV Ministerial Conference in Nairobi, UNCTAD received a more ambitious mandate that reinvigorated the application of the Havana Charter at the international level. UNCTAD Member States decided to initiate negotiations "with the objective of formulating a set of multilaterally agreed equitable principles and rules for the control of RBPs having adverse effects of international trade [the Set] (…) [and] to convene further meetings of the ad hoc intergovernmental group of experts (IGE) on RBPs which, taking into account the work of the Second Ad-hoc Group of Experts on RBPs".[3]

In 1978, the UN General Assembly decided to convene a conference on RBPs. In two sessions held in November-December 1979 and April 1980 under the auspices of UNCTAD, the remaining issues on international trade were resolved.[4] The United Nations Conference on Restrictive Business Practices (UNCRBP)[5] was concluded on 22 April 1980, with the adoption of a resolution that approved a "Set of Multilaterally Agreed Equitable Principles and Rules for the Control of Restrictive Business Practices".[6] The Set has been valid for over thirty-five years, with seven review conferences organized every five years.

Following the UN Conferences on Restrictive Business Practices, the UNCTAD has been able to assist developing countries and economies in transition in the

---

communicate to the Secretary General information concerning laws, measures and policies adopted by them in respect of such RBPs.

3 Official Archive of the United Nations, 'Proceedings of the UNCTAD. Fourth Session. Volume I, Report and Annexes' (United Nations Secretariat 1977) TD/218 (Vol I) P. 13.

4 Official Archive of the United Nations, 'United Nations General Assembly Resolution 33/153' (1978) <www.un.org>.

5 The UNCRBP deserves particular attention because it is the first global negotiation to produce a compact on the control of restrictive business practices since formal international discussions on the issue began in 1946. Moreover, the UNCRBP participants compounded their surprise by producing a lengthy and intricate text despite their strikingly diverse political philosophies coming from different regional groupings, developed, developing countries as well as the socialistic block. See Dale A Oesterle, 'United Nations Conference on Restrictive Business Practices' (1981) 14 Cornell International Law Journal 1.

6 UN, 'THE UNITED NATIONS SET OF PRINCIPLES AND RULES ON COMPETITION' <http://unctad.org/en/docs/tdrbpconf10r2.en.pdf> accessed 17 February 2017.

implementation of competition policies and law through its three pillars: (1) the Intergovernmental Group of Experts (IGE) on Competition Law and Policy and its Model Law on Competition; (2) research and analysis; and (3) technical assistance and capacity building work, all of which are vital in building laws and policies. Major UNCTAD ministerial conferences and review conferences of the UN Set on Competition have consistently endorsed the UN Set since 1980.

In 2010, the UNCTAD has received a clear mandate in the area of international cooperation in cartel enforcement to further intensify efforts to fight against cross-border anticompetitive practices at the international level. To this end, secretariat reports discussed at the 2012, 2013, 2014 IGEs have focused on the following topics: cross-border anticompetitive practices and the challenges for developing countries and economies in transition;[7] modalities and procedures for international cooperation in competition cases involving more than one country;[8] the impact of cartels on the poor;[9] and informal cooperation among competition authorities in specific cases.[10]

At the fifteenth session of the IGE in October 2016, Member States have instructed the UNCTAD Secretariat to prepare a background note on enhancing international cooperation in the investigation of competition cross-border cases. The background note was subsequently presented at the IGE in July 2017 and the note was ultimately endorsed by the BRICS countries in the quest for finding the best available tools to enhance international cooperation in cartel investigations.[11]

2. THE WORK OF THE ICN IN THE AREA OF INTERNATIONAL CARTEL ENFORCEMENT COOPERATION

The creation of the ICN was prompted by the contradictory transatlantic assessments of a global merger GE/Honeywell case in 2001.[12] The ICN, which was envisaged to promote best global practices for mergers, was officially

7 UNCTAD, 'Cross-Border Anticompetitive Practices: The Challenges for Developing Countries and Economies in Transition' (2012) TD/B/C.I/CLP/16.

8 UNCTAD, 'Modalities and Procedures for International Cooperation in Competition Cases Involving More than One Country' (2013) TD/B/C.I/CLP/21.

9 UNCTAD, 'The Impact of Cartels on the Poor' (2013) TD/B/C.I/CLP/24/Rev.1 <http://unctad.org/meetings/en/SessionalDocuments/ciclpd24rev1_en.pdf> accessed 25 February 2017.

10 UNCTAD, 'Informal Cooperation among Competition Agencies in Specific Cases' (2014) TD/B/C.I/CLP/29.

11 UNCTAD, 'Report of the Intergovernmental Group of Experts on Competition Law and Policy on Its Fifteenth Session' (2016) TD/B/C.I/CLP/40 <http://unctad.org/meetings/en/SessionalDocuments/ciclpd40_en.pdf> accessed 17 February 2017.

12 Marie-Laure Djelic and Thibaut Kleiner, 'The International Competition Network: Moving towards Transnational Governance' [2006] Transnational Governance: Institutional Dynamics of Regulation 287, P. 16.

invoked on 25 October 2001, when high-level officials from 13 countries and the EU announced the creation of the network. During that time, it was observed that "the ICN has undeniably had a promising and rapid start, with concrete steps taken and already some positive outcomes. In particular, the promotion of global 'best practices' around certain issues, like mergers, has been seen as a clear success and revealing the strength of a flexible network".[13]

The ICN's Working Group on Cartels produced a detailed manual on anti-cartel enforcement, on chapter-by-chapter basis, to be applied at domestic and regional levels by its members. The ICN developed 10 independent but coordinated chapters on anti-cartel enforcement dealing with key practical issues such as how to conduct an inspection (Chapter 1);[14] how to draft and implement an effective leniency policy for the newly set up competition authorities (Chapter 2).[15] Chapter 3 is observed to be an important chapter as it is critical for many competition authorities and it is on how to gather digital evidence;[16] as well as key aspects in the areas of the initiation of cartel investigation.[17]

Many ICN members have praised the best practices included in Chapter 5 as the process in executing an investigative strategy remains critical for many young and small competition authorities and relevant for technical assistance purposes.[18] Other chapters such as the one dealing with "Interviewing Techniques";[19] "Cartel Case Resolution"[20] and "Cartel Awareness, Outreach & Compliance" (2012);[21] remain important to specific authorities wishing to gain public support in the

---

13 Ibid P. 18.

14 ICN, 'Anti-Cartel Enforcement Manual Chapter 1: Searches Raids and Inspections' (2009) <www.internationalcompetitionnetwork.org/uploads/library/doc340.pdf> accessed 17 February 2017.

15 ICN, 'Anti-Cartel Enforcement Manual Chapter 2: Drafting and Implementing an Effective Leniency Policy' (2014) <www.internationalcompetitionnetwork.org/uploads/library/doc1005.pdf> accessed 17 February 2017.

16 ICN, 'Anti-Cartel Enforcement Manual Chapter 3: Digital Evidence Gathering' (2014) <www.internationalcompetitionnetwork.org/uploads/library/doc1006.pdf> accessed 17 February 2017.

17 ICN, 'Anti-Cartel Enforcement Manual Chapter 4: Cartel Case Initiation' (2010) <www.internationalcompetitionnetwork.org/uploads/library/doc628.pdf> accessed 17 February 2017.

18 ICN, 'Anti-Cartel Enforcement Manual Chapter 5: Investigative Strategy and Interviewing' (2008) <www.internationalcompetitionnetwork.org/uploads/library/doc344.pdf> accessed 17 February 2017.

19 ICN, 'Anti-Cartel Enforcement Manual Chapter 6: Interviewing Techniques' (2008) <www.internationalcompetitionnetwork.org/uploads/library/doc345.pdf> accessed 17 February 2017.

20 ICN, 'Anti-Cartel Enforcement Manual Chapter 7: Case Resolution' (2011) <http://internationalcompetitionnetwork.org/uploads/library/doc834.pdf> accessed 17 February 2017.

21 ICN, 'Anti-Cartel Enforcement Manual Chapter 8: Cartel Awareness, Outreach and Compliance' (2012) <http://internationalcompetitionnetwork.org/uploads/library/doc835.pdf> accessed 17 February 2017.

fight against cartels. Another important chapter is Chapter 9 as it discusses the topic of "International Cooperation and Information Sharing".[22]

As can be seen, the ICN Manual provides the most relevant best practices and techniques employed by mature agencies at various stages of anti-cartel enforcement. Evidence have shown that the ICN best practices have been proven to be effective and successful in practice. For the purpose of this research, the chapter on "International Cooperation and Information Sharing" is important for competition agencies as it reviews the main trends and practices of the mature competition agencies. It covers types of information, the ability to share information, tools for international cooperation, methods of information sharing (informal, formal, as well as international organisations and technical assistance work), uses of information, prospective challenges and finally examples of cooperation.[23]

Another important product that the ICN produced was a survey that assessed international cooperation in competition cases. The survey was done in collaboration with the OECD in 2013 and there were 57 participating countries (out of which 31 were OECD members) took part in the survey. The survey revealed that, within the period of 2007–2012, a majority of non-OECD countries had little experience in international cooperation cases.[24] Notably, more than half of the respondents of the survey were from Europe, while Africa accounted for 7%, Asia 13%, and Americas 16%. The survey showed that there was low participation of non-OECD countries in the survey. The low participation raises concerns as it could lead to problem of cooperation given the fact that there are a number of young and small competition agencies remain in Africa, the Americas, and Asia.[25]

In 2015, the Japan Fair Trade Commission (JFTC) submitted a proposal entitled "Proposal for establishing the ICN Framework for promotion of sharing non-confidential information for Cartel Enforcement" (ICN Framework)[26] to the

---

22 ICN, 'Anti-Cartel Enforcement Manual Chapter 9: International Cooperation and Information Sharing' (2013) <www.internationalcompetitionnetwork.org/uploads/cartel%20wg/icn_chapter_on_international_cooperation_and_information_sharing.pdf> accessed 17 February 2017.

23 ICN, 'Anti-Cartel Enforcement Manual Chapter 9: International Cooperation and Information Sharing' (n 35) 9.

24 OECD & ICN, 'Secretariat Report on the OECD/ICN Survey on International Enforcement Co-Operation' (2013) International Enforcement Co-operation P. 9 <www.oecd.org/daf/competition/InternEnforcementCooperation2013.pdf> accessed 25 February 2017.

25 Eleanor M Fox, 'Competition Policy: The Comparative Advantage of Developing Countries' (2016) 79 Law and Contemporary Problems 69.

26 ICN, 'Proposal for Establishing the ICN Framework for Promotion of Sharing Non-Confidential Information for Cartel Enforcement' (2015) <www.internationalcompetitionnetwork.org/uploads/library/doc1043.pdf> accessed 17 February 2017.

ICN to strengthen information sharing amongst ICN members. The idea behind the ICN Framework is to enable competition agencies to initiate investigations on international cartel cases within their own jurisdictions.[27] The investigation would be based on the exchange of information that the Initiating Agency (Initiating Agency) could get from a peer agency that has already investigated the same cartel case in its own jurisdiction (Peer Agency).[28] In the ICN framework, participating competition authorities can register and then assigned liaison officers to coordinate requests for cooperation. This arrangement can facilitate cooperation between the case team officers of the requesting competition authority and its peer authority as they can communicate directly without unnecessary intermediaries and reduce bureaucracy at the cross-border level. Overall, the ICN Framework underscores the importance of information sharing between competition agencies which fosters coordination in cross-border enforcement and avoids parallel proceedings.

In addition to the above, the ICN has produced further reports to foster convergence in national practices, Examples include the compilation of "Good Practices" from the Anti-Cartel Enforcement Manual of the ICN Cartel Working Group Anti-Cartel Templates,[29] Leniency Waiver Templates and an accompanying Explanatory Note.[30] Additional ICN productions on cartel enforcement are "Defining hard core cartel conduct: effective institutions, effective penalties";[31] "Cooperation between Competition Authorities in Cartel Investigations";[32] Cartel Settlements Report;[33] "2010 Trends and Developments

27 Toshiyuki Nambu, 'Proposal for Establishing the ICN Framework for Promotion of Sharing Non-Confidential Information for Cartel Enforcement' (2014 ICN Cartel Workshop, Taipei, Taiwan, 2 October 2014) <www.ftc.gov.tw/icncartel2014/pdf/2014.10.02.%20Plenary%20III%20%20%20Toshiyuki%20Nambu%20JFTC.pdf>.

28 Toshiyuki Nambu, 'Proposal for Establishing the ICN Framework for Promotion of Sharing Non-Confidential Information for Cartel Enforcement' (2014 ICN Cartel Workshop, Taipei, Taiwan, 2 October 2014) <www.ftc.gov.tw/icncartel2014/pdf/2014.10.02.%20Plenary%20III%20%20%20Toshiyuki%20Nambu%20JFTC.pdf>.

29 ICN, 'Compilation of "Good Practices" from the Anti-Cartel Enforcement Manual of the ICN Cartel Working Group' (ICN Cartel Working Group Subgroup 2: Enforcement Techniques 2011) <www.internationalcompetitionnetwork.org/uploads/library/doc756.pdf> accessed 17 February 2017.

30 ICN, 'Waivers of Confidentiality in Cartel Investigations – Explanatory Note' <www.internationalcompetitionnetwork.org/uploads/library/doc1012.pdf> accessed 17 February 2017.

31 ICN (ed), *Defining Hard Core Cartel Conduct: Effective Institutions, Effective Penalties* (Office for Official Publ of the European Communities 2005).

32 ICN (ed), *Co-Operation between Competition Agencies in Cartel Investigations: Report to the ICN Annual Conference, Moscow, May 2007* (EUR-OP 2007).

33 ICN, 'Cartel Settlements. Report to the ICN Annual Conference Kyoto, Japan' (2008) <www.internationalcompetitionnetwork.org/uploads/library/doc347.pdf> accessed 17 February 2017.

in Cartel Enforcement";[34] the online compilation of cartel awareness materials;[35] and the worldwide Leniency Program links.[36]

Despite the extensive reports produced by ICN, there were various requests expressed by several competition agencies to continue cooperation on fundamental principles of fair and effective procedures. Hence, the ICN Steering Group established a Framework on Competition Agency Procedures to promote agreed upon principles while minimizing the administrative burden for participants operating in different legal regimes and enforcement systems and within different resource constraints.[37]

Pursuant to the ICN's long recognition on the importance of fair and effective procedures, the International Framework on Competition Agency Procedures (CAP) was launched in 2019. The framework focuses on the implementation tool to enhance basic fairness principles among all competition authorities. Based on the "opt-in framework" concept from previous ICN frameworks, the ICN introduced a cooperation process with enhanced transparency provisions. The previous ICN frameworks were designed with the aim to promote enforcement cooperation in cartels and mergers whereby participating agencies can engage in dialogues to better understand each other's processes while allowing participants to publish their procedural rules.[38]

3. THE GUIDING POLICIES AND PROCEDURES UNDER SECTION F OF THE UN SET ON COMPETITION (GPPSF)

Throughout the period 2017–2019, UNCTAD Member States set up the UNCTAD Discussion Group on International Cooperation (DGIC) to discuss ways and means to improve international cooperation under the UN Set on

---

34 ICN, 'Trends and Developments in Cartel Enforcement' (9th Annual ICN Conference, Istanbul, Turkey, 29 April 2010) <www.internationalcompetitionnetwork.org/uploads/library/doc613.pdf> accessed 17 February 2017.

35 ICN, 'Cartel Awareness & Outreach' <www.internationalcompetitionnetwork.org/working-groups/current/cartel/awareness.aspx> accessed 17 February 2017.

36 ICN, 'Leniency Materials. Country/Organization + Link(s) to Leniency Program Materials' <www.internationalcompetitionnetwork.org/working-groups/current/cartel/awareness/leniency.aspx> accessed 17 February 2017.

37 ICN, 'ICN Framework on Competition Agency Procedures' (2019) <https://www.internationalcompetitionnetwork.org/wp-content/uploads/2019/04/ICN_CAP.pdf> accessed 5 January 2020.

38 ICN, 'New ICN-Led Framework to Promote Fair and Effective Agency Process' (2019) <https://www.internationalcompetitionnetwork.org/wp-content/uploads/2019/04/CAP_PR.pdf> accessed 5 January 2020.

Competition. Pursuant to paragraph 9 of the Agreed conclusions of the 16th session of Intergovernmental Group of Experts on Competition Law and Policy (5–7 July 2017), Member States requested the UNCTAD secretariat to facilitate the establishment of the DGIC as follows:

> "9. Requests the UNCTAD secretariat to facilitate Member States to establish a discussion group on international cooperation, open to Member States participation on a voluntary basis, to pursue the exchanges and the debate on the modalities for facilitating cooperation under Section F of the Set of Multilaterally Agreed Equitable Principles and Rules for the Control of Restrictive Business Practices and report to the seventeenth session of the Intergovernmental Group of Experts."[39]

Section F entitled "international measures" of the UN Set on Competition was adopted in 1980 and it has been reaffirmed seven times in the 5-year review conferences. The UN Set remains the only multilateral framework on Competition up to date after the attempts of the WTO to include a chapter on Competition Policy back in the 1990s with the adoption of the so-called "Singapore Issue."

At the sixteenth session of the IGE in July 2017, the UNCTAD Secretariat prepared a background note on enhancing international cooperation in the investigation of competition cross-border cases.[40] The session was led by the Russian Federation and during that session, Member States requested the UNCTAD Secretariat to facilitate the establishment of a discussion group on international cooperation. The discussion was open to Member States to participate on a voluntary basis. The objection of the session was to pursue the exchange and debate on the modalities for facilitating cooperation under Section F of the Set of Multilaterally Agreed Equitable Principles and Rules for the Control of Restrictive Business Practices and report to the seventeenth session of the Intergovernmental Group of Experts in July 2018.[41]

By mid-2018, the Discussion Group released a report of its activities which includes the preparation of a survey report entitled "obstacles to international cooperation." The survey received participation from more than 50 agencies

39 Agreed Conclusions of the Sixteenth Session of the Intergovernmental Group of Experts on Competition Law and Policy. Geneva Switzerland (5–7 July 2017). Available at: http://unctad.org/en/Pages/MeetingDetails.aspx?meetingid=1275

40 UNCTAD, 'Enhancing International Cooperation in the Investigation of Cross-Border Competition Cases: Tools and Procedures' (2017) TD/B/C.I/CLP/44 <http://unctad.org/meetings/en/SessionalDocuments/ciclpd44_en.pdf> accessed 16 May 2017.

41 See paragraph 9 of the Agreed Conclusions. UNCTAD, 'Report of the Intergovernmental Group of Experts on Competition Law and Policy on Its Sixteenth Session' (2017) TD/B/C.I/CLP/47 <http://unctad.org/meetings/en/SessionalDocuments/ciclpd47_en.pdf> accessed 3 March 2018.

worldwide which have provided their inputs.[42] The UNCTAD survey report has three main parts: the first part concerns a pre-assessment of the responding authority with respect to the willingness to cooperate with foreign peers as well as the factors surrounding international cooperation. The second part assesses critical factors that a competition agency faces when engaged in international cooperation activities. The survey classified three types of factors: awareness, legal and practical aspects that facilitate a quicker response from competition authorities. The third part looked at the future of cooperation and suggestions that each member of the group could put forward.[43]

Another section was included in order to request participating competition authorities to provide ideas on what they view as a way forward on the issue of international cooperation at the global level while considering the specific needs of younger and smaller agencies. Against this backdrop, Member States decided to renew the mandate of the Discussion Group until July 2019.[44]

3.1. ADOPTION OF THE "GUIDING POLICIES AND PROCEDURES UNDER SECTION F OF THE UN SET ON COMPETITION" (GPPSF) IN JULY 2019

At the 1st meeting of the Discussion Group in October 2018, Member States decided to establish a drafting committee composed by 10 Member States to propose a consolidated text that was discussed at the 18th session of the IGE in July 2019. By June 2019, the Drafting Committee finalized a document entitled "Guiding Policies and Procedures under Section F of the UN Set on Competition" (hereinafter known as 'GPPSF').[45]

The GPPSF was the result of intensive consultations which include virtual as well as direct meetings among various UN Member States between October 2018 and June 2019. The consultations also received- valuable feedback from UN observers. In April 2019, the UN Secretariat organized an Ad Hoc Expert Group Meeting in Geneva, Switzerland, under the header "International Cooperation

42 'Report of the Discussion Group on International Cooperation' (Intergovernmental Group of Experts on Competition Law and Policy 17th Session 11–13 July 2018 2018) Agenda Item 3e of the IGE 2018 <https://unctad.org/meetings/en/SessionalDocuments/ciclp17th_UNCTAD_rep_en.pdf> accessed 14 January 2019.

43 Ibid P. 3 of the Survey at annex 2.

44 UNCTAD Secretariat, 'Report of the Intergovernmental Group of Experts on Competition Law and Policy on Its Seventeenth Session' (2018) TD/B/C.I/CLP/52 <https://unctad.org/meetings/en/SessionalDocuments/ciclpd52_en.pdf> accessed 15 January 2019.

45 UNCTAD Drafting Committee, 'Guiding Policies and Procedures under Section F of the UN Set on Competition' (13 June 2019) <https://unctad.org/meetings/en/SessionalDocuments/ccpb_compl_%20Guiding_Policies_Procedures.pdf> accessed 29 July 2019.

in Competition Law Enforcement: Challenges and Opportunities for Younger and Smaller Agencies in Developing Countries and Countries with Economies in Transition".[46] The meeting proved essential in advancing the negotiation of the text of the GPPSF. The supporting work of selected competition authorities from Japan, the United States, the Russian Federation, Austria and Italy as well as observers from the UK and Belgium[47] were instrumental in reaching a consensus on the different provisions covered by the GPPSF.[48]

The GPPSF[49] was agreed upon at the latest UNCTAD Intergovernmental Group of Experts on Competition Law and Policy held in July 2019 in Geneva.[50] Despite the existence of multiple international cooperation frameworks, competition authorities still encounter obstacles as indicated in the survey that UNCTAD carried out in 2018 under the work of the DGIC.[51]

In light of the above, the GPPSF were then conceived to be a framework that promote mutual trust and understanding with regard to each Member States' legal framework; to facilitate contact with other authorities; to clarify what is possible in the existing scheme, especially for younger authorities with no actual experience of cooperation. These Guidelines are NOT binding, but competition authorities can use it as a practical "guide" in communicating with other authorities in practice.

The GPPSF has three main sections: (1) Guiding principles; (2) Toolkit for Cooperation in Competition Cases; and (3) The role of UNCTAD in facilitating cooperation under section F of the UN Set on Competition.[52]

---

46 UNCTAD Secretariat, 'Unctad.Org | Ad Hoc Expert Group Meeting on Competition Law and Policy' (8 April 2019) <https://unctad.org/en/pages/MeetingDetails.aspx?meetingid=2075> accessed 29 July 2019.

47 From the UK, Mr. Simon Holmes from Oxford University and Nicholas Frey from Freshfields took part in the meeting. From Brussels, Mr. David Anderson from Bryan Cave Leighton Paisner contributed actively to the deliberations of the meeting in Geneva.

48 UNCTAD Secretariat, 'Report of the Meeting of the UNCTAD Ad Hoc Expert Meeting on Competition International Cooperation' (8 April 2019) <https://unctad.org/meetings/en/SessionalDocuments/Report%20of%20the%20UNCTAD%20Ad%20hoc%20Expert%20meeting%20on%20Competition%20%2010%20May%202019.pdf> accessed 15 April 2019.

49 UNCTAD Drafting Committee, 'Guiding Policies and Procedures under Section F of the UN Set on Competition' (13 June 2019) <https://unctad.org/meetings/en/SessionalDocuments/ccpb_comp1_%20Guiding_Policies_Procedures.pdf> accessed 29 July 2019.

50 The way the DGIC operated for preparing the GPPSF was through the set up of a drafting committee (DC) composed by 10 Member States: Austria, Ecuador, Italy, Japan, Kazakhstan, Mexico, Russia, South Africa and the United States (USDOJ and USFTC). The mandate of the DC was to consolidate one single negotiating text that would be subject of DGIC deliberations.

51 'Report of the Discussion Group on International Cooperation' (n 19).

52 UNCTAD Drafting Committee (n 48).

The first section of the Guiding Principles refers to the following items:

a. It provides the benefits of cooperation between national and regional competition authorities.
b. It underlies the importance to provide tools for developing countries and economies in transition when they would like to engage in international cooperation schemes with other mature agencies worldwide.
c. It defines that cooperation is based on mutual trust between agencies and it is built over time through a number of ways and means that international development partners can facilitate such as UNCTAD, OECD and ICN.
d. It recognizes that there is significant flexibility in the way authorities may seek to cooperate with each other in particular through a number of formal and informal cooperation schemes.
e. It emphasizes that a key requisite of successful cooperation in competition cases is the ability to provide effective and credible assurances that shared information will be maintained in confidence and will be used only for purposes that the sharing authorities have permitted.

The second section entitled "Toolkit for Cooperation in Competition Cases" of the GPPSF touches upon the following:

a. It highlights the importance of having full flexibility between the authorities in initiating cooperation based on each authority's relevant domestic law and policy, or mutual agreement and understanding.
b. It provides useful information about how cooperation among authorities can be crystallized in practice through:
   - Initial contacts
   - Further communication among authorities
   - Timing alignment
   - Exchange of information, confidentiality and waivers of confidentiality
   - Discussions on substance and case resolution

The final section of the GPPSF deals with the possible role of the UNCTAD Secretariat in facilitating cooperation under Section F. As such, the UNCTAD Secretariat can assist authorities with:

a. developing confidentiality provisions and promote mutual trust among authorities that will support more effective cooperation;
b. providing publicly available legal texts and guidelines that are relevant to cooperation, such as confidentiality rules, rules concerning investigations, and data protection rules in other jurisdictions; and
c. maintaining a list of contact persons who may facilitate international cooperation at each Member State's authority, including where appropriate

by identifying contacts for particular types of conduct (e.g., mergers, cartels) and identifying linguistic abilities among contacts.

Finally, in circumstances where competition agencies indicate its preference to enter into consultations under Section F.4 of the UN Set, the requesting authority may ask the UNCTAD Secretariat for:

a. assistance with preparing the request for consultation;
b. advice on procedural matters within the scope of the consultation;
c. the provision of mutually agreed conference facilities by the Secretary-General of UNCTAD, if needed;
d. guidance, especially for authorities from developing countries and countries with economies in transition, with regard to confidentiality assurances and any use of information shared in the course of such consultation, if necessary, based on work products listed in the ANNEX;
e. interpretation of the UN Set provisions; and
f. upon specific request and consent by all authorities involved, participation in the consultation.

Since the adoption of the GPP in October 2020, UNCTAD secretariat has received two specific requests for facilitation of cooperation under Section F of the UN Set, based on the Section III. 21 of the GPP, from competition authorities in developing countries.

Regarding one of the requests, which UNCTAD Secretariat received in December 2020, a competition authority from a developing country has not been able to obtain key information from a company based in a different country in conducting its investigation against abuse of dominant position, although the alleged abusing practice by the foreign company affects their national market.

The competition authority sent a request for information to a subsidiary of the foreign company established in their jurisdiction, however, the subsidiary failed to reply to the request stating that the requested information is owned and controlled by its parent (foreign based) company. The competition authority also sought the support from the competition authority of the jurisdiction of the parent company, but due to the lack of cooperation agreements between them, no exchange of information was possible.

Another request received by UNCTAD Secretariat in May 2021 also refers to an anti-competitive case investigation by the competition authority of a regional economic organisation against a foreign-based multinational company. Without existing cooperation agreements between competition authorities in countries where the company is registered and operates its business, the competition authority is struggling to obtain the necessary information to advance in its investigation.

Both of those two requests concern investigation cooperation and exchange of information between competition authorities without formal cooperation agreements such as MOUs; requesting competition authorities require information regarding companies involved in the alleged violation, which exist outside of their jurisdictions, and seek cooperation with other competition authorities which have jurisdictions over those companies.

These requests brought to light specific challenges that developing countries face in requesting information from counterparts in cartel cases. Requests related to Section 21 (iii) The provision of mutually agreed conference facilities by the Secretary-General of UNCTAD and Section 21(vi) Participation in the consultation, upon specific request and consent by all authorities involved. Thanks to these requests, it has been brought to light that what is needed is a more practical guide to render the process easier and more concrete for competition authorities.

4. HOW THE GPPSF CAN BE CAPITALISED ON/ BUILD UPON ICN EFFORTS IN INTERNATIONAL COOPERATION

The future cooperation between UNCTAD and ICN is highly recommended in order to respond to the growing demands of the digital economy and its resulting challenges faced by agencies. Smaller and younger agencies are more vulnerable to the emerging threats associated with the digital economy such as algorithmic collusion. Hence the young agencies should take a more proactive approach to tackle those future and potential rising threats.

The ICN provides a platform for smaller agencies to learn from the experience of more mature agencies and to provide avenue for the mature agencies to cooperate with the smaller agencies. On the other hand, UNCTAD provides assistance, guidance and tools to face the uncertainties of tomorrow's economy. Therefore, the amalgamation of UNCTAD's technical expertise and the ICN's enabling platform of cooperation on an international scale seems timely and relevant to help smaller agencies face emerging challenges in a proactive manner.

ICN's efforts in providing mechanisms for younger and smaller agencies are instrumental but require further reinforcements and incentives for the Members States to rely on this system. There are three main reasons as to why UN mechanism could strengthen the work of the ICN with the particularities and effectiveness of its framework.

(1) **Young and small agencies' trust and confidence in UNCTAD's work on competition law and policy:** Taking into account "UNCTAD's long tradition of representing the interests of developing countries, its legitimacy as part of the U.N. system, and its continued focus on the linkage between competition and development"[53], young and small competition agencies have expressed their appreciation on the work of the UN in assisting them (through the government) in the enactment of their competition laws and capacity building efforts in strengthening their capacities and institutions to deal with competition law and policy implementation at large.

UNCTAD has largely supported the efforts of countries in their development for a number of historical, political and economic considerations.[54] There is an underlying trust that each countries and its respective young and small agencies, would place its faith in UNCTAD and UN. Notably, UN instruments related to competition has a long history which involved several jurisdictions, such as the establishment of Committee III on Restrictive Business Practices (RBPs) at the first session of the preparatory committee of the United Nations Conference on Trade and Employment (UNCTAE) in Church House, Dean's Yard, London, in February 1946.[55]

(2) **Wider membership in the UN:** ICN membership is an asset but not all major economies are part of this network.[56] In order to maximise the opportunities for cooperation, it would be important to view UN's expanded network under the auspices of UNCTAD. The network covers all ICN members as well as all major economies which are not affiliated with ICN.[57]

53 Ioannis Lianos, 'The Contribution of the United Nations to the Emergence of Global Antitrust Law' (Social Science Research Network 2009) SSRN Scholarly Paper ID 1398918 P. 42 <https://papers.ssrn.com/abstract=1398918> accessed 31 January 2017.

54 Marc Williams, 'Third World Cooperation: The Group of 77 in UNCTAD' (Burns & Oates 1991).

55 Pierre Horna, 'Seventy Years of Work on Competition Law and Policy in the United Nations (1946–2016)' [2016] *Sofia Competition Forum Newsletter* 23.

56 "The most notable jurisdiction with a competition law and no representation in the ICN is China, which has three national competition agencies (MOFCOM, NDRC, and SAIC). China participates in the work of the OECD Competition Committee as an observer and is a member of UNCTAD. The Chinese agencies have not discussed their intentions concerning ICN membership". Hugh Hollman and William Kovacic, 'The International Competition Network: Its Past, Current and Future Role' in Paul Lugard (ed), *The International competition network at Ten: origins, accomplishments and aspirations* (Intersentia 2011) P. 275 Note 3.

57 At the latest UNCTAD meeting of October 2016, 22 delegates from China attended the meeting. See UNCTAD, 'List of Participants of the Intergovernmental Group of Experts on Competition Law and Policy Fifteenth Session Geneva, 19–21 October 2016' (2016) TD/B/C.I/

UNCTAD's experience in addressing broad interest across regions with different development and priority needs might be an asset in the growing membership of the ICN so as to avoid fissures throughout the choice of ICN topics addressed in its regular meetings.[58]

(3) **Additional advocacy activities in the multilateral arena:** The ICN Advocacy & Implementation Network Support Program (AISUP) provides valuable work in encouraging ICN member agencies to implement ICN products. AISUP also promotes more efficient and effective antitrust enforcement worldwide by enhancing convergence and cooperation.[59] AISUP's efforts can be further enhanced by promoting ICN work products to wider audiences such as at the UNCTAD's annual sessions of the UNCTAD Intergovernmental Group of Experts on Competition Law and Policy where competition agencies from the developing world are often present.

In addition to that, there has been extensive scholarship on the emergence of the UN Set, which was adopted by the United Nations General Assembly in 1980.[60] Among the different matters covered by the UN Set, Section F of the UN Set, which relates to international measures and voluntary consultations, has been the unlikely section to be explored.[61] Interestingly, recent discussions have called for Section F's potential to be unleashed for the benefit of the vast majority of

---

CLP/INF.6 <http://unctad.org/meetings/en/SessionalDocuments/ciclpinf6_en.pdf> accessed 17 February 2017.

58 "Assembling a portfolio of projects that suits a network's members arises from expansions of membership. As a competition policy network grows, it may be difficult to pick topics that command broad interest across the network. Fissures may emerge on the basis of regional differences (e.g., competition agencies in the island economies of the Caribbean may have needs that are alien to the landlocked nations of Central Asia) or wide gaps in experience. In addition to, or as a substitute for their participation in the large, multinational networks, some countries might choose to focus resources competition initiatives undertaken in the context of regional networks such as ASEAN, CARICOM, and COMESA… "Hollman and Kovacic (n 54).

59 See ICN, 'Activity Report on ICN Advocacy and Implementation Network Support Program (AISUP) 2011–2012' (2012) <www.internationalcompetitionnetwork.org/uploads/library/doc814.pdf> accessed 8 May 2017.

60 Joel Davidow, 'The UNCTAD Restrictive Business Practices Code' (1979) 13 The International Lawyer 587; Joel Davidow and Lisa Chiles, 'The United States and the Issue of the Binding or Voluntary Nature of International Codes of Conduct Regarding Restrictive Business Practices' (1978) 72 The American Journal of International Law 247; Wolfgang Fikentscher, 'United Nations Codes of Conduct: New Paths in International Law' (1982) 30 The American Journal of Comparative Law 577; Steven L Snell, 'Controlling Restrictive Business Practices in Global Markets: Reflections on the Concepts of Sovereignty, Fairness, and Comity' (1997) 33 Stan. J. Int'l L. 215; Sigmund Timberg, 'Restrictive Business Practices as an Appropriate Subject for United Nations Action' (1955) 1 Antitrust Bulletin 409.

61 Initially, UNCTAD was required to play a role in dispute settlement but after active discussions during the December 1979, delegations did not agree to have a binding resolution but a set of principles whereby affected countries would go on consultations with no prior commitment to binding arbitration or conciliation. Stuart E Benson, 'UN Conference on

young and small competition regimes worldwide[62], particularly by an important UN Member State.[63] Section F of the UN Set on Competition was originally conceived to address the harmful effects of a cross-border cartel impacting a company seeking for enforcement actions with the competition agency in its own jurisdiction.[64] Section F.4 describes a voluntary consultation scheme, which bears similarities to the ones contained in the 1976 OECD Guidelines and the voluntary consultations in the old General Agreement on Tariffs and Trade (GATT).[65]

4. Consultations:

(a) Where a State, particularly of a developing country, believes that a consultation with another State or States is appropriate in regard to an issue concerning control of restrictive business practices, it may request a consultation with those States with a view to finding a mutually acceptable solution. When a consultation is to be held, the States involved may request the Secretary-General of UNCTAD to provide mutually agreed conference facilities for such a consultation;
(b) States should accord full consideration to requests for consultations and, upon agreement as to the subject of and the procedures for such a consultation, the consultation should take place at an appropriate time;
(c) If the States involved so agree, a joint report on the consultations and their results should be prepared by the States involved and, if they so wish, with the assistance of the UNCTAD secretariat, and be made available to the Secretary-General of UNCTAD for inclusion in the annual report on restrictive business practices.[66]

According to the abovementioned provision, there are four key elements for its implementation as highlighted below[67]:

Restrictive Business Practices' (1980) 74 The American Journal of International Law 451, P. 452.

62 In October 2016 at the 15th session of the IGE on Competition Law and Policy, the Russian Delegation to the United Nations submitted a key note speech delivered by the Head of the Federal Antimonopoly Service *FAS* whereby it was mentioned the need to further enhance the usefulness of Section F of the UN Set when it comes to investigation of cross-border competition cases. UNCTAD, 'Report of the Intergovernmental Group of Experts on Competition Law and Policy on Its Fifteenth Session' (n 16) P. 4.

63 As a result of consultations, in May 2017, the Russian Federation proposed a toolkit to operationalize section F of the UN Set. Russian Federation Website FAS, 'FAS Russia's Draft Toolkit on International Cooperation Is Now Available for Public Discussion | Федеральная Антимонопольная Служба – ФАС России' (5 May 2017) <http://en.fas.gov.ru/press-center/news/detail.html?id=49965> accessed 8 May 2017.

64 UN, 'THE UNITED NATIONS SET OF PRINCIPLES AND RULES ON COMPETITION' <http://unctad.org/en/docs/tdrbpconf10r2.en.pdf> accessed 17 February 2017.

65 Dale A Oesterle, 'United Nations Conference on Restrictive Business Practices' (1981) 14 Cornell International Law Journal 1, P. 44.

66 UN (n 63).

67 See Costa Rica's submission to the Sixth Review Conference of 2010 whereby it was proposed specific modalities for the implementation of the voluntary consultations provided for in

1. An issue concerning the control of "restrictive business practices": The content of the term "restrictive business practice" used in Section F4(a) can be found in Section B(i)1 of the UN Set. Restrictive business practices are deemed to include, inter alia, "acts or behaviour of enterprises which, through an abuse or acquisition and abuse of a dominant position of market power, limit access to markets or otherwise unduly restrain competition, having or being likely to have adverse effects on international trade". Section D of the UN Set also elaborates on the meaning of "restrictive business practices", particularly Sections D3 and D4, concerning horizontal coordinated conduct between enterprises and conduct abusive of market power, respectively. The list contained in Sections D3 and D4 are non-exhaustive, allowing for the addition of further anti-competitive practices.

2. The nature of consultations: Two points can be made with regard to the nature of the consultations. Firstly, it should be emphasised that Consultations under the UN Set are voluntary and Member States entering negotiations strive to find mutually agreed solutions.[68] Secondly, while Sections B and D address the actions of private enterprises, the Consultations are on a "State-to-State" level. This is in line with the idea that consultations are cooperative in nature and do not directly seek the resolution of a case by a third party.[69]

3. Full consideration to consultations: The parties can request and agree upon the proceeding and substance. While consultations are voluntary in nature, Member States should be required to give full consideration to the request and should be encouraged to enter into the proceeding to explore, and if possible reach, mutually agreeable solutions. If a Member State declines to participate in the consultations, it would be expected that a reasoned response would be filed to explain its decision. Responses filed will help to improve future requests and make consultations more meaningful. Participation of the corresponding Member States in the proceedings will strengthen consultation as a valid and effective mechanism to address cross-border competition issues. If the Member States agree to enter into consultation, they have to agree on the subject and on the procedures of the consultation.[70] This makes the procedure

---

Section F (4) of the Set. The proposed modalities included a number of requirements for the application, the envisaged elements to be included in the response of the request and the possible extension of the UNCTAD secretariat's participation. See UNCTAD, 'Report of the Sixth United Nations Conference to Review All Aspects of the Set of Multilaterally Agreed Equitable Principles and Rules for the Control of Restrictive Business Practices' (2011) TD/RBP/CONF.7/11 <http://unctad.org/en/Docs/tdrbpconf7d11_en.pdf> accessed 17 February 2017.

68 Oesterle (n 64) 43.

69 See Philippe Brusick, 'UN Control of Restrictive Business Practices – A Decisive First Step' (1983) 17 Journal of World Trade Law 337.

70 Proceedings should be optional to the States entering into consultations. In other words, the States may agree on different procedures. If the States decide to do so, they should still

more complex as it will be an additional agenda for the Member States to discuss and agree on. This would also compel the Member States to reinvent the wheel for every consultation. It is worth to note that the Sixth UN Conference of 2010 did not instruct UNCTAD to design a procedure for the implementation of the Consultation. Nevertheless, despite the presentation of the modalities by a Member State,[71] and with the adoption of the GPPSF as described *Supra*, there is a prospect of adopting Guiding Principles and Procedures for the implementation of the Section F. of the UN Set for the Eighth during the UN Conference of 2020. This view is based on the text adopted by the 18th Session of the IGE on Competition Law and Policy in July 2019.[72]

4. Joint report to be prepared by the States with the assistance of UNCTAD: Once the requesting Member State and the corresponding State(s) agree to enter into voluntary consultations, they may agree on specific mutually reciprocal solutions and this process could be crystallised in a joint report. Given the UNCTAD's expertise and knowledge, the Member States may also request UNCTAD's assistance in seeking possible solutions and drafting the report. The conference may want to instruct UNCTAD to bring such assistance when requested by the Member States.

---

be able to get assistance from UNCTAD. Secondly, the proceeding should be as simple as possible with basic signals to light the path for the States to explore and reach mutually agreeable solutions. The proceeding must be respectful of local laws. States entering into consultations will try to find mutually agreeable solutions that are also consistent with their own local law. Thus, the proceeding should also be respectful of local laws. At the Sixth Review Conference of Nov 2010, UNCTAD Member States of the 6th Review Conference in 2010 believed that there were benefits of having a "default" set of procedural rules to implement the consultations pursuant to section F.4. The reasons referred to included (a) the consultations would offer the State another mechanism for cooperation, in addition to formal and informal networks and technical assistance; (b) having such rules would provide predictability for the State members; and (c) UNCTAD could have a role in providing conference facilities, technical assistance and monitoring the agreements, if requested by the parties. Several delegates said that the participation of UNCTAD as an impartial third party would add value to the mechanism and help to legitimize the participation of the States in the consultations before the stakeholders in their own country. While some States may be able to share confidential information, the proceedings must also guarantee such confidentiality. UNCTAD may assist the States in the definition of what information should or should not be shared or in ways to present information while preserving the confidential component, if the States request such assistance. Finally, the proceedings should be to implement Consultations as a cooperation procedure, not as a conflict resolution forum. It also follows that UNCTAD may provide conference facilities and assistance if the States request so, but UNCTAD shall not act as a judge, nor as an arbitrator. See UNCTAD, 'Report of the Sixth United Nations Conference to Review All Aspects of the Set of Multilaterally Agreed Equitable Principles and Rules for the Control of Restrictive Business Practices' (n 65).

71 See UNCTAD, 'Contribution from Costa Rica – COMPILATION OF THE CONTRIBUTIONS SUBMITTED FOR THE CONFERENCE' (Sixth UN Conference to review the UN Set on Competition Policy Geneva, 8 – 12 November 2010) <http://unctad.org/en/Docs/tdrbpconf7contributions_en.pdf> accessed 17 February 2017.

72 UNCTAD Drafting Committee (n 48).

5. RECOMMENDATIONS: TOWARDS A VOLUNTARY CONSULTATION MECHANISM UNDER SECTION F.4 OF THE UN SET OF COMPETITION

As discussed earlier, Section F.4 of the UN Set provides key elements that could potentially facilitate the signing-up of new members to this ICN Framework beyond the 33 members, and thereby adding to the consequent sharing of non-confidential information. If the purpose of the ICN framework is to have the key features of section F.4 of the UN Set to be successfully implemented, younger or smaller agencies would be willing to enter into voluntary consultations. The stages of cooperation of these consultations are detailed as per below:

Stage 1: In accordance with the ICN framework, participating agencies can register a liaison officer who would lead the communications with the other agencies.[73] The incentive for the mature agency's liaison officer to cooperate would be the possibility of having common enforcement interests with the small or young agency, which is seeking sharable information. In order to reduce bureaucracy and middle person(s) in the process, it is advisable that the liaison officer and the case team leader to be the same person. Case team leaders who are fully involved in the case should also be at the forefront of communications with his/her foreign counterpart in order to prevent delays and miscommunication concerning critical information. This is important to ensure efficiency and trust. It has been said that: "co-operation is more likely when the organisations involved are few in number and uncertainty can thereby be reduced". This would also prevent having several officers in the agency possessing sensitive information, addressing concerns between international officers and case officers protecting their turfs.

Stage 2: When applying Section F of the UN Set[74] and the GPPSF,[75] participating agencies would need to voluntarily agree on the subject matter and the specific procedures for each consultation. Since both the subject matter and the procedures for the consultation are usually intertwined, the participating competition agencies will have to provide assurance of control over the mechanism. Previous agreement on the subject matter/s and the procedures would also prevent outright refusal to respond or provide information. In the absence of any overwhelming concern, it would be unreasonable for an agency to suddenly back-paddle as to what it wants to share or discuss. This is a critical

[73] ICN, 'Proposal for Establishing the ICN Framework for Promotion of Sharing Non-Confidential Information for Cartel Enforcement' (n 27).

[74] UN (n 63).

[75] UNCTAD Drafting Committee (n 48).

stage as ICN framework might need this feature in order to bolster trust in the system based on reciprocity principles between the participating agencies.

While some participating agencies may be able to share information, the proceedings must also guarantee confidentiality. In the absence of an international definition on confidential information, it is important to design specific procedures for organizing consultations and to provide a definition on what information should or should not be shared. The definition should also provide explanation on what to investigate and how to present information while preserving the confidential component in accordance with domestic laws. The goal should be to implement consultations as a cooperation procedure, not as a conflict resolution forum.

Stage 3: Once the subject matter and the procedures are established, the lead case team officers can provide information to each other in the following categories of agency sharable information: (1) information on the existence of an investigation; (2) theories about harm, markets, or remedies; and (3) industry background. These three categories do not constitute confidential information, as these were not provided by companies and are not protected by domestic laws. The ICN framework provides a detailed workflow that could be established at each competition agency for harmonised cooperation.

Stage 4: If the participating agencies come to a consensus, the process could be crystallised in a joint report that would monitor and record the consultations and the outcome of these communications. In the circumstances where the consultations do not result in successful delivery of non-confidential sharable information, it can be an indication to the ICN Member States that the system is progressing. The fact that attempts to communicate were monitored and recorded could eventually yield concrete results. In addition to that, the joint report could promote more discussions on how international cooperation could be approved, by being presented at the annual conferences of the ICN. The joint report could also be submitted as an item to be discussed at the annual meetings of the UNCTAD Intergovernmental Group of Experts on Competition Law and Policy. It is pointed out that the process of sharing the experience of the participating agencies could build trust and confidence in the system as the other UN Member States can appreciate these results. Illustration 1 below suggests the workflow of the four stages presented above and the key features of this tool for cooperation:

Illustration 1. Reinforcing the ICN Framework to foster international cooperation in case investigations

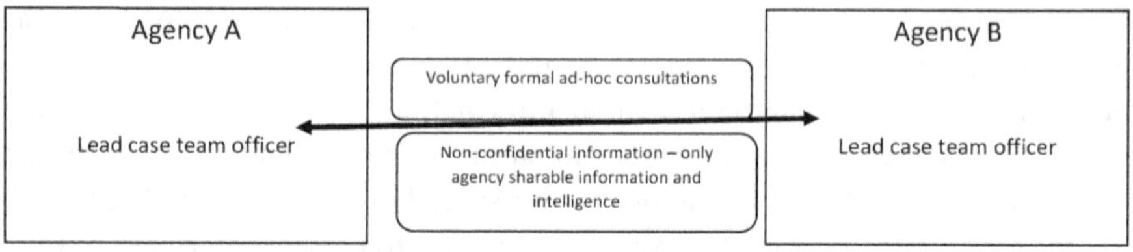

Source: Own elaboration based on the Japan proposal of 2015.

Illustration 1 introduces the term "voluntary formal ad-hoc consultations" as a result of considering the key features of Section F.4 of the UN Set. This system will build trust, enhance confidence and ease cooperation amongst competition authorities.

The application of the consultations contemplated in Section F.4 of the UN Set into the ICN Framework could help to achieve the cooperation required between competition agencies in different countries to fight international anticompetitive. The mechanisms provided by the UN could provide additional methods to strengthen the existing ICN framework.

It is highlighted that the two systems can nourish each other and the use of provisions from one system need not cause friction. One should view it as a benefit to use the best methods from each other to create a greater and more efficient system as a whole. Beyond this, however, there are some caveats that also need to be considered in the use of this tool:

(1) Entering into consultations with another Member State would eventually mean that the issue would move from "a mere legal problem to a more political realm in which the outcome would depend on the relative bargaining power of the two states and the degree to which the two states wish to protect the respective interest of private companies doing business within their borders". However, the world has changed since the adoption of the UN Set in 1980 and the specific elements of Section F.4 will eventually bring additional positive results of the ICN Framework, as it was proposed by Japan in 2015.

(2) Responses at the regional level to foster competition laws in different regional groupings also try to address the same problems that the UN Set wished to solve in 1980, which has consistently been ineffective due to national difficulties in the implementations. Since many young and small competition regimes are located in developing countries and economies-in-transition, conventional wisdom suggests that any international cartel

regulation would interfere with their domestic economic policies such as industrial policy among other things. It is pointed out that there has been a historic resistance from the developing world to implement Section F of the UN Set. This has undermined the UN's efforts to implement effective international cartel regulation.

(3) Not having a pre-existing commitment for authorities in the respective jurisdictions to cooperate with each other or to jointly perform investigation of alleged anti-competitive conducts exacerbates the problem rendering majority of small and young competition regimes with few options to address their problems. There is a concern that this may result in the small and young agencies using mature competition laws to supplant their own laws in regulating their own markets.

6. CONCLUSION

In sum, the enabling roles of international cooperation at a broader level, which include collaboration, coordination, and other types of international cooperation have gained momentum since the adoption of the UN Set on Competition, work in the IGE and other international bodies, including the International Competition Network (ICN) and the Competition Commission of the Organisation for Economic Cooperation and Development (OECD).

At UNCTAD, the Member States have been deciding gradually since 2016 to move forward in providing a more comprehensive and practical guidance on how to trigger cooperation amongst competition agencies, especially between younger and mature agencies.

The GPPSF agreed upon in July 2019 signifies a step forward that requires further dissemination at the national and regional levels for the period 2019–2020. The promotion of GPPSF is expected to continue until the 8th Review Conference of the UN Set decides to include this document as an annex to the UN Set on Competition. Most importantly, further cooperation can only be achieved through the practical use and implementation of the GPPSF. The recent triggering of the GPP demonstrates the need for further cooperation and the relevance of this instrument to support developing countries with a sustainable and practical instrument.

Younger agencies may benefit positively from such implementation because of the trickle-down effect which can result in a more pro-active approach by the agencies towards the impact and harmful effects of cross-border anticompetitive practices in their domestic jurisdictions. Such steps remain to be seen in the future. To continue to raise awareness of other Member States and/or regional organizations competition authorities, particularly from the developing world and countries with economies in transition, the UNCTAD Secretariat could organize in partnership with ICN further informative sessions on the substantive and procedural matters of the GPP, in cooperation with Member States' competition authorities, beyond the regular activities of UNCTAD Intergovernmental Group of Experts (IGE) on Competition Law and Policy. The ICN is a vital platform to promote the relevance of the GPP to Member States and support its implementation.

The cooperation between UNCTAD and the ICN could confer positive changes for smaller agencies by integrating UNCTAD's technical expertise and the international cooperation platform offered by the ICN.

ICN'S EVOLUTION FROM START-UP TO GLOBAL LEADER

Leah McCoy*

ICN's emergence on the global scene and impressive evolution over the last two decades can be readily compared to that of a successful technology start-up company. Twenty years ago, a core group of leading international competition agencies recognized that a changing global economy established a need for increased collaboration and convergence on competition enforcement efforts and priorities. Like early investors in a start-up, these founding agencies broke new ground with a bold vision for reshaping a piece of the world – in this case, the piece focusing on global competition enforcement. Like a start-up, ICN's success in its early years relied heavily on the investors' commitment to the mission.

Now, two decades old, the ICN has grown into a mature organization with over 130 member agencies and market-leading status in fostering collaboration and convergence among competition agencies worldwide. As the ICN enters its next decade, it is important to keep that start-up mindset and dedication to the mission to perpetuate the organization's success in confronting new challenges. This article examines, from the perspective of the U.S. Department of Justice, Antitrust Division (DOJ), the characteristics of the ICN that helped it succeed over the last two decades, how the ICN has repeatedly risen to face the challenges of a quickly-growing global antitrust community, and ways in which it can continue to remain relevant going forward while remaining dedicated to its original mission.

1. MEETING THE NEEDS OF THE COMPETITION COMMUNITY

A primary way that tech start-ups remain relevant is by constantly identifying and responding to evolving customer needs. This is one of ICN's strengths: like a successful start-up, it continuously finds ways to remain on the forefront of

* Leah McCoy is an International Counsel at the U.S. Department of Justice, Antitrust Division. The views expressed in this article are her own and do not necessarily reflect the views of the U.S. Department of Justice.

emerging competition issues and to engage competition agencies in examining those issues. Over the last two decades, ICN has consistently created practical work product for agencies that positively affects competition enforcement in the real world.

Notable examples include the ICN's efforts relating to merger investigations. In our increasingly global world, competition agencies are – now more than ever – faced with proposed mergers whose implications ripple across jurisdictions. In response, the ICN Merger Working Group has focused on creating a robust set of practical resources on international cooperation in merger investigations. These resources provide voluntary, flexible frameworks and practical guidance to competition agencies dealing with difficult questions of how to conduct merger reviews when multijurisdictional issues are at play. Recent examples include the Merger Working Group's "Recommended Practices for Merger Notification & Review Procedures" addressing interagency enforcement cooperation, revised in 2018;[1] the "Practical Guide to International Enforcement Cooperation in Mergers," published in 2015;[2] as well as the "Model Confidentiality Waiver."[3]

In DOJ's experience, international cooperation has proven to be invaluable in multijurisdictional merger reviews, and ICN resources like these have been critical in fostering such cooperation. The model confidentiality waiver, in particular, has facilitated the routine exchange of information in merger investigations – something that was nearly unheard of twenty years ago. The DOJ numbers tell a compelling story. In 2000, DOJ did not even keep formal records tracking cooperation, and in its annual report to the OECD that year, DOJ noted cooperation with only one other agency, on three of its significant mergers.[4] Moreover, this cooperation was at a relatively high level, with little exchange of detailed or confidential information. By contrast, today DOJ frequently coordinates with counterpart agencies on the timing of reviews, investigative

---

1 Recommended Practices of the Merger Working Group, *Recommended Practices for Merger Notification & Review Procedures*, Int'l Competition Network (2002 – 2018), https://www.internationalcompetitionnetwork.org/wp-content/uploads/2018/09/MWG_NPRecPractices2018.pdf.

2 Practical work of the Merger Working Group, *Practical Guide to International Enforcement Cooperation in Mergers*, Int'l Competition Network (2018), https://www.internationalcompetitionnetwork.org/wp-content/uploads/2018/05/MWG_GuidetoInternationalEnforcementCooperation.pdf.

3 Practical work of the Merger Working Group, *Waivers of Confidentiality in Merger Investigations*, Int'l Competition Network (2015) [hereinafter "model confidentiality waiver"], https://www.internationalcompetitionnetwork.org/wp-content/uploads/2018/05/MWG_ModelWaiver.pdf.

4 Submission of the United States, *Annual Report on Competition Policy Development in the United States from October 1, 1999 – September. 20, 2000*, pp. 15–18, (May 27, 2001), Organisation for Economic Co-operation and Development [hereinafter "OECD"], https://www.ftc.gov/sites/default/files/documents/reports_annual/2001-report/2001-annreport-competpolicydevel-us-oct-1999-sept-2000.pdf

actions and theories, and the development of compatible (or at least non-conflicting) remedies. In fiscal year 2021 alone, for instance, DOJ cooperated with 13 different counterpart agencies on 21 different merger matters. Through these exchanges, DOJ has enhanced its collective understanding of competitive conditions and reached better results for consumers and competition. These efforts have also helped to reduce burdens on merging parties and to increase consistency in outcomes across jurisdictions.

One particularly noteworthy example of successful international cooperation is the review of the 2018 Bayer/Monsanto merger, a deal involving two of the largest agricultural companies in the world. Due to the breadth of the parties' product portfolios and the global span of their operations, the transaction raised competition concerns in numerous jurisdictions. Aided by confidentiality waivers, DOJ closely coordinated its review with thirteen other agencies, including the European Commission, Canada, and Brazil. This close coordination extended to crafting a remedy that worked across jurisdictions, and that entailed a historic divestiture with global scope. In another example, DOJ conducted its investigation of the proposed (and ultimately abandoned) 2016 Halliburton/Baker Hughes merger in close cooperation with several competition agencies, including Australia and South Africa. In both these matters, as in others, DOJ found that cooperation allowed each agency to reach its own independent decision on how to proceed, but to do so more effectively and efficiently than working alone.

The ICN also has played a key role in fostering convergence relating to cartel enforcement – particularly efforts aimed at hard-core cartel activity and leniency programs – over the last two decades. In 1999, DOJ hosted the first-ever international meeting of cartel investigators and prosecutors, an event that ultimately led to the annual ICN Cartel Workshop. This workshop continues to bring investigators and prosecutors together each year to exchange ideas and discuss experiences. Perhaps more important than this annual in-person opportunity for discussion, these workshops have allowed agencies to develop close "pick-up-the-phone" relationships that serve as the basis for ongoing cooperation. ICN's continued efforts in this space have bolstered the ability of competition agencies to detect and prosecute international cartel activity, including by providing both expanded access to foreign-located evidence and witnesses and expanded coordination on investigative efforts such as dawn raids and compulsory requests for documents. Importantly, the collaboration within ICN has helped to establish a worldwide consensus on the fight against international cartels, as most countries have now adopted legislation prohibiting hard-core cartels and implemented leniency programs. The heightened, worldwide commitment to the prosecution of cartels has created a significant deterrent for cartel activity that benefits everyone.

Given the proliferation of leniency programs, the ICN is now threatened with becoming a victim of its own success in some ways. A very real new challenge is how competition agencies can maintain incentives for companies to apply for leniency when such a decision could mean applying to (and subjecting oneself to the follow-on processes in) a dozen or more agencies across the globe. This challenge provides yet another example of ICN's ability to meet the evolving needs of competition agencies that a rapidly changing global environment creates. ICN's Cartel Working Group is actively confronting the issue of managing global leniency in a variety of ways. For instance, it surveyed stakeholders in the global cartel enforcement community and issued a thoughtful report entitled "Good practices for incentivising leniency applications" in 2019.[5] In 2020, it released the "Guidance on Enhancing Cross-Border Leniency Cooperation," which is designed to provide a detailed, practical "checklist" for agencies to use in coordinating with other agencies when there is a cross-border leniency applicant.[6] This document addresses key areas of coordination with the two parallel aims of bolstering enforcement and reducing disincentives for applicants. DOJ hopes that, like the guidance materials on international merger cooperation, the guidance on leniency coordination will lead to a real change in competition agency practice, such as increased coordination on activities including witness interviews and calculation of fines.

2. EMPLOYING A FLEXIBLE STRUCTURE FOR ENGAGEMENT

Much like the digital platforms that dominate the minds of competition agencies today, another key feature of ICN is its innovative "virtual" model, which allows agencies to engage broadly at relatively low cost. Without a standing secretariat or permanent staff, the leadership and work of ICN remains largely member-driven. Though the organization is consensus-based, ICN products are not legally binding, giving ICN flexibility to take on cutting edge issues.

ICN also creates direct agency-to-agency engagement between competition enforcers, rather than government-to-government engagement, which builds consensus and promotes convergence on competition policy with relatively

5 Practical work of the Cartel Working Group, *Good practices for incentivising leniency applications,* Int'l Competition Network (Apr. 30, 2019), https://www.internationalcompetitionnetwork.org/wp-content/uploads/2019/05/CWG-Good-practices-for-incentivising-leniency.pdf.

6 Practical work of the Cartel Working Group, *Guidance on Enhancing Cross-Border Leniency Cooperation*, Int'l Competition Network (June 2020), https://www.internationalcompetitionnetwork.org/wp-content/uploads/2020/07/CWG-Leniency-Coordination-Guidance.pdf.

minimal bureaucratic red tape. Further, the flexible structure enables competition agencies to engage with other stakeholders from the world of competition enforcement, including private practitioners, academics, and industry participants, through participation of approved Non-Governmental Advisors ("NGAs"). While competition agencies will always drive the ICN agenda, NGAs provide a welcome and diverse perspective, and they help to facilitate more comprehensive discussion and analysis. Looking forward to the next decade, ICN's focus on maintaining this nimbleness and flexibility will ensure that it is effectively serving its members.

3. EMBRACING NEW TOOLS AND CHANGE

Perhaps the most significant characteristic of ICN ensuring its vitality over the last two decades has been its willingness to adapt and evolve. The 2019 Framework on Competition Agency Procedures ("CAP") is a prominent example of this adaptability.[7]

The CAP is a unique and novel instrument in many ways. Essentially, the CAP is a multilateral arrangement sponsored by ICN, under which participating competition agencies commit to a set of fundamental procedural fairness principles and agree to participate in cooperation and review mechanisms. By its legal nature, the CAP is a memorandum of understanding among participating competition agencies. While it is not legally binding, it reflects actual commitments by its participants. The CAP sits under the ICN umbrella, but is not governed by the ICN Steering Group. Importantly, the CAP is open to all national, multinational, and customs territory-specific competition agencies, including both ICN members and non-ICN member agencies.

The CAP came to the ICN through a rather untraditional process. It is based on the proposal for a Multilateral Framework on Procedures ("MFP"), which was developed by a diverse group of leading competition agencies from around the world. The goal of the MFP initiative was to identify fundamental procedural norms that are truly universal, and to achieve commitment from participating agencies to abide by these norms. The initiative was animated by principles that are widely accepted across the globe and that most competition agencies already recognized in some form. The substantive provisions set forth in the proposal included fundamental principles such as non-discrimination; transparency and predictability; notice of investigation, meaningful and timely engagement, and

---

7 ICN Framework for Competition Agency Procedures, Apr. 3, 2019, International Competition Network, https://www.internationalcompetitionnetwork.org/wp-content/uploads/2019/04/ICN_CAP.pdf.

focused information requests; timely resolution; confidentiality protections; conflict of interest protections; proper notice of alleged violation(s), access to information, and opportunity to defend; access to counsel and privilege; written enforcement decisions and public access to decisions; and availability of independent review of enforcement decisions.

Following the introduction of the MFP initiative to the broader competition community in 2018, there was unanimous support for the substantive principles it set forth from agencies all over the world. Several agencies indicated a preference for implementing the text within ICN in order to take advantage of existing institutions and processes and reduce administrative burdens on participants. Such implementation appeared quite challenging at the time. Historically, ICN has focused on issuing recommendations and guidance to its member agencies. The MFP initiative, however, was designed to reflect actual commitments by its participants, combined with meaningful review and cooperation mechanisms. It went far beyond anything ICN had done in the past. Nevertheless, over several months the negotiating group worked closely and tirelessly with the ICN chair and the ICN Steering Group to find ways to implement within an ICN instrument both the strong substantive norms contained in the MFP proposal and the meaningful adherence, cooperation, and review mechanisms.

The text that resulted from this process, the CAP, incorporates the substantive principles of the original MFP and combines these principles with adherence, cooperation, and review provisions that resemble the parallel mechanisms proposed under the MFP. It captures these universal principles, using language versatile enough to cover both common law as well as civil law jurisdictions, administrative as well as prosecutorial systems, and older as well as younger competition agencies. The ICN Steering Group adopted the final text of the CAP on April 3, 2019 – less than four months from circulation of the initial draft of the CAP in the Steering Group – and the CAP became open for competition agencies from around the world to join as participants on May 1, 2019, with 52 initial founding signatories.

The successful development of the CAP is a testament to ICN's willingness to embrace change and to creatively address global concerns. These efforts reflect strong leadership by the ICN Chair and the hard work of the whole Steering Group, as well as the thoughtfulness and mutual respect that was critical to developing the initial MFP proposal, and which ultimately helped facilitate implementation through an ICN instrument. The CAP marked a significant achievement for the many competition agencies involved in its development, for the ICN, and for the broader competition community. Dozens of agencies from around the world, including non-ICN member agencies, have already joined the

CAP. In addition to being a momentous substantive achievement, adoption of the CAP illustrates a feature key to ICN's success: a procedural adaptability that allows it to conquer new frontiers. As ICN continues to promote and expand CAP in the new decade, DOJ looks forward to the benefits that will undoubtedly arise from enhancing international procedural due process norms across the global antitrust community – and to participating in ongoing ICN efforts to embrace change in furtherance of cooperation and convergence.

And, of course, probably the most notable example of ICN's adaptability has been the organization's response to the covid-19 pandemic. While the pandemic has created unprecedented challenges for agencies around the globe, it has also provided an opportunity for ICN members to develop new and creative ways to collaborate. In 2020, the US hosted ICN's first ever virtual annual conference, which allowed a record number of attendees to participate. In September 2021, the ICN Promotion & Implementation group hosted an interactive, virtual skills workshop with 200 attendees from over 60 different jurisdictions. In November 2021, Portugal organized ICN's first hybrid Cartel Workshop with both in-person and virtual participants.

The challenges brought on by the pandemic also highlight the importance of ICN and international collaboration. As the pandemic closed borders, disrupted global supply chains, and created shortages of key medical equipment, governments around the world were looking for solutions. Competition enforcers answered that call. Agencies adapted procedures to facilitate production of lifesaving medical devices, provided key expertise and guidance to legislators, and ramped up enforcement efforts to ensure that no companies or individuals were taking advantage of the emergency situation, among other things. Throughout, ICN members turned to each other for advice and assistance in navigating these new challenges. ICN working groups adapted work plans, including hosting webinars on covid-19 responses and developing new work product focused on pandemic-related issues, such as the Cartel Working Group's ongoing project related to crisis cartels.

4. WHERE TO NEXT?

It is a challenging, but exciting, time to be a part of the global competition community. ICN enters its third decade during a resurgence of popular interest in competition law. Spurred in part by grassroots populist movements and a backlash against the tech industry, governments around the globe are rethinking competition policy. Comprehensive competition law reforms have been proposed in many ICN jurisdictions, including here in the United States. Over the next few years, competition agencies will play a starring role in the ongoing debate about the role of competition enforcement, the meaning of consumer welfare, and the future of competition law. And, of course, all of this is occurring against the backdrop of the ongoing global pandemic. In this context, the ICN continues to remain as relevant today as it was when it began two decades ago.

ICN is no longer a start-up. It is a significant platform in the competition space, and its work product can – and often does – have substantial, positive impacts on competition policy and enforcement. As it continues to grow and evolve, ICN must take care to avoid losing its hard-earned significance by detouring into public policy areas outside of competition. From the beginning, ICN's mission has been "All Competition, All The Time." Because of this mantra, the ICN is unique among its peers, being the only global organization devoted solely to competition law enforcement. Staying true to this mission while also being agile and adaptable has ensured the organization's importance and relevance to the global competition community over the last two decades. Like all established market players, the challenge for ICN in the coming decades will be to continue on its innovative path while maintaining its focus squarely on its founding purpose. DOJ looks forward to being a part of this journey.

GOVERNANCE DESIGN OF THE REGULATORY NETWORK: THE ICN AS AN EXPERIMENTALIST NETWORK?

Yane SVETIEV

1. INTRODUCTION

The International Competition Network ("ICN") was formed at a time of great enthusiasm for transnational regulatory networks ("TRNs") among both regulatory practitioners[1] and scholars.[2] Observers extolled the benefits of TRNs vis-à-vis the traditional model of cooperation under international law, which is based around formal treaties and international organisations. The champions of networks considered treaties to be difficult and slow to negotiate, often gravitating around the lowest common denominator, rather than ambitious international norms. The enforcement of formal international norms, even with an international organisational bureaucracy, was itself viewed as highly ineffective, operating subject to the constraints of state consent, diplomatic protection and international adjudication. Moreover, treaties and organisations did not always keep pace with the evolution of transnational cooperation problems and challenges, while the renegotiation and evolution of treaty norms was itself difficult and slow.

Direct networking of regulators was different and more agile, because it was supported by common interest among specialists, informal, voluntary and flexible.[3] Regulators' tasks are often quite complex and so they need to learn how to regulate: the best teachers are other regulators who have faced similar problems, attempted to resolve them and either succeeded or failed in their efforts. The flexibility of networks means that deliberations can quickly be

---

1 C James, 2002, "Reconciling Divergent Enforcement Policies: Where Do We Go From Here?", in B. Hawk, ed., *International Antitrust Law & Policy: 2001*, at 5 (Fordham Corporate Law Institute).

2 AM Slaughter, 2004, *A New World Order* (Princeton University Press); K Raustiala, 2002, "The Architecture of International Cooperation: Transgovernmental Networks and the Future of International Law", *Virginia Journal of International Law* 43:1, at 88–89.

3 Slaughter, 2004, above, at 48–49.

refocused to emergent problems for which current rules or practices may not offer adequate guidance. Finally, informality was also a virtue because the output of TRNs was not binding.[4] Therefore there was no need to agree on lowest common denominator rules, TRNs could aim to identify and endorse the current best practices for enforcement and implementation. Then it was up to individual jurisdictions to decide whether to "opt in" to the norms endorsed by a TRN, where the top international regulatory experts in the particular field of regulation participate and where the voice of all participants can be heard.

The ICN clearly fits the foregoing criteria and, perhaps unsurprisingly, it has been hailed as a new and promising form of international cooperation in competition law. It was formed after repeated failures to create a formal international antitrust cooperation regime, at an earlier time via the Havana Charter[5] and much later following the European Union's initiative[6] under the auspices of the World Trade Organisation ("WTO"), with competition law being one of the so-called "Singapore Issues" for the Doha Round of trade negotiations.[7] The repeated failures reflected a "resistance to rules"[8] and harmonisation with respect to international antitrust.[9] This resistance to common antitrust rules as part of the WTO framework was justified differently in different jurisdictions. Some jurisdictions (such as the US) were of the view that they had developed the optimal set of antitrust rules and enforcement practices and did not wish to have them watered down or subject to oversight by an international regime. Others – mainly developing countries – faced uncertainty about how an international obligation to enact and enforce competition law and policy would affect their ability to implement public policy and, in particular, to pursue developmental goals as their key policy priority.[10] In the face of resistance to binding rules, an

---

4 Ibid.

5 See e.g. S Snell, 1997, "Controlling Restrictive Business Practices in Global Markets: Reflections on the Concepts of Sovereignty, Fairness, and Comity", *Stanford Journal of International Law* 33:215, at 221–232.

6 European Commission, Report by the Group of Experts on Competition Policy in the New Trade Order: Strengthening International Cooperation and Rules, COM (95) 359 final (July 12, 1995); European Commission, XXVI Report on Competition Policy 1996 235–36 (1996). See C Damro and T Guay, 2016, *European Competition Policy and Globalization* (Springer).

7 See, B Zanettin, 2002, *Cooperation Between Antitrust Agencies at the International Level* (Hart/Bloomsbury).

8 Y Svetiev, 2015, "Scaling experimentalism: from convergence to informed divergence in transnational competition policy", in J Zeitlin (ed), *Extending Experimentalist Governance: The EU and Transnational Regulation* (Oxford University Press) (as described by Simon Evenett).

9 M Bode and O Budzinski, 2005, "Competing Ways Towards International Antitrust: The WTO versus the ICN", in Frank Collumbus (ed), *New Developments in Antitrust* (Nova Publishing).

10 M Gal, 2010, "Regional competition law agreements: an important step for antitrust enforcement", *University of Toronto Law Journal* 60:239.

informal network based on mutual learning, exchange and voluntary adoption seemed not only a feasible, but perhaps also an optimal compromise.[11]

Numerous scholars and practitioners have examined the operation of the ICN, its achievements and shortcomings, and already in its first decade lauded its success as a form of voluntary cooperation in international antitrust.[12] Given the ambition of the network's scope (covering all substantive aspects of antitrust and enforcement practices) and the breadth of its membership, it may be quite difficult to provide a comprehensive assessment and label the ICN as either an overall success or failure. Moreover, as observers have noted, assessing success or failure also requires developing metrics by which outcomes can be evaluated.[13] In this contribution I wish to argue that both for the purposes of assessing its contribution and evolving its design, it is important to reflect upon the governance design model that the ICN embodies as a network, as well as the model to which it might aspire in its third decade.[14]

To further such reflection, I will point to at least three different models of regulatory networks that incorporate the benefits of flexibility identified above, including the information and exchange network, the soft convergence network and the experimentalist network. I will also aim to identify the extent to which the ICN architecture matches onto or has evolved vis-à-vis those models. The ultimate purpose of this contribution is to provide at least some normative guidance about the desirability of these three models for the evolution of the ICN. I will argue that the experimentalist model is normatively attractive for the ICN framework of cooperation, however I will also point out that the current ICN architecture would need to be augmented for this network to play an experimentalist functionality in the elaboration of international antitrust norms and practices.

2. GOVERNANCE DESIGN MODELS FOR THE REGULATORY NETWORK

2.1. INFORMATION AND EXCHANGE

The literature identifies the information and exchange network as the least ambitious and fairly common model for TRNs. These networks are based

11 James, 2002, above.

12 E Fox, 2009, "Linked-In: Antitrust and the Virtues of a Virtual Network", *International Lawyer* 43:151, at 173 ("[T]he ICN has been dramatically successful. ... It has carved out a space for itself that no other enterprise or project could have achieved. Its own success may have overtaken calls for a global framework for antitrust proper.").

13 JH Verdier, "Transnational Regulatory Networks and Their Limits", *Yale Journal of International Law* 34:113, at 161.

14 Cf W Kovacic, H Hollman and P Grant, 2011, "How Does Your Competition Agency Measure Up?", *European Competition Journal* 7: 25.

on a common regulatory interest. In the face of the need for learning and at least minimal coordination, regulators may often spontaneously form information and exchange TRNs to cope with similar problems, particularly when such problems have a transnational dimension.[15] Given that the object of cooperation is to exchange information and learn from mutual experience, such networks do not typically have any rule-making ambition. The discussions and exchanges in such a TRN may well affect how a regulatory authority official in a specific jurisdiction exercises her regulatory mandate in analysing a specific case, but only if she finds the exchange to be persuasive and useful. Going to a TRN meeting for regulatory officials is like going to a seminar[16] – an official may or may not learn something useful during such a meeting that is applicable to her daily work. To the extent that officials learn something useful about how to analyse dominant firm conduct or assess merger efficiencies, and to the extent that such learning is consistent with the domestic legislation and regulatory framework in their own jurisdiction, such learning may be incorporated in decision-making practices in specific cases. Alternatively, an official may continue doing what she did before – consistent with her own authority's established routines and relevant local rules and precedents – but at least she will better understand how some other jurisdictions approach similar problems. Even in the latter case, exchange within the network might be regarded as useful in promoting mutual understanding even in simply comprehending the differences as between jurisdictions in approaching similar antitrust problems.

Early descriptions of the ICN and its goals, at least to some extent, match the information and exchange model of TRNs. Pursuant to its Establishment Memorandum, the ICN was intended as an informal network that would provide a venue for "structured dialogue" among "leaders of antitrust agencies" aiming to create a "common competition culture"[17] without any rule-making or codification ambition. Similarly, Fox described the founding vision of the ICN as a "voluntary forum" for "sharing of views and experiences, for close cooperation, and for exploration of common issues", which may "facilitate the sharing of information and experience, facilitate cooperation, and work towards consensus rules, principles, methodologies and procedures".[18]

While such limited ambition can be seen as an advantage of an information and exchange network, it also presents some shortcomings. Perhaps the most obvious drawback is the fact that it may be very difficult to establish any metrics for the

15 Slaughter, 2004, above, at 52.

16 Ibid. ("brainstorming" new approaches).

17 International Competition Network, Memorandum on the Establishment and Operation of the International Competition Network (2001) ("ICN Establishment Memorandum").

18 Fox, 2009, above, at 160.

success or otherwise of the operation of such a network.[19] While a network such as the ICN is not an international organisation, it is formed by public authorities and its operations are principally funded by public funds to organise meetings, as well as to finance officials' participation in such meetings and ICN deliberations. If the ICN has no ways of assessing the achievement of those goals, participation in such a network may be difficult to justify. As some scholars have argued, participation may simply be viewed as a travel perk that can be enjoyed by national competition officials without being able to demonstrate how it advances the public purpose with which they are charged.[20]

An information and exchange network may be seen to offer particular advantages for newer antitrust jurisdictions whose officials need to learn from more experienced enforcers, and from each other, about how to approach specific competition problems. They might even learn about specific enforcement initiatives pursued by their regulatory peers from other jurisdictions that can provide them with a template for local enforcement. While this type of learning may not be easy to measure or make explicit, surely it is useful for both authorities. The more experienced official ensures the spread of good practices to other jurisdictions, while the official from a new adopter jurisdiction learns how to apply such good practices. Further, this form of learning and diffusion also minimises the risk of clashing approaches between different jurisdictions in similar cases. Indirectly it may promote the goal of norm convergence, to the extent that some degree of harmonisation is viewed as the goal for international cooperation regimes.

As I have argued elsewhere, there are some doubts about whether unstructured information and exchange as between regulatory officials is either an effective or a legitimate form of learning in regulatory network, such as the ICN.[21]

Beginning with the question of effectiveness, it is true that – as many officials have pointed out both in public pronouncements and in research interviews – the ICN structure, including its regular annual meetings and other events, provides antitrust officials with the occasion to meet and maintain contacts with their counterparts from other jurisdictions, including prominent and well-respected competition regulators and practitioners.[22] It also seems to be the case that officials try to use ICN meetings as a way of developing direct relationships

19 Raustiala, 2002, above, at 55.

20 Ibid, at 62.

21 Y Svetiev, 2012, "The limits of informal international law: enforcement, norm generation, and learning in the ICN", in J Pauwelyn, R Wessel, and J Wouters (eds) *Informal international lawmaking* (Cambridge University Press).

22 Y Svetiev, 2010a, "Partial Formalization of the Regulatory Network", available at SSRN: https://ssrn.com/abstract=1564890; ICN Establishment Memorandum, above.

with other officials, whom they can call up if they are faced with a difficult and unfamiliar problem. Moreover, regulatory officials have also used the ICN framework to establish more structured exchanges around specific problems whereby officials from an established antitrust jurisdiction seek to provide assistance to officials from a newer authority.[23]

However, this form of unstructured learning and diffusion faces numerous constraints. First, there may be a considerable difference between the nature of the problems faced by a new adopter compared to the problems faced by an authority in a more established antitrust jurisdiction. Even if the problems might be framed around familiar antitrust categories, such as anticompetitive agreements or dominant firm conduct, the underlying economic, social and legal context in which these problems arise may be quite different in one country compared to another.[24] As Rodriguez and Menon have argued, conduct that may look like a cartel to an established antitrust enforcer, may well be a mechanism supplementing or correcting a specific market failure or even legal failure in a new adopter jurisdiction.[25] Moreover, cartel-like conduct may reflect pre-established local networks of production and distribution or even arise due to the local regulatory structure. If the new antitrust adopters simply accept the practices and analytical categories of established regimes, they may not correct a problem in the operation of the market, but instead compound it.[26] Otherwise, if she recognises the difference in context, an official from a recent adopter might regard the experiences of the established jurisdiction as irrelevant to her own context, but that might be a missed opportunity to try to understand how competition policy tools might be used to improve current economic performance in that jurisdiction.[27]

Secondly, if antitrust regulators use the ICN as a venue for unstructured and informal learning, and incorporate such learning into their decision-making practices, this may raise legitimacy concerns. After all, the antitrust laws of many jurisdictions have fairly similar broad formulations prohibiting anticompetitive agreements, dominant firm abuse and mergers that lessen competition. Such statutory formulations typically do not provide guidance to regulators or courts about the specific types of conduct that are prohibited or allowed by competition

23 Svetiev, 2010a, above.

24 Ibid.

25 A Rodriguez and A Menon, 2016, "The Causes of Competition Agency Ineffectiveness in Developing Countries", *Law & Contemporary Problems* 79:37, at 61–63.

26 Ibid. (as such competition law enforcement may undermine "surviving institutional organizations" that overcome "historical resource limits and institutional constraints" and are precompetitive and economically advantageous).

27 Y Svetiev and L Wang, 2016, "Competition Law Enforcement in China: Between Technocracy and Industrial Policy", *Law & Contemporary Problems* 79:187, at 220.

law, let alone how to remedy competition problems. The open texture of the language used, as well as the fact intensive nature of inquiry involved in applying most antitrust rules, both combine to give competition authority officials considerable discretion in making assessments and deciding cases. To the extent that the exercise of such discretion can be affected by informal and relatively non-transparent exchanges with transnational peers, this may be seen as quite problematic from a domestic point of view.[28] Do we know whether the advice provided and experiences shared by a transnational regulatory peer are specifically affected by normative and public policy choices made in her own jurisdiction? How do such choices compare to the normative and public policy decisions in the jurisdiction of the official who is doing the learning? Even in the unlikely event that there are no relevant differences between the local economic contexts, different normative and public policy choices between the two jurisdictions may make such unstructured learning illegitimate if it is not subject to scrutiny by domestic actors.[29]

In light of the above observations, the unstructured learning and exchange network model may lead to two other concerns – hegemony and lack of innovation. By hegemony we mean that the established models of competition law and enforcement become the standard to which new adopters tend to converge for reasons of tradition, technical assistance or other "selling" tactics. Some may regard such hegemony as undesirable in itself.[30] Moreover, hegemony of the established antitrust models (such as the US and EU) also tends to limit innovation in tailoring antitrust tools to the specific problems in production and exchange faced by recent antitrust adopters.[31] As Eleanor Fox has argued, developing countries may have "a comparative advantage in designing competition systems that are well adapted to their nations and to the modern world" because they are "not constrained by path dependence" as "their competition systems are sufficiently young and unformed".[32] If unstructured learning and exchange favours the perspectives of established jurisdictions, then new adopters of antitrust may well lose the chance to develop that advantage in tailoring antitrust to their own needs and problems.

---

28 Svetiev, 2010a, above (in purely informal learning and exchange "the norms or the oft-unstated beliefs, assumptions or approaches … are treated as entirely tacit knowledge, which cannot be made explicit nor scrutinized").

29 Verdier, 2009, above, at 115.

30 Interview with official of the Consumer Unity and Trust Society (CUTS) (NGO official suggesting that the framing of discussions within the ICN constitutes an "abuse of dominance by Western economies").

31 Rodriguez and Menon, 2016, above.

32 E Fox, 2016, "Competition Policy: The Comparative Advantage of Developing Countries", *Law & Contemporary Problems* 79: 69, at 71–73.

2.2. SOFT CONVERGENCE

Following its founding, the ICN clearly moved beyond the information and exchange network model relying on purely informal diffusion. In particular, from its early meetings the ICN sought to formalise mechanisms to structure discussion as a way of both developing concrete guidance for participating agencies and subjecting that guidance to deliberative scrutiny, not least by seeking input about relevant examples and practices from a broader and hopefully more representative set of jurisdictions.[33] The deliberations of the ICN were organised around working groups focusing on specific antitrust issues, which in itself could help to give voice to a broader set of relevant experiences, apart from those of established jurisdictions. Moreover, the ICN working groups have been developing recommended practices that jurisdictions may decide to adopt either through domestic legislation or that participating authorities may incorporate in their decision-making practice in exercising their mandate and regulatory discretion. As such, the ICN's ambition was that through a combination of the authoritativeness of its recommendations, peer pressure and the emergence of a common competition culture[34], it may produce convergence towards those recommendations, even in the absence of formal enforcement mechanisms.[35]

This second model of cooperation, based on soft convergence to recommended practices, does provide some advantages over the unstructured information and exchange diffusion model discussed above. First, it provides a more transparent model of learning by subjecting the selection of recommended practices to a process of public scrutiny, discussion and deliberation. This means that the representatives of a broader set of jurisdictions can, at least in principle, contribute their own experiences and enforcement examples and participate in the selection of the recommendations. The process of selecting recommended practices can also, at the very least, put on the record alternative approaches, as well as the reasons why some jurisdictions follow alternatives to the rules and practices that are ultimately endorsed by the ICN.[36]

---

33 Verdier, 2009, above, at 131, argued the ICN is among the "relatively formal" networks, which produce "a steady and increasing output of readily available documents, hold[] frequent meetings, and publiciz[e] their activities through the Internet and in professional and academic circles."

34 D Tarullo, 2000, "Norms and Institutions in Global Competition Policy", *American Journal of International Law* 94:479, at 495 speaks of "cognitive convergence".

35 M Coppola, 2011, "ICN Best Practice: Soft Law, Concrete Results", *Competition Policy International Antitrust Chronicle* July (1).

36 D Zaring, 2006, "Best Practices", 81 *New York University Law Review* 81:294, at 297 (best practices regulation could be a form of "localism or subsidiarity" by contrast to "mandating a one-size-fits-all" scheme).

To the extent that opting into ICN recommended practices is voluntary, under the soft convergence model we can also develop possible metrics through which to assess the success and efficacy of the ICN. For example, some authors have sought to quantify the number of jurisdictions that have adopted the ICN recommended practices into their domestic legislation or administrative practice in different fields.[37] Where a particular jurisdiction decides to adopt ICN recommended practices in its domestic legislation, this also means that domestic political or legislative bodies have endorsed such practices as consistent with local public policy priorities, attenuating the legitimacy concerns associated with purely informal learning and diffusion.

Writing towards the end of the first decade of the ICN's operation and reflecting upon its on-going role, Hollman and Kovacic suggested a model of the ICN that pursued international antitrust standardisation through three stages, including (i) "continuing decentralized experimentation" as jurisdictions test rules, methods, and techniques; (ii) "identification of superior practices"; and (iii) voluntary opting into superior practices. In particular, they suggested that the ICN can play a role in facilitating mutual understanding of the operation of individual systems, identifying superior practices, monitoring the "extent of opting-in" by ICN members into the recommendations, and promoting interoperability between antitrust systems where divergences persist.[38]

Notwithstanding the advantages of this model of evolution for the ICN compared to the pure information and exchange model discussed above, the soft convergence model still presents some limitations in terms of its operation in practice.

For one, we may wonder about the extent to which the soft convergence model addresses the problems of hegemony of the established antitrust regimes as a constraint on tailoring and innovation by new adopters for a number of reasons. First, while the above vision for the ICN operations envisages continued decentralised experimentation with different jurisdictions testing new rules, methods and techniques, given that the competition laws of many new adopters are transplanted, they may often be dormant, in the sense of not being actively

37 E.g. J Rowley and A Campbell, 2005, "Implementations of the International Competition Network's Recommended Practices for Merger Review: Final Survey Report on Practices IV-VII", *World Competition* 28:533; M Coppola and C Lagdameo, 2011, "Taking stock and taking root: a closer look at implementation of the ICN recommended practices for merger notification and review procedures", in P Lugard (ed), *The International Competition Network at Ten: Origins, Accomplishments and Aspirations* (Intersentia).

38 H Hollman and W Kovacic, 2011, "The International Competition Network: Its Past, Current and Future Role, *Minnesota Journal of International Law* 20:274. Very similar language is reflected in a document "The ICN's Vision for its Second Decade" prepared by the ICN Steering Group for the 10th annual ICN meeting in The Hague.

enforced.[39] Moreover, where new adopters enforce the laws, they may tend to simply copy both the approaches and even specific interventions of agencies from established jurisdictions.[40] In fact, some authors have shown that where a jurisdiction attempts to domesticate competition law by engaging different stakeholders in deliberation about the formulation of the goals of competition law, specific competition rules, as well as in specific enforcement initiatives, there is both a quicker uptake of the competition law locally and a tendency to develop innovative approaches that take into account local characteristics and needs.[41]

Secondly, the working groups that steer the ICN's production of normative output are formed around pre-existing antitrust categories known from the established regimes (the US and EU), such as anticompetitive practices, unilateral conduct and mergers. Similarly the guidance around enforcement mechanisms and analytical tools is developed largely around the analytical categories and existing practices of established antitrust systems and the working groups are still, to this day, principally chaired by agencies from developed industrialised economies or by "rule promoting" jurisdictions.[42] The working groups seek to incorporate input from a more representative set of jurisdictions through questionnaires about existing practices that provide the basis for ICN deliberations. However, it is not clear to what extent agency officials from new adopters think that they have relevant experiences to share or have the resources available to dedicate to sharing such experiences as part of ICN discussions so that such survey responses can be regarded as representative.[43]

Thirdly, there is the problem associated with the open-textured nature of competition law rules and the fact-intensive nature of competition decision-making. This combination of factors allows a great deal of leeway about how different facts and policy considerations are weighed in actual decision-making by agencies and their formulation of remedies. As a result, the mere adoption of ICN recommended practices by specific jurisdictions does not tell us much about how their agencies (or courts) actually decide cases. It is not clear whether the current ICN architecture has the mechanisms through which to shine

39 See generally, D Berkowitz, K Pistor and JF Richard, 2003, "Economic Development, Legality, and the Transplant Effect", *European Economic Review* 47:165, at 167.

40 Zaring, 2006, above, at 325–26, 330, points out that best practice recommendations work through "copying" or "keeping up with the Joneses" leads to entrenchment rather than innovation.

41 Svetiev 2010a, above (with reference to South Africa); L Wang and I Krizic, 2017, "Beyond Legal Transplant: China's 'Shopping Around' Approach and Formation of Anti-Monopoly Law" *World Competition* 40:505 (China); Svetiev and Wang, 2016, above (China).

42 U Aydin, 2021, "Rule-takers, Rule-makers, or Rule-promoters? Turkey and Mexico's Role as Rising Middle Powers in Global Economic Governance", *Regulation & Governance* 15:544.

43 See generally, Svetiev, 2010a, above.

a light on the specifics of antitrust decision-making by individual agencies and to subject it to scrutiny as part of the ICN's deliberations. A participating agency may, for example, misunderstand or make an error in applying an ICN recommended practice in a particular case. Alternatively, a participating agency may be subject to capture from local interests and distort the application of an ICN recommended practice.[44] Finally, a participating agency may find that a recommended practice is a poor fit to its local enforcement context and decide to reformulate and adapt it in its decision-making in a way that might be useful also to other agencies in the network.[45]

It follows from the foregoing discussion that if the objective of the ICN is to select superior practices drawing on a more representative set of examples from its members, as well as to track the extent to which there is voluntary opt in to common norms, it is necessary for there to be a mechanism for reviewing the implementation of such practices in actual decision-making.[46] Such a mechanism would make the actions of individual participating agencies observable to their peer agencies and it would help to characterise such actions as either compliant or not with ICN recommendations as a true indicator of convergence.[47]

Based on such arguments, as well as the selection of recommended practices for the design of leniency programmes for cartel detection, Steven van Uytsel has argued that the ICN should institutionalise a review mechanism that can be used both in the development and monitoring of implementation of recommended practices.[48] He points out that agencies may tend to overstate the efficacy of existing practices they employ in the enforcement of competition law and that there may be a considerable discrepancy between formal adherence to certain practices and their actual application. One possible format for institutionalising such a mechanism that we can observe in practice in the operation of many TRNs is that of peer review. After being apparently pioneered by the Organisation for Economic Cooperation and Development ("OECD")[49], the use of peer review has grown exponentially in recent years in international organisations, transnational agency networks, and other global or regional cooperation fora. Efforts to strengthen the global

44 Svetiev, 2010a, above.

45 Fox, 2009, above, at 172–173 (advocating for the principle of legitimate difference and the benefits of diversity versus conformity).

46 Svetiev, 2010a, above.

47 Svetiev, 2012, above.

48 S Van Uytsel, 2014, "The international competition network, its leniency best practice and legitimacy: An argument for introducing a review system", in M Fenwick, S Van Uytsel, S Wrbka (eds), *Networked Governance, Transnational Business and the Law* (Springer).

49 F Pagani, 2002, "Peer Review as a Tool for Co-operation and Change: an Analysis of an OECD Working Method", *African Security Review* 11:15.

financial architecture in the face of crisis[50], to cope with climate change[51] and even terrorism[52], or to promote good governance[53], use variants of peer review for both general policy-making and regulatory action.

As I argue elsewhere[54], in the face of the growing use of peer review as part of transnational regulatory networks, it is important to recognise that such review can perform different functionalities. It can, of course, be a mechanism through which agency practices and decision-making are examined in greater detail by their regulatory peers, as a way of both assessing the degree of convergence and exerting peer pressure for further convergence towards voluntary norms.[55] Slaughter, for example, argued that informal means of cooperation among regulatory peers, such as reputation, collegiality and socialisation, may be more effective at achieving convergence than the usual formal enforcement mechanisms of international law.[56] However, agencies are composed of multiple officials, who change over time and only some of whom participate in transnational networks for peer pressure to be effective.[57] Moreover, as we discussed above, competition decision-making is fact intensive and dependent on other domestic actors, apart from agencies, such as legislators, the executive or the judiciary.[58] Given such a landscape, to create effective convergence pressures in transnational networks, peer review has been viewed by some scholars as a collegial monitoring mechanism that can aid informal compliance through reputation and socialisation.[59]

---

50 E.g. Art. 6.1 of the Financial Stability Board (FSB) Charter, FSB Framework for Strengthening Adherence to International Standards, but also the G-20 Mutual Assessment Process aimed at mutual policy assessment in the face of shared growth objectives.

51 E.g. UNFCCC, The multilateral assessment process under the International Assessment and Review Process, COP Decision 1/CP.16; G-20 Voluntary Peer Reviews on Inefficient Fossil Fuel Subsidies That Encourage Wasteful Consumption, subsequently also adopted in the Asia Pacific Economic Cooperation (APEC) forum.

52 R Bossong, 2012, "Peer Reviews in the Fight Against Terrorism: A Hidden Dimension of European Security Governance", *Cooperation and Conflict* 47:519.

53 African Peer Review Mechanism (hosted by the African Union): see https://au.int/en/organs/aprm, conducts peer reviews based on four thematic areas including Democracy and Political Governance, Economic Governance and Management, Corporate Governance, Broad-based Sustainable Socio-economic Development.

54 This discussion draws on Chapter 3 of Y Svetiev, 2020, *Experimentalist Competition Law and the Regulation of Markets* (Hart/Bloomsbury).

55 G Dimitropoulous, 2015, "Compliance Through Collegiality: Peer Review in International Law", *Loyola Los Angeles International and Comparative Law Review* 37:275.

56 Slaughter, 2004, above, at 196–203.

57 Verdier, 2009, above, at 165.

58 Svetiev, 2012, above.

59 T Conzelmann, 2008, "Beyond the Carrot and the Stick: State Reporting Procedures in the WTO and the OECD" in J Jutta, B Reinalda and B Verbeek (eds), *International Organizations and Policy Implementation* (Routledge); Dimitroupoulos, 2015, above.

Transnational peer review can also be used as a mechanism of technocratic governance based on theories of delegation that propose isolating decision-makers responsible for market regulation from political influence, so as to build specialised expertise and resolve time inconsistency problems of political decision-making.[60] Market regulatory agencies, such as competition authorities, are deliberately isolated from direct political control as a way of ensuring that they build expertise necessary for regulating particular sectors, while stabilising policy commitments to provide regulatory certainty. On this view, TRNs and peer review can further enhance the autonomy of technocratic agencies, by building professionalism and a common set of values among participating regulatory officials, as a further buffer from political interference.

Proponents of trustee or technocratic governance argue that it is more legitimate than the general soft convergence model discussed above because network deliberations are focused on a narrow objective, such as the efficient operation of markets through competition law. From this perspective, peer review in a specialised regulatory field such as competition law, aims to promote best practices of effective enforcement to deliver a specific and narrowly defined public policy mandate (such as the use of specific tests for identifying market power or effective mechanisms to uncover cartels that are inimical to the efficient operation of markets). Technocratic peer review is not suitable for decision-making that involves distributive effects or that requires trading off of different policy objectives, which is the subject for executive, legislative or even judicial decision-making. While the ICN, particularly in its first decade of operation, had sought to limit attention to technical issues and questions of pure coordination which seemingly do not raise normative or distributive issues[61], as authors have pointed out, maintaining this distinction is not always so easy in practice.[62]

There are also models of transnational peer review that are not necessarily focused on convergence. For instance, transnational peer review can be used as a source of scientific input strengthening the scientific basis for the selection of regulatory practices at the transnational level. Van Uytsel himself points to academic evaluations of existing leniency practices, suggesting that they were suboptimal, which could have been brought to bear in the selection of leniency best practices within the ICN. It can even be used to strengthen the scientific basis for individual agency decisions by providing them access to scientific expertise beyond their national borders, without necessarily leading

60 G Majone, 2001, "Two Logics of Delegation: Agency and Fiduciary Relations in EU Governance", *European Union Politics* 2:103.

61 Fox, 2009, above, at 159–160.

62 Ibid, at 169–170, Verdier, 2009, above, at 123–124.

to normative convergence across different jurisdictions.[63] Some authors have suggested that in competition law networks social scientific expertise – and in particular economic expertise – provides the main basis of deliberations.[64]

Transnational peer review can also be used as a global administrative law discipline to assess whether the decision-making procedures of agencies – particularly in the exercise of functions that have transnational impact – complies with commonly-accepted public law principles, such as legality, transparency, participation and rationality.[65] In their seminal contribution on the emergence of global administrative law, Kingsbury, Steward and Krisch[66] identified at least five areas of consequential regulatory decision-making in the global administrative space which can produce an accountability deficit since such decision-making falls outside established national or international oversight mechanisms. These authors suggest that the need for legitimation of such decision-making leads to the emergence of global administrative law mechanisms, including rules and procedures that help to ensure the accountability of global administration through assuring compliance with the administrative law values of transparency, participation, rationality and legality. Again, this public law version of transnational peer review is not concerned with convergence to common substantive norms or practices, but may be used to assess adherence to procedural norms about the conduct of agency decision-making, provision of hearings and reason-giving.

Finally, peer review of the implementation of best practices through agency decision-making has also been identified as a key element of experimentalist governance. Experimentalist governance provides yet another potentially attractive model for the evolution of the ICN to which we now turn.

2.3. ICN AND THE EXPERIMENTALIST REGULATORY NETWORK MODEL

An emergent literature over the past decade or so has suggested that various fields of regulation, particularly in the European Union, have disclosed an

63 Cf J Ruhl and J Salzman, 2006, "In Defense of Regulatory Peer Review", *Washington University Law Review* 84:1.

64 D Gerber, 2007, "Two Forms of Modernization in European Competition Law", *Fordham International Law Journal* 31:1235 has argued, for example, that economics provides the common language for the operation of the ECN.

65 B Kingsbury, N Krisch and R Stewart, 2005, "The Emergence of Global Administrative Law", *Law & Contemporary Problems* 68: 15.

66 Ibid.

experimentalist governance architecture.[67] Furthermore, scholars have also traced various pathways through which the experimentalist governance model has extended to global regulatory regimes.[68] As mentioned above, peer review is an essential component of experimentalist governance. However, experimentalist peer review is a mechanism for promoting local tailoring of norms and regulatory innovation, rather than one for either soft convergence or technocratic governance.

Experimentalist (recursive) governance results where decision-makers face considerable uncertainty about the means through which to achieve desired policy outcomes. Such uncertainty – even in highly technical fields – can result from uncertainty about policy preferences, or due to an absence of scientific or expert consensus, or due to decision-makers' doubts about the suitability of decision-making practices and templates for achieving even well-defined policy goals in a specific local context. For example, there can be uncertainty about the type of competitive rivalry that can produce desired economic outcomes in a specific jurisdiction, as well as the interaction between competition and other policies.[69] There can also be doubts about how best practice templates can be transplanted into settings with differing local circumstances.[70] Similarly, there can be uncertainty about the suitability of existing best practices in the face of unpredictable dynamic changes in the market environment (due to technological developments as well as changes in consumer preferences).[71]

In the face of uncertainty about the selection of mechanisms to achieve certain goals, one mode of proceeding is to specify a set of commonly agreed framework goals at the central level (e.g. the ICN) and grant autonomy to local units (e.g. individual jurisdictions and agencies) to tailor solutions to advance those goals as best as they see fit. Local actors (such as national agencies) must tailor those solutions taking into account the existing state of scientific and regulatory knowledge, as well as the local circumstances they are faced with. In return for such autonomy, experimentalist governance formalises obligations for local actors to report their interventions to a central clearinghouse and subject them to peer review. In particular, it is not only the design of specific interventions that is subjected to peer review, but also the actual implementation of

67 See generally, C Sabel and J Zeitlin, 2010, *Experimentalist Governance in the EU: Towards a New Architecture* (Oxford University Press).

68 J Zeitlin (ed), 2015, *Extending Experimentalist Governance? The European Union and Transnational Regulation* (Oxford University Press); G de Búrca, R Keohane and C Sabel, 2013, "New Modes of Pluralist Global Governance" *NYU Journal of International Law and Politics* 45:723.

69 E.g., M Gal, 2009, *Competition Policy for Small Market Economies* (Harvard University Press).

70 E.g., Rodriguez and Menon, 2016, above.

71 See e.g. Y Svetiev, 2007, "Antitrust Governance: The New Wave of Antitrust", *Loyola University of Chicago Law Journal* 38: 593.

interventions. The combination of monitoring implementation and peer review allows regulatory decision-makers to focus their attention on the effects of their interventions (a discipline that is often lacking in a systematic way in domestic competition law enforcement). Experimentalist peer review of implementation efforts also enhances knowledge within the transnational network about how commonly identified practices touch down in the local context, allowing network participants to learn from the implementation efforts of their peers, as well as allowing network members to (recursively) adjust the common norms or even the commonly identified objectives.

Notwithstanding some tendency in the literature to assimilate experimentalist peer review with the other types of peer review identified above, this brief discussion suggests a number of key distinctions. Broad participation (beyond narrow epistemic communities of knowledge) in experimentalist peer review is crucial in the problem-solving and monitoring stages so as to understand the effects, including possible unintended consequences, of specific implemented solutions. As such, experimentalist peer review is not a tool of self-governance of a closed community (as in the technocratic view). This also means that while collegiality, professionalism, reputation and other informal bonds of trust may facilitate inter-agency interactions in a network, they can also be an impediment to experimentalist peer review to the extent that they blunt searching review and constructive input.[72]

Furthermore, it follows that experimentalist peer review is not principally concerned with the formal adoption of, or compliance with, network-endorsed regulatory best practices. To detect and evaluate experimentalist peer review a number of specific features must be identified. First, peer review should be focused on both the design *and the effects* of concrete problem-solving interventions, rather than the adoption of certain legislative texts or verification of the use of certain analytical or decision-making practices. As such, both transnational networks and national authorities must develop mechanisms for both identifying and evaluating the effects of specific interventions, which is a challenging discipline. Secondly, to stimulate policy innovation and contextualisation, the deliberative discourse in experimentalist peer review ought not be focused on harmonisation or convergence.[73] Thirdly, experimentalist peer review would not be closed to participation to the (competition) epistemic community, but it would seek to provide openings for stakeholders and affected parties to participate in both problem-solving and monitoring of implemented solutions.

---

72 Cf N Stame, 2008, "The European Project, Federalism and Evaluation" *Evaluation* 14:117; Dimitropoulos, 2015, above.

73 Svetiev, 2012, above.

If we observe the design of the enforcement and cooperation procedures in the EU, as well as the formalisation of the European Competition Network ("ECN") through EU Regulation 1/2003 (the "EU Regulation"), we can detect at least the key elements of experimentalist governance.[74] First, the EU Regulation decentralised the enforcement of EU competition rules, so that apart from the European Commission such rules can also be enforced by national competition authorities. Secondly, the EU Regulation imposes an obligation on national authorities to report enforcement actions pursuant to EU law to the Commission and ECN members.[75] Thirdly, the EU Regulation charges an Advisory Committee for Anticompetitive Practices and Dominant Positions (the "Committee") composed of representatives of all participant enforcement authorities to conduct a form of peer review of all draft decisions of the European Commission and proposed decisions of the national authorities may also be placed on the Committee's agenda for discussion.[76] Moreover, the ECN has also created various topical working groups within which details of the implementation of cases and remedies are also reviewed. Such working groups also provide a venue for the discussion and issuance of guidance documents, as well as overall policy review.[77] Finally, while both the European Commission and national authorities have emphasised the importance of maintaining the coherence of EU competition law even within the decentralised enforcement structure, observers suggest that national enforcement does in fact maintain local characteristics and reflect local priorities.[78] In fact, there have even been efforts to stimulate divergent enforcement remedies, combined with monitoring and peer review of the effects of those remedies.[79]

---

74 Y Svetiev, 2010b, "Networked Competition Governance in the EU: Delegation, Decentralisation or Experimentalist Architecture?", in C Sabel and J Zeitlin eds., *Experimentalist Governance in the European Union: Towards a New Architecture* (Oxford University Press).

75 Regulation 1/2003, Art. 11(4) (a national authority must inform the European Commission of its intent to adopt a decision under EU competition law and the information is made available to other authorities in the ECN); Art. 15(2) (Member States must report any written judgments of national courts applying EU competition law).

76 Regulation 1/2003, Art. 14.

77 K Dekeyser and D. Dalheimer, 2005, "Cooperation within the European Competition Network – Taking Stock after Ten Months of Case Practice", in P Lowe and M Reynolds (eds), *Antitrust Reform in Europe: A Year in Practice* (IBA).

78 For a recent account with respect to inter-firm agreements, see O Brook, 2019, "Struggling with Article 101 (3) TFEU: Diverging Approaches of the Commission, EU Courts, and Five Competition Authorities", *Common Market Law Review* 56:121.

79 G Cipolla, 2015, "Hotel Online Booking Sector: The Commitments of Booking and the Most Favored Nation Clauses: A Case Conducted in Cooperation with other National Competition Authorities", *Italian Antitrust Review* n. 3; see also ECN, 2016, *Report on the monitoring exercise carried out in the online hotel booking sector by the EU Competition Authorities*, available at https://ec.europa.eu/competition/ecn/hotel_monitoring_report_en.pdf.

The key attractive feature of the experimentalist network stems from the fact that it allows for differentiation and local tailoring in the implementation of competition law, however at the same time divergence is disciplined by reporting and peer review and, as such, can contribute to joint learning and the evolution of common norms. At its inception, as discussed above, the ICN was principally focused on informal diffusion and normative convergence among different antitrust jurisdictions, starting from the technocratic low hanging fruit (such as merger notifications) and proceeding towards more contested areas of competition policy (such as the treatment of unilateral conduct).[80] While it is true that, particularly in its second decade, ICN steering officials as well as national representatives increasingly recognised the limits of the convergence discourse and promoted the idea of informed divergence in areas where convergence was not possible[81], there are a number of features of its architecture that limit the ICN's evolution into an experimentalist network. The first is the fact that there is no requirement of regular reporting of interventions to disclose how participating authorities apply common norms in specific situations. The second is the absence of an institutionalised mechanism of peer review of the design and effects of such interventions by participating authorities.

To begin with the peer review element of an experimentalist regulatory network, one reform option would be to formalise and implement such a review mechanism as part of the ICN architecture, as suggested by Van Uytsel. However, in studying the transnational governance of forestry and logging, Zeitlin and Overdevest have pointed out that a transnational experimentalist regime can be assembled by linking together a set of different institutional components that perform different functionalities and that may be hosted in different forums.[82] Thus, while the ICN does not have a peer review mechanism, at least two other forums for antitrust cooperation incorporate such a functionality, including the OECD Competition Committee[83] and the United Nations Conference for Trade and Development Intergovernmental Group of Experts ("UNCTAD IGE") on Competition Policy.[84] While these peer review frameworks were not designed with experimentalist governance in mind and peer review is typically voluntary, a large number of countries have subjected their competition policy frameworks to searching peer review in one or both of these mechanisms.

80 Fox, 2009, above, at 159.

81 Svetiev, 2012, above (referring to J Fingleton, Chair-Elect, ICN Steering Group, Closing Speech to the Eighth ICN Conference in Zurich, Switz. (June 5, 2009)).

82 C Overdevest and J Zeitlin, 2014, "Assembling an Experimentalist Regime: Transnational Governance Interactions in the Forest Sector", *Regulation & Governance* 8: 22.

83 OECD, Country reviews of competition policy frameworks, https://www.oecd.org/daf/competition/countryreviewsofcompetitionpolicyframeworks.htm

84 UNCTAD, Voluntary Peer Review of Competition Law and Policy, https://unctad.org/en/Pages/DITC/CompetitionLaw/Voluntary-Peer-Review-of-Competition-Law-and-Policy.aspx

For example, the UNCTAD IGE on competition law and policy was formalised in light of uncertainty about the suitability of existing competition law templates for developing countries, to provide a specific venue for the exploration of appropriate competition rules tailored to the needs of developing countries.[85] The UNCTAD IGE also created its own peer review framework – notwithstanding the existence of the OECD one – precisely with the same goal in mind. At the same time, however, UNCTAD's peer review followed the OECD approach of basing such reviews on "country reports", which are focused on the overall competition law and policy framework of a particular jurisdiction. The country reports typically describe the general legal and administrative framework for competition enforcement in the reviewed jurisdictions, testing observed rules practices in the reviewed jurisdiction vis-à-vis pre-existing templates for competition law and enforcement. While the reports note problems that have been identified in competition enforcement in the reviewed jurisdiction, and may even list specific enforcement exercises and cases decided in the reviewed jurisdiction, the focus is principally on specific legal outcomes, rather than evidence about the effects of specific interventions on the operation of local markets. In such overall country assessments, both the reasons for and effects of any divergent local enforcement choices may not come to the fore, particularly as a possible source of learning from difference by the network participants.[86] The limited participation of local market stakeholders is another factor that enhances the technocratic tone of peer review deliberations.

The other feature of experimentalist governance that is absent in the ICN architecture is the obligation to regularly report competition interventions to the ICN as a prelude to evaluating and reviewing the design and effects of such interventions. While the ICN has introduced an Agency Effectiveness Working Group "to identify key elements of a well-functioning competition agency and good practices for strategy and planning, operations, and enforcement tools and procedures", the working group does not appear to have such a broad mandate of systematic reporting and review. Moreover, as mentioned earlier, the ICN working groups develop (and revise) recommended practices only occasionally and typically on the basis of voluntary questionnaire responses. Experimentalism instead relies on continuous and systematic reporting and peer

85 B Wardhough, 2014, *Cartels, Markets and Crime* (Cambridge University Press), at 273–274; see also A Ezrachi and H Qaqaya, 2012, "UNCTAD's Collaborative Information Platform, *Concurrences* N° 4-2012 art. N° 49298: 204.

86 See Svetiev, 2020, above. This discussion draws on Chapter 5 in *Experimentalist Competition Law and the Regulation of Markets*, where I suggest that the episodic studies based on specific topics that are presented at the annual meetings of UNCTAD's IGE on competition law have, to a much greater extent, the character of experimentalist peer reviews, because they present specific enforcement interventions on a similar problem by different jurisdictions and compare both the design and the observed effects of such intervention with stakeholder participation.

review (instead of occasional review, or review only in cases of major failure) so as to learn from contextualised implementation and revise common rules and practices in an on-going way.[87]

However, should the ICN seek to institute reforms and create such obligations of systematic reporting of national competition law interventions, it would face the obvious practical constraint presented by the size and heterogeneity of its membership. The ICN aims to provide a broad-based global network for the world's competition authorities[88] so that its membership currently counts more than 140 agencies. It follows that incorporating the foregoing experimentalist disciplines in the ICN architecture in a systematic way presents significant challenges of scale even if just for information gathering, let alone for the systematic review and comparison of implementation outcomes.

One helpful development in that respect may be the growth of regional competition law agreements over recent decades.[89] Some of these agreements, drawing on the EU's experience, provide institutions for extraterritorial enforcement, modelled on the European Commission (such as the Caricom Commission and the Secretariat of the Andean Community), while others are limited to the reporting of laws and practices and information sharing.[90] The EU itself not only encourages the formation of regional competition fora, but sometimes even seeks to participate in them, leading to exercises of reporting and review of implementation similar to the ones in the ECN.[91] Similarly, jurisdictions have sometimes formed thematic cooperation clusters, focusing on specific enforcement issues that are of particular interest to them.[92] One model for the experimentalist evolution of the ICN could thus be as a "network of networks"[93], whereby it provides both a venue for the creation of clusters of shared enforcement context (on a regional or thematic basis) for different participant authorities and a clearinghouse platform for the dialogue between different clusters based on disciplined reporting and review of cluster experiences.

---

87 See C Sabel, 2004, "Beyond principal-agent governance: experimentalist organizations, learning and accountability", in E Engelen en M Sie Dhian Ho eds., *De Staat van de Democratie: Democratie Voorbij de Staat* (Amsterdam University Press); see also B Bender, 2014, "Experimentalist Governance in the European Competition Network", in J Bailleux and A Vauchez eds., *Exploring the Transnational Circulation of Policy Paradigms* (EUI RSCAS), at 13.

88 ICN Establishment Memorandum, above.

89 See e.g. Gal, 2010, above.

90 Svetiev, 2012, above.

91 Ibid., at 192.

92 Svetiev, 2010a, above; C Damro and T Guay, 2012, "Transatlantic Merger Relations: The Pursuit of Cooperation and Convergence", *Journal of European Integration* 34:643.

93 L Viellechner, 2009, "The Network of Networks: Karl-Heinz Ladeur's Theory of Law and Globalization", *German Law Journal* 10: 515.

3. CONCLUSION

In this essay, I have sought to draw on the literature on transnational governance to reflect upon the governance design model of the ICN. My key argument is that in contemplating the evolution of the network in its third decade, it is important to consider the question of a normatively desirable design model, as well as institutional reforms that such a design model may entail and evaluation metrics. I have argued that both the informal information and exchange model and the soft convergence model face efficacy and legitimacy challenges, particularly in giving a voice to and meeting the needs of new adopters of antitrust, including (but not limited to) developing countries. I have argued that the experimentalist model is normatively desirable from that perspective, however for it to be institutionally feasible it may require reconceptualising the ICN as a network of networks.

CONCLUSION

CHINA'S COMPETITION LAW AND POLICY IN AN INTERNATIONAL COMPARATIVE CONTEXT

Huang YONG[*], Nell Lixia ZHOU[**], and Tang JINGLUN[***]

1. INTRODUCTION

In this section, we briefly discuss the background of China's competition law. In order to fully understand China's Anti-Monopoly Law (AML), an overview of the evolution of the Chinese market economy and the tradition of the rule of law is required. China transitioned from a classic command economy to a socialist market economy; but it is also a young, emerging jurisdiction of anti-monopoly law. The framework, rules, and enforcement mechanisms of China's AML are still being shaped even to this day and may further develop and evolve. All this has given rise to some unique challenges to China's AML.

According to GDP statistics from the International Monetary Fund (IMF), China is the second largest economy in the world and is therefore a powerful entity in the globalizing world economy including in regard to the formulation of global economic governance arrangements and rule-making. Questions about how the market system operates and in particular how competition law and policy operate often lie at the heart of the seemingly perpetual negotiations, conflicts, agreements and compromises that constitute rule-making in international trade, investment and other negotiations, whether bilateral, plurilateral or multilateral. In this context it should be noted that, as this article suggests, China's market arrangements and its competition law and policy are broadly tending to converge with most international norms. It also suggests that the development of China's market arrangements and its competition law and policy must revolve around efforts to align China as much as possible with international rules, although this inevitably will be a gradual process.

* Director of Competition Law Center of University of International Business and Economics (UIBE), Professor of School of Law, UIBE.

** Senior Researcher of UIBE Competition Law Center, Associate Professor of School of International Studies, UIBE.

*** Research fellow of UIBE Competition Law Center.

The priorities for China's socialist market economy at this stage remain: (i) to reform the economic system by focusing on improving the system of property rights protection and market-based factor distribution; and (ii) to give the market a decisive role in the allocation of resources.

There are two important challenges facing China's market: how to ensure a healthy and sustainable development of the market; and how to break administrative monopolies. The fair competition review system, the principle of competitive neutrality, and the efforts to improve the business climate all discussed in this paper could help in this regard.

In such a market context, it is worth examining some of the unique challenges on interface of the Chinese AML and the market, industry, and consumers. Such studies in turn could inspire in-depth discussions on some of the fundamental questions about the AML. China's AML and anti-monopoly enforcement agencies deal with daunting challenges. However, in seeking to meet the challenges, China's competition enforcement agencies may be grappling with the same or similar constraints that competition enforcement agencies in other jurisdictions are faced with, including scarce resources, experience, technology and procedures.

This article appears not only on the twentieth anniversary of the creation of the ICN, but also at the start of the second decade of China's AML. Although the Chinese anti-monopoly enforcement agency is yet to become an ICN member, the opening-up and internationalization of the Chinese market, and the fact that analytical methodologies in the field of competition law are tending to converge, makes the challenges and solutions in China's anti-monopoly enforcement identical, if not closely analogous to many decisions and topics within the ICN. The interactions between Chinese competition officials, scholars, companies, attorneys and their international counterparts will certainly better educate China to approach China-specific challenges with the benefit of global perspectives, and thus promote the internationalization of the Chinese market and the development of the AML. Such engagement could also enable international practitioners to include Chinese perspectives in approaching competition issues in their own jurisdictions. We expect to see the further unfolding of the relationships between market, competition and law in an ever-changing economic globalization.

2. A YOUNG JURISDICTION: THE HEALTHY EVOLUTION OF CHINA'S AML

In this section, we trace the evolution of China's Antimonopoly Law. As an economy in transition, China has but 26 years of experience in running a socialist market economy, and 11 years in implementing the AML. Therefore, both in terms of its market economy and AML's history, China is a very young jurisdiction. In terms of the establishment and development of rules and mechanisms, China's market and AML are moving in the right direction. Among the most salient achievements of the Chinese market and the enforcement of AML are the status conferred on competition policy and the corresponding adoption of the rule of law. This remains the likely future direction ahead for the next few foreseeable years.

China's modern economic reforms began in late 1978. The essence of the reforms was to open up the economy to international trade and investment and to bring about domestic reforms that were broadly pro-market and ultimately pro-competition. Even in the earliest periods of the modern reform there was reference to the need for more competition in China, particularly with respect to competition between the different regions of China. When the first session of the Eighth National People's Congress Standing Committee (NPCSC), a top legislative institution in China, took place in March 1993, the NPCSC adopted a line in the Chinese Constitution which stated, 'China practices a socialist market economy'. As a result, since 1993 China officially has had a market-oriented economy. Soon thereafter a process of drafting an anti-monopoly law was established, culminating in the 2008 AML. In the meantime, and in order to start establishing the market system, the first law against unfair competition was passed in September 1993. It incorporated provisions on regulating designated transactions by public undertakings, local protectionism by the government and its affiliated bodies, as well as predatory pricing and bid rigging by undertakings.[1] After the implementation of this law, there were calls by academia for the removal or refinement of these clauses. These clauses were not abolished until the revision of AUCL in Nov 2017, which means that the competition-related provisions in AUCL had been coexisting with AML since its implementation in 2008 for nearly a decade. Additionally, even Article 14 of the Price Law (currently in force) contains provisions to prohibit collusion in pricing and predatory pricing.[2] Scholars have called for the Price Law to be amended in order to improve its alignment with the AML. It was proposed that price-related exceptions, agreements to restrict competition, and abuse of dominant market position be the purview of the AML.[3] Thus, there is increasing clarity on the scope of jurisdiction of anti-monopoly rules in China.

---

1 See the Law against Unfair Competition (1993 Revision). Available at www.gov.cn/banshi/2005-08/31/content_68766.htm.

2 Huang Yong, and Wu Baiding. *Improve the Legal System of Pricing and Foster the Pricing Reform in Accordance with the Law – A Study on the Pathways of Revising the Price Law.* Price Theory and Practice, 2014 Issue 11.

3 Huang Yong, and Wu Baiding. *Improve the Legal System of Pricing and Foster the Pricing Reform in Accordance with the Law – A Study on the Pathways of Revising the Price Law.* Price Theory and Practice, 2014 Issue 11.

The AML itself is far from sufficient to address all the competition concerns arising from a great variety of business and government conduct in the market. It needs to be supplemented by criteria for analysis and determination and be supported by enforcement mechanisms and procedures. Experience gained since the implementation of the AML suggests that the analytical framework on anti-monopoly is still a work in progress, while also anti-monopoly enforcement systems and processes are still being further developed.

In terms of standards and procedures, following the implementation of the AML, the State Council promulgated the Provisions on the Thresholds for Prior Notification of Concentrations of Undertakings in 2008.[4] Additionally, the Supreme People's Court issued the Provisions on Issues concerning the Application of Law in the Trial of Civil Dispute Cases Arising from Monopolistic Conduct in 2012.[5] The State Council Anti-Monopoly Commission (AMC)[6] enacted in 2009 the Guidelines on the Definition of Relevant Market.[7] Finally, the three former anti-monopoly enforcement agencies issued from 2008 to 2017 a total of 12 departmental rules, 3 regulatory documents and 10 guidelines including Measures on Review of Concentration of Undertakings, Provisions against Price Fixing and Provisions on the Prohibition of Monopolistic Agreements. Meanwhile, the new enforcement mechanisms and the accompanying new rules have opened a new chapter for China's AML.

In late August 2017, 10 years after the adoption of the AML, a study on the revision of the AML officially launched.[8] In March 2018, close to the 10th anniversary of the implementation of the AML, a sweeping reform of state institutions took place in China. The anti-monopoly enforcement powers previously shared by the National Development and Reform Commission (NDRC), the Ministry of Commerce (MOFCOM), and the State Administration for Industry and Commerce (SAIC) were consolidated under the newly formed State Administration for Market Regulation (SAMR). Concurrently, the proposed revision of the AML was formally included in the legislative plan of

---

4 Article 21 of the AML provides, "the thresholds for notification of concentration of undertakings shall be set by the State Council", which is the top executive body in China.

5 See Supreme People's Court of China: www.court.gov.cn/fabu-xiangqing-3989.html.

6 The AMC was set up by the State Council in accordance with Article 9 of the AML. The AMC is responsible for drafting relevant competition policy, and investigating, reviewing and publishing updates on the competitive landscape, among other activities of organization, coordination and guidance on anti-monopoly.

7 In China, academics have conducted discussions over the legal hierarchy of the anti-monopoly guidelines, which was thought to be lower than the administrative laws and regulations, yet higher than the departmental rules. See Hao Junqi, and Liu Weijun. *A Discussion over the Functions of the Anti-monopoly Guidelines.* Price Supervision and Anti-Monopoly in China, September 1, 2017.

8 *The Study on the Revision of the AML Officially Launched.* China Intellectual Property, September 1, 2017.
Available at www.chinaipmagazine.com/news-show.asp?21078.html.

the incumbent NPCSC. Between the second half of 2018 and the third quarter of 2019, the SAMR introduced a flurry of regulations on enforcement authority, substantive rules and procedures[9], and completed the drafting of four anti-monopoly guidelines. These included the Guideline on Automotive Industry, leniency for horizontal agreements and IPR related issues, and Commitment mechanisms; with the hope of unifying the enforcement of AML once they are officially issued.

In terms of procedures, AML enforcement forms part of the general Chinese administrative enforcement system. Based on general administrative procedural rules, competition enforcement agencies have also issued a number of special rules and regulations, supplementing anti-monopoly enforcement in the events of conflict. The specific antitrust procedural rules prevail over the general administrative rules.

With the consolidation of the three competition agencies into one single regulator at the central level, the same structural integration of the provincial bureaus was also completed by November 2018. We have also observed changes on the judicial procedures. Thus, the decision on Issues of Litigation Procedures of IPR cases (Patents etc) which states that appeal cases of antimonopoly cases will be within the jurisdiction of the IP Tribunals SPC. This elevation of the adjudication level will enhance the professionalism and authoritativeness of the adjudication of the antitrust cases.

China's judicial procedures for anti-monopoly enforcement have also recently undergone changes. The sixth meeting of the 13th NPCSC on October 26th, 2018 passed the Decision on several issues concerning judicial procedures for patent and other intellectual property cases, which stipulated that appeals in monopoly cases should be directly heard by the Intellectual Property Tribunal of the Supreme People's Court (SPC). Before this, appeal cases had to go through two tiers of municipal and provincial courts before they could finally be appealed to the SPC. Elevating appeal in the trial hierarchy is conducive to increasing the professionalism and authority of anti-monopoly judicial cases.

---

9 E.g. Notice of SAMR on the Empowerment of AML Enforcement, Interim Provisions on Prohibiting Monopoly Agreements, Interim Provisions on Prohibiting Abuse of Dominant Market Positions, Interim Provisions on Prohibiting the Acts of Eliminating or Restricting Competition by Abuse of Administrative Power, Template Agreement on Entrusting Monitoring Trustee, Guiding Opinions on Regulating the Titles of Cases on the Notification of Concentration of Business Operators, Guiding Opinions on Notification for Simple Cases of Concentration of Business Operators, Explanation on Implementing the Notification Form of the Anti-Monopoly Review of Concentration of Undertakings, Guidelines for the Anti-monopoly Review for Concentration of Business Operators, Guiding Opinions on the Notification Documents and Materials of the Concentration of Business Operators, Guiding Opinions on the Notification of Concentration of Business Operators, etc.

China's AML, in terms of rules, standards, systems and procedures, is still in a state of change even in its second decade, but the first decade of AML implementation has generated a great deal of valuable experience and has made China more understanding of and adapted the Chinese regime more to the international landscape of competition law enforcement. Since the implementation of the AML, the enforcement agencies have closed more than 100 cases of monopolistic agreement, dozens of cases of abuse of dominant market position, and nearly 3000 cases of concentration of undertakings. In addition to routine anti-monopoly enforcement, the enforcement agencies have also investigated and processed nearly 200 cases of abuse of administrative power to eliminate or restrict competition, which has effectively checked undue government intervention in the market. In the same period, Chinese courts also closed several hundred anti-monopoly civil lawsuits, involving various sectors such as transportation, insurance, pharmaceutical, food, household appliances, power, and ICT.

In view of the particularity of the Chinese market, some have expressed concerns that China's AML may be influenced by protectionism[10], or does not comply with the principle of due process, or that it may serve China's special policy agenda.[11] On the one hand, administrative procedures can provide necessary judicial relief. On the other hand, China is an economy in transition, one of the most important pillars of the international economy, and a young jurisdiction of competition law in the world. Given these characteristics, China must constantly improve its market, the AML and its enforcement infrastructure. It requires the enforcement agencies and judicial authorities responsible for implementing the AML to build up case experience and industry know-how in the process of interacting with domestic and international markets, so as to further drive the AML to move in the right direction.

3. MATURING OF THE MARKET: FUNDAMENTAL ROLE OF COMPETITION POLICY

3.1. A BASELINE VIEW ON CHINA'S COMPETITION POLICY

This section discusses fundamental features of China's competition policy.

Establishing and strengthening the fundamental role of competition policy is of great importance to China today. As an economy in transition, China sees the

10 See Yong, Z. (2004). Will Protectionists Hijack China's Competition Law?, *International Financial Law Review* 23(1), 21–21.

11 See Foster, A. L. (2017). Navigating the Unique Features of China's Competition Landscape, *Antitrust* 31(2), 79–86.

establishing of a sophisticated and robust market system as a current priority. According to the World Bank's four dimensions of "competition policy", the first is opening the market; the second is embedding competition principles in broader public policies; the third is reforming the competition framework and its implementation; and the fourth is fostering competitive neutrality in markets with reduced direct state participation.[12] Three of the four dimensions are directed at government conduct.[13] Both definitions of the World Bank and the European Union deem that a competition legal system is a part of competition policy. However, in China, Article 9 of AML states that "doing research to formulate related competition policy" is the primary statutory duty of the Anti-Monopoly Commission (AMC) of the State Council. As a result, it can be said that Chinese competition policy is rooted in the Chinese competition legal system. Accordingly, it boils down to whether we adopt the approach of setting up competition policy at a national-level first and only then lay out the corresponding legal system, or to release a law first with the hope of bringing about a radiating effect of generating awareness of a broader sense of competition policy. The latter must, in our view, be adopted given the level of maturity of the Chinese market and roadmap of rule of law in China.

3.2. ESTABLISHMENT AND REINFORCEMENT OF THE FUNDAMENTAL ROLE OF CHINA'S COMPETITION POLICY

A country's competition policy is often equated with its competition law statutes. But a wider and better view is that a country needs to have a comprehensive competition policy (including a competition law) which addresses many sources of restrictions on competition that cannot all be addressed by a statute. This includes, for example, government laws and government practices that are anticompetitive. It is in in this context that we should look at the fundamental role of China's competition policy.

China's competition policy in this field has been the result of a series of practical developments from theoretical research to a mindset shift. Industrial policy has long been regarded as the dominant economic policy in China. Government agencies are more accustomed to tackle and combat administrative abuse of power to eliminate competition either by issuing a "red headed document"[14];

12 See the World Bank. Markets and Competition Policy. Available https://www.worldbank.org/en/topic/competition-policy.

13 Despite the fact that the formulation and implementation of laws can be regarded as conduct of the state and government, yet this statement is not appropriate under this specific context.

14 "Red-headed documents" generally refer to non-legislative documents such as measures, instructions, and orders issued by government agencies. Such documents have traditionally

or by issuing notices, meeting minutes, etc: which unfortunately, however, have not achieved their desired effect. In contrast, the AML, as an embodiment of competition policy, contained prohibitive provisions on the abuse of administrative power to eliminate or restrict competition, and achieved some initial progress in practice, but it still fell short of the expectations of the system and the economic reality of the market.[15] In essence the law alone was insufficient to deal with government restrictions on competition.

It left an institutional gap for competition policy to fill in regulating administrative monopoly and in coordinating industrial policy amid reforms of the market economic system. In short, competition policy was marginalized and did not receive enough attention. As time passed the actual or presumed benefits of industrial policy in promoting economic growth were seemingly diminishing and the adverse effects of industrial policy on China's industrial and corporate competitiveness; transformation and upgrade on the value chain; and national innovation strategy, became more significant.[16] In 2013, the Third Plenum of the 18th CPC Central Committee adopted the Decision of the CPC Central Committee on "Major Issues Concerning Comprehensively Deepening Reform", which explicitly called for "the market to play a decisive role in resource allocation". Since 2015, a series of policy documents have been issued by the CPC Central Committee and the State Council[17] to stress the important role

---

been important tools for administrative bodies at different levels to implement administrative activities. These documents are called red-headed because the upper half of the document cover would show in red the name of the public authority issuing the document. It is similar for notices and meeting minutes.

15 From a legal standpoint, this is mainly because the AML enforcement agencies only have the power to recommend corrective actions against administrative monopoly, but not the powers to enforce them. According to Article 51 of the AML, the administrative agencies and organizations mandated by laws and regulations to manage public affairs shall be ordered to rectify by their superior authorities if they have abused their administrative powers to eliminate or restrict competition. Anti-monopoly enforcement agencies may recommend corrective actions in accordance with the law to upper-level authorities. Where laws and administrative regulations provide otherwise on administrative agencies and organizations mandated by laws and regulations with the function of managing public affairs abusing their administrative powers to eliminate or restrict competition, such other provisions shall apply. In reality, the issuers of many policy documents (or the superseding legal basis of lower-level documents) rank higher than the agencies that are actually responsible for AML enforcement.

16 Huang Yong. A Study on the Legal Guarantee of the Fundamental Role of China's Competition Policy, *Business and Economic Law Review* 2018 Issue 1.

17 The policy documents issued by the CPC Central Committee and the State Council may carry less authority than those adopted by the CPC plena, but they usually concern the detailed implementation of the latter and are more elaborate and actionable. For example, the statement of "strengthening the role of competition policy and industrial policy in guiding innovation" in the Opinions of the CPC Central Committee and the State Council on Deepening the Institutional and System Reform and Accelerating the Implementation of the Innovation-Driven Strategy is the concretization of the line "giving the market a decisive role in allocating resources and better discharging the role of the government" in the document adopted by the Third Plenum of the 18th CPC Central Committee. In addition,

of competition policy in a modern market economy from different perspectives and in varying degrees and to mandate "further steering innovation with competition and industrial policies"[18], "promoting effective alignment between industrial policy and competition policy"[19], "progressively affirming the fundamental role of competition policy" and "accelerating the establishment of a process to coordinate competition policy with other policies such as industrial and investment policies".[20]

From existing behind the scenes to going front and center, competition policy began playing an increasingly important role in shaping national economic policies. In 2017, the report of the 19th CPC National Congress once again emphasized the reform of the economic system, which focuses on improving the property rights system and market-oriented allocation of factors of production so as to enable the market to play a decisive role in the allocation of resources.

The fundamental role of competition policy needs to be further strengthened today. The decision of the CPC Central Committee on "Major Issues Concerning Comprehensively Deepening Reform" clearly required "improving the mechanism for coordinating economic policies such as fiscal, monetary, industrial and regional policies". When competition policy is at odds with industrial, fiscal, investment or trade policy, the question of which policy should prevail was not answered formally in the document of the plenum of the CPC Central Committee, the venue for considering the relationship between competition policy and other policies.[21] On October 31, 2019, the Fourth Plenum of the 19th CPC Central Committee adopted the Decision of the CPC Central Committee on major issues concerning adherence to and improvement of socialism with Chinese characteristics, the advancement of the national governance system, and the modernization of the governance capabilities; which explicitly called for "strengthening the fundamental role of competition

---

following the issue of policy documents by CPC Central Committee and the State Council, party committees and government agencies will most likely formulate more detailed policy implementation documents throughout the hierarchy, thereby breaking down the policy step by step into specific actions.

18 See the Several Opinions of the CPC Central Committee and the State Council on Deepening the Reform of Systems and Mechanisms to Accelerate the Implementation of Innovation-driven Development Strategies.
Available at www.gov.cn/xinwen/2015-03/23/content_2837629.htm.

19 See the Notice of the State Council on Approving and Forwarding the Opinions of the National Development and Reform Commission on the Pivotal Work of Deepening the Reform of the Economic System in 2015.
Available at www.gov.cn/zhengce/content/2015-05/18/content_9779.htm.

20 See the Several Opinions of the CPC Central Committee and the State Council on Advancing the Pricing Mechanism Reform. Available at www.gov.cn/xinwen/2015-10/15/content_2947548.htm.

21 Same as 18.

policy".[22] This was the first time that the CPC Central Committee had, by way of its highest-level programmatic document[23], acknowledged the fundamental role of competition policy, which provides more powerful guidance and assurance for future coordination of competition policy with other economic policies. We have reasons to expect that there will be an implementation scheme to deliver the fundamental role of competition policy in the near future.

3.3. EVOLVING COMPONENTS OF CHINA'S COMPETITION POLICY

Apart from its rising status, another feature of China's competition policy was the further concretization of its components, an example being the principle of competitive neutrality. Competitive neutrality is a policy that originated in Australia and then was widely espoused by the OECD. It refers to the fact that in many countries State Owned Enterprises have some 'artificial' advantages over the private sector – they may pay less tax; they may be less regulated; they may receive subsidized inputs e.g. energy inputs; they may receive cheaper credit. This gives them what is often seen as an unfair advantage over the private sector. Arguably, it also distorts resource allocation which should flow to the most efficient operators – not the ones whose costs are lower because of government subsidies. Competitive neutrality is especially important in the Chinese context because of the large role that state-owned enterprises play in the economy.

In 2017, the market regulation plan under China's "Thirteenth Five-Year Plan"[24] already started "implementing a competitive neutrality

22 See the Decision of the CPC Central Committee on Major Issues Concerning Adherence to and Improvement of Socialism with Chinese Characteristics, the Advancement of the National Governance System, and the Modernization of the Governance Capabilities (adopted at the fourth Plenary Sessions of the 19th CPC Central Committee). Available at http://politics.people.com.cn/n1/2019/1106/c1024–31439479.html.

23 It refers to the document adopted by the CPC Central Committee plenum mentioned earlier. The document adopted by the CPC Central Committee plenum is called "the highest-level programmatic document" because such a document would carry the utmost authority in China. Typically the title of such a document contains the word "decision". The Decision adopted by the CPC Central Committee plenum provides forward guidance for various activities in China for an extended period of time (usually counted in 5–10 year terms).

24 Since 1953, China has developed a tradition of formulating a five-year plan (FYP) every five years. The 13th FYP falls between 2016 and 2020 in China. The FYP, as a form of state intervention in economic development, was however not a Chinese invention, nor was it unique to China. In an interview with Xinhua News Agency in 2016, Professor A. Michael Spence of Stanford University stated that China has benefited enormously from sticking to the FYP. This experience is worth learning from for the West. During the implementation phase, the State Council would break down the main objectives and tasks proposed in the FYP down to each region and government department according to their respective terms of reference, make clear the agencies accountable for the binding targets, break down the

system".[25] In 2018, China's Central Bank Governor and the Minister of SAMR also referred to competitive neutrality in public speeches.[26] The State Council's 2019 Government Work Report[27] clearly required that, "pursuant to the principle of competitive neutrality, enterprises, regardless of ownership structure, should be treated equally in terms of access to resources, entry permit, license to operate, government procurement and bidding and tendering."[28]

Equal treatment for all enterprises – both private companies and companies owned by the State – must be understood in the context of the broader legal framework. For example, China's Company Law requires enterprises to take on corporate social responsibility[29], and making profits is part of such social responsibility.[30] Another view is that social responsibility should include public policy goals such as protecting the environment.[31] In any event, state-owned enterprises often have internal processes for implementing national economic and social policies, whereas the corresponding mechanisms in

---

binding targets down to each region, establish a "public reporting system" for the fulfillment of the binding targets, include the fulfillment of binding targets into the comprehensive assessment and performance review on economic and social development for reach region and department, and organizes nationwide implementation.

25 See the Notice of the State Council on Issuing the Plan for Market Regulation during the 13th Five-Year Plan Period (ND [2017] 6). Available at www.gov.cn/zhengce/content/2017–01/23/content_5162572.htm.

26 At the G30 International Banking Seminar, Mr. Yi Gang, Governor of the People's Bank of China (PBoC) highlighted the necessity of further accelerating domestic reform and opening up and reinforcing the protection of IPR. In the meantime, he stressed the consideration of treating state-owned enterprises (SOEs) by the principle of competitive neutrality. In an interview with the Xinhua News Agency, former Minister of SAMR, Mr. Zhang Mao, highlighted the importance of adhering to the principle of competitive neutrality and implementing the regulation, taxation and debt neutrality in treating SOEs and private-owned enterprises (POEs).

27 Typically, in the first quarter (usually March) of each year, the State Council would report before the National People's Congress (NPC) on the government's work in the past calendar year and propose the government's work priorities for the coming year. The NPC reviews the report. Members of the CPPCC (Chinese People's Political Consultative Conference allows for participation in and consultation on political affairs. It is consulted on important national and regional policies and other important political, economic, cultural and social matters prior to decision, and on important matters during the implementation of the decision) would comment on the report. After the report is adopted by the NPCSC, it will translate into specific tasks for the central and sub-national governments for the coming year.

28 See 2019 Government Work Report. Available at www.gov.cn/premier/2019–03/16/content_5374314.htm.

29 See Article 15 of the Company Law of the People's Republic of China, "Companies engaging in the business shall comply with the provisions of laws and administrative regulations ... and bear social responsibilities."

30 Zhang Weiying. Making Money is the Social Responsibility of Corporate, *Discovery* 2007 Issue 11.

31 See Branson, D. M. (2002). Corporate Social Responsibility Redux, *Tulane Law Review* 76(5–6), 1207–1226.

private enterprises are geared towards making profits without breaking the law. This is an issue that needs to be studied in the implementation of competitive neutrality in China. In addition, the commitment of the Chinese government to a pro-business environment is another dimension of competition policy.[32] If competitive neutrality is the embodiment of the content of competition policy, the FCRS (Fair Competition Review System) to be addressed below is how competition policy is being institutionalized.

4. THE RULE OF LAW IN COMPETITION: THE AML AND THE FAIR COMPETITION REVIEW SYSTEM

In this section we discuss the AML 2008 and its relationship to wider questions of competition policy.

4.1. LIMITATIONS OF THE AML AGAINST ADMINISTRATIVE MONOPOLY

The fair competition review system China set up in 2016 is not only a useful tool under competition policy, but also an important hallmark of the establishment and fortification of the fundamental role of competition policy in the Chinese market economy more generally. Even though a whole chapter in the AML is dedicated to the regulation of abuse of administrative powers which can eliminate or restrict competition, previous attempts to break administrative monopolies through the implementation of the AML were unsuccessful. This was because: (i) the administrative enforcement of the AML lacked both force and breadth in regulating administrative monopoly; and (ii) China's Administrative Procedure Law did not offer any direct litigation recourse against the widespread "red-headed documents" in China that concerned market players.[33]

---

32 The 2019 Government Work Report has indicated a large gap between the business environment and the expectation of market entities. In this regard, in 2019, the State Council issued the Regulation on Optimizing the Business Environment.

33 According to Article 53 of the Administrative Procedure Law of the People's Republic of China, when a case is brought against an administrative action, an accompanying request may be made for the regulatory document concerned to be reviewed. This means that the law does not mandate the court to directly review regulatory documents without an administrative decision being made. Article 53 also stipulates that "rules" promulgated by various ministries under the State Council are not within the scope of incidental review.

4.2. FAIR COMPETITION REVIEW SYSTEM: BACKGROUND AND PROCESS

In China, the term Fair Competition Review relates to a review of all government laws and practices at a national, state and local level that affect competition and that most often sit outside the reach of a standard competition law. The internationally recognized prototype of the Fair Competition Review system comes from the National Competition Policy that Australia adopted in the 1990s. However, China recognized these issues soon after the 1978 reforms and took some actions to remove anti-competitive restrictions between the various regions of China. It was not until 2016 that the Fair Competition Review became a tangible system, with both substantive rules and enforcement procedures. Essentially, the Fair Competition Review system provides for a process of reviewing (at least in principle) all anti-competitive laws and regulations at all levels of government, although the implementation would be a large challenge for any country, and it must necessarily proceed step by step.

Early in the reform and opening-up process in 1980, the Interim Provisions of the State Council on Developing and Protecting Socialist Competition stated, "to the extent that industrial, transportation, financial and trade regulators and other relevant agencies have in their current rules and regulations provisions that are prejudicial to competition, they must modify such provisions to facilitate competition. It is illegal to take administrative measures to protect backwardness, curb progress, and impede the normal flow of goods. Such behaviors must be stopped."[34]

Even many years later, the practical challenge of excess planning in the socialist market economy was not addressed fully. In 2012, the 18th National Congress of the CPC emphasized the need to show greater political courage and wisdom; seize the opportunity to deepen reforms in important areas; resolutely remove all ideological and institutional barriers to scientific development; build a complete, compliant, and effective system; and make all aspects of the system more mature and stable.[35] The Third Plenum of the 18th CPC Central Committee[36] adopted

34 Now repealed.

35 Hu Jintao: Firmly March on the Path of Socialism With Chinese Characteristics and Strive to Complete the Building of a Moderately Prosperous Society in All Respects – Report to the Eighteenth NCCPC. *People's Daily*, November 18, 2012, 1st Edition.

36 Since the reform and opening up started in 1978, people have been inferring the guiding policies and work priorities of the new leaderships of CPC by paying close attention to what issues discussed, what decisions made, what measures taken and what signals revealed on the third Session of the CPC Central Committee, which is of great significance in implementing relevant work for an extended period of time up to 10 years. The documents of CPC Central Committee plena have no immediate legal force, but they can form the basis of legislation and thus carry tremendous weight in China. The future direction of socialism with Chinese

the Decision of the CPC Central Committee on major issues concerning comprehensively deepening reform, which emphasized "deepening economic reform to give the market a decisive role in the allocation of resources; committing to and improving the basic economic system; accelerating the improvement of the modern market system, a macro regulatory system and an open economy system; accelerating the transformation of economic growth model". It also said, "economic reform is a priority in the comprehensive reform. The critical pieces are to properly manage the relationship between the state and the market, give the market a decisive role in the allocation of resources and better discharge the role of the government. Having the market decide on the allocation of resources is an established law of the market economy. This law must be followed for the health of the socialist market economy. Efforts must be made to address the flaws of the market system, excess government intervention and lax regulation. Market-oriented reforms must proceed proactively and steadily both in terms of breadth and depth. Direct government allocation of resources must be reduced significantly to allow for the allocation of resources in accordance with market rules, market prices, and market competition to maximize benefits and efficiency; while cleaning up and abolishing various regulations and practices that hinder a unified market and fair competition, banning and punishing all types of illegal implementation of preferential policies, resisting local protectionism, and opposing monopoly and unfair competition."[37]

In March 2015, the Opinions of the CPC Central Committee and the State Council on "Deepening the Institutional and System Reform" and "Accelerating the Implementation of the Innovation-Driven Strategy" were circulated, which proposed "exploring the implementation of a fair competition review system." In May, the State Council approved and circulated the Opinions of the National Development and Reform Commission (NDRC) on the "Priorities of Deepening Economic Reform" in 2015, which identified "promoting effective coordination between industrial policy and competition policy, establishing and streamlining the fairness and competitiveness review mechanisms for industrial policy" as reform priorities. In June, the State Council issued the Opinion on policy

---

characteristics is steered by the CPC, which also leads the people to formulate and enforce the Constitution and laws. The senior-most steering organization of the CPC is its National Congress which takes place every five years and the Central Committee it produces. The plenary session of each Central Committee is referred to as "the xth plenum of the XXth CPC Central Committee". The documents adopted at the plenum embody the will of the CPC leadership. After a document is adopted, the measures proposed therein will be implemented through party committees and government agencies at various levels, and a considerable part will drive the creation of new legal frameworks.

37 See the Decision of the CPC Central Committee on Some Major Issues Concerning Comprehensively Deepening the Reform, *People's Daily*, November 16, 2012, 1st Edition. Available at http://politics.people.com.cn/n/2013/1115/c1001–23559207.html.

measures to vigorously promote mass entrepreneurship and innovation, which called for "expediting the introduction of a fair competition review system and creating a unified, transparent, orderly and streamlined market environment", and made clear that the NDRC and the former Legislative Affairs Office (LAO) of the State Council should lead the development of a fair competition review system. In October, the Opinions of the CPC Central Committee on Advancing Pricing Reforms proposed "gradually affirming the fundamental role of competition policy" and underscored again the need to "expedite efforts to establish a coordination mechanism between competition policy and industrial and investment policies, implement a fair competition review system and create a unified, open, competitive and orderly market system." In June 2015, China started drafting rules around a fair competition review system. On June 14, 2016, the State Council formally issued the Opinion on "Establishing a Fair Competition Review System in the Development of the Market System", subjecting policymakers issuing policy measures to direct economic activities to fair competition review as of July 1, 2016.[38]

The fair competition review system prescribes 18 rules to be strictly observed by policymakers in devising policy papers that affect market players. These rules revolve around criteria for market access and exit, free flow of goods and materials, effects on the costs of production and operation, and effects on the activities of production and operation. On October 27, 2017, the NDRC and four other government agencies issued the Implementation Rules for the Fair Competition Review System (Interim), which further refined the "Four Criteria" and "18 Must Nots" into dozens of specific situations. It can be seen from the above that a not inconsiderable effort has gone into spelling out of the approach that underlies under the operation of a Fair Competition Review system.

4.3. FAIR COMPETITION REVIEW SYSTEM: ASSESSMENT AND OUTLOOK

The language of the articulated rules suggests the fair competition review system was conceived out of the AML, but the legal nature of the fair competition review system remains a policy paper, which means it is not legally binding. Therefore, by its nature, it is more fitting to characterize the fair competition review system as a compliance process established within the government to prevent violations of the AML. At the same time, the OECD Competition Assessment Toolkit mentions that the government's inclusion of both existing policies and new policies into the scope of competition review would depend on

[38] Li Qing. Review and Prospect on China's Competition Policy, *Competition Policy Research*, 2018 Issue 2.

substantial political will.[39] Such a view may suggest that deciding on the scope of competition review is not the only matter of political will: the methodology, process and effect of competition review also depend on substantial political will. In the absence of strict liability constraints, the Chinese government also recognizes that the implementation of the fair competition review system may risk becoming "an empty machine and a rubber stamp" and lack "real grit".[40] That being said, it is clear that the political will to enforce the fair competition review system has so far increased. The 2019 State Council Government Work Report required "reforming and improving the systems of fair competition review and just supervision; and expediting the overhaul of regulations and practices that hinder a unified market and fair competition".[41]

Although the central government has included the implementation and further improvement of the fair competition review system in the government work report, local governments are not necessarily on the same page. Of the 23 provinces, 5 autonomous regions, and 4 municipalities on the Chinese mainland, in the three years following the implementation of the fair competition review system, 32 provincial governments have issued a total of 96 government work reports. Statistics show in these 96 government work reports, the expression "fair competition review system" only appeared 9 times.[42] Not only that, some provincial government work reports also contained language of local protectionism and allocation of resources by the government. For example, one province's 2019 government work report reads "supporting local financial institutions to become bigger and stronger", "promoting city commercial banks, rural commercial banks, rural credit cooperatives ... to serve local private firms and small and micro enterprises, etc.". Such language can easily give rise to practices of market access restrictions and local protectionism and seem to have little place in a country with a full-blooded commitment to competition policy. The fair competition review system has the role of regulating industrial policy. Only when it covers the entire process from the formulation of industrial policy to implementation through government budget can it serve its true purpose. Of all the provinces on the Chinese mainland, only the People's Congress of Beijing included a statement on implementing the fair competition review system in its

39 OECD Competition Assessment Toolkit: Vol.1 Principles, P32. Available at www.oecd.org/daf/competition/assessment-toolkit.htm.

40 See SAMR: Overall Progress on the Implementation of the Fair Competition Examination System in 2018. Available at www.samr.gov.cn/jjj/gpjzsc/201902/t20190215_282277.html.

41 See 2019 Government Work Report. Available at www.gov.cn/premier/2019-03/16/content_5374314.htm.

42 See the websites of Provincial People's Congresses. It is noteworthy that this paper only takes account of relevant statistics at provincial level, which does not include municipal and county levels. Thereby, the attitude toward the implementation of the fair competition examination system at municipal and county levels has yet to be inferred precisely.

Economic and Social Development Report and Fiscal Budget and Final Accounts Report. The full coverage and deep penetration of the fair competition review system will still take time.

The effective implementation of fair competition review needs to be supported by professional legal and economic analysis. The SAMR has issued guidelines on independent assessment of fair competition review[43], which serve as a professional and technical assurance for fair competition review. Conversely, to live up to its purpose of disciplining industrial policy, the fair competition review system needs to be integrated into the national governance system. With its implementation, the fair competition review system is no longer simply a stand-alone process. Rather, it has been integrated into other institutional documents, especially in the fiscal domain. On July 26, 2019, the Ministry of Finance issued the Notice on "Promoting Fair Competition in Government Procurement and Improving the Business Climate".[44] The Notice mandates "strict implementation of the fair competition review system" and reaffirms the disciplinary power of fair competition review on industrial policy.

Based on the above-mentioned, a short summary of the fair competition review system on the Chinese mainland would be that it is still a work in progress, while there are encouraging developments, as well as areas of concern. In any event, the establishment and implementation of the fair competition review system in and of itself was a big step forward in China's deepening reform of the market-oriented economic system.

What should be noted in this regard is that SAMR released on 2 Jan 2020 a draft version of the revision of AML, which not only added provisions on fair competition review system but contained changes on provisions concerning administrative monopoly. However, history indicates there will likely be significant changes in this law before it can be finalized. The equivalent provisions of the 2008 AML were changed more times than any other provisions over its 14-year drafting process. Hence, it is premature to discuss this in detail in this paper.

5. CHINA'S MARKET CLIMATE AND SPECIAL CHALLENGES TO THE AML

This section reviews some of the challenges that arise in the context of the changing economic environment of China.

43 See the Announcement by SAMR on Issuing the Guidelines on the Implementation of Independent Assessment in the *Fair Competition Review* (No. 6, 2019).

44 See the Notice by the Ministry of Finance on Promoting Fair Competition in Government Procurement and Improving the Business Climate (No. 38 of the Ministry of Finance, 2019).

It must be emphasized that to understand China's AML, one must first look at the Chinese market and rule of law. China's market continues to expand, and the functioning of the rule of law continues to improve. Against this background, new questions have emerged as to the current analysis of the AML in the areas of big data and intellectual property. They have become in some respects unique to China, but the thinking that relates to these kind of questions can still be traced back to the fundamental questions of the AML, i.e., the relationships between anti-monopoly and the market, between anti-monopoly and industrial development, and between anti-monopoly and the protection of private rights, among others.

5.1. AML AND MARKET OPENING-UP AND EXPANSION

What is the purpose of the anti-monopoly policy and what are its objectives? Only when we can answer this question with a fair amount of certainty, can we draw a rational conclusion and ask the next question.[45] The stated legislative purposes of antitrust laws in various jurisdictions suggest that the primary value is in protecting competition. Competition is the most immediate goal and object of protection as proclaimed by antitrust laws across various jurisdictions. Antitrust legislation vows to protect competition in the market process. Since the object of protection for antitrust legislation lives in the market, whether antitrust legislation can protect competition by opening and expanding the market becomes a matter of discussion. And this matter is particularly important for China as an economy in transition.

Take the challenges of big data as an example. In the age of digital economies, big data technologies that integrate data, algorithms and artificial intelligence, have engendered a series of market forces and other competitive interests.[46] Concerns over personal information and privacy protection are on the minds of scholars, courts and enforcement agencies across various antitrust jurisdictions. The globalization of markets often makes the challenges to competition law in multiple jurisdictions similar, but while such challenges may appear common to competition law, they also show specificity.[47] However, when these concerns relate to specific areas or businesses, one will find the benefits of digitally-

45 See Robert H. Bork. *Antitrust Paradox – A Policy at War with Itself.* 66 (1978).

46 From the perspective of this paper, the global concerns on the competition of big data at present mainly include algorithm collusion, personalized pricing and market power attained by the data itself. Some competition issues engendered by the Internet platforms are also regarded as competition issues in relation to big data, e.g. network neutrality.

47 At the China Competition Policy Forum hosted in Beijing on August 1, 2018, Mrs. Maureen Ohlhausen introduced the "acquisitions of small companies" in the digital economy to indicate the existence of specificity arising from the common circumstances; See Tang Jinglun. Achievements, Challenges and Solutions of China's Competition Policy and Anti-

enabled businesses for promoting China's market opening and competition.[48] This cannot be overlooked in the analysis and application of China's AML in big data settings. It is a current challenge to the enforcement of antitrust legislation in many jurisdictions.

In China, digital payment is often a case in point. On August 27, 2013, Alipay, Alibaba's digital payment service, issued a statement where it said it would be discontinuing all offline POS (Point of Sale)[49] business and will follow up with all the affected merchants to minimize disruption to their normal business, due to "well-understood reasons". A press commentary claimed that Alipay's move was in response to China UnionPay's threats of "blocking" third party payments.[50] In China, the financial services industry, including mobile payment, is highly regulated. A senior executive of Alibaba later made the following statement after the "E-commerce Development" session at the 2018 World Economic Forum in Davos: "you would go to jail if you were to offer financial services without a license".[51] Now, applications such as Alipay and WeChat Pay not only could facilitate inter-bank payments and overseas spending by the Chinese through inexpensive currency settlements, they could also allow consumers to pay water, electricity and gas bills online in the comfort of their home[52], top up travel cards, and even allow students to pay tuition fees and recharge meal cards to use in school cafeterias and shops. Not only was the financial services industry disrupted, the telecommunications industry also felt the threat from the digital economy. Many Internet companies started offering sim cards with personalized packages and affordable data and call plans a few years ago. When WeChat was

---

Monopoly Law Enforcement in the New Era – An Overview of the 2018 China Competition Policy Forum. *China Competition Policy Research* 2018 Issue 3.

48 As aforementioned, the optimization of economic system, opening-up and competition of the market still lie at the heart of China's efforts in deepening reform.

49 POS is a kind of multi-functional terminal. Installed in special credit card merchants and accepting outlets, it is linked to the internet by computer connections. It has the functionalities of automatic transfer of E-fund. It also supports consumption, pre-authorization, balance inquiry and money transfer. In China, to engage in offline POS payment business, companies are required to cooperate with China UnionPay, which is set up by Central Bank under the approval of the State Council, the Central Government. The third-party payment software of Alibaba, Alipay, launched its own POS business without approval and didn't seek cooperation with China UnionPay. It eventually had to close all related businesses because of this non-compliance.

50 Kan Xingwen. UnionPay vs Alipay: Digital Payment Has Triggered "Blocking" Storm, *China Internet Weekly* 2013 Issue 18.

51 Keynote speech delivered by Jack Ma, former President of Alibaba, at the dialogue in the 2018 Winter Davos.

52 The significance of this phenomenon lies within the fact that monopolistic behaviors achieved by public service enterprises appear more frequently in China, thereby SAMR has specifically issued the Notice on Deepening the Implementations of Special Law Enforcement Actions to Regulate Public Enterprises in Restricting Competition and Achieving Monopolistic Behaviors, so as to promote the AML enforcement in the field of public service.

launched, its top feature of the year was largely about displacing the otherwise expensive phone calls and text messages.[53]

Similar developments have occurred elsewhere. Canada's competition policy report on the digital economy also speaks of innovations by deregulating the banking system.[54] Another example is the restrictions around the world on online taxi hailing apps such as Uber and Didi Chuxing. When institutions make the market uncompetitive, it becomes a legitimate question whether it is possible to create and foster new competition for the market through the implementation of antitrust legislation. If antitrust legislation, in addition to direct protection of competition by preventing and stopping monopolistic conduct, could also include case-specific factors for examining areas of technology that could potentially disrupt a monopolistic industry, it would be in the interest of the country's market development: but in any event, any such benefit needs to be based on the legality and sensibility of antitrust analysis.

5.2. AML AND INDUSTRY TRANSFORMATION AND UPGRADE

In the age of innovation, China is graduating from a player in the global value chain to a player in the global innovation ecosystem. Protecting intellectual property rights and encouraging innovation have become national strategies.[55] In an innovative economy, industrial structures are highly modular and sophisticated. The division of labor between enterprises is not confined to the production and manufacturing, but rather extends from manufacturing to product design and development.[56] However, as industries evolve, the technology roadmap may not be a linear, one-directional line, and industrial know-how may switch discontinuously between different knowledge systems.[57] This is the case with technology and intellectual property rights that protect technology. The scholars and practitioners in China have produced many thought-provoking studies and conclusions on this matter.

---

53 In China, sending short messages by mobile phones has been charged at 0.1 RMB per piece for years. Earlier, SIM card packages would normally include services in resemblance to "100 pieces of messages for 5 RMB". The reason why people preferred text messages rather than phone calls is because the former was considered cheaper than the latter.

54 See the Competition Policy in the Digital Era released by the Competition Bureau Canada in August 2019.

55 See the State Council, Outline of the National Intellectual Property Strategy (2018). Available at www.wipo.int/wipolex/en/text.jsp?file_id=125982.

56 Sebastian K Fixson, Jin-Kyu Park (2008). The Power of Integrality: Linkages between Product Architecture, Innovation, and Industry Structure, *Research Policy* 37(8), 1296–1316.

57 Joern Huenteler, Tobias S Schmidt, Jan Ossenbrink, Volker H Hoffmann (2016). Technology Life-cycles in the Energy Sector – Technological Characteristics and the Role of Deployment for Innovation, *Technological Forecasting and Social Change* 104, 102–121, 2016.

Many discussions on China's anti-monopoly activities and intellectual property protection go beyond the AML and focus also on draft anti-monopoly guidelines on intellectual property protection and the departmental rules issued by the former State Administration for Industry and Commerce (SAIC) on the implementation of the AML in relation to intellectual property.[58] Pursuant to these rules and draft guidelines, intellectual property may constitute an essential facility for undertakings to enter relevant markets or carry out manufacturing and operating activities. Applying the doctrine of essential facilities to intellectual property is problematic, as the history of anti-monopoly shows that even monopolists, in most cases, could refuse to share the essential facility that they own with potential competitors.[59]

Whether the doctrine of essential facilities will be universally applied in anti-monopoly enforcement depends on how well enforcement agencies observe, understand and analyze industrial development. Intellectual property and innovation take place on different iterative and non-iterative paths.

Enforcement agencies ought to understand the life cycle of technology and the novelty of innovation, look for certainty amid these uncertainties, and develop enforcement strategies that are commensurate with economic and industrial development. Taking the first punitive decision is difficult for enforcement agencies, because if penalties are imposed in all similar situations, it may give rise to the risk of overcorrection and create a disincentive for corporate innovation. If only some companies in largely identical circumstances and with similar effects are penalized and others are not, it would undermine the reputation of a country's business climate due to selective enforcement. During such a transitional period, the implementation of antitrust legislation in jurisdictions such as China needs to be based on a delicate balance between the protection and limitation of intellectual property rights in order to achieve the shared pro-innovation agenda of competition and intellectual property protection.

5.3. AML AND CONSUMER WELFARE

Currently in the enforcement of antitrust legislation, there is a tendency of using the degree of rights protection as a measure of consumer welfare. The Facebook

58 See the Anti-monopoly Guidelines for the Abuse of Intellectual Property Rights (Draft for Comments. December 31, 2015) by the AMC. Available at www.gov.cn/xinwen/2015-12/31/content_5029970.htm. Also see the Provisions of SAIC on Prohibiting the Abuse of Intellectual Property Rights to Preclude or Restrict Competition (Order No. 74 of the SAIC on April 7, 2015).
Available at http://gkml.samr.gov.cn/nsjg/fldj/201905/t20190530_301699.html.

59 Huang, Y.; Wang, E.; Zhang, R. (2015). Essential Facilities Doctrine and its Application in Intellectual Property Space under China's Anti-monopoly Law, *George Mason Law Review* 22(5), 1103–1126.

case in Germany is one such example, which regards the degree of protection of the platform of user privacy as the reason constituting abuse of market dominant position. But at the same time, the chief executive of a Chinese Internet company said that the Chinese are more open or less sensitive to privacy issues. They tend to oblige when privacy is being traded for convenience or efficiency.[60] The state of California in the United States promulgated the Data Privacy Protection Act after the EU's GDPR, but they are not completely aligned on the matter of competitive analysis. Both legislations consider the protection of rights as a factor in competition analysis.

Although it is unclear whether the protection of individual rights is a reasonable and feasible measure of consumer welfare in competitive analysis, it is certain that consumer welfare is an all-encompassing idea in economics. Joseph Stiglitz's definition is relevant in this context: according to him, welfare comprises income, consumption and wealth, health, education, individual activities including work, political voice and governance, social connections and relationships and security.[61] Some scholars, however, believe that the study of antitrust legislation is underpinned by a partial equilibrium framework, which cannot accommodate welfare analysis, but only surplus analysis.[62] Surplus refers to the difference between the willingness to pay and the purchasing price. Therefore, even if individual rights are included in the framework of competitive analysis, a comprehensive analysis and measurement should still be necessary.

The situation in China is somewhat different. On the one hand, China does not have a legislative tradition of protecting personal information and privacy. Even though China is currently codifying the Civil Code, the protection of personal information and privacy was only mentioned briefly in the personality rights volume of the third Civil Code draft submitted for review in April 2019. On the other hand, there is disequilibrium in the flow of information and data within and between public rights versus private rights. To use an analogy, while companies are caught in disputes over the flows of information and data, Beijing and other regions have promulgated the Administrative Measures on the Platform to Share and Exchange Government Information Resources to facilitate the exchange of information among government agencies, including personal information collected by different agencies in the discharge of public service functions. Therefore, for China, the relationship between the protection

60 Keynote speech delivered by Robin Li, CEO of Baidu, at the 2018 China Development Forum, March 26, 2018.

61 Joseph E. Stiglitz et al. *Report By The Commission on The Measurement of Economic Performance and Social Progress 14–15 (2009).* Available at www.stiglitz-sen-fitoussi.fr/documents/rapport_anglais.pdf.

62 Jonathan B. Baker. Economics and Politics: Perspectives on the Goals and Future of Antitrust, 81 *Fordham L. Rev.* 2175, 2178 n. 9 (2013).

of individual consumer rights and the order of competition remains unclear. It is generally believed that defining property rights should come before the market, and before competition, but in China's industrial development, it appears the market and competition are defining the boundaries of those rights.

6. OUTLOOK ON THE AML: INTERNATIONAL CONVERGENCE OF SUBSTANCE AND PROCEDURES

In this section of the paper we look to the future.

Recognizing the need for economic and industrial development and for continuous improvement of consumer lifestyle, China has further liberalized and expanded its market. The Chinese market and industries now interact more frequently with their international counterparts. Hence, the sections above touch upon some peculiar issues in Chinese Antimonopoly Law, but the way of addressing these issues boils down eventually to the fundamental questions and concepts of competition law.

Therefore, the challenges to China's AML are the same as those faced by antitrust laws of other jurisdictions. China's anti-monopoly enforcement agency is not yet a member of the ICN, but discussions informed by Chinese issues and international perspectives will help provoke new ideas for markets and antitrust laws and contribute to the pursuit of "better practices" among anti-monopoly enforcement agencies.

6.1. EXPERIENCE CURVE AND PROFESSIONALIZATION

China's AML is now in its 11th year of implementation. The changes to the anti-monopoly enforcement regime in 2018 allowed for some of the enforcement experience of the three former agencies to be merged and passed down, and for some personnel previously from organizations other than anti-monopoly to join the new agency. In addition to this, although the power for anti-monopoly enforcement is generally granted to local enforcement agencies, after the consolidation local enforcement agencies will face the same challenges as their central enforcement agency in human resources, enforcement experiences, etc. Building up experience in AML enforcement also requires the deep integration of anti-monopoly enforcement agencies.

Professionalism in the implementation of the AML is largely reflected in final judgments and administrative penalty decisions. In the civil judgment for the high-profile case of Qihoo 360 vs. Tencent (abuse of dominant market position), the Supreme People's Court gave 80,000 words of analysis about the facts and grounds.[63] By contrast, the punitive decision itself issued by administrative agencies provides less thorough and less compelling arguments. Nonetheless, the reasons stated by administrative agencies in their decision are becoming increasingly deep and elaborate. For example, the punitive decision in the Tetra Pak case provides a detailed statement of the relevant analytical models and reasons.[64]

6.2. IMPROVEMENT OF ANTI-MONOPOLY ENFORCEMENT PROCEDURES

Fair procedures in anti-monopoly enforcement help uphold the fundamental principle of social justice, improve the accuracy of decisions, promote economic growth, protect government credibility, and prevent the abuse of power and corruption. At the same time, a comparison of anti-monopoly enforcement procedures in China, the European Union and the United States can display differences in the design of procedures across these jurisdictions. But despite these differences, they all speak to the commitment to fairness and transparency in the procedures and professionalism and rationality in decision-making.[65]

Although Chinese anti-monopoly enforcement agencies are neither members of the ICN nor parties to the CAP, one can see that China's anti-monopoly enforcement procedures are in line with the various CAP principles on top of having due process and professional and rational decision-making.[66]

---

63 See the No. 4 Civil Judgement of the third Civil Court of the Supreme People's Court (2013).

64 See the No. 10 Notice on the Case of Tetra Pak's Abuse of Market Dominant Position, 2016.

65 Statements and conclusions come from an ongoing joint research project "Due Process in Antitrust Enforcement: China, Europe, and the U.S." conducted by the authors of this paper in cooperation with Christopher Yoo, Professor of University of Pennsylvania and Thomas Fetzer, Professor of University of Mannheim. During the process of joint research, the team has organized several seminars, attended by judges, law enforcement officers, academics, lawyers and representatives from enterprises in three different jurisdictions.

66 According to the non-discrimination principles, e.g. Interim Provisions on Prohibiting Monopoly Agreements and Interim Provisions on Prohibiting Abuse of Dominant Market Positions, An anti-monopoly law enforcement institution shall treat all operators equally when investigating into and handling monopoly agreements; An anti-monopoly law enforcement institution shall treat all operators equally when investigating into and handling abuse of dominant market positions; Also, in accordance with the transparency and predictability principles, and Article 2 of the Interim Provisions on the Procedures for Administrative Punishments for Market Supervision and Administration, the market regulatory departments shall impose administrative punishments under the principles

Furthermore, China's anti-monopoly enforcement is subject to the judicial review of administrative procedures. For example, in 2018, Chinese courts at all levels closed 913,000 first-instance administrative cases, a year-on-year increase of 46.2%.[67] Among these, there are only 5 cases challenging the administrative decisions of the antitrust enforcement agencies. Up to now, there is not a single antitrust administrative case in which a company that was penalized managed to overturn the decision. Administration by law is a key performance indicator for institutions and officials. Therefore, the deterrence from administrative procedures creates a huge incentive for administrative agencies to perform their duties in accordance with the law. At the same time, the harmonization between administrative enforcement criteria and judicial review criteria also require more cases being tried with administrative procedure so as to identify potential loopholes and gradually enable alignment and convergence.

The key to understanding China's anti-monopoly enforcement procedures is finding the contours of enforcement procedures under China's rule of law and understanding and evaluating the performance of enforcement agencies in the implementation process. Compared with the European Union and the United States, China's anti-monopoly enforcement procedures were not developed from the ground up but have rather evolved from the general administrative enforcement procedures. The Administrative Penalty Law provides the skeleton. Enforcement agencies may have prescribed specific procedures for anti-monopoly enforcement, but those fragmented institutional arrangements failed to make the enforcement procedures a holistic and independent process.[68] However, our observation is that the procedures for anti-monopoly enforcement in relation to administrative enforcement against violation of laws on unfair competition, pricing and advertising are nonetheless more progressive in terms of the breath of its legal instruments and the quality of arguments. As the newly consolidated enforcement agency continues to go down the learning curve, we could see further improvements in procedures in the future.

---

of impartiality and openness. On one hand, on the basis of Article 45 of the Interim Provisions on the Procedures for Administrative Punishments for Market Supervision and Administration, when the investigation of a case is terminated and concluded, the case handling institution shall develop an investigation termination report, and file it with the examination institution along with the materials on a same case. On the other hand, where a business operator has any objection to the decision of administrative punishments shall institute administrative actions to the Court.

67 Zhou Qiang: Work Report of the Supreme People's Court – at the First Sessions of the 13th NPC, March 9, 2018.

68 According to Article 77 of the Interim Provisions on the Procedures for Administrative Punishments for Market Supervision and Administration, the procedures of imposing administrative punishments against the acts in violation of the Anti-Monopoly Law of the People's Republic of China shall be governed by the special provisions of the market regulatory department under the State Council. Where there are no provisions in the special provisions, these Provisions shall apply, by mutatis mutandis.

6.3. RESOURCE CONSTRAINTS AND INSTITUTIONAL RESPONSE

Whether to achieve a more refined and professional analysis of the undertakings, or to better protect procedural rights, further investment in enforcement resources is a must. As Professor Kovacic argues, the pursuit of "best practices" requires the pursuit of "better practices" as the stepping stone, and the means to the end is not invariable. The assumption that there is a clear and fixed solution to the question risks overlooking the imperfections of our knowledge and obscuring how competition authorities must continue to work in order to adapt to the dynamic environment characterized by industrial vitality and new trading phenomena, as well as to the continuous evolution of the affiliated organizations that are instrumental to the enforcement of competition policy.[69]

China reformed the infrastructure for AML enforcement in 2018, but the effects of institutional reforms are yet to be observed and evaluated. On the one hand, from the previous anti-monopoly enforcement agencies, no independent, higher-level authority has emerged as many had expected in the academic community.[70] On the other hand, some Chinese scholars believe that the competition among the three former enforcement agencies actually contributed to the professionalism and credibility of anti-monopoly enforcement in China.[71] For anti-monopoly enforcement in China, the reality is that the enforcement powers previously shared among the three departments in the three agencies are now exclusively held by one department of an agency directly under the State Council. A rough estimate suggests that after the consolidation from three to one agency, the staff size in anti-monopoly enforcement at the central government level was reduced by about two-thirds. Yet the number of cases continued to rise, and market players and theorists now expect more professionalism on the part of the enforcement agency. This will inevitably exert more pressure on the enforcement agency.

To resist such pressure, the anti-monopoly enforcement agency must consider how best to allocate the limited resources, both to ensure the running of the

---

69 See Kovacic, W. E. (2005). Achieving Better Practices in the Design of Competition Policy Institutions, *Antitrust Bulletin* 50(3), 511–518.

70 As stated in an article written by Wang Jian in 2013, the AMC of State Council shall be reformed to integrate the scattered anti-monopoly administrative enforcement power at present and eventually transit to the mechanism of power-exclusive. See Wang Jian. The Shared or Exclusive Mechanism of Power – the Model of Power Distribution of China's Anti-Monopoly Law Enforcement Agencies and Its Solutions. *Tribune of Political Science and Law.* 2013 Issue 3.

71 See Li Jian. Competition among China's Anti-Monopoly Law Enforcement Agencies – The Behavior Model, Law Enforcement Effect and Overcome of Rigid Authority, *The Jurist* 2018 Issue 1.

agency and uncompromised progress on the cases. It also needs to recognize higher expectations of the agency in terms of professionalism and procedures as a result of the rising number of administrative cases. Likewise, scholars and practitioners are looking to pick up issues and developments that merit their analysis and study.

7. CONCLUSIONS AND OUTLOOK

Since the inception of reform and opening-up, China has endeavored to improve its market, competition policy, and the governance by competition law. Due to the globalization of markets and competition law, inevitably analytical pathways, methodologies and criteria may need to converge, and anti-monopoly enforcement procedures may need to be aligned. The natural convergence of market mechanisms and competition rules also makes it important for China's competition rules to be harmonized with international norms. Whether it is done through consensus on substantive rules, or through an effective process for procedural alignment, the success largely depends on a well-recognized international organization. Some scholars in China have proposed to create an International Competition Organization (ICO)[72], but we think it would be difficult to achieve. For example, before the MFP (Multinational Framework on Procedures) was accepted as the CAP, EU Competition Commissioner Margrethe Vestager raised the issue of the relationship between the MFP and other international organizations such as the ICN and OECD, drawing particular attention to whether MFP at that time was intent on setting up a new organization. Therefore, it can be said that the success of the ICN in bringing together different stakeholders makes it difficult for the proposed ICO to materialize as expected.

As Chinese scholars, we respect the discussions in the ICN and believe that such discussion and dialogues will aid China's implementation of the AML, but whether the Chinese anti-monopoly enforcement agencies can readily heed the findings of the ICN depends exactly on what these findings contain. In addition to this, China's current priorities in competition policy, the experience and resource constraints of China's anti-monopoly enforcement agency, and the genesis and evolution of China's anti-monopoly enforcement procedures beg the question whether such findings are still beneficial for China and whether they can readily apply to China without unintended side effects. Therefore, we are hoping that the discussions at the ICN not only help identify problems in China's AML enforcement, but also offer solutions to address the root causes of the

72 See Yu Li. Suggestions on Fostering the Establishment of an International Competition Organization (ICO), *Competition Policy Research* 2019 Issue 4.

problems. This naturally requires the ICN working groups to think and discuss with more inputs from China.

In writing this article, while presenting the challenges to AML enforcement in China, we also thought about what the right direction for ICN efforts going forward is. We admit to having a personal interest in having these efforts benefit the improvement of China's market mechanism and AML enforcement. In the paper commemorating the 10th anniversary of the ICN, Professor Fox suggested that the further success of the ICN would depend on how the organization implements these research findings.[73] Professor Kovacic also suggested that the ICN should extend its terms of reference from substantive to procedural.[74] It is worth celebrating that the ICN has succeeded in these regards in its second decade. In addition to professionalization and procedural fairness, how do we achieve credibility and authority for anti-monopoly enforcement agencies? How can anti-monopoly enforcement agencies allocate their resources most precisely and efficiently to adapt to different institutional set-up and team structure and even to the handling of different cases? This paper sheds lights on some of these questions as we brace up for the third decade at the ICN.

POSTSCRIPT

It has now been more than two years since the completion of this paper, and in that time the development of competition policy and law in China has corroborated some of the points made in this paper. China is both a new antitrust jurisdiction and a young market economy in transition, and the optimal implementation of competition law cannot be achieved without the improvement of competition policy in the market. Over the past two years, China has continued to take actions to strengthen the basic status of competition policy. "Strengthening the basic status of competition policy" has not only formed a separate section in China's 14th five-year Plan document, it has also been written into the current revised draft of Anti-monopoly Law. The 21st meeting of the Comprehensive deepening Reform Committee of the CPC Central Committee examined and adopted the Opinions on strengthening Anti-monopoly and further promoting the implementation of Fair Competition Policy. The Standing Committee of the National People's Congress (NPC), top legislator in China, has conducted a special study on the management and

73 Eleanor M. Fox. Linked-In: Antitrust and the Virtues of a Virtual Network. The International Competition Network: Its past, Current and Future Role. *The International Competition Network at Ten*. Edited by Paul Lugard. (105–132).

74 Hugh M. Hollman, William E. Kovacic (2011). The International Competition Network: Its Past, Current and Future Role. *The International Competition Network at Ten*. Edited by Paul Lugard. (51–90).

reform of financial subsidies nationwide. The establishment of the State Anti-Monopoly Bureau (its official English name is yet to be released) has enriched the resources for anti-monopoly enforcement, promoted the formation of a more regular enforcement pattern, and significantly enhanced the ability of anti-monopoly enforcement agencies to combat administrative monopoly practices. In light of the above, the development of China's competition policy is sustaining and further expanding, and this continues to bring about market improvements, which in turn enables the anti-monopoly law to play an increasingly important role in China.

THE TIMES THEY ARE A-CHANGING: WHAT ICN FOR THE NEXT DECADE?

Alessandra TONAZZI*

1. INTRODUCTION

Twenty years after its foundation the International Competition Network ("ICN") can claim many achievements. If in 2001 someone questioned whether a virtual network could become a lasting reality and a significant reference point for the antitrust community, the developments of the last ten years and the adaptive response to the Covid-19 pandemic have eliminated any doubt. When compared to the views and comments after the ICN's first ten years of activity, it seems fair to say that many of the expectations have been met and that the positive sentiments expressed on that occasion can be confirmed.[1]

The ICN has constantly increased its outreach and membership,[2] adding to the diversity of its composition by also including *Non-governmental advisors* ("NGAs"), and it has continued developing Recommendations and Best Practices, widely considered as the "gold standard" for competition agencies.[3] Its events, both the Annual Conferences and the Working Group Workshops are widely, and increasingly, attended.[4]

---

* Director, European and International Affairs at the Autorità Garante della Concorrenza e del Mercato (AGCM – the Italian Competition Authority). The opinions expressed in this paper are solely those of the author and cannot be interpreted as reflecting those of the agency. I am grateful to Michele Pacillo for his comments on an earlier version.

1 See Lugard, P. (ed.), *The International Competition Network at Ten – Origins, Accomplishments and Aspirations*, Cambridge, Antwerp, Portland, Intersentia, 2011.

2 The ICN today is a mature network with 141 competition agencies (117 in 2011) from 128 jurisdictions (103 in 2011). Latest entries include members as diverse as the competition authorities of Nigeria, Oman, French Polynesia, United Arab Emirates, Bangladesh and New Caledonia.

3 In particular, it is worth highlighting the adoption of three new Recommended Practices on very relevant issues such as competition assessment (2014), predatory pricing analysis (2014) and investigative process, (2019) and a new chapter on efficiency in merger analysis (added to the Recommended Practices on Merger Analysis) (2017). it would be difficult to list all the other guidance documents, templates, webinar that it has produced.

4 In the pre Covid-19 era, the Annual Conferences were attended, on average by more than 500 participants and the Workshops have seen a constant increase from around 80 to 120 participants.

While the world was closing down due to the outbreak of the Covid-19 crisis, the virtual nature of the ICN allowed its members to share information and experiences about the impact of the pandemic on the enforcement of competition law. The Steering Group reacted immediately to support its members by issuing a statement on the importance of competition law in times of crisis and its flexibility in accounting for disrupted markets.[5] The virtual nature of the ICN meant that its events could still take place during the pandemic, although in an online format, but it was soon recognized the importance for a virtual network of having in-person meetings: for this reason, the ICN has been the first international organization to experiment with holding events in the hybrid format, thus bringing back in person networking and ensuring at the same time inclusiveness for participants not allowed to travel due to pandemic-related restrictions.

Just before the outbreak of the Covid-19 crisis, the ICN had achieved a significant step towards global convergence, with the adoption, in 2019, of the ICN Framework for Competition Agency Procedures ("CAP") an opt-in implementation framework open to all ICN members and other competition authorities. The CAP contains fundamental procedural fairness principles that reflect a broad consensus within the global competition community across different legal and institutional frameworks. By signing on to the CAP, participants demonstrate that they are willing to adhere to these principles and cooperate in the implementation of the CAP.[6] This is an important achievement in the ICN's evolution because, for the first time, agencies have committed to best practices by also adopting implementation mechanisms.

One might argue that the ICN should simply continue on this track to keep being successful. However, the last ten years have significantly changed the environment in which competition law is enforced. The consequences of the economic recessions brought about by the financial crisis together with the pace and sometimes disruption brought by digitalization of the economy have somehow affected the trust in competitive markets. Furthermore, the enforcement of competition law at the global level has become, itself, more complex, as the number of countries adopting a competition law has continued to grow and competition cases show an increasing level of complexity. Besides, the pandemic, by deepening economic and social inequalities, has resulted in greater reliance on State intervention and disillusion on market mechanisms.

---

5 See "ICN Steering Group Statement: Competition during and after the COVID-19 Pandemic", April 8, 2020, available at the following link: https://www.internationalcompetitionnetwork.org/featured/statement-competition-and-covid19/

6 On 5 June 2019, the ICN held the inaugural meeting of the participants in the CAP in Paris. The first-term CAP Co-chairs were confirmed as: (i) the Australian Competition and Consumer Commission, (ii) the German Bundeskartellamt, and (iii) the United States Department of Justice, Antitrust Division.

In this essay I would like to identify three areas where the ICN will face challenges in the next decade and present some ideas for discussion.

2. A CHANGING LANDSCAPE FOR COMPETITION ENFORCEMENT AND POLICY

When comparing the landscape surrounding competition law enforcement policy at the beginning of the last decade with the landscape today, the changes look quite significant. In 2011, when ICN members and NGAs were meeting in The Hague for the Annual Conference, while the world economy was still in the aftermath of its worst economic crisis since the end of World War Two, the general discussion about the economic crisis did not seem to challenge the role of competition law or the activity of competition agencies.

In recent years, however, stagnant economies combined with the disruptive effects of globalization and digitalization have put at the center of the general political and economic debate themes such as inequality and fairness and questioned, at times, even the belief of the previous decade that competitive markets would ultimately provide wealthier economies and therefore a positive outcome for the majority of citizens.[7]

This debate has not remained limited to politicians, economists and sociologists but it has also affected the competition community, as some have argued that the increased level of concentration and economic power of large corporations is linked to an under enforcement of competition law.[8] At the same time, new challenges have emerged with respect to the role of digital platforms and the assessment of their conduct from a competition point of view and new issues, such as the use of algorithms and data, have raised questions about the appropriateness of the analytical framework and tools at the disposal of competition agencies.[9] The Covid-19 crisis has added a new dimension to the debate: competition agencies are now dealing with the consequences of the increasing role of the State in the economy, and advising governments on how competition policy can contribute to foster economic recovery in the long term.

---

7 Baker, J and Salop, S., "Antitrust, Competition Policy, and Inequality", 25 February 2015, available at SSRN: https://ssrn.com/abstract=2567767 or http://dx.doi.org/10.2139/ssrn.2567767.

8 See Shapiro, C., "Antitrust in a Time of Populism", *International Journal of Industrial Organization*, Volume 61, November 2018, Pages 714–748.

9 Competition Policy International, *Hipster Antitrust*, Antitrust Chronicle, Volume 1, Spring 2018.

It is difficult to do justice to the debate that has taken, and is still taking, place on these issues and that is certainly not the objective of this essay. The question that I would like to address is instead how this debate may affect the activity and projects that the ICN will embrace in the coming years.

The success of the ICN can be explained, in part, by the fact that the network has focused solely on competition. The welcoming message on the ICN website recites *"All competition, all the time"*. This has worked very well for members because, with respect to other international fora, in the ICN the projects are chosen only on the basis of their relevance from the competition agencies' point of view, with the contribution of NGAs, and are not affected by other policy goals. Indeed, the ICN was created exactly for this purpose, to provide a home to competition experts to discuss global competition policy issues and exchange experiences and best practices, without the presence of government representatives who could bring the consideration of other policy objectives. Besides, the practical approach adopted in the Working Groups has proven to be particularly apt to meet the needs of new and younger agencies.

While this "narrow" focus has been the strength of the ICN in its first twenty years, allowing convergence on substantive rules and procedures and increasing confidence of newer agencies in enforcing the law and applying investigative and analytical techniques developed by the ICN, it may be a limitation in this changed landscape: competition policy, if it aspires to be relevant on the political agenda, needs to dialogue with other relevant policy objectives such as privacy and environment.[10]

Especially in light of the relevance of the current debate, which is not limited to mature agencies but affects competition agencies around the world in a similar way, there would be benefits for its members if the ICN embraced some overarching projects, endorsed by the Steering Group, that complement the work, mainly organized by area of enforcement, undertaken by the Working Groups. Such projects, of a policy nature, may take different forms and though they might not necessarily result in Recommendations or guidance, they could nevertheless provide a forum for discussion for the ICN members and, where possible, elaborate some policy directions. For instance, what does the ICN have to say on the current debate on Big Tech? What could be its added value? If there is a need of a global response to how digitalization has revolutionized our economy and society, what could the contribution from the ICN be?[11]

---

10 See Mundt, A. "Entering the ICN's Third Decade", opening speech at the 2021 ICN annual conference, October 2021.

11 See Eleanor Fox, "Happy Birthday, ICN", *Competition Policy International*, ICN Columns, December 2021.

It should be recognized that the ICN has recently made important efforts in tackling broader issues that intersect competition policy. Already in 2015–2016 the ICN Chair initiated a "Town Hall" discussion series for all members and NGAs on topics at the intersection of competition and other policies. In these teleconferences, heads of agencies discussed general policy issues and potential new topics that the ICN might deal with and which were not yet covered by the regular planning of the Working Groups.[12] More recently, the ICN has launched a new format, one to one interviews with heads of agencies discussing cutting edge issues such as competition enforcement in the digital economy.[13]

The ICN has also engaged in projects that resulted in written reports both in the form of Steering Group Strategic Projects and Special Projects chosen by the agency hosting the ICN Annual Conference.[14] Among the topics that could be addressed by future initiatives are, for instance, the issues related to the digital economy and more specifically digital platforms, for example with respect to the role that regulation and competition could respectively play in addressing some of the conducts that competition agencies are currently analyzing. Some of these topics, in particular those linked to the digital economy, have increasingly been addressed both at Annual Conferences and Workshops[15] and many new projects adopted by the Working Groups[16] are already analyzing the issues related to digitalization.

The added value of an overarching approach that could be developed in strategic projects adopted by the Steering Group would be to offer a more general and systematic view, especially on topics that do not immediately fall in one of the enforcement areas covered by the Working Groups. While there is certainly no single vision on how these issues should be addressed – for example what the role of regulation should be versus competition enforcement or what the analytical framework should be for some novel issues – there would be merit in having a

---

12 The initiative continued in 2016–2017 with two meetings addressing the topics: "What can competition authorities do for open markets?" and "Addressing public restraints on competition".

13 See ICN Virtual Spotlight, 13 Dec 2021, Andreas Mundt, President Bundeskartellamt and ICN Chair, and Rod Sims, Chair Australia Competition and Consumer Commission and ICN Vice Chair, discussed on the future direction of competition enforcement in the digital economy. The interview video is available at: https://www.internationalcompetitionnetwork.org/news-events/spotlightdec2021/

14 This has been the case, in the past for example of some Steering Group Special Projects such as Regulation and Competition in Telecom Markets, the ICN Special Project on International Cooperation. Other Special Projects have addressed for example Consumer welfare.

15 For example, the Special Project on Online Vertical Restraints, proposed by the ACCC for the 2015 ICN Annual Conference in Sydney.

16 For example, the project on "Cartels and Big Data" of the Cartel Working Group and the project on "Assessing Dominance in Digital Era" of the Unilateral Conduct Working Group.

discussion within the ICN where competition agencies and NGAs might share common views as well as diverging approaches.

In this perspective, the ICN Steering Group has launched an initiative aimed at analyzing the topic of the intersection between competition, consumer and data protection policies.[17] The global nature of the digital economy and the collection and use of data mean that the tension and interaction between competition, consumer and privacy law arise internationally. However, there are significant differences in the way that ICN member jurisdictions approach these functions. To capture these different approaches, the ICN has produced a document outlining the zones of mutual support and those of tensions at the intersection of the three policy areas and discussed agencies approaches with the ultimate objective to deliver an "agency considerations document", which is intended to be a practical tool in addressing these issues. Other important initiatives regard sustainability[18] and international cooperation, which I will discuss in section 3.

It would be important, of course, to avoid overlaps or duplication with the work already done by other organizations that address similar or complementary issues (although with different areas of focus) and have many common participants. The ICN should try instead to exploit synergies and complementarities by engaging in joint work and projects when feasible and useful.[19]

These policy projects could be complemented by advocacy to respond to some of the attacks that competition agencies – or even the concept of competition itself – are now facing. If competition is "under fire"[20] the ICN could well provide its members with tools and arguments to counter-attack. Competition authorities today face the challenge of being criticized on many fronts – because they are not doing enough, because they are doing too much or because they are not taking into account the implications of their decisions in other policy areas (for example industrial policy).

---

17 See the Scoping Paper, available at: https://www.internationalcompetitionnetwork.org/wp-content/uploads/2020/05/SG-Project-comp-cp-priv-scoping-paper.pdf and the Issues Identification Paper, available at https://www.internationalcompetitionnetwork.org/portfolio/intersection-project-issues-paper/.

18 See the ICN "Sustainable development and competition law", Survey Report, October 2021, prepared by the Hungarian Competition Authority on the occasion of the 2021 IC annual conference. Available at: https://icn2021budapest.hu/site/assets/docs/spec_project/sustainability_survey%20REPORT%20(2ndEd%202021%2009%2030)%20final%20PUBLIC.pdf.

19 In this respect the fact that the ICN has now both a ICN/OECD and ICN/UNCTAD liaison should facilitate coordination and avoid duplication of work.

20 See OECD Global Forum December 2019, at the following link: www.oecd.org/competition/globalforum/competition-under-fire.htm.

The Advocacy Working Group has supported the advocacy efforts of member agencies by sharing experiences and learning from each other, and by agencies around the world developing a consistent message regarding the benefits of effective competition policy.[21] In particular, after the economic crisis, as part of its Benefits Project, the Advocacy Working Group collated many examples and arguments explaining the benefits of competition to different stakeholders. This work might be updated to take stock of new messages developed, for example, with respect to digitalization or to respond to the economic challenges created by the pandemic.[22]

There may also be room for the ICN to discuss whether to take a bolder step and play a more visible role in the global competition policy debate by issuing consensus-based high-level resolutions on important competition policy issues or competition hot topics, such as the benefits of competition or competition in times of crisis.

3. GLOBALIZATION AND INTERNATIONAL COOPERATION IN ENFORCEMENT

The need for international cooperation has increased over the last decade and will certainly be a central issue for competition authorities in the years to come. The increasing number of countries adopting competition law and the increase in international trade are both driving this need.[23]

Cooperation in competition law enforcement is currently at a crossroads, due to the challenges brought by (i) the globalization of markets, (ii) the digitalization of markets, and (iii) the proliferation of new national and regional competition regimes. Those phenomena have brought international enforcement cooperation back again on the international policy agenda, since there is a need to develop effective responses to these challenges. Globalization and digitalization have made effective and efficient international cooperation not only desirable, but necessary.[24]

---

21 See the Advocacy Working Group Benefits project, at the following link: https://www.internationalcompetitionnetwork.org/working-groups/advocacy/benefits-of-competition/.

22 The AWG Special Project in Singapore, for example, addressed the topic of Advocacy in Digitalized Markets.

23 See Both, G, "Drivers of International Cooperation in Competition Law Enforcement", *World Competition* 38, no. 2, 2015: 301–320.

24 Mundt, A., "International Competition Convergence Pathways, Challenges, and Prospects for Success", *Forty-third Annual Fordham Competition Law Institute Conference on International Antitrust Law & Policy*, 2017.

The globalization of markets together with the growth in international trade has led to the proliferation of cross-border competition cases. The number of international cartel cases had increased from around 10-per-year in 1994, to about 80 in 2017.[25] The trend is no different when looking at the number of cross-border mergers, accounting for almost half (47%) of the value of all mergers' and 36% in volume.[26] This means that, approximately, one third of all merger reviews require a significant level of cooperation between at least two international antitrust counterparts.[27]

On the other hand, the digitalization of the economy increased the necessity of international cooperation for two reasons. Firstly, the majority of firms operating in digital markets are large businesses operating across borders, which makes cooperation crucial to collecting evidence and potentially aligning remedies and sanctions. Secondly, competition enforcement against digital firms often involves novel and complex issues (such as algorithmic collusion, network effects, two-sided markets and artificial intelligence) which may increase the potential for conflicts between competition enforcers both in terms of methodologies and outcomes.[28]

The establishment of the ICN was, in itself, an acknowledgment that, in an increasingly globalized world, competition agencies should find ways to better cooperate. The facilitation of international cooperation was one of the ICN's high-level goals outlined in the Memorandum on the Establishment and Operation of the ICN.[29]

The focus of the ICN's activity has been on the development of the highest possible degree of convergence on substantive analysis. This convergence applies equally to cases dealt with on a national basis and has led to a platform for greater case cooperation, through its promotion of shared standards and procedures.

In the area of merger review, for example, substantial improvements in international cooperation in multijurisdictional mergers have been achieved through the work of the ICN Merger Working Group.[30] The Recommended

25 Connor, J.M., "The Private International Cartels (PIC) Data Set: Guide and Summary Statistics", July 2016, available at SSRN: http://ssrn.com/abstract=2821254.

26 See Baker Mckenzie's Cross-border M&A Index Q2 2017, available at: https://www.mergermarket.com/info/baker-mckenzie-cross-border-ma-index-q2–2017.

27 Similarly, Pecman, J, "International Privacy Enforcement Meeting, Ottawa", 4 June 2015, available at: www.competitionbureau.gc.ca/eic/site/cb-bc.nsf/eng/03957.html.

28 See Capobianco, A and Nyeso, A, "Challenges for Competition Law Enforcement and Policy in the Digital Economy" 1 JECL & Pract 1, 2017;

29 See Section 1 (ii) of ICN Operational Framework, available at: https://www.internationalcompetitionnetwork.org/wp-content/uploads/2018/07/ICNOperationalFramework.pdf

30 According to the OECD Report on International Enforcement Cooperation

Practices for Merger Notification and Review Procedures, developed initially between 2002 and 2005, mainly focused on convergence in notification thresholds and procedures, but they already included a chapter on interagency enforcement cooperation.[31] It soon became clear that the recommendation to cooperate should also be complemented by practical tools and the ICN developed a model waiver on international cooperation[32] which has been used and adopted as a standard by many agencies. More recently the Merger Working Group produced a practical guide to international enforcement cooperation in mergers[33], which provides a useful step by step support on how to cooperate in a merger review case.

The Cartel Working Group has also produced guidance on cooperation with respect to investigations tackling international cartels. This guidance is aimed at facilitating information sharing between agencies and coordination in the application of leniency programs to preserve the effectiveness of investigations.[34]

One of the key benefits of the ICN is the way in which it fosters personal relationships between competition enforcers as they work together on ICN projects or meet at ICN Workshops. These "pick up the phone" relationships make closer and more effective case cooperation more likely and easy. To give stability and continuity to these relationships and facilitate contacting the right person at another agency the ICN has adopted two Frameworks, one for merger review cooperation and the other for sharing non-confidential information in cartel enforcement, where contact points for participating agencies are collected and constantly updated.[35]

Mindful of the need to have an overarching approach to the issue of international cooperation that complemented the approach of the Working Groups focused on enforcement areas, in 2012 the ICN Steering Group approved a project on International Cooperation to assess the areas where significant work had to be developed following the identification of international cooperation as a strategic

31 The RP on N&P were first adopted in 2002. They already contained a Section devoted to interagency enforcement cooperation that was updated in 2018 using some of the work that had been developed by the ICN Merger Working Group and in particular the Best Practices Recommended Practices for Merger Notification & Review Procedures, Rp X. Interagency Enforcement Cooperation (2018).

32 See "Waivers of Confidentiality in Merger Investigations: Model Confidentiality Waiver" (2005).

33 See: "Practical Guide to International Enforcement Cooperation in Mergers" (2015).

34 See the "Guidance on Enhancing Cross-Border Leniency Cooperation" (2020), "International Cooperation & Information Sharing in Cartel Investigations" (2013) and "Cartel Leniency Waiver Templates and Explanatory Note" (2014).

35 See: "ICN Framework for Merger Review Cooperation" (2012) and "ICN Framework for Sharing Non-Confidential Information In Cartel Enforcement" (2012), available at: https://www.internationalcompetitionnetwork.org/frameworks/.

theme. At around the same time the Organisation for Economic Co-operation and Development ("OECD") also identified international enforcement cooperation as a strategic area of work and the two organizations joined forces in conducting a comprehensive survey on the current state of international cooperation. This extensive survey resulted in an OECD Report that contained a vast amount of information on the experiences of the 53 respondents in international enforcement cooperation and served as the basis for updating the OECD Recommendation on International Enforcement Cooperation adopted in 2014. The ICN produced a separate but complementary Report that focused on priority topics for future ICN work related to cooperation.

In 2019 the ICN and the OECD decided to continue the joint work on international enforcement cooperation by jointly administering a new Survey of OECD and ICN members aimed at updating the information collected from the previous survey and understanding the changes that took place in the intervening years in international cooperation enforcement as well as the areas of improvement that could be addressed in future work. The two organizations this time further advanced their cooperation that extended to the drafting of a joint report, published in 2021.[36] With respect to the 2012 report the new report outlines more clearly the next steps that the two organizations could undertake in order to improve enforcement cooperation.

To this aim the ICN Steering Group established a dedicated group intended to improve coordination and oversight of the ICN's cooperation work across its working groups and engage with other international organizations, such as the OECD and UNCTAD, doing work in this area. Building on the findings of the OECD/ICN report, this special group is working on possible future areas of focus in the next decade of the ICN, in close relationship with the OECD. It is an important opportunity for the ICN to offer its unique contribution to the current impasse on international cooperation in competition enforcement, by providing solutions to ease the legal obstacles to international cooperation and improve transparency and mutual trust between competition agencies and businesses.

The results of the OECD/ICN Report could also serve as a starting point to discuss the role of the two organizations in fostering the adoption of a multilateral cooperation instrument. The previous survey underlined the legal challenges that competition agencies, especially those who do not belong to a regional network, face in enforcement cooperation. More work in this area could

[36] See OECD/ICN (2021), OECD/ICN Report on International Co-operation in Competition Enforcement, https://www.internationalcompetitionnetwork.org/portfolio/oecd-icn-report-on-international-co-operation-in-competition-enforcement-2021/

start from the successful cases of cooperation provided by the survey and could possibly explore examples, in other areas of enforcement, where multilateral cooperation instruments have been created and implemented.[37]

It is worth mentioning that in 2019 the United Nations Conference on Trade and Development ("UNCTAD") also adopted Guiding Policies and Procedures concerning international cooperation under Section F of the United Nations Set on Competition.[38] These guidelines are particularly targeted to developing countries and countries with economies in transition with little or no experience in international cooperation and aim to provide them with practical tools and methods of cooperation. The guidelines outline: the benefits and costs of cooperation, in what circumstances cooperation is beneficial, the importance of mutual trust, the different levels of cooperation that might be appropriate for each case, the importance of safeguarding confidential information.

It is interesting to observe that an increasing number of younger and smaller agencies are showing an interest in becoming more involved in international enforcement cooperation and are indicating that they would like to discuss instruments that would facilitate such cooperation. This is not surprising. More mature or large agencies have already developed many ways – be these bilateral agreements or regional networks – of cooperating on cross border cases, while younger agencies do not necessarily have the experience, resources or skills to sustain significant enforcement cooperation.

The ICN should, therefore, continue embracing international enforcement cooperation as one of its main goals and keep providing members with tools and examples to facilitate cooperation.[39] The results of the ICN/OECD new Survey has already identified the areas that are more relevant for members and it has also provided examples of successful cases of cooperation that may serve as a basis to develop further guidance.

---

37 Pecman and Pham, in a recent article on international enforcement cooperation, provide an interesting example of the IOSCO, the international body that brings together the world's securities regulators ensuring the implementation of a multilateral agreement for the securities sector, Pecman J., Pham, D. "The Next Frontier of International Cooperation in Competition Enforcement" in Charbit, N. and Ahmad, S. *Standing up for Convergence and Relevance in Antitrust, Frédéric Jenny Liber Amicorum, mai 2019, Revue Concurrences N° 2-2019, Art. N° 90048.*

38 The Discussion Group on International Cooperation that drafted the Guiding Principles made efforts to avoid (i) duplication with existing recommendations of ICN and OECD (in this regard, the UNCTAD Guidelines are consistent with ICN recommendations and provide links to all ICN relevant materials).

39 In the ICN Training on Demand a new module has been recently released on international enforcement cooperation.

4. READYING THE ICN FOR THE CHALLENGES OF ITS THIRD DECADE

The achievements of the ICN are particularly remarkable when considering that it is a virtual network and that all its projects, events, work products are sustained with the decentralized efforts of its member agencies and the contribution of the NGAs. Much of its work is conducted by telephone, video-conferencing and e-mail and work products are made freely available on the ICN website. The principles of *"inclusiveness, openness and transparency, welcoming competition agencies small and large, young and old"* inform the organization as well as its working methods.

The structure of the ICN outlined in its operational framework is rather simple. The Steering Group, Chair and Vice Chairs provide high-level guidance and oversight on the work of the Working Groups.[40] There is no permanent Secretariat although the Canadian Competition Bureau provides administrative support to the Steering Group and ICN members.

The core of the activity of the ICN is in its Working Groups. Throughout the "ICN year" and on the basis of the Workplans approved at the Annual Conference the Working Group co-chairs coordinate their projects. This ensures a focus on the main areas of competition enforcement (cartel, mergers, unilateral conduct) and advocacy, as well as on the internal organization and design of competition agencies (agency effectiveness). The planning process of the projects has a "bottom up" approach that ensures that the topics selected are close to the interests of competition agencies. The approach is usually very "hands on" in a way that is rather unique to the ICN. Both the Cartel and Merger Working Groups have, for example, developed handbooks that provide practical guidance on how to carry on a cartel case (dawn, raids, interviews, etc.) or a merger review (investigative techniques, role of economics and economic evidence, etc.). The Workshops, hosted by competition agencies, have a very practical approach and they are mainly targeted at case-handlers. The agenda often includes the analysis of hypothetical cases.[41]

There are many advantages in this decentralized organization and in the focus on practical issues, but there are also a few drawbacks, both from a substantial and from an organizational point of view. From a substantial point of view there

---

40 See ICN Operational Framework, available at: https://www.internationalcompetitionnetwork.org/wp-content/uploads/2018/07/ICNOperationalFramework.pdf.

41 See for example the Unilateral Conduct Workshop hosted by the Mexican COFECE in 2019 that discussed two hypothetical scenarios to address issues related to market definition involving digital platforms and the assessment of a tying conduct in the digital markets.

might be a risk that the projects and topics addressed in the Working Groups remain linked only to specific enforcement areas and rarely touch upon broader overarching issues. Sometimes topics that do not fall immediately in one of the WG find difficulty in being addressed.[42] The operational risk is that even when more policy oriented overarching projects are embraced – for example as a result of the discussion in the Steering Group – there might be difficulties in giving them an operational follow up.

Furthermore, as the ICN becomes a more complex organization, where the increase in the number of members has also implied more diversity in the level of experience and more complex management of projects and events, there are increasing challenges in ensuring coordination and effectiveness.

The governance and working methods of the ICN have been re-evaluated in a consultation, carried out in 2011, that resulted in the ICN Vision for its Second Decade, addressing both what the ICN did (high level goals and future work) and how it did it (participation, working procedures, and governance).[43]

On that occasion, members and NGAs were generally supportive of the way in which the ICN operated but some suggestions were made for improving the ICN's working methods, in particular in order to maximize inclusiveness, openness and transparency, and to help ensure that participation in the ICN represents an efficient use of its members' limited resources.

Many steps were taken to follow up on these suggestions especially in the direction of inclusiveness and transparency. For example, a growing number of member agencies were involved in the leadership of the Working Groups,[44] in hosting events or in participating in projects and webinars. The ICN Steering Group devoted significant efforts to making its discussions more transparent.

However, the skeleton structure of the ICN has remained largely unchanged and the occasion of beginning the third decade might provide a new opportunity to reflect on how the ICN organization and working methods might be improved in order to ensure coordination and effectiveness.

The roles in the organization – except for some high-level ones such as the Chair, Vice Chair – are not personal, and are usually attributed to agencies rather than

---

42 A good example is the vertical project that many agencies wanted to address but could not find a home and it was eventually entrusted to the Unilateral Conduct Working Group.

43 See ICN Second Decade Report, available at: https://www.internationalcompetitionnetwork.org/wp-content/uploads/2018/09/ICN2dDecade2016.pdf.

44 On the organizational side a number of guidance documents were adopted aimed at facilitating the management of Working Groups' activity and organization of the ICN events.

individuals. However, behind the agency there is usually a person, or more than one, providing the engagement and activity required by the role. This may have effects on the continuity or even undermine the institutional memory of the ICN. While people changing jobs or positions is a normal occurrence in every organization, in a virtual network such as the ICN this can negatively affect the effectiveness of the network.

The third decade might, therefore, be a good time for the ICN to revisit and update its Operational Framework and discuss whether to introduce some changes to its organization and working methods. And indeed, the ICN has launched a consultation process to gather inputs and ideas with a view of building its vision for its third decade.[45]

In particular, one aspect that is not currently addressed in the Operational Framework is the mechanism that stands between the Steering Group and the Working Groups and connects these two levels in the organization. There are already, in the ICN, agencies performing the roles of Secretariat, supporting the Steering Group and ICN members, and a Horizontal Coordinator helping enhance coordination across the ICN's working groups (for example in relation to the scheduling of calls and events and projects). The coordination of Working Group co-Chairs is now more structured, through regular conference calls where horizontal issues are discussed.

However, all these solutions have some limits because the tasks that come with this operational coordination are too burdensome to only rest with one agency, but the Working Group co-Chairs coordination involves too many agencies to take rapid decisions.[46]

Possible ideas for improvement might include strengthening the coordination roles, setting up a small coordination group, creating rotating roles attached to specific management tasks (communication, event coordination, etc.). These are just initial ideas for discussion and member agencies could offer many more. One of the virtues of a virtual network is the possibility to think creatively about its structure and organization.

In discussing new organizational solutions, it will be important to preserve a certain degree of flexibility, as this is a feature that has allowed the ICN to adapt to changing needs while the network expanded and evolved into an established

45 See ICN press release "Quality, Spirit and Professionalism, International Competition Network discusses digital economy and announces full self-evaluation of ICN", 18 September 2020, available at: https://www.internationalcompetitionnetwork.org/featured/news-release-icn-2020-annual-conference/

46 At the moment there are around 20 agencies involved as co-Chairs of Working Groups.

institution. It will also be important to ensure that, while building a more solid structure to sustain its activities and meet new challenges, the ICN does not lose one of its most important characteristics: the sense of "ownership" that members feel for the network. Competition agencies belonging to the ICN feel committed to ensure its functioning because, differently from other organizations, the ICN cannot be separated by its members. The agencies are not "represented" in the ICN, they belong to it and, to a certain extent, they "own" it.

5. CONCLUSIVE REMARKS

If "All Competition, All the time" has been the motto for the ICN in its first twenty years, allowing the development of converging investigative and analytical frameworks for competition agencies, the new landscape of the third decade may demand more from the organization if it wants to be a player in the global political agenda: it may require to dialogue more intensively with other policy areas and concerns that drive the policy landscape and the global economy, in order to avoid being seen as an isolated network of technical experts. The question for the third decade is therefore how the ICN should embrace this dialogue and what kind of contribution it can be expected to deliver to the broader political debate on the role of competition policy.

At the same time, the ICN has to provide innovative solutions to attract the attention of and increase the participation from its worldwide membership, for instance by discussing topics and issues of relevance for newer members, building their capacity through the help of existing regional networks and other international organizations, and enhancing their ability to cooperate with the other members of the network. Despite the impressive efforts made by the ICN in recent years, the majority of its members are still not active enough in the life of the ICN.

Finally, one might wonder if this virtual organization will be sufficient in the longer run to address the challenges discussed above. Should the ICN ever consider establishing some sort of brick and mortar structure (or maybe hybrid as the current times seem to suggest)? This, maybe, is a discussion for the fourth decade.

THE ROLE OF THE INTERNATIONAL COMPETITION NETWORK IN THE DIGITAL ERA

Alejandra Palacios* and Heidi Sada**

1. INTRODUCTION

The International Competition Network ("ICN") has become an important global actor and an imperative reference for competition authorities and competition law practitioners around the world. Throughout its 20 years of existence it has produced an impressive list of work products – created by consensus and in accordance with the needs and best practices of its membership – that have served as a compass to overcome the challenges of competition analysis caused by the changes that markets have experienced over the years. The role of the ICN in the digital era will not be different.[1]

The first section of this essay describes the evolution of the ICN's work products. The initial ICN products were created in a period of increasing internationalisation and globalisation of markets, thus their main focus was to promote convergence across merger regimes, and later to facilitate international cooperation in anti-cartel activity and unilateral conduct, among other topics. It also addresses – as an example of the importance of the ICN in helping less experienced agencies get up to speed – the benefits that COFECE and competition policy in Mexico have gained as a result of COFECE's participation in the ICN. The second section deals with the new challenges that the competition community faces in an era of increasing digitalisation of markets, and discusses how the experiences of several jurisdictions are relevant contributions for the ICN's work in this area and argues that the ICN is an excellent forum to discuss and work towards addressing the pressing issues of the digital era on competition law enforcement and advocacy.

* Former Chairwoman of the Mexican Federal Economic Competition Commission (COFECE).

** Executive Director of International Affairs at COFECE.

2. THE INTERNATIONAL COMPETITION NETWORK THROUGHOUT THE YEARS

Over 20 years ago, national and regional competition regimes were burgeoning around the world. Most of these regimes resulted from the increasing economic globalisation that gained impetus during the 1990s. Globalisation and the emergence of jurisdictions with competition law systems created challenges for companies operating internationally. Inconsistent or conflicting provisions and competition authorities' decisions became an important risk, particularly in relation to merger control. This called for the creation of multilateral initiatives to help generate consensus and convergence towards accepted competition principles and best practices across the global competition community.[1]

One of the multilateral institutions that emerged was the ICN. It was founded in October 2001 in New York by the competition authorities of 14 jurisdictions,[2] as a virtual network of competition agencies. It was also notably open to competition experts belonging to international organisations, practitioners of competition law, representatives from consumer and industry associations, and members of the academic community, collectively known in ICN jargon as "non-governmental advisers" or "NGAs".

As mentioned, in its early beginnings, the ICN focused on the global demands of a period marked by an increased internationalisation of markets, where companies operating worldwide faced many challenges, particularly with regard to merger control compliance in transnational transactions. Thus, the ICN created a Merger Working Group to facilitate ready access to merger control laws worldwide, the preparation of templates to facilitate comparisons between merger control regimes and to compile available information on the costs and burdens of multijurisdictional merger reviews. Perhaps the most visible and important projects undertaken then by the Merger Working Group pertained to the notification of proposed mergers and merger regulations. Guiding principles and recommended practices were developed focusing on the definition of a merger transaction, the nexus between the transaction and the reviewing jurisdiction, the definition of thresholds, timing of merger notifications, review

1 *See* Roebling, George, Ryan, Stephen A., Sjöblom, Dan. (Autumn 2003), 'The International Competition Network (ICN) two years on: concrete results of a virtual network', *Competition Policy Newsletter*, Number 3, 37–40.

2 The 14 founding agencies were from the following jurisdictions: Australia, Canada, the European Union, France, Germany, Israel, Italy, Japan, Mexico, South Africa, South Korea, the United Kingdom, the United States and Zambia;Roebling, George, Ryan, Stephen A., Sjöblom, Dan. (Autumn 2003), 'The International Competition Network (ICN) two years on: concrete results of a virtual network', Competition Policy Newsletter, Number 3, 37–40.

periods, requirements for the initial notification, and review of merger control, amongst other things.[3]

In these early years, the ICN created working groups in charge of capacity building and advocacy. The main purpose of the former group was to share the expertise of well-established agencies with those that were still building up their capacity to implement a credible competition policy. To this end, the products focused on successful capacity building and competition policy implementation in developing transition economies. These included reports on the role of the judiciary in the implementation of competition policy, lessons learned from the experience of young competition agencies and findings related to technical assistance for newer competition agencies, amongst others.

The Advocacy Working Group developed work products that facilitated the promotion of newly adopted competition legislation and helped to create key messages that would foster a culture of competition within jurisdictions.[4]

In the following years, in addition to mergers, advocacy and capacity building, the ICN approach expanded to cover other themes such as anticompetitive practices. The ICN created a Cartel Working Group to address the challenges of anti-cartel enforcement, including the prevention, detection, investigation and punishment of cartel conduct. Over time, this group has produced numerous reports, manuals, information sharing mechanisms and, most notably, leniency waiver templates.[5] In particular, the leniency waiver templates have facilitated international cooperation in cartel investigations, allowing communication between agencies and the potential coordination of procedural aspects between the competition authorities involved in the particular case.

Later on, the ICN turned its attention towards single firm abuses of dominance by creating the Unilateral Conduct Working Group, in order to examine the challenges involved in analysing the unilateral conduct of dominant firms and of firms with substantial market power. This was to facilitate a greater understanding of the issues involved in analysing unilateral conduct, and promote greater convergence and sound enforcement of laws governing these conduct. One of the outstanding results of this work is the document for recommended practices to assess substantial market power.

---

3 *See* Idem; The ICN Merger Working Group webpage provides a comprehensive list of work products at: https://www.internationalcompetitionnetwork.org/working-groups/merger/

4 The ICN Advocacy Working Group webpage provides a comprehensive list of work products at: https://www.internationalcompetitionnetwork.org/working-groups/advocacy/

5 The ICN Cartel Working Group webpage provides a comprehensive list of work products at: https://www.internationalcompetitionnetwork.org/working-groups/cartel/

Even though the ICN approached several topics pertaining to institutional capacity from the beginning,[6] one of its more recent working groups focuses on Agency Effectiveness. This group was created in 2007 to identify key elements of a well-functioning competition agency and good practices for strategy and planning, operations, and enforcement tools and procedures. It provides a forum for sharing agency operational experience and practices, encourages agencies to evaluate their effectiveness and improve the quality of agency operation and procedures, and develop operational guidance for an effective agency. It has already produced guiding principles for procedural fairness and recommended practices for the investigative process.[7]

As mentioned, the ICN started as a group of agencies from 14 jurisdictions. By the end of 2021 the geographical representation of the ICN members covered 140 members from 131 jurisdictions. Clearly, the ICN has experienced exponential growth and expansion. During the two decades of its existence, the ICN has produced an impressive list of reports, manuals, guiding principles, recommended practices and templates. Despite being criticised during its early years for the non-binding nature of these products, its "soft-law" approach has proven to be one of its strengths: jurisdictions can adapt the knowledge conveyed to their specific needs since the principles are well-founded and general in nature. However, national competition laws do not always allow for the exact and/or full adoption of these products. For example, the ICN anti-cartel enforcement manual is an important guide for effective cartel investigations, however, for COFECE, the usefulness of its section on international cooperation is constrained by the limits imposed on exchange of information by our national laws relating to confidentiality.

Moreover, the success of the ICN relies not only upon factors such as its flexibility, its consensus based approach and the voluntary and non-binding nature of its work products. It is more relevant that the ICN has created significant work products and documents to meet the needs of its membership, facing the challenges posed by the evolution of markets and their contexts.

In the Mexican case, for example, the ICN's products have substantially contributed to enhancing the effectiveness of competition policy. Many improvements to the Mexican competition regime have sought to converge with the ICN guiding principles, recommended practices and other work products, such as manuals, reports and templates. Examples of this include:

---

6 The Capacity Building and Competition Policy Implementation Group was in place between 2003 and 2007.

7 The ICN Agency Effectiveness Working Group webpage provides a comprehensive list of work products at: https://www.internationalcompetitionnetwork.org/working-groups/agency-effectiveness/

- The Immunity and Penalty Reduction Program introduced into the competition law in 2006 was designed to follow the ICN anti-cartel enforcement manual.[8] Moreover, the good practices included in the manual were used as input for designing the programme's guidelines[9] and have also recently used in the Draft Regulatory Provisions of the program that were publicly consulted upon in 2019. In addition, COFECE's Market Intelligence Unit, which resides in the Investigative Authority, frequently follows the applicable good practices established in the manual's chapter on searches, raids and inspections.
- International cooperation related to immunity applications prompted COFECE's request for waivers. The ICN leniency waiver template has been regularly used by COFECE's Investigative Authority when cooperating in international cartel investigations with immunity applicants.[10]
- For mergers, the ICN confidentiality waiver model has served as a guide when parties allow COFECE to exchange confidential information with staff from other competition authorities.[11] Moreover, the practical guide to international enforcement cooperation in mergers has also been helpful in making clear for COFECE when to cooperate with other agencies and which types of information can be exchanged, both with waivers and without them.[12]
- The planning and design of COFECE's advocacy strategy was heavily influenced by ICN work products, such as the practical tool for explaining the benefits of competition to businesses, which provides good practices for approaching and communicating with the business community.[13] Moreover, the recommended practices on competition assessment are a tool used regularly by the Commission when conducting such assessments on national and local proposed and existing regulation.

---

8 ICN Anti-Cartel Enforcement Manual: https://www.internationalcompetitionnetwork.org/working-groups/cartel/investigation-enforcement/

9 GUIA-003/2015: Guía del Programa de Inmunidad y Reducción de Sanciones at: https://cofece.mx/wp-content/uploads/2017/11/guia_programa_inmunidad.pdf.

10 ICN Leniency waiver templates and explanatory note (2014) at: https://www.internationalcompetitionnetwork.org/portfolio/leniency-waiver-template/

11 ICN Model Confidentiality Waiver for Mergers at: https://www.internationalcompetitionnetwork.org/portfolio/model-confidentiality-waiver-for-mergers/

12 ICN Practical Guide to International Enforcement Cooperation in Mergers at: https://www.internationalcompetitionnetwork.org/wp-content/uploads/2018/05/MWG_GuidetoInternationalEnforcementCooperation.pdf

13 ICN Recommended Practices for Competition Assessment at: https://www.internationalcompetitionnetwork.org/working-groups/advocacy/comp-assessment/. The ICN Explaining the Benefits of Competition to Businesses at: https://www.internationalcompetitionnetwork.org/portfolio/explaining-the-benefits-of-competition-to-business/. COFECE. (2015). *Working Together for a Competition Culture*, Mexico: COFECE: https://www.cofece.mx/cofece/ingles/attachments/article/38/Working_together_for_a_competition_culture.pdf

- Furthermore, ICN guiding principles and good practices for market studies have served as a guide when conducting market studies. A recent example of this was its use in the Study on Competition in the Federal Passenger Transportation Market in Mexico.[14]

As mentioned, the ICN has been addressing and working on each of the issues that demanded immediate attention over the years. Today the most pressing issue that calls for the attention of agencies around the world has to do with the rapid digitalisation of markets. The next section describes some of the challenges that digital markets pose to competition authorities and how the ICN can facilitate the approach to these markets.

3. THE ROLE OF THE ICN IN THE DIGITAL ERA

Since its creation, the ICN has positioned itself as a key forum for both competition authorities and practitioners to share experiences and knowledge, enabling international cooperation and the identification of elements for consensus and convergence in matters of competition enforcement.

Today, the ICN and international cooperation are more important than ever, as national and international markets face an accelerated transformation which may be traced to an ever-growing digitalisation of human, commercial and economic activities. For this obvious reason, the focus of the ICN will turn to the analysis of digital markets.

Digital markets are characterised by swift change and innovation, which often result in dynamic efficiencies a positive trait of competitive markets. In many ways, digitalisation is transforming traditional markets, by providing more information and facilitating access to it, allowing customers to compare prices, as well as the quality of goods and services. Moreover, digital platforms are creating new markets, providing new ways for acquiring goods and services, in many cases, reducing transaction costs and lowering prices, and creating a collaborative economy.

However, several aspects specific to digitalised markets present new challenges for the competition community. For example, digital platforms increasingly dominate key industries, taking advantage of network externalities and

14 ICN Market Studies Work webpage at: https://www.internationalcompetitionnetwork.org/working-groups/advocacy/market-studies/. COFECE. (2019). Estudio de competencia en el autotransporte federal de pasajeros at: https://www.cofece.mx/estudios-economicos-estudio-de-competencia-en-el-autotransporte-federal-de-pasajeros/

economies of scale in the use of consumer data. This consumer data or "Big Data" improves understanding of customers and therefore helps to create a variety of innovative services to better satisfy their needs. Nonetheless, its accumulation, together with anticompetitive behavior, may result in leverage or abuse of market power, entry barriers, lock-in effects, foreclosure and even "killer acquisitions".

In addition, digitalisation and growing computational capacity through more sophisticated algorithms have made it easier to generate, collect and process large amounts of information. However, these algorithms are also serving as tools to make strategic commercial decisions, such as price determination, even without clear human intervention.

The challenges faced today have posed several questions to the international competition community. Some of the most frequently asked include:

1. How well equipped are competition authorities to address the digital markets of the twenty-first century?;
2. Are current competition analytical and methodological tools (such as market definition and the assessment of market power) adequate?;
3. Is market definition for platforms so different from that of traditional one-sided markets?;
4. How are markets defined and market power determined in markets with products priced at (apparently) zero?;
5. Should thresholds or other criteria for compulsory merger notification be modified and if so how?;
6. What other considerations should competition authorities take into account when positioning theories of harm (for example, data and privacy considerations)?; and
7. How must sector regulation be designed to truly harness the advantages that digital markets may bring about for consumers?

In this sense, the ICN plays a salient role in the digital age. The ICN can foster analysis and discussion about the aforementioned questions and promote best international practices for the analysis of digital markets.

Recently, we have seen a tendency by some jurisdictions at the forefront of the topic to enact, or design and propose, regulations for certain digital platforms, those that could be considered as gatekeepers' in certain markets. These include the 10th amendment to the German Competition Law, passed on January 2021, focused on regulating firms with "paramount significance for competition across markets" with measures such as prohibitions on self-preferencing practices and on strategic use of data, as well as fostering data portability and interoperability.[15] By the same token, in December 2020, the European Commission proposed the Digital Markets Act (DMA),[16] which aims to be an *ex ante* regulation for incumbents considered gatekeepers, with potential transparency obligations, aggregated data for business users, self-preferencing prohibitions, among others. Also in December 2020, the Digital Markets Taskforce of the United Kingdom, proposed regulation for firms with "strategic market status" focused on a mandatory Code of Conduct.[17] The development and discussions regarding these proposals enrich the experience on digital markets worldwide.

Also, high profile cases using traditional antitrust tools have arisen in recent years. Examples include the Facebook vs Bundeskartellamt case,[18] confirmed by Federal Tribunals in Germany, a case where the German Competition Authority considered that the imposition of non-transparent terms and conditions on users' data constituted abuse of dominance; as well as other cases around the world, like the Federal Trade Commission's antitrust lawsuit against Facebook for possibly abusing its excessive market power to eliminate threats to its dominance in the United States' personal social networking market;[19] the United States' Department of Justice's antitrust lawsuit against Google's monopolisation of the digital advertising market and search engines by signing exclusive agreements with Apple and setting Google as the default search engine on Android;[20] and the European Commission's investigation to assess Amazon's use of sensitive data from independent retailers who sell on its marketplace.[21]

All of these will serve as references to be included in ICN work products as similar efforts for legal modifications and enforcement cases will increasingly

---

15 Bundeskartellamt (2021). Amendment of the German Act against Restraints of Competition at: https://www.bundeskartellamt.de/SharedDocs/Meldung/EN/Pressemitteilungen/2021/19_01_2021_GWB%20Novelle.html.

16 European Commission (2020). Digital Markets Act at: https://eur-lex.europa.eu/legal-content/EN/TXT/PDF/?uri=CELEX:52020PC0842&from=en.

17 CMA (2020). A new pro-competition regime for digital markets. Advice of the Digital Markets Taskforce at: https://assets.publishing.service.gov.uk/media/5fce7567e90e07562f98286c/Digital_Taskforce_-_Advice.pdf.

18 Bundeskartellamt (2019). Bundeskartellamt prohibits Facebook from combining user data from different sources at: https://www.bundeskartellamt.de/SharedDocs/Meldung/EN/Pressemitteilungen/2019/07_02_2019_Facebook.html.

19 According to the FTC, Facebook control prices or exclude competition; significantly reduce the quality of its offering to users without losing a significant number of users; exclude competition by driving actual or potential competitors out of business, keeps high switching costs among others. FTC (2021). Facebook, Inc., FTC v. at: https://www.ftc.gov/system/files/documents/cases/ecf_75-1_ftc_v_facebook_public_redacted_fac.pdf.

20 Justice Department Sues Monopolist Google For Violating Antitrust Laws at: https://www.justice.gov/opa/press-release/file/1328941/download.

21 CE (2019). Antitrust: Commission opens investigation into possible anti-competitive conduct of Amazon at: https://ec.europa.eu/commission/presscorner/detail/es/IP_19_4291.

emerge in other jurisdictions. With the help of the ICN, less experienced agencies will be able to use the outcome of cases of the aforementioned competition agencies as a starting point when dealing with digital markets.

In COFECE's case, for example, these experiences have been useful in creating a digital taskforce that will develop a strategy to approach Mexican digital markets. Inspired on other agencies experiences, in March 2020 we published COFECE's Digital Strategy,[22] a document with the next steps facing the challenges of the digital economy. In August of same year, we created the Digital Markets General Directorate, a specialised unit for the analysis of the development of the digital economy and its repercussions on the processes of competition.

As mentioned, one of the key purposes of the ICN is to share the expertise of well-established agencies (who have issued decisions or advocacy documents related to traditional and digital markets) with those that are still building up their capacity to conduct competition analysis, but who will surely be confronted with the challenges posed by the digitalisation era. However, in this new digital context, it is fair to say that such matters are new for all competition agencies. Therefore, some younger jurisdictions have had experiences with digital markets that may also be useful to others.

A pioneering example of the above, from a less developed agency, is COFECE's advocacy effort of 2015, where we recommended that the new business model of transport network companies (or "TNCs", for example, Uber, Cabify, and Easy Taxi) be allowed to operate in local markets, without undue restrictions on competition. After this recommendation, thirteen Mexican states modified their legal framework, or issued new regulations, to recognise and allow the operation of TNCs, potentially avoiding rules inhibiting or outright prohibiting them.[23] The Commission was one of the first jurisdictions to advocate this type of issues (i.e. how new digital markets can create important competitive pressure on traditional markets and its incumbents) and its efforts were later replicated by other countries.

More recently, in 2019 the ICN Unilateral Conduct Working Group organised its first ever workshop dealing entirely with digital markets.[24] Given the importance and the rise of the digital platform usage worldwide, this workshop was of extreme relevance to ICN members in discussing issues surrounding the assessment of unilateral conduct in the context of these technologies. This

22 Https://www.cofece.mx/wp-content/uploads/2020/03/EstrategiaDigital_ENG_V10.pdf

23 OPN-0082015 at: https://www.cofece.mx/CFCResoluciones/docs/Mercados%20Regulados/V6/16/2042252.pdf

24 2019 UCWG Workshop Mexico City webpage at: https://www.cofece.mx/uc-workshop2019/

workshop fostered a lively and dynamic discussion on market definition, the market power of digital platforms and on tying in digital markets. Participants discussed hypothetical cases which allowed them to conduct practical competition analysis in markets related to technologies that might be part of our daily lives, such as those connecting potential dating partners and apps for smart-wears. This workshop was hosted by COFECE and is an example of initial approaches by the ICN with the digital economy.

Another example of the ICN's work in digital markets is the report on recent advocacy experiences. This outlines how the members' advocacy strategies and approaches have changed in consideration of the digital economy. Findings are expected to allow further development of guiding principles, best practices or recommendations on advocacy in digital markets.[25]

Annual conferences have also served to showcase the ICN's efforts to advance the issue. In recent years, their plenaries and breakout sessions have had a marked tendency towards digital topics. For example, in 2016 the Competition Commission of Singapore presented the findings of a special project that sought to better understand advocacy experiences in disruptive innovation. Later in 2019, the Superintendence of Industry and Commerce of Colombia presented a report on competition policy and creative industries with a digital economy approach to develop innovative solutions. As of 2020, the ICN virtual conference organised by the competition agencies of the United States included plenaries on big data and cartelisation, digital mergers, digital strategies of competition agencies and advocacy in the digital age.

Thus, future products, workshops and annual conferences are likely to have a greater emphasis on the challenges that agencies already face, and will continue to face, when conducting competition analysis in the digital era. Examples of this are the Steering Group's on going special project on the "Intersection Between Competition, Consumer Protection and Privacy", the Unilateral Conduct Working Group performing a multi-year project on "Assessing dominance in the digital age"; the Merger Working Group's series of webinars on digital mergers; the Cartel Working Group's project on "Big Data and Cartels", and the Agency Effectiveness Working Group's organisational design products, with a focus on knowledge management in a digital era. The 2021 virtual program of the annual conference organised by the Hungarian competition authority foresees sessions on anti-cartel enforcement and abuse of dominance in the digital era, as well as on digitalisation and agency effectiveness.

---

25 ICN AWG. (2019). Advocacy Working Group Report on ICN Member's Recent Experiences (2015–2018) in Conducting Competition Advocacy in Digital Markets at: https://www.internationalcompetitionnetwork.org/wp-content/uploads/2019/06/AWG_AdvDigitalMktsReport2019.pdf

In conclusion, the ICN will continue to serve as a fundamental forum for the discussion of emerging issues related to competition in digital markets – like the assessment of dominant platforms, access to data, interdisciplinary cooperation among competition authorities and other regulators, to mention just a few. COFECE, like most ICN members, is keen and willing to contribute to (and learn from) the ICN's role in the digital era.

November 2021

THE ECONOMICS OF INTERNATIONAL COMPETITION POLICY: NEW CHALLENGES IN THE LIGHT OF DIGITIZATION?

Oliver BUDZINSKI*

1. INTRODUCTION

The debate whether competition on international, intercontinental and global markets requires an international competition policy regime is about 100 years old. For a long time, solutions were envisioned in the context of international organizations governing the relations of sovereign nations, like the League of Nations or, after the Second World War, the global trading system since the 1990s under the umbrella of the World Trade Organization (WTO).[1] However, the implementation of binding global competition rules or enforcement agencies always failed. Thus, national competition authorities (and international ones like the European Union), which are bound to territorially defined jurisdictions that cover only a part of the relevant geographic markets, have to deal with companies competing on international and intercontinental scales. Twenty years ago, competition authorities from countries all around the world decided to form an informal cooperative forum in order to facilitate cooperation among competition authorities and create a "soft" process of convergence of competition rules, practices, and enforcement styles: the International Competition Network (ICN).[2]

---

* Prof. Dr. Oliver Budzinski is Professor of Economic Theory at Ilmenau University of Technology, Institute of Economics and Institute of Media and Mobile Communication, Germany. Email: oliver.budzinski@tu-ilmenau.de. I thank *Sarah Kraus* for valuable editorial assistance.

1 See with comprehensive references O. Budzinski, *The Governance of Global Competition*, Cheltenham: Elgar, 2008, 134–142; O. Budzinski, "International Antitrust Institutions", in R. D. Blair and D. D. Sokol (eds.), *The Oxford Handbook of International Antitrust Economics*, Vol. 1, Oxford: Oxford University Press, 2015, 129–130.

2 I have elsewhere discussed the fundamental pros and cons, success stories and limits of the ICN approach. See O. Budzinski, "The International Competition Network – Prospects and Limits on the Road towards International Competition Governance", (2004) 8 *Competition and Change*, 243–266; O. Budzinski, *The Governance of Global Competition*, Cheltenham: Elgar,

Among the permanent challenges for every competition policy regime, the ever-changing phenomenon of market competition provides the most fundamental one. The very thing that competition laws and authorities aim to protect and to provide an institutional framework for is subject to permanent evolution, for instance, through innovative company behavior, changing consumption habits, new technologies, etc. The ubiquitous process of digitization represents the currently most prominent challenge for competition policy regimes.[3] Most recently, four of the more relevant competition regimes have commissioned detailed expert reports on how competition laws and policies need to change in order to cope with the effects of digitization. *Kerber* provides an excellent summary and comparison of these reports, demonstrating similarities like an identified need for substantial changes as well as considerable differences with respect to the suggested solutions.[4] Furthermore, virtually every other active competition policy regime is discussing reform needs and options in the face of digitization as well. The implications of the considerable changes brought by digitization also affect international competition policy. First, competition on online markets and particularly competition on markets for digitized goods is inherently global and geographically limited only by limits to internet access. The business behavior of companies like Alphabet-Google, Facebook (including Instagram and WhatsApp), Amazon, WeChat, Apple, Spotify, etc. is notoriously difficult to isolate regarding a certain national territory. Second, market structures on these markets are often narrow on a global scale and, accordingly, international market power by those companies is often higher than before, inter alia, because of direct and indirect network effects as well as data-based business

---

2008, 142–148; O. Budzinski "International Antitrust Institutions", in R. D. Blair and D. D. Sokol (eds.), *The Oxford Handbook of International Antitrust Economics*, Vol. 1, Oxford: Oxford University Press, 2015, 130–139. See about the origin and development of the ICN generally also the chapters in P. Lugard, *The International Competition Network at Ten*, Antwerp: Intersentia, 2011. New empirical analyses about the records of the ICN present, inter alia, H. Abu Karky, "The Impact of the International Competition Network on Competition Advocacy and Global Competition Collaboration", (2019) 40 *European Competition Law Review*, 490–501; C. Townley, M. Tavares and M. Guidi, *Influence in the International Competition Network (ICN): Who Seeks It, How Do They Do This and Why?* 2019, available at SSRN: https://papers.ssrn.com/sol3/papers.cfm?abstract_id=3415067 (accessed 11 November 2019).

3 See, inter alia, O. Budzinski and A. Stöhr, "Competition Policy Reform in Europe and Germany – Institutional Change in the Light of Digitization", (2019) 15 *European Competition Journal*, 15–54; O. Budzinski and B. A. Kuchinke, "Industrial Organization of Media Markets and Competition Policy", in B. von Rimscha (ed.), *Handbook Economics and Management of Media and Communication*, Berlin: DeGruyter 2020; O. Budzinski, S. Gaenssle and A. Stöhr, "Outstanding Relevance across Markets: A New Concept of Market Power?" (2020) 17 *Concurrences*, 38-43.

4 See W. Kerber, *Updating Competition Policy for the Digital Economy? An Analysis of Recent Reports in Germany, UK, EU, and Australia*, (2019), available at SSRN: http://dx.doi.org/10.2139/ssrn.3469624.

models.[5] Third, antitrust policies and practices, which used to work quite well to remedy market power and preserve consumer welfare, may now display and cause opposite effects because the nature of consumption has changed.[6]

As these developments influence the (in-)effectiveness of national competition policies towards international anticompetitive arrangements and behavior, the effects of digitization provide challenges for the ICN in the transition to its third decade as well. This paper aims to discuss how digitization changes the needs for international competition policy from an economic perspective (sections 2–5). Furthermore, it concludes some implications for the ICN's third decade.

2. CROSS-BORDER EXTERNALITIES OF NATIONAL COMPETITION POLICIES

If the geographical area of competition exceeds the geographical scope of competition rules and policy, the occurrence of cross-border externalities becomes likely even if all competition policy regimes in all jurisdictions would execute their competition policy according to the same law, the same standards, and the same underlying economic theories. Competition policy regimes are most typically inbound-focused in the sense that they address every anticompetitive conduct or arrangement that restricts competition within their borders, i.e., harms domestic (consumer) welfare. This so-called *effects doctrine* rules that anticompetitive arrangements or conducts are subject to national competition laws whenever they affect domestic markets irrespective of their geographic origin.[7] At the same time, anticompetitive effects originating from domestic companies but adversely affecting 'only' markets abroad are usually not subject to national competition laws. Consequently, each jurisdiction tends to focus only on domestic effects, ignoring possible effects abroad.

Economic theory derives that differences in the economy and market conditions between countries, like for instance an asymmetric allocation of producers

---

5 See O. Budzinski and B. A. Kuchinke, "Industrial Organization of Media Markets and Competition Policy", in B. von Rimscha (ed.), *Handbook Economics and Management of Media and Communication*, Berlin: DeGruyter 2020.

6 See for instance the striking example discussed by O. Budzinski, S. Gaenssle and P. Kunz-Kaltenhäuser, "How Does Online Streaming Affect Antitrust Remedies to Centralized Marketing? – The Case of European Football Broadcasting Rights", (2019) 14 *International Journal of Sport Finance*, 147–157.

7 See inter alia, J. P. Griffin, "Extraterritoriality in U.S. and EU Antitrust Enforcement", (1999) 67 *Antitrust Law Journal*, 159–199; E. M. Fox, "Can We Solve the Antitrust Problems by Extraterritoriality and Cooperation? Sufficiency and Legitimacy", (2003) 48 *The Antitrust Bulletin*, 355–376; O. Budzinski, *The Governance of Global Competition*, Cheltenham: Elgar, 2008, 32–49, 168–173.

and consumers across jurisdictions within a relevant international market or different sizes of domestic (partial) markets, already represent sufficient conditions to generate cross-border negative externalities.[8] Even if there is no difference in laws, standards, and theories, the decisions of national authorities cannot be fully compatible with each other, thus causing frictions in the protection of competition on the supranational markets. Even if national competition authorities act in the best interest of protecting competition, the inbound focus and the accompanying ignorance of effects on competition abroad lead to a reduction of global welfare compared to a situation where the geographic scope of anticompetitive effect and regulating regime were congruent. Note that negative externalities from national competition policy decisions can be both due to under-enforcement and over-enforcement, always compared to what would be the optimal decision to the affected country abroad.[9]

The problem of cross-border externalities is aggravated when national competition regimes intentionally seek to harm other countries in order to increase their domestic welfare – or, more often, the rents of powerful national lobbies and vested interests. Strategic competition policy represents a strategy like strategic trade policy and belongs to the so-called beggar-my-neighbor policies, seeking to redirect rents from foreign to domestic parties.[10] In competition policy, the attempt to create so-called 'national champions', i.e. domestic companies with market power on international markets, belongs to such strategies. The policy intention here is that domestic companies may exploit consumers in foreign countries (welfare loss abroad) with the profits ending up

8 See P. P. Barros and L. M. Cabral, "Merger Policy in Open Economies", (1994) 38 *European Economic Review*, 1041–1055; K. Head and J. Ries, "International Mergers and Welfare under Decentralized Competition Policy", (1997) 30 *Canadian Journal of Economics*, 1104–1123; D. J. Neven and L.-H. Röller, "The Allocation of Jurisdiction in International Antitrust", (2000) 44 *European Economic Review*, 845–855; A. Tay and G. Willmann, "Why (no) Global Competition Policy is a Tough Choice", (2005) 45 *The Quarterly Review of Economics and Finance*, 312–324; J. Haucap, F. Müller and C. Wey, "How to Reduce Conflicts over International Antitrust", (2006) 23 *Conferences on New Political Economy*, 307–343; P. Mehra, "Supranational Agency: A Solution for Conflict in International Mergers", (2011) 27 *Homo Oeconomicus*, 545–574.; J. P. Choi and H. Gerlach, "International Antitrust Enforcement and Multimarket Contact", (2012) 53 *International Economic Review*, 635–657; J. P. Choi and H. Gerlach, "Multi-Market Collusion with Demand Linkages and Antitrust Enforcement", (2013) 61 *The Journal of Industrial Economics*, 987–1021; H. Beinlich, V. Nocke and N. Schutz, "Merger Policy in a Quantitative Model of International Trade", 2020 130 *Economic Journal* 393–421, https://doi.org/10.1093/ej/uez061.

9 See H. Beinlich, V. Nocke and N. Schutz, "International Aspects of Merger Policy: A Survey", (2017) 50 *International Journal of Industrial Organization*, 415–429.

10 See E. M. Fox, "Antitrust and Regulatory Federalism: Races Up, Down, and Sideways", (2000) 75 *New York University Law Review*, 1781–1807; O. Budzinski, *The Governance of Global Competition*, Cheltenham: Elgar, 2008, 53–64; M. De Stefano and M. Rysman, "Competition Policy as Strategic Trade with Differentiated Products", (2010) 18 *Review of International Economics*, 758–77; M. Motta and M. Ruta, "A Political Economy Model of Merger Policy in International Markets", (2012) 79 *Economica*, 115–136.

'at home' (domestic welfare gain). A permissive merger control towards domestic mergers accompanied by a strict approach towards mergers between foreign companies would serve such a purpose as would selective non-enforcement of anti-cartel rules towards domestic companies, domestic antitrust exceptions for so-called (and however picked) "key" industries or exempting pure export cartels from an otherwise effective cartel prohibition. According to economic theory, strategic competition policies (like strategic trade policies) decrease world welfare due to (deliberately) causing negative externalities but regularly do not increase overall domestic welfare or the welfare of domestic consumers. Instead, only some domestic parties, i.e. powerful companies or industries, benefit – at the expense of both foreign and domestic consumers. The reasoning underlying strategic competition policy then merely serves the purpose to conceal successful lobbyism activities in an imperfect political decision process.[11]

Cross-border externalities from diverging and mutually incompatible decisions of national competition authorities regarding the same case may cause jurisdictional conflicts, in particular (but not only) in the case of strategic competition policy.[12] Literature lists an impressive number of jurisdictional conflicts on competition policy issues involving a multitude of countries.[13] For instance, the European antitrust authorities' challenge of the mergers between the US companies Boeing and McDonnell Douglas as well as GE and Honeywell caused negative externalities on trade and diplomatic relations between the two jurisdictions.[14]

---

11 See, inter alia, W. Kerber and O. Budzinski, "Competition of Competition Laws: Mission Impossible?", in R. A. Epstein and M. S. Greve (eds.), *Competition Laws in Conflict – Antitrust Jurisdiction in the Global Economy*, Washington, D.C.: AEI Press, 2004, 31–65.

12 See N. Campbell and M. J. Trebilcock, "International Merger Review – Problems of Multi-Jurisdictional Conflict", in E. Kantzenbach et al. (eds.), *Competition Policy in an Interdependent World Economy*, Baden-Baden: Nomos, 1993; N. Campbell and M. J. Trebilcock, "Interjurisdictional Conflict in Merger Review", in L. Waverman, W. S. Comanor and A. Goto (eds.), *Competition Policy in the Global Economy*, London: Routledge, 1997; D. J. Neven and L.-H. Röller, "On the Scope of Conflict in International Merger Control", (2003) 3 *Journal of Industry, Competition and Trade*, 235–249; J. Haucap, F. Müller and C. Wey, "How to Reduce Conflicts over International Antitrust", (2006) 23 *Conferences on New Political Economy*, 307–343; H. Beinlich, V. Nocke and N. Schutz, "International Aspects of Merger Policy: A Survey", (2017) 50 *International Journal of Industrial Organization*, 415–429.

13 See, inter alia, H. Klodt, *Towards a Global Competition Order*, Berlin: Liberal, 2005, 45–65; O. Budzinski, *The Governance of Global Competition*, Cheltenham: Elgar, 2008, 40–49.

14 See E. M. Fox, "Antitrust Regulation Across National Borders – The United States of Boeing versus the European Union of Airbus", (1998) 16 *The Brookings Review*, 30–32; W. E. Kovacic, "Transatlantic Turbulence: The Boeing-McDonnell Douglas Merger and International Competition Policy", (2001) 69 *Antitrust Law Journal*, 805–874; R. J. Reynolds and J. A. Ordover, "Archimedean Leveraging and the GE/Honeywell Transaction", (2002) 70 *Antitrust Law Journal*, 171–198.; D. J. Gerber, "The European Commission's GE/Honeywell Decision: US Responses and their Implications", (2003) 1 *Journal of Competition Law (ZWeR)*, 87–95.

The ongoing process of digitization implies more international and intercontinental markets as well as broader international markets. Probably, only digital markets where digital goods are traded can become truly global markets because as soon as physical goods are involved, costs of geographic distance play some role (even if they are ordered digitally) and limit the geographic reach of markets. And, at the same time, the decrease and eventual absence of costs of distance limit the scope for truly national or regional markets. It would be a gross over-exaggeration to claim that *all* markets are going to be digital and global, however, the number of purely digital markets with (almost) global scope is increasing. Moreover, the digital elements of the trade of physical goods facilitate its internationalization as well. Therefore, the likelihood of mutually incompatible decisions because of differences in the economy and market conditions between countries increases and, thus, problems from cross-border externalities caused by national competition policies become more relevant and more pressing. In particular, the asymmetry of the allocation of producers and consumers has increased with the (almost worldwide) dominance of US-based companies like Alphabet-Google, Amazon, Facebook, Apple, Netflix, and others in markets like search engines, social media services, online marketplaces, shopping comparisons services, streaming, etc. The current wave of national antitrust proceedings against the mentioned internet giants in a multitude of jurisdictions is likely to cause welfare-decreasing externalities from under- and over-enforcement just as the preceding period of no national antitrust interventions against obvious anticompetitive conduct by these companies decreased welfare through under-enforcement.

Furthermore, a new uprising of strategic competition policies appears to be on the horizon, fuelled by a general comeback of protectionist policies, (not only) driven by the US. In the EU, for instance, politicians are calling for reforming competition policy to promote "European Champions" or allowing exemptions from merger control for "strategic industries".[15] While one of the cases motivating these – so far unsuccessful – new initiative is firmly rooted in traditional industries (the Siemens-Alstom-merger), similar patterns of reasoning are surfacing with respect to the digital economy and the (real or perceived) dominance by American firms. Furthermore, the merger-and-acquisition activities by Chinese government funds cause concerns about strategic intentions and, consequently, debates about establishing defense measures in competition law and policy.

15 See for a discussion with further references O. Budzinski and A. Stöhr, "Public Interest Considerations in European Merger Control Regimes", (2019) 25 *Ilmenau Economics Discussion Papers*.

In summary, the problem of cross-border externalities from national competition policies is likely to significantly increase due to the process of digitization.

3. COSTS AND BURDEN OF MULTIPLE PROCEDURES

If national competition authorities treat antitrust cases in international markets each by each in a non-coordinated way, then multiple competition policy procedures of the same case are conducted parallel to each other. Global players often face antitrust proceedings with respect to mergers and acquisitions, cartel offences, or abuse of market power from (sometimes by far) more than twenty jurisdictions at the same time on the same case and conduct. These multiple procedures cause administration and transaction extra costs that reduce welfare in all affected jurisdictions. First, costs for taxpayers increase if virtually the same facts of the case are investigated in a parallel effort by multiple competition authorities. Most of the doubling, tripling and multiplying of investigation costs merely increases the 'production costs' of competition policy without yielding additional 'output', insights or benefits. Second, if companies face multiple procedures, they have to provide information to multiple competition authorities in multiple languages with multiple legal experts of multiple law systems and by paying multiple notification, submission and consultancy fees. Thus, the transaction costs for companies accompanying an international merger, cooperation agreement or strategy exert a relevant burden on companies.[16] While this may represent a welcome additional deterrence of anticompetitive arrangements and conduct, the additional costs from multiple procedures also fall on unproblematic and procompetitive cases, thus discouraging some beneficial strategies and arrangements.[17] In balance, it seems difficult to argue that there is no harm for welfare from additional administrative and transactional costs burdened on taxpayers and companies.

The ICN has been active in developing best practices for many elements of antitrust procedures and, through this soft and voluntary process of harmonization, seeks to alleviate the burden from multiple procedures.

16 See for an impressive overview ICN, *Report on the Costs and Burdens of Multijurisdictional Merger Review*, Napoli, (2002), www.internationalcompetitionnetwork.org/costburd.doc (accessed 15 January 2004).

17 See, inter alia, S. J. Evenett, "How Much Have Merger Review Laws Reduced Cross-Border Mergers and Acquisitions?", in J. W. Rowley (ed.), *International Merger Control: Prescriptions for Convergence*, London: International Bar Association, 2002; J. De Loecker et al., "Merger Review: Hoe Much of Industry Is Affected in an International Perspective", (2008) 8 *Journal of Industry, Competition and Trade*, 1–19.

However, since the ICN as a voluntary cooperation network of competition authorities cannot allocate cases to one single jurisdiction, the results of these efforts are limited – but still highly valuable. Obviously, the effects of digitization further increase the burden from multiple procedures because of the increase in international and intercontinental business activities. In the absence of more far-reaching cooperation towards an international competition policy regime,[18] the ICN way becomes even more valuable and necessary because of the increase in multiple procedure cases. However, as I argue in section 5, the process of digitization is also likely to increase the diversity of competition policies. Since especially the dealing with data-based business models and strategies also requires new procedures, the soft harmonization process will likely be challenged here. It may be considered, though, that in the absence of powerful agencies vis-à-vis the global digital giants, multiple costs of national procedures may recapture some of the deterrence effect lost by the asymmetry of power.

Notwithstanding, altogether the problem of the costs for companies and taxpayers from multiple procedures can be expected to aggravate with the ongoing digitization of the economy.

4. LOOPHOLES IN THE PROTECTION OF COMPETITION

Protecting competition requires an effective competition policy regime. While – also thanks to the activities of the ICN – more and more countries (but not all) possess competition laws and enforcement agencies nowadays, not all these regimes are effective and sufficiently powerful. In theory, the inbound-focused effects doctrine allows every country to protect competition in its domestic markets as well as within its part of international markets. However, whether a national competition authority is also able to effectively enforce its competition law against global player companies from abroad, depends on several factors: (i) a national competition policy regime must exist, (ii) the national competition authorities must be workable (and not just paper tigers), and (iii) the relevance

18 See, inter alia, E. M. Fox, "Antitrust and Regulatory Federalism: Races Up, Down, and Sideways", (2000) 75 *New York University Law Review*, 1781–1807; L. M. Cabral, "An Equilibrium Approach to International Merger Policy", (2005) 23 *International Journal of Industrial Organization*, 739–751, L. M. Cabral, "Competition Policy in the Global Era", (2017) 51 *New Zealand Economic Papers*, 100–108; H. First, "Evolving Toward What? – The Development of International Antitrust", in J. Drexl (ed.), *The Future of Transnational Antitrust: From Comparative to Common Competition Law*, Berne: Staempfli/Kluwer, 2003; O. Budzinski, *The Governance of Global Competition*, Cheltenham: Elgar, 2008; O. Budzinski "International Antitrust Institutions", in R. D. Blair and D. D. Sokol (eds.), *The Oxford Handbook of International Antitrust Economics*, Vol. 1, Oxford: Oxford University Press, 2015, 119–146.

of the domestic markets must be high enough to make international companies comply with rulings of the national competition authorities. Ultimately, domestic enforcement power against antitrust violations from abroad relies on the power to restrain access to domestic markets, be it by monetary sanctions on domestic turnovers or be it by blocking domestic sales altogether. Thus, when facing rulings or sanctions by a national competition authority, any international company must weigh the importance of that national market for its business with the costs of complying with the national (antitrust) laws. In tendency, comparatively wealthy industrialized countries enjoy a lot of power to enforce their competition laws, whereas comparatively poorer developing countries struggle.[19] Consequently, loopholes arise in particular where companies competing on international or intercontinental markets restrict competition with negative effects only in smaller and poorer countries. Then, the inbound-focused regimes of the more powerful countries do not capture the negative effects and the smaller authorities are not sufficiently powerful to effectively combat the incoming anticompetitive arrangements and conduct. The literature offers an impressive list of examples.[20]

Notwithstanding, umbrella effects limit the scope of the loopholes (albeit not eroding them). Smaller competition policy regimes benefit from decisions by larger authorities effectively combating an anticompetitive arrangement that would also have affected the smaller regimes' jurisdiction. If European or American antitrust authorities, for instance, break up a cartel or prohibit a merger because it adversely affected consumers in their domestic markets, this arrangement becomes ineffective in most cases also for the smaller competition policy regime's domestic markets. Thus, competition on their markets is indirectly protected by the actions of the bigger regimes and, to some extent, the smaller regimes may hide under the umbrella of the big regimes. However, if a certain arrangement or conduct only affects markets in smaller competition policy regimes, no umbrella effects provide relief.

The ICN is contributing to the reduction of such loopholes through its activities to empower smaller competition policy regimes and increase their effectiveness. In the course of the process of digitization, more and more powerful (American, Chinese, etc.) companies confront smaller regimes and it will be interesting to

---

19 See M. S. Gal, "Antitrust in a Globalized Economy: The Unique Enforcement Challenges Faced by Small and Developing Jurisdictions", (2009) 33 *Fordham International Law Journal*, 1–56.

20 See F. Jenny, "Competition Law and Policy: Global Governance Issues", (2003) 26 *World Competition*, 609–624; F. Jenny, "International Cooperation on Competition: Myth, Reality and Perspective", (2003) 48 *The Antitrust Bulletin*, 973–1003; M. C. Levenstein and V. Y. Suslow, "Contemporary International Cartels and Developing Countries: Economic Effects and Implications for Competition Policy", (2004) 71 *Antitrust Law Journal*, 801–852.

witness whether empowered and more effective regimes of smaller and poorer countries will be able to enforce their antitrust laws against internet giants. However, there is reason for skepticism. As far as we can observe by now, the digital economy seems to go along with a shift in the type of anticompetitive conduct. Digital companies do not seem to engage in cartels as much as traditional industries – so far, at least. Mergers are an issue but often it is about so-called *killer acquisitions* of potential future competitors (i.e. taking upcoming mavericks off the market) and not so often mega-mergers among equals. The most relevant type of antitrust violation relevant for the digital economy, however, appears to be the abuse of market power. Due to direct and indirect network effects, market power positions are more likely to surface in the digital economy and the decrease of the costs of geography (i.e. costs of distance) implies that powerful positions are often international in nature.[21] Consequently, smaller competition policy regimes will be confronted more often with particularly powerful companies (enjoying strong market power with an almost global reach). Unfortunately, strategies abusing market power represent an area of competition policy, where umbrella effects often do not occur because a certain practice (e.g. access or use of personalized data, forced bundling and tying, or some types of remedies against an artificial blocking of compatibility) may be prohibited in one country but still be executed in another.

In summary, problems of loopholes for internationally powerful companies with respect to smaller and poorer competition policy regime are likely to increase through digitization.

5. DIVERSITY OF SOCIETIES AND ECONOMICS

Real-world competition regimes differ not only with respect to their economy and market structures (section 2), their intentions (section 2), their procedures (section 3), and their power towards multinational companies (section 4). They

21 Note that there is no automatism or inevitability for dominant positions to emerge in digital markets. Competition among online platforms is possible and desirable and economic research is pointing out (and further researching) the conditions for sustainable competition among online services, like for instance compatibility and inter-operability, low switching costs, multi-homing, etc. See, inter alia, J. Haucap and U. Heimeshoff, "Google, Facebook, Amazon, eBay: Is the Internet Driving Competition or Market Monopolization?" (2014) 11 *International Economics and Economic Policy*, 49–61; J. Haucap and T. Stühmeier, "Competition and Antitrust in Internet Markets", in J. Bauer and M. Latzer (eds.), *Handbook on the Economics of the Internet*, Elgar: Cheltenham, 2016, 183–210; O. Budzinski and A. Stöhr, "Competition Policy Reform in Europe and Germany – Institutional Change in the Light of Digitization", (2019) 15 *European Competition Journal*, 15–54; O. Budzinski and B. A. Kuchinke, "Industrial Organization of Media Markets and Competition Policy", in B. von Rimscha (ed.), *Handbook Economics and Management of Media and Communication*, Berlin: DeGruyter 2020.

also (i) pursue different goals and standards and (ii) apply different economic theories, concepts and methods. Firstly, different countries and societies want their competition policy to achieve different goals and measure pro- and anticompetitiveness of arrangements and conduct according to different standards. Even though economic science points to welfare as the preferable ultimate goal of competition policy and is predominantly skeptical about adding other goals, democratic societies entail the right to trade some degree of efficiency or (economic-material) welfare against goals they view to be important (like market integration, economic development, fairness, high employment, international competitiveness, climate policy, etc.) – at least if there is transparency about the welfare costs of doing so. And, furthermore, even within economics it is not perfectly clear what the 'right' welfare standard is: consumer welfare vs. total welfare; allocative welfare vs. dynamic welfare, protection of the competitive process vs. maximizing efficiency, etc.[22]

Secondly, there is no and there cannot be a consensus on a unifying theory of competition within economics.[23] This is particularly true with respect to both the evolution of science (theory innovation and development) and the dynamics of the phenomenon, market competition, itself: companies innovate on pro- as well as on anticompetitive behavior. Therefore, different competition policy regimes will legitimately base their theories of competitive harm on diverging economic approaches – probably not always but at least in some of the cases. Consequently, the dividing line between procompetitive and anticompetitive arrangements and conduct will not be exactly the same in each jurisdiction. The same is true for investigational and analytical methods, which also change in line with scientific evolution and market dynamics.

Altogether, the diversity of societies and economics justifies some diversity of competition policy regimes. There is no one-size-fits-all model for each country and jurisdiction and for all times. This limits the scope for reducing the problems discussed in section 2 and 3.[24] Moreover, it points to a benefit of having some diversity, even in terms of welfare. If several competition regimes

---

22 See, inter alia, J. Farrell and M. L. Katz, "The Economics of Welfare Standards in Antitrust", (2006) 2 *Competition Policy International*, 3–28; W. Kerber, "Should Competition Law Promote Efficiency? Some Reflections of an Economist on the Normative Foundations of Competition Law", in J. Drexl et al. (eds.), *Economic Theory and Competition Law*, Cheltenham: Elgar, 2009; V. J. Vanberg, "Consumer Welfare, Total Welfare and Economic Freedom: On the Normative Foundations of Competition Policy", in J. Drexl et al. (eds.), *Competition Policy and the Economic Approach*, Cheltenham: Elgar, 2011; G. J. Werden, "Consumer Welfare and Competition Policy", in J. Drexl et al. (eds.), *Competition Policy and the Economic Approach*, Cheltenham: Elgar, 2011.

23 See O. Budzinski, "Monoculture versus Diversity in Competition Economics", (2008) 32 *Cambridge Journal of Economics*, 295–324.

24 Notwithstanding, there *is* ample scope for reduce the burdens and welfare losses of uncoordinated national competition policies – just not to zero.

experiment with different theories and methods, then this offers scope for dynamic institutional learning. In case of diversity, competition regimes learn from their own successes and failures and, additionally, they learn from other regimes' successes and failures. This mutual learning speeds up the learning process, offers potential to dynamically improve competition policy, and thus increases welfare.[25] This is particularly true if there is no ultimate academic consensus and if new ideas, concepts, and solutions need to be injected into the policy process in the course of time. However, these fundamental benefits of a system with decentralized elements do not imply that the same case must be exposed to multiple procedures and conflicting decisions. Instead, sophisticated lead-jurisdiction models offer scope for combining welfare benefits of competition policy coordination with welfare gains from mutual institutional learning and diversity.[26]

Throughout its first two decades, the ICN has employed its best practice approach to contribute to less diverging interpretations of goals, concepts and theories among competition authorities. This was particularly done by aiming to develop a common competition culture among the participating antitrust agencies and by developing and suggesting informal standards for the use of economic theories and methods in competition policy proceedings.

Goals, theories and methods of competition policy are particularly affected by the process of digitization. With respect to goals, the digital economy leads to a stronger amalgamation between consumer welfare pursued by competition policy and consumer welfare pursued by consumer protection policy.[27] The German Facebook case represents a striking example: the German competition

25 See W. Kerber and O. Budzinski, "Towards a Differentiated Analysis of Competition of Competition Laws", (2003) 1 *Journal of Competition Law (ZWeR)*, 411–448.

26 See N. Campbell and M. J. Trebilcock, "International Merger Review – Problems of Multi-Jurisdictional Conflict", in E. Kantzenbach et al. (eds.), *Competition Policy in an Interdependent World Economy*, Baden-Baden: Nomos, 1993; N. Campbell and M. J. Trebilcock, "Interjurisdictional Conflict in Merger Review", in L. Waverman, W. S. Comanor and A. Goto (eds.), *Competition Policy in the Global Economy*, London: Routledge, 1997; M. J. Trebilcock and E. Iacobucci, "National Treatment and Extraterritoriality: Defining the Domains of Trade and Antitrust Policy", in R. A. Epstein and M. S. Greve (eds.), *Competition Laws in Conflict: Antitrust Jurisdiction in the Global Economy*, Washington, D.C.: AEI Press, 2014; O. Budzinski, *The Governance of Global Competition*, Cheltenham: Elgar, 2008; O. Budzinski, "An International Multilevel Competition Policy System", (2009) 6 *International Economics and Economic Policy*, 367–389; O. Budzinski, "Lead Jurisdiction Concepts: Prospects and Limits for Rationalizing International Competition Policy Enforcement", (2018) 18 *Global Economy Journal*, doi.org/10.1515/gej-2016–0025.

27 See, inter alia, S. Bhattacharya and M. C. Buiten, "Privacy as a Competition Law Concern? Lessons from Facebook/WhatsApp", in *Essays in Law and Economics in Honour of Roger Van den Bergh*, Antwerp: Intersentia, 2018, 115–134; M. C. Buiten, "Regulating Data Giants: Between Competition Law and Data Protection Law", in K. Mathis (ed.), *New Developments in Competition Law and Economics*, Berlin: Springer, 2018, 265–294.

authority investigated, inter alia, whether a permanent violation of data protection and privacy standards (as a part of consumer protection policy) can constitute an abuse of market power and, respectively, can be interpreted as an indication for existing market power.[28] Similar questions on the interface of antitrust policy and consumer protection policy are discussed in many countries including the consolidation of agency competencies in these two areas. Furthermore, the rise of the digital economy is accompanied by the emergence and innovation of new business strategies. Next to platform strategies, these are in particular data-based strategies like zero-priced service offers financed by revenues from sophisticated analyses of the personalized data collected from the service's users and data-based individualized search and recommendation systems. These market phenomena require new economic concepts and theories and express themselves in innovative pro- and anticompetitive arrangements and conduct.[29] Some features of digital markets like the paying-with-data character further require new methods for analysis since "classical" price- and turnover-based measures may not work adequately anymore. Obviously, economic theory is developing parallel to the new market phenomena and there are considerable dynamics of new insights.

With respect to the diversity issue, the process of digitization entails pros and cons. On the pro side, the diversity of competition policy regimes allows for a process of experimenting for adequate rules for competition in a digitized world. Different concepts and methods can be applied and mutual learning, which is particularly fruitful in times of considerable change, can help antitrust authorities to get to grips with the challenges from the digital economy. On the contra side, however, regimes are drifting away from each other. While the understanding of competition and the borderline between pro- and anticompetitive arrangements and conduct is converging regarding traditional industries, it may be diverging with respect to digital industries. Germany, for instance, introduced significant changes to their competition law, especially introducing novel concepts and policies against the abuse of dominance in digital ecosystems, in their recent competition law reform.[30] Moreover, the European Union is, at the time of writing, completing the implementation of a special regulation of large online service providers (the so-called Digital Markets

28 See on the case R. Podszun, "Regulatory Mishmash? Competition Law, Facebook and Consumer Protection" (2019) 8 *Journal of European Consumer and Market Law*, 49-52; O. Budzinski, M. Grusevaja and V. Noskova, "The Economics of the German Investigation of Facebook's Data Collection" (2021) 5 *Market and Competition Law Review*, 43-80.

29 See for a contemporary overview O. Budzinski and B. A. Kuchinke, "Industrial Organization of Media Markets and Competition Policy", in B. von Rimscha (ed.), *Handbook Economics and Management of Media and Communication*, Berlin: DeGruyter 2020.

30 See, inter alia, O. Budzinski, S. Gaenssle and A. Stöhr, "Outstanding Relevance across Markets: A New Concept of Market Power?" (2020) 17 *Concurrences*, 38-43.

Act) who departs significantly from various antitrust policy traditions.[31] In the U.S., about a dozen bills compete within the legislative system to become new regulations of digital ecosystems. Shall killer acquisitions of small maverick start-ups without considerable turnover by internet giants be prohibited? Do transaction-value-based thresholds capture these mergers? How to include concepts of economic dependence into competition law, based on what theories and by using which methods?[32] These and many other relevant questions will be answered by different competition policy regimes in different ways. And before the process of mutual learning from parallel experimentation has not taken place, it will be difficult to derive best practices. Theoretical and empirical economics provide some guidance but due to the significant underlying dynamics (both of market behavior and of economic insights), the scientific learning process is not concluded yet as well. And, of course, this development entails a feedback loop to the issues discussed in section 2: the increasing divergence of approaches is likely to create more incompatible decisions and more jurisdictional conflicts.

6. THE ROLE OF THE ICN IN ITS THIRD DECADE

Altogether, the process of digitization entails several challenges for international competition policy: an increase of externalities and jurisdictional conflicts, increasing costs from multiple procedures, more loopholes, and generally diverging regimes. In particular, if these developments are accompanied by a revival of strategic competition policies, the current "system" of national competition policy regimes dealing with international and intercontinental business behavior may face tough times. On the other hand, only a decentralized system of competition policies offers the necessary openness and flexibility to deal with the underlying dynamics of the markets themselves as well as of the academic knowledge about the digital economy.

Thus, the process of digitization is already challenging and will further challenge the role of the ICN in its third decade. Its fundamental approach to identify best practices and create a soft harmonization process by peer pressure towards adapting the published (and consensual) best practices rests on experience with the targeted industries and the surfacing pro- and anticompetitive strategies and arrangements. However, the novel character of business models and strategies

31 See, inter alia, R. Podszun, P. Bongartz and S. Langenstein, "Proposals on how to Improve the Digital Markets Act" (2021) https://ssrn.com/abstract=3788571 (last accessed 29.9.2021); O. Budzinski and J. Mendelsohn, "Regulating Big Tech: From Competition Policy to Sector Regulation?" (2022) 71 *ORDO* forthcoming.

32 See, inter alia, P. Bougette, O. Budzinski and F. Marty, "Exploitive Abuse and Abuse of Economic Dependence: What Can We Learn from an Industrial Organization Approach?" (2019) 129 *Revue d'Economie Politique*, 261–286.

– pro- and anticompetitive ones – in the digital economy implies that best practices are not yet found. As a consequence, the ICN needs to move forward from focusing on comparing existent policies towards developing and pondering new solutions. And it is already starting to embrace such approaches on its way into its third decade. It will be interesting to see how the ICN will be able to withstand the uprising of uncooperative and strategic policy approaches that quickly may include more strategic competition policies as well.

Still, while the ICN approach is definitely superior to an uncoordinated approach, scientific insight from economics favor an enhanced integration of competition policy regimes vis-á-vis the increasing international and intercontinental character of competition. Concepts for reducing the (welfare) costs of multiple and conflicting proceedings and decisions as well as for closing loopholes without jeopardizing a beneficial diversity and openness have been proposed.[33] However, it remains unclear whether a window of opportunity to move towards such scenarios will emerge sometime along the ICN's third decade and whether the ICN can play the role of a facilitator for enhanced cooperation solutions in such a scenario.

33 See O. Budzinski, *The Governance of Global Competition*, Cheltenham: Elgar, 2008; O. Budzinski, "An International Multilevel Competition Policy System", (2009) 6 *International Economics and Economic Policy*, 367–389; O. Budzinski, "Lead Jurisdiction Concepts: Prospects and Limits for Rationalizing International Competition Policy Enforcement", (2018) 18 *Global Economy Journal*, doi.org/10.1515/gej-2016–0025.

DEVELOPMENTS AND PROSPECTS FOR THE DISCUSSION AND REGULATION OF "ABUSE OF SUPERIOR BARGAINING POSITION" IN THE DIGITAL AGE

Kazuyuki SUGIMOTO*

1. INTRODUCTION

It is said that recent rapid developments of the digital economy have been changing the ways of businesses dramatically in various industries, providing small and/or local but innovative businesses with a greater chance of competing than ever, and also offering consumers more choices for goods and services than ever, leading to tremendous social welfare gain. However, many consumers and businesses might have suffered from the anticompetitive conduct of newly emerging digital giants, which took advantage of some unique features of the digital economy, such as direct and indirect network effects, data-driven innovation, and superb developments of algorithms and artificial intelligence, AI. Competition authorities around the world are facing new challenges and struggling to find effective ways to address them in a timely manner.

It is essential to examine how to address the conduct of large digital platforms. The regulation of abuse of dominance has been one of the traditional ways to respond to the conduct of dominant players in defined relevant markets. However, it is also said that such ways have some limits when it comes to effectively dealing with these issues in the digital market.

On the other hand, the regulation of abuse of superior bargaining position[1] has gathered attention because it can be another way to effectively eliminate

---

* Former Chairman, Japan Fair Trade Commission. Views expressed here (as of February 2020) are personal and do not necessarily represent those of the Japan Fair Trade Commission.

1 See ICN Task Force for Abuse of Superior Bargaining Position (2008), *ICN Special Program for Kyoto Annual Conference – Report on Abuse of Superior Bargaining Position*, www.internationalcompetitionnetwork.org/wp-content/uploads/2019/11/SP_ASBP2008.pdf, p. 3 ("Abuse of Superior Bargaining Position" typically includes, but is not limited to, a situation

anticompetitive conduct that suppresses businesses that are dependent on big giants in the digital market.

The regulation of abuse of superior bargaining position was discussed at the ICN Kyoto Annual Conference, which was hosted by the Japan Fair Trade Commission ("JFTC"), to explore its availability as one of the competition law tools.

To celebrate the twentieth anniversary of the ICN, which is the second turning point of the organization, this article touches upon the discussion on abuse of superior bargaining position at the Kyoto Annual Conference and mentions some subsequent developments in major ICN member jurisdictions. The article also explores the role, which should be played by the ICN in the discussion on the regulation of abuse of superior bargaining position among other various competition issues in the digital market.

2. DISCUSSION AT THE ICN KYOTO ANNUAL CONFERENCE

2.1. OVERVIEW OF THE SPECIAL PROGRAM ON ABUSE OF SUPERIOR BARGAINING POSITION

In April 2008, the JFTC hosted the 7th ICN Annual Conference in Kyoto. During the conference, many participants enjoyed the panel discussion on abuse of superior bargaining position, which was the Special Program, as well as other discussions in plenary and breakout sessions led by ICN Working Groups. The theme of the Special Program was proposed by the JFTC, the longest-standing competition agency handling this issue in the world. ICN members also supported the proposal as the conference was thought to be an effective opportunity to deepen mutual understanding among ICN members on this regulation. At this time, most of the members had not adopted or not applied this regulation so actively as one of the tools of competition law and policy. In June 2007, one year before the Annual Conference, a task force[2] was organized for the Special Program to prepare for the panel discussion.

---

in which a party makes use of its superior bargaining position relative to another party with whom it maintains a continuous business relationship to oblige the second party to act contrary to its interests, such as to unjustly, in light of normal business practices, cause the other party to provide money, service or other economic benefits. A party in the superior bargaining position does not necessarily have to be a dominant firm or a firm with significant market power.).

2 The task force was comprised of 15 competition authorities: Armenia, Austria, Belgium, Brazil, Canada, European Union, France, Germany, Japan, Latvia, Pakistan, Russia, Slovak Republic and the United States (DOJ and FTC).

Based on the presumption that there were various views and rules on whether or how to address the issues concerning abuse of superior bargaining among jurisdictions, the task force conducted a questionnaire survey which asked "What does 'abuse of superior bargaining position' mean in business-to-business relations in your jurisdiction?". Those jurisdictions where such practices are regulated were then asked "How are such practices regulated, and why?". Those jurisdictions where such practices are not regulated were asked "Why are such practices not regulated?". The task force drafted a report[3] based on the responses from 32 jurisdictions.

The report was submitted to the Kyoto Annual Conference. Panelists from jurisdictions with various policies on this issue had active discussions at the Special Program Session. There were different points of view between countries with specific provisions regulating abuse of superior bargaining position and those which apply their contract laws to such conduct.

2.2. REPORT OF THE SPECIAL PROGRAM

The Special Program report summarized views of all of the surveyed jurisdictions on how to address abuse of superior bargaining position.

Seven of the 32 survey respondents reported that they had specific provisions relevant to the concept of abuse of superior bargaining position within competition law or other law. The reasons offered by these jurisdictions for their specific provisions included: "to protect competition from negative effects of contract terms that would not occur in the absence of abuse of superior bargaining position"; "to prevent negative competitive effects by non-dominant firms that may distort competition by exercising market power only to a certain extent and only in relation to certain undertakings"; and "to protect against exploitation of trade partners".

However, 24 survey respondents reported that they did not recognize abuse of superior bargaining position as an independent legal concept in their jurisdictions. Among the reasons offered by these jurisdictions were: "reluctance to interfere with the contractual freedom between private parties"; "abuse of superior bargaining position-type conduct is not considered anticompetitive in the absence of market impact"; "contract disputes involve private harm and case-by-case circumstances that are effectively dealt with through private enforcement"; and "general competition law is sufficient to assure competition".

---

3 See *supra* note 2.

2.3. PANEL DISCUSSION OF THE SPECIAL PROGRAM

At the panel discussion of the Special Program at the ICN Kyoto Annual Conference, Frederic Jenny, Chairman of the OECD Competition Committee, led the panel as moderator. Agency representatives from France, New Zealand, Russia, the United States and Indonesia as well as one Japanese NGA, Tadashi Shiraishi, Professor at University of Tokyo, were panellists. The aim of the panel was to share understanding about the differences between member jurisdictions' responses to abuse of superior bargaining position.

The panel presented two hypothetical cases. The first case was that of a retailer, which was not dominant but that was an influential party in a market, forcing its suppliers to offer monetary contributions, dispatch their employees to the retailer and provide it with other economic benefits. The second case was that of a bank that demanded small and medium-sized companies, which were in a business relationship with and relying on the bank, to purchase junk bonds as a condition for loans to the companies.

Panelists from Japan and France stated that provisions related to abuse of superior bargaining position could be applied to the two hypothetical cases in their jurisdictions. The Russian representative mentioned that provisions on abuse of dominance could be applied in his jurisdiction. However, speakers from New Zealand and the United States, which did not recognize specific provisions relevant to the concept of abuse of superior bargaining position, nor other provisions of competition law that could be applied to it, said that abuse of superior bargaining position was not a competition problem, and that competition authorities should not intervene in such cases.

In response to the comments from New Zealand's and the United States' agency representatives, the Japanese NGA mentioned that it was necessary to examine the issue according to the circumstances of each country and area, considering that in some jurisdictions it was a heavy burden to file a civil action, sector regulation was not well equipped and aggrieved parties were reluctant to bring a lawsuit which would reveal their identity. Based on these situations, he argued that we should not necessarily decide that competition law could not be applicable to abuse of superior bargaining position. There was one comment from the audience that the prohibition of abuse of superior bargaining position was necessary to ensure level playing fields between large companies and small and medium-sized companies.

As described above, different views were expressed by the panelists. The Program played a significant role in inspiring international discussion on the issue. When discussing what kind of conduct the regulation of abuse of market dominance could be applied to, or the boundaries of the regulation, some experts have mentioned the discussion at the Special Program of the Kyoto Annual Conference.[4] We can say that the regulation of abuse of superior bargaining position has been attracting further attention as a result of the discussion at the Kyoto Annual Conference.

3. DEVELOPMENTS IN ICN MEMBER JURISDICTIONS AFTER THE KYOTO ANNUAL CONFERENCE

Although some jurisdictions were reluctant to recognize regulation of abuse of superior bargaining position within the framework of competition law at the ICN Kyoto Annual Conference, there have been developments in various jurisdictions which have introduced such regulation in order to address increasing buying power or market power of the buying side.

To name but a few, Australia replaced the Trade Practices Act 1974[5] with the Competition and Consumer Act 2010, which prohibits unconscionable conduct by parties making use of their relative bargaining strength. Thailand revised its competition law in 2018, introducing a prohibition of conduct of operators that results in damage to other business operators by unfairly utilizing superior bargaining power.[6] In the United Kingdom, the Groceries Supply Code of Practice[7], which exclusively regulates the relationship between supermarkets and their suppliers, was introduced in 2009, and there have been cases based on this code.

Furthermore, other ICN member authorities have been increasingly engaged in enforcement activities against abuse of superior bargaining position. For instance, the German competition law prohibits undertakings with relative

---

4 Frederic Jenny (2008), *Abuse of Dominance, Submission to the Ad-Hoc Expert Group on the Role of Competition Law and Policy in Promoting Growth and Development Geneva, 15 July 2008*, https://unctad.org/meetings/en/Contribution/CCPB_AdHoc2014_Cont_WTORAAM_en.pdf.

5 Australian Competition and Consumer Commission (2010), *Stronger powers means better protection for consumers*, www.accc.gov.au/media-release/stronger-powers-means-better-protection-for-consumers.

6 Section 57 of the TRADE COMPETITION ACT B.E.2560 stipulates that "No business operator shall undertake any conduct resulting in damage on other business operators in one of the following ways: ... (2) by unfairly utilizing superior market power or superior bargaining power...", otcc.or.th/ewt_dl_link.php?nid=404&lang=EN.

7 See the Paragraph 3 an Paragraph 5 of the Groceries Supply Code of Practice, https://www.gov.uk/government/publications/groceries-supply-code-of-practice/groceries-supply-code-of-practice.

market power from requesting a trading partner, including but not confined to small and medium sized companies, to grant them advantages without any objective justification[8] when the requested trading partner depends on them. Under this legal regime, the Bundeskartellamt issued a decision in July 2014 stating that EDEKA Zentrale AG & Co.KG, a food retailer, demanded suppliers to provide it with rebates and thereby violated the provision, which prohibits retailers from inducing their suppliers to grant them benefits without any objective justification.[9]

As mentioned earlier, in Australia where the Competition and Consumer Act 2010 introduced the prohibition on unconscionable conduct by the parties making use of the relative bargaining strength, the Australian Competition and Consumer Commission ("ACCC") has taken action using the provision. In May 2014, the ACCC instituted proceedings in the Federal Court of Australia against Coles Supermarkets Australia Pty Ltd and Grocery Holdings Pty Ltd (together "Coles") alleging that Coles engaged in unconscionable conduct in relation to its suppliers, taking advantage of its superior bargaining position by, amongst other things, seeking payments when it had no legitimate basis to do so.[10] In December 2014, the ACCC's claim was held by the Federal Court.[11]

Furthermore, in Korea and Taiwan, which have already recognized the regulation of abuse of superior bargaining position, there has been continuous active enforcements. In February 2013, the Korea Fair Trade Commission issued a cease and desist order to three large companies and system integration operators. This included Lotte Data Communication Company Co., Ltd., who were fined for abusing their bargaining power in their credit card transactions with Value Added Network ("VAN") service providers, unilaterally raising fees paid by VAN service providers or changing bidding conditions during their contract terms.[12] The Taiwan Fair Trade Commission issued a cease order to

---

8 See the Section 19 and Section 20 of the Act against Restraints of Competition, www.gesetze-im-internet.de/englisch_gwb/englisch_gwb.html.

9 Bundeskartellamt (2014), *Bundeskartellamt takes decision of principle in food retail case – EDEKA's demands on suppliers were abusive*, www.bundeskartellamt.de/SharedDocs/Meldung/EN/Pressemitteilungen/2014/03_07_2014_edeka.html.

10 Australian Competition and Consumer Commission (2014), *ACCC takes action against Coles for alleged unconscionable conduct towards its suppliers*, www.accc.gov.au/media-release/accc-takes-action-against-coles-for-alleged-unconscionable-conduct-towards-its-suppliers.

11 Australian Competition and Consumer Commission (2014), *Court finds Coles engaged in unconscionable conduct and orders Coles pay $10 million penalties*, www.accc.gov.au/media-release/court-finds-coles-engaged-in-unconscionable-conduct-and-orders-coles-pay-10-milli on-penalties.

12 Korea Fair Trade Commission (2013), *Large Firms Fined for Forcing Fees from Credit Card VAN Operators*, www.ftc.go.kr/solution/skin/doc.html?fn=90fbeb64952a27c96f6a5f24be0b2 19c4afb8ce84bad0a42d32a1dfcf5640d51&rs=/fileupload/data/result/BBSMSTR_0000000024 02/.

President Chain Store Corporation and imposed an administrative fine on it for not fully disclosing important conditions of their franchise agreements and other restrictions to its franchisees in writing.[13]

In Japan, abuse of superior bargaining position has been regulated as one of the unfair trade practices. Incidents of this have been subject to cease and desist orders. In 2009, the Antimonopoly Act was amended and the surcharge payment order was introduced in order to enhance the deterrent effect of the regulation.

Since then, the JFTC has taken severe legal action against companies including surcharge payment orders. Examples of such companies include an operator of discount stores (DIREX Corporation)[14], an operator of supermarkets (RALSE Company, Limited)[15], an operator of electrical appliance stores (EDION Corporation)[16] and an operator of toy stores (Toys"R"Us-Japan, Ltd.).[17] In these cases, violators demanded that suppliers in an inferior bargaining position dispatch their employees to the violators' stores, provide monetary contributions and accept returns of goods by making use of their superior bargaining positions over the suppliers unjustly in light of normal business practices.

As described above, competition authorities have been paying much more attention than ever to the regulation of abuse of superior bargaining position since the discussion at the Kyoto Annual Conference in 2008.

4. SIGNIFICANCE OF THE REGULATION OF ABUSE OF SUPERIOR BARGAINING POSITION IN THE DIGITAL AGE

The regulation of abuse of superior bargaining position does not focus on the market position of violators but rather on the relative position in business

---

[13] Taiwan Fair Trade Commission (2017), *March, 2017 [Decisions]*, www.ftc.gov.tw/internet/english/doc/docDetail.aspx?uid=179&docid=15081.

[14] Japan Fair Trade Commission (2014), *The JFTC issued Cease and Desist Order and Surcharge Payment Order to DIREX Corporation*, www.jftc.go.jp/en/pressreleases/yearly-2014/June/140605.html.

[15] Japan Fair Trade Commission (2013), *The JFTC issued Cease and Desist Order and Surcharge Payment Order to RALSE Company, Limited*, www.jftc.go.jp/en/pressreleases/yearly-2013/july/130703.html.

[16] Japan Fair Trade Commission (2012), *The JFTC issued Cease and Desist Order and Surcharge Payment Order against EDION Corporation*, www.jftc.go.jp/en/pressreleases/yearly-2012/feb/individual-000465.html.

[17] Japan Fair Trade Commission (2011), *The JFTC issued Cease and Desist Order and Surcharge Payment Order against Toys"R"Us-Japan, Ltd.*, www.jftc.go.jp/en/pressreleases/yearly-2011/dec/individual-000456.html.

relationships. The aim of the regulation is to prevent companies with market power (the superior company) from hindering free and independent decisions of dependent companies (the inferior company). The situation where inferior companies are forced to accept unfair trade terms and unfair disadvantages imposed by superior companies causes the hold-up problems such as inhibiting inferior companies' investments and R&D incentives. Abuse of superior bargaining position also leads to the enhancement of market power.

Moreover, in the digital age it has become particularly necessary for competition authorities to respond to anticompetitive concerns brought about by digital platforms. It has been pointed out in recent years that the regulation of abuse of superior bargaining position or similar regulations are essential to tackle these concerns.

The JFTC conducted a market survey in order to find out whether there were anticompetitive problems in trade practices between online retail platforms and app stores from the viewpoint of Japanese competition law and policy. In October 2019, the JFTC published a report[18], which argued that one of the competition concerns caused by the digital platforms was the abuse of superior bargaining position.[19]

Prior to this report in October 2019, the JFTC requested public comments on its "Guidelines Concerning Abuse of a Superior Bargaining Position in Transactions between Digital Platform Operators and Consumers that Provide Personal Information, etc." In December 2019, the JFTC published the final version of the Guidelines based on the submitted public comments. The aim was to clarify the regulation of abuse of superior bargaining position in relation to acquiring or utilizing personal information in transactions between digital platforms and the consumers who are requested to provide their information to these platforms.[20]

---

18 Japan Fair Trade Commission (2019), *Report regarding trade practices on Digital Platforms Chapter 1&3 in PDF*, www.jftc.go.jp/en/pressreleases/yearly-2019/October/191031Chapter1and3.pdf.

19 Ibid p. 3 ("In this way, the concentration of data on a digital platform supported by the network effect and economics of scale may involve switching costs and lock-in effects. Because of these characteristics of a digital platform, a digital platform operator may be in a superior position over business partners. In particular, a digital platform operator that has a strong position in the market is likely to be in a superior position over many business partners.
It can be said that a digital platform operator with a superior position is able to impose disadvantages on their business partners. Actually, in surveys conducted so far, there have been a certain number of responses suggesting dissatisfaction at changes in trade conditions.").

20 Japan Fair Trade Commission (2019), *Release of "Guidelines Concerning Abuse of a Superior Bargaining Position in Transactions between Digital Platform Operators and Consumers*

The European Union and Australia have been trying to address concerns caused by digital platforms by utilising the regulation of abuse of superior bargaining position or similar regulations. In the report[21] published by the European Commission based on the market study regarding "platform to business" practices in digital platforms, it was reported that dozens of small and medium-sized enterprises were highly dependent on digital platforms[22] and a significant proportion of users had experienced problems in their transactions with them.[23] Based on this survey result, the European Union introduced the regulation on promoting fairness and transparency for business users of online intermediation services ("P2B regulation") as an ex-ante regulation in June 2018.[24] The P2B regulation states that the aim of the regulation is to address concerns caused by digital platforms on the premise that they have superior bargaining power, which enables them to unfairly harm the legitimate interests of their business users.[25] In the case of restriction, suspension or termination of services, certain digital platforms are obliged to inform their users about these. It can be inferred that the P2B regulation is introduced to focus on superior bargaining position.

---

that Provide Personal Information, etc.", www.jftc.go.jp/en/pressreleases/yearly-2019/December/191217_DP.html.

21 European Commission (2017), *Business-to-business relations in the online platform environment final report*, op.europa.eu/en/publication-detail/-/publication/04c75b09–4b2b-11e7-aea8–01aa75ed71a1/language-en.

22 Ibid p. xviii-xix ("As can be observed from the above, platform business practices can have a serious, at times negative impact on business users, including their business models and business strategies. The study has found that the most important practices influence business users' turnover (in some cases dramatically), their product selection and product development decisions (also by discouraging them from selling or developing specific products), their employment decisions and their marketing choices (i.e. what products should be sold on what platform). Beyond the individual business user level, it can be argued that some of the platforms' practices may have a significant (distortive) impact on the competition between the companies and innovation. These findings match a broader signal received from business users that they are highly dependent on platforms, notwithstanding actual or potential multi-homing.").

23 Ibid p. ix ("A total of 46% of business users responded that they have experienced problems and disagreements with the platforms in the course of their business relationship. Among the business users with more than half of turnover generated via online platforms (heavy users), the share of those that experienced problems is significantly higher (75%). Out of those who have experienced problems 21% indicated that they occurred often over the course of the business relationship. For heavy users of online platforms, a significantly higher share (32%) have experienced problems often.").

24 *Regulation (EU) 2019/1150 of the European Parliament and of the Council of 20 June 2019 on promoting fairness and transparency for business users of online intermediation services (Text with EEA relevance)*, eur-lex.europa.eu/legal-content/EN/TXT/PDF/?uri=CELEX:32019R1150&from=EN.

25 Ibid p. 1 ("given that increasing dependence, the providers of those services often have superior bargaining power, which enables them to, in effect, behave unilaterally in a way that can be unfair and that can be harmful to the legitimate interests of their businesses users and, indirectly, also of consumers in the Union.").

The ACCC conducted an inquiry into digital platforms and published the final report in July 2019.[26] The final report acknowledged the significant information asymmetries and bargaining power imbalances in the relationship between consumers and digital platforms, which left consumers in a weak position to negotiate with digital platforms for the collection, use and disclosure of their personal data, which resulted in unfair contract terms.[27] The ACCC proposed to the government that these unfair terms must be prohibited.[28]

As observed in the market study by the JFTC, the European Commission and the ACCC, the bargaining power imbalance in the relationship between digital platforms and their business users and consumers has been drawing greater attention. In deterring and correcting such conduct by digital platforms as unfairly imposing disadvantages on consumers and their business users, the regulation of abuse of market dominance, which considers factors such as market share, has some limitations regarding the coverage of its application. Alternatively, the regulation of abuse of superior bargaining position, which focuses on the fact that users or trading partners are in an inferior position and have no choice but to accept unfair contract terms, can be an effective tool to address concerns specifically found in digital markets. For example, in a case where there is certain competition between more than two platforms which exert superior bargaining power on consumers and business users, the regulation of abuse of superior bargaining position seems to be much more effective than the regulation of abuse of dominance to address abusive conduct by digital platforms.

Thus, there has been an increasing necessity for competition authorities and NGAs at international fora, such as the ICN, to actively discuss the significance of regulating abuse of superior bargaining position in the age of digitalization.

5. CONCLUSION

The ICN has been playing a significant role in promoting convergence of competition law and policy for many years. It is essential that the ICN continues

---

26 Australian Competition and Consumer Commission (2019), *Digital platforms inquiry – final report*, www.accc.gov.au/system/files/Digital%20platforms%20inquiry%20-%20final%20report.pdf.

27 Ibid p. 497 ("Due to the significant information asymmetries and bargaining power imbalances in the relationship between consumers and digital platforms, consumers are unable to negotiate a bargain with digital platforms for the collection, use and disclosure of their personal data. This bargaining imbalance results in terms within the consumer bargain that are potentially unfair contract terms (UCTs) under the ACL.").

28 Ibid. p. 497 ("Amend the Competition and Consumer Act 2010 so that unfair contract terms are prohibited (not just voidable). This would mean that civil pecuniary penalties apply to the use of unfair contract terms in any standard form consumer or small business contract.").

to play this role after marking its 20th anniversary. As competition authorities are required to tackle digitalization, we should examine the effectiveness of various tools for tackling competition issues brought about by digital platforms.

At the time of the Kyoto Annual Conference in 2008, some Japanese experts said that regulation of abuse of superior bargaining position was a peculiar tool employed by the JFTC and a few limited authorities, and not one commonly used by other competition authorities around the world. However, as described above, we have seen newly established regulations concerning abuse of superior bargaining position and active enforcements in the Asia-Pacific region and in Europe. The regulation of abuse of superior bargaining position is becoming established as an effective tool for ensuring a free and fair competitive environment. Moreover, as abuse of superior bargaining position by digital platforms is becoming conspicuous, the effectiveness of the regulation as one of the enforcement tools seems to be increasing.

The ICN must play a key role in sharing the experiences of each jurisdiction through workshops and other events to deepen the common understanding of how to effectively regulate abuse of superior bargaining position in the digital age.

THE AUTHORS

Alejandra Palacios

Alejandra Palacios is a Senior Fellow at the Price School of Public Policy at the University of Southern California (USC) and Affiliate to the USC Marshall Initiative on Digital Competition. She chaired the Mexican antitrust agency, COFECE, from September 2013 until September 2021. Alejandra was the first woman to preside over the agency, with an eight-year tenure following an original four-year appointment and a subsequent reelection. With more than 15 years of experience as a public policy expert and Ministry level government official, she has proposed and advanced regulatory solutions in several markets in Mexico, including the opening of the telecom, airline, financial, energy, transport, and health sectors.

Under Palacio's tenure as Chair of COFECE, directing a team of 450 professionals, the agency handled unprecedented antitrust cases for legacy industries. The agency is internationally lauded for its effective competition advocacy efforts and is acknowledged as one of the twenty leading competition authorities in the world, according to the Global Competition Review. She also served as the Vice President of the International Competition Network, the premier global organization on antitrust, composed of 140 competition authorities from around the world, and as member of the Board of the Competition Committee of the Organization for Economic Cooperation and Development (OECD).

Prior to COFECE she served as Deputy Director of Economic Regulation Research at the Mexican Institute of Competitiveness, a highly regarded center for applied investigation in Mexico and a Lecturer at the Economics Department of Instituto Tecnologico Autonomo de Mexico (ITAM).

Palacios obtained her bachelor's degree in Economics from the ITAM, graduating in the top 1% with the highest honors. She also holds a Master′s in Business Administration from ITAM and a Master′s in Public Administration and Public Policy from the Centro de Investigacion y Docencia Economicas (CIDE), also graduating with highest honors.

Alejandra is member of the Trilateral Commission, as well as of the Mexican chapter of the International Women′s Forum (IWF).

Alessandra Tonazzi

Alessandra Tonazzi is the Director of International and European Relations at the Italian Competition Authority (AGCM). Her present role involves

representation of the ICA in international fora (ICN, ECN, OECD and UNCTAD), the promotion of international cooperation with other competition agencies through multilateral organizations and bilateral agreements and the co-ordination of the Authority's international projects, including technical assistance programs on competition policy and enforcement and reviews of national competition laws and policy. From October 2012 to April 2013 she was seconded to the Competition Division of the OECD where she worked on the OECD strategic project on International Enforcement Co-operation. She currently co-chairs, on behalf of the Authority, the International Competition Network Cartel Working Group. She is a member of the ICN Steering Group and in March 2018 she has been appointed ICN/UNCTAD liaison to coordinate the work of the two organizations. She is currently a Bureau Member and Vice Chair of the OECD Committee on Consumer Policy.
She holds a PhD in Economics from the University of Rome and a MSc in Economics from Warwick University. She graduated in Law and Economics from the University "La Sapienza" in Rome.

Allan Fels
Professor Allan Fels AO has attended all ICN conferences. He chaired the Australian Competition and Consumer Commission and its predecessor bodies from 1989 until 2003. Following that he was Dean of the Australia and New Zealand School of Government from 2003 until 2013 and has been involved in numerous government bodies and inquiries since 2003. Professor Fels took part in the ICPAC hearings of 1998, attended all preliminary meetings about the ICN and was a member of the ICN Steering Committee from its foundation until 2003.

Andreas Mundt
Andreas Mundt has been President of the German Bundeskartellamt (Federal Cartel Office) since December 2009. In September 2013 Andreas Mundt was elected to be the new Steering Group Chair of the International Competition Network. Since 2010 he has been a Member of the Bureau of the OECD Competition Committee.
After qualifying as a lawyer following studies at the University of Bonn and the University of Lausanne, Switzerland, Andreas Mundt entered the Federal Ministry of Economics where he worked from 1991 to 1993. He then joined the staff of the Free Democratic Party in the German Parliament from 1993 to 2000, where he was in charge of the portfolio of labour and social law.
In 2000 Andreas Mundt joined the Bundeskartellamt as rapporteur, with responsibility for banking and card payment systems issues. He was Head of the International Section of the Bundeskartellamt from 2001 to 2005 and Director of General Policy from 2005 to 2009.

Anne Riley

Anne Riley retired in 2019 as Head of Royal Dutch Shell's (now Shell plc's) global antitrust group, which she led since September 1992 (having practiced as an antitrust lawyer since 1985) and was a member of Shell's Group Ethics and Compliance Office Leadership Team until her retirement.

Anne is Co-Chair of the International Chamber of Commerce (ICC) Task Force on Antitrust Compliance and Advocacy (which produced the ICC Antitrust Compliance Toolkit in 2013 and the SME Compliance Toolkit in 2015, and which engages in antitrust advocacy around the world). Anne is currently a Non-Governmental Adviser (NGA) to the European Union (DG COMP) for the International Competition Network.

Anne (individually) and her team (collectively) have received many antitrust awards and accolades including, in September 2019, an award on behalf of the ICC from the Society of Corporate Compliance and Ethics for the ICC's contributions to Antitrust Compliance. In March 2022, Anne co-edited the Concurrences book "Perspectives on Antitrust Compliance", along with co-editors Professor Andreas Stephan and Anny Tubbs.

Aranka Nagy

Aranka Nagy is Senior Associate at CMS Cameron McKenna Nabarro Olswang LLP, Hungarian Branch Office. Previously, she was a member of the Hungarian Competition Authority (GVH) in various positions, involving mergers and international relations. She participated in the special project of the GVH as the host of the 20th ICN Annual Conference in 2021.

Csaba Kovács

Csaba Kovács is Deputy Head of the Competition Economics and Market Research Section of the Hungarian Competition Authority (GVH), where he has been a member in various positions since 1992. He participated in the special project of the GVH as the host of the 20th ICN Annual Conference in 2021.

Cynthia Lagdameo

Cynthia Lewis Lagdameo is Counsel for International in the U.S. Federal Trade Commission's Office of International Affairs. Ms. Lagdameo works with the International Competition Network and is co-chair of the ICN Chairs Working Group. Ms. Lagdameo is former co-chair of the ICN's Unilateral Conduct Working Group and Merger Notification and Procedures Subgroup. Ms. Lagdameo is responsible for bilateral cooperation and case coordination and works on technical assistance programs, providing training to foreign agencies in substantive legal principles, analytical framework, and investigative techniques.

Prior to joining the FTC in 2007, Ms. Lagdameo was an attorney at the U.S. Department of Justice's Antitrust Division. She was a member of the Foreign

Commerce Section from 2002 to 2007, where she coordinated the Section's work on the ICN. From 2000 to 2001, she served on the Telecommunications Task Force, where she worked on merger investigations and was lead staff attorney responsible for advising the Federal Communications Commission on whether a Bell Operating Company had met legal requirements designed to open local telecommunications markets to competition. From 1998 to 2000, Ms. Lagdameo was counsel to the International Competition Policy Advisory Committee, responsible for multijurisdictional merger review issues. Ms. Lagdameo began her career as an attorney at Skadden, Arps, Slate, Meagher & Flom in New York and Brussels.

Ms. Lagdameo obtained her law degree from the Georgetown University Law School, where she graduated Magna Cum Laude. Ms. Lagdameo is a member of the Editorial Board of the Journal of Antitrust Enforcement an active member of the American Bar Association, serving as Co-Chair of the Dominance Divergence Task Force, a Vice-Chair of the Section of Antitrust Law's Membership Committee (2014 to 2017), Consumer Protection Committee (2012 to 2014), Pricing Conduct Committee (2009 to 2012), and International Committee (2002 to 2007).

Duy D Pham

Duy Pham is Legal Counsel for the Hong Kong Competition Commission. He has previously worked for the Canadian Competition Bureau, U.S. Federal Trade Commission, World Bank and Blake, Cassels & Graydon LLP. He obtained his J.D. from the University of Ottawa Faculty of Law and his LL.M. from the Georgetown University Law Center.

Eddy De Smijter

Eddy De Smijter is Head of the International Relations Unit in DG Competition at the European Commission since October 2016.

He joined the European Commission in 2001 as a member of the team that negotiated Regulation 1/2003 on the implementation of the EU competition rules. After the adoption of the Regulation, Eddy De Smijter stayed within the unit responsible for the European Competition Network until his move, in 2005, to the team that is responsible for the Commission's policy on private enforcement of the EU antitrust rules. In that capacity, he was leading the team that on behalf of the Commission negotiated with the European Parliament and the Council, the Directive on antitrust damages actions. Today, he is leading the Commission team in the legislative negotiations on the Foreign Subsidies Regulation.

Eleanor M. Fox

Eleanor M. Fox is the Walter J. Derenberg Professor of Trade Regulation at New York University School of Law. She is an expert in antitrust law and international

and comparative competition policy, particularly including European law, developing countries' law, and globalization and markets. She was a partner in the New York law firm Simpson Thacher & Bartlett. She served as a member of President Carter's antitrust review commission. She was a member of President Clinton's International Competition Policy Advisory Committee, which proposed a global competition initiative that was to become the International Competition Network. Fox is a non-governmental advisor to the ICN.
Fox was awarded an honorary doctorate degree from the University of Paris-Dauphine in 2009. She was awarded an inaugural Lifetime Achievement award in 2011 by the Global Competition Review for "substantial, lasting and transformational impact on competition policy and practice." She received the inaugural award for outstanding contributions to the competition law community in 2015 by ASCOLA, the world network of professors of antitrust law and economics. She was awarded the Lifetime Achievement Award of the Antitrust & Economic Regulation Section of the Association of American Law Schools in 2017.

Elizabeth F. Kraus

Elizabeth F. Kraus is Deputy Director for International Antitrust at the U.S. Federal Trade Commission. She leads the team that coordinates the FTC's international antitrust policy, bilateral cooperation and case coordination work, and represents the FTC in multilateral fora, actively participating in the International Competition Network and the OECD Competition Committee.
Liz previously served as Counsel to the Director of the FTC's Bureau of Competition and, prior to that, as Counsel for Multilateral Affairs for the Bureau's International Antitrust Division, where she represented the FTC in a number of international fora related to competition policy and law enforcement. Prior to joining the FTC in 2002, Liz practiced EU competition law in the Brussels office of Weil, Gotshal & Manges LLP, focusing on merger-related work in the telecommunications and Internet technology fields. She was a Fulbright Scholar to the European Union, received a Master's degree in European Legal Studies from the College of Europe, Bruges, Belgium, and holds a J.D. from Georgetown University Law Center and a B.A. from Dartmouth College. Liz serves as a member of the American Bar Association's Antitrust Law Section leadership.
Liz has been engaged in the ICN since its inception, from helping to establish the ICN's strategic direction, to leading ICN initiatives on international cooperation, to developing key work product, including the ICN Recommended Practices on Merger Notification and Procedures, Unilateral Conduct, and Investigative Process.

Eyad Maher Dabbah

Eyad Dabbah holds the chair in competition law and policy and is the founder and director of the Institute for Competition and Consumers (ICC) (previously the Interdisciplinary Centre for Competition Law and Policy), Queen Mary University of London. He is the author of several books dealing with national, regional and global competition law and policy, including: The *Internationalization of Antitrust Policy* (Cambridge, 2003 – translated into Chinese in 2008); *International and Comparative Competition Law* (Cambridge, 2010); and *Competition Law and Policy in the Middle East* (Cambridge, 2007). He is also the General Editor (with Paul Lasok QC) of *Merger Control Worldwide* (Cambridge, 2005 and 2012) and (with Barry Hawk) of *Anti-cartel Enforcement Worldwide* (Cambridge, 2009).

Eyad is also the author of a work outside the field of competition law, *A Promising Middle East* (2014). Eyad acts as special counsel and consultant to several governments, international organisations (including the OECD, United Nations and the World Bank) and large businesses and is involved in the training of government officials, judges, lawyers and economists in the field of competition law. He has acted as special counsel in notable cases –specifically in the areas of abuse of dominance and mergers – and led teams of advisors from major law firms. Eyad also specialises in trade and anti-dumping matters and has handled major antidumping complaints and disputes involving both business firms and countries. Between 2012 and 2017, Eyad served as the Chairman of the Anti-dumping Tribunal of Israel. He was the Series Editor (with Barry Hawk) for Antitrust and Competition at Cambridge University Press (from 2006–2017) and is a barrister of the Middle Temple.

Filip Kubík

Filip Kubík has worked in the International Relations Unit in DG Competition at the European Commission since September 2017. He develops and coordinates DG Competition's policy contributions to the International Competition Network, the OECD, and UNCTAD. Further, he is DG Competition's desk for bilateral relations with the United States of America.

He joined the European Commission in 2005 as a case handler in the Telecommunications Antitrust Unit. In 2008, he moved to DG Competition's policy team that developed the Commission's initiative on private enforcement of the EU antitrust rules. In that position, he co-drafted the Directive on antitrust damages actions, took part in the negotiations leading to the Directive's adoption, and subsequently managed DG Competition's efforts in monitoring and facilitating the Directive's implementation in EU Member States.

Graeme Jarvie

Graeme Jarvie is the International Affairs Director at the Swedish Competition Authority (SCA). In his role he is responsible for coordinating the Authority's work on international cooperation. He has worked with international affairs since he joined the Authority in 2012. During his time at the SCA, Graeme has had significant experience of the ICN's work while acting as co-chair of the Unilateral Conduct Working Group, the Advocacy Working Group and latterly the Agency Effectiveness Working Group. Among other things he coordinated the drafting of the Unilateral Conduct Working Group's workbook chapter on Tying and Bundling, as well as the revision of the Advocacy Working Group's Market Studies Handbook. Graeme has participated as a speaker at various international conferences and workshops. Graeme studied law at Glasgow University and qualified as a solicitor in Scotland before taking his master's degree in European Law at Stockholm University.

Guy Pinsonnault

Guy Pinsonnault is a Partner in McMillan's Competition, White Collar Defence and Government Investigations Groups. His practice includes the full range of competition, white-collar crime and Canadian business regulation, litigation and advisory work, with a particular focus on Canadian and international cartel and commercial crime matters.

Prior to joining McMillan, Guy was the General Counsel, Competition Law Section, Public Prosecution Service of Canada, from 2004 to 2012. His work as the senior prosecutor at the Competition Bureau focused mainly on the prosecution of criminal cartel matters, as well as bid-rigging and fraudulent misrepresentation, in many of the major contested competition prosecutions in that period. He also provided extensive advice in the development of the Competition Bureau policies and programs in the criminal field (e.g. the Immunity and Leniency Programs) and advised on Bureau policies and practices for search and seizure, wiretaps, immunity and plea agreements.

Guy has extensive criminal and competition law experience dealing with local, national and cross-border corporate crime investigations. His practice involved foreign corrupt practices, fraud, commercial crime and other white-collar offences. His work included multi-jurisdictional files for the Competition Bureau with the United States Department of Justice Antitrust Division, as well as the RCMP Commercial Crime Division, the Integrated Proceeds of Crime Unit, and the Province of Quebec anti-corruption unit (UPAC). He has appeared before Superior courts, the Federal Court, the Court of Appeal of Quebec and the Supreme Court of Canada.

From 1990 to 2004, Guy was a prosecutor with Federal Prosecution Services, Justice Canada, where he prosecuted gang related drug cases, proceeds of crime and criminal organization offences, as well as criminal tax evasion.

The International Competition Network invited Guy to participate as a non-governmental advisor at the Cartel Workshop in 2013 (Cape Town, Africa), 2014 (Taipei, Taiwan), 2015 (Cartagena, Colombia), 2016 (Madrid, Spain), 2017 (Ottawa) and 2018 (Tel Aviv, Israel).

Heidi Sada

In 2006, Ms. Heidi Sada joined the extinct Mexican Federal Competition Commission (CFC or Commission) working in the General Directorate of Competition Advocacy and since 2008 she held the position of Deputy General Director of International Affairs. During 2014 to 2016 she worked as Competition Expert in the Competition Division of the Organization for Economic Co-operation and Development (OECD). Then from 2017 to 2018 she worked as an Advisor at the Telecommunications and Information Technologies Branch of the Mexican State Oil Company, Petróleos Mexicanos (PEMEX). In 2019, she rejoined the Mexican Federal Economic Competition Commission, COFECE, as Executive Director of International Affairs.

In the academic arena, Ms. Sada is a professor at the Tecnológico de Monterrey, where she has taught the subjects of Quantitative Techniques for Social Sciences, Strategic Foresight and Public Goods. She has a PhD in Social and Political Sciences from Universidad Iberoamericana, holds a Master's Degree in Global Management from the University of Phoenix in Arizona, and a Bachelor in Engineering from Tecnológico de Monterrey.

Huang Yong

Dr. and Professor HUANG Yong is Director of the Competition Law Centre of the University of International Business & Economics (UIBE) and a law professor. Currently he is also a member of the Expert Advisory Committee under the Anti-Monopoly Commission of State Council.

Professor HUANG was elected to serve in the Beijing Municipal People's Congress, sitting in the Congress' Financial and Economic Committee. Moreover, he serves as the Chief Researcher of Judicial Case Research Institute of the Supreme People's Court Anti-Monopoly Law, Researcher of Center for Judicial Protection of Intellectual Property Rights of Supreme People's Court. Professor HUANG also serves as expert of the State Administration of Market Regulation, SAMR, Legal Adviser to the State-owned Assets Supervision and Administration Commission of the State Council, Member of Expert Committee of China Consumer Association, Vice-Chairman of the Competition Committee of the International Chamber of Commerce China, etc.

Professor HUANG received his LL.B. degree from Peking University, his LL.M. and PhD degrees from the University of International Business & Economics. He was a visiting scholar in the University of Connecticut School of Law from 1996 to 1997.

James F. Rill

James Rill is Senior Counsel in the Washington, DC office of Baker Botts L.L.P. During his career, James Rill has played a uniquely important role in the development of global antitrust. From 1989 to 1992, Mr. Rill served as Assistant Attorney General (AAG) of the U.S. Department of Justice (DOJ)

Antitrust Division, during which time the DOJ and Federal Trade Commission (FTC) for the first time issued joint Horizontal Merger Guidelines. It was also an important time for the expansion of competition law internationally and for U.S. relations with other competition regimes. As AAG, Mr. Rill directed structural impediment talks with the Japanese government, using competition law to ensure market access; assisted newly liberated Eastern European countries in their efforts to establish new free-market systems; and helped negotiate a landmark antitrust cooperation agreement between the United States and the European Union.

In 1997, then-Attorney General Janet Reno and Assistant Attorney General for antitrust Joel Klein appointed Mr. Rill as co-chair of the International Competition Policy Advisory Committee (ICPAC) to advise the DOJ regarding international antitrust policy in the 21st century. Foremost among ICPAC's recommendations was its proposal to create a global competition forum for competition authorities throughout the world to confer on competition law issues. That recommendation was the impetus for establishing the International Competition Network in 2001, which in the past 20 years has contributed significantly to worldwide convergence of competition law and policies.

Mr. Rill served as Chair of the American Bar Association's Section of Antitrust Law from 1987–1988 and over the years has been a mentor and trusted advisor to many in the leadership of the Section and U.S. enforcement agencies.

Jana Seidl

Jana Seidl is a Senior Associate in the Washington, DC office of Baker Botts L.L.P., where she is a member of the antitrust and competition practice. Jana represents some of the world's leading companies in connection with mergers across various jurisdictions' competition regimes, as well as private and government litigation in the U.S.

Jana is a Non-Governmental Adviser to the International Competition Network and has previously published on issues of global convergence with particular focus on international due process norms advanced by the ICN and other organizations. Jana is active in the American Bar Association's Section of Antitrust Law, currently serving as a Vice Chair for the Section's Podcast Committee and as a member of the Young Lawyer Taskforce, having previously been the Co-Coordinator for the Section's Young Lawyer Representative Program.

John Pecman

John Pecman is a Senior Business Advisor in the Antitrust/Competition & Marketing group at Fasken. He served as a Commissioner of Competition at the Competition Bureau Canada from 2013–2018. Having served at the Competition Bureau as an investigator, manager and executive, John's pubic service career spanned over 34 years.

As Commissioner, John was a member of the executive bodies of the International Competition Network (ICN) and the Organization for Economic Co-operation and Development (OECD) Competition Committee. He also served as the first ICN-OECD Liaison to ensure coordination of the work by these two international bodies. Currently, John is a Non-Governmental Advisor to the ICN, a member Business at the OECD, Competition Committee, and a member of the ABA Antitrust Section Policy Task Force. John began his work with the leadership of the ICN in 2007 as co-chair of the Cartel Sub-Group Working Group, co-chairing and speaking at the annual workshops, and directing the development of chapters for the ICN Enforcement Manual.
John holds an M.A. from McMaster University in economics. He is currently a Senior Fellow with the CD Howe Institute, Competition Committee and a TMX Industry Professor for DeGroote Business School at McMaster University.

Kazuyuki Sugimoto
Kazuyuki Sugimoto was Chairman of the Japan Fair Trade Commission ("JFTC") from 2013 to 2020. Before joining the JFTC, he was a professor of the Graduate School of Public Policy, University of Tokyo. He had an extensive 35 year-long career at the Ministry of Finance, where he held the position of Administrative Vice Minister of Finance. He holds an LLB degree from the University of Tokyo and an MA degree from the University of Cambridge. Under his leadership, the JFTC was a member of the Steering Group, a Co-Chair of the Unilateral Conduct Working Group (2020-), a Co-Chair of the Merger Working Group (2017–2020), a Co-Chair of the Cartel Working Group Subgroup 1 (2014–2017) and a Co-Chair of the Cartel Working Group (2011–2014) at the ICN. As the Co-Chair of the MWG, the JFTC hosted the 2018 ICN Merger Workshop in Tokyo under the theme "Merger Review in the 2020s: Do Digitalization and Globalization Change the Analysis?"

Leah McCoy
Leah McCoy is an attorney in the International Section at the U.S. Department of Justice Antitrust Division. She began her career at the DOJ in 2008. Prior to joining the International Section, she worked as a trial attorney in the Washington Criminal 2 Section and the Transportation, Energy, and Agriculture Section. Ms. McCoy also served as an attorney advisor in the Criminal Division of the U.S. Department of Justice, where she handled matters involving criminal and civil asset forfeiture and money laundering. Ms. McCoy is a graduate of Georgetown Law and Texas Tech University.

Marcus Bezzi
Marcus has been an Executive General Manager at the Australian Competition and Consumer Commission (ACCC) since early 2009. From 2009 until July 2021 he was responsible for various enforcement functions in the ACCC including

cartels and competition enforcement. He is currently responsible for the ACCC's Specialist Advice and Services Division and Legal Service. As well as overseeing the provision of legal services and economic advice to the ACCC, he oversees the ACCC's international work, intelligence and data analytics and infocentres.
Marcus has been an active participant in the International Competition Network for more than ten years. He represents the ACCC in steering group meetings and as a co-chair at the ICN Competition Agencies Procedures (CAP) project. He has previously represented the ACCC in its role as a co-chair of the ICN Unilateral Conduct Working Group (2016 – 2019) and as a co-chair of the ICN Cartel Working Group between 2009 and 2019. In addition to contribution to the work of the ICN Cartel and Unilateral Conduct workgroups, Marcus has been involved in organizing cartel workshops, Unilateral Conduct Working Group workshops and the ICN Annual Conference in Sydney in 2019.
Marcus has a background as a government and private sector lawyer in Australia and the UK.

Margarida Matos Rosa
Margarida Matos Rosa is President of the Portuguese Competition Authority (Autoridade da Concorrência), serving as Steering Group member at the ICN. She is also responsible for the ICN/OECD liaison regarding competition matters. She previously worked for the Portuguese Securities Markets Commission (CMVM) and, in the private sector, for BNP Paribas, Santander Investment and UBS Bank. Margarida Matos Rosa holds an M.P.A. from Princeton University and an undergraduate degree in Economics from Université Catholique de Louvain (Belgium).

Maria Coppola
Maria Coppola is counsel for international antitrust at the U.S. Federal Trade Commission. She is responsible for the agency's enforcement and policy work with Europe. She is an adjunct professor at George Mason University's Antonin Scalia Law School.
Prior to her current position, she was responsible for the FTC's participation in the International Competition Network, and continues to be an active participant in the ICN's Merger Working group. In 2010–2011, Ms. Coppola was the Victor Kramer fellow at Harvard Law School, researching and writing on transgovernmental networks, based on her work with the ICN.
Ms. Coppola's experience is enriched by work at two other competition agencies. In 2012–2013, she was seconded to Mexico's Federal Competition Commission and in 2008 and 2009 she was seconded to the U.K. Office of Fair Trading.

Martin Mandorff
Martin leads the Market Abuse Unit at the Swedish Competition Authority. Before that he was Deputy Chief Economist. Prior to joining the Authority he

worked as a Senior Consultant at Bates White LLC in Washington D.C. Martin participates actively in the ICN UCWG, contributing to its webinar series and participating in workshops. He holds a Ph.D. in Economics from the University of Chicago.

Mateusz Błachucki

Mateusz Błachucki is an associate professor in the Department of Administrative Law of Institute of Law Studies, Polish Academy of Sciences. He is a member of the Scientific Council of the Institute. He holds a Habilitation in Law (2019), PhD in law (2011), M.A. (Hons) in Law (2002) and M.A. in Economics (2003). He is an assistant editor of Polish Case Law Review. The author and editor of several monographs, inter alia, 1) International Cooperation of Competition Authorities within Transnational Administrative Networks (forthcoming 2022); 2) International Cooperation of Competition Authorities in Europe: From Bilateral Agreements to Transgovernmental Networks, Warsaw 2021; and 3) Polish Competition Law. Commentary, Case Law and Texts, Warsaw 2013 and various articles in the field of competition law, transnational administrative law and administrative procedures published in Polish and international legal journals.

Mateusz serves also as an advisor to the President of the Office for Competition and Consumer Protection (Polish competition authority). His main duties include conducting complex merger and sanctioning investigations and representing the Polish authority before the courts in competition cases. Member and active participant of the ICN Merger Working Group since 2005. He is responsible for international cooperation in merger control and serves as an expert in working groups devoted to competition protection and cooperation in various international fora, i.e. ECN, MWG (UE), ECA and OECD Competition Committee.

Mattia Guidi

Mattia Guidi is assistant professor of political science at the Department of Social, Political and Cognitive Studies of the University of Siena. His research focuses on delegation and institutions, independent regulatory agencies, EU competition policy and EU macroeconomic governance. He has published articles on several international journals, including JCMS: Journal of Common Market Studies, Regulation & Governance, European Union Politics, European Political Science Review, Acta Politica, Comparative European Politics, and book chapters for Palgrave MacMillan and Routledge. His monograph "Competition policy enforcement in EU member states" (2016) is published by Palgrave MacMillan in the European Administrative Governance series.

Michal Halperin

Michal Halperin was the Director General of the Israel Competition Authority from March 2016 until July 2021 and is currently Senior Fellow at Harvard

Kennedy School (M-RCBG). For the past 25 years Ms. Halperin has been practicing law, specializing in antitrust law. In the beginning of her professional career she worked at a leading Israeli commercial law firm and after five years, she joined as a partner. In 2000 she moved to Boston and served as special advisor to Mintz, Levin, Cohn, Ferris, Glovsky & Popeo law firm. After returning to Israel in 2002, Ms. Halperin served for four and a half years as Chief Legal Counsel and Deputy Director General at the Israel Competition Authority. In 2007, Ms. Halperin joined a leading Israeli law firm as a partner where she established and lead the firm's Antitrust Department.

Michele Pacillo

Mr Michele Pacillo is an official for international antirust affairs at the Italian Competition Authority (AGCM) since 2014. He is responsible for the AGCM participation in multilateral organizations (e.g., ECN, OCED and ICN), as well as bilateral cooperation with other competition agencies. Before joining the AGCM, he worked at the Irish Competition Authority in the merger division and in the policy division during the period 2005–2009. He has been involved in all ICN activities since 2005, co-leading several projects in the Merger, Advocacy and Unilateral Working Groups. In particular, he coordinated the drafting of international merger review guidelines and best practice such as ICN Merger Guidelines Workbook (2006), the sections on barriers to entry and expansion of the ICN Recommended Practices on Merger Analysis (2008–2009) and the chapter on "The Role of Economists and Economic Evidence in Merger Analysis" (2013) of the Investigative Techniques Handbook for Merger Review of the ICN Merger Working Group. He represented the AGCM at the ICN annual conference in 2017 Porto, in the ICN Merger Workshop in Washington (2017), the ICN Advocacy Workshop in Mexico City (2016) and the Merger Workshops in New Delhi (2014) and Brussels (2015), and involved as moderator in breakout sessions. He graduated in Economics from Bocconi University, Italy, and holds a MSc in Economics from University of York, England, and a Postgraduate Diploma in EU Competition Law from King's College, London.

Neil Campbell

Neil is the Co-Chair of McMillan's Competition and International Trade Law groups. His competition law experience includes over 300 merger clearances under the Competition Act and/or the Investment Canada Act, including the Ultramar/Coastal and American Iron and Metal/SNF cases before the Competition Tribunal, as well as the Novartis/Alcon, Coca-Cola/CCE and Quebecor/Transcontinental consent agreements; over 25 domestic or international cartel cases and related class actions including optical disc drives, vitamins, air cargo, chocolate confectionery, foreign exchange, car carriers and auto parts; and a wide range of unilateral conduct proceedings, including

UCDA v IBC, Paradise Pharmacy v Novartis and several abuse of dominance investigations which were closed by the Competition Bureau. Neil also advises on marketing, distribution, grey marketing and joint venture issues.

Neil has appeared in the courts of Ontario and BC and the Federal Court on competition-related matters and was counsel to the Philips and Lite-On defendants in the appeal of the optical disc drives certification decision to the Supreme Court of Canada (Godfrey v. Toshiba Corp). He has represented parties before the Competition Tribunal, Canadian International Trade Tribunal and Canadian Transportation Agency. He acted as special counsel to the Competition Bureau on BHP Billiton / Potash Corp and to the Canadian Radio-Television and Telecommunications Commission on two foreign ownership reviews.

Neil is a non-governmental adviser to the International Competition Network. He has been a member of the ICN's Unilateral Conduct Working Group and its Cartel Working Group. In December 2019, he presented on the CWG's Webinar on Damages Claims.

Neil is the global contributing editor for Getting the Deal Through: Cartel Regulation and has published Merger Law and Practice and numerous articles on competition, trade and investment matters. He is a member of the CD Howe Institute's Competition Policy Council, the MLex Antitrust Advisory Board, and the editorial advisory board of the IBA's Business Law International journal.

He is ranked as one of the Global Elite competition lawyers by Who's Who Legal and received the "Dealmaker of the Year" award from Global Competition Review in 2016.

Nell Lixia Zhou

Dr Nell Lixia ZHOU is a senior researcher of Competition Law Center of UIBE and an associate professor of UIBE. She has extensively undertook the academic projects from competition agencies as well as other governmental agencies and businesses on diverse themes of antitrust law. She also published books and articles on the frontier competition issues. She is the legal consultant of WBG's Project on Competition Reforms for China and she wrote reports for WBG on Competitive Neutrality, Fair Competition Review Mechanism (FCRM), Chinese government subsidies, Chinese SOEs etc. She also wrote reports on FCRM, national subsidies etc. for DG COMP.

She is a vocal representative of the Chinese antitrust community in the international stage in voicing the latest development both academically and in practice in antitrust issues. She is now the only academic NGA from China for ICN since 2016. She is also an invited scholar for the UNCTAD Research Partnership Platform on Competition and Consumer Protection laws and Policies. She is a contributor of the ICC Leniency Brochure and a translator of the ICC Compliance Toolkit Chinese version. She is also an expert consultant for the Competition Committee of the China Chamber of International Commerce.

She obtained her Master of Law on International Business Law in 2004 from Law School of UIBE and LLM on Banking and Financial Law from Law School from UCL(University College London). She got her PH.D in Law degree on International Business Law from Law School of UIBE in 2011. She is qualified lawyer since 2002 (Chinese Bar).

Oliver Budzinski

Oliver Budzinski is Professor (Chair) of Economic Theory and Director of the Institute of Economics at Ilmenau University of Technology in Germany (since 2012). In 1999, he received his Ph.D. in Economics from Leibniz-University of Hanover, Germany, and thereafter was on post-doc positions at Marburg University, Germany, New York University, U.S., and the University of Duisburg-Essen, Germany. He held a professorship at the University of Southern Denmark, Campus Esbjerg, from 2008 to 2012. His research interests cover competition economics and antitrust policy as well as media economics, institutional economics, law & economics, and sports economics. In these fields, Oliver Budzinski has published more than 50 papers in academic journals, 3 books and 4 edited volumes, and more than 40 chapters in conference proceedings, handbooks, and other collected volumes. Among them, there are numerous contributions to the topic international competition policy and, more specifically, the role of the International Competition Network.

Paul O'Brien

Paul O'Brien is Counsel for International Antitrust in the Office of International Affairs at the U.S. Federal Trade Commission. Mr. O'Brien is the lead attorney for the FTC's participation in the International Competition Network and contributes to other bilateral and multilateral efforts. Mr. O'Brien has chaired the ICN's Merger Working Group, Agency Effectiveness Working Group, and Promotion and Implementation team. He has led projects in every ICN working group, including drafting recommended practices, reports, and manuals; coordinating many ICN teleseminars; and helping organize more than a dozen ICN workshops. Mr. O'Brien has a JD and LL.M. (International & Comparative Law) from Georgetown University Law Center.

Mr. O'Brien joined the FTC in 2012 from the US Department of Justice, Antitrust Division's Foreign Commerce Section. At the Antitrust Division, he was responsible for ICN participation across all enforcement areas and other aspects of international policy. He also previously served as a Special Assistant to the Directors of Civil and Criminal Enforcement in the Division and as a Trial Attorney in an enforcement section that handled merger review.

Paulo Burnier da Silveira

Paulo is a Senior Competition Expert at the Organization for Economic Cooperation and Development (OECD) and Manager of the OECD Regional

Center for Competition in Latin America. He is also a former Commissioner at the Brazilian Competition Authority (CADE) and former head of CADE's International Unit, with an active participation in ICN activities during 2011–2019. He holds a PhD from the University of Paris and is a Law Professor at the University of Brasilia.

Pierre Horna

Dr Horna has been a Legal Affairs officer at the Competition and Consumer Policies Branch of the United Nations Conference on Trade and Development (UNCTAD) for more than 15 years. He has been responsible for the design, formulation and implementation of technical assistance and capacity building programmes on competition and consumer protection policies in the ASEAN, Balkan, CIS (ex-Soviet Union countries) and Latin American regions. He has actively assisted governments and policymakers in the design and implementations of competition and consumer protection policies regimes as well as drafted several legal assessment reports on competition laws for many developing countries and transition economies. He was a visiting Research Fellow at Oxford's Centre for Competition Law and Policy at Oxford University during 2017. He earned his PhD Degree in International Law at the Graduate Institute, Switzerland (2017) and Master of Laws in International Business Law from Leiden University, the Netherlands (2002–2003), and studies on e-commerce and consumer protection at Buckingham University, England (2001). Dr. Horna recently published a book with Hart Publishing in 2020 entitled: *Fighting Cross-Border Cartels: The Perspective of the Young and Small Competition Authorities.*

Randolph Tritell

Randolph Tritell is the Director of the U.S. Federal Trade Commission's Office of International Affairs, where he is responsible for coordinating the FTC's international antitrust and consumer protection policies and the FTC's involvement in cases that raise international issues. He represents the FTC in multilateral fora including the International Competition Network – where he serves on the Steering Group and has been involved in projects on mergers, unilateral conduct, and procedural fairness among others – and the OECD Competition Committee. He is also responsible for the FTC's negotiation and implementation of international cooperation agreements and relevant provisions of trade agreements.

Prior to joining the FTC, Mr. Tritell was a partner with Weil, Gotshal & Manges LLP, practicing in New York and in Brussels where he opened the firm's office. Mr. Tritell began his career at the FTC, serving in various positions including Assistant to the Director of the Bureau of Consumer Protection, Attorney Advisor to Commissioner Terry Calvani, and Executive Assistant to the Chairman. Mr. Tritell obtained his law degree from the University of

Pennsylvania Law School. He co-chairs the ABA Section of Antitrust Law's International Comments and Policy Committee and serves on the advisory board of the Journal of Antitrust Enforcement and the Fordham Competition Law Institute.

Rod Sims

Rod Sims served as Chair of the Australian Competition and Consumer Commission (ACCC) from 2011 until his term as Chair ended in March 2022.

Rod has extensive business and public sector experience. Immediately prior to his appointment to the ACCC he was the Chairman of the Independent Pricing and Regulatory Tribunal of New South Wales, a Commissioner on the National Competition Council and was also a Director of Port Jackson's Partners Limited, where he advised the CEOs and Boards of some of Australia's top 50 companies on commercial corporate strategy over many years. Prior to joining the ACCC, he was also a Director of various private sector companies, some based in Asia and Europe.

During the late 1980s and early 1990s, Rod worked as the Deputy Secretary in the Australian Government's Department of Prime Minister and Cabinet responsible for economic, infrastructure and social policy and the Cabinet Office. He also worked as Deputy Secretary in the Department of Transport and Communications. From 1988 – 90 he was the Economic Adviser to Australia's Prime Minister.

Rod was Chair of the ACCC when it hosted the 2015 Annual Meeting of the ICN in Sydney, and in 2017 when the ACCC was presented with an international award by ICN and the World Bank for the ACCC's role in elevating competition policy to the national economic agenda. He was also a Vice-Chair of the ICN Steering Group with a focus on cooperation in relation to digital economy issues and Asia Pacific liaison.

Rod Sims holds a first class honours degree in Commerce from the University of Melbourne and a Master of Economics from the Australian National University.

Shira Gillat

Ms. Shira Gillat joined the Israel Competition Authority as Director of International Affairs in 2018. She oversees ICA's affairs vis-à-vis the ICN and the OECD, as well as manages and develops ICA's network of peer competition authorities, worldwide. Prior to joining ICA, Ms. Gillat worked at the Competition & Antitrust Department, of Fischer Behar Chen Well Orion and Co law firm, where she specialized in competition & antitrust law, anti-dumping and complex litigation. Ms. Gillat provided legal counsel to major domestic and international corporations in a broad array of antitrust matters, including in complex civil litigation, class actions, and in proceedings before the ICA. Ms. Gillat also provided legal counsel to companies with regard to anti-dumping matters, including general counsel, and administrative proceedings. Ms. Gillat obtained her law degree, and an additional degree in philosophy (cum laude), from the Tel Aviv University. She is a member of the Israel Bar Association (2009 to date).

Siún O'Keeffe

Siún O'Keeffe is Manager of the Academy at the Netherlands ACM. ACM's Academy organises training and educational courses for ACM's employees, and advises the Board on learning and development. From July 2020 to June 2021, Siún was (Acting) Manager of the Competition & Markets unit of ACM's Legal Service. In 2022, Siún is chair of the Contact Network for BEREC (Body of European Regulators for Electronic Communications).

Prior to becoming manager at the Academy, Siún was Senior Strategy Advisor at ACM, from 2013 to 2018 and Senior International Advisor at the Netherlands Competition Authority (NMa), from 2008 to 2013. From 2008 to 2018, Siún was active in the ICN, during which time the Netherlands authority was co-chair of the Cartels Working Group, member of the Steering Group and host of the 2011 Annual Conference.

From 2003 to 2008, Siún worked as case-handler at the NMa. An Irish lawyer, Siún lectured European and Competition law from 1993 to 2002 at the Universities of Limerick in Ireland and Nijmegen in the Netherlands. She studied Law at University College Cork, College of Europe, Bruges, and King's Inns, Dublin.

Tang Jinglun

Aaron Jinglun Tang is doctoral student of the Law School of the University of International Business & Economics (UIBE) and a research fellow of UIBE Competition Law Centre. Aaron is assistant of member of Beijing Municipal People's Congress. Before the reform of national anti-monopoly law enforcement agencies, Aaron once worked as an intern for a half year in the Price Supervision & Inspection and Antimonopoly Bureau of the National Development and Reform Commission. As a doctoral student major in competition law Aaron has published several articles on China competition policy, competition law enforcement and Fair Competition Review Mechanism. In 2017, Aaron's paper was rewarded by Competition Law Committee of China Economic Law Society as the 5th China Youth Competition Law Top 10 Thesis.

Tembinkosi Bonakele

Tembinkosi Bonakele has been the Commissioner of the South African Competition Commission since 2013. He was appointed Deputy Commissioner in 2008, and prior to that worked as head of mergers, head of compliance, and senior legal counsel respectively. Mr Bonakele is an admitted attorney and holds a BJuris and an LLB from the University of Fort Hare and an MBA from Gordon Institute of Business Science, University of Pretoria. He is an adjunct

visiting professor of law at Wits Law School, an adjunct professor in the Business School of Nelson Mandela University, an Associate of the European Summer School and Conference in Competition and Regulation of Athens University of Economics and Business, a Fellow of the University of Johannesburg's Centre for Competition, Regulation and Economic Development and a Board Member of the University of Stellenbosch's Centre for Competition Law and Economics. He is a Ph.D. candidate and teaching fellow at the University University College London and a member of the 2020 Cohort of the Atlantic Fellows for Racial Equity (AFRE); a decade-long investment of The Atlantic Philanthropies designed to identify and advance solutions to anti-black racism in the United States and South Africa by supporting a diverse group of leaders committed to combatting prejudice and overcoming legacies of slavery, Jim Crow and apartheid.
He has published widely in academic journals and writes for newspapers and business magazines on competition matters. He has recently co-edited a book titled 'Competition Law for the New Era'. Mr Bonakele currently serves as the Chairperson of the African Competition Forum, is a member of the BRICS competition forum and Vice Chair of the International Competition Network Steering Group.

Yane Svetiev
Yane Svetiev is Associate Professor of Law at the University of Sydney Law School (Australia) and Fernand Braudel Fellow at the Law Department and the Robert Schuman Centre of the European University Institute. He works in the areas of market regulation, competition law and regulatory private law with a specific focus on institutional and remedial design. He has previously held appointments at the European University Institute in Florence (Italy) and at Brooklyn Law School (New York, USA). During his doctoral studies at Columbia University, he also practiced as a litigation associate with Cravath, Swaine and Moore in New York. His book *Experimentalist Competition Law and the Regulation of Markets* was published by Hart/Bloomsbury in 2020. His current research funded by the Australian Research Council focuses on the use of transnational peer review in market regulation.

THE EDITORS

Paul Lugard

Paul Lugard is a partner in the Brussels office of Baker Botts L.L.P., where he is a member of the firm's antitrust and competition practice. Paul has practiced in the international competition law field for more than 25 years and concentrates on complex merger review proceedings and investigations into alleged anticompetitive business practices. He has also counselled some of the world's leading companies on strategic cooperation agreements, platform competition, distribution agreements and technology licensing agreements. His areas of experience include the application of the antitrust laws to high technology sectors, and the energy sector. Paul has assisted clients in oil and gas, LNG, human and animal health, consumer electronics, fast moving consumer goods, medical imaging, telecommunications and in various online industries.

Paul is active in the development of international competition policy. He has served as a Non-Governmental Advisor (NGA) to the International Competition Network (ICN) for more than 15 years. He is a Vice Chair of the Business and Industry Advisory Committee to the OECD (BIAC) and the immediate past Chair of the ICC Competition Commission. Mr. Lugard was a senior vice president and the Head of Antitrust at Royal Philips Electronics from 2005 until 2012.

David Anderson

Dave Anderson is a partner in Bryan Cave Leighton Paisner's Antitrust & Competition Law team and leads the firm's Brussels office. He is a US/UK/Belgian national, qualified to practice in the US, Belgium, Ireland and the UK. Dave has practiced in the international competition law field for over 25 years and focuses on EU and international aspects of mergers, acquisitions, joint ventures, restrictive practices, cartels and abuses of dominant positions. Dave also advises on EU regulatory law, public affairs and Brexit. He serves clients worldwide across a range of industries and he has specialist expertise in the technology/digital, transportation, energy and consumer goods sectors. Dave has served as a non-governmental adviser (NGA) since the ICN's founding and is a European Commission NGA. He also advises the UN Conference on Trade and Development (UNCTAD) and national competition authorities on competition law reform and agency capacity building in Europe, Africa, Asia and South America. Dave is recognized as a leading international competition lawyer by

Global Competition Review, Chambers Global and Legal 500. He holds a Juris Doctor from American University (Washington DC; Magna Cum Laude), an MA from University College London (First Class Honours) and a BA from St Olaf College (Phi Beta Kappa).

Paul Culliford

Paul is a New Zealand qualified Senior Associate based in Bryan Cave Leighton Paisner's Brussels office, where he specialises in antitrust and competition law. Prior to joining BCLP, Paul spent four years practising competition law with one of New Zealand's leading law firms. Paul's experience covers all areas of competition law, including merger control, restrictive practices, investigations and general compliance.

Avani Joshi

Avani Joshi is an Associate at Cyril Amarchand Mangaldas. After receiving her undergraduate law degree in India, Avani earned her Master of Laws degree at University College London as a JN Tata Scholar in 2018, specialising in competition law. She has previously been an editor for the UCL Journal of Law and Jurisprudence. Avani deals with a broad spectrum of antitrust issues, gaining experience at law firms across India and in Brussels and London.

INDEX

D

www.ingramcontent.com/pod-product-compliance
Lightning Source LLC
LaVergne TN
LVHW020647300926
849161LV00004B/846

* 9 7 8 1 9 3 9 0 0 7 0 9 4 *